The Book of Man

The
Book
of Man

Readings on the Path to Manhood

William J.
BENNETT

with Christopher Beach

NELSON
BOOKS

An Imprint of Thomas Nelson

Published in Nashville, Tennessee, by Nelson Books. Nelson Books and Thomas Nelson are registered trademarks of Thomas Nelson, Inc.

Thomas Nelson, Inc., titles may be purchased in bulk for educational, business, fund-raising, or sales promotional use. For information, please e-mail SpecialMarkets@ThomasNelson.com.

Unless otherwise noted, Scripture quotations are taken from HOLY BIBLE: NEW INTERNATIONAL VERSION®. © 1973, 1978, 1984 by International Bible Society. Used by permission of Zondervan Publishing House. All rights reserved.

Scripture quotations marked NKJV are from THE NEW KING JAMES VERSION. © 1982 by Thomas Nelson, Inc. Used by permission. All rights reserved.

ISBN 978-1-59555-539-7 (Paperback)

The Library of Congress has catalogued the hardcover edition as follows:

Bennett, William J. (William John), 1943–
  The book of man / William J. Bennett.
    p. cm.
  ISBN 978-1-59555-271-6
  1. Men—Conduct of life. 2. Character—Case studies. I. Title.
  BJ1601.B46 2011
  808.8'035211—dc23

2011026714

Printed in the United States of America

13 14 15 16 17 QG 7 6 5 4 3 2 1

—— ❧ ——

To our sons, John and Joseph, who are becoming the kind of men we hoped, prayed, and worked for. Know that others will say of each of you, following Homer, that the son is far better than the father, and he makes glad the heart of his mother.

Contents

2 MAN AT WORK 89

3 MAN IN PLAY, SPORTS, AND LEISURE 169

4 MAN IN THE POLIS 251

5 MAN WITH WOMAN AND CHILDREN 367

6 MAN IN PRAYER AND REFLECTION 459

Introduction

The purpose of this book is to explore and explain what it means to be a man. In these pages you will find a variety of sources that offer a coherent, defensible, and appealing notion of manhood. The selections range from ancient to modern, and in sum they carry timeless instruction. Taken together, they present an ideal of manhood both suitable and practical for today. In a variety of life's contexts, these readings define what a man should be, how he should live, and the things to which he should aspire.

For boys to become men they need to be guided through advice, habit, instruction, example, and correction. It is true in all ages. Someone once characterized the two essential questions Plato posed as: Who teaches the children, and what do we teach them? Each generation of men and women has an obligation to teach the younger males (and females, of course) coming behind them. When they fail in that obligation, trouble surely follows.

There is trouble with men today. For example, after studying today's workforce data, author and commentator David Brooks observed that "in 1954, about 96 percent of American men between the ages of 25 and 54 worked. Today that number is around 80 percent. One-fifth of all men in their prime working ages are not getting up and going to work."

Men, American men in particular, are increasingly dependent on the government dole rather than the fruits of their own labor. As Brooks pointed out, the result is worrisome: "There are probably more idle men now than at any time since the

Great Depression, and this time the problem is mostly structural, not cyclical. These men will find it hard to attract spouses. Many will pick up habits that have a corrosive cultural influence on those around them."

In his article, "Broken Families, Broken Economy," Mitch Pearlstein observes a similar phenomenon. "Under normal circumstances, boys grow up and marry the women who become the mothers of their children. If, however, they reach adulthood unable to hold a job, stay sober, or keep out of jail, they quickly find that desirable women have little interest in hitching themselves to them," Pearlstein writes. "In communities where marriage is vanishing, it cannot be revived unless millions of boys (and girls) get their lives in decent order. Aimless or felonious men are not the only reason for the decline of marriage, but they are a sizable one." Considering that, in 1970, 80 percent of twenty-five- to twenty-nine-year-old men were married and in 2007 only 40 percent were, Pearlstein's and Brooks's assessments are tragically accurate.

Other commentators, like *National Review* editor Rich Lowry, have written recently about the working class in America. Lowry noted that "the working class is getting cut off from the richest sources of social capital: marriage, two-parent families, and church-going. More people are falling into a lower class characterized by men who can't make a minimal living and single women with children."

But the decline in foundational virtues—work, marriage, and religion—affects more than the lower class. It appears to affect the upper reaches of the wealthiest also. For instance, we once believed that wealth and success for men were connected to and were a product of diligence and virtue. We are not so sure anymore.

Walter Russell Mead, the accomplished cultural essayist, put it this way about some of America's elite men: "What a surprise! We raised a generation of bright kids without a foundation in religion, and they've grown up and gone to Wall Street. We never told them that the virtuous life was both necessary and hard, that character was something that had to be built step by step from youth, that moral weakness was both contemptible and natural: and we are shocked, shocked! when, placed in proximity to large sums of loose cash, they grab all they can." In short, from the top to the bottom of American society we have a problem with a good number of our men.

One such symptom is the collapse of what is known as the code of men, or the code of a gentleman. There was once a common understanding in our society among men that there are standards of action and behavior to which men should hold themselves. Men, the code dictates, among other things, keep their word, whether in writing or not, men do not take advantage of women, men support their children, and men watch their language, especially around women and children. The code of men is fading.

In his essay, "The Crisis of Manliness," Waller Newell laments, "As a culture we have never been more conflicted about what we mean by manhood." Many of our men today suffer from *Fight Club* syndrome. Newell explains, "Under-fathered young men, many from broken homes, [are] prone to identify their maleness with aggression because they have no better model to go by . . . [I]f young men are cut off from the positive tradition of manly pride their manliness will reemerge in crude and retrograde forms."

So, one might argue that in our time there is especially a need for guidance, and the important role of men for boys is particularly acute. Of course there are successes, and every day great boys are raised to be great men. But there are too many other cases as well. Confusion regarding manhood abounds, including confusion about a proper understanding of virility. Fathers are missing from boys' lives in devastatingly high numbers. Children are exposed to a dizzying array of cultural signals about what it means to be a man, signals both good and bad. Our society is moving forward so rapidly that it has forgotten much good from the past. And women are beginning to take the place of men in many ways. Women have now surpassed men in several categories that reflect economic and cultural standing. In American colleges, for every two men who graduate with a bachelor of arts degree, three women receive a BA. Women now dominate thirteen of the fifteen job categories expected to grow the most in the coming decade. This has led some to ask: Do we even need men?

So what's wrong? Increasingly, the messages to boys about what it means to be a man are confusing. The machismo of the street gang calls out with a swagger. Video games, television, and music offer dubious lessons to boys who have been abandoned by their fathers. Gay culture often parades itself in a flamboyant display and challenge to traditional masculinity. Some coaches and drill sergeants bark, "What kind of man are you?" but don't explain. The flickering cinema screen is filled with stories of men who refuse to grow up. Some thirty-year-olds, suspended in a state of permanent adolescence, stay stoned on marijuana and refuse to take responsibility in relationships.

Men, some obsessed with sex, treat women as toys to be discarded when things get complicated. Through all these different and conflicting signals, our boys must decipher what it means to be a man, and for many of them it is harder to figure out.

Many rightly decry a deficit in manhood among our boys and men. And many, especially girls and women, parents, teachers, coaches, and adults in authority observe problems among boys and men. Why are there so many boys and men who are irresponsible, unmotivated, unchivalrous, selfish, and lazy? Why do so many boys and men spend so much time in pointless and soulless activities, inconsiderate of others, absorbed in self or mindless technology? For example, men between the ages of eighteen and thirty-four are now the biggest users of video games, with 48.2 percent of all American men using a console daily and spending an average of two hours and thirty-four minutes per day on it, according to a 2007 Nielsen survey (Nielsen Media, "The State of the Console," The Nielsen Company, 2007). In 2009, men spent an average of 4.54 hours per day watching television (Television Bureau of Advertising, Survey, 2009). Fashioning men has never been easy, but the difficulties seem pronounced today. One thinks of C. S. Lewis's line, "The task of the modern educator is not to cut down jungles, but to irrigate deserts."

My hope is that this book will be a healthy alternative to questionable messages that inundate boys and men every day. Let this book stand as a rough line—an approximation on the ground of our society—that helps define the extents and limits of true manhood. There is no full instruction manual or formula on how to be a man—yes, there are codes and sets of rules, like the Ten Commandments, the Boy Scout Oath, and the Navy SEAL Code—but these are axiomatic. They are general principles and do not offer context. More can and should be said. That is what I offer here. There are examples worthy of emulation, stories worth knowing, lives worth studying and remembering, and counsel worth hearing. I have tried to gather a wide sampling of material that can encourage and guide. And so, while this book cannot make you a good man, it should give you a helpful idea of what a good man is.

It is unlikely that any man cited or described in this book would dare to hold himself up as the standard of traditional masculinity and manhood. The writer of this book certainly does not. In writing this book, I do not offer myself up as any kind of role model or example. Each man portrayed here in this book falls short of the ideal in some way. Still, from each man represented here something can be learned.

This book is by no means a definitive collection. Though a hefty volume, it only scratches the surface of the wonderful library that is history, literature, philosophy, religion, and human experience. I have tried to choose readings that cover a wide range of life's stages and circumstances and current maladies.

In addition to selections from literature and history, I have included profiles of men from our own time whom I admire, both everyday men and well-known public figures. Some of them I have come to know personally, others indirectly. It is important to remember that living, breathing men who may even live close by us rank among our most compelling and vibrant examples of manhood. I present them as I know them, incompletely, but with high regard for the virtues they possess, all the while realizing the imperfections and frailty of our shared humanity.

In developed Western countries, man has unprecedented freedom to choose, to a degree heretofore unknown, a life of his own wanting and design. A mere hundred years ago, man couldn't afford to dawdle in limbo between adolescence and manhood; manhood was thrust upon him for survival. Today, more opportunity lies at his feet than ever before. Yet with this increased opportunity comes increased confusion, and the response on the part of some men has not been encouraging.

The survival of humanity once depended on a man's hands, muscles, and intellect. If he could not provide for his family, it did not survive. Today, our livelihood rests substantially on technology, microprocessors, and artificial intelligence. Men and women seem less dependent on each other for economic livelihood. This newfound freedom has provoked many men to ask the question: What does it mean to be a man today? This book argues that while the plot, actors, and scenes are constantly changing, the virtues, characteristics, and challenges of manhood remain the same today as thousands of years ago and that more than ever we need men who live like men.

———

I have organized this book into six parts. The first chapter, "Man in War," illustrates how the battlefield remains one place where manhood is still largely intact. Order, loyalty, service—the virtues of manhood—define military service. At the extreme edge of human suffering and endurance, bravery and courage, a man can find his truest, most elevated self.

"Man at Work" next explains how the definition of work has changed—from plowing fields to designing Web sites—but the principle remains: hard, fruitful work is at the heart—and should be one of the joys—of a man's life, and he should approach his occupation with devotion.

In the third chapter, "Man in Play, Sports, and Leisure," I offer examples of how men should enjoy life, but enjoy it responsibly. Athletics and hobbies are not just distractions; they can teach invaluable life lessons and mirror excellence in other endeavors.

"Man in the Polis," the fourth chapter, focuses on how and why men come together in the polis—the city, the community, the state, the society—to provide for common interests and protect the general welfare. The Reverend Martin Luther King Jr. said the highest duty in life is serving our fellow man. As much as we take from the polis, we must put back in.

Many women today wonder where the "real men" are, especially when it comes to fulfilling their responsibilities as husbands and fathers. The fifth chapter, "Man with Woman and Children," illuminates in important ways that how a man treats a woman and how well he fathers his children constitute the essence of manhood.

Over the last several decades, church attendance surveys show that fewer and fewer men attend church. The sixth and final chapter of this book, "Man in Prayer and Reflection," describes why prayer and reflection are a man's internal GPS system, and why neglecting the examined or prayerful life is like going on a journey without a map or a compass.

In looking through this volume, you'll find that most of the selections are examples of positive thought and action. In other words, they point to maxims, models, and standards of behavior. So I mean them to be. Tragedies and other examples of vice are always instructive in reminding us of paths to avoid. But men, in our time above all, need lifting up, so I have concentrated on readings that will raise the sights and aspirations of boys and men.

One of my most treasured possessions is a picture taken many years ago when I was a young father. It is a picture of me at the beach and on my shoulder I'm carrying my older son, John, who was three years old. I love it partly for obvious reasons of sentiment, but also for another reason. The picture represents one of those moments when I might have played the role of a father well. It is an inspiration and a reminder and it lifts me up, as I lifted up my son on that day.

In the same way, I hope this book will lift up you and the ones you love. I hope it will help you learn and remember what it is to be a man.

The examples in this book are just a fraction of the countless stories, accounts, and lessons of and about men spread throughout literature, history, and the human story. I invite readers to send me stories—things you have read, heard, or experienced that had a lasting impact on your life and improved your understanding of what it means to be a man.

Let's Bring Back Heroes

WILLIAM J. BENNETT

To begin with, I wish to set the stage with a piece on heroism. Men are called to be heroes in ways both big and small in every area of their lives, all the areas we cover in this book—war, work, and play; civic life, family life, and prayer life. What follows is a piece I wrote more than forty years ago and one whose message serves as a foundation for the pieces to follow. Whether we take up the sword, the plow, the ball, the gavel, our children, or our Bibles, we must always do it like the men we are called to be.

As a child growing up in Brooklyn, New York, I had many heroes. The one I remember best was Gary Cooper, as Marshal Will Kane, in *High Noon*. I saw the movie when I was nine years old and Coop, as Will, is still special to me. He wasn't the roughest, toughest guy in the world in that movie, his courage wasn't the macho callousness of Clint Eastwood's "Dirty Harry" or the "Man with No Name"; that was the stuff of his antagonists: the Miller brothers. Will was worth admiring for other things, in language I was to learn later—for his courage and compassion and sense of what deserved to be loved and protected. In addition to Will, because my family and teachers thought it worth their time, I was exposed to a variety of other heroes and heroines: Lou Gehrig, Roy Campanella, Edmund Hillary, Tamsen Donner, Abraham Lincoln, Esther, and Odysseus; and later on, in college, to Mother Courage and Socrates, Martin Luther King Jr. and Justice Holmes.

In all of them it is fair to say that there was a certain nobility, a largeness of soul, a hitching up of one's own purposes to larger purposes, to purposes beyond the self, to something that demanded endurance sacrifice or courage or resolution or compassion; it was to nurture ~ing because one had a sense of what deserved to be loved and

Qualities Worth Striving For

From childhood through adolescence and into early adulthood, people I knew went to the trouble of pointing out to me individuals who possessed qualities of human excellence that were worth imitating and striving for. Eventually, I learned that heroes and their qualities were to be found closer to home and that there were neighbors, friends, and even members of my family who possessed these qualities.

In a recent survey of twelve hundred junior high school children, the most popular response to the question "Who is your hero?" was "None." Nobody. Other answers far down the line in this and other polls have revealed the devaluation of the hero, at least. Students today cite rock musicians, Evel Knievel, and the bionic man and woman. This suggests—and my own informal poll and the reports of friends of mine who are teachers have confirmed my suspicion—that heroes are out of fashion. For some reason, perhaps for no reason, many of us think it is not proper to have heroes; or worse, that there aren't any—or only shabby ones.

Such a fad is dangerous because it puts children's ideals, aspirations, and their notions of self-worth in jeopardy. Children need to know what deserves to be emulated and loved and nurtured, but knowing these things is not transmitted by their genes; these things must pass, through education, from generation to generation.

The Worst Aha! of All

We have been too much suckered by what is called "the reality of technique," or what I call the Aha! theory of human behavior. The Aha! theory of behavior assumes that the most real aspects of anything are those that are base and are concealed from the eye. Aha!—you may appear to be an honest lawyer, but that is only a devious approach to get my business; Aha!—teacher, you may appear to have an interest in my child but you are merely putting me on in order to get me to tell the principal how fine you are so you can get a raise; or the worst Aha! of all: Aha!—Dad, you may try to make me believe that you're doing it for my good, but you are really just doing it to manipulate me, to show you have power over me.

Think about it: How is it that the worst somehow gains more reality than the best? How is it that baseness, insensitivity, callous indifference, hardness, sadism are more real than pride and honor and compassion and courage and sacrifice? Even if they are more prevalent—and I am not sure they are—that just won't do; reality doesn't depend on a majority vote.

We have become so interested in raking muck that we scarcely lift our eyes from it. Watergate, "demythologizing," phony sophistication, believing that every good action has an ulterior and crass motive, the rise of the anti-hero, and a variety of other forces have made the hero invisible to us.

In 1950, in his Nobel Prize acceptance speech, William Faulkner mentioned with disdain authors who write "not of the heart but of the glands." He reminded his audience that the basest of all things is to be afraid and that the writer must leave "no room in his workshop for anything but the old verities and truths of the heart . . . lacking which any story is ephemeral and doomed—love and honor and pity and pride and compassion and sacrifice." He echoed Yeats's well-known prophecy about a time, perhaps our time, when "the ceremony of innocence is drowned" and "the best lack all conviction." It is hard to have convictions without ideals. Heroes instantiate ideals.

Real heroes, not the bionic types who do it with wires, may be fictional or factual as long as they embody character, as long as they possess qualities that we instantly recognize as true to human life and worth human attention.

DESIRABLE REAL EXAMPLES

In education, rather than squabble for innovation on the one hand and a return to basics on the other, we ought to encourage something that is both: an innovation and a return to the basics of aspiration. Along with emphasis on sound arithmetic and spelling, even on sociology for the first-grader, we should tell some stories, true stories, about heroes. We should offer our students and ourselves some real examples, not only of human corruption, degradation, and duplicity, but also of the qualities we think men and women can and should possess.

Along with true accounts of Carlos the Jackal, we should recall the truth of Yonatan Netanyahu, the young philosophy student who died at Entebbe. Every community, even Sodom and Gomorrah, has one individual in it who might be identified to students as worth admiring. This could be done even as students are taught to engage in the now honored practice of suspecting the motives of everyone else. I think the time taken for this exercise will be worth it. And it's possible that if we don't take the time, our children, taught as they have been to doubt, will live the consequences of not knowing what they may safely believe.

I

Man in War

Spanning twenty-seven years, the Peloponnesian War between Athens and Sparta in ancient Greece forever transformed the landscape of the ancient world. Considered one of the world's first great wars, the Athenians and Spartans fought a bloody and horrific war for freedom. After the first series of battles and amid great sorrow and loss, the Athenian leader Pericles faced his fellow countrymen and delivered his famous funeral oration to memorialize and immortalize the Athenian lives lost.

Of his fallen comrades, said the great Pericles: "For heroes have the whole earth for their tomb; and in lands far from their own, where the column with its epitaph declares it, there is enshrined in every breast a record unwritten with no tablet to preserve it, except that of the heart. These take as your model and, judging happiness to be the fruit of freedom and freedom of valor, never decline the dangers of war."

Pericles' eulogy immortalized the virtuous ideals of war—the idea of sacrificing one's self for liberty, happiness, and state. Pericles understood that he was asking the men of Athens to leave their homes and families behind to die a painful death on the battlefield. He assured them that their death was not in vain. Because of their stoicism and sacrifice, their progeny would live to enjoy the precious right of liberty.

The history of man is rife with war of all kinds, but Pericles' message remains timeless. The actors and plots might change, from the ancient barbaric crusades of Genghis Khan to today's high-tech, super-trained military operations; but *men* still fight wars. At its core, war has, and always will be, a horrific act of violence between fellow men. The Greek philosopher Plato famously noted, "It is only the dead who have seen the end of war." By definition, war is one of man's most dangerous acts. To engage in war is to risk everything, including your life.

This is why history has long wrestled with the concept of war. What is *casus belli*? What is a just war? From Aristotle to Aquinas, civilized man has sought to define war as a means of preventing it. Yet, where laws and morals fail, war becomes the answer. It is the last resort for men to solve disputes and settle differences. In essence, war captures the best and worst traits of mankind.

As for the latter, war unleashes the worst violence man is capable of. Living through the American Revolution, Thomas Jefferson admitted, "I have seen enough of one war never to wish to see another." Even if you haven't experienced war firsthand, you can understand the loss, the chaos, and the pain that emanate from broken families, blackened landscapes, and shattered psyches. Behind every war are men using their God-given intellects to plot and scheme the death and torture of other men. What started with hand-to-hand combat developed to spears to swords to bullets to bombs. As cruel as it sounds, war breeds its own culture of war. It should come as no shock that there has never been an extended period of world peace in human history.

With the worst of war, however, also comes the best of men. Often the darkest of moments and the worst of times bring out the finest in men. We will forever remember George Washington crossing the ice-capped Delaware River, the brave men storming the death-trap beaches of Normandy, and the tired, bloodied soldiers raising the flag over Iwo Jima. War provokes the highest virtues of man's soul: honor, fortitude, service, and sacrifice. It is no wonder that the greatest moments of manhood are often found in battle.

What is it about combat that would make a young man leave his home and family to risk death for a cause that is not entirely his own? What is war that a man would fall on an enemy grenade to save his comrades? Simply put, war restores in man the belief that there are some things worth fighting and dying for; things like love, liberty, and faith. Furthermore, it instills in men a notion of priorities (what Augustine called the *ordo amorum*, the order of the loves) and responsibility for the protection of the individual, the family, and the polis. Famous World War II general George S. Patton said, "Battle is the most magnificent competition in which a human being can indulge. It brings out all that is best; it removes all that is base ... duty is the essence of manhood."

The fight between life and death has a way of turning boys into men and transforming mobs of untrained civilians into intelligent, coordinated military units. About the nature of war, H. G. Wells said, "One lives in a higher order of being." Philosopher William James taught that combat revived the "martial values" in men and forced on them "intrepidity, contempt of softness, surrender of private interest, obedience to command." There may be no better trial by fire for a man's character than to subject himself to the rigors and abuses of war.

As iron sharpens iron, so also does war whet the rough edges of a man's soul. British minister Sydney Smith, quoted often by Teddy Roosevelt, recognized that "there are seasons in human affairs when qualities, fit enough to conduct the common business of life, are feeble and useless . . . [when] God calls all the passions out in their keenness and vigor for the present safety of mankind . . . all the secret strength, all the invisible array of the feelings—all that nature has reserved for the great scenes of the world when the usual hopes and aids of man are gone." When laws and morals fail, the strength and fortitude of human passions become nature's protector.

The test of war's virtue can be seen in its fruits—men like George Washington, Teddy Roosevelt, Robert E. Lee, Ulysses S. Grant, and countless others. These great men surrendered their own volitions to a higher cause, whether family, faith, or state. They did not fear death because they recognized the honor in serving and protecting a cause above their own. "It is sweet and fitting to die for one's country," said the ancient Roman poet Horace.

Having said that, today's modern man remains mostly immune to war or combat. A vast majority of our generation's young men will never don a military uniform or take orders from a military commander. Let us never take war lightly, however, or take our military protection for granted. John Stuart Mill, the British philosopher, said, "War is an ugly thing, but not the ugliest of things. The decayed and degraded state of moral and patriotic feeling which thinks that nothing is worth war is much worse. A man who has nothing for which he is willing to fight, nothing which is more important than his own personal safety, is a miserable creature and has no chance of being free unless made and kept so by the exertions of better men than himself."

Some of the worst atrocities committed by mankind were done in the name of war. When entrusted in the wrong hands, the power of war has been the instrument of death for the world's worst men. But, remember, when civility, diplomacy, and the rule of law fail, it is only through war that good conquers evil and freedom crushes tyranny. As Oliver Wendell Holmes Jr. told Harvard students in 1895, "War, when you are at it, is horrible and dull. It is only when time has passed that you see that its message was divine." Learn from men at war, pray for peace, but always be ready to fight.

Profile: Donovan Campbell

Donovan Campbell has always pursued excellence. After he graduated with honors from Princeton University, he finished first in his class in the Marines' basic officer course and later went on to graduate from Harvard Business School. Campbell served two combat deployments in Iraq and another in Afghanistan. He spent a little more than six months in Ramadi, Iraq, at the height of the violence, from March to September 2004. For his outstanding service in that war-torn city he was awarded the Combat Action Ribbon and a Bronze Star with Valor. His book, *Joker One*, is an account of his tour in Ramadi. Here, from an interview on my radio show, Campbell describes what he learned about leadership, sacrifice, heroism, and courage in his tenure there, embodying to the fullest what the U.S. Marine Corps stands for.

N o person was ever honored for what he received," wrote Calvin Coolidge. "Honor has been the reward for what he gave."

For Donovan Campbell, a captain in the U.S. Marine Corps who served in Ramadi during some of the most vicious fighting of Operation Iraqi Freedom, giving wasn't on his mind when he first enrolled in the Marine Officer Candidates School after his junior year at Princeton University. In fact, he was mostly focused on taking.

"I need to do something to get serious about my job and career after Princeton," Campbell recalls thinking, "but I wasn't ready to do a desk job. My mind-set at the time was, 'what will differentiate me from the other middle-of-the-rank students?'"

To Campbell, the Marines seemed like an ideal situation. He would use the honor and character building of military service as a springboard to worldly success.

"So I decided to enroll in Marine Officer Candidates School—that will show toughness—that will show that I'm dedicated, I have perseverance, and [it] will really stand out on a résumé. But I didn't get it at the time—it was mainly about me."

What Campbell did get was a rude awakening.

"Unsurprisingly, after ten weeks of being screamed at, bored, having my head shaved, and being terrified sometimes, I decided there was no way I would be a Marine. And I went back to senior year thinking, 'Fortunately I've crossed that one off the list—what else is there?'

"But as the year went on, the more I thought seriously about who I wanted to become. I'm a Christian and I had starting taking my faith more seriously—I knew my faith called me to do more than serve myself. It called me to put my words into action by serving others. I wanted something that would grow me up and allow me to give back."

So Campbell made the decision to join the Marines.

"If I join the Corps I can serve, I can give back. When I say I'm a Christian, people will know it means something to me because I'm sacrificing at least four years of my life. I knew I was young, I knew I wanted to learn to lead and I didn't see any way to do it [other] than to lead. I didn't want to spend fourteen hours per day in a cubicle behind a computer. I also knew I could have a little a bit of an adventure. So I accepted the commission I had earned the previous summer and became an officer in the Marine Corps the day I graduated."

Flash forward to the city of Ramadi, Iraq, 2004. One morning every minaret from every mosque in the city started yelling "Jihad! Jihad! Jihad!" Pause. "Jihad! Jihad! Jihad!" That day, violence exploded all across Ramadi. Campbell's unit ended up with sixteen Marines killed in action and dozens wounded. In the course of the day's events, three squads were separated from each other and were taking heavy casualties during house-to-house fighting. Shortly after the fighting started, Campbell, who had just fallen asleep after a thirty-six-hour extended night patrol with his platoon, was awakened by a young Marine informing him of the situation: "You need to go rescue them!" So Campbell, sleeping with his boots still on, rolled out of bed, marshaled his men, and headed straight for the gunfire. For Campbell, it was one of his greatest tests of leadership in the midst of battle.

"When you're in that situation as a young leader, all you can think is *Where are my guys? Where are the bad guys?* It's so chaotic and confusing. All you can do is try to figure out where the fighting is coming from and where all your people are.

"I don't think you're ever in control of the situation, you just do your best to manage the chaos to [the] best of your ability, keep your men safe, and achieve your mission. But keeping your men safe isn't the only objective, although you hope and pray you can do that. Otherwise why would you leave the states?"

For Campbell, the difficulty of keeping his men safe was exacerbated by the nature of urban warfare. One of the most important aspects of the mission was to limit civilian casualties, an extremely difficult task given the high population density of the city. This meant limiting the weaponry that could be used against the enemy—a decision that placed his troops in danger but was a necessary component of the mission.

"We had to do the best we could to protect civilians, in addition to finding those who wanted to kill us on a daily basis, so we voluntarily limited some of the tools we could use. We never fired artillery in the city, rarely used tanks; we didn't bring to bear the heaviest weapons we could in order that we wouldn't kill people indiscriminately. So we generally fought house to house with only what we can carry on our backs."

Complicating the issue was the ever-present uncertainty of who were friends and who were enemies. Often it took restraint to hold fire.

"It doesn't matter whether you think people love you or are against you. What matters is what you have to do. You cannot shoot indiscriminately. We made the choice as young leaders to risk our own lives and our men's lives more often than not, and it was very hard to err on the side of not shooting. Often the decision to not shoot is far harder than to shoot."

But not every lesson in leadership happened amid hellacious fighting. Captain Campbell learned quickly that the smallest things make the biggest difference.

"Originally, my thinking as a leader was, *I need to make big decisions well, show heroism in combat, give the occasional great speech.* But I didn't realize that my men watched everything. It didn't matter what I did with larger decisions if I wasn't consistent in smaller ones."

Before shipping out to Ramadi, Campbell and his men were stationed in Kuwait on a base that had very rudimentary facilities. Marines couldn't call home very often. There were two phones, but their use was restricted—one for Marines, one for emergencies. Eventually, officers began taking liberties with the emergency phone.

"Officers were calling home every two or three days, but my guys could only call every two to three weeks. One day one of my Marines, one of the best Marines I've ever met, pulled me aside . . . and said, 'We notice that you use the cell phone a lot and we don't use it as often.' I felt about six inches tall at that point."

———

The U.S. Marines are known the world over for their lethal capabilities in warfare. But some of Campbell's proudest moments revolve around witnessing his men's acts of mercy, at their mortal expense.

One day while on patrol, a rocket from a group of insurgents had missed its target—Campbell's platoon—and hit directly in the middle of a group of children. The carnage of so many children slaughtered was ghastly, "A macabre tableaux from hell," as Campbell described it. In spite of the attendant danger, the first reaction of the platoon was to rush to the children's aid. The unit's doctors started working feverishly to help the wounded, not even bothering to put on latex gloves. The instinct of the Marines to help the wounded, even at great harm to themselves, was in full view that day.

"My guys were phenomenal—I love them so much. There's a moment of decision when something like that happens. We could have shut all the doors and driven away, knowing that it would have gotten us out of the line of fire and preserved us all, or [we could] jump out of the Humvee, run toward the fire, and help those who need help. And we just jumped out of Humvees and started tending the wounded. I took part of the platoon and pursued part of those who attacked us but we couldn't get them.

"When I came back I faced another decision: Do we stay and wait for Iraqis to come with [an] ambulance for the children, or do we leave? If we stayed we would be there for a while and we would get attacked again. Ten minutes in the same place you will get attacked. But I made the decision to stay there and help them."

Then, Campbell, in a decision questioned by many military officers, directed his men to stay despite the risk.

(At this point, Campbell couldn't hold back the tears.)

"That's what the U.S. Marines do.

"We're not in this just to protect ourselves. I lost a man as a result of that, but I think it was the right call."

Human beings have always shown an ability to form unbreakable bonds in the midst of the most desperate circumstances. Suffering produces camaraderie. One of the most distinguishing features of Campbell's time in Iraq was the concern that his men showed for him and for one another—"I was one man trying to take care of forty, but I had forty trying to take care of me."

After leading a unit through so much chaos and bloodshed in only a few months, Campbell, who by his own estimation was clinically depressed through much of his tour in Ramadi, experienced a crisis of faith.

"You keep asking yourself why and don't get any good answers. Eventually I questioned if there is a God and why he allows such evil to exist. My faith took a beating, but I had an immature faith. I was too often in it to see what God could give to me, not what I could give to God."

In the end, the few and the proud proved themselves to be just that. After months of killing and misery, those bonds that had been forged between Marines in the most terrible of circumstances proved more meaningful, more real, than the horrors that Campbell experienced.

"Part of what brought me back was seeing my men's love for each other, how such a beautiful thing could exist even in such a horrifying context. There is good and beauty even in the worst places. I am more humble now, and I don't think I will ever understand a magnificent and transcendent God."

Semper Fi.

Always Faithful.

"Saint Crispin's Day Speech"

WILLIAM SHAKESPEARE

Although Shakespeare wrote this almost two hundred years after the Battle of Agincourt (1415), it remains one of the finest fictional interpretations of what manhood looks like in war. During the Battle of Agincourt between the English and French, morale in the English line was dangerously low as they stared at an overwhelming force of heavily armored, highly skilled French knights. King Henry V, rising to the occasion, reminded his men of the honor and glory in their cause. His speech—including the very famous line, "We few, we happy few, we band of brothers"—rallied the English troops and carried them to victory. As a result, the French princess Catherine married Henry V, and France and England were at peace for the remainder of Henry's short life.

Westmoreland. *O that we now had here*
But one ten thousand of those men in England
That do no work to-day!

King. *What's he that wishes so?*
My cousin Westmoreland? No, my fair cousin;
If we are mark'd to die, we are enow
To do our country loss; and if to live,
The fewer men, the greater share of honour.
God's will! I pray thee, wish not one man more.
By Jove, I am not covetous for gold,
Nor care I who doth feed upon my cost;
It yearns me not if men my garments wear;
Such outward things dwell not in my desires.
But if it be a sin to covet honour,
I am the most offending soul alive.
No, faith, my coz, wish not a man from England.
God's peace! I would not lose so great an honour
As one man more methinks would share from me
For the best hope I have. O, do not wish one more!
Rather proclaim it, Westmoreland, through my host,
That he which hath no stomach to this fight,
Let him depart; his passport shall be made,

And crowns for convoy put into his purse;
We would not die in that man's company
That fears his fellowship to die with us.
This day is call'd the feast of Crispian.
He that outlives this day, and comes safe home,
Will stand a tip-toe when this day is nam'd,
And rouse him at the name of Crispian.
He that shall live this day, and see old age,
Will yearly on the vigil feast his neighbours,
And say "To-morrow is Saint Crispian."
Then will he strip his sleeve and show his scars,
And say "These wounds I had on Crispian's day."
Old men forget; yet all shall be forgot,
But he'll remember, with advantages,
What feats he did that day. Then shall our names,
Familiar in his mouth as household words—
Harry the King, Bedford and Exeter,
Warwick and Talbot, Salisbury and Gloucester—
Be in their flowing cups freshly rememb'red.
This story shall the good man teach his son;
And Crispin Crispian shall ne'er go by,
From this day to the ending of the world,
But we in it shall be remembered—
We few, we happy few, we band of brothers;
For he to-day that sheds his blood with me
Shall be my brother; be he ne'er so vile,
This day shall gentle his condition;
And gentlemen in England now-a-bed
Shall think themselves accurs'd they were not here,
And hold their manhoods cheap whiles any speaks
That fought with us upon Saint Crispin's day.

——— ❧ ———

Response to the Archbishop of Canterbury

COLIN POWELL

During an address to the World Economic Forum in Davos, Switzerland, on January 26, 2003, Secretary of State Colin Powell defended the U.S. government's use of military force against Saddam Hussein. Without direct military intervention, the complete disarmament of Iraq would not be possible, argued Powell. In a question-and-answer period after the speech, former Archbishop of Canterbury George Carey challenged Powell if he felt the United States and its coalition had given enough thought to the use of "soft power"—nonmilitary and diplomatic force as a means of disarming Saddam Hussein—instead of what seemed to him to be the preferred American way: the use of "hard power"—military force. Here is Powell's response.

There is nothing in American experience or in American political life or in our culture that suggests we want to use hard power. But what we have found over the decades is that unless you do have hard power—and here I think you're referring to military power—then sometimes you are faced with situations that you can't deal with.

I mean, it was not soft power that freed Europe. It was hard power. And what followed immediately after hard power? Did the United States ask for dominion over a single nation in Europe? No. Soft power came in the Marshall Plan. Soft power came with American GIs who put their weapons down once the war was over and helped all those nations rebuild. We did the same thing in Japan.

So our record of living our values and letting our values be an inspiration to others I think is clear. And I don't think I have anything to be ashamed of or apologize for with respect to what America has done for the world.

We have gone forth from our shores repeatedly over the last hundred years and we've done this as recently as the last year in Afghanistan and put wonderful young men and women at risk, many of whom have lost their lives, and we have asked for nothing except enough ground to bury them in, and otherwise we have returned home to seek our own, you know, to seek our own lives in peace, to live our own lives in peace. But there comes a time when soft power or talking with evil will not work where, unfortunately, hard power is the only thing that works.

"Character of the Happy Warrior"

WILLIAM WORDSWORTH

William Wordsworth (1770–1850) was an English poet who helped usher in the Romantic movement, publishing some of the era's finest verses, none more striking than those contained in the work he coauthored with Samuel Coleridge entitled *Lyrical Ballads*. In this simple poem, Wordsworth illustrates the characteristics that embody a fighting man: virtue, honor, and a big heart.

Who is the happy Warrior? Who is he
That every man in arms should wish to be?
—It is the generous Spirit, who, when brought
Among the tasks of real life, hath wrought
Upon the plan that pleased his boyish thought:
Whose high endeavours are an inward light
That makes the path before him always bright:
Who, with a natural instinct to discern
What knowledge can perform, is diligent to learn;
Abides by this resolve, and stops not there,
But makes his moral being his prime care;
Who, doomed to go in company with Pain,
And Fear, and Bloodshed, miserable train!
Turns his necessity to glorious gain;
In face of these doth exercise a power
Which is our human nature's highest dower;

Controls them and subdues, transmutes, bereaves
Of their bad influence, and their good receives:
By objects, which might force the soul to abate
Her feeling, rendered more compassionate;
Is placable—because occasions rise
So often that demand such sacrifice;
More skilful in self-knowledge, even more pure,
As tempted more; more able to endure,
As more exposed to suffering and distress;
Thence, also, more alive to tenderness.
—'Tis he whose law is reason; who depends
Upon that law as on the best of friends;
Whence, in a state where men are tempted still
To evil for a guard against worse ill,
And what in quality or act is best
Doth seldom on a right foundation rest,
He labours good on good to fix, and owes
To virtue every triumph that he knows:
—Who, if he rise to station of command,
Rises by open means; and there will stand
On honourable terms, or else retire,
And in himself possess his own desire;
Who comprehends his trust, and to the same
Keeps faithful with a singleness of aim;
And therefore does not stoop, nor lie in wait
For wealth, or honours, or for worldly state;
Whom they must follow; on whose head must fall,
Like showers of manna, if they come at all:
Whose powers shed round him in the common strife,
Or mild concerns of ordinary life,
A constant influence, a peculiar grace;
But who, if he be called upon to face
Some awful moment to which Heaven has joined

Great issues, good or bad for human kind,
Is happy as a Lover; and attired
With sudden brightness, like a Man inspired;
And, through the heat of conflict, keeps the law
In calmness made, and sees what he foresaw;
Or if an unexpected call succeed,
Come when it will, is equal to the need:
—He who, though thus endued as with a sense
And faculty for storm and turbulence,
Is yet a Soul whose master-bias leans
To homefelt pleasures and to gentle scenes;
Sweet images! which, wheresoe'er he be,
Are at his heart; and such fidelity
It is his darling passion to approve;
More brave for this, that he hath much to love:—
'Tis, finally, the Man, who, lifted high,
Conspicuous object in a Nation's eye,
Or left unthought-of in obscurity,—
Who, with a toward or untoward lot,
Prosperous or adverse, to his wish or not—
Plays, in the many games of life, that one
Where what he most doth value must be won:
Whom neither shape of danger can dismay,
Nor thought of tender happiness betray;
Who, not content that former worth stand fast,
Looks forward, persevering to the last,
From well to better, daily self-surpast:
Who, whether praise of him must walk the earth
For ever, and to noble deeds give birth,
Or he must fall, to sleep without his fame,
And leave a dead unprofitable name—
Finds comfort in himself and in his cause;
And, while the mortal mist is gathering, draws

His breath in confidence of Heaven's applause:
This is the happy Warrior; this is He
That every Man in arms should wish to be.

"The Campaigns of Alexander the Great"

ALEXANDER THE GREAT, TOLD BY ARRIAN, THE ROMAN HISTORIAN

In 324 BC, after returning from a campaign in Persia, Alexander the Great led a troop of war-weary men who were anxious to get home. Though his plans of conquest were far from complete, Alexander decided to allow disabled veteran soldiers to return to their families in Macedonia. The rest of his able-bodied men were, understandably, disgruntled and dissatisfied with their fate. To both chastise and encourage his men, Alexander told them of his own sacrifice and perseverance throughout the campaign. This evident dedication, passion, and devotion to the cause made Alexander one of the most esteemed military rulers in history.

My countrymen, you are sick for home—so be it! I shall make no attempt to check your longing to return. Go whither you will; I shall not hinder you. But, if go you must, there is one thing I would have you understand—what I have done for you, and in what coin you have repaid me . . .

Perhaps you will say that, in my position as your commander, I had none of the labors and distress which you had to endure to win for me what I have won. But does any man among you honestly feel that he has suffered more for me than I have suffered for him? Come now—if you are wounded, strip and show your wounds, and I will show mine. There is no part of my body but my back which has not a scar; not a weapon a man may grasp or fling the mark of which I do not carry upon me. I have sword-cuts from close fight; arrows have pierced me, missiles from catapults bruised my flesh; again and again I have been struck by stones or clubs—and all for your sakes; for your glory and your gain. Over every land and sea, across river, mountain, and plain, I led you to the world's end, a victorious army. I married as you married, and many of you will have children related by blood to my own. Some of you have owed money—I have paid your debts, never troubling to inquire how they were incurred, and in spite of the fact that you earn good pay and grow rich from the sack of cities. To most of you I have given a circlet of gold as a memorial for ever and ever of your courage and of my regard. And what of those who have died in battle? Their death was noble, their burial illustrious; almost all are commemorated at home by statues of bronze; their parents are held in honor, with all dues of money and service remitted, for under my leadership not a man among you has ever fallen with his back to the enemy.

Profile: Joshua Marcellino

War should not be taken lightly. Despite what we read in books and see in movies, war is a horrible act. The men who go to war do not return the same. The story of Joshua Marcellino illustrates the effect war has on a man's psyche. As the adage goes, that which doesn't kill you, only makes you stronger. I came across Joshua and his story through my radio show, *Morning in America*.

Before Joshua Marcellino became a corporal in the U.S. Marine Corps and lost his innocence, he was the oldest of six children—brother to Elyse, Cassie, Jeremiah, Johnson, and Josiah—and son to Jerry and Dawn.

His father was from Los Angeles, California, played football at the University of Hawaii, "got saved," and became a Reformed Baptist pastor. His mother came from a Louisiana farm, had a classically trained voice, and held sway over the home with a spark of French-Cajun elegance.

Jerry led a church in Laurel, Mississippi—a town with tall pine trees, hot summers, and more than a few quiet roads. Dawn sang on Sundays and enrolled the children in the private Christian school.

Joshua could grow a beard while his classmates were teasing out fuzz—blame his Italian heritage—made decent grades in school, and while he was never the tallest on the court or the fastest on the field, Joshua never stopped competing. He wielded a foil, a saber, and an épée at a young age, fencing his way to the Junior Olympics.

Boys playing soldier runs deep in the American psyche—but Joshua seemed to live for a higher struggle. Camouflage, flight simulators, and civil war strategy games—Joshua ate and drank warfare. Put the VHS copy of *The Battle of Midway*—filmed on the ground in shaky black and white—on repeat; Joshua couldn't get enough of the Stars and Stripes.

September 11 happened when Joshua was in high school, cementing the future that people could see coming, and a boy playing with guns turned quickly into a man shipping off to Parris Island, pushed to the cracking point by screaming drill instructors.

"You have to want it, this life, and you better want it bad," said Joshua, "because they're going to do everything they can to break you."

And then there was war. Joshua deployed in February 2007. Members of the church made T-shirts with "We're praying for you" and his Marine Corps picture, put his name in the bulletin each week, and kept writing him in Iraq.

But that's the person Joshua was—before he hit the ground in Iraq.

Corporal Joshua Marcellino served in Lima Company, 3rd Battalion, 23rd Marines, 4th Marine Division—in the town of Haditha in Anbar Province. There were eight hundred to nine hundred missions in nine months. Days that he was on detail, it was up at 5:30 in the morning, stay up till 11:00 at night. There were sweeps for bombs—IEDs—detaining suspects, and the pressure that at every moment, the person watching you on patrol might make the phone call that would result in your death.

"No one wears any uniforms. They watch you for it every single day, and when they go into town, they tell their buddy. If you looked like you weren't paying attention, they would pass that on . . . If you went the same way, turned in the same spot, even more than once, there'd be a bomb next time and you'd be killed."

And then there was the time in between.

"War isn't what I thought it would be. It was boring. There was so much of the hurry up and wait. You'd go do a mission, and your blood would be pumping. Then there'd be a month and a half before anything else happened . . . Marines are a different breed; we're made to go after people. If you're not killing someone or being killed, you're not happy."

War makes a man different. The change comes in different ways. There can be the things one is forced to do, one is forced to see—the strain of fighting an enemy without uniform or respect for human life—and change can come looking in the faces and at the bodies of the least of the members of humanity.

"Innocence gets killed in war. No matter how much you try to keep it, it just dies," Joshua said, then paused. "There were so many kids getting killed."

From the time of his youth, Joshua heard and believed in a faith that made much of kids. Christ told the little ones to come unto him. Joshua's own church saw children as a blessing and was brimming with squealing toddlers, grubby-faced youngsters playing games of tackle football outside, and families that needed fifteen-passenger vans.

But on this continent, things were different, and the images burned into Joshua's mind.

"You'd be in combat, and you'd see a kid get hurt, or you'd find one on the ground. You'd want to run up, check on the kids, and make sure they're okay. You wanted to try and help them, but they would set bombs in kids' bodies, in the dead ones . . .

"You'd have a guy run up with his kid, blood shooting everywhere out of the kid's body, asking for help, so you'd say, yeah, let's take him to the hospital, and then he'd run past you, and explode himself.

"There was this one time, they took this child—mentally retarded—and they filled his wheelchair with bombs on it, and then they told him to go toward the Marines . . . And then you have to try and decide what to do."

Those images don't leave his mind when a serviceman returns home.

"You put your whole life and effort into helping these people, try to give them something better; you watch people die, and then you leave."

No one moment defines that shift, that loss of innocence in Joshua. In many ways, he's still the same person who left Laurel in 2007. He still is a Christian. He says that the struggle in Iraq was as much spiritual as physical: "Each day you realized God is in control of every second, and if it's my last day—oh well. In civilian life, you don't see prayer answered every day, but when you're in combat you see prayer answered."

He helped in the handover of power to the Iraqi people, watched as the Anbar Province woke out of the depths of lawlessness and defeat and was transformed into a jewel of order and stability.

But like so many of the veterans coming home from wars in the last few years, Joshua returned changed. In some it comes in violent fits, sleeplessness, and other neurological disorders, but in Joshua, the lurking effects of combat stress came in what he calls "a fog," one that made living and interacting on a college campus anything but easy.

"The hardest thing was putting up with civilians . . . I was in a fog for almost two years before I became myself again. I didn't want to talk to people; I just wasn't the same. People would try to talk to you about it, and they'd want to understand, but they couldn't understand—they hadn't been through that. They didn't know what it was like, and it would just make me mad."

Joshua found some rest in working with his hands on his grandfather's farm in Louisiana.

Now, when he's on campus or at a soccer game and sees the American flag flying it brings back somber and bitter memories.

"I really love my flag, but it's different. I just know that when it looks like the world is going to collapse, if you go anywhere else, you're going to think that America is the greatest thing on earth."

For Joshua, warfare was different from the films and stories. There wasn't this "band of brothers" mentality that had defined previous generations of servicemen; rather it was an immediate, day-to-day, hour-by-hour struggle for survival.

"All you knew [was that] if I survived this day, and if my buddy makes it through with me, it's a good thing."

And when that struggle was over and the soldiers came home, well, each one went their separate ways and just didn't talk about what had happened.

"It's different," said Joshua, who won't pursue a career in the military. "Things are different, and freedom, freedom just has a different taste to it."

Joshua Marcellino graduated from Belhaven University in Jackson, Mississippi, in 2011.

"Concord Hymn"

Ralph Waldo Emerson

In this elegant tribute to the citizen-soldiers of the Revolutionary War, Ralph Waldo Emerson (1803–1882) penned the famous phrase "the shot heard round the world." He wrote this poem—sung as a hymn at a July 4, 1837, ceremony to mark the completion of the Concord Monument in Massachusetts—to remember the valiant resistance of American Minutemen to British forces on April 19, 1775.

> *By the rude bridge that arched the flood,*
> *Their flag to April's breeze unfurled,*
> *Here once the embattled farmers stood,*
> *And fired the shot heard round the world.*
> *The foe long since in silence slept;*
> *Alike the conqueror silent sleeps;*
> *And Time the ruined bridge has swept*
> *Down the dark stream which seaward creeps.*
> *On this green bank, by this soft stream,*
> *We set to-day a votive stone;*
> *That memory may their deed redeem,*
> *When, like our sires, our sons are gone.*
> *Spirit, that made those heroes dare*
> *To die, and leave their children free,*
> *Bid Time and Nature gently spare*
> *The shaft we raise to them and thee.*

"This Was Their Finest Hour"

WINSTON CHURCHILL

As Hitler and Mussolini prepared to crash down upon Britain, all eyes looked to the cornerstone of resistance, the stalwart and indefatigable, Winston Churchill. As Churchill addressed the House of Commons on June 18, 1940, Europe was in retreat. Holland, Luxembourg, and Belgium had fallen. The French government had fled Paris, and now Adolf Hitler turned his eyes toward Britain. The coming Nazi storm suffocated the

British people in a vise grip that left many arguing over past mistakes and the future, and even starting to doubt their trademark resolve.

With a slow growl that never rose beyond a gentle roar, Churchill delivered a masterful speech. Rumbling through an exposition of the past, Churchill was an example of magnanimity, looking to the urgency of the present, rather than shifting blame over past mistakes. Possessing a clear, unflinching vision of the present plight, the lighthouse of Britain stood in the creeping night and dared Hitler to extinguish its spirit.

It was a call dyed in the colors of the Union Jack, the moral fabric of that nation, a powerful reminder for Britain to "brace itself for its duty" and a call to rise to a greatness that would echo throughout history.

Now I put all this aside. I put it on the shelf, from which the historians, when they have time, will select their documents to tell their stories. We have to think of the future and not of the past. This also applies in a small way to our own affairs at home. There are many who would hold an inquest in the House of Commons on the conduct of the Governments—and of Parliaments, for they are in it, too—during the years which led up to this catastrophe. They seek to indict those who were responsible for the guidance of our affairs. This also would be a foolish and pernicious process. There are too many in it. Let each man search his conscience and search his speeches. I frequently search mine.

Of this I am quite sure, that if we open a quarrel between the past and the present, we shall find that we have lost the future . . .

. . . There remains, of course, the danger of bombing attacks, which will certainly be made very soon upon us by the bomber forces of the enemy. It is true that the German bomber force is superior in numbers to ours; but we have a very large bomber force also, which we shall use to strike at military targets in Germany without intermission. I do not at all underrate the severity of the ordeal which lies before us; but I believe our countrymen will show themselves capable of standing up to it, like the brave men of Barcelona, and will be able to stand up to it, and carry on in spite of it, at least as well as any other people in the world. Much will depend upon this; every man and every woman will have the chance to show the finest qualities of their race, and render the highest service to their cause. For all of us, at this time, whatever our sphere, our station, our occupation or our duties, it will be a help to remember the famous lines:

"He nothing common did or mean, Upon that memorable scene."

I have thought it right upon this occasion to give the House and the country some indication of the solid, practical grounds upon which we base our inflexible resolve to continue the war. There are a good many people who say, "Never mind. Win or lose, sink or swim, better die than submit to tyranny—and such a tyranny." And I do not dissociate myself from them. But I can assure them that our professional advisers of the three Services unitedly advise that we should carry on the war, and that there are good and reasonable hopes of final victory. We have fully informed and consulted all the self-governing Dominions, these great communities far beyond the oceans who have been built up on our laws and on our civilization, and who are absolutely free to choose their course, but are absolutely devoted to the ancient Motherland, and who feel themselves inspired by the same emotions which lead me to stake our all upon duty and honor. We have fully consulted them, and I have received from their Prime Ministers, Mr. Mackenzie King of Canada, Mr. Menzies of Australia, Mr. Fraser of New Zealand, and General Smuts of South Africa—that wonderful man, with his immense profound mind, and his eye watching from a distance the whole panorama of European affairs—I have received from all these eminent men, who all have Governments behind them elected on wide franchises, who are all there because they represent the will of their people, messages couched in the most moving terms in which they endorse our decision to fight on, and declare themselves ready to share our fortunes and to persevere to the end. That is what we are going to do.

We may now ask ourselves: In what way has our position worsened since the beginning of the war? It has worsened by the fact that the Germans have conquered a large part of the coast line of Western Europe, and many small countries have been overrun by them. This aggravates the possibilities of air attack and adds to our naval preoccupations. It in no way diminishes, but on the contrary definitely increases, the power of our long-distance blockade. Similarly, the entrance of Italy into the war increases the power of our long-distance blockade. We have stopped the worst leak by that. We do not know whether military resistance will come to an end in France or not, but should it do so, then of course the Germans will be able to concentrate their forces, both military and industrial, upon us. But for the reasons I have given to the House these will not be found so easy to apply. If invasion has become more imminent, as no doubt it has, we, being relieved from the task of maintaining a large army in France, have far larger and more efficient forces to meet it.

If Hitler can bring under his despotic control the industries of the countries he has conquered, this will add greatly to his already vast armament output. On the other hand, this will not happen immediately, and we are now assured of immense, continuous and increasing support in supplies and munitions of all kinds from the United States; and especially of aeroplanes and pilots from the Dominions and across the oceans coming from regions which are beyond the reach of enemy bombers.

I do not see how any of these factors can operate to our detriment on balance before the winter comes; and the winter will impose a strain upon the Nazi regime, with almost all Europe writhing and starving under its cruel heel, which, for all their ruthlessness, will run them very hard. We must not forget that from the moment when we declared war on the 3rd September it was always possible for Germany to turn all her Air Force upon this country, together with any other devices of invasion she might conceive, and that France could have done little or nothing to prevent her doing so. We have, therefore, lived under this danger, in principle and in a slightly modified form, during all these months. In the meanwhile, however, we have enormously improved our methods of defense, and we have learned what we had no right to assume at the beginning, namely, that the individual aircraft and the individual British pilot have a sure and definite superiority. Therefore, in casting up this dread balance sheet and contemplating our dangers with a disillusioned eye, I see great reason for intense vigilance and exertion, but none whatever for panic or despair.

During the first four years of the last war the Allies experienced nothing but disaster and disappointment. That was our constant fear: one blow after another, terrible losses, frightful dangers. Everything miscarried. And yet at the end of those four years the morale of the Allies was higher than that of the Germans, who had moved from one aggressive triumph to another, and who stood everywhere triumphant invaders of the lands into which they had broken. During that war we repeatedly asked ourselves the question: "How are we going to win?" And no one was able ever to answer it with much precision, until at the end, quite suddenly, quite unexpectedly, our terrible foe collapsed before us, and we were so glutted with victory that in our folly we threw it away.

We do not yet know what will happen in France or whether the French resistance will be prolonged, both in France and in the French Empire overseas. The French Government will be throwing away great opportunities and casting adrift their future if they do not continue the war in accordance with their treaty obligations, from which we have not felt able to release them. The House will have read the historic declaration in which, at the desire of many Frenchmen—and of our own hearts—we have proclaimed our willingness at the darkest hour in French history to conclude a union of common citizenship in this struggle. However matters may go in France or with the French Government, or other French Governments, we in this Island and in the British Empire will never lose our sense of comradeship with the French people. If we are now called upon to endure what they have been suffering, we shall emulate their courage, and if final victory rewards our toils they shall share the gains, aye, and freedom shall be restored to all. We abate nothing of our just demands; not one jot or tittle do we recede. Czechs, Poles, Norwegians, Dutch, Belgians have joined their causes to our own. All these shall be restored.

What General Weygand called the Battle of France is over. I expect that the Battle of Britain is about to begin. Upon this battle depends the survival of Christian civilization. Upon it depends our own British life, and the long continuity of our institutions and our Empire. The whole fury and might of the enemy must very soon be turned on us.

Hitler knows that he will have to break us in this Island or lose the war. If we can stand up to him, all Europe may be free and the life of the world may move forward into broad, sunlit uplands. But if we fail, then the whole world, including the United States, including all that we have known and cared for, will sink into the abyss of a new Dark Age made more sinister, and perhaps more protracted, by the lights of perverted science.

Let us therefore brace ourselves to our duties, and so bear ourselves that if the British Empire and its Commonwealth last for a thousand years, men will still say, "This was their finest hour."

— ❦ —

David and Goliath

1 Samuel 17:1–58 NKJV

The story of David and Goliath is strikingly different from the epic war stories of ancient myth and legend. Unlike Beowulf or Achilles, David was a humble shepherd who was not trained in warfare and battle. Yet his bravery and courage allowed him to stand for a cause greater than his stature, and face a fearsome giant with confidence.

Now the Philistines gathered their armies together to battle, and were gathered at Sochoh, which belongs to Judah; they encamped between Sochoh and Azekah, in Ephes Dammim. And Saul and the men of Israel were gathered together, and they encamped in the Valley of Elah, and drew up in battle array against the Philistines. The Philistines stood on a mountain on one side, and Israel stood on a mountain on the other side, with a valley between them.

And a champion went out from the camp of the Philistines, named Goliath, from Gath, whose height was six cubits and a span. He had a bronze helmet on his head, and he was armed with a coat of mail, and the weight of the coat was five thousand shekels of bronze. And he had bronze armor on his legs and a bronze javelin between his shoulders. Now the staff of his spear was like a weaver's beam, and his iron spearhead weighed six hundred shekels; and a shield-bearer went before him. Then he stood and cried out to the armies of Israel, and said to them, "Why have you come out to line up for battle? Am I not a Philistine, and you the servants of Saul? Choose a man for yourselves, and let him come down to me. If he is able to fight with me and kill me, then we will be your servants. But if I prevail against him and kill him, then you shall be our servants and serve us." And the Philistine said, "I defy the armies of Israel this day; give me a man, that we may fight together." When Saul and all Israel heard these words of the Philistine, they were dismayed and greatly afraid.

Now David was the son of that Ephrathite of Bethlehem Judah, whose name was Jesse, and who had eight sons. And the man was old, advanced in years, in the days of Saul. The three oldest sons of Jesse had gone to follow Saul to the battle. The names of his three sons who went to the battle were Eliab the firstborn, next to him Abinadab, and the third Shammah. David was the youngest. And the three oldest followed Saul. But David occasionally went and returned from Saul to feed his father's sheep at Bethlehem.

And the Philistine drew near and presented himself forty days, morning and evening.

Then Jesse said to his son David, "Take now for your brothers an ephah of this dried grain and these ten loaves, and run to your brothers at the camp. And carry these ten cheeses to the captain of their thousand, and see how your brothers fare, and bring back news of them." Now Saul and they and all the men of Israel were in the Valley of Elah, fighting with the Philistines.

So David rose early in the morning, left the sheep with a keeper, and took the things and went as Jesse had commanded him. And he came to the camp as the army was going out to the fight and shouting for the battle. For Israel and the Philistines had drawn up in battle array, army against army. And David left his supplies in the hand of the supply keeper, ran to the army, and came and greeted his brothers. Then as he talked with them, there was the champion, the Philistine of Gath, Goliath by name, coming up from the armies of the Philistines; and he spoke according to the same words. So David heard them. And all the men of Israel, when they saw the man, fled from him and were dreadfully afraid. So the men of Israel said, "Have you seen this man who has come up? Surely he has come up to defy Israel; and it shall be that the man who kills him the king will enrich with great riches, will give him his daughter, and give his father's house exemption from taxes in Israel."

Then David spoke to the men who stood by him, saying, "What shall be done for the man who kills this Philistine and takes away the reproach from Israel? For who is this uncircumcised Philistine, that he should defy the armies of the living God?"

And the people answered him in this manner, saying, "So shall it be done for the man who kills him."

Now Eliab his oldest brother heard when he spoke to the men; and Eliab's anger was aroused against David, and he said, "Why did you come down here? And with whom have you left those few sheep in the wilderness? I know your pride and the insolence of your heart, for you have come down to see the battle."

And David said, "What have I done now? Is there not a cause?" Then he turned from him toward another and said the same thing; and these people answered him as the first ones did.

Now when the words which David spoke were heard, they reported them to Saul; and he sent for him. Then David said to Saul, "Let no man's heart fail because of him; your servant will go and fight with this Philistine."

And Saul said to David, "You are not able to go against this Philistine to fight with him; for you are a youth, and he a man of war from his youth."

But David said to Saul, "Your servant used to keep his father's sheep, and when a lion or a bear came and took a lamb out of the flock, I went out after it and struck it, and delivered the lamb from its mouth; and when it arose against me, I caught it by its beard, and struck and killed it. Your servant has killed both lion and bear; and this uncircumcised Philistine will be like one of them, seeing he has defied the armies of the living God." Moreover David said, "The LORD, who delivered me from the paw of the lion and from the paw of the bear, He will deliver me from the hand of this Philistine."

And Saul said to David, "Go, and the Lord be with you!"

So Saul clothed David with his armor, and he put a bronze helmet on his head; he also clothed him with a coat of mail. David fastened his sword to his armor and tried to walk, for he had not tested them. And David said to Saul, "I cannot walk with these, for I have not tested them." So David took them off.

Then he took his staff in his hand; and he chose for himself five smooth stones from the brook, and put them in a shepherd's bag, in a pouch which he had, and his sling was in his hand. And he drew near to the Philistine. So the Philistine came, and began drawing near to David, and the man who bore the shield went before him. And when the Philistine looked about and saw David, he disdained him; for he was only a youth, ruddy and good-looking. So the Philistine said to David, "Am I a dog, that you come to me with sticks?" And the Philistine cursed David by his gods. And the Philistine said to David, "Come to me, and I will give your flesh to the birds of the air and the beasts of the field!"

Then David said to the Philistine, "You come to me with a sword, with a spear, and with a javelin. But I come to you in the name of the LORD of hosts, the God of the armies of Israel, whom you have defied. This day the LORD will deliver you into my hand, and I will strike you and take your head from you. And this day I will give the carcasses of the camp of the Philistines to the birds of the air and the wild beasts of the earth, that all the earth may know that there is a God in Israel. Then all this assembly shall know that the LORD does not save with sword and spear; for the battle is the LORD's, and He will give you into our hands."

So it was, when the Philistine arose and came and drew near to meet David, that David hurried and ran toward the army to meet the Philistine. Then David put his hand in his bag and took out a stone; and he slung it and struck the Philistine in his forehead, so that the stone sank into his forehead, and he fell on his face to the earth. So David prevailed over the Philistine with a sling and a stone, and struck the Philistine and killed him. But there was no sword in the hand of David. Therefore David ran and stood over the Philistine, took his sword and drew it out of its sheath and killed him, and cut off his head with it.

And when the Philistines saw that their champion was dead, they fled. Now the men of Israel and Judah arose and shouted, and pursued the Philistines as far as the entrance of the valley and to the gates of Ekron. And the wounded of the Philistines fell along the road to Shaaraim, even as far as Gath and Ekron. Then the children of Israel returned from chasing the Philistines, and they plundered their tents. And David took the head of the Philistine and brought it to Jerusalem, but he put his armor in his tent.

When Saul saw David going out against the Philistine, he said to Abner, the commander of the army, "Abner, whose son is this youth?"

And Abner said, "As your soul lives, O king, I do not know."

So the king said, "Inquire whose son this young man is."

Then, as David returned from the slaughter of the Philistine, Abner took him and brought him before Saul with the head of the Philistine in his hand. And Saul said to him, "Whose son are you, young man?"

So David answered, "I am the son of your servant Jesse the Bethlehemite."

Profile: Rick Rescorla

On September 11, 2001, extremist Islamic terrorists murdered nearly three thousand innocent people in the worst terror attack on American soil in history. It changed the lives of Americans forever and the grief of the nation seemed unbearable. But out of the ashes of destruction came stories of real American heroes: men and women who triumphed over evil even in the darkest hour. One of those men was Rick Rescorla. He treated everyone with love—his wife, his children, and the total strangers he saved on September 11. His story, as told here through the lens of his widow, Susan Rescorla, is one that the world should never forget.

At 8:46 a.m. on September 11, 2001, American Airlines Flight 11 struck World Trade Center Tower 1. Across the street at Tower 2, more than twenty-seven hundred employees of Morgan Stanley were told by building officials to stay calm and remain in the building. Rick Rescorla was in charge of security at Morgan Stanley and ignored the official warning. Rick began the evacuation of all Morgan Stanley employees in Tower 2 and one thousand employees in Tower 5.

Panic spread quickly as workers saw smoke pouring out of Tower 1. Rescorla urged them to remain calm and began singing "God Bless America" and Cornish military songs over his bullhorn:

> *Men of Cornwall stop your dreaming;*
> *Can't you see their spearpoints gleaming?*
> *See their warriors' pennants streaming*
> *To this battlefield.*
> *Men of Cornwall stand ye steady;*
> *It cannot be ever said ye*
> *for the battle were not ready;*
> *Stand and never yield!*

He told them to "be proud to be an American . . . everyone will be talking about you tomorrow."

At 9:03 a.m., United Airlines Flight 175 struck Tower 2. Rescorla had rescued almost all of Morgan Stanley's employees, but there were still others in the building. As other workers warned Rescorla that he had to evacuate now, he calmly replied, "As soon as I make sure everyone else is out." Rescorla was last seen on the tenth floor of Tower 2 heading up the stairs to rescue more employees.

Because of his response, all but six of Morgan Stanley's twenty-seven hundred World Trade Center employees survived the September 11 attacks. Four of those six were Rescorla and three deputies who followed him back into the building—Wesley Mercer, Jorge Velazquez, and Godwin Forde.

To those who knew Cyril Richard Rescorla, it was as if his entire life had prepared him for these few precious minutes. "He lived by a code. He had his own philosophy and he used to say to me, 'You declare what you're about when you're young and you try to stay on that road so that at the end of your life you knew you did the very best you could,'" said his widow, Susan.

Born in Hayle, Cornwall, Britain, in 1939, Rescorla grew up in the headquarters of the 175th Infantry Regiment of the U.S. 29th Infantry Division. As a child, Rescorla admired the U.S. soldiers and wanted to be one himself. "They are a special breed of people down in Cornwall," explained Susan. "They weren't little kids playing in the house, they were out running around from the time they were two or three years old with no raincoats and no boots. He was strong; he was rugged. His childhood friends said to me that you could tell that he was a leader from the beginning; this was something that was innate."

In 1957, Rescorla enlisted in the British Army and served with distinction in Cyprus and Rhodesia. Susan recounted, "When I met a couple of his men whom he was in Rhodesia with, they said if you were to meet twenty men . . . ten or fifteen years later who would you remember? You would remember Rick Rescorla."

After his service in Britain, Rescorla moved to the United States. As a platoon leader in the 2nd Battalion of the United States Army in Vietnam, Rescorla again distinguished himself as a fearless leader. He often sang military hymns to calm his soldiers, just as he did decades later on September 11. He returned from Vietnam with a Silver Star, the Bronze Star with Oak Leaf Cluster, a Purple Heart, and the Vietnamese Cross of Gallantry.

In 1972, Rescorla married his first wife, Betsy. They had two children and moved around from South Carolina to Chicago to New Jersey while Rescorla worked various security jobs. In 1992, Rescorla warned the Port Authority of New York City, the owners of the World Trade Center, about the possibility of someone using a truck bomb to attack the pillars of the towers in the basement parking garage. They ignored him, and in 1993 terrorists used that exact method. Rescorla was vital in the evacuation of the building and was the last man out.

After the 1993 attack failed, Rescorla believed there would be another attack and this time it could be a plane used as a gigantic missile crashing into the towers. Rescorla even recommended to Morgan Stanley that the company leave Manhattan and relocate to New Jersey. He was ignored again. But at his insistence, Rescorla had all employees, including senior executives, practice emergency evacuations every three months.

In 1997, Rescorla became director of security for Morgan Stanley with its headquarters in the World Trade Center. After a battle with prostate cancer and his divorce from Betsy, Rescorla met Susan and the two married in 1999.

On that infamous September morning, Rescorla called Susan to tell her what was happening. "I was hysterical," recalled Susan. " 'Stop crying,' he said. 'I have to get my people out.' " Susan described how very methodically, calmly, and lovingly he explained the situation to her. " 'If something should happen to me I want you to know that you made my life,' he told me. And then of course I said that to him and the phone went dead."

"He had to finish his mission. He had to do what they call in the military—doing the last sweep—making sure that everyone was out," explained Susan.

Rick's remains were never found after the collapse of the towers. Susan's marriage was cut off after only two years, but it was an unforgettable two years. "He was a man for all seasons . . . he was giving and thoughtful and our relationship was as if we had known each other forever and ever. We were inseparable and wanted to spend every moment together when we were not working," remembered Susan.

"I don't want America to forget Rick Rescorla, but even more than that I don't want America to forget what happened on 9/11," said Susan.

Funeral Oration

PERICLES

For almost half a century, tensions had steadily risen between the city-state of Athens and the rest of the Greek world. After leading the Greeks to a decisive victory over Persian forces in 480 BC, Athens had exercised hegemonic control over all of Greece, becoming an economic and military powerhouse, often disregarding the welfare of her allies. Meanwhile, Sparta, a militaristic city-state in the southern part of the Peloponnese, grew increasingly alarmed at the growth of Athenian military power and adventurism in foreign affairs. After Athens levied economic sanctions on Megara, a Spartan ally, in 432/433, BC, Sparta could no longer tolerate what they perceived as Athenian arrogance and declared war.

Beginning in 431, the Peloponnesian War would rage across Greece, Macedon, and Sicily for twenty-seven years. Athens possessed almost inexhaustible economic resources and manpower, but Sparta refused to quit. Finally, in the seventeenth year of the war, the disastrous Athenian naval expedition to seize the rich colony of Syracuse, on Sicily, marked the beginning of the end. Although Athens would fight on for ten more years, the Peloponnesian War gradually came to an end, with Sparta emerging as the dominant power in the Greek world.

Striding up a raised platform, before all of Athens, the Athenian general Pericles measured and weighed each of his words. Known throughout the state for his clarity of mind and grace of tongue, the orator earned the great privilege of speaking on this most solemn of days, the day of the funeral ceremony honoring those who had been killed in the first year of the war between Athens and Sparta. The commander of the Athenian forces at the onset of the war would have been unable to imagine that this conflict would rage on for twenty-six more years, but as he prepared his magnificent funeral oration, he could not have missed the sobriety of the situation. Many Athenians had died in the first year alone, and he himself would be dead the next year, a victim of a lethal plague that swept Athens.

Custom held that three days before this traditional funeral ceremony, the bones of the dead had been laid out in a tent. Friends and family brought offerings to their fallen relatives, and then, on the third day, the bones were cradled in cypress coffins—one left empty for the unknown soldiers—and brought in solemn procession to the public sepulcher. All the while, the women would wail and cry for those lost.

Then a man, chief among virtue and wisdom in the community, would be called on to deliver a final oration over those lost. The words delivered by Pericles, son of Xanthippus, were some of the most eloquent ever uttered in the memory of fallen warriors. His words are a history lesson to the forgetful, a reminder of the nobility of the Athenian experiment in democracy and the character of those men who had struggled and fallen. Pericles focused on the resilience and accomplishments of the city-state to remind his audience that it was worth protecting and even dying for. His last sentence is immortal.

Indeed if I have dwelt at some length upon the character of our country, it has been to show that our stake in the struggle is not the same as theirs who have no such blessings to lose, and also that the panegyric of the men over whom I am now speaking might be by definite proofs established. That panegyric is now in a great measure complete; for the Athens that I have celebrated is only what the heroism of these and their like have made her, men whose fame, unlike that of most Hellenes, will be found to be only commensurate with their deserts. And if a test of worth be wanted, it is to be found in their closing scene, and this not only in cases in which it set the final seal upon their merit, but also in those in which it gave the first intimation of their having any. For there is justice in the claim that steadfastness in his country's battles should be as a cloak to cover a man's other imperfections; since the good action has blotted out the bad, and his merit as a citizen more than outweighed his demerits as an individual. But none of these allowed either wealth with its prospect of future enjoyment to unnerve his spirit, or poverty with its hope of a day of freedom and riches to tempt him to shrink from danger. No, holding that vengeance upon their enemies was more to be desired than any personal blessings, and reckoning this to be the most glorious of hazards, they joyfully determined to accept the risk, to make sure of their vengeance, and to let their wishes wait; and while committing to hope the uncertainty of final success, in the business before them they thought fit to act boldly and trust in themselves. Thus choosing to die resisting, rather than to live submitting, they fled only from dishonor, but met danger face to face, and after one brief moment, while at the summit of their fortune, escaped, not from their fear, but from their glory.

So died these men as became Athenians. You, their survivors, must determine to have as unfaltering a resolution in the field, though you may pray that it may have a happier issue. And not contented with ideas derived only from words of the advantages which are bound up with the defense of your country, though these would furnish a valuable text to a speaker even before an audience so alive to them as the present, you must yourselves realize the power of Athens, and feed your eyes upon her from day to day, till love of her fills your hearts; and then, when all her greatness shall break upon you, you must reflect that it was by courage, sense of duty, and a keen feeling of honor in action that men were enabled to win all this, and that no personal failure in an enterprise could make them consent to deprive their country of their valor, but they laid it at her feet as the most glorious contribution that they could offer. For this offering of their lives made in common by them all they each of them individually received that renown which never grows old, and for a sepulcher, not so much that in which their bones have been deposited, but that noblest of shrines wherein their glory is laid up to be eternally remembered upon every occasion on which deed or story shall call for its commemoration. For heroes have the whole earth for their tomb; and in lands far from their own, where the column with its epitaph declares it, there is enshrined in every breast a record unwritten with no tablet to preserve it, except that of the heart. These take as your model and, judging happiness to be the fruit of freedom and freedom of valor, never decline the dangers of war. For it is not the miserable that would most justly be unsparing of their lives; these have nothing to hope for: it is rather they to whom continued life may bring reverses as yet unknown, and to whom a fall, if it came, would be most tremendous in its consequences. And surely, to a man of spirit, the degradation of cowardice must be immeasurably more grievous than the unfelt death which strikes him in the midst of his strength and patriotism!

Comfort, therefore, not condolence, is what I have to offer to the parents of the dead who may be here. Numberless are the chances to which, as they know, the life of man is subject; but fortunate indeed are they who draw for their lot a death so glorious as that which has caused your mourning, and to whom life has been so exactly measured as to terminate in the happiness in which it has been passed. Still I know that this is a hard saying, especially when those are in question of whom you will constantly be reminded by seeing in the homes of others blessings of which once you also boasted: for grief is felt not so much for the want of what we have never known, as for the loss of that to which we have been long accustomed. Yet you who are still of an age to beget children must bear up in the hope of having others in their stead; not only will they help you to forget those whom you have lost, but will be to the state at once a reinforcement and a security; for never can a fair or just policy be expected of the citizen who does not, like his fellows, bring to the decision the interests and apprehensions of a father. While those of you who have passed your prime must congratulate yourselves with the thought that the best part of your life was fortunate, and that the brief span that remains will be cheered by the fame of the departed. For it is only the love of honour, that never grows old; and honour it is, not gain, as some would have it, that rejoices the heart of age and helplessness.

"Before Action"

W. N. HODGSON

William Noel Hodgson (1893–1916) was an English poet of World War I. During the war, he published stories and poems under the pen name Edward Melbourne. Hodgson volunteered for the British Army at the outbreak of World War I. He was killed on the first day of the Battle of the Somme while attacking German trenches near Mametz. He is probably best remembered today for his poem "Before Action," which was written two days before he died.

By all the glories of the day
And the cool evening's benison,
By that last sunset touch that lay
Upon the hills where day was done,
By beauty lavishly outpoured
And blessings carelessly received,
By all the days that I have lived
Make me a soldier, Lord.
By all of man's hopes and fears,
And all the wonders poets sing,
The laughter of unclouded years,
And every sad and lovely thing;
By the romantic ages stored
With high endeavor that was his,

By all his mad catastrophes
Make me a man, O Lord.
I, that on my familiar hill
Saw with uncomprehending eyes
A hundred of Thy sunsets spill
Their fresh and sanguine sacrifice,
Ere the sun swings his noonday sword
Must say goodbye to all of this;—
By all delights that I shall miss,
Help me to die, O Lord.

"Battle Is a Joyous Thing"

JEAN DE BRUEIL

This ancient passage eloquently illustrates how combat can bring out the best qualities in men. Instead of focusing on fear and death, the French knight Jean de Brueil said that the virtues of battle—loyalty, bravery, and duty—make men immune to cowardice.

Battle is a joyous thing. We love each other so much in battle. If we see that our cause is just and our kinsmen fight boldly, tears come to our eyes. A sweet joy rises in our hearts, in the feeling of our honest loyalty to each other; and seeing our friend so bravely exposing his body to danger in order to fulfill the commandment of our Creator, we resolve to go forward and die or live with him on account of love. This brings such delight that anyone who has not felt it cannot say how wonderful it is. Do you think someone who feels this is afraid of death? Not in the least! He is so strengthened, so delighted, that he does not know where he is. Truly, he fears nothing in the world!

The Navy SEAL Creed

The U.S. Navy's Sea, Air, and Land teams, commonly known as Navy SEALs, are one of the elite branches of the United States military. As the special operations forces of the navy, the SEALs execute the most dangerous and important intelligence and combat missions. Members of the SEALs have always lived by an unspoken creed of courage and duty. It takes a special commitment both physically and mentally to become a SEAL and deserve the privilege of wearing the Trident. In 2005, a formal creed was created to honor these men and their commitment to each other and their country. These men represent the highest order of military expertise and their creed attests to the values that make them so great and so deservedly esteemed.

In times of war or uncertainty there is a special breed of warrior ready to answer our Nation's call. A common man with uncommon desire to succeed. Forged by adversity, he stands alongside America's finest special operation forces to serve his country, the American people, and protect their way of life. I am that man.

My Trident is a symbol of honor and heritage. Bestowed upon me by the heroes that have gone before, it embodies the trust of those I have sworn to protect. By wearing the Trident I accept the responsibility of my chosen profession and way of life. It is a privilege that I must earn every day.

My loyalty to Country and Team is beyond reproach. I humbly serve as a guardian to my fellow Americans always ready to defend those who are unable to defend themselves. I do not advertise the nature of my work, nor seek recognition for my actions. I voluntarily accept the inherent hazards of my profession, placing the welfare and security of others before my own.

I serve with honor on and off the battlefield. The ability to control my emotions and my actions, regardless of circumstances, sets me apart from other men. Uncompromising integrity is my standard. My character and honor are steadfast. My word is my bond.

We expect to lead and be led. In the absence of orders I will take charge, lead my teammates and accomplish the mission. I lead by example in all situations. I will never quit. I persevere and thrive on adversity. My Nation expects me to be physically harder and mentally stronger than my enemies. If knocked down, I will get back up, every time. I will draw on every remaining ounce of strength to protect my teammates and to accomplish our mission. I am never out of the fight.

We demand discipline. We expect innovation. The lives of my teammates and the success of our mission depend on me—my technical skill, tactical proficiency, and attention to detail. My training is never complete.

We train for war and fight to win. I stand ready to bring the full spectrum of combat power to bear in order to achieve my mission and the goals established by my country. The execution of my duties will be swift and violent when required yet guided by the very principles that I serve to defend.

Brave men have fought and died building the proud tradition and feared reputation that I am bound to uphold. In the worst of conditions, the legacy of my teammates steadies my resolve and silently guides my every deed. I will not fail.

Profile: Nathan Bruckenthal

At the onset of Operation Iraqi Freedom in 2003, Americans knew that the brave men and women of the United States Army, Navy, Marines, and Air Force would be asked to make tremendous sacrifices in order to safeguard the United States and the world from violence and tyranny. But when contemplating the risks and sacrifice asked of those who serve, we too often forget the members of the U.S. Coast Guard, who are often omitted in praise of the military but deserve a respect similar to that given to the other branches. The Coast Guard's mission is broader in scope than many of us realize, as they play a critical role in the defense of our country at home and the assistance of operations abroad. This profile focuses on a man, Nathan Bruckenthal, who was devoted to the service of his family and his country, rarely thinking of himself.

There is a photograph of Petty Officer Nathan Bruckenthal, taken at an unknown date in his time in the Coast Guard. In the photo Bruckenthal, standing a stout six-foot-two, two hundred twenty pounds, gazes wistfully at the camera. Sunglasses dangle around his neck. Behind him, the ocean stretches into the distance. It is hard to imagine what he could be thinking.

In another time, Nathan Bruckenthal grew up in his hometown of Ridgefield, Connecticut, dreaming of becoming a police officer or firefighter. He played football in high school, but wasn't a great student. Still, Bruckenthal was well-liked and had an inclusive streak, helping out at school with a club called LINK—"Let's Include New Kids." It made sense. Bruckenthal himself had at other times lived in Hawaii and Virginia after his parents divorced as a child and perhaps knew the pain of exclusion in a new school.

A year and a half out of high school, often serving as a volunteer firefighter but lacking direction, he joined the Coast Guard in 1999, knowing that the experience would help him get some college education so that he could make it above sergeant as a policeman in his hometown. He first served on an eighty-two-foot patrol boat out of Montauk, New York, before being shipped out to Neah Bay, Washington, or, as Bruckenthal recalled, "the end of the world." It was cold, rainy, and boring.

Still, Neah Bay wasn't all bad for Bruckenthal. He met his wife, Pattie, who was in college studying the Makah Indian Tribe and got on a civilian tour of the Neah Bay Station, a tour led by Bruckenthal. Locals recalled Bruckenthal as a man who loved to help others.

"Volunteering was the first thing he did; he helped the community," Joe McGimpsey, a resident of Neah Bay and member of the Makah Tribe, told the *Seattle-Post Intelligencer.*

"Nate gave unconditionally and that is why he was so loved in this community," recalled Neah Bay Police Chief T.J. Greene.

After terrorists attacked the World Trade Center in 2001, Bruckenthal headed east to New York, where he assisted in funerals for two firefighters and a police officer killed on that day. He extended his time into October, using up his leave time to stay at ground zero for a few weeks, passing out food and water to firefighters, police officers, and construction workers helping to clean up the site.

By 2003, Bruckenthal was destined for Iraq, serving on a Coast Guard unit that boarded vessels traveling through the waters around offshore oil rigs. Bruckenthal was excited, accepting the risks involved but describing himself as feeling "on a high horse."

"He was very honored to do anything that the Coast Guard asked him," said Petty Officer Daniel Burgoyne, who was Bruckenthal's shipmate, friend, and neighbor in Dania Beach, Florida. "He was a true patriot. He loved serving his country."

In 2004, Bruckenthal signed up for another tour, destined to be a hundred days. Before this tour, Pattie became pregnant with the couple's first child, Harper, and Bruckenthal couldn't wait to come home. After all, he had already missed both of the couple's first two wedding anniversaries because of his duty in Iraq.

But in the early evening hours of April 24, 2004, a small vessel approached an oil rig in the Persian Gulf. Bruckenthal, trained as part of a unit who boarded suspicious vessels, was accompanied by one other Coast Guardsman and five sailors from the United States Navy. The unit took off in pursuit of the vessel with Bruckenthal eventually leading the operation to board it.

As the crew was poised to board the boat, an explosion was detonated—a suicide bomb. Bruckenthal was killed by the force of the blast. Two Navy petty officers also died as a result of the waterborne attack: PO1 Michael J. Pernaselli, 27, of Monroe, New York, and Christopher E. Watts, 28, of Knoxville, Tennessee. Three other Navy sailors were injured, as was Joseph T. Ruggiero, USCG, 23, from Revere, Massachusetts, who received the Purple Heart.

For his heroics, Bruckenthal was awarded the Bronze Star with Valor, the Purple Heart, and the Global War on Terrorism Expeditionary Medal.

Glenn Grahl, one of Bruckenthal's commanding officers, remembered him by saying, "Nate was jovial, he was intense, and he was a dedicated professional."

Nathan Bruckenthal became the first member of the U.S. Coast Guard to be killed in wartime action since the Vietnam War. But it wasn't his death that made him special.

From "Bivouac of the Dead"

Theodore O'Hara

Lines from Theodore O'Hara's elegiac poem "Bivouac of the Dead" are inscribed on memorials in some of the nation's oldest cemeteries. O'Hara, a poet-soldier, served in the military from the Mexican War through the Civil War. These verses originally memorialized the heroes of the Mexican War, but their sentiments so captivated the nation that they were reprinted in graveyards across the country. Quartermaster General Montgomery C. Meigs (1816–1892) recognized the poem's solemn appeal and directed that lines from "Bivouac" grace the entrance to Arlington National Cemetery.

> *The muffled drum's sad roll has beat*
> *The soldier's last tattoo;*
> *No more on Life's parade shall meet*
> *That brave and fallen few.*
> *On fame's eternal camping ground*
> *Their silent tents to spread,*
> *And glory guards, with solemn round*
> *The bivouac of the dead.*
> *No rumor of the foe's advance*
> *Now swells upon the wind;*
> *Nor troubled thought at midnight haunts*
> *Of loved ones left behind;*
> *No vision of the morrow's strife*
> *The warrior's dreams alarms;*
> *No braying horn or screaming fife*
> *At dawn shall call to arms.*
> *Their shriveled swords are red with rust,*
> *Their plumed heads are bowed,*
> *Their haughty banner, trailed in dust,*

Is now their martial shroud.
And plenteous funeral tears have washed
The red stains from each brow,
And the proud forms, by battle gashed
Are free from anguish now.
The neighing troop, the flashing blade,
The bugle's stirring blast,
The charge, the dreadful cannonade,
The din and shout, are past;
Nor war's wild note, nor glory's peal
Shall thrill with fierce delight
Those breasts that nevermore may feel
The rapture of the fight.
Like the fierce Northern hurricane
That sweeps the great plateau,
Flushed with triumph, yet to gain,
Come down the serried foe,
Who heard the thunder of the fray
Break o'er the field beneath,
Knew the watchword of the day
Was "Victory or death!"
Long had the doubtful conflict raged
O'er all that stricken plain,
For never fiercer fight had waged
The vengeful blood of Spain;
And still the storm of battle blew,
Still swelled the glory tide;
Not long, our stout old Chieftain knew,
Such odds his strength could bide.
Twas in that hour his stern command
Called to a martyr's grave
The flower of his beloved land,
The nation's flag to save.

By rivers of their father's gore
His first-born laurels grew,
And well he deemed the sons would pour
Their lives for glory too.
For many a mother's breath has swept
O'er Angostura's plain—
And long the pitying sky has wept
Above its moldered slain.
The raven's scream, or eagle's flight,
Or shepherd's pensive lay,
Alone awakes each sullen height
That frowned o'er that dread fray.

—— ❧ ——

Profile: Red Falvey

Today we remember them as the Greatest Generation: the millions of Americans who survived the Great Depression, served in World War II, and made America the most powerful nation on the earth. They came from all different races, classes, and areas of the country, but they were united in their belief of service and sacrifice to country. Red Falvey was one of those men we are all indebted to. I found Red and his story through my radio show, *Morning in America*.

All Red Falvey wanted for his twenty-first birthday was the right to jump out of planes, to see the ground rushing up, feel terror for a few short seconds, then pull the cord and watch the parachute billow above and the world swing below him—but now he was standing in front of the recruiter, and the stern-faced man with the notepad asked if there was anything wrong with his body.

"I can't touch my left shoulder."

The recruiter's face crinkled up, "Aw, you'll never get in. To get into airborne, you have to be 110 percent and there's no way that they're going to let you in."

Red Falvey walked out of the recruiting station, discouraged but not defeated.

It was August 2, 1942, and the boy from Yonkers, New York—who broke his arm climbing a tree—was a patriot. On December 7, 1941, when the crackle of the radio interrupted his life and President Roosevelt called him to battle, he knew what he had to do.

It was on that day of infamy when he was calling on the girl that he would someday marry and be with for fifty-four years—Leona Swarthouse—that bigger news came rolling over the airwaves. Falvey couldn't point out Pearl Harbor on a map, but one thought kept turning in his mind: *Those silly little fools, do they have any idea what they've done? Don't they know we'll wipe them up in a week?*

Growing up, Falvey spent much of his free time at the airfields, watching the barnstorming tours of planes with his brothers. He knew he wanted to be up in the air. Regardless of what any army recruiter told him, Falvey wanted to be airborne. Despite his injured arm, Falvey proved the recruiters wrong and successfully enlisted in the 506th Infantry Regiment (known today as the popular Band of Brothers).

The 506th Regiment was an experiment, a test to see whether men could be better trained by being wholly devoted to the sky, rather than starting with thirteen weeks with feet on the ground.

"We had to save time, the brass were trying to hurry things along and get us ready for combat," said Falvey. "There was nothing easy about that training and so many of those boys couldn't handle the intensity. They washed out."

It's a fitting term of the service—"washing out"—because before the boys of the 506th could ever break over the beaches of Normandy, they had to beat against the trials of Fort Benning, Georgia—and more than a few were not equal to the task.

"If you hesitate, even for a second, they will wash you out." Falvey repeated the mantra daily, this gospel of the boot camp drilled into his skull, silencing any fear with the knowledge of his duty.

And so Falvey found himself standing at the edge of a roaring plane, second on the line to jump, listening to Charles Rhinehart in front of him—a fellow who always seemed to need a few extra seconds to screw up the nerve to step into the sky—beg Falvey to push him out of the plane.

Falvey pushed and Rhinehart thanked him, but before the two would go up in the sky again, Falvey pulled the shrinking man aside.

"That's it, if you're going to do this again; you've got to find someone else. I can't take care of you up there."

But Rhinehart conquered his fear, jumping his way through the entire tour of Normandy and surviving the war.

"No one wanted to be washed out," said Falvey. "But there were two thousand men who made the regiment, and we had another five thousand who washed out."

Anyone knew these men had ample opportunity to fall behind. Daybreak runs—Falvey didn't finish first, but never finished last—were screaming races up mountains and jumps that tested all God-given sense of fear.

And then there was the march across Georgia for jump training.

"No one quite knew how bad it was. We had heard about a Japanese squad that set a record for marching. So we decided to beat it. It was 118 miles in three days, in the summer, in a full field pack. It was miserable and even the blisters had blisters."

Red Falvey never claims to be special, but he didn't wash out.

"Our regiment was America," said Falvey. "It was fellows who had college educations; it was fellows who had come off the farm."

And there is the little-understood truth about history. There are the images that stand out in textbooks: Washington crossing a frozen Delaware, John Paul Jones returning a call for surrender with "I have not yet begun to fight," and Alvin York single-handedly capturing one hundred thiry two Germans in World War I. But alongside those faces leading the charge, there are the oft-overlooked men who follow, the men who forge ahead against the cold, and the men who continue when all others stop.

"We just felt we were special. That's what they pushed into us. We were so very proud of our boots and our jumpsuits . . . You know they blew us up and we ate it up. They told us how good we were, how good we had to be."

While men doing extraordinary things laid the cornerstone of America, men who simply refused to give up built this country's foundations.

Red Falvey never gave up.

"One fellow had to be taught how to put a tie on; he'd never worn one in his life. It was a cross section, all across society, just a piece of America. This is the way it was across the entire company and it was marvelous."

This cross section of America was trained for war and heading out of the Hudson

River, when the men turned and saw the Statue of Liberty, emerging out of the early morning fog.

"There's our girl," said Falvey. "This is what it's all about, and we're going to protect her."

And so the boys went to England. They saw the bombed countryside, the families living by thousands down in the depths of the subway, and they met a people who refused to give up, refused to surrender, and refused to complain.

"My heart went out to them, it was such a mess in England, but they never complained, I never heard them cry or moan."

The 506th came to England for a reason though, and when night fell on June 5, the boys were ready to jump into the fray.

Falvey took a Thompson and a few grenades and strapped in with the thirteen thousand other soldiers preparing for the jump. People kept quiet in the early hours of June 6. The plane took off, Falvey sitting behind Captain Hester on the line, and the vast armada of planes rolled through the sky over the channel.

The time in the air was short. It only took eleven minutes to fly across the Cherbourg Peninsula, but hell can come quickly.

As the men huddled in the back of the plane, waiting for a signal to jump, the night turned bright and antiaircraft fire began shaking the sky. One plane was hit, exploding into a ball of fire. "They trained so hard, and so long, and they never had a chance." Another jolted, started dropping to the ground. The boy from Yonkers kept praying—"Oh, dear Lord, those boys never had a chance"—that he'd get to jump.

The green light came on—Falvey jumped.

Hugging the back of Captain Hester the short ride down, Falvey hit the ground just outside Saint-Martin-de-Varreville. His company was six miles from where they should have been on the Cherbourg Peninsula, scattered across the unfamiliar countryside, and the earth was still wrapped in darkness.

"The original plan was that we'd assemble on this big field," said Falvey. "Each team with their light would be on a different part of the field and get to the second causeway. None of that ever happened. We were scattered out all over hell."

Hell had come to France.

"Good heavens, it was the 6th of June and there wasn't a single leaf left on a tree," said Falvey. "The British and Americans had destroyed the area; all that was left was bomb craters."

Falvey and the other men knew where the roads should have been, but things had been obliterated. They slowly worked their way along a dirt road, flanked by hedgerows, and then they came upon the German.

He was lying there in the road, dead, with his motorbike beside him.

Major Horton barked out, "Falvey, stick 'em. See if he's dead."

Falvey refused.

"Major, you know he's dead."

A twisted bit of bravado was what passed for humor in a war zone. Whether it was the first dead German, one of the men drinking wine with a French family for hours in the predawn, or a German grenade that Falvey toted as a trophy—the men kept their sanity by laughing in the fields of death.

It wasn't till the next day that Falvey came into combat.

"When it started, I was leaning over a hedgerow, just firing, trying to spread fire. I couldn't see much, but I kept firing . . . There were other times that I had a bead on a German, and I don't think he got up. At Normandy, I don't remember killing anyone."

It was a different type of warfare in World War II, and while there were those men who stormed machine gun nests and lobbed grenades into strongholds, there were also those who followed orders, kept calm, and just kept marching on.

Even when faced with the horrors of death.

"I remember when I encountered my first dead American," said Falvey. "He was in this grotesque position, and I, oh gosh . . . it was awful. I just bent down. I tried to straighten him out, and it scared me; because of the rigor mortis, nothing moved or straightened out. It was horrible, and terrible."

But Falvey didn't shrink back, serving from the beaches of Normandy to the peaks of Hitler's Eagle's Nest. He eventually was brought home, after his time in service, to help spearhead a victory bond drive. After the Armistice, Falvey went to work for the railroad. He married Leona Swarthouse in 1948. The two were married until her death in 2002 and had three children, Richard, Sandra Lee, and Kurt.

Falvey never claimed to be something great on his own strength. But by joining more than eleven million other U.S. citizens serving in the U.S. forces during World War II, Falvey attained a higher standard of nobility: a class of people who sought to serve their country, rather than themselves—a quiet knighthood that did not need medals or praise to know they had fulfilled their duty. Soldiers, like Falvey, who did not relish the horrors of war, but who still said, "We knew we had a job to do and that nothing was going to happen with that war until they put us in."

The recruiter tried to keep Falvey out of airborne. He couldn't fire his gun with his right hand. He never finished first during the training or earned any great medals during combat. But Falvey answered the call of his country, went to war, and didn't turn away. He came back to the United States and served his family and loved his wife.

Red Falvey was a man who served at war, but knew how to live at peace. He couldn't touch his left shoulder, but he never washed out. He served.

"Be Ye the Avengers of Noble Blood"

WILLIAM THE CONQUEROR

It was an October morning in 1066 when Duke William of Normandy stepped in front of his seven thousand troops. Control over England was up for grabs, and the Norman believed that his relative Edward the Confessor had named him successor to the throne of England. And so when Earl Harold of Wessex was elected king instead, William challenged the newly crowned King Harold II at Hastings. The morning of the battle, William called his men into the struggle with a speech that still speeds the heart and rousts men into action today. At the end of the fight, King Harold II was slain, and William of Normandy took over the throne and the title "William the Conqueror."

Normans! bravest of nations! I have no doubt of your courage, and none of your victory, which never by any chance or obstacle escaped your efforts. If indeed you had, once only, failed to conquer, there might be a need now to inflame your courage by exhortation; but your native spirit does not require to be roused. Bravest of men, what could the power of the Frankish King effect with all his people, from Lorraine to Spain, against Hastings my predecessor? What he wanted of France he took, and gave to the King only what he pleased. What he had, he held as long as it suited him, and relinquished it only for something better. Did not Rollo my ancestor, founder of our nation, with our fathers conquer at Paris the King of the Franks in the heart of his kingdom, nor had the King of the Franks any hope of safety until he humbly offered his daughter and possession of the country, which, after you, is called Normandy.

Did not your fathers capture the King of the Franks at Rouen, and keep him there until he restored Normandy to Duke Richard, then a boy; with this condition, that, in every conference between the King of France and the Duke of Normandy, the duke should wear his sword, while the King should not be permitted to carry a sword nor even a dagger. This concession your fathers compelled the great King to submit to, as binding for ever. Did not the same duke lead your fathers to Mirmande, at the foot of the Alps, and enforce submission from the lord of the town, his son-in-law, to his own wife, the duke's daughter? Nor was it enough for you to conquer men, he conquered the devil himself, with whom he wrestled, cast down and bound him with his hands behind his back, and left him a shameful spectacle to angels. But why do I talk of former times? Did not you, in our own time, engage the Franks at Mortemer? Did not the Franks prefer flight to battle, and use their spurs? While you—Ralph, the commander of the Franks having been slain—reaped the honour and the spoil as the natural result of your usual success. Ah! Let any one of the English whom, a hundred times, our predecessors, both Danes and Normans, have defeated in battle, come forth and show that the race of Rollo ever suffered a defeat from his time until now, and I will withdraw conquered. Is it not, therefore, shameful that a people accustomed to be conquered, a people ignorant of war, a people even without arrows, should proceed in order of battle against you, my brave men? Is it not a shame that King Harold, perjured as he was in your presence, should dare to show his face to you? It is amazing to me that you have been allowed to see those who, by a horrible crime, beheaded your relations and Alfred my kinsman, and that their own heads are still on their shoulders. Raise your standards, my brave men, and set neither measure nor limit to your merited rage. May the lightning of your glory be seen and the thunders of your onset heard from east to west, and be ye the avengers of noble blood.

Profile: Alvin York

Alvin York (1887–1964) was one of the great American heroes of World War I. He went from a poor, backwoods Tennessee boy to a national celebrity almost overnight. After his heroics in the war, the offers for movies, advertisements, and books poured in, but York turned them all down. He never sought the spotlight or fame. He served his country and went home to help his community.

Alvin Cullum York was born in a two-room log cabin near Pall Mall, Tennessee, on December 13, 1887, the third of eleven children. The York family was anything but wealthy. Alvin's father, William, worked as a blacksmith to provide for the family. Alvin and his brothers would gather and harvest their own food, while their mother knit all the family clothing.

The York sons could only attend school a total of nine months before they were forced to withdraw from school and help sustain the family farm and hunt small game to feed the family. Naturally, guns were a major part of the Yorks' livelihood. Hunting was more of a necessity than a sport in the mountains, and Alvin quickly acquired a reputation as the best marksman and hunter in the county. Shooting matches were popular in Fentress County, Tennessee, and Alvin often outshot all his opponents.

When Alvin was only twenty-four years old, his father passed away. Being the oldest remaining son at home, Alvin was left to help his mother raise his younger siblings. So he took a job on a railroad construction crew and another working as a logger. It wasn't long before the hard work and pressure began to affect Alvin. In the few years building up to World War I, he became a violent alcoholic who often fought in saloons and was arrested several times. In his own words, he was "hog-wild."

Alvin's mother, a devout Protestant, tried her hardest to persuade Alvin to repent and change his ways. Sadly, her pleas fell on deaf ears until one unfortunate night. In the winter of 1914, Alvin and his friend Everett Delk got in a fight with other saloon patrons after an evening of heavy drinking. The incident ended with Delk beaten to death inside the saloon. The event was painful enough for Alvin that he finally followed his mother's advice and became a pacifist and stopped drinking alcohol. He was baptized as a Christian in the Wolf River in early 1915.

Having completely changed his ways, York later wrote, "I am a great deal like Paul [the apostle], the things I once loved I now hate."

Only two years after his conversion, Alvin York was drafted into the United States Army to serve in World War I. Being a Bible-believing pacifist but also a proud patriot and supporter of his country, York was torn over his proper duty in the war. At first he tried to get an exemption based on his religious convictions. When he registered for the draft, he answered the question "Do you claim exemption from draft (specify grounds)?" by writing, "Yes. Don't Want To Fight."

York filed four appeals on religious grounds; all were rejected. Still wrestling in his mind over the virtue of war, he was miserable during his first weeks of military service. He remained silent about his uncertainties until he found out he would be assigned to a combat unit headed to Europe. His company commander sent him to see battalion commander General George Edward Buxton. He and York spent hours discussing the Bible's teachings about war.

Ultimately, Buxton gave him a ten-day pass to return home and think things through. Buxton agreed to discharge him if he hadn't changed his mind by the time he returned.

York spent two days in the Tennessee mountains soul searching and asking for God's wisdom. One biblical verse in particular weighed heavily on his heart: "Blessed are the peacemakers." Gradually, York came to the epiphany that the only way to keep peace in this world would be to engage the Germans on the terms they understood—war.

York returned to duty in April 1918, and shortly afterward his division set sail for France. In late June, they were commissioned to serve on the Western Front. Life in the trenches was anything but comfortable. Bullets constantly whizzed overhead, bombs dropped from above, and you never knew when the enemy would charge your trench without warning. In his off hours, York read his Bible. In his diary he wrote, "The only thing to do was to pray and trust God."

On October 8, 1918, York's division was part of the Meuse-Argonne offensive in northeast France. After his regiment was pinned down by enemy machine-gun fire, York spearheaded a seven-man unit designed to silence the machine guns and allow the regiment to push forward. His squad had already taken two casualties when York found himself face-to-face with a German machine-gun company with just a rifle and a pistol.

Using his rifle, York picked off any Germans who popped their heads above the trenches. Then, when six Germans rushed him with bayonets, he grabbed his pistol and killed all six. He quickly positioned himself at the end of the German trench and began mowing down Germans as they stood in line. When the dust settled and the fight ended, 25 Germans were dead. Stunned and scared, the remaining 132 Germans surrendered to York and his unit.

Describing the fight in his diary, York said,

> There were over thirty of them in continuous action, and all I could do was touch the Germans off just as fast as I could. I was sharpshooting. I don't think I missed a shot. It was no time to miss. In order to sight me or to swing their machine guns on me, the Germans had to show their heads above the trench, and every time I saw a head I just touched it off. All the time I kept yelling at them to come down. I didn't want to kill any more than I had to. But it was they or I. And I was giving them the best I had. (Sergeant York Patriotic Foundation: "Sgt. Alvin C. York's Diary: October 8, 1918")

York's heroics elevated him to the heights of an American hero. He was later promoted to sergeant and received the Congressional Medal of Honor along with fifty other decorations and honors. When he returned to the United States, York was offered hundreds of thousands of dollars for endorsements, newspaper articles, and movie roles. Being the simple Tennessee man that he was, York wrote, "They offered so much money that it almost takened my breath away."

In the end, York refused the money and returned home to Tennessee. Looking beyond himself and his own personal gains, he believed God had chosen him to "bring the benefits of an industrial society to his neighbors . . . [and that] the war had been part of God's plan to prepare him for a life of service [to his neighbors]." He said, "My ambition . . . is to devote my time improving conditions here in the mountains."

Fentress County had no full-time elementary school. His people lacked well-built roads, schools, libraries, homes, and modern farming techniques. To raise the standard of living in the Tennessee mountains, York set up the Alvin C. York Foundation to improve education with an elementary school, an industrial school, and a Bible school. In 1929, the York Agricultural Institute opened its doors to provide vocational training. Of all his accomplishments, York considered this to be his greatest.

Remarks on the Fortieth Anniversary of D-Day

RONALD REAGAN

Standing in front of the U.S. Rangers Monument and overlooking the beaches of Normandy, on June 6, 1984, President Ronald Reagan (1911–2004) delivered this speech to memorialize the sacrifice of the Allied forces of World War II, especially "the boys of Pointe du Hoc." Reagan's words eloquently recount an "impossible" battle won by the champions of the free world. While Reagan's speech reflected on the virtues of a generation of freedom fighters, it also reaffirmed America's commitment to freedom and democracy for our future generations.

We're here to mark that day in history when the Allied armies joined in battle to reclaim this continent to liberty. For four long years, much of Europe had been under a terrible shadow. Free nations had fallen, Jews cried out in the camps, millions cried out for liberation. Europe was enslaved and the world prayed for its rescue. Here, in Normandy, the rescue began. Here, the Allies stood and fought against tyranny, in a giant undertaking unparalleled in human history.

We stand on a lonely, windswept point on the northern shore of France. The air is soft, but forty years ago at this moment, the air was dense with smoke and the cries of men, and the air was filled with the crack of rifle fire and the roar of cannon. At dawn, on the morning of the 6th of June, 1944, two hundred and twenty-five Rangers jumped off the British landing craft and ran to the bottom of these cliffs.

Their mission was one of the most difficult and daring of the invasion: to climb these sheer and desolate cliffs and take out the enemy guns. The Allies had been told that some of the mightiest of these guns were here, and they would be trained on the beaches to stop the Allied advance.

The Rangers looked up and saw the enemy soldiers at the edge of the cliffs, shooting down at them with machine guns and throwing grenades. And the American Rangers began to climb. They shot rope ladders over the face of these cliffs and began to pull themselves up. When one Ranger fell, another would take his place. When one rope was cut, a Ranger would grab another and begin his climb again. They climbed, shot back, and held their footing. Soon, one by one, the Rangers pulled themselves over the top, and in seizing the firm land at the top of these cliffs, they began to seize back the continent of Europe. Two hundred and twenty-five came here. After two days of fighting, only ninety could still bear arms.

And behind me is a memorial that symbolizes the Ranger daggers that were thrust into the top of these cliffs. And before me are the men who put them there. These are the boys of Pointe du Hoc. These are the men who took the cliffs. These are the champions who helped free a continent. And these are the heroes who helped end a war. Gentlemen, I look at you and I think of the words of Stephen Spender's poem. You are men who in your "lives fought for life and left the vivid air signed with your honor."

I think I know what you may be thinking right now—thinking "we were just part of a bigger effort; everyone was brave that day." Well everyone was. Do you remember the story of Bill Millin of the 51st Highlanders? Forty years ago today, British troops were pinned down near a bridge, waiting desperately for help. Suddenly, they heard the sound of bagpipes, and some thought they were dreaming. Well, they weren't. They looked up and saw Bill Millin with his bagpipes, leading the reinforcements and ignoring the smack of the bullets into the ground around him.

Lord Lovat was with him—Lord Lovat of Scotland, who calmly announced when he got to the bridge, "Sorry, I'm a few minutes late," as if he'd been delayed by a traffic jam, when in truth he'd just come from the bloody fighting on Sword Beach, which he and his men had just taken.

There was the impossible valor of the Poles, who threw themselves between the enemy and the rest of Europe as the invasion took hold; and the unsurpassed courage of the Canadians who had already seen the horrors of war on this coast. They knew what awaited them there, but they would not be deterred. And once they hit Juno Beach, they never looked back.

All of these men were part of a roll call of honor with names that spoke of a pride as bright as the colors they bore; [t]he Royal Winnipeg Rifles, Poland's 24th Lancers, the Royal Scots' Fusiliers, the Screaming Eagles, the Yeomen of England's armored divisions, the forces of Free France, the Coast Guard's "Matchbox Fleet," and you, the American Rangers.

Forty summers have passed since the battle that you fought here. You were young the day you took these cliffs; some of you were hardly more than boys, with the deepest joys of life before you. Yet you risked everything here. Why? Why did you do it? What impelled you to put aside the instinct for self-preservation and risk your lives to take these cliffs? What inspired all the men of the armies that met here? We look at you, and somehow we know the answer. It was faith and belief. It was loyalty and love.

The men of Normandy had faith that what they were doing was right, faith that they fought for all humanity, faith that a just God would grant them mercy on this beachhead, or on the next. It was the deep knowledge—and pray God we have not lost it—that there is a profound moral difference between the use of force for liberation and the use of force for conquest. You were here to liberate, not to conquer, and so you and those others did not doubt your cause. And you were right not to doubt.

You all knew that some things are worth dying for. One's country is worth dying for, and democracy is worth dying for, because it's the most deeply honorable form of government ever devised by man. All of you loved liberty. All of you were willing to fight tyranny, and you knew the people of your countries were behind you.

The Americans who fought here that morning knew word of the invasion was spreading through the darkness back home. They fought—or felt in their hearts, though they couldn't know in fact, that in Georgia they were filling the churches at 4:00 a.m. In Kansas they were kneeling on their porches and praying. And in Philadelphia they were ringing the Liberty Bell.

Something else helped the men of D-day; their rock-hard belief that Providence would have a great hand in the events that would unfold here; that God was an ally in this great cause. And so, the night before the invasion, when Colonel Wolverton asked his parachute troops to kneel with him in prayer, he told them: "Do not bow your heads, but look up so you can see God and ask His blessing in what we're about to do." Also, that night, General Matthew Ridgway lie on his cot, listening in the darkness for the promise God made to Joshua: "I will not fail thee nor forsake thee."

. . . Here, in this place where the West held together, let us make a vow to our dead. Let us show them by our actions that we understand what they died for. Let our actions say to them the words for which Matthew Ridgway listened: "I will not fail thee nor forsake thee."

Strengthened by their courage and heartened by their [valor] and borne by their memory, let us continue to stand for the ideals for which they lived and died.

From *The Apology*

PLATO

During Socrates' trial, the jury asked how it was that the philosopher Socrates could be so willing to pursue his metaphysical exploration even when his very life was threatened. Socrates explained that he believed some things were of more importance than life and death. He compared his philosophical exploration of the truth to a great warrior's determination on the battlefield.

Someone will say: And are you not ashamed, Socrates, of a course of life which is likely to bring you to an untimely end? To him I may fairly answer: There you are mistaken: a man who is good for anything ought not to calculate the chance of living or dying; he ought only to consider whether in doing anything he is doing right or wrong—acting the part of a good man or of a bad. Whereas, according to your view, the heroes who fell at Troy were not good for much, and the son of Thetis above all, who altogether despised danger in comparison with disgrace; and when his goddess mother said to him, in his eagerness to slay Hector, that if he avenged his companion Patroclus, and slew Hector, he would die himself—"Fate," as she said, "waits upon you next after Hector"; he, hearing this, utterly despised danger and death, and instead of fearing them, feared rather to live in dishonor, and not to avenge his friend. "Let me die next," he replies, "and be avenged of my enemy, rather than abide here by the beaked ships, a scorn and a burden of the earth." Had Achilles any thought of death and danger? For wherever a man's place is, whether the place which he has chosen or that in which he has been placed by a commander, there he ought to remain in the hour of danger; he should not think of death or of anything, but of disgrace. And this, O men of Athens, is a true saying.

From "The Soldier's Faith"

Oliver Wendell Holmes Jr.

Serving as associate justice on the Supreme Court of the United States from 1902 to 1932, Oliver Wendell Holmes Jr. is one of the most widely cited U.S. Supreme Court justices in history. This speech was given on Memorial Day, May 30, 1895, at a meeting called by the graduating class of Harvard University. President Theodore Roosevelt's admiration for this speech played a large role in Holmes's eventual nomination to the U.S. Supreme Court. Holmes used this speech to offer an introspective look into the heart of a soldier, saying famously, "We have shared the incommunicable experience of war; we have felt, we still feel, the passion of life to its top." During his senior year of college, Holmes enlisted for the Union in the Civil War. He saw action and suffered wounds at the Battle of Ball's Bluff, Antietam, and Fredericksburg.

When I went to the war I thought that soldiers were old men. I remembered a picture of the revolutionary soldier which some of you may have seen, representing a white-haired man with his flint-lock slung across his back. I remembered one or two examples of revolutionary soldiers whom I have met, and I took no account of the lapse of time. It was not long after, in winter quarters, as I was listening to some of the sentimental songs in vogue, such as—

Farewell, Mother, you may never
See your darling boy again,

that it came over me that the army was made up of what I should now call very young men. I dare say that my illusion has been shared by some of those now present, as they have looked at us upon whose heads the white shadows have begun to fall. But the truth is that war is the business of youth and early middle age. You who called this assemblage together, not we, would be the soldiers of another war, if we should have one, and we speak to you as the dying Merlin did in the verse which I have just quoted. Would that the blind man's pipe might be transformed by Merlin's magic, to make you hear the bugles as once we heard them beneath the morning stars! For you it is that now is sung the Song of the Sword:—

The War-Thing, the Comrade,
Father of Honor,
And Giver of kingship,
The fame-smith, the song master.
Priest (saith the Lord)
Of his marriage with victory

. . .

Clear singing, clean slicing;?
Sweet spoken, soft finishing;?
Making death beautiful
Life but a coin
To be staked in a pastime
Whose playing is more
Than the transfer of being;
Arch-anarch, chief builder,
Prince and evangelist,
I am the Will of God:
I am the Sword.

War, when you are at it, is horrible and dull. It is only when time has passed that you see that its message was divine. I hope it may be long before we are called again to sit at that master's feet. But some teacher of the kind we all need. In this snug, over-safe corner of the world we need it, that we may realize that our comfortable routine is no eternal necessity of things, but merely a little space of calm in the midst of the tempestuous untamed streaming of the world, and in order that we may be ready for danger. We need it in this time of individualist negations, with its literature of French and American humor, revolting at discipline, loving flesh-pots, and denying that anything is worthy of reverence—in order that we may remember all that buffoons forget. We need it everywhere and at all times. For high and dangerous action teaches us to believe as right beyond dispute things for which our doubting minds are slow to find words of proof. Out of heroism grows faith in the worth of heroism. The proof comes later, and even may never come. Therefore I rejoice at every dangerous sport which I see pursued. The students at Heidelberg, with their sword-slashed faces, inspire me with sincere respect. I gaze with delight upon our polo players. If once in a while in our rough riding a neck is broken, I regard it, not as a waste, but as a price well paid for the breeding of a race fit for headship and command.

We do not save our traditions, in our country. The regiments whose battle-flags were not large enough to hold the names of the battles they had fought vanished with the surrender of Lee, although their memories inherited would have made heroes for a century. It is the more necessary to learn the lesson afresh from perils newly sought, and perhaps it is not vain for us to tell the new generation what we learned in our day, and what we still believe. That the joy of life is living, is to put out all one's powers as far as they will go; that the measure of power is obstacles overcome; to ride boldly at what is in front of you, be it fence or enemy; to pray, not for comfort, but for combat; to keep the soldier's faith against the doubts of civil life, more besetting and harder to overcome than all the misgivings of the battlefield, and to remember that duty is not to be proved in the evil day, but then to be obeyed unquestioning; to love glory more than the temptations of wallowing ease, but to know that one's final judge and only rival is oneself: with all our failures in act and thought, these things we learned from noble enemies in Virginia or Georgia or on the Mississippi, thirty years ago; these things we believe to be true.

"Life is not lost", said she,
"for which is bought Endless renown."
We learned also, and we still believe, that love of country is not yet an idle name.

Deare countrey! O how dearly deare
Ought thy rememberance, and perpetuall band
Be to thy foster child, that from thy hand
Did commun breath and nouriture receave!
How brutish is it not to understand
How much to her we owe, that all us gave;
That much to her we owe, that all us gave;
That gave unto us all, whatever good we have!

As for us, our days of combat are over. Our swords are rust. Our guns will thunder no more. The vultures that once wheeled over our heads must be buried with their prey. Whatever of glory must be won in the council or the closet, never again in the field. I do not repine. We have shared the incommunicable experience of war; we have felt, we still feel, the passion of life to its top.

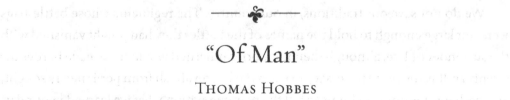

"Of Man"

THOMAS HOBBES

Thomas Hobbes (1588–1679) was an English philosopher and political theorist whose monumental work *Leviathan* is one of the most foundational and thoroughly argued defenses of monarchy and a piercing look into the nature of man and the world in which he lives. In this selection, Hobbes attempts to give an explanation for why men enter into conflict with each other. He concludes that it is ungoverned equality that brings men into irreconcilable conflict. Hobbes' view of life and man is both dark and powerful. The last words of this essay capture Hobbes' view of human nature: a state of war. He is no Pollyanna.

Nature hath made men so equal in the faculties of body and mind as that, though there be found one man sometimes manifestly stronger in body or of quicker mind than another, yet when all is reckoned together the difference between man and man is not so considerable as that one man can thereupon claim to himself any benefit to which another may not pretend as well as he. For as to the strength of body, the weakest has strength enough to kill the strongest, either by secret machination or by confederacy with others that are in the same danger with himself.

From this equality of ability ariseth equality of hope in the attaining of our ends. And therefore if any two men desire the same thing, which nevertheless they cannot both enjoy, they become enemies; and in the way to their end (which is principally their own conservation, and sometimes their delectation only) endeavour to destroy or subdue one another. And from hence it comes to pass that where an invader hath no more to fear than another man's single power, if one plant, sow, build, or possess a convenient seat, others may probably be expected to come prepared with forces united to dispossess and deprive him, not only of the fruit of his labour, but also of his life or liberty. And the invader again is in the like danger of another.

And from this diffidence of one another, there is no way for any man to secure himself so reasonable as anticipation; that is, by force, or wiles, to master the persons of all men he can so long till he see no other power great enough to endanger him: and this is no more than his own conservation requireth, and is generally allowed. Also, because there be some that, taking pleasure in contemplating their own power in the acts of conquest, which they pursue farther than their security requires, if others, that otherwise would be glad to be at ease within modest bounds, should not by invasion increase their power, they would not be able, long time, by standing only on their defence, to subsist. And by consequence, such augmentation of dominion over men being necessary to a man's conservation, it ought to be allowed him.

Again, men have no pleasure (but on the contrary a great deal of grief) in keeping company where there is no power able to overawe them all. For every man looketh that his companion should value him at the same rate he sets upon himself, and upon all signs of contempt or undervaluing naturally endeavours, as far as he dares (which amongst them that have no common power to keep them in quiet is far enough to make them destroy each other), to extort a greater value from his contemners, by damage; and from others, by the example.

So that in the nature of man, we find three principal causes of quarrel. First, competition; secondly, diffidence; thirdly, glory.

The first maketh men invade for gain; the second, for safety; and the third, for reputation. The first use violence, to make themselves masters of other men's persons, wives, children, and cattle; the second, to defend them; the third, for trifles, as a word, a smile, a different opinion, and any other sign of undervalue, either direct in their persons or by reflection in their kindred, their friends, their nation, their profession, or their name.

Hereby it is manifest that during the time men live without a common power to keep them all in awe, they are in that condition which is called war; and such a war as is of every man against every man. For war consisteth not in battle only, or the act of fighting, but in a tract of time, wherein the will to contend by battle is sufficiently known: and therefore the notion of time is to be considered in the nature of war, as it is in the nature of weather. For as the nature of foul weather lieth not in a shower or two of rain, but in an inclination thereto of many days together: so the nature of war consisteth not in actual fighting, but in the known disposition thereto during all the time there is no assurance to the contrary. All other time is peace.

Whatsoever therefore is consequent to a time of war, where every man is enemy to every man, the same consequent to the time wherein men live without other security than what their own strength and their own invention shall furnish them withal. In such condition there is no place for industry, because the fruit thereof is uncertain: and consequently no culture of the earth; no navigation, nor use of the commodities that may be imported by sea; no commodious building; no instruments of moving and removing such things as require much force; no knowledge of the face of the earth; no account of time; no arts; no letters; no society; and which is worst of all, continual fear, and danger of violent death; and the life of man, solitary, poor, nasty, brutish, and short.

"The Charge of the Light Brigade"

Alfred, Lord Tennyson

"The Charge of the Light Brigade" describes a disastrous charge of British cavalry led by Lord Cardigan against Russian forces during the Battle of Balaclava on October 25, 1854, in the Crimean War (the area of modern-day Ukraine). Tennyson's evocative poem immortalized the charge as a symbol of war at its most honorable and its most tragic.

> *Half a league half a league,*
> *Half a league onward,*
> *All in the valley of Death*
> *Rode the six hundred:*
> *'Forward, the Light Brigade!*
> *Charge for the guns' he said:*

Into the valley of Death
Rode the six hundred.
'Forward, the Light Brigade!'
Was there a man dismay'd?
Not tho' the soldier knew
Some one had blunder'd:
Theirs not to make reply,
Theirs not to reason why,
Theirs but to do & die,
Into the valley of Death
Rode the six hundred.
Cannon to right of them,
Cannon to left of them,
Cannon in front of them
Volley'd & thunder'd;
Storm'd at with shot and shell,
Boldly they rode and well,
Into the jaws of Death,
Into the mouth of Hell
Rode the six hundred.
Flash'd all their sabres bare,
Flash'd as they turn'd in air
Sabring the gunners there,
Charging an army while
All the world wonder'd:
Plunged in the battery-smoke
Right thro' the line they broke;
Cossack & Russian
Reel'd from the sabre-stroke,
Shatter'd & sunder'd.
Then they rode back, but not
Not the six hundred.
  Cannon to right of them,

Cannon to left of them,
Cannon behind them
Volley'd and thunder'd;
Storm'd at with shot and shell,
While horse & hero fell,
They that had fought so well
Came thro' the jaws of Death,
Back from the mouth of Hell,
All that was left of them,
Left of six hundred.
When can their glory fade?
O the wild charge they made!
All the world wonder'd.
Honour the charge they made!
Honour the Light Brigade,
Noble six hundred!

"We Shall Fight on the Beaches"

WINSTON CHURCHILL

"We Shall Fight on the Beaches" is the common title given to this speech delivered by British prime minister Winston Churchill to the House of Commons of the British Parliament on June 4, 1940. This was the second of three major war speeches given during the Battle of France in World War II. The others were designated as the "Blood, Toil, Tears, and Sweat" speech of May 13 and the "This Was Their Finest Hour" speech of June 18. Taken all together, Churchill's series of speeches are considered some of the most rhetorically motivating proclamations in modern history. His task was to rally the British people to prepare to fight the Axis powers, even to the death. We know how the story ends, but these speeches capture the urgency and passion of the moment in which freedom and democracy hung in the balance.

I have, myself, full confidence that if all do their duty, if nothing is neglected, and if the best arrangements are made, as they are being made, we shall prove ourselves once again able to defend our Island home, to ride out the storm of war, and to outlive the menace of tyranny, if necessary for years, if necessary alone.

At any rate, that is what we are going to try to do. That is the resolve of His Majesty's Government—every man of them. That is the will of Parliament and the nation.

The British Empire and the French Republic, linked together in their cause and in their need, will defend to the death their native soil, aiding each other like good comrades to the utmost of their strength.

Even though large tracts of Europe and many old and famous States have fallen or may fall into the grip of the Gestapo and all the odious apparatus of Nazi rule, we shall not flag or fail.

We shall go on to the end, we shall fight in France, we shall fight on the seas and oceans, we shall fight with growing confidence and growing strength in the air, we shall defend our Island, whatever the cost may be, we shall fight on the beaches, we shall fight on the landing grounds, we shall fight in the fields and in the streets, we shall fight in the hills; we shall never surrender, and even if, which I do not for a moment believe, this Island or a large part of it were subjugated and starving, then our Empire beyond the seas, armed and guarded by the British Fleet, would carry on the struggle, until, in God's good time, the New World, with all its power and might, steps forth to the rescue and the liberation of the old.

Ares: Greek God of War

HOMER

The *Iliad* is an epic poem by the ancient Greek poet Homer. Set during the fabled Trojan War, the *Iliad* recounts the battles and events during a quarrel between King Agamemnon, commander of the Achaeans, and the warrior Achilles as they fight to win back Helen from Paris of Troy. Much like other Greek mythology, the *Iliad* glorifies men and gods in battle and lauds the stoic, courageous warrior who rules the battlefield. According to Greek tradition, Ares is the god of war. Described as a menacing and terrifying figure, Ares rules the battlefield often unjustly—killing whomever he pleases. In this excerpt, Athena—the goddess of wisdom, warfare, and skills—tricks Ares. He flees to complain to Zeus, the father of the gods, but Zeus chides him for being the worst of the gods—an allegory to describe the chaos and injustice in war.

> *So speaking she laid hand on Sthenelus*
> *And pulled him back and from the driver's place*
> *Forced to the ground, who sped in haste away.*
> *Then on the car beside the godlike chief*
> *Eager the goddess stept; and loudly groaned*
> *The oaken axle with unwonted weight,*
> *Bearing a goddess dread and peerless man.*
> *The whip and reins Pallas Athene took,*
> *And turned on Ares first the firm-hoofed steeds.*
> *He even now huge Periphas had slain,*
> *The best by far of all Aetolia's host,*
> *Ochesius' noble son—him had he slain,*
> *That blood-stained Ares, when Athene came*
> *With helm of Hades dark around her drawn,*
> *To be of mighty Ares all unseen.*
> *But soon as man-destroying Ares saw*
> *The godlike Diomedes, there he left*
> *Huge Periphas to lie where at the first*
> *He slew him and bereft of life: but he*
> *Straight at steed-taming Diomedes rushed.*
> *And when the twain advancing drew anigh,*
> *First Ares o'er the yoke and horses' reins*
> *Lunged out with brazen lance, in haste to slay:*
> *But with her hand Athene, stern-eyed maid,*
> *Seizing the spear, aside and from the car*
> *Thrust it away to spend an idle speed.*

Then second Diomedes good in fray
Attacked with brazen lance: which with strong force
Pallas Athene drove deep in the flank
Below the ribs, where round the loins was girt
The girdle: there the hero with true aim
Wounded the god, and rent his comely skin,
And back drew out the shaft.
Then roared amain the brazen
Ares, loud as thousands nine
May roar, or thousands ten on battle plain
Of men who meet in shock of martial fray.
And fear and trembling was on all, alike
On Trojan and Achaian host, so loud
Roared Ares, that insatiate god of war.
And as the air is dark with thunder clouds,
In sultry heat, when threatening swells the wind;
So brazen Ares to Tydides' sight
Darkling was seen, as all in clouds enwrapt
To the wide heaven he took his upward way.
And swiftly came he to the gods' abode,
Olympus steep, and sate him down beside
Zeus Cronides in grief of heart, and showed
The ambrosial blood down flowing from the wound;
While thus in winged words he made his moan:
"O Father Zeus, seems it not shame to thee,
Such foul destruction wrought? The worst alway
We gods have suffered from each other's spite,
While doing mortals pleasure. And with thee
We all now quarrel: who begatst a maid
Mad, baneful, ever set on wrongful work.
For we the rest who in Olympus dwell
Obey thee, and each god submissive bows:
But her thou checkest nor by word nor deed,

But loosest free, because she is thy child,
Destroying plague. And Tydeus' son but now,
Presumptuous Diomedes, she hath loosed
Madly to rage against immortal gods.
Cypris first wounded he upon the wrist,
Smiting her close; then on myself he rushed
Like one divine: but me my swift feet bare
Away: else had I long felt anguish there
Amid foul heaps of slain, or faint in swoon
Lain dead in life beneath his trenchant blows."
To whom with sternest glance cloud-gathering Zeus:
"Sit not by me, thou shifting weather-vane,
With whining plaint! Hateful to me art thou
Above all gods who in Olympus dwell.
For alway strife thou lov'st and wars and fights.
Thy mother's mood is thine, that brooks no check,
Nor yields—thy mother Herd's mood; whom I
Scarce by my words can tame. Wherefore I deem
'Tis by her prompting that thou suffer'st now.
Yet will I not endure that longer thus
Thou be in pain; for thou art son of mine,
To me thy mother bare thee: surely else—
Destroyer as thou art—hadst thou been born
Of other god, thou hadst long since been hurled
Below the rebel sons of Uranus."

Profile: John Leone

Today the United States military is an all-volunteer force. Service is no longer a requirement for all citizens, which means that those who enter the armed forces make the conscious decision to do so. As John Leone's story shows, this decision is never easy. I was introduced to John's story through my radio show.

No father wants to see his son die.

After a twenty-two-year career in the Air Force—whether sweating through the Vietnam War in Guam or steeling himself to count body bags during the first Gulf War—John Leone was no stranger to the military. But when his son wanted to join the Marines, the paternal instincts started kicking in . . . hard.

"He told me that he was going to join the Marines," said John. "And my first reaction was, 'Are you crazy?'"

There is nothing easy about mixing parenting and patriotism. The bonds of family and country intersect and overlap, and while a mother might bleed red, white, and blue, the thought of her child walking into harm's way never comes without a tear. It's rarely easier on the father.

Maternal bonds run strong, but ask any father what it feels like to see his son—carrying all the memories of a first game of catch, camping trips, and Christmas mornings—prepare to go to war.

And so John told his son Mike, "You know you don't have to do this."

It was in the short years after 9/11. A sense of duty and defense had gripped the hearts and imaginations of high school students—kids suddenly felt that it was right to rise to the call of their attacked homeland—and Mike was no exception.

"Mike said, 'No, Dad, it's going to be fun,'" said John. "And I thought, *he doesn't know what it's going to be like, he has no idea.* So I said, 'Do you know what kind of hardships will be there, do you know what's going to happen?'"

"C'mon, Dad, it can't be that bad."

"Wait a minute, son, I did it, I've lived that life."

Mike paused for a second, "Yeah, but you're old. You have no idea what you're talking about."

The conversation stopped there. John hoped that his son would get over this "fad," but Mike went through his junior year and entered his senior year in high school. He came home one day, six months from graduation, and told his father that he'd been talking to a Marine recruiter.

"I was like, 'Are you nuts?'" said John.

John had served in Vietnam and Guam.

"They knew that we were going to have duty here in the states trying to make sure that people knew what had happened to their kids," said John. "You don't know who you're going to have to call up and say, 'I hate to inform you that your kid is . . .'"

The possibility of losing his son haunted John. While he always felt that serving in the military was honorable and noble, there are certain images and fears that stick with fathers.

"I just wanted him to make sure that he knew what he was getting into."

John and Mary Lou argued with Mike, but their son was enamored with the life, the training, and the image of what it means to be a Marine. The camaraderie and sense of purpose that permeates every level of that branch of service can be intoxicating to a boy who wants to become a man.

Thanksgiving came around and Mike was excelling in his studies. One day he came home from school with a photo of the flag being raised at Iwo Jima, given to him by the recruiter. Mike told his father that he was preparing to sign his contracts.

"Son, do you know what you're going to be facing?" asked John.

"Yeah."

John took Mike away from his mother—he believed some things aren't meant to be said in front of women—and continued pressing his son.

"You may go to the front lines. You're going to see heads blown off, you're going to see bodies disintegrated, and you're going to see horrible things. Son, are you ready for this?"

Mike looked at his father and replied, "Yeah, yeah, Dad, it's no big deal."

John stopped everything. "Look at me, look at me in my face."

When a father locks eyes with his son, everything else fades away and things get serious.

"Are you ready to die for your country? Are you ready to give it all up?"

The question shocked Mike. He took a step back, shuddering. No recruiter, no person had ever asked him point-blank if he was ready to die. "What?" he asked.

John spoke again, calmly, but with force: "You can get excited about the uniform and the military—it's exciting, I know—but when you get in, it's more than the friends you'll make. You're going to probably go over to either Iraq or Afghanistan and there's a strong chance that you could die."

Mike stood there, silent, so John asked again, "Are you ready to die for your country?"

Finally his son said, quietly, "I never thought of it that way."

Mike left his father, went into his room, and locked the door.

For three days, Mike would come home from school, walk upstairs, lock his door, and just think. His parents would only see him briefly, at meals, and then Mike would go back upstairs and lock the door.

On the third day, Mike finally came out of his room.

"Dad?"

Something was different about Mike. John had never seen his son this somber, this serious, and this resolute.

The two men walked outside, away from Mike's mother.

Mike looked his father straight in the eye and said, "Dad, you asked me if I was ready to die for my country. Well, I now know I am. I love this country and I'm willing to do whatever it takes to get the job done, and if that means dying for my country, then that's what it will be. This is what I want."

Tears were quivering in both men's eyes. They stood there for a moment, then embraced and hugged.

John whispered, "You know I'll support you 110 percent. I'm proud of you for joining, and you should become the best Marine you can be. You will be serving in the greatest military organization in the world."

They had to go back inside and tell Mike's mother. Mary Lou cried, distraught over the thought of her baby dying.

"He's a man now," said John. "He can't just sit back and watch something greater than the both of us. He needs to know that we support him. He's going to see things that are going to be difficult for him. We're going to do this the right way and make sure that he's the best he can be."

Mike entered boot camp in February 2005 and graduated in May. In 2006, he entered his first tour of duty in Iraq. Four years of active duty and two tours later, Mike returned safely to his family with the Navy Commendation Medal. As of this writing, Mike remains in the Marine Corps Reserves.

John serves as the department chair of the religion department for St. Anthony Catholic High School in San Antonio, Texas. He and Mary Lou live in Schertz, Texas.

❖

From *Beowulf*

UNKNOWN SAXON POET, TRANSLATED BY FRANCIS B. GUMMERE

The character of Beowulf has long been admired and esteemed as a picture of antiquated manhood and courage. Set in a pre-Anglo-Saxon Scandinavian culture, the epic poem *Beowulf* relates the story of King Hrothgar of Denmark. A young Geatish warrior named Beowulf comes to the aid of Hrothgar when his country is beset by the aggressive swampland demon Grendel. He slays the demon, but then encounters the rage of Grendel's bereaved mother. In parts XIX and XX, Beowulf and Hrothgar discuss the dangers and challenges that will be present in dealing with the wrath of Grendel's mother.

> *Beowulf spake, bairn of Ecgtheow:*
> *"Sorrow not, sage! It beseems us better*
> *friends to avenge than fruitlessly mourn them.*
> *Each of us all must his end abide*
> *in the ways of the world; so win who may*
> *glory ere death! When his days are told,*
> *that is the warrior's worthiest doom.*
> *Rise, O realm-warder! Ride we anon,*
> *and mark the trail of the mother of Grendel.*
> *No harbor shall hide her—heed my promise!*
> *—enfolding of field or forested mountain*
> *or floor of the flood, let her flee where she will!*
> *But thou this day endure in patience,*
> *as I ween thou wilt, thy woes each one."*
> *Leaped up the graybeard: God he thanked,*
> *mighty Lord, for the man's brave words.*
> *For Hrothgar soon a horse was saddled*
> *wave-maned steed. The sovran wise*

stately rode on; his shield-armed men
followed in force. The footprints led
along the woodland, widely seen,
a path o'er the plain, where she passed, and trod
the murky moor; of men-at-arms
she bore the bravest and best one, dead,
him who with Hrothgar the homestead ruled.

On then went the atheling-born
o'er stone-cliffs steep and strait defiles,
narrow passes and unknown ways,
headlands sheer, and the haunts of the Nicors.
Foremost he fared, a few at his side
of the wiser men, the ways to scan,
till he found in a flash the forested hill
hanging over the hoary rock,
a woful wood: the waves below
were dyed in blood. The Danish men
had sorrow of soul, and for Scyldings all,
for many a hero, 'twas hard to bear,
ill for earls, when Aeschere's head
they found by the flood on the foreland there.
Waves were welling, the warriors saw,
hot with blood; but the horn sang oft
battle-song bold. The band sat down,
and watched on the water worm-like things,
sea-dragons strange that sounded the deep,
and nicors that lay on the ledge of the ness—
such as oft essay at hour of morn
on the road-of-sails their ruthless quest,—
and sea-snakes and monsters. These started away,
swollen and savage that song to hear,
that war-horn's blast. The warden of Geats,

with bolt from bow, then balked of life,
of wave-work, one monster; amid its heart
went the keen war-shaft; in water it seemed
less doughty in swimming whom death had seized.
Swift on the billows, with boar-spears well
hooked and barbed, it was hard beset,
done to death and dragged on the headland,
wave-roamer wondrous. Warriors viewed
the grisly guest.

Then girt him Beowulf
in martial mail, nor mourned for his life.
His breastplate broad and bright of hues,
woven by hand, should the waters try;
well could it ward the warrior's body
that battle should break on his breast in vain
nor harm his heart by the hand of a foe.
And the helmet white that his head protected
was destined to dare the deeps of the flood,
through wave-whirl win: 'twas wound with chains,
decked with gold, as in days of yore
the weapon-smith worked it wondrously,
with swine-forms set it, that swords nowise,
brandished in battle, could bite that helm.
Nor was that the meanest of mighty helps
which Hrothgar's orator offered at need:
"Hrunting" they named the hilted sword,
of old-time heirlooms easily first;
iron was its edge, all etched with poison,
with battle-blood hardened, nor blenched it at fight
in hero's hand who held it ever,
on paths of peril prepared to go
to folkstead of foes. Not first time this

it was destined to do a daring task.
For he bore not in mind, the bairn of Ecglaf
sturdy and strong, that speech he had made,
drunk with wine, now this weapon he lent
to a stouter swordsman. Himself, though, durst not
under welter of waters wager his life
as loyal liegeman. So lost he his glory,
honor of earls. With the other not so,
who girded him now for the grim encounter.

"In Flanders Fields"

LIEUTENANT COLONEL JOHN MCCRAE

To this day, Lieutenant Colonel John McCrae's "In Flanders Fields" remains one of the most moving war poems ever penned. Major McCrae, a surgeon attached to the 1st Field Artillery Brigade, spent seventeen days treating injured men in the Ypres Salient.

McCrae later reflected on his service, writing, "I wish I could embody on paper some of the varied sensations of that seventeen days . . . Seventeen days of Hades! At the end of the first day if anyone had told us we had to spend seventeen days there, we would have folded our hands and said it could not have been done."

McCrae was especially moved by one death. On May 2, 1915, a shell burst killed a young friend and former student, Lieutenant Alexis Helmer of Ottawa, and McCrae performed the funeral ceremony for him.

The next day McCrae released his sorrows by writing this poem. In the nearby cemetery, McCrae could see the wild poppies scattered throughout the fields and it inspired the serene words of this poem.

The poem was almost not published. McCrae didn't like his work and threw the poem away, but a fellow officer retrieved it and sent it to newspapers in England. *Punch* published it on December 8, 1915.

In Flanders fields the poppies blow
Between the crosses, row on row,
    That mark our place; and in the sky
    The larks, still bravely singing, fly
Scarce heard amid the guns below.
We are the Dead. Short days ago
We lived, felt dawn, saw sunset glow,
    Loved, and were loved, and now we lie
In Flanders fields.

Take up our quarrel with the foe:
To you from failing hands we throw
    The torch; be yours to hold it high.
    If ye break faith with us who die
We shall not sleep, though poppies grow
In Flanders fields.

Horatius at the Bridge

LIVY

Around 510 BC, the city of Rome was in upheaval and soon to be invaded by the Etruscans at the command of their lord, Lars Porsena. The Roman army, overwhelmed by the force of the enemy soldiers, began to flee. Only Horatius Cocles was left to defend the bridge to the city. For its bold tenacity, Horatius' stand is remembered as one of the most valiant in ancient history.

By this time the Tarquins had fled to Lars Porsena, king of Clusium. There, mixing advice with their entreaties, "They sometimes besought him not to suffer them, who were descended from the Etrurians, and of the same blood and name, to live in exile and poverty; at other times they advised him not to let this commencing practice of expelling kings pass unpunished. That liberty has charms enough in itself; and unless kings defend their crowns with as much vigour as the people pursue their liberty, that the highest must be reduced to a level with the lowest; there will be nothing exalted, nothing distinguished above the rest; and hence there must be an end of regal government, the most beautiful institution both among gods and men."

Porsena, thinking that it would be an honour to the Tuscans both that there should be a king at Rome, and especially one of the Etrurian nation, marched towards Rome with a hostile army. Never before on any other occasion did so great terror seize the senate; so powerful was the state of Clusium at the time, and so great the renown of Porsena. Nor did they only dread their enemies, but even their own citizens, lest the common people, through excess of fear, should, by receiving the Tarquins into the city, accept peace even if purchased with slavery . . .

Some parts seemed secured by the walls, others by the interposition of the Tiber. The Sublician bridge well nigh afforded a passage to the enemy, had there not been one man, Horatius Cocles (that defence the fortune of Rome had on that day), who, happening to be posted on guard at the bridge, when he saw the Janiculum taken by a sudden assault, and that the enemy were pouring down from thence in full speed, and that his own party, in terror and confusion, were abandoning their arms and ranks, laying hold of them one by one, standing in their way, and appealing to the faith of gods and men, he declared, "That their flight would avail them nothing if they deserted their post; if they passed the bridge and left it behind them, there would soon be more of the enemy in the Palatium and Capitol than in the Janiculum; for that reason he advised and charged them to demolish the bridge, by their sword, by fire, or by any means whatever; that he would stand the shock of the enemy as far as could be done by one man." He then advances to the first entrance of the bridge, and being easily distinguished among those who showed their backs in retreating from the fight, facing about to engage the foe hand to hand, by his surprising bravery he terrified the enemy. Two indeed a sense of shame kept with him, Sp. Lartius and T. Herminius, men eminent for their birth, and renowned for their gallant exploits. With them he for a short time stood the first storm of the danger, and the severest brunt of the battle.

But as they who demolished the bridge called upon them to retire, he obliged them also to withdraw to a place of safety on a small portion of the bridge still left.

Then casting his stern eyes round all the officers of the Etrurians in a threatening manner, he sometimes challenged them singly, sometimes reproached them all; "the slaves of haughty tyrants, who, regardless of their own freedom, came to oppress the liberty of others."

They hesitated for a considerable time, looking round one at the other, to commence the fight; shame then put the army in motion, and a shout being raised, they hurl their weapons from all sides on their single adversary; and when they all stuck in the shield held before him, and he with no less obstinacy kept possession of the bridge with firm step, they now endeavoured to thrust him down from it by one push, when at once the crash of the falling bridge, at the same time a shout of the Romans raised for joy at having completed their purpose, checked their ardour with sudden panic.

Then Cocles says, "Holy father Tiberinus, I pray that thou wouldst receive these arms, and this thy soldier, in thy propitious stream." Armed as he was, he leaped into the Tiber, and amid showers of darts hurled on him, swam across safe to his party, having dared an act which is likely to obtain more fame than credit with posterity.

The state was grateful towards such valour; a statue was erected to him in the comitium, and as much land was given to him as he ploughed around in one day. The zeal of private individuals also was conspicuous among the public honours. For, amid the great scarcity, each person contributed something to him according to his supply at home, depriving himself of his own support.

"Duty, Honor, Country"

GENERAL DOUGLAS MACARTHUR

General Douglas MacArthur served as the chief of staff of the army from 1930 to 1937 and was named commander of the Southwest Pacific arena during World War II. His wartime heroics are responsible in large part for the United States victory over Japan. This address by General MacArthur to the cadets of the U.S. Military Academy in accepting the Sylvanus Thayer Award on May 12, 1962, is a lasting tribute to the ideals that inspired that great American soldier. Reflecting on his wartime experience, MacArthur instructed the cadets to define their lives by duty, honor, and country—a code by which all men should live.

General Westmoreland, General Grove, distinguished guests, and gentlemen of the Corps!

As I was leaving the hotel this morning, a doorman asked me, "Where are you bound for, General?" And when I replied, "West Point," he remarked, "Beautiful place. Have you ever been there before?"

No human being could fail to be deeply moved by such a tribute as this [Thayer Award]. Coming from a profession I have served so long, and a people I have loved so well, it fills me with an emotion I cannot express. But this award is not intended primarily to honor a personality, but to symbolize a great moral code—the code of conduct and chivalry of those who guard this beloved land of culture and ancient descent. That is the animation of this medallion. For all eyes and for all time, it is an expression of the ethics of the American soldier. That I should be integrated in this way with so noble an ideal arouses a sense of pride and yet of humility which will be with me always.

Duty, Honor, Country: Those three hallowed words reverently dictate what you ought to be, what you can be, what you will be. They are your rallying points: to build courage when courage seems to fail; to regain faith when there seems to be little cause for faith; to create hope when hope becomes forlorn.

Unhappily, I possess neither that eloquence of diction, that poetry of imagination, nor that brilliance of metaphor to tell you all that they mean.

The unbelievers will say they are but words, but a slogan, but a flamboyant phrase. Every pedant, every demagogue, every cynic, every hypocrite, every troublemaker, and I am sorry to say, some others of an entirely different character, will try to downgrade them even to the extent of mockery and ridicule.

But these are some of the things they do. They build your basic character. They mold you for your future roles as the custodians of the nation's defense. They make you strong enough to know when you are weak, and brave enough to face yourself when you are afraid. They teach you to be proud and unbending in honest failure, but humble and gentle in success; not to substitute words for actions, not to seek the path of comfort, but to face the stress and spur of difficulty and challenge; to learn to stand up in the storm but to have compassion on those who fall; to master yourself before you seek to master others; to have a heart that is clean, a goal that is high; to learn to laugh, yet never forget how to weep; to reach into the future, yet never neglect the past; to be serious, yet never to take yourself too seriously; to be modest so that you will remember the simplicity of true greatness, the open mind of true wisdom, the meekness of true strength. They give you a temper of the will, a quality of the imagination, a vigor of the emotions, a freshness of the deep springs of life, a temperamental predominance of courage over timidity, of an appetite for adventure over love of ease. They create in your heart the sense of wonder, the unfailing hope of what next, and the joy and inspiration of life. They teach you in this way to be an officer and a gentleman.

And what sort of soldiers are those you are to lead? Are they reliable? Are they brave? Are they capable of victory? Their story is known to all of you. It is the story of the American man-at-arms. My estimate of him was formed on the battlefield many, many years ago, and has never changed. I regarded him then as I regard him now—as one of the world's noblest figures, not only as one of the finest military characters, but also as one of the most stainless. His name and fame are the birthright of every American citizen. In his youth and strength, his love and loyalty, he gave all that mortality can give.

He needs no eulogy from me or from any other man. He has written his own history and written it in red on his enemy's breast. But when I think of his patience under adversity, of his courage under fire, and of his modesty in victory, I am filled with an emotion of admiration I cannot put into words. He belongs to history as furnishing one of the greatest examples of successful patriotism. He belongs to posterity as the instructor of future generations in the principles of liberty and freedom. He belongs to the present, to us, by his virtues and by his achievements. In twenty campaigns, on a hundred battlefields, around a thousand campfires, I have witnessed that enduring fortitude, that patriotic self-abnegation, and that invincible determination which have carved his statue in the hearts of his people. From one end of the world to the other he has drained deep the chalice of courage.

As I listened to those songs [of the glee club], in memory's eye I could see those staggering columns of the First World War, bending under soggy packs, on many a weary march from dripping dusk to drizzling dawn, slogging ankle-deep through the mire of shell-shocked roads, to form grimly for the attack, blue-lipped, covered with sludge and mud, chilled by the wind and rain, driving home to their objective, and for many, to the judgment seat of God.

I do not know the dignity of their birth, but I do know the glory of their death. They died unquestioning, uncomplaining, with faith in their hearts, and on their lips the hope that we would go on to victory. Always, for them: *Duty, Honor, Country*; always their blood and sweat and tears, as we sought the way and the light and the truth.

And twenty years after, on the other side of the globe, again the filth of murky foxholes, the stench of ghostly trenches, the slime of dripping dugouts; those boiling suns of relentless heat, those torrential rains of devastating storms; the loneliness and utter desolation of jungle trails; the bitterness of long separation from those they loved and cherished; the deadly pestilence of tropical disease; the horror of stricken areas of war; their resolute and determined defense, their swift and sure attack, their indomitable purpose, their complete and decisive victory—always victory. Always through the bloody haze of their last reverberating shot, the vision of gaunt, ghastly men reverently following your password of: *Duty, Honor, Country*.

The code which those words perpetuate embraces the highest moral laws and will stand the test of any ethics or philosophies ever promulgated for the uplift of mankind. Its requirements are for the things that are right, and its restraints are from the things that are wrong.

The soldier, above all other men, is required to practice the greatest act of religious training—sacrifice.

In battle and in the face of danger and death, he discloses those divine attributes which his Maker gave when he created man in his own image. No physical courage and no brute instinct can take the place of the Divine help which alone can sustain him.

However horrible the incidents of war may be, the soldier who is called upon to offer and to give his life for his country is the noblest development of mankind.

You now face a new world—a world of change. The thrust into outer space of the satellite, spheres, and missiles marks the beginning of another epoch in the long story of mankind. In the five or more billions of years the scientists tell us it has taken to form the earth, in the three or more billion years of development of the human race, there has never been a more abrupt or staggering evolution. We deal now not with things of this world alone, but with the illimitable distances and as yet unfathomed mysteries of the universe. We are reaching out for a new and boundless frontier.

We speak in strange terms: of harnessing the cosmic energy; of making winds and tides work for us; of creating unheard synthetic materials to supplement or even replace our old standard basics; to purify sea water for our drink; of mining ocean floors for new fields of wealth and food; of disease preventatives to expand life into the hundreds of years; of controlling the weather for a more equitable distribution of heat and cold, of rain and shine; of spaceships to the moon; of the primary target in war, no longer limited to the armed forces of an enemy, but instead to include his civil populations; of ultimate conflict between a united human race and the sinister forces of some other planetary galaxy; of such dreams and fantasies as to make life the most exciting of all time.

And through all this welter of change and development, your mission remains fixed, determined, inviolable: it is to win our wars.

Everything else in your professional career is but corollary to this vital dedication. All other public purposes, all other public projects, all other public needs, great or small, will find others for their accomplishment. But you are the ones who are trained to fight. Yours is the profession of arms, the will to win, the sure knowledge that in war there is no substitute for victory; that if you lose, the nation will be destroyed; that the very obsession of your public service must be: *Duty, Honor, Country.*

Others will debate the controversial issues, national and international, which divide men's minds; but serene, calm, aloof, you stand as the Nation's war-guardian, as its lifeguard from the raging tides of international conflict, as its gladiator in the arena of battle. For a century and a half you have defended, guarded, and protected its hallowed traditions of liberty and freedom, of right and justice.

Let civilian voices argue the merits or demerits of our processes of government; whether our strength is being sapped by deficit financing, indulged in too long, by federal paternalism grown too mighty, by power groups grown too arrogant, by politics grown too corrupt, by crime grown too rampant, by morals grown too low, by taxes grown too high, by extremists grown too violent; whether our personal liberties are as thorough and complete as they should be. These great national problems are not for your professional participation or military solution. Your guidepost stands out like a tenfold beacon in the night: *Duty, Honor, Country.*

You are the leaven which binds together the entire fabric of our national system of defense. From your ranks come the great captains who hold the nation's destiny in their hands the moment the war tocsin sounds. The Long Gray Line has never failed us. Were you to do so, a million ghosts in olive drab, in brown khaki, in blue and gray, would rise from their white crosses thundering those magic words: *Duty, Honor, Country.*

This does not mean that you are war mongers.

On the contrary, the soldier, above all other people, prays for peace, for he must suffer and bear the deepest wounds and scars of war.

But always in our ears ring the ominous words of Plato, that wisest of all philosophers: "Only the dead have seen the end of war."

The shadows are lengthening for me. The twilight is here. My days of old have vanished, tone and tint. They have gone glimmering through the dreams of things that were. Their memory is one of wondrous beauty, watered by tears, and coaxed and caressed by the smiles of yesterday. I listen vainly, but with thirsty ears, for the witching melody of faint bugles blowing reveille, of far drums beating the long roll. In my dreams I hear again the crash of guns, the rattle of musketry, the strange, mournful mutter of the battlefield.

But in the evening of my memory, always I come back to West Point.

Always there echoes and re-echoes: *Duty, Honor, Country.*

Today marks my final roll call with you, but I want you to know that when I cross the river my last conscious thoughts will be of The Corps, and The Corps, and The Corps.

I bid you farewell.

"War Sonnets"

RUPERT BROOKE

Rupert Brooke was a popular English poet during World War I. His "War Sonnets" remain Brooke's best-loved and most well-known poetry because of the beautiful imagery he uses to memorialize his fallen comrades. His deep love of his country is profoundly moving and the admiration he shows for the English cause is the ultimate patriotism. This excerpt from "The War Sonnets" contains one of the most moving lines of war poetry, "If I should die, think only this of me: That there's some corner of a foreign field that is for ever England."

III. The Dead

Blow out, you bugles, over the rich Dead!
   There's none of these so lonely and poor of old,
     But, dying, has made us rarer gifts than gold.
These laid the world away; poured out the red
Sweet wine of youth; gave up the years to be
   Of work and joy, and that unhoped serene,
     That men call age; and those who would have been,
Their sons, they gave, their immortality.

Blow, bugles, blow! They brought us, for our dearth,
   Holiness, lacked so long, and Love, and Pain.
Honour has come back, as a king, to earth,
   And paid his subjects with a royal wage;
And Nobleness walks in our ways again;
   And we have come into our heritage.

IV. The Dead

These hearts were woven of human joys and cares,
   Washed marvellously with sorrow, swift to mirth.
The years had given them kindness. Dawn was theirs,
   And sunset, and the colours of the earth.
These had seen movements, and heard music; known
   Slumber and waking; loved; gone proudly friended;
Felt the quick stir of wonder; sat alone;
   Touched flowers and furs and cheeks. All this is ended.

There are waters blown by changing winds to laughter
And lit by the rich skies, all day. And after,
 Frost, with a gesture, stays the waves that dance
And wandering loveliness. He leaves a white
 Unbroken glory, a gathered radiance,
A width, a shining peace, under the night.

V. The Soldier

If I should die, think only this of me:
 That there's some corner of a foreign field
That is for ever England. There shall be
 In that rich earth a richer dust concealed;
A dust whom England bore, shaped, made aware,
 Gave, once, her flowers to love, her ways to roam,
A body of England's, breathing English air,
 Washed by the rivers, blest by suns of home.

And think, this heart, all evil shed away,
 A pulse in the eternal mind, no less
 Gives somewhere back the thoughts by England given;
 Her sights and sounds; dreams happy as her day;
 And laughter, learnt of friends; and gentleness,
In hearts at peace, under an English heaven.

Profile: Audie Murphy

More than four million people visit Arlington National Cemetery every year. The most popular site is the grave of President John F. Kennedy. The second most visited site is the simple grave marker of Audie Murphy, the most decorated combat soldier of World War II.

He wanted to join the Marines, but he was too short. The paratroopers wouldn't have him either. Reluctantly, he settled on the infantry, enlisting to become nothing less than one of the most decorated heroes of World War II. He was Audie Murphy, the baby-faced Texas farm boy who became an American legend. Murphy grew up on a sharecropper's farm in Hunt County, Texas. Left at a very young age to help raise ten brothers and sisters when his father deserted their mother, Audie was only sixteen when his mother died. He watched as his brothers and sisters were doled out to an orphanage or to relatives.

Seeking an escape from that life in 1942, he looked to the Marines. War had just been declared and, like so many other young men, Murphy lied about his age in his attempt to enlist. But it was not his age that kept him out of the Marines; it was his size. Not tall enough to meet the minimum requirements, he tried to enlist in the paratroopers, but again was denied entrance. Despondent, he chose the infantry.

Following basic training Murphy was assigned to the 15th Regiment, 3rd Infantry Division in North Africa preparing to invade Sicily. It was there in 1943 that he first saw combat, proving himself to be a proficient marksman and highly skilled soldier. His performance consistently demonstrated how well he understood the techniques of small-unit action. He landed at Salerno to fight in the Volturno River campaign and then at Anzio to be part of the Allied force that fought its way to Rome. Throughout these campaigns, Murphy's skills earned him advancements in rank. Also many of his superior officers were being transferred, wounded, or killed. After the capture of Rome, Murphy earned his first decoration for gallantry.

Shortly thereafter his unit was withdrawn from Italy to train for Operation Anvil-Dragoon, the invasion of southern France. During seven weeks of fighting in that successful campaign, Murphy's division suffered forty-five hundred casualties, and he became one of the most decorated men in his company. But his biggest test was yet to come.

On January 26, 1945, near the village of Holtzwihr in eastern France, Lieutenant Murphy's forward positions came under fierce attack by the Germans. Against the onslaught of six panzer tanks and 250 infantrymen, Murphy ordered his men to fall back to better their defenses. Alone, he mounted an abandoned burning tank destroyer and with a single machine gun contested the enemy's advance. Wounded in the leg during the heavy fire, Murphy remained there for nearly an hour, repelling the attack of German soldiers on three sides and single-handedly killing fifty of them. His courageous performance stalled the German advance and allowed him to lead his men in the counterattack, which ultimately drove the enemy from Holtzwihr. For this, Murphy was awarded the Medal of Honor, the nation's highest award for gallantry in action.

By the war's end, Murphy had become the nation's most decorated soldier, earning an unparalleled twenty-eight medals, including three from France and one from Belgium. Murphy had been wounded three times during the war; yet, in May 1945, when victory was declared in Europe, he still had not reached his twenty-first birthday.

Audie Murphy returned to a hero's welcome in the United States. His photograph appeared on the cover of *Life* magazine and he was persuaded by actor James Cagney to embark on an acting career. Still very shy and unassuming, Murphy arrived in Hollywood with only his good looks and—by his own account—"no talent." Nevertheless, he went on to make more than forty films. His first part was just a small one in *Beyond Glory* in 1948. The following year he published his wartime memoirs, *To Hell and Back*, which received good reviews. Later he portrayed himself in the 1955 movie version of the book. Many film critics, however, believe his best performance was in *Red Badge of Courage*, Stephen Crane's Civil War epic.

After nearly twenty years he retired from acting and started a career in private business. But the venture was unsuccessful, eventually forcing him into bankruptcy in 1968. Murphy, who once said that he could only sleep with a loaded pistol under his pillow, was haunted by nightmares of his wartime experiences throughout his adult life. In 1971, at the age of forty-six, he died in the crash of a private plane near Roanoke, Virginia.

Audie Murphy is buried in Arlington National Cemetery, just across Memorial Drive from the Memorial Amphitheater. A special flagstone walkway has been constructed to accommodate the large number of people who stop to pay their respects to this hero. At the end of a row of graves, his tomb is marked by a simple, white, government-issue tombstone, which lists only a few of his many military decorations. The stone is, as he was, too small.

2

Man at Work

On September 7, 1903, in the middle of economic panic on Wall Street, President Theodore Roosevelt addressed an anxious crowd at the Labor Day Parade in Syracuse, New York. Facing a looming depression, Roosevelt spoke on what he knew best, inspiring the workers of America. "Far and away the best prize that life has to offer is the chance to work hard at work worth doing," said Roosevelt. His words still echo today. Work, if pursued correctly, can be one of the most rewarding and fulfilling activities a man can undertake.

Whether it is earning a living for our families and ourselves, taking out the trash, or doing homework, work occupies much of our waking lives. Yet we seldom stop to ask ourselves what our occupation means to us or why we do it. What do you want to be when you grow up? What do you do for work? How you answer these questions may determine how you will spend much of your life.

As men mature, school can become harder and the workweek gets longer. Soon enough, we all learn that work is a necessary, unavoidable part of life. It does not stop on the weekend, when the school bell rings, or at retirement. The early English settlers of Jamestown, Virginia, learned this the hard way when they decided not to do their share of work for the colony. To solve the problem, Captain John Smith, their leader, made a new rule: *If you don't work, you don't eat.* The men's perspective changed very quickly.

The attitude you take in your approach to work is vital. Often, your job will be tedious, burdensome, and primarily serve the interests of someone else. The more time you spend working, the less time you have for playing, and it becomes easy to live for the weekend. Vacation and recreation become the escape from work. The thought of such a reward enables many a man to endure long and grueling days in an occupation he dislikes.

As is often the case, life can become separated between livelihood and leisure. In one, man receives money for his efforts; in the other, he receives satisfaction from his earnings. The two are both dependent on each other, but we act as if they are two separate worlds—the workweek and the weekend. Why not search for a life that connects both, what Aristotle called "the ideal life"? Here's one test: When you think of what brings you happiness, do you think of work or do you think of leisure activities, such as hobbies or recreations? Why not both?

Eric Liddell, a Scottish athlete who won the men's four hundred meters in the 1924 Summer Olympics, said, "When I run, I feel God's pleasure." After the Olympics, Liddell returned to his work as a missionary in China, one of the greatest sacrifices a man can make through work.

In a telling confession, the Irish playwright George Bernard Shaw once said, "The harder I work the more I live." The reward for work can go far beyond the paycheck and there is much satisfaction to be found in a job well done. Aristotle observed that "pleasure in the job puts perfection in the work." A worthy goal is to find the same type of enjoyment in your life's labors.

Remember, the word *vocation* comes from the Latin root "to call." Your "calling" is your life's work. It can be done enthusiastically or carelessly, cheerfully or grudgingly. Approached the right way, a man's labor can be both his vocation and his *avocation*. Done improperly, his work can be what philosopher Leo Strauss deemed a "joyless quest for joy." It's up to you. Your occupation can be a means to an end, or it can be an end in itself.

The lesson here is to find something you love to do, whatever it might be, and do it to the best of your ability. As parents, we often tell our kids to get good grades, go to a good school, and get a good job. But, is that the best advice we can give? Not every student is the next Rhodes Scholar, *nor wants to be.* Not every man is the next Bill Gates, *nor wants to be.* Different people are attracted to different types of work. I'm not saying to lower your expectations; instead, I'm saying to be the best at what you love and don't let image, status, or jealousy steer you away from that. "Every calling is great," said Oliver Wendell Holmes, "when greatly pursued."

That being said, sometimes, even often, people have to choose work they don't enjoy to accomplish other worthy ends. Fathers and mothers clean offices, drive cabs at night, take in sewing and take other second jobs so they can provide for their family or send a child through college. And for young people, often your first job is not going to be something you necessarily love or want to do for its own sake, but it ought to be a step toward a job you will enjoy. Often the long-term goal of the job you really love is reached by taking a few jobs you know you're not going to love.

Remember, no matter the job, no matter the calling, there can be purpose in it. Jimmy Buffett, the hardworking singer of songs about leisure, has a song entitled "It's My Job," the chorus of which runs, "It's my job to be better than the rest, and that makes the day for me." Singer, songwriter, trucker, physician, attorney, trash collector, carpenter, you name it—there is, or can be, meaning in our work.

Needless to say, one area we often neglect is manual labor. Hard physical labor is what men did for many centuries. Some still do. Before the Industrial Revolution, almost all work was physical work, but since the inventions of the assembly line, robotics, and computers, man finds himself being "modernized," drawn away from open-air fields and shops and more into offices and cubicles.

What's changed, too, is that a majority of today's workforce has shifted to what we call a knowledge-based economy. But that does not mean that blue-collar work is mindless and enervating, while white-collar work is intellectually superior and therefore more rewarding. George Orwell once said, in retrospect almost prophetically, "[C]ease to use your hands and you have lopped off a huge chunk of your consciousness."

Despite what popular culture might convey, we know there is something intrinsically satisfying in being able to plant your own garden, repair your own house, and fix your own car. Recently, a friend of mine was recovering from life-threatening cancer. His doctor told him that he could not work, exercise, or enjoy the other fruits of life—all things that men pride themselves on. I asked him what hurts the most to be without. "Work," he said. "I don't feel like a man. Work has more to do with me being a man than sex or muscle."

The truth is that work satisfies more than just material needs. It quenches an innate yearning for order, importance, and regularity. French writer Albert Camus believed that "without work, all life goes rotten. But when work is soulless, life stifles and dies." Find fulfillment and enjoyment in your work, not aside from it. As the following excerpts and accounts will illustrate, manhood is incomplete without acknowledging the importance of, and doing, good work.

Profile: Terry Toussaint

Whether you like it or not, you will spend a majority of your life at work. The attitude you approach this work with determines whether you will enjoy your job or hate waking up and going to work. Terry Toussaint of Fort Valley, Georgia, is a sanitation worker who loves his job. His happiness is not determined by his paycheck or job title but by the mind-set he carries with him every day. His story is humbling and one we can all learn from. He is a listener to my radio show.

He calls himself the "proud sanitation worker."

While Terry Toussaint's official title is "supervisor of the Fort Valley Sanitation Department," he prefers the shorter, more direct term. He is not ashamed of his work or the stereotypes that go along with it.

"I've never heard a sanitation worker say 'I'm a proud sanitation worker,' but I am. I really am," said Toussaint.

The title is a tribute to Martin Luther King Jr. On March 18, 1968, King spoke to a crowd of street sweepers in Memphis, Tennessee. He told them, "If it falls your lot to be a street sweeper, sweep streets like Michelangelo painted pictures, like Shakespeare wrote poetry, like Beethoven composed music; sweep streets so well that all the host of heaven and earth will have to pause and say, 'Here lived a great street sweeper, who swept his job well.'"

King's earth-moving words spoke to a generation of Americans in need of direction and guidance. The aftershock of his wisdom is still felt today, even in the small rural town of Fort Valley, Georgia, where Toussaint oversees the city's sanitation department. For a town of roughly eight thousand people, Toussaint is in charge of keeping the town clean, whether it's clearing fallen trees, roadkill, or garbage.

"It's all about cleanliness. We service every aspect, be it businesses, schools, or

whatever. It's just a sense of pride in keeping that flow going, keeping the trash moving. I pride myself in my job, I like my job," Toussaint said.

In fact, Toussaint likes his job so much he hasn't missed a day of work in years.
"It's all part of my work ethic," Toussaint explained.

Growing up in Florida, Toussaint had every reason *not* to adhere to a strict work
ethic. "I haven't seen my dad since sixth grade. I had to look around at the positive men
or positive role models, not only in my family but that were around me all the time."

These role models manifested themselves in the form of Toussaint's uncles, his
mother, his grandmother, and later the U.S. Army. After his service in the military,
Toussaint landed in Miami and found a job as an operator for Bell South.

In 2002, Toussaint's life came to a screeching halt. While driving his SUV,
another car cut him off, forcing his vehicle into a death spiral, rolling twice across
the highway and finally landing on its back with the wheels in the air. Miraculously,
Toussaint kicked out the door and walked out of the wreck without a scratch.

Afterward his beloved grandmother called him and said, "Well, this goes to show
you that God is not ready for you yet; you still have some work to do."

Two months later, Toussaint's grandmother passed away.

Toussaint has never forgotten her words. "I feed off of that every day. The work
ethic and the spirit, it's all rolled up into one."

After the accident, his outlook on life changed dramatically. "I try to keep a positive spirit and a positive attitude toward life because there's so much bad stuff going
on in the world," he said.

"I'm vertical and breathing," he joked. "Whatever happens after that is icing on
the cake."

With a newfound lease on life, Toussaint went back to work. After several years
of hard work and perfect attendance, there was an opportunity for promotion at Bell
South. Despite his best efforts, Toussaint failed to land the job and soon after moved
to Georgia, where he landed a job as a supervisor of the streets department in Fort
Valley.

Initially, Toussaint cleaned gutters and fixed potholes and curbs. Some might
call it a demotion, but he calls it "hitting the ground running." After eight months,
the director saw the potential in Toussaint and promoted him to supervisor of the
sanitation department.

"There are a lot of people out here like myself—who may not have credentials on paper but are positive people who have good spirits and mean well—that folks don't even know about," Toussaint said.

April 20, 2010, as Toussaint was driving his city truck, he noticed a sheriff deputy's car stopped several feet in front of a four-way intersection. As he drove closer, he noticed a man in the back of the police car, kicking his way out and then escaping across the highway.

Toussaint jumped out of his car and rushed up to the sheriff. "Officer, do you need help?"

"Yes," said the officer, who was not fast enough to catch the escaping convict. Toussaint took off running. Two or three blocks down the street he lost the man in a wooded section. That's where his military training kicked in—he stopped and listened. It was the height of summer, and Toussaint could hear branches cracking and leaves rustling. Seconds passed and he heard the convict start to move again.

"I caught him and held him down to the ground. I pulled out my cell phone and dialed 911," Toussaint said. With one hand on his phone and the other on the back of the inmate, he restrained his prisoner until the police arrived.

To top off his story, Toussaint added, "To this day, no one has acknowledged what I did." Not the police, not the local news, and not even the sheriff.

But don't call him a hero; it's part of his duty, he said. "If it were to happen tomorrow, I would do it again. I feel like we are all city employees and whether it's law enforcement or not, [or] fire department, I feel that it was my civic duty to intervene and help this law enforcement officer capture this inmate."

For Toussaint, it's all part of the day's job. At fifty years old, he starts every day at 4:45 a.m. and never misses a day of work. He makes every day count. Toussaint lives out the words of Martin Luther King Jr.

"I'll always be the best that I can be at [whatever job I have]," Toussaint boasted. His attitude, not his job or status, defines who he is as a man. He describes himself as "financially strapped and morally rich."

For the proud sanitation worker of Fort Valley, Georgia, work is more than a paycheck, more than a means to an end. It's a chance to appreciate life and what he's been given. Whatever his calling might be, he takes pride in his work and does it to the best of his ability. One day the world will look back at Fort Valley, Georgia, and say, "Here lived a great sanitation worker, who did his job well."

"You keep swinging at that ball and you know that eventually you're going to hit it. And that's the attitude that I have," Toussaint said. "A lot of folks strike out and give up and walk to the dugout with their heads down. But you know what, the guy who's going to make it is the guy who goes back up to the plate with that vigor and says, 'I'm going to hit that ball this time,' no matter how many strikes you might get. Always stay positive because you know what, that next pitch is the one that you might knock out of the ball park.

"I hit it out of the park every day that I get up."

Since the writing of this profile Terry Toussaint has moved on to work construction in South Carolina, driving hours to his job every day and still bringing the same commitment and selflessness to his work.

"Work"

Eliza Cook

Work can often feel trivial, boring, and insignificant. This poem reminds us that whatever our work may be we can always find value and worth in a job well done.

> *Work, work, my boy, be not afraid;*
> *   Look labor boldly in the face;*
> *Take up the hammer or the spade,*
> *   And blush not for your humble place.*
> *There's glory in the shuttle's song;*
> *   There's triumph in the anvil's stroke;*
> *There's merit in the brave and strong,*
> *   Who dig the mine or fell the oak.*

— ❧ —

"The Plough Boy"

KATE DOUGLAS WIGGIN AND NORA ARCHIBALD SMITH

With the right mind-set, a hard day's work and a good night's sleep can be just as rewarding as a day of play.

> *Where winds blow pure and freely,*
> *And blossoms load the air,*
> *And green leaves wave their leafy boughs*
> *And all around looks fair;*
> *I ply my daily labor,*
> *And work till night has come,*
> *And then return contented*
> *To rest myself at home.*

— ❧ —

"How Do You Tackle Your Work?"

EDGAR A. GUEST

Many mornings we wake up and dread going to work. Other times we find ourselves just going through the motions to get our job done. We must remember, however, that success comes from confidence and a can-do attitude, no matter how menial our work might feel.

> *How do you tackle your work each day?*
> *Are you scared of the job you find?*
> *Do you grapple the task that comes your way*
> *With a confident, easy mind?*

Do you stand right up to the work ahead
Or fearfully pause to view it?
Do you start to toil with a sense of dread
Or feel that you're going to do it?
You can do as much as you think you can,
But you'll never accomplish more;
If you're afraid of yourself, young man,
There's little for you in store.
For failure comes from the inside first,
It's there if we only knew it,
And you can win, though you face the worst,
If you feel that you're going to do it.
Success! It's found in the soul of you,
And not in the realm of luck!
The world will furnish the work to do,
But you must provide the pluck.
You can do whatever you think you can,
It's all in the way you view it.
It's all in the start you make, young man:
You must feel that you're going to do it.
How do you tackle your work each day?
With confidence clear, or dread?
What to yourself do you stop and say
When a new task lies ahead?
What is the thought that is in your mind?
Is fear ever running through it?
If so, just tackle the next you find
By thinking you're going to do it.

The Gift of God

ECCLESIASTES 3:10–15 NKJV

Instead of worrying about what the future holds, the Bible reminds us to enjoy the life and work that has been given to us. Find contentment in what has been given to you because you do not know what tomorrow will bring.

I have seen the God-given task with which the sons of men are to be occupied. He has made everything beautiful in its time. Also He has put eternity in their hearts, except that no one can find out the work that God does from beginning to end. I know that nothing is better for them than to rejoice, and to do good in their lives, and also that every man should eat and drink and enjoy the good of all his labor—it is the gift of God.

> *I know that whatever God does,*
> *It shall be forever.*
> *Nothing can be added to it,*
> *And nothing taken from it.*
> *God does it, that men should fear before Him.*
> *That which is has already been,*
> *And what is to be has already been;*
> *And God requires an account of what is past.*

From *Two Years Before the Mast*

RICHARD HENRY DANA

Richard Dana's travel narrative tells the story of one young man's trials serving at sea. Dana described vividly what life and work are like on board a ship. It's a brutal and nonstop existence that should be a sobering example of what working hard can look like. In life, as on board a ship, there is always more work to be done.

Before I end my explanations, it may be well to define a day's work, and to correct a mistake prevalent among landsmen about a sailor's life. Nothing is more common than to hear people say, "Are not sailors very idle at sea? What can they find to do?" This is a natural mistake, and, being frequently made, is one which every sailor feels interested in having corrected. In the first place, then, the discipline of the ship requires every man to be at work upon something when he is on deck, except at night and on Sundays. At all other times you will never see a man, on board a well-ordered vessel, standing idle on deck, sitting down, or leaning over the side. It is the officer's duty to keep everyone at work, even if there is nothing to be done but to scrape the rust from the chain cables. In no state prison are the convicts more regularly set to work, and more closely watched. No conversation is allowed among the crew at their duty, and though they frequently do talk when aloft, or when near one another, yet they stop when an officer is nigh.

With regard to the work upon which the men are put, it is a matter which probably would not be understood by one who has not been at sea. When I first left port, and found that we were kept regularly employed for a week or two, I supposed that we were getting the vessel into sea trim, and that it would soon be over, and we should have nothing to do but to sail the ship; but I found that it continued so for two years, and at the end of the two years there was as much to be done as ever. As has often been said, a ship is like a lady's watch, always out of repair. When first leaving port, studding-sail gear is to be rove, all the running rigging to be examined, that which is unfit for use to be got down, and new rigging rove in its place; then the standing rigging is to be overhauled, replaced, and repaired in a thousand different ways; and wherever any of the numberless ropes or the yards are chafing or wearing upon it, there "chafing gear," as it is called, must be put on. This chafing gear consists of worming, parcelling, roundings, battens, and service of all kinds,—rope-yarns, spun-yarn, marline, and seizing-stuffs. Taking off, putting on, and mending the chafing gear alone, upon a vessel, would find constant employment for a man or for two men, during working hours, for a whole voyage.

The next point to be considered is, that all the "small stuffs" which are used on board a ship—such as spun-yarn, marline, seizing-stuff, etc.—are made on board. The owners of a vessel buy up incredible quantities of "old junk," which the sailors unlay, and, after drawing out the yarns, knot them together, and roll them up in balls. These "rope-yarns" are constantly used for various purposes, but the greater part is manufactured into spun-yarn. For this purpose, every vessel is furnished with a "spun-yarn winch"; which is very simple, consisting of a wheel and spindle. This may be heard constantly going on deck in pleasant weather; and we had employment, during a great part of the time, for three hands, in drawing and knotting yarns, and making spun-yarn.

Another method of employing the crew is "setting-up" rigging. Whenever any of the standing rigging becomes slack (which is continually happening), the seizings and coverings must be taken off, tackles got up, and, after the rigging is bowsed well taut, the seizings and coverings be replaced, which is a very nice piece of work. There is also such a connection between different parts of a vessel, that one rope can seldom be touched without requiring a change in another. You cannot stay a mast aft by the back stays, without slacking up the head stays, etc. If we add to this all the tarring, greasing, oiling, varnishing, painting, scraping, and scrubbing which is required in the course of a long voyage, and also remember this is all to be done in addition to watching at night, steering, reefing, furling, bracing, making and setting sail, and pulling, hauling, and climbing in every direction, one will hardly ask, "What can a sailor find to do at sea?"

If, after all this labour,—after exposing their lives and limbs in storms, wet and cold,—

> "Wherein the cub-drawn bear would couch,
> The lion and the belly-pinched wolf
> Keep their furs dry,"—

the merchants and captains think that the sailors have not earned their twelve dollars a month (out of which they clothe themselves), and their salt beef and hard bread, they keep them picking oakum—ad infinitum. This is the usual resource upon a rainy day, for then it will not do to work upon rigging; and when it is pouring down in floods, instead of letting the sailors stand about in sheltered places, and talk, and keep themselves comfortable, they are separated to different parts of the ship, and kept at work picking oakum. I have seen oakum stuff placed about in different parts of the ship, so that the sailors might not be idle in the snatches between the frequent squalls upon crossing the equator. Some officers have been so driven to find work for the crew in a ship ready for sea, that they have set them to pounding the anchors (often done) and scraping the chain cables. The "Philadelphia Catechism" is,

"Six days shalt thou labour and do all thou art able, And on the seventh,—holystone the decks and scrape the cable."

This kind of work, of course, is not kept up off Cape Horn, Cape of Good Hope, and in extreme north and south latitudes; but I have seen the decks washed down and scrubbed when the water would have frozen if it had been fresh, and all hands kept at work upon the rigging, when we had on our pea-jackets, and our hands so numb that we could hardly hold our marline-spikes.

I have here gone out of my narrative course in order that any who read this may, at the start, form as correct an idea of a sailor's life and duty as possible. I have done it in this place because, for some time, our life was nothing but the unvarying repetition of these duties, which can be better described together. Before leaving this description, however, I would state, in order to show landsmen how little they know of the nature of a ship, that a ship-carpenter is kept constantly employed, during good weather, on board vessels which are in what is called perfect sea order.

The "Parable of the Talents"

MATTHEW 25:14–30 NKJV (ALSO IN LUKE 19:12–28)

Jesus used the parable of the talents to illustrate to his disciples the value of stewardship. When a man left home, he gave three of his workers different amounts of money according to their abilities. Two of the servants invested the money, while the other did nothing with it. This lesson teaches that we must take what talents we are blessed with and put them to work.

For the kingdom of heaven is like a man traveling to a far country, who called his own servants and delivered his goods to them. And to one he gave five talents, to another two, and to another one, to each according to his own ability; and immediately he went on a journey. Then he who had received the five talents went and traded with them, and made another five talents. And likewise he who had received two gained two more also. But he who had received one went and dug in the ground, and hid his lord's money. After a long time the lord of those servants came and settled accounts with them.

So he who had received five talents came and brought five other talents, saying, "Lord, you delivered to me five talents; look, I have gained five more talents besides them." His lord said to him, "Well done, good and faithful servant; you were faithful over a few things, I will make you ruler over many things. Enter into the joy of your lord." He also who had received two talents came and said, "Lord, you delivered to me two talents; look, I have gained two more talents besides them." His lord said to him, "Well done, good and faithful servant; you have been faithful over a few things, I will make you ruler over many things. Enter into the joy of your lord."

Then he who had received the one talent came and said, "Lord, I knew you to be a hard man, reaping where you have not sown, and gathering where you have not scattered seed. And I was afraid, and went and hid your talent in the ground. Look, there you have what is yours."

But his lord answered and said to him, "You wicked and lazy servant, you knew that I reap where I have not sown, and gather where I have not scattered seed. So you ought to have deposited my money with the bankers, and at my coming I would have received back my own with interest. So take the talent from him, and give it to him who has ten talents.

For to everyone who has, more will be given, and he will have abundance; but from him who does not have, even what he has will be taken away. And cast the unprofitable servant into the outer darkness. There will be weeping and gnashing of teeth."

Profile: Gac Filipaj, the Janitor Turned Classicist

Homer. Herodotus. Sophocles. Plato. Aristotle. Demosthenes. Cicero. Virgil. Horace. Tacitus. Set foot on Columbia University's campus, and these names gaze down at you from the front of the Butler Library building, an impressive neoclassical structure completed in 1946. They resound through the ages as ballasts of truth and wisdom.

But would you believe that these days Columbia's most distinguished practitioner of Greek and Latin, the language of the historic greats, is also one of its janitors?

Like generations of immigrants before him, Gac Filipaj came to America in search of a better life. In 1992, the then thirty-two-year-old Filipaj arrived in New York City after fleeing his war-scarred homeland of the former Yugoslavia, where he had been a part-time law student. In Yugoslavia, Filipaj couldn't attend classes in person because of his responsibilities on his family's farm. Instead, he had studied in his spare time, and would take a train eight hours overnight to school at exam time. Said Filipaj, "Eventually I began rooming with a friend near campus, but the fighting in Yugoslavia prevented me from finishing my degree."

In America, Filipaj found work as a janitor. Many would scoff at, or refuse, such a downshift in prestige, going from studying law to cleaning bathrooms. But Filipaj saw his position as an opportunity. He settled in the Bronx and started taking English classes at night at a local high school.

After several years, Filipaj's English improved enough for him to take classes at Columbia. Because Columbia offered free tuition for its employees, Filipaj attended the School of Continuing Education, and later, the School of General Studies. But he also continued to work full-time at his janitorial position, fitting in one or two classes per semester around his eight-hour shift. Word by word, test by test, day by day, Filipaj worked toward his bachelor's degree.

When the time came to declare a major, he chose classics, the close study of Greek and Roman authors in their original languages. But why? "Latin is an interesting language," he said, "and their culture, Greco-Roman culture, is very interesting."

In addition to being interesting, classics is also a very difficult subject. To excel in it requires plenty of personal discipline, perseverance, and many hours of memorization and translation work. So Filipaj would go to class in the mornings, work from 2:30 to 11:00 p.m., and then head home to hit the books. "I had some very difficult moments," he said. "Some days, I was so tired."

But his perseverance paid off. In 2012, at age fifty-two, Filipaj finally completed the necessary one hundred and twenty four credit hours of coursework at Columbia, qualifying him for a bachelor of arts.

At his commencement ceremony, a reporter asked Filipaj if he planned to take any time off. He said he would take two days off, then get back to work.

Filipaj told reporters that in the future he would like to pursue graduate school in classics. He would also like to find another job. But Filipaj recognizes that the dignity of work lies in the act itself. Despite being a janitor, his self-worth isn't defined by his profession. "I think I'm going to stay at Columbia," he said. "If I can get a job better than cleaning, good. If not, there is nothing shameful about that work."

Still, Filipaj has his sights set as high as he ever has. "I would say that I have fulfilled half of my dream—going to graduate school would complete it."

His name may never appear on a library, but in his own way, Gac Filipaj is a master of Greek and Latin.

"The Strenuous Life"
THEODORE ROOSEVELT

History remembers Teddy Roosevelt as the United States' twenty-sixth president and national hero for his service in the Rough Riders in the Spanish-American War. But Roosevelt was much more; through his actions, words, and ideals he transformed himself into an icon of virtuous American masculinity. In the following three excerpts from some of his most memorable speeches, he champions hard work as a way of life over the life of luxury and idleness.

In a speech to members of the Hamilton Club in Chicago, Theodore Roosevelt attacks the notion that the goal of life is to achieve "easy peace" and leisure. Rather, Roosevelt argues that the noble man seeks the strenuous life, the life of hard work. It is through this alone that he can make the world, the nation, and himself great. Roosevelt's message is clear: The purpose of life is to create order out of a disorderly world through hard work and determination.

The timid man, the lazy man, the man who distrusts his country, the over-civilized man, who has lost the great fighting, masterful virtues, the ignorant man, and the man of dull mind, whose soul is incapable of feeling the mighty lift that thrills "stern men with empires in their brains"—all these, of course, shrink from seeing the nation undertake its new duties; shrink from seeing us build a navy and an army adequate to our needs; shrink from seeing us do our share of the world's work, by bringing order out of chaos in the great, fair tropic islands from which the valor of our soldiers and sailors has driven the Spanish flag. These are the men who fear the strenuous life, who fear the only national life which is really worth leading. They believe in that cloistered life which saps the hardy virtues in a nation, as it saps them in the individual; or else they are wedded to that base spirit of gain and greed which recognizes in commercialism the be-all and end-all of national life, instead of realizing that, though an indispensable element, it is, after all, but one of the many elements that go to make up true national greatness. No country can long endure if its foundations are not laid deep in the material prosperity which comes from thrift, from business energy and enterprise, from hard, unsparing effort in the fields of industrial activity; but neither was any nation ever yet truly great if it relied upon material prosperity alone. All honor must be paid to the architects of our material prosperity, to the great captains of industry who have built our factories and our railroads, to the strong men who toil for wealth with brain or hand; for great is the debt of the nation to these and their kind. But our debt is yet greater to the men whose highest type is to be found in a statesman like Lincoln, a soldier like Grant. They showed by their lives that they recognized the law of work, the law of strife; they toiled to win a competence for themselves and those dependent upon them; but they recognized that there were yet other and even loftier duties—duties to the nation and duties to the race.

In this life we get nothing save by effort. Freedom from effort in the present merely means that there has been stored up effort in the past. A man can be freed from the necessity of work only by the fact that he or his fathers before him have worked to good purpose. If the freedom thus purchased is used aright, and the man still does actual work, though of a different kind, whether as a writer or a general, whether in the field of politics or in the field of exploration and adventure, he shows he deserves his good fortune. But if he treats this period of freedom from the need of actual labor as a period, not of preparation, but of mere enjoyment, even though perhaps not of vicious enjoyment, he shows that he is simply a cumberer of the earth's surface, and he surely unfits himself to hold his own with his fellows if the need to do so should again arise. A mere life of ease is not in the end a very satisfactory life, and, above all, it is a life which ultimately unfits those who follow it for serious work in the world.

The work must be done; we cannot escape our responsibility; and if we are worth our salt, we shall be glad of the chance to do the work—glad of the chance to show ourselves equal to one of the great tasks set modern civilization. But let us not deceive ourselves as to the importance of the task. Let us not be misled by vainglory into underestimating the strain it will put on our powers. Above all, let us, as we value our own self-respect, face the responsibilities with proper seriousness, courage, and high resolve.

I preach to you, then, my countrymen, that our country calls not for the life of ease but for the life of strenuous endeavor. The twentieth century looms before us big with the fate of many nations. If we stand idly by, if we seek merely swollen, slothful ease and ignoble peace, if we shrink from the hard contests where men must win at hazard of their lives and at the risk of all they hold dear, then the bolder and stronger peoples will pass us by, and will win for themselves the domination of the world. Let us therefore boldly face the life of strife, resolute to do our duty well and manfully; resolute to uphold righteousness by deed and by word; resolute to be both honest and brave, to serve high ideals, yet to use practical methods. Above all, let us shrink from no strife, moral or physical, within or without the nation, provided we are certain that the strife is justified, for it is only through strife, through hard and dangerous endeavor, that we shall ultimately win the goal of true national greatness.

"The Work Is What Counts"

THEODORE ROOSEVELT

In his September 8, 1902, speech to the Brotherhood of Locomotive Firemen in Chattanooga, Tennessee, Roosevelt praised the railroad men for their hard work under immense pressure.

Your work is hard. Do you suppose I mention that because I pity you? No; not a bit. I don't pity any man who does hard work worth doing. I admire him. I pity the creature who doesn't work, at whichever end of the social scale he may regard himself as being. The law of worthy work well done is the law of successful American life. I believe in play, too—play, and play hard while you play; but don't make the mistake of thinking that that is the main thing. The work is what counts, and if a man does his work well and it is worth doing, then it matters but little in which line that work is done; the man is a good American citizen. If he does his work in slipshod fashion, then no matter what kind of work it is, he is a poor American citizen.

"No Man Is Happy If He Does Not Work"

THEODORE ROOSEVELT

In 1903, speaking to the men of the YMCA in Topeka, Kansas, Roosevelt argued that work and love are the two most powerful forces for the betterment of mankind.

Work, the quality which makes a man ashamed not to be able to pull his own weight, not to be able to do for himself as well as for others without being beholden to any one for what he is doing. No man is happy if he does not work. Of all miserable creatures the idler, in whatever rank of society, is in the long run the most miserable. If a man does not work, if he has not in him not merely the capacity for work but the desire for work, then nothing can be done with him. He is out of place in our community. We have in our scheme of government no room for the man who does not wish to pay his way through life by what he does for himself and for the community. If he has leisure which makes it unnecessary for him to devote his time to earning his daily bread, then all the more he is bound to work just as hard in some way that will make the community the better off for his existence. If he fails that, he fails to justify his existence.

Work, the capacity for work, is absolutely necessary; and no man's life is full, no man can be said to live in the true sense of the word, if he does not work. This is necessary, and yet it is not enough. If a man is utterly selfish, if utterly disregardful of the rights of others, if he has no ideals, if he works simply to gratify himself, small is his good in the community. I think even then he is probably better off than if he is an idler, but he is of no real use unless together with the quality which enables him to work he has the quality which enables him to love his fellows, to work with them and for them for the common good of all.

Saving Time

SENECA

Seneca the Younger, a Roman philosopher and statesman, wrote 124 letters of advice and wisdom at the end of his life. In these letters, Seneca gave Lucilius tips on how to become a more devoted Stoic. Lucilius was, at that time, the governor of Sicily. Seneca's writings give us valuable insights into daily life in ancient Rome. Two thousand years later, his practical advice for managing our time and work still rings true.

Therefore, Lucilius, do as you write me that you are doing: hold every hour in your grasp. Lay hold of today's task, and you will not need to depend so much upon tomorrow's. While we are postponing, life speeds by. Nothing, Lucilius, is ours, except time. We were entrusted by nature with the ownership of this single thing, so fleeting and slippery that anyone who will can oust us from possession. What fools these mortals be! They allow the cheapest and most useless things, which can easily be replaced, to be charged in the reckoning, after they have acquired them; but they never regard themselves as in debt when they have received some of that precious commodity—time! And yet time is the one loan which even a grateful recipient cannot repay.

Profile: Incwell

It's not always important where you come from in life; it's where you are headed. This is the story of Craig Carozza-Caviness, born into the crime and drug culture of urban Washington DC, who rose above his lowly beginnings through hard work and dedication to music—his vehicle to escape—and built a successful life of his own. I came across his compelling story via my radio show.

Craig Carozza-Caviness isn't like his father.

His grandmother, Shirley Carozza, knows it, and reminds the twenty-five-year-old singer he's someone entirely different from her son.

"He's good. So much better than his father and his uncles," said Shirley.

Why?

"I didn't want to step out of line," said Craig. "My father and uncles were bad. Robbing banks, time in jail. But I never wanted to hurt her [his grandmother]."

Still living with his grandparents, Craig spends his time behind a microphone, not on a street corner, and peddles lyrics instead of drugs. Icon Jay-Z may have made a name for himself as a "businessman," but Craig doesn't rap from behind a bulletproof vest. He's proving being a man, even a businessman, doesn't hinge on selling life in the cellblocks or glamorizing the street.

Craig learned the ABCs of crime at the age of four when his father was murdered.

"I grew up in the rent houses over off Georgia Avenue in Washington DC," said Craig, who became "Incwell" on the bills for the shows he now sells out. "My father was murdered when I was four and my mom, well, they were both into the street life. So I moved when I was five or six with my grandparents."

Incwell's genesis isn't unusual. In America, broken families spawn countless beginnings just like the beginnings of this quiet-spoken singer from Silver Spring, Maryland. Whether across the street, a short drive across the tracks, or in the newspaper behind the stretched yellow-tape photographs—Incwell's start is repeated on the concrete of Washington DC, in the housing complexes of Laurel, Mississippi, and in the water-stained slums of New Orleans.

But the finish, the finish is different. Just how did Incwell stay out of trouble?

Two things: hard work and tough grandparents.

Start with the home.

"They've been around since I was three or four," said Incwell, of his grandmother Shirley and his Italian step-grandfather, Michael Carozza. "It's been an absolute blessing. They were strict but very loving. My grandmother was the anchor to keep me out of trouble."

From the rubble of his birth family, Incwell found a solid foundation with his grandparents. Heavy amounts of love coupled with curfews and an emphasis on education marked the Carozzas, and they enrolled Incwell in Saint Bernadette's Catholic School.

"He wasn't a huge fan of school, didn't like to study or do homework," said Shirley. "But he always loved community work—working with autistic children and interning in group homes—and loved volunteering. It was tough for him to be interested in some of his jobs, but he never stopped looking for work, even if he hated the jobs."

There's a tattoo on Incwell's arm, "SDS." It stands for the "Sun Don't Shine boy," because Incwell knew that being the man of his family meant working, even when times were hard and the sun wasn't shining—he had to, people depended on him.

And whether it was a drug-addicted mother, bouncing back and forth between jail and the streets; an alcoholic half-brother, calling in the middle of the night from jail; or cousins who thought that time behind bars was cool, Incwell didn't complain. He stayed out of trouble and kept working hard to help support the rest of his family.

"You have to take responsibility for what you're doing," said Incwell. "It's not always our fault, and there are bad situations around us, but you choose what you make of life."

Incwell struggled in college, moving between four schools in three years.

"It was my fault, I wasn't doing what I should have been doing," said Incwell. "I'm ashamed of myself."

But even treading water at school, Incwell never listened to the sirens calling him to follow in his father's footsteps, even when the footsteps followed him. Coming back from an evening in Georgetown, the sixteen-year-old Incwell was riding in the back of a car with some friends when the lights flashed.

"I'm sitting in the back-seat, not involved, and my man was like 'Dog, I got weed under the seat,'" said Incwell. "The police took us in and locked us up for a few hours. That was the wake-up call."

Incwell went to work as the end of college marked the beginning of music. The motivation that the young artist couldn't find for the books came out behind the microphone and the soundboard. Calling himself the "rebirth of the flower child," Incwell mixes his growing-up stories with a big live-band sound, referencing rock and roll, soul, and more than a little Motown.

He doesn't use profanity. He said, "I wanted to let my grandmother hear the songs. You ostracize large amounts of people by using profanity because many people won't understand that it's part of the art . . . It's kind of like my shows . . . my friends bring their mothers to the shows."

Nothing comes easy for Incwell. Always writing—with more than one thousand tracks sitting in his library—he's only made one album, 2009's *Phantasmagoria*. There was a huge disappointment when a record deal with Lava Records (a subsidiary of Atlantic) fell through in 2003, but he didn't stop writing or working.

Incwell explained, "This is what I'm supposed to do. You know, I always think about quitting. I thought about quitting last night. I think about it on a weekly basis, but if I quit, what can I do? I can't quit this. This is my life."

"He's come through a lot of adversity," said Shirley. "I'm so happy to see the man he's become."

From "Works and Days"

HESIOD

Loved at home and abroad, Hesiod's works have become a staple in what is now known as "ancient Greek wisdom literature." Full of wisdom and advice, Hesiod desired to instruct the men of his day on how to live the "good life." In a letter of advice to his slothful brother Perses, Hesiod wrote that work is the universal lot of man, but that if a man works hard and is industrious with his time, then he will never see want. Hesiod followed this by instructing men in how to be successful in their labor.

Do not put your work off till tomorrow and the day after; for a sluggish worker does not fill his barn, nor one who puts off his work: industry makes work go well, but a man who puts off work is always at hand-grips with ruin.

If your heart within you desires wealth, do these things and work with work upon work.

Pass by the smithy and its crowded lounge in winter time when the cold keeps men from field work—for then an industrious man can greatly prosper his house—lest bitter winter catch you helpless and poor and you chafe a swollen foot with a shrunk hand. The idle man, who waits on empty hope, lacking a livelihood, lays to heart mischief-making; it is not a wholesome hope that accompanies a needy man who lolls at ease while he has no sure livelihood.

Avoid shady seats and sleeping until dawn in the harvest season, when the sun scorches the body. Then be busy, and bring home your fruits, getting up early to make your livelihood sure. For dawn takes away a third part of your work, dawn advances a man on his journey and advances him in his work—dawn which appears and sets many men on their road, and puts yokes on many oxen.

But do you at any rate, always remembering my charge, work, high-born Perses, that Hunger may hate you, and venerable Demeter richly crowned may love you and fill your barn with food; for Hunger is altogether a meet comrade for the sluggard. Both gods and men are angry with a man who lives idle, for in nature he is like the stingless drones who waste the labour of the bees, eating without working; but let it be your care to order your work properly, that in the right season your barns may be full of victual. Through work men grow rich in flocks and substance, and working they are much better loved by the immortals. Work is no disgrace: it is idleness which is a disgrace. But if you work, the idle will soon envy you as you grow rich, for fame and renown attend on wealth. And whatever be your lot, work is best for you, if you turn your misguided mind away from other men's property to your work and attend to your livelihood as I bid you. An evil shame is the needy man's companion, shame which both greatly harms and prospers men: shame is with poverty, but confidence with wealth.

From *The Sea-Wolf*

JACK LONDON

Jack London was an American author and naturalist who wrote during the early 1900s. Famous for novels such as *White Fang* and *The Call of the Wild*, London captured the adventurous spirit of innocence and adventure in his wilderness tales. *The Sea Wolf*, one of London's earlier novels, portrays the collision of two separate lives: the sedentary life of intellectual pursuits and the life of hard work and toil by seal hunters. On this stage London wrestles with the purpose of life and the possibility of objective goodness existing in a difficult world. The triumph of Humphrey Van Weyden's hardworking altruistic optimism over the materialistic utilitarianism of Wolf Larsen beautifully proclaims the nobility of man and his need for perseverance and work as well as strong moral foundations.

The novel traces the progress of a scrawny intellectual man in his midthirties from an inexperienced, weak individual to a hard worker. Humphrey Van Weyden is recovered from the wreck of the sinking *Martinez* ferryboat by the *Ghost*, a sealing schooner destined for the Japanese hunting grounds. The ship is captained by the infamous Wolf Larsen, an indomitable, self-willed man, who desires only to further his own ends. The *Ghost* had recently lost a sailor, and deeming the situation fortuitous, Larsen forces Humphrey to work on the *Ghost* as a cabin boy. It is at this intersection that Humphrey's sedentary life of idleness and intellectual pursuits is exposed and ridiculed.

W hat do you do for a living?"

I confess I had never had such a question asked me before, nor had I ever canvassed it. I was quite taken aback, and before I could find myself had sillily stammered, "I—I am a gentleman."

His lip curled in a swift sneer.

"I have worked, I do work," I cried impetuously, as though he were my judge and I required vindication, and at the same time very much aware of my arrant idiocy in discussing the subject at all.

"For your living?"

There was something so imperative and masterful about him that I was quite beside myself—"rattled," as Furuseth would have termed it, like a quaking child before a stern school-master.

"Who feeds you?" was his next question.

"I have an income," I answered stoutly, and could have bitten my tongue the next instant. "All of which, you will pardon my observing, has nothing whatsoever to do with what I wish to see you about."

But he disregarded my protest.

"Who earned it? Eh? I thought so. Your father. You stand on dead men's legs.

You've never had any of your own. You couldn't walk alone between two sunrises and hustle the meat for your belly for three meals. Let me see your hand."

His tremendous, dormant strength must have stirred, swiftly and accurately, or I must have slept a moment, for before I knew it he had stepped two paces forward, gripped my right hand in his, and held it up for inspection. I tried to withdraw it, but his fingers tightened, without visible effort, till I thought mine would be crushed. It is hard to maintain one's dignity under such circumstances. I could not squirm or struggle like a schoolboy. Nor could I attack such a creature who had but to twist my arm to break it. Nothing remained but to stand still and accept the indignity. I had time to notice that the pockets of the dead man had been emptied on the deck, and that his body and his grin had been wrapped from view in canvas, the folds of which the sailor, Johansen, was sewing together with coarse white twine, shoving the needle through with a leather contrivance fitted on the palm of his hand.

Wolf Larsen dropped my hand with a flirt of disdain.

"Dead men's hands have kept it soft. Good for little else than dish-washing and scullion work."

"I wish to be put ashore," I said firmly, for I now had myself in control. "I shall pay you whatever you judge your delay and trouble to be worth."

He looked at me curiously. Mockery shone in his eyes.

"I have a counter proposition to make, and for the good of your soul. My mate's gone, and there'll be a lot of promotion. A sailor comes aft to take mate's place, cabin-boy goes for'ard to take sailor's place, and you take the cabin-boy's place, sign the articles for the cruise, twenty dollars per month and found. Now what do you say? And mind you, it's for your own soul's sake. It will be the making of you. You might learn in time to stand on your own legs, and perhaps to toddle along a bit."

As the voyage continues Humphrey begins to learn the way of the sea and to become accustomed to the work of a sailor. In time a mutiny breaks out against Wolf Larsen. Humphrey is made first mate after this outbreak. The responsibility and demanding nature of the position continues to chisel away at his uncalloused hands.

My hands bothered me a great deal, unused as they were to work. The nails were discoloured and black, while the skin was already grained with dirt which even a scrubbing-brush could not remove. Then blisters came, in a painful and never-ending procession, and I had a great burn on my forearm, acquired by losing my balance in a roll of the ship and pitching against the galley stove. Nor was my knee any better. The swelling had not gone down, and the cap was still up on edge. Hobbling about on it from morning till night was not helping it any. What I needed was rest, if it were ever to get well.

Rest! I never before knew the meaning of the word. I had been resting all my life and did not know it. But now, could I sit still for one half-hour and do nothing, not even think, it would be the most pleasurable thing in the world. But it is a revelation, on the other hand. I shall be able to appreciate the lives of the working people hereafter. I did not dream that work was so terrible a thing. From half-past five in the morning till ten o'clock at night I am everybody's slave, with not one moment to myself, except such as I can steal near the end of the second dog-watch. Let me pause for a minute to look out over the sea sparkling in the sun, or to gaze at a sailor going aloft to the gaff-topsails, or running out the bowsprit, and I am sure to hear the hateful voice, "'Ere, you, 'Ump, no sodgerin'. I've got my peepers on yer."

"Hump," he [Wolf Larsen] said, "I beg pardon, Mr. Van Weyden, I congratulate you. I think you can now fire your father's legs back into the grave to him. You've discovered your own and learned to stand on them. A little rope-work, sail-making, and experience with storms and such things, and by the end of the voyage you could ship on any coasting schooner."

Profile: Coach Ken

High school football in Texas is in a league of its own. The packed stadiums, thousands of fans, and intense pressure make it feel more like professional football than an organized group of teenagers. As a high school football coach in Texas, Coach Ken Purcell has a responsibility not only to develop players and win games, but also to teach his athletes the skills and work ethic that will make them successful on more than just the football field. Coach Ken and I talk regularly on my radio show.

Coach Ken Purcell races the sunrise to work.

Sometime between 6:05 and 6:10 a.m.—depending on whether Sonic opens on time for the coach to get his cup of unsweet tea (with ice)—Coach Purcell walks into his office, high up in the C. H. Collins Athletic Complex in Denton, Texas. Then, as the first rays of light start trickling across the football field and into his perch in the north end zone, Purcell maps out his playbook for the day's work.

"There are always long-term and short-term goals," said Purcell. "When I was coaching a team, the long-term was to win state championship, but you can't talk long-term every day, so you have to ask, what am I going to accomplish every day?"

Purcell started working on a tractor in fourth grade, when he was hired to help plow a twelve-hundred-acre field for one dollar an hour. It's been thirty-eight years since Purcell first stepped on the field as an offensive coordinator for the Tahoka Bulldogs in the little town of Tahoka, Texas. One year at Tahoka, nine years at Plano, and then another fourteen at Allen. There were winning seasons, a few rings, and then Coach Purcell put away the clipboard in 1996. This man wasn't done teaching though. Coach Purcell took over the athletic director position for the Denton Independent School District. That's where he's stayed, "coaching coaches."

"We've got 213 coaches on staff," said Purcell. "When I interview a coach, I ask him why he wants to coach, and if he says 'I love football,' that's not the answer I'm looking for. The answer I want is, 'I love kids, I love student athletes.'"

Purcell also loves his wife, Teresa—they've been married for more than forty years—and his two sons, Sean and Shannon, who both coach and teach as well.

"I just couldn't persuade them against following me," he said with a laugh.

And Coach Purcell taught those kids, those student athletes, about more than winning. He taught them how to work, and ultimately, how to live.

"If we're not teaching values, then we're wasting too much money on a game," said Purcell. "The old-school mentality is that winning is everything, and that doesn't float anymore, because what happens when you lose? You've got to have something to fall back on."

So, just what are those values that Coach Ken Purcell tries to make sure get emblazoned into the helmets and heads of the players in Denton?

"We want to make sure that each player learns discipline, pride, poise, class, accountability, and decision-making skills," said Purcell. "These are things you need to succeed regardless of what you do in life."

And part of this imparting of success comes in teaching these players just not to quit.

"Part of being a man means that you have integrity," said Purcell. "It means that you honor your commitments, you follow through on what you say you're going to do."

For Purcell this meant following through on taking a job in a small town, even after being offered a position at a larger school. For his players this meant not quitting on the team with three weeks left to go in the season.

Practically though, this coach sees athletics as a key to more than just success on the field. "A study a few years ago showed that 95 percent of Fortune 500 company's CEOs have athletics in their background. I don't think that's a coincidence," said Purcell. "Athletics teach things . . . . I get phone calls from athletes I coached twenty years ago who are now successful businessmen, thanking me for the things they learned in our athletic program."

Purcell and the other coaches in Denton lead by example, working seventy to eighty hours a week while they coach sports and teach classes. There is no punching the clock, no checking out at the end of the day. These coaches stay at the school until the job is done, whatever the time might be.

"I grew up in ranching and agriculture. Coaching in Texas is very similar in work ethic. You work until the work is done," said Purcell. "It's a bit like cattle or the wheat harvest. When the wheat harvest comes in, you just have to get it in. The wheat is ripe; you've got to get it cut. Wheat harvesters will cut it all night to get it done, and as a coach, you have to prepare for the opponent over the weekend."

Starting with the sunrise and ending with the final whistle, Purcell continues to see that preparation pays off in his life and in the thousands of players who walk across his field.

"A Humorist's Confession"

MARK TWAIN

Samuel Clemens (1835–1910), otherwise known as Mark Twain, was an American humorist, novelist, lecturer, and journalist famous across the world for his playful stories of boyhood adventurism and his humorous cultural commentary. Producing a substantial body of work in his time, Twain is a credible source to anyone who wants to better their work ethic. In this excerpt from an interview with the *New York Times*, published in November 26, 1905, Mark Twain reminds us that it is best to pursue a line of work that we actually enjoy.

Mark Twain will be 70 years old on Thanksgiving Day, and he has never done a day's work in his life. He told me so himself, sitting in one of the cheerful, spacious rooms of the old-fashioned stately New York house which he will probably call his city home as long as he lives. I probably started upon hearing this unlooked-for statement from the lips of the good, gray humorist, for he repeated emphatically:

"No, Sir, not a day's work in all my life. What I have done I have done, because it has been play. If it had been work I shouldn't have done it.

"Who was it who said, 'Blessed is the man who has found his work'? Whoever it was he had the right idea in his mind. Mark you, he says his work—not somebody else's work. The work that is really a man's own work is play and not work at all. Cursed is the man who has found some other man's work and cannot lose it. When we talk about the great workers of the world we really mean the great players of the world. The fellows who groan and sweat under the weary load of toil that they bear never can hope to do anything great. How can they when their souls are in a ferment of revolt against the employment of their hands and brains? The product of slavery, intellectual or physical, can never be great."

— ❧ —

"Psalm of Life"

HENRY WADSWORTH LONGFELLOW

Henry Wadsworth Longfellow (1807–1882) was the most-loved American poet of the nineteenth century. Author of such works as "Paul Revere's Ride," "Evangeline," and "The Song of Hiawatha," Longfellow entranced the world with his beautiful work, which often carried a bit of wisdom or a command to appreciate life's beauty. In the "Psalm of Life," Longfellow reminds us that our purpose is not in pursuing mere creature comforts, but in striving to make the world the way we want it. He tells us that in a world where nothing is promised, the only thing to do is to strive and pray, "life is earnest."

TELL ME NOT, IN MOURNFUL NUMBERS,
 Life is but an empty dream!—
For the soul is dead that slumbers,
 And things are not what they seem.
Life is real! Life is earnest!
 And the grave is not its goal;
Dust thou art, to dust returnest,
 Was not spoken of the soul.

Not enjoyment, and not sorrow,
 Is our destined end or way;
But to act, that each to-morrow
 Find us farther than to-day.

Art is long, and Time is fleeting,
 And our hearts, though stout and brave,
Still, like muffled drums, are beating
 Funeral marches to the grave.

In the world's broad field of battle,
*   In the bivouac of Life,*
Be not like dumb, driven cattle!
*   Be a hero in the strife!*

Trust no Future, howe'er pleasant!
*   Let the dead Past bury its dead!*
Act,—act in the living Present!
*   Heart within, and God o'erhead!*

Lives of great men all remind us
*   We can make our lives sublime,*
And, departing, leave behind us
*   Footprints on the sands of time;*

Footprints, that perhaps another,
*   Sailing o'er life's solemn main,*
A forlorn and shipwrecked brother,
*   Seeing, shall take heart again.*

Let us, then, be up and doing,
*   With a heart for any fate;*
Still achieving, still pursuing,
*   Learn to labor and to wait.*

"The Spiritual Value of Work"

MARK JUDGE

In times of economic hardship, finding or keeping a job can be difficult
and frustrating. Being without a steady occupation can leave you feeling

empty and paralyzed. In this personal confession, Mark Judge loses his job as a journalist and gets a new job as an usher at a museum. Despite settling for a lower-paying occupation, Judge discovers the spiritual value of work and the fulfillment it can bring.

The recession has been bad for the economy, and a disaster for us journalists. But it's been good for my soul.

After a twenty-year career as a writer and journalist, I'm now an usher. Actually, I'm a Visitor Services Representative for the Terra Cotta Warriors exhibit at the National Geographic Society. My job is to check coats, tear tickets, politely herd people to proper locations and [in] general do whatever needs to be done for the 2,000–3,000 people who come through the museum every day to see the Terra Cotta Warriors—life-sized, 2,000-year-old Chinese clay figures who have been the winter buzz of Washington. The figures, some 8,000 total (the Geographic has fifteen on display) were built by artisans around 200 BC. They were done at the order of China's first dictator, Qin Shi Huang, and no two are alike. Their purpose was to both usher the emperor into the afterlife and protect him.

So I'm kind of a gopher, making people happy and protecting the protectors of the emperor. It's a temporary job, and one that I didn't necessarily have to take. What made me do so was the cancer that I was diagnosed with last year. After six months of chemotherapy, I felt unwilling to do anything that seemed petty, micromanaged, or aesthetically dead. I simply could not be the guy in the movie *Office Space*, losing a small piece of his mind day by day while the boss passive-aggressively asked him to cancel his weekend plans—again—so he can come in and push papers.

And, for the first time in months, I felt strong. To be sure, the chemo had caused some nerve and tissue damage, and according to my doctor it would take about a year for that to wear off. I would also be on a maintenance drug Rituxan that was new and experimental. For all I knew, it would turn me into the Hulk. But none of that was anything like the dreary, deadening fatigue I felt in the months leading up to December 2008, when I was diagnosed with cancer. No matter what happens in life, there is usually a sense of security that, if all else should fail, you still have your working body. You can change careers, move to a different state, botch a relationship, but at the end of the day you won't starve. You can wash dishes or fold clothes. But when your body itself begins to weaken and you don't know why, a desperation sets in. You don't feel well enough to work, yet you don't know why. When I was diagnosed, I was actually relieved. Anything was better than living like that.

There is also a spiritual malaise that sets in when you can't work. One of my heroes is Pope John Paul II, who had penetrating insights into the connection between work and spirituality. In 1940, when Poland was under Nazi occupation, the twenty-year-old Karol Wojtyla went to work at the Zakrzowek quarry breaking up limestone. Up until then the future pope had believed, as he was taught as a boy, that hard work was a penalty of original sin. Yet seeing the dignity of the older workers, he came to a different conclusion. As Catholic intellectual George Weigel puts it in "Witness to Hope": "[The pope saw that] work, with all its rigors and hardships, was a participation in God's creativity, because work touched the very essence of the human being as a creature to whom God had given dominion over the earth."

The question was, what kind of work would I do after my recovery? My father had worked at National Geographic. His was a grand life of travel and discovery and adventure. Yet it wasn't 1965 anymore, or even 1995. Magazines and newspapers were laying people off. I checked the Web site, where I saw an ad for "visitor service representatives" for the five months that Terra Cotta would be in Washington. I had been an usher—I mean visitor services representative—at movie theaters years before. My dad had worked on the ninth floor as the associate editor. I would be on the first floor, saying things like "Sorry sir, no reentry without a ticket stub." It was a long way down.

Or was it? While I'm convinced that bohemian raptures about freedom and escaping The Man are most often excuses for the self-indulgent, there was something to be said for doing work that wasn't abstract—that didn't involve information technology or accounting, or sitting in front of a computer all day trying to make money off of other people's money. There was something to be said for work that allowed you to be inside your own body, like Adam plowing the fields of the Lord. After the cancer it would be an affirmation of health, of joy, of the simple goodness of doing simple, physical things—especially in the service of helping others experience something marvelous. It would be like that powerful scene at the climax of the movie *Wall Street*, when onetime Wall Street titan Bud Fox, played by Charlie Sheen, has been arrested for insider trading. On a rainy morning in Central Park, he explains to his former mentor Gordon Gekko, who preached that "greed is good," that he had lost his soul. He wasn't a destroyer of worlds. "Maybe I'm just Bud Fox," he said. It also didn't hurt that National Geographic pays a good wage and treats its workers well, and that my coworkers, mostly students half my age, are smart and engaging.

In March, the job will end and, God willing, something else, something permanent, will begin. I will take leave of the warriors who have kept watch for two millennia, knowing that I am better in body and soul. I have passed through the shadow, but some pain, the pain that we all endure as fallen creatures, will remain. But I will be changed, I think. My ambitions are not what they once were. One night after work I was riding the subway home to Maryland. I felt spent. But I also felt alive. As the train came into Maryland and up from the underground, I saw the lights of home. On my iPod was a U2 song, "Moment of Surrender":

> *I was speeding on the subway*
> *Through the station of the cross*
> *Every eye looking every other way*
> *Counting down 'til the pain would stop*
> *At the moment of surrender*
> *Of vision over visibility*
> *I did not notice the passers-by*
> *And they did not notice me*

From *The Future of the American Negro*

BOOKER T. WASHINGTON

Booker T. Washington (1856–1915) is an important cultural figure in African American history. Washington was a former slave turned successful businessman and founder of the Tuskegee Institute, an institution of higher learning for African Americans. After the Civil War he dedicated his life to helping freed slaves learn the necessary skills to enter society as competitive and helpful citizens. In the following excerpts taken from *The Future of the American Negro* and *Up from Slavery*, Washington reminds us that hard work is the key to success because it creates a good reputation. With it a good man can better provide for himself, his family, and his community. Washington's advice for the African American community is still sound advice for any association of people working together today— be it a company, a sports team, or the American people as a whole.

A race, like an individual, has got to have a reputation. Such a reputation goes a long way toward helping a race or an individual; and, when we have succeeded in getting such a reputation, we shall find that a great many of the discouraging features of our life will melt away.

You cannot keep back very long a race that has the reputation for doing perfect work in everything that it undertakes. Then we want to get a reputation for being industrious. Now, remember these three things: Get a reputation for being skilled. It will not do for a few here and there to have it: the race must have the reputation. Get a reputation for being so skilful, so industrious, that you will not leave a job until it is as nearly perfect as any one can make it. And then we want to make a reputation for the race for being honest,—honest at all times and under all circumstances. A few individuals here and there have it, a few communities have it; but the race as a mass must "get it."

The social lines that were once sharply drawn between those who laboured with the hands and those who did not are disappearing. Those who formerly sought to escape labour, now when they see that brains and skill rob labour of the toil and drudgery once associated with it, instead of trying to avoid it, are willing to pay to be taught how to engage in it. The South is beginning to see labour raised up, dignified and beautified, and in this sees its salvation. In proportion as the love of labour grows, the large idle class, which has long been one of the curses of the South, disappears. As people become absorbed in their own affairs, they have less time to attend to everybody else's business.

And then we want to get a reputation for being thoughtful. This I want to emphasize more than anything else. We want to get a reputation for doing things without being told to do them every time. If you have work to do, think about it so constantly, investigate and read about it so thoroughly, that you will always be finding ways and means of improving that work. The average person going to work becomes a regular machine, never giving the matter of improving the methods of his work a thought. He is never at his work before the appointed time, and is sure to stop the minute the hour is up. The world is looking for the person who is thoughtful, who will say at the close of work hours: "Is there not something else I can do for you? Can I not stay a little later, and help you?"

A person who goes at an undertaking with the feeling that he cannot succeed is likely to fail. On the other hand, the individual who goes at an undertaking, feeling that he can succeed, is the individual who in nine cases out of ten does succeed. But, whenever you find an individual that is ashamed of his race, trying to get away from his race, apologizing for being a member of his race, then you find a weak individual. Where you find a race that is ashamed of itself, that is apologizing for itself, there you will find a weak, vacillating race. Let us no longer have to apologize for our race in these or other matters. Let us think seriously and work seriously: then, as a race, we shall be thought of seriously, and, therefore, seriously respected.

———— ❧ ————

From *Up From Slavery*

BOOKER T. WASHINGTON

Some people may say that it was Tuskegee's good luck that brought to us this gift of fifty thousand dollars. No, it was not luck. It was hard work. Nothing ever comes to me, that is worth having, except as the result of hard work. When Mr. Huntington gave me the first two dollars, I did not blame him for not giving me more, but made up my mind that I was going to convince him by tangible results that we were worthy of larger gifts. For a dozen years I made a strong effort to convince Mr. Huntington of the value of our work. I noted that just in proportion as the usefulness of the school grew, his donations increased. Never did I meet an individual who took a more kindly and sympathetic interest in our school than did Mr. Huntington. He not only gave money to us, but took time in which to advise me, as a father would a son, about the general conduct of the school.

— ❧ —

From *The Way to Wealth*

BENJAMIN FRANKLIN

Benjamin Franklin (1706–1790) was one of America's Founding Fathers and one of the most brilliant men of his day. Franklin was a paragon of the American work ethic. Published yearly from 1734 to 1747, *Poor Richard's Almanack* is Franklin's widely admired collection of timeless proverbs reminding one to work hard and for the right reasons. In 1758, Franklin published *The Way to Wealth*, a compilation of some of the money-related aphorisms contained in *Poor Richard's Almanack* during the previous 25 years. In this excerpt, Franklin argues that industry, attention to one's own business, and frugality are essential to acquiring wealth.

So what signifies wishing and hoping for better times[?] We may make these times better if we bestir ourselves. *Industry need not wish*, as Poor Richard says, and *he that lives upon hope will die fasting. There are no gains, without pains,* then *help hands, for I have no lands,* or if I have, they are smartly taxed. And, as Poor Richard likewise observes, *he that hath a trade hath an estate,* and *he that hath a calling hath an office of profit and honor;* but then the trade must be worked at, and the calling well followed, or neither the estate, nor the office, will enable us to pay our taxes. If we are industrious we shall never starve; for, as Poor Richard says, *at the working man's house hunger looks in, but dares not enter.* Nor will the bailiff nor the constable enter, *for industry pays debts, while despair encreaseth them,* says Poor Richard. What though you have found no treasure, nor has any rich relation left you a legacy, *diligence is the mother of good luck,* as Poor Richard says, and *God gives all things to industry.* Then *plough deep, while sluggards sleep, and you shall have corn to sell and to keep,* says Poor Dick. Work while it is called today, for you know not how much you may be hindered tomorrow, which makes Poor Richard say, *one today is worth two tomorrows;* and farther, *have you somewhat to do tomorrow, do it today.* If you were a servant, would you not be ashamed that a good master should catch you idle? Are you then your own master, *be ashamed to catch yourself idle*, as Poor Dick says. When there is so much to be done for yourself, your family, your country, and your gracious king, be up by peep of day; *let not the sun look down and say, inglorious here he lies.* Handle your tools without mittens; remember that *the cat in gloves catches no mice*, as Poor Richard says. 'Tis true there is much to be done, and perhaps you are weak handed, but stick to it steadily, and you will see great effects, for *constant dropping wears away stones*, and *by diligence and patience the mouse ate in two the cable*; and *little strokes fell great oaks*, as Poor Richard says in his almanac, the year I cannot just now remember.

Sloth, by bringing on diseases, absolutely shortens life. *Sloth, like rust, consumes faster than labor wears, while the used key is always bright*, as Poor Richard says. But *dost thou love life, then do not squander time, for that's the stuff life is made of*, as Poor Richard says. How much more than is necessary do we spend in sleep! forgetting that *the sleeping fox catches no poultry*, and that *there will be sleeping enough in the grave*, as Poor Richard says. If time be of all things the most precious, *wasting time* must be, as Poor Richard says, *the greatest prodigality*, since, as he elsewhere tells us, *lost time is never found again*, and what we call *time-enough, always proves little enough*: let us then be up and be doing, and doing to the purpose; so by diligence shall we do more with less perplexity. *Sloth makes all things difficult, but industry all easy*, as Poor Richard says; and *he that riseth late, must trot all day, and shall scarce overtake his business at night*. While *laziness travels so slowly, that poverty soon overtakes him*, as we read in Poor Richard, who adds, *drive thy business, let not that drive thee*; and *early to bed, and early to rise, makes a man healthy, wealthy and wise.*

———————

This doctrine, my friends, is reason and wisdom; but after all, do not depend too much upon your own industry, and frugality, and prudence, though excellent things, for they may all be blasted without the blessing of heaven; and therefore ask that blessing humbly, and be not uncharitable to those that at present seem to want it, but comfort and help them. Remember Job suffered, and was afterwards prosperous.

"Charmides"

PLATO

Alfred North Whitehead said, "All western philosophy consists of footnotes to Plato." Plato founded the Academy in Athens, the first institution of higher learning in the Western world. In this dialogue Plato examines the virtue of Temperance. In the discussion that follows, Socrates and his friend Critias discover that work is best if one is employed doing noble and useful things.

SOCRATES: What! I asked; do you mean to say that doing and making are not the same?

CRITIAS: No more, he replied, than making or working are the same; thus much I have learned from Hesiod, who says that "work is no disgrace." Now do you imagine that if he had meant by working and doing such things as you were describing, he would have said that there was no disgrace in them—for example, in the manufacture of shoes, or in selling pickles, or sitting for hire in a house of ill-fame? That, Socrates, is not to be supposed: but I conceive him to have distinguished making from doing and work; and, while admitting that the making anything might sometimes become a disgrace, when the employment was not honourable, to have thought that work was never any disgrace at all. For things nobly and usefully made he called works; and such makings he called workings, and doings; and he must be supposed to have called such things only man's proper business, and what is hurtful, not his business: and in that sense Hesiod, and any other wise man, may be reasonably supposed to call him wise who does his own work.

Profile: George Gershwin

Music has long tamed, as well as inflamed, many a boy's spirit and soul. Here, in a brief account, is the discovery of music by one of America's greatest composers. We see how music enchanted, infused, and calmed a soul. It straightened out a life and gave our country a gift. It's a wonderful story. Only one question remains—when he does what he does, is Gershwin playing or working?

In 1893, the *New York Times* described the Lower East Side of the city as the "eyesore of New York." To the patrician editors at the newspaper, that part of the city teemed with Slavic and Jewish immigrants, many of whom spoke no English and had no job, and often crowded in filthy and dangerous tenement buildings, specifically constructed by slumlords to house the mass of foreigners now swelling the city. Two million immigrants of Russian and Jewish background had come to the United States from Russia in the 1890s, many fleeing the threat of pogroms in their native land. But a better life hardly seemed to be the case for what amounted to one-fourth of the city's population.

But for all the quotidian hardscrabble circumstances that most residents of the Lower East side experienced, the neighborhood could not suppress the enterprising spirit and tireless work ethic of the millions of residents who lived there. One of these residents was Moshe Gershowitz, who had arrived in America in 1890, having lost the address of his uncle, his only contact in America, and whose only meal that first day was bought with his winnings in a card game. Though Gershowitz wasn't tenement-poor, he was by no means rich, working a succession of dozens of odd jobs when he could find work, and moving his family more than twenty-five times over the years in search of a suitable place to call home after being evicted from the last one.

In 1898, the same year they earned their citizenship, Moshe and his wife, Rose, a fellow immigrant, had their second of four children, Yakob. Although teachers remembered him as "a nice lad—modest and retiring," Yakob Gershovitz (renamed George Gershwin to assimilate into American culture) was a troublemaking boy more interested in mischief than in music. By Gershwin's own account, as a young-ster roaming the streets of New York, "music never really interested me, and I really like to spend my time with the boys, making somewhat of a nuisance of myself in the streets." He liked to fight, break windows, set fires, and steal food from street ven-dors. Moshe himself predicted that George would "grow up to be a bum."

But one day, young George became entranced.

"I stood outside a penny arcade listening to an automatic piano leaping through Rubenstein's Melody in F . . . To this day I can't hear the tune without picturing myself standing outside that arcade on 125th St., standing there barefoot and in over-alls, drinking it all in avidly."

Gershwin became almost instantly smitten by music. Some time around 1908, he heard a schoolmate's violin recital of Dvorak's *Humoresque*—"a flashing revela-tion of beauty," he recalled—and never looked back. That very day, Gershwin, in the pouring rain, raced over to the home of the performer, a boy named Max Rosen, and waited more than an hour for him to come home. Max's first advice for George was discouraging—he encouraged him to forget about music because he had no real talent. In spite of Rosen's doubts, Gershwin and Rosen became fast friends, bonding over their mutual love of music. George also began to keep a scrapbook of musical ideas and articles.

A little later, Gershwin began to play the piano whenever he could, mostly bang-ing around on an old player piano at a friend's home. It is easy to picture a young boy, perhaps scuffed and dirty from playing in the street, earnestly asking to play the keyboard, knowing he must play well, knowing that too much dissonance from his still-clumsy fingers might cause him to lose his precious privileges in a guest's home. Gershwin's desire for access to the piano caused him to develop more social graces—courtesy, not overstaying one's welcome, and punctuality.

In addition, George began running errands for a local piano store in exchange for some secret practice time. Even at a young age, the canvas of roaring, ascen-dant, hopeful New York became the emotional touchstone for Gershwin's music. He said, "I was becoming acquainted with that which later I was to interpret—the soul of the American people. Having been born in New York and grown up among New Yorkers, I have heard the voice of that soul. It spoke to me on the streets, in school, at the theater. In the chorus of city sounds I heard it." This included the nascent sounds of jazz, which had started to emerge from Harlem. George was playing a lot.

By 1910, the Gershwin family had prospered enough to afford a piano, intending it for George's brother, Ira, a studied and serious boy, unlike his rabble-rousing brother. But as soon as the piano got into the apartment, eleven-year-old George proceeded to lower the stool and tickle the ivories, to the delight and absolute shock of the entire family. Nobody had known about his musical forays. It was quickly decided that George would become the one taking lessons, "with no argument from me," remembered Ira.

Soon enough the piano completed George's life change. "Studying the piano made a good boy out of a bad one. It took the piano to tone me down. It made me more serious. I was a changed person six months after I took it up," he said.

Socrates, in Plato's *Republic*, recognized the intoxicating effects of music and Gershwin's experience mirrored almost exactly what the old Athenian already knew: "Musical training is a more potent instrument than any other, because rhythm and harmony find their way into the inward places of the soul, on which they mightily fasten, imparting grace."

In spite of George's talents, the Gershwin parents were generally uninterested in his pursuit. "Whatever I know about music, I've wrenched out for myself. I had no parents to stand over me and encourage me in the little tunes I used to make up. No one ever urged me on by telling me that Mozart was a great composer when he was 11," Gershwin said. His self-motivation is a testament to his determination to become a great musician—a quality inspired by music itself!

Gershwin was undeterred in his enthusiasm and started taking lessons. Around 1913, his teacher, Charles Hambitzer, wrote: "I have a new pupil who will make his mark in music if anybody will. The boy is a genius, without a doubt; he's just crazy about music and can't wait until it's time to take his lesson. No watching the clock for this boy! He wants to go in for the modern stuff, jazz and whatnot. But I'm not going to let him for awhile. I'll see that he gets a firm foundation in the standard music first."

At fifteen, Gershwin dropped out of school to be a songwriter full time. He eventually became bored writing popular songs for others and studied several more years with talented teachers.

Although dropping out of school was often a necessity in earlier times, it was classic Gershwin to take up new challenges. "In person my brother was a good deal like his music: vibrant, dynamic, honest, and if I may, charming," Ira said. "Although most of it was devoted to the piano and his music, it was a continual source of amazement to me that he found time to engage in so many other activities. He was a fine painter, a good golfer, a discerning and courageous art collector, an excellent photographer, a wonderful dancer. George lived fast, moved fast, studied hard, and learned fast."

For Gershwin, the ideas of play and work became indistinguishable from each other. Gershwin was completely immersed in his music, so much so that he never married. His sister described him as "lonely inside himself." His commitment to his craft is admirable, but such fervent devotion can have a downside.

Eventually Gershwin went on to become one of the most respected composers of the twentieth century, known for his compositional techniques and fusion of jazz sounds with classical forms. His 1924 composition *Rhapsody in Blue* is considered a landmark work, a fitting ode to the struggles and triumphs of early twentieth-century America that Gershwin lived through. The dreamlike yet epic themes of the composition largely come from Gershwin's own experience in those environs—from the Lower East Side to the most ornate concert halls in the world, Gershwin lived the American dream. Gershwin captured another element of America with his highly original 1935 work *Porgy and Bess*, an African American love story set in the 1920s in South Carolina. Gershwin described it as "an American folk opera."

Gershwin later reflected on the link between his music and his country: "True music must repeat the thought and aspirations of the people and the time. My people are Americans. My time is today."

"Chuck Yeager Breaks the Sound Barrier"

FROM *AMERICAN PATRIOT'S ALMANAC* BY WILLIAM J. BENNETT
AND JOHN T. CRIBB

Many of the great scientific achievements of our time came through trial and error, with great danger and even death involved. From airplanes to skyscrapers to spaceships, we have brave men and women to thank for risking life and limb for technological advancements. One such man is Chuck Yeager. Because of his courage and determination, American scientists were able to finally break the sound barrier and develop the technology needed for jets and high-speed aircraft. Here, literally, is a breakthrough worker.

Until October 14, 1947, no one knew if a plane could fly faster than the speed of sound. Aircraft approaching Mach 1 shook violently, as if hitting an invisible wall. Only a year earlier, British pilot Geoffrey De Havilland had died when his plane broke apart flying close to the speed of sound. Scientists theorized that as a plane reached high speeds, sound waves piled up around it, creating a "sound barrier" that held it back.

After World War II the U.S. military and Bell Aircraft developed the X-1, a "bullet with wings" designed to punch a hole through the sound barrier. The test pilot for the rocket-powered plane was twenty-four-year-old Captain Chuck Yeager. A decorated combat ace, Yeager had cheated death more than once. During the war, he'd been shot down over France but eluded the Nazis with the help of the French Resistance, made it back to his squadron, and returned to the skies.

By mid-October 1947 Yeager had flown the X-1 several times over the Mojave Desert, edging closer to the sound barrier. On October 14 he climbed into the plane with two cracked ribs from a fall off a horse—an injury he kept secret so he wouldn't be grounded. A giant B-29 carried the X-1 to twenty thousand feet and released it. The plane stalled and dropped five hundred feet while Yeager struggled to bring it under control. He fired his rocket engines, climbed to forty-two thousand feet, leveled off, and fired a rocket again.

Then it happened. The shaking suddenly stopped. "I was so high and so remote, and the airplane was so very quiet that I might have been motionless," Yeager later recalled. But the needle on the speed gauge jumped off the scale. On the ground below, engineers heard the thunder of a sonic boom. Chuck Yeager had punched through the sound barrier.

From *Democracy in America*

ALEXIS DE TOCQUEVILLE

After the American Revolution, French historian and political commentator Alexis de Tocqueville ventured to America to observe and record its
customs and try to describe what made this new country so great and
unique. What stood out to de Tocqueville, as he says in the following passage, is the work ethic and attitude that early Americans displayed in all
areas of life.

Among a democratic people, where there is no hereditary wealth, every
man works to earn a living, or has worked, or is born of parents who have
worked. The notion of labor is therefore presented to the mind on every
side as the necessary, natural, and honest condition of human existence. Not only is
labor not dishonorable among such a people, but it is held in honor: the prejudice is
not against it, but in its favor. In the United States a wealthy man thinks that he owes
it to public opinion to devote his leisure to some kind of industrial or commercial
pursuit, or to public business. He would think himself in bad repute if he employed
his life solely in living. It is for the purpose of escaping this obligation to work that
so many rich Americans come to Europe, where they find some scattered remains of
aristocratic society, among which idleness is still held in honor.

Equality of conditions not only ennobles the notion of labor in men's estimation,
but it raises the notion of labor as a source of profit. In aristocracies it is not exactly
labor that is despised, but labor with a view to profit. Labor is honorific in itself,
when it is undertaken at the sole bidding of ambition or of virtue. Yet in aristocratic
society it constantly happens that he who works for honor is not insensible to the
attractions of profit. But these two desires only intermingle in the innermost depths
of his soul: he carefully hides from every eye the point at which they join; he would
fain conceal it from himself. In aristocratic countries there are few public officers
who do not affect to serve their country without interested motives. Their salary is
an incident of which they think but little, and of which they always affect not to

think at all. Thus the notion of profit is kept distinct from that of labor; however they may be united in point of fact, they are not thought of together.

In democratic communities these two notions are, on the contrary, always palpably united. As the desire of well-being is universal—as fortunes are slender or fluctuating—as every one wants either to increase his own resources, or to provide fresh ones for his progeny, men clearly see that it is profit which, if not wholly at least partially, leads them to work. Even those who are principally actuated by the love of fame are necessarily made familiar with the thought that they are not exclusively actuated by that motive; and they discover that the desire of getting a living is mingled in their minds with the desire of making life illustrious.

As soon as, on the one hand, labor is held by the whole community to be an honorable necessity of man's condition, and, on the other, as soon as labor is always ostensibly performed, wholly or in part, for the purpose of earning remuneration, the immense interval which separated different callings in aristocratic societies disappears. If all are not alike, all at least have one feature in common. No profession exists in which men do not work for money; and the remuneration which is common to them all gives them all an air of resemblance. This serves to explain the opinions which the Americans entertain with respect to different callings. In America no one is degraded because he works, for every one about him works also; nor is any one humiliated by the notion of receiving pay, for the President of the United States also works for pay. He is paid for commanding, other men for obeying orders. In the United States professions are more or less laborious, more or less profitable; but they are never either high or low: every honest calling is honorable.

Profile: Michel Faulkner

Many of the inner cities of America are a battleground for men, both physically and spiritually. Between drugs, violence, and crime, men are pressured from all sides with negative influences. One man leading the charge to save these men is Michel Faulkner. His battleground is Harlem, New York City, and he is fighting every day to bring a light to the darkness.

Working not for himself, but for the benefit of others, Faulkner's life is a
shining example of the virtue of service. I first featured him and his story
on my radio show, *Morning in America*.

Call Michel Faulkner a Renaissance man.
Raised in the suburbs of Washington DC by his mother, a hairdresser,
and his stepfather, a police officer, Faulker displayed a gift for talent on the
football field at an early age. Faulkner attended Virginia Tech on a football scholarship, becoming a four-year starter and a freshman All-American.

After college, Faulkner took to the gridiron for the New York Jets of the NFL,
although he lasted only one season due to injury. Undaunted, Faulkner felt the demands
God was putting on his life and returned to Virginia Tech in 1983 for an MA in education and career counseling. Eventually he was hired as the assistant dean of students,
and later vice-president of urban ministry, at Liberty University. In 1988 he moved back
to New York City to work as a pastor, with a focus on spreading the gospel to some of
the city's most impoverished and desperate residents—the homeless, the imprisoned,
the AIDS victims. It was a far less glamorous beginning than his first trip to New York.

One of Faulkner's heroes, Booker T. Washington, once said, "The man or woman
who is not a servant accomplishes nothing."

Faulkner, fifty-three, doesn't have to worry.

"I could talk football all day and it wasn't going to change anyone's life. But the
minute that I mentioned God, some people huddled closer and listened, and other
people were like, 'I don't have time for this.' It became clear to me that the most
significant impact I could have on a person's life was to do it in a way that was connecting faith and everyday life."

To that end, Faulkner has spent the entirety of the last three decades cease-
lessly entrenched on the front lines of urban social reform, letting the gospel drive
his work. Beginning in the early nineties, he worked on Mayor Rudy Giuliani's Task
Force on Police Community Relations, on the city board of education's HIV/AIDS
Task Force, and as regional chaplain for the New York State Office of Children and
Family Services, among other positions. As the head of the New York Youth Leaders
Network, he coordinated the efforts of more than three thousand youth workers in
the city.

These days, Faulkner makes the cultivation of leadership skills one of his main missions. In 2005, he launched his own nonprofit organization, the Institute for Leadership, which trains leaders in government and private life to apply biblical principles in their planning and decision making, in addition to providing practical skills such as money management and job training for the disadvantaged.

"I want to keep encouraging other people to come and be a part of the equation that's going to make a difference; we need all Americans to do that . . . and not to do it and say what's in it for me, but understand the collective good that we need to do as citizens."

Faulkner particularly has a heart for young men, and wants to see adult men assert themselves as guardians of social and civic decency in an age of moral relativism.

"The problem is right now that men are afraid are to be men. We are afraid to confront that kid on the train that's cursing; we're afraid to say to him that's not the way we're supposed to behave. We get into this whole live and let live, but live and let live does not mean I let people do whatever they want to do because I want to do whatever I want to do."

Although Faulkner was raised in a religious atmosphere, he understands the temptations facing men. In college especially, even the strongest young men can stumble. "If it feels good I'll do it; if it feels real good I'll do it twice," he said, describing the mentality that too many men fall prey to.

Faulkner abhors the culture of dependence on government that has harmed the population of America's inner cities in the last half-century. "We don't need government handouts. What we need is a hand up to build strength in this community," he said.

Many Americans agree, but there's something about a black man living in Harlem who says it.

And then does something about it.

"I'm not dependent on the government to bring about the American dream. It's not the government's dream," he said. "The thing that makes America great is that we can come with all of these divergent ideas and come together for the collective good of the people—a government of the people, for the people, and by the people."

In 2010, Faulkner challenged powerful incumbent Charles Rangel in the U.S. House of Representatives for the seat belonging to the 15th District of New York, Harlem.

"Running for Congress is a sense of my duty as a citizen and as a patriot. I didn't run as a religious leader; I ran as a person who loves the community, loves God, loves people, loves his country, and feels like we're headed down some paths that aren't good and rather than curse the darkness, I want to light some candles."

Although his bid was unsuccessful, Faulkner relished the opportunity as a chance to run, and said he would do it again. Since 2006, Faulkner, who is married with three children, has been the pastor of New Horizons Church in Harlem. His daily routine begins at 5:00 a.m., praying for an hour and a half. With titanic challenges facing him, he depends on God to shepherd him through his work.

"Being a Christian, there was no immunity agreement that I wouldn't have crisis. Faith is not the absence of conflict, but the presence of God in the midst of conflict."

To the outsider, a lifetime ministering to the poor and the lost of the concrete jungle of New York can seem impossibly discouraging. There are myriad challenges of raising funding, identifying which programs work, and managing personnel. There are long hours and little pay. Your office is the ghetto, the penitentiary, the AIDS clinic, the soup kitchen.

But don't feel sorry for Michel Faulkner.

"I thank God he's called me to Harlem."

From *Middlemarch*

George Eliot

Mary Ann Evans, more famously known by her pen name George Eliot, was an English Victorian novelist who wrote *Adam Bede*, *The Mill on the Floss*, and her magnum opus *Middlemarch*. Evans successfully dealt with the tough societal issues facing Victorian England with the unique voice of a woman author in a dominantly male-driven world. She is my favorite novelist.

In this first excerpt, Caleb Garth, a hardworking man who struggles to provide for his family, reflects on the joy and value of work. His is the life of a simple man, what we call a "common man," and he is a profoundly good, simple man.

Caleb Garth often shook his head in meditation on the value, the indispensable might of that myriad-headed, myriad-handed labor by which the social body is fed, clothed, and housed. It had laid hold of his imagination in boyhood. The echoes of the great hammer where roof or keel were a-making, the signal-shouts of the workmen, the roar of the furnace, the thunder and plash of the engine, were a sublime music to him; the felling and lading of timber, and the huge trunk vibrating star-like in the distance along the highway, the crane at work on the wharf, the piled-up produce in warehouses, the precision and variety of muscular effort wherever exact work had to be turned out,—all these sights of his youth had acted on him as poetry without the aid of the poets, had made a philosophy for him without the aid of philosophers, a religion without the aid of theology. His early ambition had been to have as effective a share as possible in this sublime labor, which was peculiarly dignified by him with the name of "business;" and though he had only been a short time under a surveyor, and had been chiefly his own teacher, he knew more of land, building, and mining than most of the special men in the county.

————

After fighting day-to-day to provide for his family's welfare, Caleb Garth receives the news that he has been offered a job that will significantly help his family in their financial troubles.

Mrs. Garth's eyes were now drawn towards her husband, who was already deep in the letter he was reading. His face had an expression of grave surprise, which alarmed her a little, but he did not like to be questioned while he was reading, and she remained anxiously watching till she saw him suddenly shaken by a little joyous laugh as he turned back to the beginning of the letter, and looking at her above his spectacles, said, in a low tone, "What do you think, Susan?"

She went and stood behind him, putting her hand on his shoulder, while they read the letter together. It was from Sir James Chettam, offering to Mr. Garth the management of the family estates at Freshitt and elsewhere, and adding that Sir James had been requested by Mr. Brooke of Tipton to ascertain whether Mr. Garth would be disposed at the same time to resume the agency of the Tipton property. The Baronet added in very obliging words that he himself was particularly desirous of seeing the Freshitt and Tipton estates under the same management, and he hoped to be able to show that the double agency might be held on terms agreeable to Mr. Garth, whom he would be glad to see at the Hall at twelve o'clock on the following day.

"He writes handsomely, doesn't he, Susan?" said Caleb, turning his eyes upward to his wife, who raised her hand from his shoulder to his ear, while she rested her chin on his head. "Brooke didn't like to ask me himself, I can see," he continued, laughing silently.

"Here is an honor to your father, children," said Mrs. Garth, looking round at the five pair of eyes, all fixed on the parents. "He is asked to take a post again by those who dismissed him long ago. That shows that he did his work well, so that they feel the want of him."

"Like Cincinnatus—hooray!" said Ben, riding on his chair, with a pleasant confidence that discipline was relaxed.

"Will they come to fetch him, mother?" said Letty, thinking of the Mayor and Corporation in their robes.

Mrs. Garth patted Letty's head and smiled, but seeing that her husband was gathering up his letters and likely soon to be out of reach in that sanctuary "business," she pressed his shoulder and said emphatically—

"Now, mind you ask fair pay, Caleb."

"Oh yes," said Caleb, in a deep voice of assent, as if it would be unreasonable to suppose anything else of him. "It'll come to between four and five hundred, the two together." Then with a little start of remembrance he said, "Mary, write and give up that school. Stay and help your mother. I'm as pleased as Punch, now I've thought of that."

No manner could have been less like that of Punch triumphant than Caleb's, but his talents did not lie in finding phrases, though he was very particular about his letter-writing, and regarded his wife as a treasury of correct language.

There was almost an uproar among the children now, and Mary held up the cambric embroidery towards her mother entreatingly, that it might be put out of reach while the boys dragged her into a dance. Mrs. Garth, in placid joy, began to put the cups and plates together, while Caleb pushing his chair from the table, as if he were going to move to the desk, still sat holding his letters in his hand and looking on the ground meditatively, stretching out the fingers of his left hand, according to a mute language of his own. At last he said—"It's a thousand pities Christy didn't take to business, Susan. I shall want help by-and-by. And Alfred must go off to the engineering—I've made up my mind to that." He fell into meditation and finger-rhetoric again for a little while, and then continued: "I shall make Brooke have new agreements with the tenants, and I shall draw up a rotation of crops. And I'll lay a wager we can get fine bricks out of the clay at Bott's corner. I must look into that: it would cheapen the repairs. It's a fine bit of work, Susan! A man without a family would be glad to do it for nothing."

"Mind you don't, though," said his wife, lifting up her finger.

"No, no; but it's a fine thing to come to a man when he's seen into the nature of business: to have the chance of getting a bit of the country into good fettle, as they say, and putting men into the right way with their farming, and getting a bit of good contriving and solid building done—that those who are living and those who come after will be the better for. I'd sooner have it than a fortune. I hold it the most honorable work that is." Here Caleb laid down his letters, thrust his fingers between the buttons of his waistcoat, and sat upright, but presently proceeded with some awe in his voice and moving his head slowly aside—"It's a great gift of God, Susan."

"That it is, Caleb," said his wife, with answering fervor. "And it will be a blessing to your children to have had a father who did such work: a father whose good work remains though his name may be forgotten." She could not say any more to him then about the pay.

"The Four Chaplains of World War II"

FROM *AMERICAN PATRIOT'S ALMANAC* BY WILLIAM J. BENNETT AND JOHN T. CRIBB

The most powerful examples of work and service are those who make the ultimate sacrifice—their lives—for their profession. Firemen, police officers, soldiers, missionaries, and so on, risk their lives every day they go to work. The four chaplains in the following story were at work to save men's souls, and when the chance arrived, not in the way they were expecting, they selflessly gave their lives for their work.

In the early hours of February 3, 1943, the U.S. Army troopship *Dorchester* steamed through the icy waters of "torpedo alley" some one hundred miles off the coast of Greenland. The ship, carrying more than nine hundred men, was having a rough go of it. Winter winds screeched across the North Atlantic, and heavy seas pounded the bow. Beneath the frenzied surface lurked a German submarine.

At 12:55 a.m. a torpedo ripped into the *Dorchester*'s side, and immediately the ship started to sink. Desperate soliders rushed topside, stumbling toward lifeboats and jumping overboard.

Amid the confusion, four army chaplains worked quietly and methodically, calming the soldiers, directing them toward lifeboats, and handing out life jackets. When they ran out, they took off their own life jackets and put them on other men.

They were four chaplains of different faiths: Jewish rabbi Alexander Goode, Catholic priest John Washington, and Protestant ministers George Fox and Clark Poling. They had joined the U.S. Army to tend to the spiritual needs of the troops. Now, in this hour of urgent need, they put their courage and faith to work so others might live.

As the ship slid beneath the surface, soldiers in the lifeboats took one last look at the *Dorchester*. They saw the four chaplains standing on deck, arms linked, praying.

Rescue ships plucked 230 men from the sea, but 672 died in the freezing Atlantic. The four chaplains were not among the survivors.

"They were always together," one of the soldiers later said. "They carried their faith together." The four chaplains died as they lived, serving their country, their fellow men, and God.

From *Paradise Lost*

JOHN MILTON

John Milton (1608-1674) was an English poet and historian, considered by many to be the most significant English author since Shakespeare.

Milton's epic poem *Paradise Lost* is one of the most important works written in the English language. In this scene, Adam and Eve are in the garden of Eden, and Adam tells Eve about the life that they will live and of the roles they will play in nurturing and ordering the world through the work of their hands.

> *When Adam thus to Eve: Fair Consort, th' hour*
> *Of night, and all things now retir'd to rest*
> *Mind us of like repose, since God hath set*
> *Labour and rest, as day and night to men*
> *Successive, and the timely dew of sleep*
> *Now falling with soft slumbrous weight inclines*
> *Our eye-lids; other Creatures all day long*
> *Rove idle unimploid, and less need rest;*
> *Man hath his daily work of body or mind*
> *Appointed, which declares his Dignitie,*
> *And the regard of Heav'n on all his waies;*
> *While other Animals unactive range,*
> *And of thir doings God takes no account.*
> *To morrow ere fresh Morning streak the East*
> *With first approach of light, we must be ris'n,*
> *And at our pleasant labour, to reform*
> *Yon flourie Arbors, yonder Allies green,*
> *Our walks at noon, with branches overgrown,*
> *That mock our scant manuring, and require*
> *More hands than ours to lop thir wanton growth:*
> *Those Blossoms also, and those dropping Gumms,*
> *That lie bestrowne unsightly and unsmooth,*
> *Ask riddance, if we mean to tread with ease;*
> *Mean while, as Nature wills, Night bids us rest.*

— ❧ —

From *True Tales of Arctic Heroism in the New World*

ADOLPHUS WASHINGTON GREELY

As we see from the tireless work of Sir John Franklin and his fellow Arctic explorers, happy is the man who lives and dies knowing that he has finished some great work he set out to accomplish.

Few persons realize the accompaniments of the prolonged search by England for the northwest passage, whether in its wealth of venturesome daring, in its development of the greatest maritime nation of the world, or in its material contributions to the wealth of the nations. Through three and a half centuries the British Government never lost sight of it, from the voyage of Sebastian Cabot, in 1498, to the completion of the discovery by Sir John Franklin in 1846-7. It became a part of the maritime life of England when Sir Martin Frobisher brought to bear on the search "all the most eminent interests of England—political and aristocratic, scientific and commercial." To the search are due the fur-trade of Hudson Bay, the discovery of continental America, the cod-fishery of Newfoundland, and the whale-fishery of Baffin Bay. For the discovery of the northwest passage various parliaments offered a reward of twenty thousand pounds sterling.

An enterprise that so vitally affected the maritime policy of England, and in which the historic explorer, Henry Hudson, and the great navigator, James Cook, met their deaths, involved many heroic adventures, among which none has engaged more attention than the fateful voyage of Sir John Franklin and his men, by which the problem was solved.

The tale of the northwest passage in its last phase of discovery cannot anywhere be found in a distinct and connected form. As a record of man's heroic endeavor and of successful accomplishment at the cost of life itself, it should be retold from time to time. For it vividly illustrates an eagerness for adventurous daring for honor's sake that seems to be growing rarer and rarer under the influences of a luxurious and materialistic century.

When in 1845 the British Government decided to send out an expedition for the northwest passage, all thoughts turned to Franklin. Notable among the naval giants of his day through deeds done at sea and on land, in battle and on civic duty, he was an honored type of the brave and able captains of the royal navy. Following the glorious day of Trafalgar came six years of arctic service—whose arduous demands appear in the sketch, "Crossing the Barren Grounds"—followed by seven years of duty as governor of Tasmania. But these exacting duties had not tamed the adventurous spirit of this heroic Englishman. Deeming it a high honor, he would not ask for the command of this squadron, for the expedition was a notable public enterprise whereon England should send its ablest commander.

When tendered the command the public awaited eagerly for his reply. He was in his sixtieth year, and through forty-one degrees of longitude—from 107° W. to 148° W.—he had traced the coast of North America, thus outlining far the greater extent of the passage. But his arctic work had been done under such conditions of hardship and at such eminent [sic] peril of life as would have deterred most men from ever again accepting such hazardous duty save under imperative orders.

Franklin's manly character stood forth in his answer: "No service is dearer to my heart than the completion of the survey of the northern coast of North America and the accomplishment of the northwest passage."

Going with him on this dangerous duty were other heroic souls, officers, and men, old in polar service, defiantly familiar with its perils and scornful of its hardships. Among these were Crozier and Gore, who, the first in five and the last in two voyages, had sailed into both the ice-packs of northern seas and among the wondrous ice islands of the antarctic world.

Sailing May 26, 1845, with one hundred and twenty-nine souls in the *Erebus* and the *Terror*, Franklin's ships were last seen by Captain Dennett, of the whaler *Prince of Wales*, on July 26, 1845. Then moored to an iceberg, they awaited an opening in the middle pack through which to cross Baffin Bay and enter Lancaster Sound . . .

Knowing the virtue of labor, the captain set up an observatory on shore, built a workshop for sledgemaking and for repairs, and surely must have tested the strength and spirit of his crews by journeys of exploration to the north and to the east. It is more than probable that the energy and experiences of this master of arctic exploration sent the flag of England far to the north of Wellington Channel.

Affairs looked dark the next spring, for three of the men had died, while the main floe of the straits was holding fast later than usual. As summer came on care was given to the making of a little garden, while the seaman's sense of order was seen in the decorative garden border made of scores of empty meat-cans in lieu of more fitting material.

They had built a canvas-covered stone hut, made wind-proof by having its cracks calked, sailor-fashion, by bunches of long, reddish moss. This was the sleeping or rest room of the magnetic and other scientific observers, who cooked their simple meals in a stone fireplace built to the leeward of the main hut. Here with hunter's skill were roasted and served the sweetmeated arctic grouse savored with wild sorrel and scurvy grass from the near-by ravines.

. . . The polar winter, tedious and dreary at any time, must have been of fearful and almost unendurable length to those eager, ambitious men who, helpless and idle in their ice-held ships, knew that they had substantially finished the search which for two hundred and forty-nine years had engaged the heart and hand of the best of the marine talent of England. The winter passed, oh! how slowly, but it ended, and with the welcome sun and warmer air of coming spring there was a cheerful sense of thankfulness that death had passed by and left their circle unbroken and that "all were well."

A man of Franklin's type did not let the squadron remain idle, and it is certain that the shores of Victoria and Boothia Peninsula were explored and the magnetic pole visited and definitely relocated.

From the Crozier record, to be mentioned later, it is known that evil days followed immediately the favorable conditions set forth by Gore. Sir John Franklin was spared the agony of watching his men and officers perish one by one of exhaustion and starvation, for the record tells us that he died on the ice-beset *Erebus*, June 11, 1847, fourteen days after the erection of the Point Victory cairn. Death was now busy with the squadron, and within the next eleven months seven officers, including Gore, and twelve seamen perished, probably from scurvy.

Franklin's last days must have been made happy by the certainty that his labors had not been in vain, since it was clearly evident that he had practically finished the two labors dearest to his heart—"the completion of the survey of the northern coasts of North America and the accomplishment of the northwest passage."

"Men Wanted for Hazardous Journey"

The Antarctic continent remains one of the last frontiers of human exploration. Today, enormous steel icebreakers are the few travelers to brave the outer waters of Antarctica, dodging razor-sharp icebergs and hurricane-like storms. There are no permanent residents of Antarctica, only scientists and researchers scattered across the ice and snow for various periods of time.

For hundreds of years men have been entranced with the thought of this final frontier of Earth. Since the eighteenth century, explorers have tried to set foot on the continent. Their wooden ships, makeshift sleds, and poorly knit clothing hardly stood a chance against the deadly elements. Yet, their technological deficiencies made their journeys even more remarkable feats of human strength and will. One such story is Ernest Shackleton's Antarctic exploration in 1914.

Shackleton was one of the greatest leaders of men—the famous explorer who lost not a man during one of the most trying journeys in human history. His fellow Antarctic explorer Raymond Priestley once said, "When disaster strikes and all hope is gone, get down on your knees and pray for Shackleton." Below is a retelling of Shackleton's daunting journey, one that almost killed him and his entire crew. Men, like Shackleton and his crew, will often choose the hard path in life, believing rightly that often more will be gained from it.

In 1902, Ernest Shackleton undertook his first mission to the South Pole. Battling the extreme cold and foreign elements, Shackleton broke down with sickness and was sent home on an earlier ship. His trip was discouragingly short-lived.

Undaunted, Shackleton returned to Antarctica in 1908 on the Nimrod Expedition, determined to reach the South Pole. This time, he and his team reached a record south latitude, only 112 miles from the South Pole. Fighting starvation, Shackleton and his team survived on a mere biscuit a day toward the end of the trip. He returned to England a national hero.

After jump-starting a race for conquest of the South Pole, in 1914 Schackleton plotted his own ultimate voyage, an expedition across the Antarctic continent, infamously dubbed the "Imperial Trans-Antarctic Expedition." He would use two ships: the *Endurance* and the *Aurora*. The *Endurance* would take the main team into the Weddell Sea to the Vahsel Bay where a team of six, led by Shackleton, would commence their crossing. On the other side of the continent, the *Aurora* would approach the Great Ice Barrier laying depots [*sic*] of food and fuel for Shackleton's crew to use once they got close to the end of their journey.

Shackleton's voyage did not go as planned.

The *Endurance* departed on December 5 and became frozen solid in an ice floe deep in the Weddell Sea by the middle of January. Shackleton hoped that the ship would drift with the ice and break loose in a spring thaw; however, months ticked by and nothing loosened. Finally in November, the ice took its toll and broke a hole in the ship. Shackleton and his men abanonded the ship and remained stranded, floating on ice floes hoping to reach shore. In April, the ice floe broke in half and Shackleton ordered his men to embark in their emergency lifeboats for the nearest land.

After five harrowing days at sea, the men reached Elephant Island. According to Shackleton's diaries, this was the first time they had touched solid ground in 497 days.

However, for Shackleton and a few of his men their stay was short-lived as Elephant Island was cruelly inhospitable. The men set their sights on South Georgia Island, a small island with whaling stations where they could find food and shelter. With hypothermia and starvation setting in, they set sail in the *James Caird*, a craft no better than a small sailboat. They packed very few supplies knowing that if they didn't make it to South Georgia they would surely die. Thanks to uncanny navigation and miraculous fortune the men survived hurricane-force winds, floating ice, and nearby rocks until they finally reached the south tip of South Georgia.

Now all that stood between the men and rescue was the mountainous island of South Georgia. Shackleton took two of his men and made a death-defying thirty-six-hour journey over unknown and uncharted terrain until he and his small team finally reached the nearest whaling station. Shackleton was saved but he wasted no time outfitting a ship to return to Elephant Island to rescue his remaining men. After more than a year at sea, the crew was rescued.

Throughout the entire journey, Shackleton never lost a man in his own crew. He never reached the South Pole or completed his transcontinental expedition, but his story remains a remarkable beacon of human strength and survival. His audacity changed the course of Antarctic exploration and spurred on an entire generation of pioneers.

Before he embarked on this storied journey, Shackleton placed the following ad in a London paper looking for men to accompany him on his mission: "MEN WANTED FOR HAZARDOUS JOURNEY. Small wages, bitter cold, long months of complete darkness, constant danger, safe return doubtful. Honor and recognition in case of success."

The ad was answered by many more times the number of men than were needed. Men need bread, water, and warmth. They also long for honor in their work.

"Inaugural Address at Edinburgh University"

THOMAS CARLYLE

Thomas Carlyle (1795–1881) was a British historian and lecturer. Notable for his history on the French Revolution and for his fascination with heroes throughout history, Carlyle defined an era of British thought concerning matters of government, man, and art. In his inaugural address, April 2, 1866, on being installed as the rector of Edinburgh University, Carlyle (and Goethe) emphasized that a man—a true, hardworking, virtuous man—pushes on toward the goal, despite all obstacles or hindrances.

On the whole, I would bid you stand up to your work, whatever it may be, and not be afraid of it; not in sorrows or contradictions to yield, but to push on toward the goal.

I will wind up with a small bit of verse, which is from Goethe also, and has often gone through my mind. To me it has something of a modern psalm in it, in some measure. It is deep as the foundations, deep and high, and it is true and clear; no clearer man, or nobler and grander intellect has lived in the world, I believe, since Shakespeare left it. This is what the poet sings; a kind of road-melody or marching-music of mankind:

The future hides in it
Gladness and sorrow;
We press still thorow,
Naught that abides in it
Daunting us,—onward.

And solemn before us,
Veiled, the dark Portal;
Goal of all mortal:—
Stars silent rest o'er us
Graves under us silent!

While earnest thou gazest,
Comes boding of terror,
Comes phantasm and error;
Perplexes the bravest
With doubt and misgiving.

But heard are the Voices,
Heard are the Sages,
The Worlds and the Ages:
"Choose well; your choice is
Brief, and yet endless.

Here eyes do regard you,
In Eternity's stillness;
Here is all fulness,
Ye brave, to reward you;
Work, and despair not!"

Work, and despair not: *Wir heissen euch hoffen,* "We bid you be of hope!"—let that be my last word. Gentlemen, I thank you for your great patience in hearing me; and, with many most kind wishes, say Adieu for this time.

"On the Elevation of the Laboring Classes"

William Ellery Channing

William Ellery Channing was an important Unitarian preacher in the United States known for his passionate sermons and speeches. He did much to help the laboring classes of America, while staying far from socialism. In his speech to the Mechanic Apprentices' Library Association, William Channing defined and defended the valor and value of hard work. The goal, as this excerpt shows, is to create a balance between things in life, i.e., hard manual labor *and* study are both necessary to build true manly character.

I have faith in labor, and I see the goodness of God in placing us in a world where labor alone can keep us alive. I would not change, if I could, our subjection to physical laws, our exposure to hunger and cold, and the necessity of constant conflicts with the material world. I would not, if I could, so temper the elements that they should infuse into us only grateful sensations, that they should make vegetation so exuberant as to anticipate every want, and the minerals so ductile as to offer no resistance to our strength and skill. Such a world would make a contemptible race. Man owes his growth, his energy, chiefly to that striving of the will, that conflict with difficulty, which we call effort. Easy, pleasant work does not make robust minds, does not give men a consciousness of their powers, does not train them to endurance, to perseverance, to steady force of will, that force without which all other acquisitions avail nothing. Manual labor is a school in which men are placed to get energy of purpose and character. They are placed, indeed, under hard masters, physical sufferings and wants, the power of fearful elements, and the vicissitudes of all human things; but these stern teachers do a work which no compassionate, indulgent friend could do for us; and true wisdom will bless Providence for their sharp ministry.

I have great faith in hard work. The material world does much for the mind by its beauty and order; but it does more for our minds by the pains it inflicts; by its obstinate resistance, which nothing but patient toil can overcome; by its vast forces, which nothing but unremitting skill and effort can turn to our use; by its perils, which demand continual vigilance; and by its tendencies to decay. I believe that difficulties are more important to the human mind than what we call assistances. Work we all must, if we mean to bring out and perfect our nature.

Even if we do not work with the hands, we must undergo equivalent toil in some other direction. No business or study which does not present obstacles, tasking to the full the intellect and the will, is worthy of man.

You will see that to me labor has great dignity. It is not merely the grand instrument by which the earth is overspread with fruitfulness and beauty, and the ocean subdued, and matter wrought into innumerable forms for comfort and ornament. It has a far higher function, which is to give force to the will, efficiency, courage, the capacity of endurance, and of persevering devotion to far-reaching plans.

Alas, for the man who has not learned to work! He is a poor creature. He does not know himself. He depends on others, with no capacity of making returns for the support they give; and let him not fancy that he has a monopoly of enjoyment. Ease, rest, owes its deliciousness to toil; and no toil is so burdensome as the rest of him who has nothing to task and quicken his powers.

Profile: David Aikman

David Aikman is a best-selling author, prolific journalist, and renowned foreign policy consultant. His astounding résumé—for example, interviewing Mother Teresa and Boris Yeltsin—is the product of years of dangerous and thrilling journalist endeavors all over the world. Aikman had a knack for being in the right spot at the right time, enabling him to record some of history's most unforgettable events. His success sprang, not from luck or coincidence, but from hard work, research, and preparation. In this lengthy excerpt we see the work of a man's life take shape at his direction.

In the seconds after a gun is fired, many a man shows his true character.

Flinching is no sign of weakness. The harsh crack of the bullet exploding from the barrel can cause even the stoutest of hearts to flicker briefly. Eyelids flick shut, without choice, and a sharp ringing begins echoing down the caverns of the eardrums.

The sound shakes the soul of a man, starting from the base of the spine and racing through the entire body. He is forced to stop—to remember that he is mortal and that his days on this earth have been numbered. But when the shock leaves and the ringing in the ears quiets a bit, there is a half-second pause in the moments after the shot, where a man must ask himself, "What must I do now?"

Life rarely rewards stupidity and there is nothing honorable about risking one's safety without thought or care. Recklessness is not a trait of true manhood. But some men are called to run toward the gunshot, toward the danger, and serve so that the rest of the world can stay safe and free.

Whether it's the hell raging on the beaches of Normandy, a knife victim bleeding in an alley, or a raging fire, some men must answer to the call of danger. Seeing the need, they weigh the situation, look for the best course of action, and then act. The compulsion of duty outweighs fear. There is something different about these men—something that refuses to let them sit safely on the side while there are people who need help or while there is a job left undone.

And when asked, "Why risk your life?" the answer comes: "Because there's no other way for the job to get done."

Or, if you're longtime *Time* magazine journalist and writer David Aikman, the answer is: "I didn't sign up to be a journalist to drive buses. If you don't want to get shot, don't join the army."

———

"I think a man is a person who is willing to take risks," said Aikman. "Someone who is willing to restrain his appetite when it is appropriate—his desires—for the sake of being gracious to other people. It is a man who knows that there are physical dangers but he is willing to take the risks to encounter them when it is necessary for a particular job."

The job that David Aikman thought he was born for did not involve danger. It was supposed to be a sensible job, suitable to the disposition of an Englishman, and never would have involved Aikman hitting the ground face-first in Cambodia as bullets flew around him, and rockets exploded.

Raised in Surrey, England, Aikman went to private boarding school, and then attended Oxford University's Worcester College—earning a degree in modern languages and graduating in 1965. He planned first to apply for the diplomatic service, but when he failed the entrance exams, he accepted a job as a banker for Barclay's International.

"I had accepted a job after graduating, thinking that I would be sitting on a veranda somewhere with some sort of native fanning me with an ostrich feather," Aikman said.

But Barclay's had other plans for Aikman and they placed him "in a grubby bank, south of London, counting pound notes covered in mince meat."

These were the days when a man was hired and would be expected to start at the bottom of the bank, as a teller, and then work up the chain of authority. It would require patience and a quiet long-suffering spirit—something an Englishman should have in spades—but when the president of the bank asked Aikman how he liked the job, his reply was direct.

"It's awful."

The honesty shocked the president, shocked him so much that he decided to send this young bank teller to the United States to learn how to work on Wall Street.

Banking had not stoked Aikman's interest, but if the profession was going to be interesting anywhere, it would be interesting in the United States. After he arrived at the training center, he soon discovered that his dreams of rising above the level of the filing department were fleeting. He was stuck. He had relatives in New Jersey—Americans—and as he told them of his frustration, he began looking for some type of escape from the drudgery of Barclay's.

While Aikman had accepted a job with a bank, with dreams of exotic leisure and interesting travel, he had a deeper desire and curiosity for life that could not be sated with a nameplate on a desk in a room with no windows.

There was a compulsion lurking in his soul forcing him out of the office. It had surfaced before in his life, an adrenaline rush captivating his imagination the last year of his undergraduate degree in 1965.

Sir Winston Churchill, the lion who had defended England with every last drop of his "blood, sweat and tears," had passed away. A state funeral was arranged at St. Paul's Cathedral and as Aikman watched the preparations, sixty-five miles away at school, he felt the pull.

"I can't just watch things happen. I'm someone who wants to be in the moment, to be part of it."

So, on January 30, Aikman bundled himself into his "ramshackle fifteen-pound car" and sped off, praying each mile down the M40 that the car would hold together and he'd make it to the funeral.

He arrived early in the morning and took up a place on the sidewalk, directly across the street from St. Paul's Cathedral. This was not the university crowd that Aikman had been living alongside; these people were working-class Londoners who ground out a living, believed in the greatness of the British Empire, and had no time for the latest philosophical foolishness that might capture the younger generation.

"Can't trust this Labor government." Aikman heard murmurs as the crowd waited. "They'll sell you down the river."

It was the type of attitude Liberals might label "reactionary," but these plucky hard-nosed Londoners revered Sir Winston Churchill and the stolid, honorable Britannia that he had represented. The man who thrust his jaw out and stood up to the Third Reich and Adolf Hitler became the first politician to receive a state funeral, and the world paid tribute.

The gun carriage slowly carrying Churchill's body had been previously used for four royal funerals, and as Aikman waited, the dignitaries started passing: General de Gaulle from France, Marshal Zhukov from Russia, and representatives from more than one hundred countries. It was a solemn moment, the kind that sticks in a young man's mind.

"It was an extremely important moment. I felt that it would change history, and I wanted to be there," Aikman said.

Aikman was not only blessed to recognize those history-changing moments, but he was also infected with the need to be there when history was made. It followed him the rest of his life, surfacing after his banking career began suffocating his joy. He looked at graduate schools, wanting to expand his knowledge of the Chinese and Sino-Russian relationships. He taught Russian to beginners at the University of Washington while he pursued his studies.

Outside the campus walls, bombs were going off and Aikman's studies couldn't drown out the anger of the 1960s. Aikman had stumbled into an epicenter for unrest. College campuses seethed in a fomenting mass of angry students protesting Vietnam, occupying office buildings and holding them under siege.

By this time, Aikman had switched his major to history, studying the Russians. While reading about a student movement in the 1870s in St. Petersburg that Moscow called "back to the people," where upper-class, "cosseted" college students took a summer and went out to the peasants to try and stir up a revolution and teach them to take power, Aikman heard chants from his window.

"Pow-er to the peo-ple! Pow-er to the peo-ple!"

And something clicked in Aikman's head and turned his stomach. *These people are not very bright, not very decent but—my gosh—are they trying to do the same things as the Bolsheviks?* he thought.

He could no longer just listen to the "crude and unimaginative" spewed slogans, and Aikman decided to raise a challenge. He walked into the office of the campus newspaper and asked what it would take to get an article published. He walked out with a spot as a weekly columnist.

He wrote under the name "Francis Arouet," the pen name of the French writer Voltaire, and started documenting the exploits of the students. Aikman had become disenchanted with students who would stage elaborate protests and make grand pronouncements—signing peace treaties with North Vietnamese students—all with little practical merit.

"I was quite concerned about the extremism of the student movement, and, to be quite honest, what I felt was the stupidity of my fellow students . . . Did they really think that student signatures were going to change the war?"

The columns started piling up for Aikman, and after a friend of his father's handed three of them to the publisher of *Time* magazine, Aikman was soon on a flight to New York City. He accepted a position as a campus stringer—a part-time reporter only called into action for specific stories. Aikman was responsible for keeping *Time* tapped into the fury raging on college campuses.

Then the fury nearly burned Aikman. Working on his PhD in history, Aikman was finishing an exam and leaving a deserted classroom to head back to his tiny office. Due to radicals invading classrooms, all office buildings had been locked down, but as Aikman walked up the stairs, he passed a wild-haired student wandering down the stairs. Aikman didn't think this "hippie-like character" would have been issued keys by the university. He made it up another flight of stairs before he smelled the smoke and saw the flames.

This fellow has set fire to the building, Aikman thought, with a bit of surprise—and then took off at a sprint, hurtling down the stairs.

He burst through the doors of the building and spotted the man bolting across the grounds. Aikman pursued him along a path, and when one of his students saw him chasing the man, the student put his arm out and knocked the man to the ground. Aikman held him on the ground and—British citizenship notwithstanding—declared a citizen's arrest.

This was on a Saturday, and on the following Monday morning, four students were shot at Kent State University. The cover of *Time* highlighted student protests and Aikman's report of detaining the protestor made it into the publisher's note at the front of the magazine.

A year and a half later, in 1971, Aikman talked his way into a job in the New York bureau of *Time* and spent time at the Washington bureau. He learned the basics of journalism, how to construct an inverted pyramid sentence and how to conduct a good interview.

"I've always felt that the best interviews are almost always like very good conversations, two bright people talking about something interesting."

But for those who are to report and to write, curiosity is essential.

"There must be a willingness to report things you don't agree with, and report them fairly," said Aikman. "The best way you can tell if a reporter is a good and honest reporter is to get him to interview someone whose views he finds completely abhorrent, to report what the person says, to give the report back to the person and say, 'Is that a fair representation of your views?' If the answer is yes, then you've got a good reporter."

Aikman quickly encountered abhorrent views and was forced to prove his mettle as a good reporter. Assigned to Hong Kong for his first foreign post, he was thrust into the middle of a region torn by war in Vietnam and the advance of Communism seemingly everywhere else. He traveled to China, Burma, the Philippines, and Indochina.

Only four years after becoming a full-time reporter for *Time*, Aikman was in

Phnom Penh, the capital of Cambodia, driving along with an officer, close to infantry combat and feeling the ground rumble with the crash of rockets.

Evil lived in Cambodia. This was the time of Pol Pot and the Khmer Rouge, of piles of innocent bodies and the deaths of hundreds of thousands—genocide caused by a madman and a party slavishly devoted to Marxist-driven social engineering. Aikman had heard the gunfire. His heart pumped adrenaline and even though he would readily admit that he felt fear—he wasn't blind or ignorant—there was no question where he needed to be. Someone had to tell the story of these atrocities, to give voice to those people who might be forgotten—and he wouldn't run from the sound of gunshots.

He talked to the men perpetuating these horrors, walking up to one of the leaders of the Khmer Rouge when the opportunity presented itself.

"You have to be willing to subordinate your own disgust or antipathy to the person for the need for good reporting," said Aikman. "You've got to keep your own emotional reactions firmly under control, in order to make sure if the person says something interesting, you don't miss it, because you're fuming away over how horrible he is."

Aikman never has been a reporter who filed reports from an undisclosed safe location. His articles for *Time* were written from the heart of a man fleeing government and an ongoing atrocity.

In 1978, a *Time* essay written by Aikman, "An Experiment in Genocide," called Western leaders to account for indecision in the face of this evil. By putting himself into the crossfire, Aikman could report with eyewitness accuracy. But Aikman's stories and articles never simply mirrored the present; they always had a firm understanding of the past. His knowledge of history kept him grounded and provided a lens through which he could write with clarity.

———

Aikman's career résumé is staggering. He spent four and a half years in Hong Kong before being transferred to Berlin as the Eastern Europe correspondent during a time when dissident activity in places like Poland and Czechoslovakia was rising, and a day's work might include being tailed by the secret police.

He served as the bureau chief in Jerusalem during the leadership of Prime Minister Menachem Begin and was responsible for eleven *Time* cover stories in fifteen weeks. He was posted back to China and Beijing. He covered the Chernobyl disaster as bureau chief in Moscow. Then as the State Department correspondent, in 1989 Aikman landed a rare interview with Aleksandr Solzhenitsyn in May, and—following his sense of Chinese history and the Communist party—camped out in Tiananmen Square in June. Aikman knew the current student uprising had dramatically underestimated the willingness of the ruling Communist party to use indiscriminate force.

"I knew it wouldn't end well," said Aikman. "The government was just relentlessly opposed to being challenged, and this was just a catastrophe waiting to happen."

He knew the government, knew their history, and knew that he had to be on the scene.

On June 4, Aikman watched government forces shoot students without pity, ruthlessly suppressing what he would later call "one of the most dramatic spontaneous upsurges in support of democracy by any national movement in the 20th century."

A few months later, Aikman was on hand for the "Velvet Revolution" in Czechoslovakia in November.

Aikman has seen tragedy and talked to evil. He described interviewing a spokesperson for Hamas, who talked about blowing up children, as a physically nauseating experience. He remains a hopeful man, without the morose cynicism that infects journalists of all ages.

"Faith is the best antidote to cynicism," said Aikman. "Christians understand human nature because it is created in the image of God; it is capable of tremendous actions of good and altruism, but we're flawed."

Aikman's Christian faith has been tremendously affected by the example of the Chinese underground church and those persecuted people who back up their profession of faith with action.

"Most of them I've met have either been to prison or are willing to be arrested and go to prison for what they believe," said Aikman. "You're dealing with people of extraordinary integrity who are willing to die for their faith."

He finished his career at the Washington bureau in the early 1990s, traveling with the secretary of state and covering Russia after the Soviet Union fell. He became friends with Boris Yeltsin at this time, spotting greatness in this politico before anyone was writing about him and even saving the Russian's life on one slightly humorous occasion. When Aikman left *Time* to focus on writing books after twenty-three years as a senior correspondent, he had filed reports from five continents and more than fifty-five countries.

But he is still a humble, gracious man and speaks only quietly of his globe-stretching days.

The people he has interviewed provide his examples. He saw humility in Solzhenitsyn's strength and in Mother Teresa's love. He saw humility in Billy Graham, who would personally drive out to the airport to pick up Aikman and pepper the journalist with questions about his life.

The greatest are those who still think of themselves as the least.

In the seconds after a gunshot is fired, a man can prove his worth. But it is often not until the minutes and hours later, after the dust has settled, that the full extent of his character can be revealed. A man may withstand the hail of bullets, only to wilt in vanity under the praise of men.

Aikman never speaks too loudly. He is a gentle and gracious man who remembers that a journalist's work is telling the story of someone else. He has faced death, but he knows that a gentleman is called to do his duty despite any danger, and at the end "comes away not thinking he's any better for it."

Emerson on Labor

RALPH WALDO EMERSON

Ralph Waldo Emerson was an American lecturer, poet, and essayist who devoted a large part of his life to inspiring Americans to conquer the fields of art and literature. The following excerpts represent Emerson's invaluable insights on the value of labor in society and in our personal lives.

In the 1841 lecture, "Man the Reformer," read before the Mechanics Apprentices' Library Association, Emerson powerfully shames the institution of slavery not only for what it is but also for the way it encourages society to devalue manual labor. Emerson presents the idea that labor is necessary for the good life.

But quite apart from the emphasis which the times give to the doctrine that the manual labor of society ought to be shared among all the members, there are reasons proper to every individual why he should not be deprived of it. The use of manual labor is one which never grows obsolete, and which is inapplicable to no person. A man should have a farm or a mechanical craft for his culture. We must have a basis for our higher accomplishments, our delicate entertainments of poetry and philosophy, in the work of our hands. We must have an antagonism in the tough world for all the variety of our spiritual faculties or they will not be born. Manual labor is the study of the external world. The advantage of riches remains with him who procured them, not with the heir. When I go into my garden with a spade, and dig a bed, I feel such an exhilaration and health, that I discover that I have been defrauding myself all this time in letting others do for me what I should have done with my own hands. But not only health, but education, is in the work. Is it possible that I who get indefinite quantities of sugar, hominy, cotton, buckets, crockery ware, and letter paper, by simply signing my name once in three months to a check in favor of John Smith and Co., traders, get the fair share of exercise to my faculties by that act, which Nature intended for me in making all these farfetched matters important to my comfort? It is Smith himself, and his carriers, and dealers, and manufacturers, it is the sailor, the hidedrogher, the butcher, the negro, the hunter, and the planter who have intercepted the sugar of the sugar, and the cotton of the cotton. They have got the education, I only the commodity. This were all very well if I were necessarily absent, being detained by work of my own, like theirs, work of the same faculties; then should I be sure of my hands and feet, but now I feel some shame before my wood-chopper, my ploughman, and my cook, for they have some sort of self-sufficiency, they can contrive without my aid to bring the day and year round, but I depend on them, and have not earned by use a right to my arms and feet.

I do not wish to overstate this doctrine of labor, or insist that every man should be a farmer, any more than that every man should be a lexicographer. In general, one may say that the husbandman's is the oldest and most universal profession, and that where a man does not yet discover in himself any fitness for one work more than another, this may be preferred. But the doctrine of the farm is merely this, that every man ought to stand in primary relations with the work of the world, ought to do it himself, and not to suffer the accident of his having a purse in his pocket, or his having been bred to some dishonorable and injurious craft, to sever him from those duties; and for this reason, that labor is God's education; that he only is a sincere learner, he only can become a master, who learns the secrets of labor, and who by real cunning extorts from Nature its sceptre.

Emerson reminds us that if we learn to live off another man's dollar, instead of our own, then we will be useless to the community and will not get far in life. The true wage of labor, he argues here in his 1841 essay, "Compensation," is knowledge and virtue.

Experienced men of the world know very well that it is best to pay scot and lot as they go along, and that a man often pays dear for a small frugality. The borrower runs in his own debt. Has a man gained any thing who has received a hundred favors and rendered none? Has he gained by borrowing, through indolence or cunning, his neighbor's wares, or horses, or money? There arises on the deed the instant acknowledgment of benefit on the one part and of debt on the other; that is, of superiority and inferiority. The transaction remains in the memory of himself and his neighbor; and every new transaction alters according to its nature their relation to each other. He may soon come to see that he had better have broken his own bones than to have ridden in his neighbor's coach, and that "the highest price he can pay for a thing is to ask for it."

A wise man will extend this lesson to all parts of life, and know that it is always the part of prudence to face every claimant and pay every just demand on your time, your talents, or your heart. Always pay; for first or last you must pay your entire debt. Persons and events may stand for a time between you and justice, but it is only a postponement. You must pay at last your own debt. If you are wise you will dread a prosperity which only loads you with more. Benefit is the end of nature. But for every benefit which you receive, a tax is levied. He is great who confers the most benefits. He is base,—and that is the one base thing in the universe,—to receive favors and render none. In the order of nature we cannot render benefits to those from whom we receive them, or only seldom. But the benefit we receive must be rendered again, line for line, deed for deed, cent for cent, to somebody. Beware of too much good staying in your hand. It will fast corrupt and worm worms. Pay it away quickly in some sort.

Labor is watched over by the same pitiless laws. Cheapest, says the prudent, is the dearest labor. What we buy in a broom, a mat, a wagon, a knife, is some application of good sense to a common want. It is best to pay in your land a skilful gardener, or to buy good sense applied to gardening; in your sailor, good sense applied to navigation; in the house, good sense applied to cooking, sewing, serving; in your agent, good sense applied to accounts and affairs. So do you multiply your presence, or spread yourself throughout your estate. But because of the dual constitution of things, in labor as in life there can be no cheating. The thief steals from himself. The swindler swindles himself. For the real price of labor is knowledge and virtue, whereof wealth and credit are signs. These signs, like paper money, may be counterfeited or stolen, but that which they represent, namely, knowledge and virtue, cannot be counterfeited or stolen. These ends of labor cannot be answered but by real exertions of the mind; and in obedience to pure motives. The cheat, the defaulter, the gambler, cannot extort the benefit, cannot extort the knowledge of material and moral nature which his honest care and pains yield to the operative. The law of nature is, Do the thing, and you shall have the power; but they who do not the thing have not the power.

Ability and talent are only achieved through action and work. In 1860's "Worship," Emerson asserts that the happiest man is he who trusts the value of his own work.

I look on that man as happy, who, when there is question of success, looks into his work for a reply, not into the market, not into opinion, not into patronage. In every variety of human employment, in the mechanical and in the fine arts, in navigation, in farming, in legislating, there are among the numbers who do their task perfunctorily, as we say, or just to pass, and as badly as they dare,—there are the working-men on whom the burden of the business falls,—those who love work, and love to see it rightly done, who finish their task for its own sake; and the state and the world is happy, that has the most of such finishers. The world will always do justice at last to such finishers: it cannot otherwise. He who has acquired the ability, may wait securely the occasion of making it felt and appreciated, and know that it will not loiter. Men talk as if victory were something fortunate. Work is victory. Wherever work is done, victory is obtained. There is no chance, and no blanks. You want but one verdict: if you have your own, you are secure of the rest.

Some Fruits of Solitude

WILLIAM PENN

William Penn (1644–1718) was the founder of the commonwealth of Pennsylvania and an important religious freedoms advocate in colonial America. Through his many accomplishments, Penn learned valuable lessons about life and work. In his reflections on life, Penn wrote that work is good for the body and mind.

Love labor: For if thou dost not want it for food, thou mayest for physick. It is wholesome for thy body, and good for thy mind. It prevents the fruits of idleness, which many times comes of nothing to do, and leads too many to do what is worse than nothing . . .

A garden, an elaboratory, a work-house, improvements and breeding, are pleasant and profitable diversions to the idle and ingenious: For here they miss ill company, and converse with nature and art; whose variety are equally grateful and instructing; and preserve a good constitution of body and mind.

Selections from *Meditations*

MARCUS AURELIUS

Marcus Aurelius was one of Rome's most admirable emperors. Full of wisdom and manly virtue, Marcus Aurelius led Rome through its golden age of peace and prosperity. In *Meditations* he explains that hard work, attention to duty, and care for the good of family, the community, and the nation define what it is to be a good man.

Labour not unwillingly, nor without regard to the common interest, nor without due consideration, nor with distraction; nor let studied ornament set off thy thoughts, and be not either a man of many words, or busy about too many things. And further, let the deity which is in thee be the guardian of a living being, manly and of ripe age, and engaged in matter political, and a Roman, and a ruler, who has taken his post like a man waiting for the signal which summons him from life, and ready to go, having need neither of oath nor of any man's testimony. Be cheerful also, and seek not external help nor the tranquility which others give. A man then must stand erect, not be kept erect by others.

In the morning when thou risest unwillingly, let this thought be present—I am rising to the work of a human being. Why then am I dissatisfied if I am going to do the things for which I exist and for which I was brought into the world? Or have I been made for this, to lie in the bed-clothes and keep myself warm?—But this is more pleasant.—Dost thou exist then to take thy pleasure, and not at all for action or exertion? Dost thou not see the little plants, the little birds, the ants, the spiders, the bees working together to put in order their several parts of the universe? And art thou unwilling to do the work of a human being, and dost thou not make haste to do that which is according to thy nature?—But it is necessary to take rest also.—It is necessary: however nature has fixed bounds to this too: she has fixed bounds both to eating and drinking, and yet thou goest beyond these bounds, beyond what is sufficient; yet in thy acts it is not so, but thou stoppest short of what thou canst do. So thou lovest not thyself, for if thou didst, thou wouldst love thy nature and her will. But those who love their several arts exhaust themselves in working at them unwashed and without food; but thou valuest thy own nature less than the turner values the turning art, or the dancer the dancing art, or the lover of money values his money, or the vainglorious man his little glory. And such men, when they have a violent affection to a thing, choose neither to eat nor to sleep rather than to perfect the things which they care for. But are the acts which concern society more vile in thy eyes and less worthy of thy labour?

———

Neither the labour which the hand does nor that of the foot is contrary to nature, so long as the foot does the foot's work and the hand the hand's. So then neither to a man as a man is his labour contrary to nature, so long as it does the things of a man. But if the labour is not contrary to his nature, neither is it an evil to him.

Pensées

BLAISE PASCAL

Blaise Pascal (1623–1662) was a French mathematician, physicist, and philosopher who identified many philosophical and physical laws such as Pascal's Wager and Pascal's Law of Pressure. He believed man was created to work—that without work man is weak and incomplete, but with it man finds meaning and purpose.

Our nature consists in motion; complete rest is death . . . Nothing is so insufferable to man as to be completely at rest, without passions, without business, without diversion, without study. He then feels his nothingness, his forlornness, his insufficiency, his dependence, his weakness, his emptiness. There will immediately arise from the depth of his heart weariness, gloom, sadness, fretfulness, vexation, despair.

3

Man in Play, Sports, and Leisure

You can tell a lot about a man by the way he handles both his work and leisure time. Do you live for the weekend or do you look forward to going back to work Monday morning? I. F. Stone, editor of the *Nation*, when asked about his work, would say that he was "having so much fun he ought to be arrested."

Finding a job like that is a treasure, but very few men are fortunate enough to be in that position. Most men spend five days a week in trying, often unpleasant, and sometimes grueling labor and spend the remaining two days trying to enjoy the little leisure time they have. Work should always take priority in a man's life. It is his duty and the means by which he provides for himself and his family, but play is also a vital part of man's development and character. Whether through sports, athletics, hobbies, or the arts, our free time shapes our minds and our bodies.

In competition and sports, a man develops attributes that last long after the game or match: perseverance, the will to win, teamwork, work ethic, and self-control, to name a few. Howard Cosell, the great American sportswriter, said, "Sports is human life in microcosm." If you lose a game, do you give up and hang your head or do you press on with tenacity to win the next? If you win, do you boast and brag or do you credit your teammates and coach? The way you react on the field or the court will often mirror the way you respond in the office or the classroom.

The twentieth-century sports journalist Grantland Rice used to say, "Eighteen holes of match play will teach you more about your foe than eighteen years of dealing with him across a desk." This is true for more than just athletics. Whether it's chess, music, hunting, fishing, or mountain climbing, the way you treat games and competition can reveal your character as a man. In his "Rules for Civility," George Washington wrote, "Let your recreations be manful, not sinful."

If approached correctly, games provide happiness while also improving a man's soul. Albert Einstein remarked, "I know that the most joy in my life has come from my violin." After a hard week of work, there can be no better feeling than enjoying healthy diversions. They refresh and replenish the mind like an ice-cold drink on a hot summer day. Benjamin Franklin taught that "games lubricate the body and mind."

While we all need rest and relaxation, it becomes very easy for leisure to descend into slothfulness, laziness, and irresponsibility. Said Voltaire, the famous eighteenth-century French writer, "Work spares us from three evils: boredom, vice, and need." Television and video games, while entertaining and enjoyable, can too often become an excuse to shut off our bodies and minds. Never turn off your brain; use other parts of it. As you will notice, some of the excerpts in this chapter could be included in either the chapters on work or play. That's because some men carry into sports and games a workmanlike ethic that distinguishes them from the rest of society. And some work gives so much joy, it might as well be play. We say TGIF (Thank God It's Friday), but why not TGIM (Thank God It's Monday) too? A well-rounded man applies himself diligently to his work while also making the most out of his leisure time.

There are no better examples of this than the great men of sports. "Pistol" Pete Maravich practiced basketball eight hours a day, and when he was exhausted he would watch basketball tapes or spin the basketball on his finger, never wasting an opportunity to improve. If we all approached life that way, imagine how successful we would be. Social scientist and best-selling author Malcolm Gladwell calculated that in addition to talent and proclivity it takes ten thousand hours of practice to master an art or skill. Athletes like Jesse Owens, Jackie Robinson, Roberto Clemente, and Michael Jordan are examples of Gladwell's thesis. They push their bodies and minds to the limit and inspire us to do the same.

Whether you are playing catch in the backyard, recording music, fishing and hunting, or practicing your three-point shot, make the most of your leisure time. Exercise your mind and your body in responsible and fulfilling ways. "Leisure only means a chance to do other jobs that demand attention," said former U.S. Supreme Court Justice Oliver Wendell Holmes Jr.

Work and play are not mutually exclusive events. Don't assume that work can't be fun and play can't be laborious. "A man can never be idle with safety and advantage until he has been so trained by work that he makes his freedom from times and tasks more fruitful than his toil has been," penned Hamilton Wright Mabie, an early twentieth-century American essayist. In play, a man is free to his own devices, and a true judge of his manliness can be how, when, and where he chooses to apply his time.

Profile: "Pistol" Pete Maravich

Play, at its best, often emulates work. "Pistol" Pete Maravich, one of the all-time great basketball players, took the sport of basketball and transformed it forever through hard work and tireless practice.

In the late 1960s, a gangly kid from the small steel town of Aliquippa, Pennsylvania, changed the game of basketball forever. Behind-the-back dribbling, over-the-head passes, circus shots, head fakes, long-range shots—everything you see in today's NBA games is owed almost solely to one man: Pete Maravich.

Even before NBA stars like LeBron James, Michael Jordan, Magic Johnson, and Julius Erving were executing highlight film shots and passes, there was Pete Maravich, the original basketball showman.

Born to a Serbian American family outside the city of Pittsburgh, Maravich grew up under the tutelage of his father and coach, Press Maravich, a former pro basketball player himself. Maravich lived and breathed basketball from an early age, often practicing eight hours a day. He became notorious for developing drills and tricks with the basketball that had never been done before. He would dribble the ball between his legs and around his back at dizzying speeds, and then do it again with his opposite hand or with two basketballs.

Maravich would do anything he could think of to increase his ball handling skills and hand-eye coordination. He would dribble around the house, to school, and anywhere he could bounce a ball. His father would even drive the car while he leaned out the window practicing dribbling at different speeds!

In the eighth grade, Maravich played for the high school varsity team. He was always the best dribbler on the court, but he lacked the strength for long shots. In order to compensate, he would shoot straight from his hip, earning his famous nickname "Pistol." After becoming a highly touted prospect in high school, Maravich followed his father to Louisiana State University where his father became the new head coach.

In the 1960s, college freshman were not allowed to play at the college varsity level in the NCAA. So Maravich spent his first year of college on the freshman team, which quickly surpassed the varsity team as the most popular game on campus. So many fans would come to watch the Pistol's never-seen-before antics that the varsity games would often be nearly empty.

In 1967, Maravich joined the varsity team and took the world of college basketball by storm. For the next three years, he averaged an astronomical 44.2 points a game and led the NCAA in scoring each year. He is still the NCAA's all-time leading scorer with 3,667 points. Don't forget that Maravich played in an era when there was no three-point line. Basketball experts estimate that he could have averaged almost 57 points a game with the modern college rules.

After leaving LSU in 1970, Maravich was the third pick in that year's NBA draft and signed a $1.9 million contract with the Atlanta Hawks, one of the highest salaries at that time. Maravich's high salary and flashy style made his transition to the NBA tough. While the crowd loved him, his teammates and coach were irritated by his style. Maravich became one of the top five scorers in the league and an all-star selection, but he could never make it off losing teams. In 1980, Maravich retired from basketball after severe knee injuries kept sidelining him.

Stripped of basketball at an early age, Maravich was suddenly lost in the world. He said, "My life had no meaning at all. I found only brief interludes of satisfaction. It was as if my whole life had been about my whole basketball career." Turning to alcohol and empty soul-searching, the next few years were a low point in Pistol Pete's life. Then, in 1982, Pete found peace in Christianity.

Soon after, he became a lay pastor and traveled the country to teach basketball and relate his story. During a speech he delivered in 1982, Pete said, "There is nothing wrong with dedication and goals, but if you focus on yourself, all the lights fade away and you become a fleeting moment in life. I lived my life one way for thirty-five years, for me. And then the focus came in on who I really was."

On January 5, 1988, while playing a pickup game at a church in Pasadena, California, with a group of men, including Dr. James Dobson, Maravich collapsed and died at the age of forty from a sudden heart attack. An autopsy revealed that Maravich was born with a rare congenital defect and was missing his left coronary artery. For his entire life, his severely enlarged right coronary artery had been compensating for the defect. Dobson said that Maravich's last words, only minutes before he died, were, "I feel great."

"Do You Fear the Wind?"

Hamlin Garland

Hannibal Hamlin Garland (1860–1940) was an American poet and writer. He grew up on a farm in Wisconsin and settled in Boston, where he established a career best known for his fiction about the hardworking Midwestern farmers. In this motivational poem, Garland emphasizes that too many men are complacent in their homes, protected from the rain and the wind. He wants men to return to nature where they have to prove their manliness and survive on their own. A modern formulation of this message can be found in John Eldredge's great book *Wild at Heart*.

> *Do you fear the force of the wind,*
> *The slash of the rain?*
> *Go face them and fight them,*
> *Be savage again.*
> *Go hungry and cold like the wolf,*
> *   Go wade like the crane.*

The palms of your hands will thicken,
The skin of your forehead tan—
You'll be ragged and swarthy and weary
    But—you'll walk like a man.

"It Is a Pleasant Day"

PETER PARLEY

Too many boys spend their days inside watching TV or playing video games.
This poem is a simple reminder to enjoy the outdoors and everything it has
to offer. Whether in sports or games, the outdoors promote healthiness,
creativity, and fun in a way that surpasses staring at the television.

Come, my children, come away,
For the sun shines bright to-day;
Little children, come with me,
Birds and brooks, arid posies see;
Get your hats and come away,
For it is a pleasant day.
Every thing is laughing, singing,
All the pretty flowers are springing;
See the kitten full of fun,
Sporting in the pleasant sun;
Children too, may sport and play,
For it is a pleasant day.
Bring the hoop, and bring the ball,
Come with happy faces all;
Let us make a merry ring,
Talk and laugh, arid dance and sing;
Quickly, quickly, come away,
For it is a pleasant day.

"The Answer"

GRANTLAND RICE

Grantland Rice (1880–1954) was an early twentieth-century American sportswriter and broadcaster. His writings and broadcasts reached homes all across America. In his poem "Alumnus Football," he famously penned the line: "For when the One Great Scorer comes, / To write against your name, / He marks—not that you won or lost—/ But how you played the Game." Rice looked at sports for deeper truths than just athletic skill and talents, and he often regretted the negative influence money had on sports. In his poem "The Answer," Rice admonishes us to make the best of what we have and to never give up, no matter what the world may throw at us. No matter how hard we get knocked down, we should always get back up and keep fighting.

When the battle breaks against you and the crowd forgets to cheer,
When the Anvil Chorus echoes with the essence of a jeer;
When the knockers start their panning in the knocker's nimble way,
With a rap for all your errors and a josh upon your play.
There is one quick answer ready that will nail them on the wing;
There is one reply forthcoming that will wipe away the sting;
There is one elastic come-back that will hold them, as it should,
Make good.
No matter where you finish in the mix-up or the row,
There are those among the rabble who will pan you anyhow;
But the entry who is sticking and delivering the stuff,
Can listen to the yapping as he giggles up his cuff;
The loafer has no come-back and the quitter no reply,
When the Anvil Chorus echoes, as it will, against the sky;
But there's one quick answer ready that will wrap them in a hood,
Make good.

"Playing the Game"

ANONYMOUS

This poem summarizes how we should approach not only sports, but also life in general. Don't complain when things don't go your way; life isn't always fair. Instead, hold your head up high and play the game as best you can.

Life is a game with a glorious prize,
If we can only play it right.
It is give and take, build and break,
And often it ends in a fight;
But he surely wins who honestly tries
(Regardless of wealth or fame),
He can never despair who plays it fair,
How are you playing the game?
Do you wilt and whine, if you fail to win
In the manner you think your due?
Do you sneer at the man in case that he can
And does, do better than you?
Do you take your rebuffs with a knowing grin?
Do you laugh tho' you pull up lame?
Does your faith hold true when the whole world's blue?
How are you playing the game?
Get into the thick of it—wade in, boys!
Whatever your cherished goal;
Brace up your will till your pulses thrill,
And you dare—to your very soul!
Do something more than make a noise;
Let your purpose leap into flame,
As you plunge with a cry, "I shall do or die,"
Then you will be playing the game.

From "The Quitter"

ROBERT W. SERVICE

As the maxim goes: quitters never win, and winners never quit. Robert W. Service (1874–1958), the popular poet and writer, noted how easy it is to quit and give up, but the real men and the real winners press on even when there is no hope in sight. Nicknamed the "Bard of the Yukon," Service's writings were so emphatic that his readers often took him for a gruff, old prospector and not the bank clerk he actually was at the time. Following are the last two stanzas of one of his most famous poems "The Quitter."

"You're sick of the game!" Well, now, that's a shame.
You're young and you're brave and you're bright.
"You've had a raw deal!" I know—but don't squeal,
Buck up, do your damnedest, and fight.
It's the plugging away that will win you the day,
So don't be a piker, old pard!
Just draw on your grit; it's so easy to quit:
It's the keeping-your-chin-up that's hard.

It's easy to cry that you're beaten—and die;
It's easy to crawfish and crawl;
But to fight and to fight when hope's out of sight—
Why, that's the best game of them all!
And though you come out of each grueling bout,
All broken and beaten and scarred,
Just have one more try—it's dead easy to die,
It's the keeping-on-living that's hard.

Profile: Eddie Aikau

In the late 1970s, Eddie Aikau was at the top of the sport of surfing when he got caught in a tragic shipwreck. Aikau had the most to lose of all the crew, yet he was the first to risk his life to save the others. If you were in his position, would you do the same thing?

March 17, 2011, marked the thirty-third anniversary of the disappearance of legendary Hawaiian surfer and waterman Eddie Aikau. It was on this fateful day that he and his crew set sail from Hawaii to Tahiti on their way to reenact the twenty-four-hundred-mile ancient Polynesian migration. Eddie was only thirty-one years old and he had just won the coveted Duke Kahanamoku Invitational Surfing Championship, one of the biggest surfing competitions in Hawaii. But more important to him than any surf competition was this voyage across the great Pacific Ocean.

Immediately after they left port, Eddie and his crew encountered terrible weather with strong winds and high seas. Only five hours into their journey, their boat capsized and the entire crew was left clinging to the side of the ship for their lives. After almost an entire day of shooting off flares and trying to signal planes overhead, the cold was starting to set in and the crew was gradually drifting farther and farther from land.

Eddie realized that the longer they waited, the higher the chance would be that they would never be found. So Eddie begged the captain to let him take out the surfboard he had brought with him and try to paddle to the island of Lanai, which was twelve miles away. At first the captain resisted, but as the situation became graver he allowed Eddie to go. That was the last time Eddie was ever seen.

Late that evening, a plane overhead spotted a flare the remaining crew had sent off and soon rescue ships were on their way. Once they reached port safely, a massive search party was sent to find Eddie, but they returned empty-handed.

Today, Eddie's sacrifice and heroism are remembered by Quiksilver's big-wave competition "The Eddie" held in his name at Waimea Bay in Hawaii. In addition, the popular catchphrase "Eddie Would Go" is displayed proudly on the shirts and bumper stickers of thousands of people all across the world.

From "The American Boy"

THEODORE ROOSEVELT

From hunting to exploring to football, Theodore Roosevelt was a president who understood the importance of games, competition, and the self-improvement it fostered. In the following selection from an essay published in 1900, Roosevelt describes what it means to be an American man, and how an American boy can grow up to be one.

What we have a right to expect of the American boy is that he shall turn out to be a good American man.

The boy can best become a good man by being a good boy—not a goody-goody boy, but just a plain good boy.

I do not mean that he must love only the negative virtues; I mean that he must love the positive virtues also. "Good," in the largest sense, should include whatever is fine, straightforward, clean, brave and manly.

The best boys I know—the best men I know—are good at their studies or their business, fearless and stalwart, hated and feared by all that is wicked and depraved, incapable of submitting to wrongdoing, and equally incapable of being aught but tender to the weak and helpless.

Of course the effect that a thoroughly manly, thoroughly straight and upright boy can have upon the companions of his own age, and upon those who are younger, is incalculable.

If he is not thoroughly manly, then they will not respect him, and his good qualities will count for but little; while, of course, if he is mean, cruel, or wicked, then his physical strength and force of mind merely make him so much the more objectionable a member of society.

He can not do good work if he is not strong and does not try with his whole heart and soul to count in any contest; and his strength will be a curse to himself and to every one else if he does not have a thorough command over himself and over his own evil passions, and if he does not use his strength on the side of decency, justice and fair dealing.

In short, in life, as in a football game, the principle to follow is: Hit the line hard: don't foul and don't shirk, but hit the line hard.

"A President and His Leisure"

THEODORE ROOSEVELT

From Theodore Roosevelt's autobiography we get an inside look at the psyche and personality of one of America's most influential presidents. While Roosevelt took work very seriously, he understood the value of exercise and physical improvement. Even as president, Roosevelt always found time to run, ride, or swim in the parks around Washington DC.

But at Oyster Bay [Roosevelt's home on Long Island, New York] our great and permanent amusements were rowing and sailing; I do not care for the latter, and am fond of the former. I suppose it sounds archaic, but I cannot help thinking that the people with motor boats miss a great deal. If they would only keep to rowboats or canoes, and use oar or paddle themselves, they would get infinitely more benefit than by having their work done for them by gasoline. But I rarely took exercise merely as exercise. Primarily I took it because I liked it. Play should never be allowed to interfere with work; and a life devoted merely to play is, of all forms of existence, the most dismal. But the joy of life is a very good thing, and while work is the essential in it, play also has its place.

While in the White House I always tried to get a couple of hours' exercise in the afternoons—sometimes tennis, more often riding, or else a rough cross-country walk, perhaps down Rock Creek [a large park in Washington, DC], which was then as wild as a stream in the White Mountains, or on the Virginia side along the Potomac. Often, especially in the winters and early springs, we would arrange for a point to point walk, not turning aside for anything—for instance, swimming Rock

Creek or even the Potomac if it came in our way. Of course under such circumstances we had to arrange that our return to Washington should be when it was dark, so that our appearance might scandalize no one. On several occasions we thus swam Rock Creek in the early spring when the ice was floating thick upon it. If we swam the Potomac, we usually took off our clothes. I remember one such occasion when the French Ambassador, Jusserand, who was a member of the Tennis Cabinet, was along, and, just as we were about to get in to swim, somebody said, "Mr. Ambassador, Mr. Ambassador, you haven't taken off your gloves," to which he promptly responded, "I think I will leave them on; we might meet ladies!"

— ❦ —

"Coin Collecting"

THE NUMISMATIST

Not all boys are interested in sports and athletics, but there are other hobbies and diversions that a boy can engage in that will make him a well-rounded man. This selection talks about the value and fun in coin collecting. In this a boy can learn the value in saving and preserving valuables while also studying the time period of the coins and where and how they were made.

No other hobby, perhaps, when once commenced, possesses so great a fascination as coin collecting, and there are many things to induce one to take it up. It is a clean hobby, the specimens do not perish, it requires no vast amount of room and the tyro can commence in a very humble way, at no great risk of initial expense.

He can first collect the current coins of the realm and then either obtain those in circulation in other countries, or coins which, in remoter periods, passed in his own. If he does the former, it must of necessity give him wider and clearer views of the world, its geography, its customs and its rulers, for in those coins he has something tangible, which will do more to impress upon his memory facts in connection with countries and people, than a vast amount of study would do without them.

And what significance coins possess! They help us to build up the history of the past; they remain to us while the peoples which used them have passed away. On them we get the likeness of their rulers, their temples, their gods. They bear the impress of the character of the people. The Greek coins are things of beauty, which we have not succeeded, in many respects, in surpassing yet. The Roman coins are indicative of war. And, to come down to those of our own time and country, Britannia seated by the waves tells of our commerce and rule upon the deep.

Coins have many associations. They make us feel in touch with their time. "Yes, perhaps Shakespeare handled that one; perhaps Milton, before his eyes grew dim, saw that. That may have been one of the very mites the widow cast into the treasury; that the one Christ asked whose superscription it bore." And so they link us with the past, and are tokens of the power and yet the frailty of man.

Coney Island

THE CENTURY ILLUSTRATED MONTHLY MAGAZINE

Coney Island is a peninsula in Brooklyn that was home to one of the earliest theme parks in America, as this piece from the early twentieth century describes. With roller coasters, board games, rides, and amusements all right across from the Atlantic Ocean, Coney Island has been a famous vacation destination for New Yorkers for more than a hundred years; but some people are a bit too snobby to go there. When I was a boy growing up in Brooklyn, I would ride the subway with my mom and brother to Coney Island.

The most distant dweller from New York City has heard of Coney Island. He may not be able to name a single theater on Broadway, the Metropolitan Art Museum may be to him without form, and void; but the reputation of Coney Island as a garden of gaiety to which the city itself seems more or less an adjunct is firmly established in the remotest hamlet of the farthest frontier.

"Well, how's Coney Island this year? How about old Coney?" is the question likely to greet the New Yorker in his rural wanderings. Whereupon the dweller on Manhattan Island may suddenly find himself involved in a humiliating confession that he has not been to Coney Island this year, or for half a dozen years; that to him it is a place almost as removed as though it were an island in the South Pacific, instead of a "Land of Heart's Desire" lying close at his harbor gates. And the city man loses prestige with his questioners just in proportion as his lack of intimacy with the world-famed resort is revealed. No matter what else he claims to have seen, he cannot redeem himself. A man who lives within a ten-cent fare of Coney Island and does not go there is likely to be poor authority on any matter of recreation.

"A Nation's Pastime"
A. G. SPALDING

The influence of Albert Goodwill Spalding (1850–1915) on our national pastime cannot be understated. Originally rising to prominence as one of the greatest pitchers of the nineteenth century, Spalding then turned his attention to selling sporting goods, and the company he founded bearing his name made him a wealthy man. In 1889–1890 Spalding organized a baseball world tour, bringing the brightest stars of the game to New Zealand, Australia, Ceylon, Egypt, Italy, France, and England for a series of exhibition games. Spalding also made it his life's mission to prove that baseball was uniquely an American game, in spite of its obvious origins in older European games like cricket and rounders. In this piece, Spalding writes effusively about the effect that baseball had on soldiers during the Civil War, showing it to be an escape from the carnage that the war engendered. No sport has ever been given a grander compliment.

Growing up in Brooklyn, one of the most prized possessions a kid could have was a new can of balls to play with—"spaldeens" as we mistakenly referred to them.

No human mind may measure the blessings conferred by the game of base-ball on the soldiers of our Civil War. A National Game? Why, no country on the face of the earth ever had a form of sport with so clear a title to that distinction. Baseball had been born in the brain of an American soldier. It received its baptism in bloody days of our Nation's direst danger. It had its early evolution when soldiers, North and South, were striving to forget their foes by cultivating, through this grand game, fraternal friendships with comrades in arms. It had its best develop-ment at the time when Southern soldiers, disheartened by distressing defeat, were seeking the solace of something safe and sane; at a time when Northern soldiers, flushed with victory, were *yet* willing to turn from fighting with bombs and bullets to playing with bat and ball. It was a panacea for the pangs of humiliation to the van-quished on the one side, and a sedative against the natural exuberance of victors on the other. It healed the wounds of war, and was balm to stinging memories of sword thrust and saber stroke. It served to fill the enforced leisure hours of countless thou-sands of men suddenly thrown out of employment. It calmed the restless spirits of men who, after four years of bitter strife, found themselves all at once in the midst of a monotonous era, with nothing at all to do.

And then, when true patriots of all sections were striving to forget that there had been a time of black and dismal war, it was a beacon, lighting their paths to a future of perpetual peace. And, later still, it was a medium through which the men who had worn the blue, found welcome to the cities of those who had worn the gray, and before the decade of the sixties had died the game of baseball helped all of us to "know no North, no South," only remembering a reunited Nation, whose game it was henceforth to be forever.

— ❧ —

"Leisure"

WILLIAM HENRY DAVIES

The Welsh poet, William Henry Davies (1871–1940), lived quite a unique
life. He spent much of his life as a tramp traveling across the United

States and the United Kingdom writing about his experiences. After an unfortunate injury slowed down his travels, Davies returned to England and established himself as one of the favorite poets of his time. As you can see from the following poem, Davies' idea of leisure was to step back from the business of life and admire the beauty of creation.

WHAT IS THIS LIFE IF, FULL OF CARE,
We have no time to stand and stare.
No time to stand beneath the boughs
And stare as long as sheep or cows.
No time to see, when woods we pass,
Where squirrels hide their nuts in grass.
No time to see, in broad daylight,
Streams full of stars like skies at night.
No time to turn at Beauty's glance,
And watch her feet, how they can dance.
No time to wait till her mouth can
Enrich that smile her eyes began.
A poor life this if, full of care,
We have no time to stand and stare.

On Gardening

FRANCIS BACON

Francis Bacon (1561–1626) was an English philosopher and scientist. He has been called the father of empiricism and is famous for his contributions to modern science, for example, the scientific method. Gardening, which we usually associate as work, was seen by Bacon as one of the great pleasures of God's creation.

G od Almighty first planted a garden. And indeed it is the purest of human pleasures. It is the greatest refreshment to the spirits of man; without which, buildings and palaces are but gross handiworks. And man shall see, that when ages grow to civility and elegancy, men come to build stately sooner than to garden finely; as if gardening were the greater perfection. I do hold it, in the royal ordering of gardens, there ought to be gardens, for all the months in the year; in which things of beauty may be then in season.

"Finding Troy"

HEINRICH SCHLIEMANN

Born in Germany in 1822, Heinrich Schliemann grew up entranced by stories from the *Iliad* and the *Odyssey*. After a career in business that brought him a massive fortune, Schliemann set out to pursue his life's goal—excavating the mighty city of Troy. Dubbed a madman by the professional community, Schliemann roamed the coast of Turkey for years with copies of Homer as his guide, hoping to find the exact spot where mighty Troy once stood. In 1871, Schliemann found the spot that he posited to be the site of the city.

After two years of excavations, Schliemann unearthed the site of an ancient citadel, and some of the most magnificent finds in archaeological history, dubbing them "Priam's Treasure." Although Schliemann's methods were primitive for the time, he nonetheless made significant contributions to the science of archaeology and showed that the Homeric poems did have some elements of truth based on actual events. In this selection, Schliemann describes the great lengths he took to pursue his leisure interests, and how rewarding it was.

G reat as was my wish to learn Greek, I did not venture upon its study till I had acquired a moderate fortune; for I was afraid that this language would exercise too great a fascination upon me and estrange me from my commercial business. When, however, I could no longer restrain my desire for learning, I at last set vigorously to work at Greek in January 1856; first with Mr. N. Pappadakes, and then with Mr. Th. Vimpos of Athens, always following my old method. It did not take me more than six weeks to master the difficulties of modern Greek, and I then applied myself to the ancient language, of which in three months I learned sufficient to understand some of the ancient authors, and especially Homer, whom I read and re-read with the most lively enthusiasm.

I then occupied myself for two years exclusively with the ancient Greek literature; and during this time I read almost all the old authors cursorily, and the *Iliad* and *Odyssey* several times.

In the year 1858 I travelled to Sweden, Denmark, Germany, Italy and Egypt, where I sailed up the Nile as far as the second cataract in Nubia. I availed myself of this opportunity to learn Arabic, and I afterwards travelled across the desert from Cairo to Jerusalem. I visited Petra, traversed the whole of Syria, and in this manner I had abundant opportunity of acquiring a practical knowledge of Arabic, the deeper study of which I afterwards continued in St. Petersburg. After leaving Syria, I visited Athens in the summer of 1859, and I was on the point of starting for the island of Ithaca when I was seized with an illness which obliged me to return to St. Petersburg.

Heaven had blessed my mercantile undertakings in a wonderful manner, so that at the end of 1863 I found myself in possession of a fortune such as my ambition had never ventured to aspire to. I therefore retired from business, in order to devote myself exclusively to the studies which have the greatest fascination for me.

In the year 1864 I was on the road to visit the native island of Ulysses and the Plain of Troy, when I allowed myself to be persuaded to visit India, China and Japan, and to travel round the world. I spent two years on this journey, and on my return in 1866 I settled in Paris, with the purpose of devoting the rest of my life to study, and especially to archaeology, which has the greatest charm for me.

At last I was able to realize the dream of my whole life, and to visit at my leisure the scene of those events which had such an intense interest for me, and the country of the heroes whose adventures had delighted and comforted my childhood. I started, therefore, last summer, and visited in succession the places which still possess such living poetic memorials of antiquity.

I had not, however, the ambition of publishing a work on the subject; this I only decided upon doing when I found what errors almost all archaeologists had spread about the site once occupied by the Homeric capital of Ithaca, about the stables of Eumaeus, the Island of Asteris, ancient Troy, the sepulchral mounds of Batiea and of Esyetes, the tomb of Hector, and so forth.

Apart from the hope of correcting opinions which I hold to be erroneous, I should consider myself fortunate could I aid in diffusing among the intelligent public a taste for the beautiful and noble studies which have sustained my courage during the hard trials of my life, and which will sweeten the days yet left me to live.

"A Father to His Son, Upon Leaving for College"

JOHN D. SWAIN

After his son left for his freshman year at Yale in 1912, John Swain reflected on the things he wished he had told his son before he left. So he penned this letter of advice and admiration. Not much is known about the author, but from reading this letter you will see that he loved and cared for his son and wanted to help him find his place in the world and manage his work and leisure. Sports and other "extracurriculars" are no small part of this wise father's advice.

MY DEAR SON: I am writing a few things I meant to say to you when we took our last walk together, the day before you left for Yale. I intended to say them then and I will even confess that I shamelessly inveigled you into taking a stroll on the quiet street that I might rehearse a carefully prepared bit of Chesterfield up-to-date; but somehow I could not seem to begin,—and, after all, perhaps I can write what was in my mind more freely and plainly than I could have spoken it.

I think I had never realized before that I was getting old.

Of course I have known that my hair is causing your mother much solicitude, and that I am hopelessly wedded to my pince-nez while reading my—daily paper, and at the opera; but in some incomprehensible way I had forgotten to associate these trifles with the encroachments of time. It was the sudden realization that you were about to become a Freshman in the college from which, as it seems to me, I but yesterday graduated, that "froze the genial current of my soul," and spared you my paternal lecture.

Why, I can shut my eyes and still hear the Ivy Song, as we sang it that beautiful June morning; and yet but a few nights more and you will be locked in the deadly Rush on the same field where I triumphantly received two blackened eyes, and, I trust, gave many more!

Another thing, trifling in itself, opened my eyes to the fact of my advancing years.

My son, my loyal and affectionate boy, some day it may be yours to know the pain, the unreasonable pain that comes over a man to know that between him and his boy, and his boy's friends, an unseen but unassailable barrier has arisen, erected by no human agency; and to feel that while they may experience a vague respect and even curiosity to know what exists on your side of the barrier, you on your part would give all,—wealth, position, influence, honor—to get back to theirs! All the world, clumsily or gracefully, is crawling over this barrier; but not one ever crawls back again!

You have ever seemed happy to be with me; you have worked with me, read and smoked with me, even played golf with me; but the subtle change in your attitude, the kindling of your eye when we met young men of your age, is the keenest pain I have ever known; yet one which, God knows! I would not reproach you with.

It explains what I used to see on my father's face and did not understand.

For the tyranny of youth, my son, is the one tyranny which never has been, never can be overthrown. Nothing can displace it, nothing shake its power.

I usually beat you at golf, and occasionally at tennis; I suppose that if we were to spar together I might still make a respectable showing, and at least "save my face." It avails nothing. I am on my side of the barrier, you on yours.

It seems but a year and a day since I tucked the ball under my arm and sped down the gridiron, sustained by the yells of my partisans; and if our game lacked the machine-like precision of the mass formations you are already somewhat familiar with, it was a good game, and we were good men, and all on the right side of the barrier!

So bear with me if I pause a moment and gaze back across this inevitable gulf into the pleasant land that lies behind me,—a picture evoked by your dawning college career.

I would not have you think me regretful, or melancholy. Life has been good to me—and every age has its gifts for the man who is willing to work for them and use them temperately. And nothing is more ungraceful, more ludicrous, than the spectacle of one who attempts to linger over the pleasures of an age he had outlived, and ignore the advantages of his own time of life.

Yet, as the years bring weakness, the mind persistently drifts back to the earlier periods of life, until the aged actually enter a phase we not inaptly name "second childhood," from which Heaven forefend me!

I can still appreciate a pair of sparkling blue eyes, and I am not oblivious to the turn of a pretty shoulder; although I devoutly trust that my interest is now impersonal, and merely artistic . . .

Some fathers say to their sons upon the first home leaving,—"Beware of wine and women!" I do not.

If your home life has not taught you the virtues of a temperate, clean life, as I hope, then no words of mine can do it, and you must learn, as too many others have, from a bitter intimacy with its antithesis.

As to women, I never avoided them; I sought them out, from the time when, a red-cheeked youngster, I trudged to school beside a red-cheeked lassie—asleep these many years in the little village lot where lie so many with whom I fought and played these many years gone by.

I have no advice to offer you on this great subject; its ethics are not taught by letter. If I have any regrets, they are not for your ear, nor any man's. And if, of some women I have known, I cannot say that I lifted them up, at least of no woman can it be said that I thrust her down!

I ask of you no more than this and the guidance of your own heart; that, in the latter years, when you, too, pass over the barrier, you may not leave behind your shadows on the flower-decked meadows of your youth.

You will probably play cards in college; most men do,—I did. The gambling instinct in man is primordial. Kept under due bounds, if not useful, it is at least comparatively harmless. This is the very best that I or any honest man can say of it. I should be glad if you never cared to gamble; but I do not ask it. Assuming that you will, I do not insult you, and myself equally, by warning you against unfairness; to suppose you capable of cheating at cards is to suppose an impossibility. You could not do so without forfeiting the right ever to enter your home again. But some care-less and insidious practices, not unknown in my day and class, savor to the upright mind of cheating, without always incurring its penalties.

To play with men whom you know cannot afford to lose, and who must either cheat or suffer privation; to play when you yourself must win your bet to square your-self; that is, when you do not reasonably see how you are going to raise the money to pay providing you lose,—this is a gambler's chance to which no gentleman will ever expose his fellow players.

There is nothing heroic about these desperate casts of the die; one risks only the other fellow's money. These practices I ask and expect you to avoid.

I ask nothing of you in the way of a declared position on religion. Your mother may have demanded more of you here,—entreated more; I cannot. I ask but this; that you will give earnest, serious consideration to the fact that we exist on this planet for a shockingly brief fraction of Eternity; that it behooves every man to diligently seek an answer to the great question,—Why am I here? And then, as best he can, to live up to the ideal enjoined by his answer. And if this carries you far, and if it leads you to embrace any of the great creeds of Christendom, this will be to your mother an unspeakable joy, and perhaps not less so to me; but it is a question which cannot be settled by the mere filial desire to please.

Last of all, while you are in college, be of it and support its every healthful activity.

I ask no academic honor your natural inclinations may not lead you to strive for; no physical supremacy your animal spirits may not instinctively reach out and grasp.

You will, I presume, make the fraternity I made, and, I hope, the societies; you will probably then learn that your father was not always a dignified, bearded man in pincenez and frock coat, and that on his side of the barrier he cut not a few capers which, seen in the clear light of his summer, gain little grace. Yet, were he to live his life over again, he would cut the same, or worse.

Finally, if you make any of the teams, never quit. That is all the secret of success. Never quit!

Quitting, I like to believe, has not been a striking characteristic of our family, and it is not tolerated in our college.

If you can't win the scholarship, fight it out to the end of the examination.

If you can't win your race, at least finish—somewhere.

If your boat can't win, at least keep pulling on your oar, even if your eye glazes and the taste of blood comes into your throat with every heave.

If you cannot make your five yards in football, keep bucking the line—never let up,—if you can't see, or hear, keep plugging ahead! Never quit! If you forget all else I have said, remember these two words, through all your life, and come success or failure, I shall proudly think of you as my own dear son.

And so, from the old home-life, farewell, and Godspeed!

Your Affectionate Father.

— ❧ —

Profile: Tim Tebow

There may be no more controversial figure in sports today than Tim Tebow. He is first and foremost a man of deep conviction, faith, and character. He's also a great football player, perhaps one of the most decorated college quarterbacks of all time. But as is frequently the case in the world of sports, where success, money, and fame can often take priority over integrity and conviction, a man with Tebow's outspoken faith is an affront to many players and media personalities. And yet, he remains a man of steely conviction and faith. Tim Tebow's story is one from which we can all learn: it's the story of the battle to remain a man of conviction in the face of great criticism and pressure. His story gives us encouragement that men don't have to succumb to the popular pressures of the world. We need more men like Tim Tebow.

To say that Tim Tebow, now one of the most talked-about professional football players in the world, came from humble beginnings would be a tremendous understatement. He was born to Baptist missionaries in Manila, Philippines. His mother fell very ill when she was pregnant with Tebow, and doctors recommended she terminate the pregnancy. She decided against the doctor's wishes and carried out the pregnancy. Tim Tebow was born August 14, 1987.

To emphasize Christian teaching while continuing their mission work, Tebow's American-born parents homeschooled him and his siblings from elementary school all the way up to college. In high school, and by that time back in the States, Tebow was able to utilize a Florida law that allowed homeschoolers to compete in high school sports.

With his imposing size, speed, and athletic prowess (in many games he was actually bigger and faster than the opposing team's linebackers), Tebow often preferred rushing over passing. While unorthodox for a quarterback, it was devastatingly effective. Opposing defenses couldn't tell whether the freight train of a quarterback was going to throw the ball or run it. He went on to lead Allen D. Nease High School, in Ponte Vedra, to a state title and was twice named Florida's Player of the Year.

Tebow excelled even more at the University of Florida, becoming one of the most decorated college quarterbacks of all time. He led the Florida Gators to two national championships and won the Heisman Trophy his sophomore year, becoming the only player in college football history to throw for more than 20 touchdowns and rush for more than 20 touchdowns in the same season.

Even with all his success, Tebow never lost his roots. He was still an outspoken Christian, the humble son of missionaries. He would often place Bible verses, like John 3:16 and Proverbs 3:5–6, on his eye black during games. He even admitted publicly that he was a virgin and was saving himself for marriage.

For this, Tebow became the target of much ridicule and mockery by other players and some in the media. Jake Plummer, former Broncos quarterback, said in one interview, "I wish he'd just shut up." They'd tell him to take his "holier-than-thou" faith off the field. His critics are bothered by his faith, character, and conviction.

In the world of collegiate and professional sports, where fame is often synonymous with extravagance, showboating, partying, and womanizing, Tebow represented something dramatically different. He represented a man grounded in his faith and unwilling to yield to the pressures of the world around him.

"You and I were created by God to be so much more than normal," Tebow wrote in his book *Through My Eyes*. "Following the crowd is not a winning approach to life. In the end it's a loser's game, because we never become who God created us to be by trying to be like everybody else."

But the more vocal his faith got, the more vocal his critics got. Heading into the NFL Draft in 2010, many commentators, scouts, and coaches thought he lacked the quarterback skills to handle NFL defenses.

He was drafted with the twenty-fifth pick in the 2010 draft by the Denver Broncos. Tebow played sparingly in the 2010 season and was on the bench for the start of the 2011 season. But after the Broncos began the year 1-4, Tebow got his chance.

Down 16 points to the San Diego Chargers in the fourth quarter, Tebow passed and ran for touchdowns and nearly led a remarkable comeback. Denver lost the game, but Tebow won the starting spot the next week.

What happened next was even more remarkable. Tebow led the Broncos to six wins in their next seven games, most of which were come-from-behind fourth-quarter victories. In fact, Tebow's six come-from-behind fourth-quarter or overtime victories in his eleven career starts was the most in NFL history for any quarterback in that time span. His remarkable streak culminated in taking the Broncos to the playoffs and beating the Pittsburgh Steelers in the first round.

Tebow left his mark on the league in just his first full season. His usual touchdown celebration of bending his knee in prayer became an online sensation called "Tebowing."

For the time being, Tebow had all but silenced his critics. He was, by all accounts, the future franchise quarterback of the Denver Broncos.

But the Broncos had different plans. In the off-season, the Broncos acquired future Hall of Fame quarterback Peyton Manning. Tebow had said and done all the right things for the Broncos, but he was no longer needed. So the Broncos traded him to the New York Jets. In a new city with a new team, Tebow again found himself at the center of a quarterback controversy.

During the 2012 season, Tebow didn't start a single game. In fact, he rarely even played. He was again the subject of much gossip and criticism, even from some of his own teammates.

But through it all, Tebow remained steadfast. He supported his teammates, his coaches, and his organization, never once criticizing them. Very few men would have had the patience and selflessness he demonstrated.

At this writing, Tebow's future in the NFL is uncertain. But if we know anything from his past, the type of man and leader Tebow will be, on and off the field, is far from uncertain.

— ❧ —

Tragedy on K2

Mountain climbing is one of the most dangerous sports in the world. Beyond the physical demands and the dangerous terrain, mountaineering requires interminable will and spirit. In one of the most famous mountain climbing stories of all time, an expedition to climb K2 is pushed to the limits of survival. With the entire team facing almost certain death, one man sacrificed his life to save his team. It's stories like these that we should never forget, because they bring out the best qualities in men, in work or play.

K2 is the second-highest mountain in the world after Mount Everest. Standing at 28,251 feet tall, K2 is located on the border between China and Pakistan. K2 has the dubious title of "Savage Mountain" because of the number of people who have died trying to climb it. As of July 2010, only 302 people have completed the ascent of K2, compared with more than 2,700 climbers who have conquered Everest. At least seventy-seven people have died attempting to climb K2. This means that for every four people who have reached the summit, one has died trying—making K2 the most dangerous climb on Earth.

There are several factors that make K2 so perilous. First is the lack of oxygen due to the extremely high alititude. There is only one-third as much oxygen available at the summit of K2 as there is at sea level. The second factor is the unpredictable and violent storms that sweep across K2 and can last several days. Finally, all the climbing routes up K2 are steep, precipitous, and exposed, making the climb itself dangerous and the retreat even more dangerous. The Savage Mountain earned its name for a reason.

The first successful ascent was made on July 31, 1954, by the Italian expedition of Achille Compagnoni and Lino Lacedelli. Only one year earlier, Charles Houston led an American expedition up K2 in what became one of the most iconic and tragic climbs in mountain climbing history.

Houston and his team, the 1953 Third American Karakoram Expedition, began their ascent, establishing Camps I through III with relative ease because of good weather. They established Camp VIII at an elevation of about 25,500 feet and began their attempt to conquer the summit. It was here that things went from good to bad to tragic very quickly.

While stationed at Camp VIII, horrible storms trapped all eight members of the team for seven days. With hurricane force winds, blizzard-like snow, and rapidly depleting supplies of food and drink, their dreams of the summit hung by a thread. That thread snapped when Art Gilkey became terribly sick and needed to be evacuated.

Even though it was nearly impossible to lower their sick comrade down the side of K2, Houston and his men were determined to save their friend from certain death on the side of the mountain. When a break in the storms finally came, the team began to lower Gilkey, only be to turned away by the threat of avalanches. They retreated to Camp VIII and waited until the next day.

Furious winds and driving snow met them again the next day, but Gilkey was so sick by this time that they couldn't turn back. Foot by foot the team began the daunting task of lowering Gilkey down the steep descent of K2. All of a sudden, a mass fall began when climber George Bell slipped and fell on a patch of ice, pulling on his rope-mate Tony Streather. As they fell their rope tangled with those connecting Houston, Bell, Gilkey, and Dee Molenaar, pulling all these men off their feet as well.

Finally, all the weight came bearing down on Pete Schoening. Instantly wrapping the rope around his shoulders and ice axe, Schoening stopped the fall of all six climbers and prevented them from falling to their certain death. Amazingly, the eight-man team was still intact. Schoening's hold was an amazing act of strength and determination.

After the climbers recovered and proceeded to the tent at Camp VII, they anchored Gilkey to the ice as they prepared the tent. When the climbers returned to get him, they found no trace of him. A faint track in the snow suggesting an avalanche was the only evidence left of Gilkey. Gilkey's death, while heartbreaking and tragic, undoubtedly saved the rest of the expedition by allowing them to descend without having to carry him. Most authors and historians believe that Gilkey realized the burden he was to the team and released himself to save the team—the ultimate act of selfless sacrifice.

The remaining seven men survived a harrowing descent. Their expedition remains one of the most gripping and moving stories in mountaineering history. Their survival is a testament to the strength of human will and the incredible lengths men will go to save their fallen friends. Men at play often reveal the character beneath.

Abe Lincoln Wrestles Jack Armstrong

JOHN G. NICOLAY AND JOHN HAY

In 1831, a flat boatman named Abraham Lincoln took up residence in the frontier village of New Salem, Illinois, to try his hand at clerking in a general store. The store's proprietor, a backwoods schemer named Denton Offutt, could not help bragging about his new clerk's strength, and his talk soon landed Abe in a wrestling match with Jack Armstrong, leader of a local gang of rowdies. As many biographers have noted, the contest turned out to be an important event in the life of the future president.

The episode is a good reminder that the character a young man displays in a physical challenge often affects other spheres of his life. In this case, it helped Lincoln establish a reputation he would use to launch a career in law and politics. For better or worse, rough-and-tumble jams are part of growing up for many young men. Sometimes the outcome involves hard knocks. Still, there are lessons to be learned from such rough play.

This account of the famous wrestling match is abridged from the biography of Lincoln by John G. Nicolay and John Hay, who served as his private secretaries in the White House. The charming language is from another era but carries perennial truths.

Denton Offutt admired Abraham beyond measure, and praised him beyond prudence. He said that Abe could beat any man in the county running, jumping, or "wrastling." This proposition was not likely to pass unchallenged. Public opinion at New Salem was formed by a crowd of ruffianly young fellows who were called the Clary's Grove Boys. Once or twice a week they descended upon the village and passed the day in drinking, fighting, and brutal horse-play. If a stranger appeared in the place, he was likely to suffer a rude initiation into the social life of New Salem at the hands of these jovial savages. Sometimes he was nailed up in a hogshead and rolled down hill; sometimes he was insulted into a fight and then mauled black and blue, for despite their pretensions to chivalry they had no scruples about fair play or any such superstitions of civilization.

At first they did not seem inclined to molest young Lincoln. His appearance did not invite insolence; his reputation for strength and activity was a greater protection to him than his inoffensive good-nature. But the loud admiration of Offutt gave them umbrage. It led to dispute, contradictions, and finally to a formal banter [challenge] to a wrestling match. Lincoln was greatly averse to all this "wooling and pulling," as he called it. But Offutt's indiscretion had made it necessary for him to show his mettle.

Jack Armstrong, the leading bully of the gang, was selected to throw him, and expected an easy victory. But he soon found himself in different hands from any he had heretofore engaged with. Seeing he could not manage the tall stranger, his friends swarmed in, and by kicking and tripping nearly succeeded in getting Lincoln down.

At this, as has been said of another hero, "the spirit of Odin entered into him," and putting forth his whole strength, he held the pride of Clary's Grove in his arms like a child, and almost choked the exuberant life out of him. For a moment a general fight seemed inevitable; but Lincoln, standing undismayed with his back to the wall, looked so formidable in his defiance that an honest admiration took the place of momentary fury, and his initiation was over.

As to Armstrong, he was Lincoln's friend and sworn brother as soon as he recovered the use of his larynx, and the bond thus strangely created lasted through life. Lincoln had no further occasion to fight his own battles while Armstrong was there to act as his champion. The two friends, although so widely different, were helpful to each other afterwards in many ways.

This incident, trivial and vulgar as it may seem, was of great importance in Lincoln's life. His behavior in this ignoble scuffle did the work of years for him, in giving him the position he required in the community where his lot was cast. He became from that moment, in a certain sense, a personage, with a name and standing of his own. The verdict of Clary's Grove was unanimous that he was "the cleverest fellow that had ever broke into the settlement." He did not have to be constantly scuffling to guard his self-respect, and at the same time he gained the good-will of the better sort by his evident peaceableness and integrity.

From *War and Peace*

LEO TOLSTOY

This scene from Leo Tolstoy's famous novel *War and Peace* takes place
during Napoleon's invasion of Russia. Napoleon rides into camp, stopping
at a river for a break. Meanwhile, his troops who are gathered at the river
start playing around in the river attempting to show off their strength to
Napoleon. Their ill-planned stunts suddenly turn tragic when the current
of the river sweeps away the soldiers and kills many of them. The lesson,
although a harsh one, is that sports and games are appropriate when
practiced at the right time, for the right reasons, and in the right way.

On the thirteenth of June a rather small, thoroughbred Arab horse was
brought to Napoleon. He mounted it and rode at a gallop to one of the
bridges over the Niemen, deafened continually by incessant and raptur-
ous acclamations which he evidently endured only because it was impossible to
forbid the soldiers to express their love of him by such shouting . . . He rode across
one of the swaying pontoon bridges to the farther side, turned sharply to the left,
and galloped in the direction of Kovno, preceded by enraptured, mounted chasseurs
of the Guard who, breathless with delight, galloped ahead to clear a path for him
through the troops. On reaching the broad river Viliya, he stopped near a regiment
of Polish Uhlans stationed by the river.

"Vivat!" shouted the Poles, ecstatically, breaking their ranks and pressing against
one another to see him.

Napoleon looked up and down the river, dismounted, and sat down on a log that
lay on the bank. At a mute sign from him, a telescope was handed him which he rested
on the back of a happy page who had run up to him, and he gazed at the opposite
bank. Then he became absorbed in a map laid out on the logs. Without lifting his head
he said something, and two of his aides-de-camp galloped off to the Polish Uhlans.

"What? What did he say?" was heard in the ranks of the Polish Uhlans when one
of the aides-de-camp rode up to them.

The order was to find a ford and to cross the river. The colonel of the Polish Uhlans, a handsome old man, flushed and, fumbling in his speech from excitement, asked the aide-de-camp whether he would be permitted to swim the river with his Uhlans instead of seeking a ford. In evident fear of refusal, like a boy asking for permission to get on a horse, he begged to be allowed to swim across the river before the Emperor's eyes. The aide-de-camp replied that probably the Emperor would not be displeased at this excess of zeal.

As soon as the aide-de-camp had said this, the old mustached officer, with happy face and sparkling eyes, raised his saber, shouted "Vivat!" and, commanding the Uhlans to follow him, spurred his horse and galloped into the river. He gave an angry thrust to his horse, which had grown restive under him, and plunged into the water, heading for the deepest part where the current was swift. Hundreds of Uhlans galloped in after him. It was cold and uncanny in the rapid current in the middle of the stream, and the Uhlans caught hold of one another as they fell off their horses. Some of the horses were drowned and some of the men; the others tried to swim on, some in the saddle and some clinging to their horses' manes. They tried to make their way forward to the opposite bank and, though there was a ford one third of a mile away, were proud that they were swimming and drowning in this river under the eyes of the man who sat on the log and was not even looking at what they were doing. When the aide-de-camp, having returned and choosing an opportune moment, ventured to draw the Emperor's attention to the devotion of the Poles to his person, the little man in the gray overcoat got up and, having summoned Berthier, began pacing up and down the bank with him, giving him instructions and occasionally glancing disapprovingly at the drowning Uhlans who distracted his attention.

For him it was no new conviction that his presence in any part of the world, from Africa to the steppes of Muscovy alike, was enough to dumfound people and impel them to insane self-oblivion. He called for his horse and rode to his quarters.

Some forty Uhlans were drowned in the river, though boats were sent to their assistance. The majority struggled back to the bank from which they had started. The colonel and some of his men got across and with difficulty clambered out on the further bank. And as soon as they had got out, in their soaked and streaming clothes, they shouted "Vivat!" and looked ecstatically at the spot where Napoleon had been but where he no longer was and at that moment considered themselves happy.

— ❧ —

"The Traffic Guard"

CHRISTOPHER BEACH

Surfing takes many of life's great leisure experiences—physical exertion, travel, and nature—and combines them into one unique expression of skill and style. Christopher Beach, a colleague and the producer of my radio show, penned this essay after a surf trip to Costa Rica. With this essay, he won the Surfer *magazine writing contest. Traveling from city to city, Beach ran into a homeless American who left a lasting impression on him. It's a story of two men and the different ways they chose to express their hobbies and leisure and the different paths their lives took.*

If you're traveling by bus from northern Costa Rica to Playa Hermosa or any point south of that, your route will take you to the port city of Puntarenas, known by surfers for its fickle river mouth break that spits out one of the longest lefts in the country.

To distract visitors from the city's disfigurements, the bus stops in Puntarenas are strategically located across the street from the beautiful Pacific Ocean. Here I stood next to the main *calle* and under a small half concrete-half scrap metal, lean-to bus stop with destinations and distances painted on cinderblocks in eye-catching colors.

As is the case for many buses in Costa Rica, you pay when you get on the bus, or else there is a sign that points you to a terminal to buy a ticket. Not so for the bus from Putarenas to Hermosa. All the gringos and tourists stand in line waiting for the bus, take one step onto the bus, only to get a rude awakening from the bus driver who yells that you can't get on the bus without a ticket. So you ask him where to buy a ticket and he points you three blocks down the street. By the time you've ran and bought your ticket the bus is long gone.

So I introduce you to Robert, the resident traffic guard. He makes his living by standing at the bus stop and helping tourists get tickets, who in turn tip him 100 or 200 colones. Not a bad life for an alcoholic bum.

This being our first time through Puntarenas, my friends and I stood at the bus stop without a ticket or even knowing where to buy one. Robert approached us and in perfect English told us we needed to go buy a ticket down the block. Naturally, we tried to ignore him; he smelled of last night's trash and looked even worse. But hearing his distinct Midwestern American accent, I turned and listened to him. Turns out he was right and the first Costa Rican gutterpup I took advice from.

After tipping Robert way more than I should have, he insisted on helping us carry our board bags to the bus.

"Ya know what?" he blurted. "People normally tip me like ... 100 colones ... but you, you man, you gave me like a thousand. Do you know what that means? That means I can buy breakfast today. Thank you, man."

Rubbing his newfound fortune over and over in his hands, Robert felt compelled to share more.

Sixteen years ago he was a construction engineer in Chicago. On a whim, he ventured to Costa Rica on vacation. Once he was there, he quickly realized that this nascent Third World country was paradise for a middle-class American. The cocaine was cheap and the women were cheaper. So Robert dropped his 40-hour workweek in Middle America and moved to Costa Rica. In less than a year, he became a full-blown cocaine addict and dealer, one of the first "cocaine cowboys" of Costa Rica.

He paused for a moment, choked back a sentence and skipped ahead. "Today," Robert explained, "I've been four years without drugs." You would think that was a remarkable recovery until you saw him in his current state. His skin is dark, leathery, and wrinkled and he looks twenty years older than he probably is. He wears cut-off jean shorts, ratty open-toed sandals, a dirty gray V-neck T-shirt, and a bright yellow traffic guard bib that he probably found in the trash. It helps distinguish him, the traffic guard, from the other vagrants and bums who roam the local bus stops.

Robert reeks of alcohol and cigarettes and whatever else was in the gutter he woke up in. He hasn't shaved in months, and his beard is a vapid combination of aging white and grey and sun-bleached blonde.

"Ya know, man, I've been four years without drugs. Now I just got my cigarettes and alcohol. Ya know, if I can get enough money to buy some cigarettes and a little *guaro*, I'm happy. That's all I need, some guaro, a couple cigarettes, and maybe a beer. I like a beer from time to time, too." He paused to smile, probably the first time he's done so in a long time.

"And after that, if I can afford some breakfast, I'm happy, man. You know you made my day, man. Thank you."

As the bus pulled away and Robert faded back into the slums, I couldn't tell if I had just committed the wicked sin of "giving money to a drunk" or if I had actually made this poor soul happy.

While we spent our summer days in the shade of Costa Rica's best A-frame beachbreak barrels, Robert hid from the beating sun under the shade of Costa Rica's grungiest bus stops.

We couldn't be further apart in life, but for one coincidental meeting, we shared a glimpse of each other's world. Mine a world he once knew, and his a world I never want to know.

"The Art of Fencing"

LOUIS AND REGIS SENAC

Fencing has been a method of defense for hundreds of years. Over time the practice of sword fighting was transformed into a sport of skill, style, and form. This passage describes the grace and physical prowess the sport demands. Fencing is not as popular today as it once was, but it still remains an esteemed sport and a great exercise in discipline.

The fencer is always enthusiastic concerning his art, his "grande passion." And why is this the case? Why does he not accept his fencing pleasures philosophically and continue in the even tenor of his way? The truth is, that he has found something of great value, of undeniable fascination, and about which he believes all his friends and acquaintances should know.

Sometimes uninitiated folk marvel at the unbounded praise fencing devotees shower on their favorite diversion. They stand aloof with a superior air and occasionally condescend to show a modicum of interest in the foils.

There comes a time, however, when the supercilious one becomes infected by the fever. He dons fencing garb, grasps a foil, and makes some instructor's life one continuous round of labor for weeks at a time. Then one day he realizes that he is actually a convert to the foils and that his enthusiasm may well be said to border on the fanatical. "I came to laugh and I remained to learn," he says to himself, and delves still deeper into the mysteries of the intricate, yet unparalleled science.

It is through many rewards to its disciples that fencing holds the attention of every man and woman, even though he or she taste ever so sparingly of its cup of pleasure. First, the practice of fencing affords an exercise that is absolutely unrivaled as a natural aid to the highest form of physical development and education. (Muscles as well as brains can be educated.) Can you fail to recognize the fencer? His grace and elasticity of bearing; his elegance of manner; his calm reserve, and, withal, the keenest of eyes; his firm hand-clasp, literally vibrating with energy; the admirable poise of his head; his erect carriage, and his buoyant step set him apart from ordinary men, men of sedentary pursuits.

A Day at the Ancient Olympic Games

ANACHARSIS OF SCYTHIA

The Olympic Games are the largest collection of sporting events between countries in the entire world. Held every two years (alternating between the Summer and Winter Games), the Olympics pit country against country to crown the greatest athletes in the world in their respective sports. Many people may not know that the Olympics actually began more than two thousand years ago with the ancient Greeks. According to historical records the first Olympic Games began in 776 BC as a series of athletic competitions between the various city-states of Greece. This passage from Anacharsis of Scythia offers a first-person account of some of the earliest Olympic Games in history.

At the first dawn of day we repaired to the stadium, which was already filled with athletes, exercising themselves in preparatory skirmishes, and surrounded by a multitude of spectators; while others in still greater numbers were stationing themselves confusedly on a hill, in form of an amphitheatre, above the course. Chariots were flying over the plain; on all sides were heard the sound of trumpets and the neighing of horses, mingled with the shouts of the multitude. But when we were able to divert our eyes for a moment from this spectacle, and to contrast the tumultuous agitations of the public joy with the repose and silence of nature, how delightful were the impressions we experienced from the serenity of the sky, the delightful coolness of the air from the Alpheus, which here forms a magnificent canal, and the fertile fields, illumed and embellished by the first rays of the sun!

Learning Languages for Fun

BENJAMIN FRANKLIN

It is easy to distinguish the character of a man by the way he spends his leisure time. Ben Franklin, Mr. Self-Improvement and one of America's Founding Fathers, spent some of his free time learning foreign languages.

I had begun in 1733 to study languages; I soon made myself so much a master of the French as to be able to read the books with ease. I then undertook the Italian. An acquaintance, who was also learning it, used often to tempt me to play chess with him. Finding this took up too much of the time I had to spare for study, I at length refused to play any more, unless on this condition, that the victor in every game should have a right to impose a task, either in parts of the grammar to be got by heart, or in translations, etc., which tasks the vanquished was to perform upon honor, before our next meeting.

As we played pretty equally, we thus beat one another into that language. I afterwards with a little painstaking, acquired as much of the Spanish as to read their books also. I have already mentioned that I had only one year's instruction in a Latin school, and that when very young, after which I neglected that language entirely. But, when I had attained an acquaintance with the French, Italian, and Spanish, I was surprised to find, on looking over a Latin Testament, that I understood so much more of that language than I had imagined, which encouraged me to apply myself again to the study of it, and I met with more success, as those preceding languages had greatly smoothed my way.

From "An Autumn Effect"

Robert Louis Stevenson

The Scotsman Robert Louis Stevenson (1850–1894) was one of the premier English language writers of the nineteenth century, authoring such classics as *Kidnapped, Treasure Island*, and *Dr. Jekyll and Mr. Hyde*. Although Stevenson has not always enjoyed acclaim from modern scholars, Stevenson's fiction remains tremendously popular for its thrilling plots and subject matter, which often focus on a series of adventures. Stevenson himself was an intrepid explorer, writing a number of travelogues about his wanderings in places such as Spain, France, California, and Hawaii. In his travel essay "An Autumn Effect" (1875), Stevenson describes the freedom a solo traveler has to go wherever he pleases, and how pleasurable that freedom is.

I began my little pilgrimage in the most enviable of all humors: that in which a person, with a sufficiency of money and a knapsack, turns his back on a town and walks forward into a country of which he knows only by the vague report of others. Such a one has not surrendered his will and contracted for the next hundred miles, like a man on a railway. He may change his mind at every finger-post, and, where ways meet, follow vague preferences freely and go the low road or the high, choose the shadow or the sunshine, suffer himself to be tempted by the lane that turns immediately into the woods, or the broad road that lies open before him into the distance, and shows him the far-off spires of some city, or a range of mountain-tops, or a rim of sea, perhaps, along a low horizon. In short, he may gratify his every whim and fancy, without a pang of reproving conscience, or the least jostle to his self-respect.

Filling Days and Finding Relaxation

PLINY THE YOUNGER

Gaius Plinius Caecilius Secundus (AD 61–ca. 112), better known as Pliny the Younger, was a magistrate of ancient Rome. Pliny is known today because many of his letters survived and provide invaluable insights into the ancient world of Rome. Written more than two thousand years ago, Pliny's reflections still illustrate how easy it is for man to waste away his leisure time. In this selection Pliny comments on what he considers profitable exercises of free time and how much he looks forward to them once he has finished his work.

It is astonishing how good an account can be given, or seem to be given, of each separate day spent in Rome, yet that this is not the case with regard to a number of days in a row. If you were to ask any one, "What have you been doing to-day?" he would reply, "I have attended at the ceremony of a youth's coming of age. I have helped to celebrate a betrothal or a wedding. One has invited me to the signing of his will, another to attend a trial on his behalf, another to a consultation." These things seem indispensable at the time when they are done, but when you come to reflect that you have been doing them day after day, they strike you as mere frivolities; and much more is this the case when one has retired into the country.

For, then, the recollection steals over you, "How many days have I wasted, and in what dreary pursuits!" This is what happens to me as soon as I am in my house at Laurentum, and am reading or writing, or even merely looking after my bodily health, that stay on which the mind reposes. I hear nothing, I say nothing, which one need be ashamed of hearing or saying. No one about me gossips ill-naturedly of any one else, and I for my part censure no one, except myself, however, when my writings are not up to the mark. I am troubled by no hopes and no fears, disquieted by no rumours: I converse with myself only and with my books. What a true and genuine life, what a sweet and honest repose, one might almost say, more attractive than occupation of any kind!

Are you studying? Or fishing? Or hunting? Or uniting all these pursuits? They can all be united at my place. The lake abounds in fish, the woods which surround the lake in game, and that most profound retreat in incentives to study. However, whether you are combining them all, or engaged in any one of them, I am distressed that these pursuits are not permitted me, which I yearn for as sick people yearn for wine, baths, and spring water. Shall I never be able to break through, if unable to loosen them, these bonds which so closely confine me? Never, I imagine. For fresh business is always growing on to the old, and yet the old is not completed. So numerous are the coils, so numerous the links, so to speak, by which the chain of my occupations is daily extended.

"Angler Grover Cleveland"

A. M. STODDART

Grover Cleveland, the twenty-second and twenty-fourth president of the United States, was a dedicated fisherman. This amusing 1915 retelling of one of his fishing stories from the *Oregon Sportsman* highlights the enjoyment President Cleveland found in the outdoors.

Various stories are told of Grover Cleveland by anglers. While fishing one day, dressed in oilskins and slouch hat, Mr. Cleveland was addressed by an angler dressed in the height of fashion with:

"Hello, boatman, you've certainly got a good catch. What will you take for the fish?"

"I'm not selling them," replied the man in oilskins.

"Well," continued the persistent angler, "when do you want to take me out fishing tomorrow?"

Mr. Cleveland was plainly enjoying the joke.

"I can't make any engagement except by the season," he replied. "Will you give me as much as I made last year?"

"You're a sharp fellow," replied the angler, "but a good fisherman, and I'll accept your terms. What did you make last year?"

"Oh," replied Mr. Cleveland, "about $1,000 a week. I was President of the United States."

Mr. Cleveland was an angler who believed in conservation. He practiced leaving something for those that come after. His limit was twelve fish a day. Curious to relate, when black bass fishing he always carried a measuring stick and returned to the lake all fish less than twelve inches in length.

Profile: Milan High School and the 1954 Indiana State Championship

The underdog is one of the great motifs in sports. It's the David versus Goliath story that inspires all of us. One of the most memorable underdog stories is that of the "Hoosiers," the 1954 Milan High School State Champions. These young men were undersized and underrated, but they defeated the overwhelming odds in one of modern sport's greatest Cinderella stories.

For decades Indiana has been considered the heartland of the hardwood. John Wooden was born here, in the town of Hall, and won the state high school championship in 1927 before winning the NCAA championship with Purdue University in 1932, acquiring the nickname "The Indiana Rubber Man" for his relentless dives to the hardwood in hopes of wrestling away a loose ball. Indianapolis's own Oscar Robertson won two state high school titles in 1955 and 1956, in spite of vicious racism from fans and opponents, and eventually became the only man to ever average double-figure points, rebounds, and assists in an NBA season. The great Larry Bird, "the Hick from French Lick," is one of the all-time greatest players in collegiate and NBA history, first leading Indiana State to the 1979 NCAA championship game, and then captaining the Boston Celtics to three NBA championships in the 1980s. And Bob Knight, though not an Indianan by birth, coached the Indiana University Hoosiers to NCAA titles in 1976, 1981, and 1987.

"Basketball," said James Naismith, the inventor of the game, "was born in Massachusetts, but grew up in Indiana."

Though now considered a predominantly urban game, basketball originally gained popularity in Indiana as a welcome diversion for farming communities, who sought entertainment after the sun went down on cold winter nights. Entire towns would crowd into tiny gyms to cheer on their local boys, and high schools developed fierce rivalries with one another, in spite of their diminutive sizes.

And no team played with more ferocity than the 1954 Milan High School Indians.

Boasting an enrollment of only 161 students, the prospect of the Indians capturing the state title that year looked unlikely. Their coach was a quiet twenty-six-year-old named Marvin Wood. Wood had replaced the previous coach, described by one player as "the most popular coach in Milan's history," two seasons prior, after he had been fired for ordering new uniforms without permission. Wood had promptly installed new offensive and defensive schemes and shut out practice to outsiders, turning many residents against him. Milan's size was also an issue. The tallest of the ten boys on the team, five-foot-eleven-inch Gene White, was hardly an imposing figure.

But, as White would say nearly fifty years later, "I was raised to play whoever comes along."

In Milan, a tiny farming town tucked in the corner of the state, whoever came along was almost always familiar with one another. Assembling pickup games on gravel driveways and dirt lots, the Milan players had been competing with and against one another since childhood and had forged chemistry and basketball intelligence, which helped them overcome more athletically gifted opponents.

Milan had qualified for the state tournament the year before and made a strong showing, advancing all the way to the semifinals. Now in 1954, with the majority of the key contributors to the team returning and postseason experience under their belt, Milan seemed poised to do well. Typically, small towns like Milan could expect some degree of success in the state tournament, but almost always bowed out to powerhouse teams from larger cities like Indianapolis, Gary, and South Bend.

But Milan wasn't ready to settle.

Buoyed by Coach Wood's stifling defensive schemes, the Indians finished the regular season 19–2, ripping off a ten-game winning streak as the championship tournament approached, in which 751 schools from across the state would vie for the title.

After steamrolling through the sectional and regional rounds of the tournament, Milan entered the semifinals in Indianapolis against the Montezuma High School Aztecs, an underdog in their own right, as Montezuma had half the enrollment of Milan's 161. Nonetheless, Milan prevailed in a 44–34 triumph, then scurried back to their hotel to catch a nap before a night game against Crispus Attucks High School, whose star player, Oscar Robertson, went on to lead his team to two consecutive state championships in 1955 and 1956, and would later be voted one of the NBA's fifty greatest players in 1996.

Bobby Plump, Milan's star player, had worn himself out against Montezuma that afternoon and was struggling to get through the game versus Crispus Attucks. At halftime, Plump was wrapped up in a blanket, shivering in a cold sweat from exhaustion. His teammates told him they would hold down their slim 7-point lead, but Plump insisted on going back out and was already shooting warm-up jumpers as Coach Wood emerged out of the locker room for the second half. Plump's iron will was partly forged by a hardscrabble childhood. He was the youngest of six children, whose mother had died when Bobby was five, and was raised by his father and oldest sister. The family never had any running water, and electricity came only when Bobby was twelve. But the Plumps were close-knit, and any material deficiencies were made up for by the close comforts of family and Bobby's love for the game of basketball. No doubt inspired that day by Plump's heroics, Milan topped Crispus Attucks 65–52, advancing to play Terre Haute Gerstmeyer Tech.

In the state semifinal, Milan bested Tech by the score of 60–48, and earned the right to play the powerful Muncie Central for the championship. Muncie's gym alone could fit seven times the entire population of Milan.

It has been estimated that 90 percent of all Indiana families either watched or listened to the championship game that day—a defensive contest that featured a poor shooting performance from Bobby Plump. Sensing that his traditional strategies would not work against the mighty Muncie front line, Coach Wood resorted to dilatory tactics—holding the ball stationary for four minutes of the fourth quarter—in order to keep the game close. With three seconds left on the clock and the score tied 30–30, Plump played the hero once again, draining a jump shot as time expired to give the Indians the title. The Indiana High School Athletic Association awarded Plump the Trester Award for the player exhibiting outstanding mental attitude, sportsmanship, and character.

While plenty of underdog teams have captured titles throughout the history of sports, none have captured the popular imagination quite like the 1954 Milan Indians. Forty thousand people descended on Milan (population: 1,150) the next day as the team returned home from Indianapolis. The 1986 movie *Hoosiers* retold the story, although it did feature many variations of the true story to fit film conventions. For instance, the movie character Jimmy Chitwood, based on Bobby Plump, was eager to take—and make—the final shot. "I was a very shy kid," Bobby Plump told the *Washington Post* in 1995. "I never would have said, 'I'll make it.'" Nonetheless, *Hoosiers* helped to ingrain the Milan Indians in sporting legend forever.

All the players on the 1954 championship team went on to have fruitful careers in public and private life, with many becoming successful teachers and coaches in their own right, like starting forward Ron Truitt and reserve Glen Butte. The determination, team play, and underdog mentality that propelled them to victory in 1954 proved to be invaluable throughout their lives. In 2004, Bobby Plump told *USA Today*, "I think what 1954 did, not just for myself but for all the players and all the students and the town, is raise expectations a little bit. I think they assumed they could do things they assumed they couldn't do before."

Leo Tolstoy the Chess Player

Edward Winter

Leo Tolstoy (1828-1910) is regarded as one of the greatest writers of all time, penning classics such as *War and Peace* and *Anna Karenina*. In his leisure time, he loved to play chess. On a series of visits to Russia, a British chess writer had the opportunity to play Tolstoy several times. It is especially enjoyable to see how Tolstoy's enthusiasm for the game seems to border on the absurd, but it is not so intense that it compromises meaningful family interaction.

Count Tolstoy, who is now staying at St. Petersburg, is said to be devoting himself enthusiastically to the study of chess. It is reported that he and his wife and children are playing as if their lives depended on the results. The tables in the various rooms are marked out as chess boards, and the dogs and other pets are named after the chess pieces. This sort of thing of course cannot last.

It seems to me that Tolstoy shows an excellent sense of proportion in his way of playing chess. He does it well enough to make and to enjoy combinations, but he never sacrifices social family life for the sake of the game. Anyone may interrupt him while he is playing, and he talks and jests so that no-one who only knew the game at Yásnaya [Tolstoy's home] would consider chess unsocial. Previously I generally used to beat him; but on this occasion he won two games from me very rapidly.

Profile: Cal Ripken Jr., the Iron Man of Baseball

For sixteen straight seasons, Cal Ripken Jr. never took a day off work. In the process, he became baseball's "Iron Man" and one of the great hitters of all time. His manly example on the field carries beyond sports and into all areas of life. One might think about the success men could have if they approached their labor or leisure with Ripken's incredible work ethic.

On May 30, 1982, the Toronto Blue Jays defeated the Baltimore Orioles 6–0 at Memorial Stadium. Rookie Jim Gott pitched six innings to pick up the win, while Orioles legend Jim Palmer threw eight tough innings but came away with the loss. It was just another day in major league baseball, except for one man—the Orioles' scrawny, twenty-one-year-old third basemen who went 0-for-2 that day: Cal Ripken Jr.

Little did he know, but May 30, 1982, would mark the start of baseball's longest consecutive game streak. Ripken started that game, the next one, every game of the

1982 season, the 1983 season, the 1984 season, and so on. When his streak finally came to an end on September 20, 1998, Ripken had played a record 2,632 consecutive games—an unbelievable sixteen seasons in a row.

On the way, Ripken shattered Lou Gehrig's record of 2,130 consecutives games in 1995, making him the new "Iron Man" of baseball. He won the American League Most Valuable Player Award in 1983 and 1991, and he currently holds the Baltimore franchise records in games played, at bats, runs, hits, doubles, home runs, total bases, runs batted in and extra-base hits.

A Major League baseball season is a grueling 162-game marathon. Traveling from city to city all across America, fighting injury and sickness, professional baseball players rarely play every game of an entire season. How many of us can even say we attend work or school that many days in a row?

Ripken famously said, "As long as I can compete, I won't quit." He had a tenacity and perseverance of will that is rarely seen in life, let alone in the world of sports. Ripken once remarked, "Stubbornness is usually considered a negative, but I think that trait has been a positive for me."

The game of baseball takes incredible skill and talent—throwing 90-mph fastballs or hitting a vicious head-to-toes curveball. Ripken set hitting and fielding records of his own and is recognized as one of the greatest shortstops of all time, yet he did something great that we can all relate to—he committed himself to his work every day of his career.

He said, "Whether your name is [Lou] Gehrig or [Cal] Ripken, [Joe] DiMaggio or [Jackie] Robinson, or that of some youngster who picks up his bat or puts on his glove, you are challenged by the game of baseball to do your very best day in and day out. That's all I've ever tried to do."

Ripken's work ethic and attitude were contagious. He was one of the most respected baseball players in the league and deservedly so. The great Yankees' manager Joe Torre said, "Cal is a bridge, maybe the last bridge, back to the way the game was played. Hitting home runs and all that other good stuff is not enough. It's how you handle yourself in all the good times and bad times that matters. That's what Cal showed us. Being a star is not enough. He showed us how to be more."

— ❧ —

"In Defense of Sports"

WILLIAM J. BENNETT

I penned this essay in February 1976 at a time when a number of writers and cultural commentators were questioning the integrity of competitive sports. Below is my defense of my belief that athletics has a valuable impact in a man's life that reverberates through society as a whole. The examples are dated—recall the cultural revolution of the late sixties and early seventies—but some of the issues discussed here are still pertinent.

Competitive athletics, currently under scrutiny, is being subjected to a method of investigation that assumes the most significant aspects of anything are those concealed from the eye. Jack Scott, friend of Bill Walton and allegedly connected with Patty Hearst and the SLA, is the would-be chief muckraker and reformer of this loved part of American life. In the *New York Times* recently, Scott "revealed" that American sports is really just an instrument of monopoly capitalism whose primary purpose is to force upon men an obsession with masculinity. Scott is not alone in his efforts to tell the whole truth about our games.

A flurry of books—Scott's own *The Athletic Revolution*, Paul Hoch's *Rip Off the Big Game*, Joseph Durso's *The Sports Factory*, George Leonard's *The Ultimate Athlete*—have hit this and related themes. These books, written mostly by nonathletes, have come in the wake of books by the players themselves—*Out of Their League* by Dave Meggyesy, *They Call It a Game* by Bernie Parrish, *High for the Game* by Chip Oliver, and the early and popular *Ball Four* by Jim Bouton. Mixed in have been some works of fiction that simultaneously apotheosize and make fun of sports and athletes—the sybaritic *Semi-Tough* by Dan Jenkins and the interesting but maudlin *North Dallas Forty* by former Dallas receiver Pete Gent.

The lessons these books teach are that sports and sportsmen are exploited by a power elite; that college football players are members of a "frenzied slave market" and victims of torture and drills that resemble concentration-camp musters; that drugs and amphetamines are part of the professional athlete's steady diet; that organized athletics systematically emphasizes "cool" over character; and that athletes offer a particularly offensive and dangerous misrepresentation of the sporting life to children. Sports in America are alleged to be sexist, racist, and male-chauvinistic. America's gods of the playing field are made of clay, or lesser stuff, their strengths chemically derived, and their power and charms media-created; these drugged beasts are used and abused once a week for the pleasure and gain of corporate-boardroom masters; our adulation of these heroes leads to a national celebration of violence, causing fans to become savage in the stands, in parking lots, and at home in front of the TV.

Russell Baker wrote a few years ago that sports in America is the opiate of the people. The charge is repeated by Paul Hoch, who also denounced "industrial workers . . . so radically involved with the fates of their sports heroes that they are perfectly oblivious to the exploitative conditions in their own factories." The values of the young are distorted by our overemphasis on winning, according to these authors. Mystical insights and transcendental visions lose out in a "system" of sports instruction that puts the emphasis on "wars" of competition. The war connection is one repeatedly emphasized: interest in sports and athletics has the same roots as interest in military battle: "[We] play our games, or watch them contested, with the same ferocious tenacity with which we fight a war in Vietnam and with as little reason or sense" (Leonard Schechter, former sports editor of *Look*, quoted in *Rip Off the Big Game*). The politics of sports are "reactionary," said Jack Scott, pointing to "the conservative militaristic nature of intercollegiate athletics." Football comes close to "political fascism . . . in its cultivation of mass hysteria," according to John McMurtry, a former Canadian-league player, and "enthusiasm for sports events brings to mind the decadence of the Roman Empire," according to a "scholar" of soccer (Alex Natan, *Sport and Society*).

Is there anything good to be said for sports? These critics argue that athletics does have a purer side, a redemptive side, that needs to be rediscovered and reaffirmed. Yet the recovery of this side of the game depends upon overcoming our fixation on "winning" and on competition. Thus George Leonard in *The Ultimate Athlete* wrote of striving for a new unity in a "Game of Games that joins the limited human body with the limitless possibilities of consciousness and being"; for this "we need balance and harmony, sensitivity and the art of reconciliation—not ego, the test of manhood, the clash of force against force, the battle of God against the Devil." (Specifically, Leonard recommends such noncompetitive games as Infinity Volleyball, Mating, and Environmental Tag.) Will Hetzel, University of Maryland basketball star, was quoted by both Hoch and Scott: "Athletics can be such a beautiful thing. It's a shame to have to keep score. In fact it's a shame to have to keep score on anything in life." Meggyesy speaks of "the death culture versus the life culture" where "the life culture is trying to say something else. It's saying instead of competition let's think about cooperation." Then there is Chip Oliver's ideal:

> I have a vision of a team without coaches, without silly restrictions or rules. It would be a communal team where the players would live together, eat only the finest natural foods and practice yoga and transcendental meditation. The entire element of control from coaches would be gone. Each man would control himself so as to be his best. Each man would strive toward the goal of being good, but there would be no punishment for failure except the natural punishment of not being as good as you could be. Success would exclude failure and punishment, and winning and losing would be seen in only a relative sense. The outcome, the decision, of the game would be unimportant. The game itself, in fact, would all but disappear. The members of the team would do the Dance of Football . . . I firmly believe in a team living together like that, as brothers sharing brown rice and doing everything in the spirit of meditation, including football practice . . .

———

It should be enough simply to quote as I have been doing from the critics' abundant stores of transcendent silliness, dime-store Marxism, and countercultural blather to expose the deficiencies of their critique, but they appear to be striking a note that many are all too ready to hear. To those who are drawn to the simple-minded culture of opposition, games as games are easy targets, and the effect of a hyperbolic statement like, "we play games while children are dying," is obviously extremely arresting (even though few would consider it an effective argument against personal cleanliness to say that "while bombs are being dropped we are brushing our teeth and shampooing our hair," not to mention blowing dope or eating brown rice).

But it is one thing to attack human greed or to grieve over the fact that man is often a wolf to other men; it is another thing to contend, as these critics do, that any activity in which unattractive human qualities may appear is therefore the producer of those qualities. Grant the presence of stupidity, narrowness, exploitation, cruelty, and weakness in sports—why should it be immune to the normal afflictions of the human condition? And grant, too, that many things go on at and in games that should not be seen by children and do not deserve to be imitated by anyone. None of this, however, is consistent with the nature of sports. The eruption into violence on the field or in the stands is in fact a degradation, not a perfection, of the game. It is the opposite of the game. If sports, in George Orwell's phrase, is "war minus the shooting," as these critics seem to be saying, it comes out remarkably well in the comparison. Mike Barnicle of the *Boston Globe* has written accurately of the "pure insanity and hatred inside the Boston Garden" when the game of ice hockey "is overshadowed by the primal example of blood on ice." In Boston, too, in Fenway Park, a fan had his throat slashed in the stands last season. That this is senseless is of course obvious, but how is it that the game, and not the man who wields the knife, is held responsible? Who endorses blood-letting and the glorification of violence? Who justifies excess? (Or who, for that matter, justifies the gratuitous slaughter of civilians in war?) To ask such questions is to see the self-serving hollowness of this sort of reductive thinking. Sheer uncontrolled violence in sports, often called unnecessary roughness, unsportsmanlike conduct, is not a part of the game. On the contrary, it stops the game, nullifies the play.

No matter what else it is, sports has always been an arena in which children can grow in light of unambiguous, tangible universal standards and measures. With proper supervision and coaching, the only limits are those of an individual's abilities and the abilities of the best players of the game. Sports is still an activity in which excellence can be seen and reached for and approximated each day; sports has been relatively unaffected by the general erosion of standards in the culture at large.

Critics charge that competitive sports are not conducive to the development of character. Is this true? My own high school coach, a Marine, taught "toughness without callousness," as William James put the ideal. He taught us the difference between real strength and the mere show of strength, a lesson ignored by Scott, Leonard, Hoch, and Durso. He talked to his big linemen about not throwing their weight around in the street or in cars, about how strength was to be shown on the field against someone your own size in a fair match in pads. For coaches like that, the main issue is one of consistency of performance, which is an issue of character. The coaches who dot the pages of Scott's *The Athletic Revolution* only encourage boys to beat up hippies.

Everyone knows where the truth lies in these matters, really. It is not for nothing that the attempts to de-athleticize athletics and to deflate the country's interest in sports have met with uniform failure. Countercultural sports programs have dried up: Scott's own efforts as director of athletics at Oberlin College ended in his being forced to resign, and if trustworthy reports are to be believed, his "reforms" at Oberlin not only did not replace bad values with good ones, but themselves provided instruction in decanal authoritarianism. Dave Meggyesy "explains" such failures by saying that "the revolution" is in a period of gestation, but the fact is that the revolution has not done and cannot do what its progenitors argued it must do—replace the values of winning and competition with other and better noncompetitive values. As a nation, Americans have expressed more, not less, interest in competitive athletics since the "revolution" began, and, if anything, seem to be resisting the tendencies toward leveling in sports. More people are playing sports, going to sporting events, and watching games on TV; baseball set attendance records last year. There is more interest on the part of women in competitive sports; "new" sports—tennis and soccer—are gaining prominence, Pelé joins Namath in broad TV coverage. Even box lacrosse might make it; Hollywood's "Rollerball," with no rules, will not.

The team I now play on, a team of former athletes, is a slow-pitch softball team called the Boston Flamingos. We have pickup games with other organized nonleague teams, the Road House (because they drink there), the Boston Company (because they work there), or somebody's law-school or business-school section. Our team members threw in five dollars each and had shirts made, a dumb-looking bird standing on one leg with a bat in his teeth against a green background. The Flamingo team is made up of friends. We're not great—no semi-pro or ex-minor leaguers—but we're not bad. We catch about 80 percent of what's hit to us and hit the ball very well. We win most of the games we play and are proud when we win.

One of our occasional "competitors" is a team with no name that we have dubbed the Cambridge Persons. The reason we named them the Persons is not only that they are the kind of people who always say "person" instead of whatever is called for, but because the name suggests accurately enough their own concern to display a trendy, hip quality. The Persons cannot put away their desire for ideological purity at game time, and they make "politics" an obvious feature of their game, seeing so-called political issues in everything they do. Scott, Oliver, Hoch, even Charles Reich would be pleased with their attitude.

The team is coed; they have no "discrimination" and no "roles," and as a result, positions and batting orders are not established. Occasionally they let one of their dogs (with a name like Che or Mao) "play" a position, and as the Flamingos wait, the game is delayed while Che runs out of left field and the Persons laugh and try to look loose and noncompetitive. Some of their players are not bad—ability and good reflexes are hard to hide—but what's missing is a sense of organization born of the desire to compete and to take one's ability seriously. There simply is no team here, no coherence. Each Person does his own thing; they don't throw relays or watch the other players to adjust their movements accordingly.

The Persons are halfhearted about winning and they make little jokes and laugh and skip when a ball is hit over their head. Compared to them, the Flamingos are a winning machine; 28–3, 21–0, are common scores in our games with them. In the end the Persons must be judged, in their own terms, to be insensitive, both to the game and to one another as "players"—the cost, no doubt, of each one's being sensitive to himself exclusively as a Person. What's more interesting, I believe, is the fact that we have more fun than the Persons. We invest more in the game and the game is more of a release for us.

Playing sports and watching sports seriously as a fan possess a quality shared by only a very few activities; they are at once a doing and a relief from doing. Sports in this sense do not constitute either an exaggeration or a distortion of our lives but a willing departure from our usual sorts of responsibility with the aim of an eventual return. Charles Reich's ideal in *The Greening of America*—a laughing generation playing football in bell-bottom trousers—is one of sheer aimlessness, of distraction pure and simple, doing nothing. Serious playing and watching, on the other hand, are part of what one may do with one's time while in the business of trying to make sense of things. They are rarely, if ever, doing nothing, for sports is a way to scorn indifference, and occasionally, indeed, one can even discern in competition those elements of grace, skill, beauty, and courage that mirror the greatest affirmations of human spirit and passion.

Buster Douglas Defeats Mike Tyson, Tokyo, 1990

The experts said Mike Tyson was unbeatable; he was anointed the greatest boxer in the world, and no one could stop him. Buster Douglas had different plans. He defeated Tyson in what is considered the greatest boxing feat in history. Douglas skyrocketed to fame overnight. But his story didn't end there. The fame eventually destroyed Douglas from within, until he was fighting another great fight—this time with his life at stake.

To boxing experts, James "Buster" Douglas could have been—in the words of Marlon Brando—"a contender." His father, William, had been a heavyweight boxer, who handed down to his son the physical pedigree and pugilistic tutelage necessary to make waves in the unforgiving world of the ring. Douglas started his career off well, going 18–1–1 in twenty professional fights since 1981. But a string of losses to unspectacular opponents set him back, and in 1990 he was written off as a legitimate title contender at only twenty-nine. He had struggled with his weight, and HBO boxing commentator Jim Lampley described him as "a plodding fighter who has difficulty looking spectacular." But one night in Tokyo, Japan, Douglas stunned the boxing world.

His opponent that evening was "Iron" Mike Tyson, a brash and terrifying fighter, undefeated as a professional and known for his impossibly powerful punches and lightning quickness in the ring. Tyson had become the world's youngest heavyweight champion in 1986, and it seemed unlikely that Douglas would upset him—so unlikely, in fact, that the odds for the fight were set at 42–1.

Douglas was fighting with nothing to lose. He had the flu. The mother of his son was in the hospital. His own mother had passed away twenty-three days before the fight, and Douglas wanted to honor her memory. Douglas had trained hard for the fight, while Tyson, by his own admission, enjoyed the nightlife Tokyo had to offer.

Douglas marched into the ring, fearless, unintimidated by Tyson's fearsome gaze. As the opening bell rang, Douglas deftly landed a number of jabs on Tyson, coming at him from hard angles, fully aware that one blow from Tyson could send him to the canvas. Douglas continued to outbox Tyson in the later rounds, landing several combinations of hooks and uppercuts. When Tyson tried to counterattack, Douglas tied him up. In the eighth round, Tyson managed to land a blow to Douglas that knocked him down, and he barely escaped the count to get back up. In the ninth, Tyson went for the kill, anticipating that Douglas was still dazed from the knockdown. But Douglas held fast, heaping more punishment on Tyson than he had ever experienced.

In the tenth, Tyson succumbed to the accumulated punishment, as Douglas sent him backward to the mat, where Tyson grasped around in vain for his mouthpiece, eventually feebly sticking it in his mouth backward.

Ding Ding Ding!

Douglas's corner rushed into the ring to congratulate him. HBO boxing commentator Larry Merchant rushed over for an interview, asking what inspired Douglas to pull off the greatest upset in boxing history. Then it all came to a head for the new champ.

"My mother, my mother! God bless her heart!" Douglas sobbed.

But as Virgil wrote in his *Aeneid*—"*fama volat*"—fame flies. Douglas had a hard time facing up to the pressure of being the champ—the media requests, the hangers-on, the money, the critics, the girls, the drugs, the alcohol, the food. He gained weight and lost the title in his next fight, never to recapture it again. Douglas retired immediately afterward and for the next several years lived a sedentary lifestyle, living off his riches and contracting diabetes, pushing four hundred pounds. He was a nobody again. When he awoke from a diabetic coma in 1994, he had one thought:

"I got to get out of this pity party," he told ESPN.

Douglas decided to fight professionally yet again. He lost nearly two hundred pounds in the two years after he was hospitalized; and during his comeback attempt, he won six consecutive fights. Although he didn't get a shot at the title, he retired in 1999, contented. "I had the opportunity to change. Some people don't get that," said the forty-nine-year-old Douglas, who is married and has settled down in Columbus, Ohio. "I'm excited for the future. I want to watch my grandchildren grow up. I have a new lease on life."

Ever the fighter, Douglas continued to blaze new paths in life after retiring from the ring. He has started his own construction company and also authored his own cookbook for diabetics, *Buster's Backyard Bar-B-Q.* Douglas now has peace about his boxing journey, understanding how special his feat was, even if the success didn't last as long as he would have liked. When *Sports Illustrated* asked him in 2010 how he wanted to be remembered, Douglas answered, "Just as a man who had a dream, went after it, and achieved it."

— ❧ —

"The National Game"

Charles A. Peverelly

In its early years, professional baseball was much different than the game it is today. Players didn't make millions of dollars, games were all played during the daytime, and baseball was much more of a community sport. This excerpt traces the origins of baseball and how it became "America's Pastime." It is an unintentionally stilted, but interesting, look into the days of baseball's founding, written by Peverelly in 1866.

The game of Base Ball has now become beyond question the leading feature of the out-door sports of the United States, and to account for its present truly proud position, there are many and sufficient reasons. It is a game which is peculiarly suited to the American temperament and disposition; the nine innings are played in the brief space of two and one half hours, or less. From the moment the first striker takes his position, and poises his bat, it has an excitement and vim about it, until the last hand is put out in the ninth innings. There is no delay or suspense about it, from beginning to end; and even if one feels disposed to leave the ground, temporarily, he will generally waive his desire, especially if it is a close contest, from fear of missing some good point or clever effort of the trial.

An American assemblage cannot be kept in one locality for the period of two or three hours, without being offered something above the ordinary fun of excitement and attraction. They are too mercurial and impulsive a race not to get drowsy and dissatisfied with anything which permits their natural ardor to droop even for a brief space of time. Hence their congeniality with, and partiality for Base Ball, which game caters to their inclination and desires to a nicety; in short, the pastime suits the people, and the people suit the pastime.

It is also, comparatively, an economical recreation; the uniform is not costly, the playing implements, colors, and furnishing of a neat club-room, need not occasion an extravagant outlay when divided, pro rata, by the members of a full club . . . Base Ball does not demand from its votaries too much time or rather, too great a proportion of the day. In the long sunshiny days of summer, games are frequently commenced at for [sic] and even five o'clock in the afternoon, and completed some time before sunset. Consequently the great mass, who are in a subordinate capacity, can participate in this health-giving and noble pastime.

The game stands today in a proud and fairly-won position—scarcely requiring eulogy from any source. Dating from the years when the old Knickerbocker Club, closely followed by the Gotham, Eagle, and Empire, gave their colors to the breeze as rallying points for the lovers of the game to master at, it has grown with giant strides until its organization are the pride of numberless villages, towns, and cities, all over the land. Wherever established, it has quickly had the sentiment and good feeling of the community with it, and with scarcely an effort, achieved solid popularity. Having no debasing attributes, and being very worthy of the presence of the good and the refined, it has everywhere been countenanced and encouraged by our best citizens; and of the thousands who gather at important matches, we have always noted with sincere gratification that the lades constituted an honored proportion.

The game originated in Great Britain, and is familiarly known there as the game of Rounders . . . the merest outline of what is now termed by the American press and public The National Game.

Practice Makes Perfect

The Beatles are one of the most celebrated and successful bands in the history of rock and roll. What many people don't know about them is how they achieved their greatness. It wasn't just their ear-catching tunes and memorable rhythms. The Beatles had an unprecedented work ethic. They spent their early years playing thousands of shows in front of scant audiences. The years of practice formed them into an impeccable rock quartet poised to explode upon the world of music. Hard work can transform men from average to great, no matter what the pursuit.

Before "Beatlemania" took the world by storm, the Beatles were an unknown high school rock band from Liverpool, England. Before 1960 they had yet to record an official track and they hadn't donned their famous haircuts.

In search of more playing time and popularity, the Beatles' booking agent, Allan Williams, sent the group to Hamburg, Germany, in 1960. The local clubs of Hamburg were seedy areas frequented by gangsters and prostitutes. The entire music scene was abysmal and not anything you would naturally associate with the future kings of rock and roll.

The original members of the group—Lennon, McCartney, Harrison, Stuart Sutcliffe (bass), and Pete Best (drums)—quickly discovered that the road to success was anything but easy. (Sutcliffe left the group in 1961 and Best was replaced by Ringo Starr shortly after in 1962.) They were underpaid. They slept in unheated storerooms behind the screens of a cinema. Their equipment was shoddy and the acoustics of the clubs were wretched.

What did the Beatles gain from their Hamburg experience? One priceless thing: practice. Even though they were playing in low-life bars and clubs, by 1962 the Beatles were playing eight hours a day, seven days a week. When the "Beatles revolution" came to America, it is estimated that they had already played more than twelve hundred concerts together. Most bands don't play that much in a lifetime!

George Harrison said, "Hamburg was really like our apprenticeship, learning how to play in front of people." In his book *Outliers*, Malcom Gladwell wrote that, with talent, mastery of a skill or art often comes after ten thousand hours of practice. He estimated that the Beatles surpassed that number in their time in Hamburg, making them one of the greatest bands of all time, not primarily because of luck or talent but because of hard work.

Gladwell cited John Lennon's explanation: "We got better and more confident. We couldn't help it with all the experience we gained from playing ALL night long—it was handy being from Liverpool because we had to try even harder than the locals, put our heart and soul into our performances to get ourselves over (to Hamburg). In Liverpool we only ever did one hour sessions and we only did our best numbers—the same ones, over and over. In Hamburg we had to play for eight hours so, we really had to find a new way of playing."

When the Beatles arrived in America in 1964, they were a seamless, talented rock group. They went from playing in abysmal, alley dive bars to premiering before almost 74 million viewers, over 40 percent of the U.S. population, on the *Ed Sullivan Show*. The Beatles hadn't achieved stardom overnight. It took years of sweat and hard work for them to create a sound that was distinctly their own, and one that revolutionized rock and roll forever.

Profile: Aaron Rodgers

The NFL Super Bowl is arguably the biggest stage in all of sports. Millions of people all over the world watch the two top-rated football teams battle it out for the championship title. Many men have succumbed to the pressure and the spotlight, but not the Green Bay Packers' Aaron Rodgers. He proved his greatness as an NFL quarterback and as a man in Super Bowl XLV.

For the Green Bay Packers' quarterback Aaron Rodgers, the road to becoming Super Bowl champion and MVP was paved with speed bumps, stoplights, and sharp curves. On the field, football fans know Rodgers for his cannon of a throwing arm, his highlight-reel touchdowns, and his poise under pressure, but it's his off-the-field attitude and work ethic that make Rodgers the man he is.

Rodgers grew up playing football at Pleasant Valley High School in Chico, California, where he made a name for himself by setting single-season records as the starting quarterback. But as a senior, Rodgers stood only five foot ten and weighed 165 pounds—far too small for Division I college quarterbacks. In fact, Rodgers got only one Division I offer and it was as a walk on, so he decided to attend Butte Community College.

In his freshman year, Rodgers threw an incredible twenty-eight touchdowns while leading Butte to a 10–1 record and a NorCal Conference championship. With this newfound attention, he transferred to the University of California, Berkeley, where he led Cal to a bowl game victory and a top-five ranking nationwide. Rodgers decided to forgo his senior year at Cal and entered the NFL draft.

Rodgers was rated one of the best quarterbacks in the nation and widely regarded as a potential number one pick overall in the NFL draft. Things didn't go as planned for Rodgers, however, and he slipped all the way to the Packers with the twenty-fourth pick—a huge disappointment for such a highly touted prospect.

Starting at quarterback for the Packers was the great Brett Favre, so Rodgers spent the 2005–2007 seasons on the Packers' bench, only seeing playing time if Favre got hurt. Nevertheless, Rodgers never complained, worked hard, and waited patiently for his chance. In 2008, Favre announced his retirement and Rodgers stepped in as the starting quarterback.

Once again things didn't go as planned for Rodgers. Favre decided to return from retirement in the 2008 season and expected his starting job back. In what became a tense and ugly war of words between Favre and the Packers' organization, Favre was eventually traded to the New York Jets and the reins were officially handed to Rodgers. Despite Favre's antics and the pressure of replacing a Hall of Fame quarterback, Rodgers held his tongue, remained supportive of the organization, and never once lashed out.

After finishing 13–3 in 2007, the spotlight was on Rodgers in 2008. He played well, but the Packers finished a measly 6–10 and did not qualify for the playoffs. Skeptics wondered if the Packers had made a huge mistake by keeping Rodgers and letting Favre go. In 2009, Rodgers came back and answered his critics by leading the Packers to an 11–5 season and a playoff berth. In his first playoff game, Rodgers threw an amazing four touchdowns and passed over 400 yards, but fumbled in overtime to lose the game. His critics were back louder than ever.

In 2010, Rodgers rebounded again and came back better than ever, leading the Packers to the Super Bowl. It was the biggest game of his life, the moment that Rodgers had worked so hard for, and once again things started to go wrong. It must have felt all too familiar to Rodgers. This time his own teammates turned on him and started dropping passes—five perfect passes that could have sealed the game.

With the Super Bowl on the line and the Pittsburgh Steelers trying to make one of the greatest comebacks ever, Rodgers zipped a spiral to his wide receiver Jordy Nelson. Had Nelson caught the ball, the game would have been over, but he dropped another wide-open pass. Did Rodgers lose his cool? Did he scream and yell at his receivers? No, he ignored the drops, the pressure, and the critics, and he got back in the huddle and kept working. Remarkably, Rodgers threw the very next pass right back at Nelson, and this time Nelson caught the ball for a huge first down.

Two plays later the Packers scored another touchdown and the game was out of reach for the Steelers. After the game ESPN's Rick Reilly, recalling Rodgers's throwing again to Nelson after he had dropped a crucial pass, captured Rodgers' persona perfectly. He said, "To err is human, to forgive divine. But to forgive in the Super Bowl—is even better."

"Little Bob's First Bass"

Will H. Dilg

In this endearing short story, a father takes his son, Bob, fishing for the first time. Little Bob learns the hard way about fish preservation and "catch and release." Men should enjoy nature, and do so responsibly.

The profession of being Daddy to a small boy is a more or less serious calling, for, to use a contemporary idiom, we have to watch our step pretty carefully. As the tree is bent, so is the twig inclined; and our kids are inclined to follow in our footsteps pretty closely, sometimes.

Last year I became enthused over bass fishing in the Wabash, Tippecanoe, and tributary waters near Lafayette, and of course Bob, at four, absorbed the spirit purely by emulation. His favorite bed-time story was one concerning "Billy Bass," which had a close second a little later in the year in the tale of "Daddy Duck, Mummer Duck and Tommy Duck!" His one absorbing ambition was to get a little bigger and a little bigger, until he would be big enough to really catch a bass for himself. His mother knew not whether to second this ambition very strongly, and mustered as Exhibit A all the village ne'er-do-wells as a dire illustration of the fate that overtakes those who spend any portion at all of their time in hunting and fishing. The defense had to name all the illustrious Teddies and Grovers to prove that in rare instances the sportsman is not preordained to ignominy, and womanlike, she was still unconvinced. But Bob's bent was not thereby reduced to the extent of a single little kink. He still dreamed of catching a bass . . .

The next day being Sunday, to make good matters bad, I gathered up the family, Mother and all, and we betook ourselves into our canoe and up the river to a quiet little cove, seeking sunfish. Mother sat in the bow of the canoe, reading a magazine, while Bob and I performed the ceremony of wetting the line. Bob's tackle consisted of a stout linen carpet thread, small hook, and a float made of a large cork suspended from his dad's lancewood pole.

All was quiet along the Wabash for the space of half an hour, the Biblical limit for a woman to keep quiet, when we suddenly discovered that Bob was busy, very busy in fact. For before we could get to him he had raised a bass, a real bass, out of the water and had him dangling in the air. Now all of you hardened sinners must not believe that the fish has to get away to make a tragedy of the affair—not in the least. In another moment Bob had swung the pole in my direction and the fish was safely in the boat.

But some unregenerate legislators in Indiana had made and provided a statute to the purpose and effect that a fish of this particular breed must attain a length of ten inches in order to be considered legitimate treasure trove, and this "little whale," to use Bob's expression for it, could only muster a paltry seven. Tragedy? You who have seen your five to seven pounder vanish in the swirling water, taking with him your best fly, have no common measure of despair and grief with the youngster who, by reason of a law, recognizing no difference in attendant circumstances, must see his first bass, caught with his own hands, disappear over the side of the canoe.

—— ❧ ——

"Hunting the Grisly"

THEODORE ROOSEVELT

By now you have noticed that Theodore Roosevelt appears frequently in
this book. That is because Roosevelt's manliness is impossible to doubt.
In addition to being president of the United States, Roosevelt was a
successful naturalist, explorer, hunter, author, and soldier. He served his
country, his countrymen, and his family with unquestionable loyalty. And
if that wasn't enough to prove his valor, he hunted grizzly bears in his
free time.

I f out in the late fall or early spring, it is often possible to follow a bear's trail in
the snow; having come upon it either by chance or hard hunting, or else having
found where it leads from some carcass on which the beast has been feeding. In
the pursuit one must exercise great caution, as at such times the hunter is easily seen a
long way off, and game is always especially watchful for any foe that may follow its trail.
Once I killed a grisly in this manner . . .

One day while camped near the Bitter Root Mountains in Montana I found that
a bear had been feeding on the carcass of a moose which lay some five miles from the
little open glade in which my tent was pitched, and I made up my mind to try to get a
shot at it that afternoon. I stayed in camp till about three o'clock, lying lazily back on
the bed of sweet-smelling evergreen boughs, watching the pack ponies as they stood
under the pines on the edge of the open, stamping now and then, and switching
their tails. The air was still, the sky a glorious blue; at that hour in the afternoon even
the September sun was hot. The smoke from the smouldering logs of the camp fire
curled thinly upward. Little chipmunks scuttled out from their holes to the packs,
which lay in a heap on the ground, and then scuttled madly back again. A couple of
drab-colored whiskey-jacks, with bold mien and fearless bright eyes, hopped and
fluttered round, picking up the scraps, and uttering an extraordinary variety of notes,
mostly discordant; so tame were they that one of them lit on my outstretched arm as
I half dozed, basking in the sunshine.

When the shadows began to lengthen, I shouldered my rifle and plunged into the woods. At first my route lay along a mountain side; then for half a mile over a windfall, the dead timber piled about in crazy confusion. After that I went up the bottom of a valley by a little brook, the ground being carpeted with a sponge of soaked moss. At the head of this brook was a pond covered with water-lilies; and a scramble through a rocky pass took me into a high, wet valley, where the thick growth of spruce was broken by occasional strips of meadow. In this valley the moose carcass lay, well at the upper end.

In moccasined feet I trod softly through the soundless woods. Under the dark branches it was already dusk, and the air had the cool chill of evening. As I neared the clump where the body lay, I walked with redoubled caution, watching and listening with strained alertness. Then I heard a twig snap; and my blood leaped, for I knew the bear was at his supper. In another moment I saw his shaggy, brown form. He was working with all his awkward giant strength, trying to bury the carcass, twisting it to one side and the other with wonderful ease. Once he got angry and suddenly gave it a tremendous cuff with his paw; in his bearing he had something half humorous, half devilish. I crept up within forty yards; but for several minutes he would not keep his head still. Then something attracted his attention in the forest, and he stood motionless looking toward it, broadside to me, with his forepaws planted on the carcass. This gave me my chance. I drew a very fine bead between his eye and ear, and pulled the trigger. He dropped like a steer when struck with a pole-axe.

If there is a good hiding-place handy it is better to lie in wait at the carcass. One day on the headwaters of the Madison, I found that a bear was coming to an elk I had shot some days before; and I at once determined to ambush the beast when he came back that evening. The carcass lay in the middle of a valley a quarter of a mile broad. The bottom of this valley was covered by an open forest of tall pines; a thick jungle of smaller evergreens marked where the mountains rose on either hand. There were a number of large rocks scattered here and there, one, of very convenient shape, being only some seventy or eighty yards from the carcass. Up this I clambered. It hid me perfectly, and on its top was a carpet of soft pine needles, on which I could lie at my ease.

Hour after hour passed by. A little black woodpecker with a yellow crest ran nimbly up and down the tree-trunks for some time and then flitted away with a party of chickadees and nut-hatches. Occasionally a Clark's crow soared about overhead or clung in any position to the swaying end of a pine branch, chattering and screaming. Flocks of crossbills, with wavy flight and plaintive calls, flew to a small mineral lick near by, where they scraped the clay with their queer little beaks.

As the westering sun sank out of sight beyond the mountains these sounds of bird-life gradually died away. Under the great pines the evening was still with the silence of primeval desolation. The sense of sadness and loneliness, the melancholy of the wilderness, came over me like a spell. Every slight noise made my pulses throb as I lay motionless on the rock gazing intently into the gathering gloom. I began to fear that it would grow too dark to shoot before the grisly came.

Suddenly and without warning, the great bear stepped out of the bushes and trod across the pine needles with such swift and silent footsteps that its bulk seemed unreal. It was very cautious, continually halting to peer around; and once it stood up on its hind legs and looked long down the valley toward the red west. As it reached the carcass I put a bullet between its shoulders. It rolled over, while the woods resounded with its savage roaring. Immediately it struggled to its feet and staggered off; and fell again to the next shot, squalling and yelling. Twice this was repeated; the brute being one of those bears which greet every wound with a great outcry, and sometimes seem to lose their feet when hit—although they will occasionally fight as savagely as their more silent brethren. In this case, the wounds were mortal, and the bear died before reaching the edge of the thicket.

1980 U.S. Ice Hockey Team Miracle on Ice

One of the great lessons in sports is that victory is never guaranteed. The odds are never too great to overcome and no team is ever too great to lose. Infamously dubbed the "Miracle on Ice," the 1980 U.S. hockey team took down the Goliath Soviet Union hockey team in one of the greatest upsets ever. Its story reminds men to never give up, even if they are facing unfathomable odds.

Four days before the beginning of the 1980 Winter Olympics in Lake Placid, New York, the Soviet Union men's ice hockey team, largely composed of seasoned professional players, had embarrassed the United States in an exhibition game at Madison Square Garden in New York, racking up almost a dozen goals against an inexperienced squad of twenty-something college players. The Russians were used to Olympic dominance—since 1964, the Soviet team had gone 27–1–1 and outscored the opposition 175–44, taking four gold medals in the process. In head-to-head matchups against the United States, the cumulative score over that period was 28–7. The year before, the Soviet team had trounced a team of NHL all-stars 6–0 in the deciding third game of a three-game exhibition series.

Things looked no different at the Olympic Games. To open the tournament, the USSR took down Japan 16–0, then victimized the Netherlands 17–4, Poland 8–1, Finland 4–2, and Canada 6–4. They looked unbeatable.

But as unsurprising as the Soviets' march through the competition was, the United States was equally as surprising in a string of victories against top competition. Team USA's play mimicked the spirit of their firebrand coach, Herb Brooks, who preached physicality and team play to his team. In its first game against favored Sweden, Team USA earned a dramatic 2–2 draw by scoring with twenty-seven seconds left after pulling goalie Jim Craig for an extra attacker. Then came a stunning 7–3 victory over Czechoslovakia, considered by many to be the second-best team after the Soviet Union and a favorite for the silver medal. With its two toughest games in the group phase out of the way, the U.S. team reeled off three more wins, beating Norway 5–1, Romania 7–2, and West Germany 4–2 to go 4–0–1 and advance to the medal round from its group, along with the Swedes.

The stage was set for what became the most memorable hockey game of all time. The scrappy U.S. team took on the Russian juggernaut for the right to play in the gold medal game. Columnist Dave Anderson of the *New York Times* considered the game a formality: "Unless the ice melts, or unless the United States team or another team performs a miracle, as did the American squad in 1960, the Russians are expected to easily win the Olympic gold medal for the sixth time in the last seven tournaments."

But Coach Brooks believed in his players, and delivered an impassioned pregame address, telling them, "You were born to be a player. You were meant to be here. This moment is yours." On Friday afternoon, February 22, 1980, both teams took to the ice.

After falling behind early, the United States tied up the game, but subsequently fell behind again. Luckily, forward Mark Johnson was able to slap an errant rebound past Soviet goalie Vladimir Tretiak, as time expired in the first period, tying the game at 2. In the second, the Soviet team kept up a relentless attack, but U.S. goalie Jim Craig bravely turned away all but one of the Soviet shots, leaving the score 3–2 as the teams entered the third and final period. "He was a tower of strength for us, no question," said U.S. coach Herb Brooks. "For an American team to be successful, the catalyst has to be the goalkeeper. Craig told me yesterday, 'You wait, wait till tomorrow, Coach. You haven't seen it.'"

Early into the third period, Mark Johnson again came through in the clutch, tying the game at 3. Then, only a few minutes later, U.S. captain Mike Eruzione (which means "eruption" in Italian), blasted a shot past Soviet goalie Vladimir Myshkin, who had replaced Tretiak after the first period: 4–3 USA.

The last ten minutes presented a gleefully unexpected but impossibly difficult task: withstand the Soviet onslaught while clinging to a one-goal lead. Coach Brooks had worked his team to the bone in the weeks prior to the Olympics, hoping that top physical conditioning would prove to be as valuable to success as skill or experience. They would tap the deepest reserve of their stamina, as the Soviets swarmed into the American zone, relentlessly challenging Craig. But he stood tall that day, stopping thirty-six of the thirty-nine shots he faced during the game, while the Americans managed only sixteen. As the seconds melted off the clock, the crowd cheered louder and louder, chanting "USA!" over and over to spur on their weary heroes. At last, the United States weathered the Soviet storm, jubilantly embracing one another as the shocked Soviets stood stoically gazing at the celebration, anguished that they had let such a winnable game slip away. A team of college hockey players had taken down the mighty Soviets, putting their grit and energy against many medals, years of experience, and superior talent.

At the final buzzer, after the fans had chanted the final seconds away, fathers and mothers and friends of the United States players stormed the ice, hugging anyone they could find in red, white, and blue uniforms. Meanwhile, in the stands, most of the ten thousand fans—including about fifteen hundred standees, who paid $24.40 apiece for a ticket—shouted "USA," over and over, and hundreds outside waved American flags. During the postgame commentary, ABC Olympic sports anchor Jim McKay compared the American victory over the Soviets to a group of Canadian college football players defeating the Pittsburgh Steelers, recently crowned Super Bowl champions.

Coach Brooks raced back to the dressing room, out of the sight of the cameras, and wept.

In the locker room, Eruzione was overcome.

"It's a human emotion that is indescribable," he said.

The *Washington Post* asked if it was ecstasy.

"That's not strong enough," he said. "We beat the Russians. We beat the Russians."

Profile: Jeremy Lin

Many great athletes are born great. From an early age they demonstrate a talent, drive, or skill in such a way that it clearly separates them from the rest of their competitors, and you know they are eventually destined for greatness. One thinks of athletes like Bo Jackson or LeBron James. But for many more athletes, the pursuit of greatness is a struggle far more difficult. It takes thousands of hours of practice, and even then you may not excel or be given the chance to excel. The story of Jeremy Lin's rocketship rise to international basketball fame is a story of the latter, a battle for athletic greatness so remarkable and unexpected that it took the world by storm. Through it all, Lin's character shone through in ways that boys all around the world can emulate and that make his rise to stardom not so surprising after all.

Jeremy Lin grew up in the Northern California suburbs of Palo Alto. Early on, his parents, immigrants from Taiwan, instilled in him rigorous study habits, and he coupled that diligence with an equally zealous passion for basketball. It wasn't long before he began to excel at both academics and sports.

In his senior year of high school, Lin led Palo Alto High School to a 32-1 record and the Division II state title, upsetting vaunted powerhouse Mater Dei.

Lin's high school career was extraordinary, and yet, he did not receive a single athletic scholarship. The problem was that scouts for college programs didn't think he could cut it in the college game. While he was a standout point guard with tremendous court vision and ability, he lacked the freakish athletic ability that most college scouts look for. Scouts thought he wouldn't be able to keep up with faster and more agile college point guards.

So Lin decided to attend Harvard University, where he could play basketball and also focus on attaining an excellent academic education. To the surprise of many, he quickly became the leader of the Harvard basketball team and a nationally recognized point guard. He set numerous Ivy League records during his time at Harvard.

Yet, still the scouts doubted him. After college he went undrafted. Again, scouts didn't think he had the physical attributes to succeed in the NBA.

Not one to give up easily, Lin set out to prove himself to NBA teams, which he did, starting at the bottom, in the NBA's Summer League. Before long, Lin managed to earn himself a contract with the Golden State Warriors. Even then he rarely played for the Warriors, and bounced back and forth multiple times between the Warriors and their D-League affiliate. In the 2011 off-season, the Warriors waived Lin. He was claimed by the Houston Rockets, but only to be dropped again.

Eventually the New York Knicks acquired Lin to be a backup point guard to another backup point guard. After bouncing back and forth with New York's D-league, Lin finally got a chance to play for the Knicks after they'd lost several point guards to injury.

On February 4, 2012, Lin made his debut against the New Jersey Nets, facing off against all-star point guard Deron Williams. Lin posted a shocking twenty-five points, five rebounds, and seven assists, and led the Knicks to victory. The NBA took notice, but they thought it was an anomaly, and nothing more.

In the next game, against the Utah Jazz, Lin's task was even greater. The Knicks were without their two best players, Carmelo Anthony and Amar'e Stoudemire. Lin responded with twenty-eight points, eight assists, and another Knicks victory. Slowly the doubters were becoming believers.

A few days later, the "Linsanity," as it was dubbed, officially started to explode. Lin scored thirty-eight points and dealt seven assists, leading the Knicks to a win over the Los Angeles Lakers and outscoring future Hall of Famer Kobe Bryant. Lin's face and story papered almost every sports show and website in the world at that point. You could hardly turn on the TV or browse the Internet without hearing about Jeremy Lin and "Linsanity."

After his first five starts, Lin became the first NBA player ever to score at least twenty points and have seven assists in each game. Who was this incredible point guard who seemed to come out of nowhere?

Well, as noted earlier, Lin's success hardly came out of nowhere.

Kobe Bryant remarked after the Lakers and Knicks game, "Players playing that well don't usually come out of nowhere. It seems like they come out of nowhere, but if you can go back and take a look, his skill level was probably there from the beginning. It probably just went unnoticed."

In one game, the savvy Bryant realized what so many coaches and scouts had passed over time and time again for years: though Lin didn't have physical talent equal to NBA standards, he possessed the diligence and skill to excel at an NBA level.

Before his breakout performances, Lin was sleeping on a couch in his brother's one-bedroom apartment in Manhattan. Only weeks later he was an international basketball phenomenon, appearing on the cover of *Sports Illustrated* and other magazines around the world. He was even named in *Time* magazine's 2012 list of the "Top 100 Most Influential People in the World."

As chronicled earlier, none of this success came easy to Lin. But there was another factor that made it even more difficult: his race.

From his high school days all the way up to the NBA, Lin has been subject to terrible ethnic slurs and racial profiling from fans, other players, and even journalists. Because there are very few Asian-Americans in basketball, especially the NBA, some people wrongly think that Asian-Americans are genetically or racially inferior or that they don't belong on a basketball court. And as Lin's stature rose, the racism only got worse.

Perhaps what has made Lin so successful, in spite of his critics, is his ability to channel criticism into motivation. Like many great men throughout history, he was able to turn the worst things his critics said into fuel for improving his skill and ability.

"I know a lot of people say I'm 'deceptively athletic' and 'deceptively quick,' and I'm not sure what's deceptive," Lin said during the 2012 All-Star Weekend. "But it could be the fact that I'm Asian-American. But I think that's fine. It's something that I embrace, and it gives me a chip on my shoulder. But I'm very proud to be Asian-American and I love it."

Lin is a devout Christian, as well, and says he owes his faith in God to helping him overcome the many obstacles to his success.

"I'm not playing to prove anything to anybody," Lin said. "That affected my game last year and my joy last year . . . . I felt I needed to prove myself. Prove that I'm not a marketing tool, I'm not a ploy to improve attendance. Prove I can play in this league. But I've surrendered that to God. I'm not in a battle with what everybody else thinks anymore."

In spite of his success, Lin's career with the New York Knicks was suddenly cut short after the 2011–2012 season. No one knows for certain why the Knicks let Lin go, but perhaps they also doubted that his rise to stardom could continue.

At the time of writing this profile, Lin is the starting point guard for the Houston Rockets. He continues to thrive as a point guard in the NBA. Admittedly, some of the "Linsanity" has worn off by this time. However, Lin remains an ambassador for Asian-Americans around the world and a testament to the power of hard work and determination. He is a man who did not seek fame, but when it found him, he handled it admirably and humbly, like the man he always was.

On Leisure

SENECA

The Roman writer Seneca (ca. 4 BC–AD 65) was one of Rome's most contemplative writers. He wrote a variety of works on philosophy, morality, and virtue. He believed man should never abandon reading and that studying is how he defends his soul.

L eisure without study is death; it is a tomb for the living man. What then is the advantage of retirement? As if the real causes of our anxieties did not follow us across the seas! What hiding place is there, where the fear of death does not enter? What peaceful haunts are there, so fortified and so far withdrawn that pain does not fill them with fear? Where you hide yourself, human ills will make an uproar all around. There are many external things which compass us about, to deceive us or to weigh upon us; there are many things within which, even amid solitude, fret and ferment.

Therefore, gird yourself about with philosophy, an impregnable wall. Though it be assaulted by many engines, Fortune can find no passage into it. The soul stands on unassailable ground, if it has abandoned external things; it is independent in its own fortress; and every weapon that is hurled falls short of the mark. Fortune has not the long reach with which we credit her; she can seize none except him that clings to her. Let us then recoil from her as far as we are able. This will be possible for us only through knowledge of self and of the world of Nature. The soul should know whither it is going and whence it came, what is good for it, and what is evil, what it seeks and what it avoids . . .

This strength of heart, however, will come from constant study, provided you practise, not with the tongue but with the soul.

The Thrilla in Manila

Muhammad Ali and Joe Frazier were accustomed to the spotlight. Both burst onto the boxing scene in the sixties, knocking out opponents with lethal combinations of confidence, speed, and punching prowess. Both had earned millions of dollars. At a time when America was experiencing profound social discord, Ali, formerly Cassius Clay, converted to Islam and was imprisoned for refusing to fight in Vietnam. Frazier, meanwhile, came to represent pro-war America, later arguing that he would have fought had he not had children. After Ali's release from prison, they fought in the "Fight of the Century," a fifteen-round bloodbath in 1971 that saw Frazier retain the heavyweight championship as Ali tried to prove his pugilistic skills had not eroded. In the rematch three years later, Ali beat Frazier on a decision. Along the way, personal animosity had built to a fever pitch, as the two traded barbs in the media and even came to blows on the set of ABC's *Wide World of Sports*. The result was one of the highest-profile rivalries in sports history.

We are two," Ali declared, "of the famousest fighters in the whole world." But now, in 1975, their feud had never been so public. The place was Manila, the Philippines. An up-and-coming boxing promoter named Don King had secured the steaming island nation's capital city as the locale for the third bout of the Ali-Frazier rivalry, a fight King would dub "The Thrilla in Manila." Per usual, the lead-up to the fight was marked by a series of insults in the press.

"I want you," said Frazier, "like a hog wants slop."

"Ain't no Baptist," retorted Ali, "gonna beat no Muslim."

"I don't want to knock him out," stated Frazier to the *New York Times*, "I want to beat him, beat him."

But Ali uttered an insult that infuriated Frazier more than any other, calling him a "gorilla," with all its racial connotations, in response to Frazier calling Ali by the name Clay, which he had dropped upon converting to Islam.

With the Heavyweight Boxing Championship of the World and millions of dollars on the line (including a one-million-dollar side bet between the two), racial and religious rhetoric now stoked the two men's anger against each other as the public prepared to witness what surely would be a fight for the ages.

On Friday, October 1, at 10:45 a.m. (an unusual time for a boxing match, but ideal for international audiences who would watch via closed-circuit TV), the 225-pound Ali stepped into the ring against the 215-pound Frazier, who had once honed his boxing skills while working at a slaughterhouse. Twenty-five thousand spectators, including President Ferdinand Marcos and his wife, looked on in the stifling humidity. Ali was known for his quickness and deceptive approach—deliberately letting opponents tire themselves out by absorbing blows, then exploding in a hail of punches—a strategy he called the "rope a dope."

Frazier, on the other hand, relied on pure force and was considered the most powerful puncher at the time, more a brawler than a boxer.

Ali, however, came out with manic intent to punish Frazier, working him over intently in the first three rounds. Despite opening up cuts on Frazier's face, Frazier continued to withstand Ali's punishment. Ali grew so frustrated with Frazier's refusal to go down or stop coming forward that he screamed "You stupid chump, you!" at Frazier in the fourth round. It was now Frazier's turn to batter Ali, who had wanted to make it a short fight.

Frazier made his own assault and began punishing Ali about the body and head with his trademark left hooks. By the sixth round, Frazier had staggered Ali in turn and seemed to be gaining control of the bout. At the beginning of the seventh round, Ali reportedly whispered in Frazier's ear, "Joe, they told me you was all washed up." Frazier growled back, "They told you wrong, pretty boy."

Frazier dominated the middle rounds. Ali tried to fend Frazier off with occasional furious flurries of punches and bursts of uncontrolled activity, and even unsuccessfully tried to use the rope-a-dope technique that had defeated George Foreman nearly a year earlier, but it was all negated by Frazier's relentless aggression. Between the terrific heat inside the stadium, Frazier's assault, and his own nonchalant training leading up to the fight, it began to seem as if defeat was close at hand for Ali.

But Frazier's offensive had spent a great deal of energy, and Ali was able to mount a counteroffensive. In the eleventh round he used his speed to dance more and to unload a series of fast combinations on Frazier, which severely bruised his face by the end of the round, swelling Frazier's eyes to the point that nothing but a tiny slit remained open.

Into Round 12 the momentum continued to shift in Ali's favor, as he took advantage of Frazier's swollen eyes to hit Frazier with one hard right after another. The *New York Times* remarked that Frazier's face looked like "a swollen chocolate marshmallow." Early in Round 13, Ali landed another furious combination on Frazier, sending the injured fighter's mouthguard flying into the crowd. During the next two minutes Ali relentlessly kept after Frazier, the mouthguard not being replaced until the bell, hitting Frazier with hard combinations when Frazier wasn't throwing punches; and when Frazier did throw, Ali used the openings left to inflict yet more damage. Frazier's mouth was badly cut by the end of this round.

By the fourteenth round Frazier was virtually helpless, and although Ali was desperately tired and hurting, he was able to summon the energy once again to give Frazier a fierce beating, and once again Frazier was knocked down before the bell ended the round.

Seeing the results of Round 14, Frazier's trainer, Eddie Futch, decided to stop the fight between rounds rather than risk long-term physical consequences for Frazier in the fifteenth.

Frazier protested stopping the fight, shouting "I want him, boss," but later realized it was for the better, saying, "I wanted to go on, but I'd never go against Eddie."

Ali had put on one of the most impressive bouts of stamina in sports history, enduring hundreds of powerful punches from the hardest hitter in the sport, describing both men's condition after the match as "next to death" and declaring Frazier to be "the toughest man in the world." But Ali's indomitable will was the real story. The self-anointed "greatest fighter of all-time" backed up his tough talk with his indomitable will to win. Ali's trainer, Angelo Dundee, told the *New York Times*, "My guy sucked it up, when he looked completely out of gas, he put on another gas tank." Both men left the ring drained and exhausted and never physically the same again. That event should have been where the expression "leave it all on the field" was coined. Both men left never to be the same again, never to get back what they left in the ring that night.

"Prepared for a Rain"

WILL H. DILG

In the game of life there's always one guy who talks a big game, but never quite lives up to it. Too often he lets his ego and excitement get the best of him and forgets to do the easy essentials. We can all relate to the following hilarious sketch about several friends on a fishing trip.

If the following incident had happened to me instead of to Jesse Newton, it would have been my most tragic moment, as it was his. As it turned out, it was tragedy for him and comedy to the rest of us. That, I believe, is the usual way with life.

Jesse is an old-timer, and when he was a young man he was among the best trappers, hunters, and fishermen in his little town of Lowell, Michigan. He owns up to it himself—not only owns up to it but insists on it. But he is getting old and rheumatic, and after a week's work, feels more like staying around home than traipsing up and down a half dozen creeks looking for a trout.

His younger brother and I have "parded" on the fishing stuff for many years, and in framing up one of our Sunday trips we asked Jesse to come along. He was pleased to accept the invitation. His jointed cane "poles" had been put away years before, all wrapped in newspaper and thrown into the attic, together with the usual amount of cast-offs relegated to that part of a well-regulated home. He gathered his package and his tobacco box full of the usual junk, and when Lizzie came, Sunday at about two in the morning, he was as "peppy" as we were and "rarin" to go.

It was a great pleasure to see the years fall from him and although usually taciturn, he talked a blue streak all the thirty-five miles to the first creek. These are "grasshopper" creeks—too narrow and grass grown to get a fly to, and at many places even too overgrown with grass to get a hopper into.

We hit the first one just as it was getting light enough to find hoppers. It was a perfect morning, everything set. Jesse was as cocky as an Airedale pup and assured us that, when he got his pole to working, he would have his limit by eight, and then would have to help us catch ours. The thrill of anticipation had him and he acted about thirteen years old.

First out of the car, he got his junk from under my feet. All of a sudden, he "blew up." I have said he was quiet and unobtrusive. Right then, he was not. He sure does know lots of one-hundred-proof swear words, and I learned a great number from him in the next minute or two. Calamity had overtaken him. He had thrown his package into the grass, and after we had calmed him and had him coherent again, he showed us what he had trustingly brought thirty-five miles on a trout trip. What he had thought was his package of "poles" were two little parasols [umbrellas] belonging to his girls!

Profile: Mario Andretti

The greatest men in the world are rarely born into greatness. Mario Andretti was a poor Italian immigrant who came to the United States at a young age. He set his sights on one thing—automobile racing—and took to it with a workmanlike fervor. We might consider racing a sport, but for Andretti it was his life. Great athletes transform play into profession.

M ario Andretti is known as one of the most skilled automobile racers of all time. In more than five decades of racing, he won 111 races, and is still the only man to win the Indianapolis 500, Daytona 500, and Formula

One World Championship, setting a world record along the way for clocking in at 234.275 mph during one race. But Andretti's success did not come easily. Even today he remains a living testament to achieving—and sustaining—the American dream through hard work.

Born in a small farming community outside of Trieste, Italy, Andretti belonged to a family that had achieved success as farmers, attaining a comfortable life. Mario fell in love with racing when he was young, running around the dining room with his twin brother, Aldo, pretending to be racers. As the brothers got a little older, they raced self-constructed wooden cars down the hills around their town, startling elderly ladies.

By the end of World War II, the Andrettis' property had been ceded to Yugoslavia as part of the terms of surrender imposed by the Allies. The Andretti family's fortunes took a turn for the worse. Adapting to the Communist lifestyle proved to be a miserable experience. After three years trying to adapt, they decided to flee. For the next seven years, the family of five lived in a refugee camp northwest of Florence, Italy, sharing a single room, partitioned with blankets, with several other families. Finally, Mario's father decided to take the family to the United States in 1955—knowing nobody, speaking little English, and possessing only $125.

Mario and Aldo set to work making a name for themselves in the racing world, rebuilding an old Hudson and racing it on a little dirt track near their house in Nazareth, Pennsylvania. After Aldo suffered a major crash in 1959, their parents were angry that the boys had been racing, but Mario was unwilling to give up his dream. After spending the early sixties in East Coast regional racing circuits, in 1964 he was racing nationally in the U.S. Automobile Club and by 1965 was the youngest champion in the series' history. For the next four decades, Andretti would dominate racetracks around the world, winning in whatever American and European series he raced in.

After he left racing in 1994, Andretti kept his competitive edge alive in various business ventures: Andretti is vice chairman of a winery named Andretti Winery in Napa Valley, California, and he owns a chain of gasoline stations, a car dealership, car washes, car-care products, go-kart tracks, a clothing line, video games, and replica cars, as well as his own racing school in Las Vegas. Pixar also recruited Andretti to lend his voice to one of the characters in the movie *Cars*.

In addition to his own inner desire for excellence, Andretti keenly attributes much of his success to the opportunities America has given him. Andretti told *Auto Racing Daily*, "I'm a perfect example of living the American dream because I'm an immigrant. I was able to realize, again, what I was still dreaming about when I left Italy . . . I arrived in the States, and motor racing was the only thing in my mind— besides school, of course, at the age of 15. I started driving here at 19. I would have never had the opportunity if I would have stayed in Italy, for instance. So I did fully realize it because of what this country can provide for you."

One way Andretti decided to give back to America is through making appearances on USO tours overseas. "I think it always gives you just a great feeling to visit with the military around the world, these young individuals that obviously are out there and serving our country and sacrificing in many different ways. If we can bring a smile to their face for whatever reason, I think it's a great feeling."

— ❧ —

Piers Paul Read's *Alive: The Story of the Andes Survivors*

William J. Bennett

I strongly admired *Commentary* magazine as a young man and always longed to write for it. I asked a friend how to approach it and he said to find a topic that you think you know better than anyone else and write about it. Catholicism, football, and mountains were a large part of my youth, and remain a part of my life today. So when the book *Alive: The Story of the Andes Survivors*, the story of Catholic boys who are rugby players stuck on a mountain, was published, I rushed to write a review. This review ran in the August 1974 edition of the magazine. The ethos that defines a sports team can sometimes be important for even larger purposes. Here it enabled a life-saving rescue.

There are many opportunities for instruction about the psychology of survival in this story of sixteen Uruguayan young men who lived for seventy-one days on the frozen slopes of the Andes following the crash of their plane bound for Chile for a rugby match. Unfortunately, too many of these opportunities are sacrificed to overemphasis on the issue that has caused all the fanfare—the fact that the survivors fed from the bodies of their dead companions as a means of survival. Although recourse to this extreme measure is undeniably interesting and newsworthy, and it haunts the book as it haunts the reader's imagination, there is more to the story than anthropophagy. To be done with it, then, it should be acknowledged that there is no interesting moral problem about the violation of this taboo in these circumstances, and these religious Roman Catholic boys did not spend much time debating the merits of their decision. Although many of the boys were reluctant to eat from the bodies of the dead passengers, no one opposed the measure on principle and eventually all participated. This is not shocking, and what would be shocking, what in fact has happened in similar situations, is not present: there is no murder of the weak by the strong and no drawing of straws to see who will commit suicide to provide a source of food for the others. For the boys it is primarily a matter of mutual exhortation to overcome their strong revulsion against eating human flesh. Upon the return of the survivors, the priests who hear their confessions insist they have done nothing wrong, official Rome does not object, and even the parents of the dead understand what necessity required.

Read seems more interested in the cannibalism issue than in bringing out the significant fact that the boys who survived (there was one man of thirty-five, the others were all between eighteen and twenty-six) had some important advantages in this desperate situation. For one, many knew each other as teammates or as close friends and supporters of the rugby team and thus were able to draw upon a shared history of cooperation and teamwork. Immediately following the crash the team captain becomes the leader of the survivors. In organizing an expeditionary force to search for a way down from the mountain, these athletes decide a practice run should be made to determine the physical fitness of the members of the force. Even though the group is short on supplies and energy, three boys are sent on a practice climb up a mountain. Costly as this is, it is worth the effort. One of the expeditionaries is unable to take the difficult conditions and is justly dropped from the expeditionary team. In the first days there is another advantage for the boys. They find solace from a lone woman survivor, Liliana Methol, a thirty-five-year-old mother of four, traveling with her husband. She comforts the boys in the evenings when she gathers them around her and tells them to tell stories about themselves. For the boys she becomes mother and novia; she keeps up their spirits in the most trying first few days. Only the death of the team captain by the same avalanche that takes her life and the lives of seven others is felt as deeply by the boys. This sense of devastation experienced by the boys is instructive; it contrasts sharply with current proclamations that woman's traditional role, the role that Liliana Methol played on the mountain, is demeaning, small, inconsequential.

Read provides a vivid picture of how time is spent on the mountain. Following the team captain's death the different groups—cooks, cleaners, expeditionaries, convalescents—negotiate their different and conflicting needs in a kind of checks-and-balances polity. The inevitable tensions arise, but on the whole there is a remarkably strong sense of teamwork and cooperation; there is good humor and even several practical jokes, and all this after the boys believe the search for them has been abandoned. Survival appears less sensational in this true story than in many fictional accounts. Thaumaturgy is also missing from the story. On the long nights on the cold mountain (the temperature would drop to forty degrees below zero) there are no deep philosophical discussions of death; because death is so close there is no need to speak of it. But there is talk of God, and all are confident he is watching over them. Theological debate is absent for, as Read points out, the boys were trained by the Christian Brothers, not the Jesuits. Before going to sleep the boys say the rosary together and on the expeditions the travelers pray as they climb, one word of the Lord's Prayer for every step. As is to be expected, thoughts of food occupy the boys' minds. They imagine the finest meals they will eat if rescued and exchange tales of the best dishes they can remember. Talk of home is too painful. There is little talk or thought of sex. Physically weak and deeply religious, these Roman Catholic boys, in Read's words, feel they "have too great a need of God to offend Him."

———

In writing about the ill-fated Donner expedition across the United States in 1846 (here there was cannibalism following the murder of the victim), Bernard De Voto said: "Why, when death must be faced, do some personalities disintegrate whereas others abide by the qualities of resolution, fortitude, and courage which have persuaded the human race that it has dignity?" Neither Read, the storyteller, nor the story itself answers this pertinent question, but in the narrative there is ample material for carrying on the inquiry. One man, Parrado, known before the crash mainly as the sidekick of one of the handsome team stars, Abal, who dies in the crash, becomes in this desolate place a leader and a source of fortitude and courage for the others. The boys come to revere him. He leads the expeditions, and on the final successful expedition he carries his companion's pack up the steep mountainside, refuses to leave him lying in the snow, and gives up his share of food to him, believing him weaker. In the epilogue, Read follows Parrado upon his return home. Trying to live his new role of hero in the rich night life of Buenos Aires doesn't work. He poses for a picture with racing stars Emerson Fittipaldi and Jackie Stewart, judges a beauty contest, but soon flees the photographers and returns home to his job as a nuts-and-bolts salesman and his former friendly anonymity. Another character, the lawyer Pedro Delgado, whose professional eloquence is an initial asset in cheering the spirit of the survivors in the hours immediately following the crash, becomes the most disliked by the group of survivors. He is the least trustworthy; he takes more than his share of food and is regarded as a hoarder by the others. But unliked and unpopular in the desolation of the Andes, he becomes, to the subsequent displeasure of the boys, the sought-after spokesman of the group and darling of the press upon his return.

In the background, back in "civilization," a distressing plan is pursued. While the boys are struggling for survival these seventy-one days, their friends and parents do not give up hope despite discouragement from official reports. Motivated by strong religious faith, the parents make a terrible error in judgment that binds them all. Neglecting the facts that point to a search in the site of the actual crash, they expend their efforts in an area "divined" in the visions of the internationally known medium, Sidney Croiset, Jr. The effort expended in following his advice proves costly. One boy who survived in the fuselage for two weeks after the crash might have been saved had Croiset's advice been ignored. When his vision turns up nothing, Croiset then expresses his opinion that the survivors are dead. Fortunately, he is not listened to and the search efforts continue. Rescue finally comes as Parrado and his companion stumble off the mountain onto foothills where they are spotted by a mountain peasant.

Despite occasional disconcerting repetition (of unimportant details as well as of the cannibalism issue), the story of the Andes survivors is undeniably fascinating and Read tells it well. He is appropriately sympathetic to the boys and inappropriately forgiving toward Croiset who he argues did have some visions that corresponded with real events. His sympathy and understanding of the boys peak when they are set upon by an army of "journalists" seeking pictures and grisly particulars about the extreme measures taken to insure physical survival. But the most important lesson of the book concerns the boys' mental sustenance. It is clear that the boys are kept from mental desperation and despair by the strength of their inner resources. Deeply religious and deeply devoted to their families, they are able to live through an incredibly cruel and vicious assault on their stability and sanity largely because of the spiritual resilience that has been provided for them. Read's book is important, then, not only for what it teaches about the boys but for what it says, indirectly, about the institutions that nurtured these boys: the Church in whose faith they were raised, the families they refused to give up hope of seeing, and their teachers. These are the uncelebrated agents of rescue and heroes of the story. It is important to see that on the cold mountain the boys, although physically isolated, are not alone.

4

Man in the Polis

The word *polis* originated from the ancient Greek idea of a city-state. Instead of a city or town being ruled by a king or a small oligarchy, the Greeks developed the *polis*—a self-contained entity governed by a body of citizens. It's the root of such words as *politics*, *polity*, and *metropolis*. The idea of self-governance, autonomy, and independence passed down by the Greeks remains to this day the foundation for modern democracy.

The ancient Greeks believed that man was made as a civic being and incapable of surviving life on his own. Therefore, it was natural that a man should join into the bond of a community for his own survival. Aristotle famously remarked, "Man is by nature a political animal." As such, each man is responsible to perform his role in the polis. Through the actions of each man, the body as a whole survives. The Greeks taught the world that individual citizens should join together in common interests to form a city-state.

The idea of men coalescing into one cohesive body was passed on from the Greeks to the Romans. The equivalent word for *polis* in Latin is *civitas*, which means "citizenhood." Over time the Greek polis slowly vanished and was replaced by the conquering Roman Empire and eventually the monarchies and feudal systems of the Middle Ages. It wasn't until the seventeenth century that a communal governing movement resurged in the Enlightenment in the form of parliamentarism and anti-monarchism.

Influential thinkers of that time like Thomas Hobbes, John Locke, and Jean-Jacques

Rousseau were instrumental in reviving social contract theory—the belief that man entered into a binding communal agreement that should serve to protect his well-being in exchange for his service. Locke wrote in his "Second Treatise on Government," "Thus that, which begins and actually constitutes any political society, is nothing but the consent of any number of freeman capable of a majority to unite."

Locke and his contemporaries believed in a return to the Aristotelian idea of self-government, that all men are equals and should be governed as equals. They believed that men were not like wolves, who roamed in packs and preyed on the weaker of their kind. Instead, they viewed men more like bees where the survival of the hive is contingent on the efforts of the individuals.

Their work sparked the fire of the American Revolution. Our Founding Fathers, for example, Alexander Hamilton, James Madison, and Thomas Jefferson, relied on the teachings of Locke, Burke, and company to give birth to the most citizen-driven, representative system of government the world has ever seen.

For democracy to be successful, our Founding Fathers recognized that citizens must play their part in defending and ensuring the rights and liberties of their fellows. Samuel Adams remarked, "The liberties of our country, the freedom of our civil constitution, are worth defending against all hazards: And it is our duty to defend them against all attacks."

Essential to the survival of the polis in ancient Greece was the belief that each man would fight for his city and its well-being, whether through war, politics, or public service. The same rings true for modern democracy and self-government. "Every right implies a responsibility; every opportunity, an obligation; every possession, a duty," said John D. Rockefeller. Democracy is not free and our freedom comes at the great cost and sacrifice of many heroic men and women.

Because of these great citizens, the spirit of democracy lives on in more than just constitutions, laws, and court decisions; it is manifest in the lives of its people. Henry Wadsworth Longfellow wrote, "The life of a man consists not in seeing visions and in dreaming dreams, but in active charity and in willing service." It should be our privilege to come to the aid of our fellow man, a small price to pay for the freedoms we all enjoy.

The men who most obviously and directly live out this attitude today are those serving in the military. General Douglas MacArthur instructed his men, "Duty, Honor, Country. Those three hallowed words reverently dictate what you ought to be, what you can be, what you will be." Every day military men put their lives on the line to secure and protect the liberties and freedoms of their countrymen, and, in other ways, all of us can serve the polis.

Yet in our constitutional republic civic duty, responsibility, and service are not forced on anyone. Each man is free to make his own choices and actions. History teaches us, however, that some of the world's worst acts resulted from the activity of bad men and the inactivity of good men. Edmund Burke wrote, "All that is necessary for the triumph of evil is for good men to do nothing."

Former President Calvin Coolidge said, "No enterprise can exist for itself alone. It ministers to some great need, it performs some great service, not for itself, but for others; or failing therein, it ceases to be profitable and ceases to exist." The polis exists because it benefits each man. John Adams put it bluntly, "If we do not lay out ourselves in the service of mankind whom should we serve?"

Whom should man serve? That is the question each man must wrestle with. Should he serve himself and his own self-interests? Or should he join together in a community of men to serve his fellow man for the better of the whole? Albert Einstein once said, "It is every man's obligation to put back into the world at least the equivalent of what he takes out of it." As the following passages illustrate, men of the polis should serve God, country, and family, for that is our calling.

"Not Yours to Give"

David Crockett

David Crockett (1786–1836) was an American folk hero, frontiersman, soldier, and politician. Known by Americans familiarly as "Davy" Crockett, he represented Tennessee in the U.S. House of Representatives, served in the Texas Revolution, and died at the Battle of the Alamo.

Crockett grew up in East Tennessee, where he gained a reputation for hunting and storytelling. After being elected to the rank of colonel in the militia of Lawrence County, Tennessee, he was elected to the Tennessee state legislature in 1821. In 1826, Crockett was elected to the U.S. House of Representatives. Congressman Crockett vehemently opposed many of the policies of President Andrew Jackson, most notably the Indian Removal Act. Crockett took part in the Texas Revolution and was killed at the Battle of the Alamo in March 1836.

In his speech before the House of Representatives, "Not Yours to Give," Crockett opposed the appropriation of funds for a charitable cause, something he considered an unconstitutional measure. Instead, he advised the representatives to each contribute a week's wages to help the individual in need. Crockett's proposal is an appeal to civic virtue that American politicians ought to possess, and expresses his belief that an overreliance on government measures will rob men of their individual duty to contribute and do good works for their community. Here is a great example of civic manhood. It is redolent of contemporary debates about the purpose and responsibility of government and efforts to restrain the expansion of the federal government.

One day in the House of Representatives, a bill was taken up appropriating money for the benefit of a widow of a distinguished naval officer. Several beautiful speeches had been made in its support. The Speaker was just about to put the question before the House when Mr. Crockett arose:

Mr. Speaker—I have as much respect for the memory of the deceased, and as much sympathy for the suffering of the living, if suffering there be, as any man in this house, but we must not permit our respect for the dead or our sympathy for a part of the living to lead us into an act of injustice to the balance of the living. I will not go into an argument to prove that Congress has no power to appropriate this money as an act of charity. Every member upon this floor knows it. We have the right, as individuals, to give away as much of our own money as we please in charity; but as members of Congress we have no right so to appropriate a dollar of the public money. Some eloquent appeals have been made to us upon the ground that it is a debt due the deceased. Mr. Speaker, the deceased lived long after the close of the war; he was in office to the day of his death, and I have never heard that the government was in arrears to him.

Every man in this House knows it is not a debt. We cannot, without the grossest corruption, appropriate this money as the payment of a debt. We have not the semblance of authority to appropriate it as a charity. Mr. Speaker, I have said we have the right to give as much money of our own as we please. I am the poorest man on this floor. I cannot vote for this bill, but I will give one week's pay to the object, and, if every member of Congress will do the same, it will amount to more than the bill asks.

He took his seat. Nobody replied. The bill was put upon its passage, and, instead of passing unanimously, as was generally supposed, and as, no doubt, it would have, but for that speech, it received but few votes, and of course, was lost.

Later, when asked by a friend why he had opposed the appropriation, Crockett gave this explanation:

Several years ago I was one evening standing on the steps of the Capitol with some other members of Congress, when our attention was attracted by a great light over in Georgetown. It was evidently a large fire. We jumped into a hack and drove over as fast as we could. In spite of all that could be done, many houses were burned and many families made homeless, and, besides, some of them had lost all but the clothes they had on. The weather was very cold, and when I saw so many women and children suffering, I felt that something ought to be done for them. The next morning a bill was introduced appropriating $20,000 for their relief. We put aside all other business and rushed it through as soon as it could be done.

The next summer, when it began to be time to think about the election, I concluded I would take a scout around among the boys of my district. I had no opposition there, but, as the election was some time off, I did not know what might turn up. When riding one day in a part of my district in which I was more a stranger than any other, I saw a man in a field plowing and coming toward the road. I gauged my gait so that we should meet as he came to the fence. As he came up, I spoke to the man. He replied politely, but, as I thought, rather coldly.

I began: "Well, friend, I am one of those unfortunate beings called candidates, and—"

"Yes, I know you; you are Colonel Crockett. I have seen you once before, and voted for you the last time you were elected. I suppose you are out electioneering now, but you had better not waste your time or mine. I shall not vote for you again."

This was a sockdolager . . . I begged him to tell me what was the matter.

"Well, Colonel, it is hardly worth-while to waste time or words upon it. I do not see how it can be mended, but you gave a vote last winter which shows that either you have not capacity to understand the Constitution, or that you are wanting in the honesty and firmness to be guided by it. In either case you are not the man to represent me. But I beg your pardon for expressing it in that way. I did not intend to avail myself of the privilege of the constituent to speak plainly to a candidate for the purpose of insulting or wounding you. I intended by it only to say that your understanding of the Constitution is very different from mine; and I will say to you what, but for my rudeness, I should not have said, that I believe you to be honest . . . But an understanding of the Constitution different from mine I cannot overlook, because the Constitution, to be worth anything, must be held sacred, and rigidly observed in all its provisions. The man who wields power and misinterprets it is the more dangerous the more honest he is."

"I admit the truth of all you say, but there must be some mistake about it, for I do not remember that I gave any vote last winter upon any Constitutional question."

"No, Colonel, there's no mistake. Though I live here in the backwoods and seldom go from home, I take the papers from Washington and read very carefully all the proceedings in Congress. My papers say that last winter you voted for a bill to appropriate $20,000 to some suffers [sufferers] by a fire in Georgetown. Is that true?"

"Well, my friend, I may as well own up. You have got me there. But certainly nobody will complain that a great and rich country like ours should give the insignificant sum of $20,000 to relieve its suffering women and children, particularly with a full and overflowing Treasury, and I am sure, if you had been there, you would have done just as I did."

"It is not the amount, Colonel, that I complain of; it is the principle. In the first place, the government ought to have in the Treasury no more than enough for its legitimate purposes. But that has nothing to do with the question. The power of collecting and disbursing money at pleasure is the most dangerous power that can be entrusted to man, particularly under our system of collecting revenue by tariff, which reaches every man in the country, no matter how poor he may be, and the poorer he is the more he pays in proportion to his means. What is worse, it presses upon him without his knowledge where the weight centers, for there is not a man in the United States who can ever guess how much he pays to the government. So you see, that while you are contributing to relieve one, you are drawing it from thousands who are even worse off than he. If you had the right to give anything, the amount was simply a matter of discretion with you, and you had as much right to give $20,000,000 as $20,000. If you have the right to give to one, you have the right to give to all; and, as the Constitution neither defines charity nor stipulates the amount, you are at liberty to give to anything and everything which you may believe, or profess to believe, is a charity, and to any amount you may think proper. You will very easily perceive what a wide door this would open for fraud and corruption and favoritism, on the one hand, and for robbing the people on the other. No, Colonel, Congress has no right to give charity. Individual members may give as much of their own money as they please, but they have no right to touch a dollar of the public money for that purpose. If twice as many houses had been burned in this county as in Georgetown, neither you nor any other member of Congress would have thought of appropriating a dollar for our relief. There are about two hundred and forty members of Congress. If they had shown their sympathy for the suffers [sufferers] by contributing each one week's pay, it would have made over $13,000. There are plenty of men in and around Washington who could have given $20,000 without depriving themselves of even a luxury of life. The congressmen chose to keep their own money, which, if reports be true, some of them spend not very creditable; and the people about Washington, no doubt, applauded you for relieving them from the necessity of giving by giving what was not yours to give. The people have delegated to Congress, by the Constitution, the power to do certain things. To do these, it is authorized to collect and pay moneys, and for nothing else. Everything beyond this is usurpation, and a violation of the Constitution. So you see, Colonel, you have violated the Constitution in what I consider a vital point. It is a precedent fraught with danger to the country, for when Congress once begins to stretch it's [its] power beyond the limits of the Constitution, there is no limit to it, and no security for the people. I have no doubt you acted honestly, but that does not make it any better, except as far as you are personally concerned, and you see that I cannot vote for you."

I tell you I felt streaked . . . I could not answer him, for the fact is, I was so fully convinced that he was right, I did not want to. But I must satisfy him, and I said to him: "Well, my friend, you hit the nail upon the head when you said I did not have sense enough to understand the Constitution. I intended to be guided by it, and thought I had studied it fully. I have heard many speeches in Congress about the powers of Congress, but what you have said here at your plow has got more hard, sound sense in it than all the fine speeches I ever heard. If I had ever taken the view of it that you have, I would have put my head into the fire before I would have given that vote; and if I ever vote for another unconstitutional law I wish I may be shot."

Profile: Zuhdi Jasser

Dr. Zuhdi Jasser's record of service to his community and his country is prolific. As a former lieutenant commander in the United States Navy, Dr. Jasser served eleven years as a medical officer. A devout Muslim, Dr. Jasser founded the American Islamic Forum for Democracy (AIFD) after the terrorist attacks on September 11, 2001. He is not afraid to denounce the political extremists in Islam who threaten and attack the innocent citizens of the United States and other countries around the world. He has testified before Congress and spoken at hundreds of national events. He is a man of political courage and conviction, and I wish there were more men like him.

They called Dr. Zuhdi Jasser a dog. The cartoon was bold. Crudely drawn, it showed up in the *Muslim Voice* newspaper in Phoenix, Arizona.

Jasser was pictured down on all fours, as a canine, with a leash tied around his neck, being led by the *Arizona Republic* newspaper.

The message was clear. The ex-director of a local branch of the Islamist organization CAIR (Council on American-Islamic Relations) drew the comic. He was saying that Jasser was an instrument of the media, a token Muslim who would toe the line, say what conservatives wanted said, and had no business referring to himself as a true Muslim.

And it did more than simply mock Jasser for his unorthodox views on the role of Islam in America—the needed separation between mosque and state. In Islamic culture, calling someone a dog is one of the worst insults possible. Men are drummed out of office and polite society for racial insults and slurs far less than the one hurled at Jasser.

In his hometown, this is the reception that Jasser receives. The local imams try to marginalize him. They want him to be silent. But this soft-spoken doctor from Wisconsin, this son of Syrian immigrants, won't stop speaking. His voice rings through the radio and his face frequents television. He testifies in DC on the dangers of radical Islam.

He thinks someone within the Muslim community has to speak out, to denounce the violence, the suicide bombs, and the mentality that considers execution an acceptable punishment for blasphemy. Someone has to say that a society in which women receive half the rights of men is not acceptable.

Dr. Jasser is the founder of the American Islamic Forum for Democracy. This organization is dedicated to "the preservation of the founding principles of the United States Constitution, liberty and freedom, through the separation of mosque and state"—Jasser wants to cultivate "Jeffersonian Muslims."

This means that while Jasser prays five times a day and seeks to devotedly practice his religious beliefs, he doesn't believe that what happens at the mosque should rule the actions of the state. He believes that Muslims should be allowed to practice their beliefs alongside any other religion. According to Jasser, there is to be no institution of a state religion and no coercion or imposition of forced religious behavior. Faith is a choice, not a command.

"If we believe that faith is a choice, then you have to live in the laboratory which gives you that choice," said Jasser. "If you don't live in that laboratory, then you've negated faith and it's no longer faith; it becomes coercion and that's no longer religion."

In the laboratory of America, that seems like a clear distinction, and Jasser and many moderate Muslims claim that freedom of choice and plurality of belief can coexist. But that belief seems at odds with what shows up on the news and the daily actions of some Islamic nations around the world. The Arabic word *islam* means "submission to the will of God," and for some Muslim extremists, the will of God includes oppressing and putting to death nonbelievers.

Facing oppression and persecution isn't something new for the Jasser family. Zuhdi's father Muhammed Kais—MK for short—was a dissident in Syria, a rebellious student standing up to a dictatorship. Wracked by coups, Syria was held hostage by radicals who filled the ranks of the military. His grandfather, whom Zuhdi is named after, was a business owner who bounced in and out of house arrest. Each time Zuhdi's grandfather penned a newspaper column, even under a pseudonym, he was arrested.

And when the Jasser family came to the United States of America, they were captivated by the freedom and tolerance shown by this nation, written into the governing documents and preserved by the military. In America, the military was not a service reserved for the lower classes, but rather an honor, a sacred trust safeguarding liberty. The reason that even the highest members of Congress helped nominate individuals to the academies was to preserve core principles of freedom and justice.

"I was raised with the sense that serving in the military was the highest honor," said Jasser. "You gave back to God through charity and prayer and devotionals and being true to yourself. You are to give back to your family, children—give more than you receive—and that it was the same thing with your country as well."

Patriotism and love of country were taught to Jasser from his earliest days. His parents stressed pride in civic service, the value of hard work, and the importance of voting. Jasser attended the University of Wisconsin. Accepted into medical school, he chose to serve in the U.S. Navy as a medical officer. Jasser served on the USS *El Paso* after serving in Somalia. As a Muslim, these were formative days cementing his view of America as a liberating force for good, not a country looking for empires or colonies.

"I learned about values of Americans on board that ship," said Jasser, who earned the rank of lieutenant commander. "I learned about the diversity and the open-mindedness of the nation from the people around me."

Jasser returned to the United States and finished a residency at Bethesda Naval

Hospital. He served in the Office of the Attending Physician to the United States Congress, taking care of members of Congress and the Supreme Court, and developed relationships with some of the members of the highest government seats in the United States.

"When I served Congress, my parents realized the American dream," said Jasser. "This is a country that would allow any individual who performed well, who was honest and who worked hard and who loved this country to be rewarded and recognized for that. The pride that they had, it was an honor and a culmination of my navy years."

Jasser participated in the American experience—he saw how it worked, its merits, its shortcomings, and he's fought back as he watched the conflict develop between Islamist extremism and that set of ideals.

"Americans understand how you can have a tandem devout law and society without having a religious government," said Jasser. "Muslims don't get that."

Muslim society unites religion and government—the mosque is the state. For Jasser, this springs out of an incorrect view of the Koran, a hyper-literal reading that ignores the historical context of many of the commands.

"All religions, you need to separate history from religion," said Jasser. "The text of the Koran has a lot of practices and things that were specifically related to the time from 610 to 630. As a result, the Prophet wore three hats, he was a messenger of God, he was a head of a military, and he was a head of state." This threefold role meant to Jasser that Muhammed saw no separation of church and state.

"Scripture can be reinterpreted based on the times," said Jasser. "The Koran doesn't talk about government. It's the discussions of the Prophet that some of us reformists think are the main problem. It isn't scripture but rather oral tradition that needs to be discarded and is the main obstacle. Most of what's mainly black-and-white draconian interpretations of the Koran, are just that, interpretations. And some of those are called religious law or *sharia*. It's man's law. It's man's interpretation of God's law."

And when it comes to Islam's interaction with other religions, Jasser doesn't believe in antagonism.

"The relationship with God is not an exclusivist one," said Jasser. "There are many pathways to heaven and Islam is not the only one—Judaism and Christianity, and there are others, pathways to the same God—and I in no way believe in evangelism for our faith. I believe it's simply a personal relationship with God and whatever avenue you choose is fine."

His view apparently is not widely shared. He is pushed on whether what he calls the Muslim faith is truly the Muslim faith, or just a sanitized and modified evolution from a man not qualified to interpret the Koran.

"The beauty of America is that you have to convince me based on your reason," said Jasser. "If you have disagreement with something that I say, pull out the passage in the Koran and correct me."

The pushback against Jasser's ideas has been hard though.

"It takes a toll on the family," said Jasser. "There's the time away from daily routines, social pressures. Tribalism exists within Arabic and Muslim society. It makes things hard. Marriage is partnership and my wife sees all this investment, the time I put in, the criticism I receive, and she wonders sometimes, what return do you get on this?"

So far, even Jasser—a man endowed with what seems to be a ceaseless supply of optimism, a belief in the American capacity to change and grow—would admit any return is very small.

But he keeps fighting.

"If our ideas take hold, it threatens the entire power structure. The leaders of the mosques don't want that . . . I'll keep going forward until I know that I've succeeded, that the snowball has started going down the hill and getting larger. We're still trying to pack it together, much less roll it down the hill."

It's this type of attitude that makes Jasser just the type of man Alexis de Tocqueville might have admired. When de Tocqueville crossed the Atlantic in 1831, the twenty-five-year-old Frenchman was struck by the power of individuals working together to effect change.

"Americans of all ages, all conditions and all minds are constantly joining together in groups," wrote de Tocqueville in *Democracy in America*. "If, finally, they wish to publicize a truth or foster a sentiment with the help of a great example, they associate."

Other countries might see change pushed down from the top, through the actions of the aristocrats and wealthy—in America, even the smallest person can effect change. These associations are what have helped push change through American society. Community action committees, neighborhood organizations, and local churches all provide grassroots means for effecting very real change. It always starts small, just one person meeting with another, and, if the cause is valid, then conversation by conversation more people will come on board. Eventually a critical mass is reached, and some type of change happens.

With Jasser, the battle against the violence of radical Islam moves slowly. The insults keep flying, the hate speech fills the Internet, but he keeps talking. It's the hope that the right ears will be listening, that reason will triumph over centuries of violent tradition, and that he can persuade just one person at a time to become one of his "Jeffersonian Muslims."

It's not the easiest path, but it's the only one he can walk.

"If it was just for me selfishly, I don't have any conflict between my faith and my country," said Jasser. "If I was selfish, I would just say, these guys are crazy and hopefully our military will get them. But I'm worried about our security and that our children won't have anyone to learn from so they will learn the proper relationship with God. I'm going to have to answer to God for my actions, and so I keep on."

—— ❧ ——

The Athenian Oath

The young men of ancient Athens repeated the Athenian Oath when they reached the age of seventeen. The essence of the oath emphasizes loyalty and obligation to the *polis* and its citizens.

We will never bring disgrace on this our City by an act of dishonesty or cowardice. We will fight for the ideals and Sacred Things of the City both alone and with many.

We will revere and obey the City's laws, and will do our best to incite a like reverence and respect in those above us who are prone to annul them or set them at naught.

We will strive increasingly to quicken the public's sense of civic duty.

Thus in all these ways we will transmit this City, not only not less, but greater and more beautiful than it was transmitted to us.

"A Politician and a Hero"

RICHARD J. HINTON

Politicians don't always have the cleanest reputations. Known for patronage, corruption, and swindling, a few disreputable politicians have ruined the public's perception of many admirable public servants. Here is one story of the late Senator John P. Jones, who served from 1873 to 1903 in the United States Senate. He was not only a politician but also a hero.

I t was an election day in Nevada, back in the seventies [1870s]. The result of the election meant the reelection or defeat of John P. Jones, then and now United States Senator from that state. A witty Irishman was asked why he, a Democrat, should be so fast a friend of a rigid Republican such as the Senator then was.

"Sure," said the miner in reply, "why shouldn't I work for the man who saved my life? There's never a mining man in Nevada old enough to remember but what votes for John P. just as long as he wants a vote. It's not politics, sir, it's pure love of the man. How was it? Well, he came here first as superintendent of the Crown Point and Kaintuck [Kentucky] mines. He was liked from the first. It was him that originated eight-hour shifts—three tricks for the men in each twenty-four. But that's not what did it. One day the alarm was raised of fire in the Kaintuck, on the ten-hundred-foot level. You know, sir, how cuts, drifts, and levels are shored-up. There's wood enough down in the Comstock to build another place like 'Frisco. Now, a fire is a serious thing, especially if it gets into the metals—the ore-veins, I mean. The flame decomposes them very rapidly, and the galleries fill with poisonous gases. It was soon seen that this fire meant business.

"The first man to enter the cage was Superintendent Jones. Other men went down with him. The cage works by hydraulic pressure, and there was the danger, soon seen, that the flames might reach the pipes and prevent its working. The Senator is a big, broad-shouldered, and deep-chested man. He has the clear head sure, and no better miner is there alive than he. There was a lot of men down below when the alarm came, but they soon got up—all but nineteen; and I was one of them, foreman of the gang furdest away from the shaft, nearest to the fire. It got hold of the timbers, and in the dryest of the levels. We fought our way to air. With several others, I was soon overcome. Then the timbers behind us began to fall in, and the roof caved, increasing the gas. The last I remember distinctly was Jones's cheery voice shouting to keep up our courage.

"It was a long day and a night. The cage was fortunately able to run. Man after man among the rescuers became affected by the fumes, but the superintendent remained active and untiring. He helped to drag out and send up the men who were overcome and the men also that were rescued. Timbers were cut away, Jones at the front always—every man swears to that. Air was pumped in; water used to flood, and, step by step, the rescue party got eighteen out of the most dangerous places. I was one of the last.

"It came about that the fire took fresh hold. There was only one man left, and it was declared that life would be sacrificed in any effort to rescue him. Jones stepped on the cage. The man who run it had keeled over with the gas, and could not work. A volunteer was called for. None of the men responded. At last a boy of sixteen (Jim Hudson was his name, I think) got in. The Senator hesitated; but as there was no one else, down they went. At the mouth of the shaft there was agony; but at last the bell was heard, and up shot the cage, the gas fumes behind it, and smell of fire close to the works. It came swiftly; and when eager hands clutched at the door the boy lay huddled up; and the superintendent, scorched by the flame and gasping for breath, holding the limp figure of a man by one arm as he worked the elevator cable by the other hand, stumbled out and fell prone on the shaft-house floor. The boy was pulled out quickly, and only just in time, for the cage fell quite a distance. A few moments later all three would have died.

"The man recovered, and the boy was soon about. But the Senator long after felt the effects. Don't you think we are all right in being willing to give him a Senatorship, if we have the chance, for every one of them nineteen lives he saved?"

Thus it comes about that John P. Jones has sat in the United States Senate for over twenty-six years, and will be there for thirty if he lives to fill his term.

From *Politics*

ARISTOTLE

Long before the conception of social contract theory and democratic government, the ancient Greeks laid the foundation for Western political thought and governance. Aristotle, the famous Greek philosopher, was influential in developing the idea of the *polis*, or city-state, in which each man played a part in deciding the fate of the community. In his work *Politics*, Aristotle explains the building blocks of society and how men should rightly govern themselves.

Every state is a community of some kind, and every community is established with a view to some good; for mankind always act in order to obtain that which they think good. But, if all communities aim at some good, the state or political community, which is the highest of all, and which embraces all the rest, aims, and in a greater degree than any other, at the highest good.

Now there is an erroneous opinion that a statesman, king, householder, and master are the same, and that they differ, not in kind, but only in the number of their subjects. For example, the ruler over a few is called a master: over more, the manager of a household; over a still larger number, a statesman or king, as if there were no difference between a great household and a small state. The distinction which is made between the king and the statesman is as follows: When the government is personal, the ruler is a king; when, according to the principles of the political science, the citizens rule and are ruled in turn, then he is called a statesman.

But all this is a mistake; for governments differ in kind, as will be evident to any one who considers the matter according to the method which has hitherto guided us. As in other departments of science, so in politics, the compound should always be resolved into the simple elements or least parts of the whole. We must therefore look at the elements of which the state is composed, in order that we may see in what they differ from one another, and whether any scientific distinction can be drawn between the different kinds of rule . . .

When several villages are united in a single community, perfect and large enough to be nearly or quite self-sufficing, the state comes into existence, originating in the bare needs of life, and continuing in existence for the sake of a good life. And therefore, if the earlier forms of society are natural, so is the state for it is the end of them, and the [completed] nature is the end. For what each thing is when fully developed, we call its nature, whether we are speaking of a man, a horse, or a family. Besides, the final cause and end of a thing is the best, and to be self-sufficing is the end and the best.

Hence it is evident that the state is a creation of nature, and that man is by nature a political animal. And he who by nature and not by mere accident is without a state, is either above humanity, or below it; he is the "Tribeless, lawless, hearthless one," whom Homer denounces—the outcast who is a lover of war; he may be compared to an unprotected piece in the game of draughts.

Now the reason why man is more of a political animal than bees or any other gregarious animals is evident. Nature, as we often say, makes nothing in vain, and man is the only animal whom she has endowed with the gift of speech. And whereas mere sound is but an indication of pleasure or pain, and is therefore found in other animals (for their nature attains to the perception of pleasure and pain and the intimation of them to one another, and no further), the power of speech is intended to set forth the expedient and inexpedient, and likewise the just and the unjust. And it is a characteristic of man that he alone has any sense of good and evil, of just and unjust, and the association of living beings who have this sense makes a family and a state.

Thus the state is by nature clearly prior to the family and to the individual, since the whole is of necessity prior to the part; for example, if the whole body be destroyed, there will be no foot or hand, except in an equivocal sense, as we might speak of a stone hand; for when destroyed the hand will be no better. But things are defined by their working and power; and we ought not to say that they are the same when they are no longer the same, but only that they have the same name. The proof that the state is a creation of nature and prior to the individual is that the individual, when isolated, is not self-sufficing; and therefore he is like a part in relation to the whole. But he who is unable to live in society, or who has no need because he is sufficient for himself, must be either a beast or a god: he is no part of a state. A social instinct is implanted in all men by nature, and yet he who first founded the state was the greatest of benefactors. For man, when perfected, is the best of animals, but, when separated from law and justice, he is the worst of all; since armed injustice is the more dangerous, and he is equipped at birth with the arms of intelligence and with moral qualities which he may use for the worst ends.

"A Nation's Strength"

RALPH WALDO EMERSON

A nation is composed of thousands or millions of people of different qualities, character, and backgrounds; so what makes one nation stronger than another? Ralph Waldo Emerson, one of the most significant American essayists, poets, and philosophers of the nineteenth century, believed in the power of individualism. Emerson held that the collective strength of great and powerful men is what makes their nation great.

What builds the nation's pillars high
And its foundations strong?
What makes it mighty to defy
The foes that 'round it throng?
It is not gold. Its kingdoms grand
Go down in battle shock;
Its shafts are laid on sinking sand,
Not on abiding rock.
Is it the sword? Ask the red dust
Of empires passed away;
The blood has turned their stones to rust,
Their glory to decay.
And is it pride? Ah! that bright crown
Has seemed to nations sweet;
But God has struck its luster down
In ashes at his feet.

Not gold but only men can make
A people great and strong;
Men who for truth and honor's sake
Stand fast and suffer long.
Brave men who work while others sleep,
Who dare while others fly . . .
They build a nation's pillars deep
And lift them to the sky.

— ❧ —

Profile: A Navy SEAL

On May 1, 2011, under the cover of night, four helicopters carrying U.S. Navy SEALs took off from Afghanistan on the most important mission of their lives. Their target was a large, walled compound in Abbottabad, Pakistan, thought to be the home of Osama bin Laden, leader of the terrorist organization al-Qaeda and responsible for the deaths of thousands of innocent civilians. For almost ten years the hunt for bin Laden had gone cold. Now the SEALs had one chance at America's most wanted man.

The helicopters slipped undetected past the watch of Pakistani radar and approached the compound. A team of SEALs of the United States Naval Special Warfare Development Group (DEVGRU) fast-roped out of their Blackhawk helicopters. At approximately 1:00 a.m., local time, the SEALs blasted a hole in the concrete walls around the compound and began the raid, not knowing what they were about to encounter.

After gunning down several combatants and restraining the remaining inhabitants, the SEALs made their way to the third floor of the compound. Here they stood face-to-face with bin Laden. Their encounter lasted only seconds. A double tap—one shot to the chest and one to the skull—and bin Laden was dead. The raid lasted forty minutes. No SEALs were killed, and bin Laden had been eliminated. Once again, the U.S. Navy SEALs had proven their title as the world's most elite soldiers.

Navy SEALs operate outside the limits of modern life. They are physical specimens, highly trained to fulfill their mission at any cost. They don't ask questions and
they don't take credit. You will find them in the darkest corners of the world bringing
justice to the wicked and peace to the suffering.

We might never know the identity of the men who killed Osama bin Laden. To
them, the credit is expendable, and the cause is everything. But we do know the story
of fellow SEALs, and their stories are worth our attention, gratitude, and admiration. They teach us what boys can become and what men can do in service to their
country.

Eric Greitens, lieutenant commander, U.S. Navy SEALs, is author of *The Heart
and the Fist*. Today, Greitens travels the world to serve his country as both a humanitarian, serving afflicted people, and as a fighter, removing the afflicters.

In an interview, Greitens explained to me what makes the SEALs such an estimable and imitable group of men. "What really makes a SEAL is what they have in
their heart," Greitens said. "SEALs really have that heart that allows them even at
a moment of great challenge to be able to serve others, and it's kind of a warrior's
heart."

Service is what sets the SEALs apart, and it's a motif in Greiten's life that eventually led him to the Navy SEALs. For example, when Greitens was only sixteen
years old, his Sunday school teacher took him to a homeless shelter in downtown St.
Louis, not to give out food, but to spend the night and see what his fellow men were
experiencing. That one night left a lasting impression on him.

Fast-forward several years and Greitens has gone from the dingy, dirty homeless shelter to the impoverished countryside of Croatia. While doing humanitarian
work for the Croatian people, he came across a man who stopped him in his tracks.
Greitens still remembers what the Croatian said to him: "If you really cared about us
you would be willing to protect us."

Greitens realized there was more he could do to help these people. He went on
to become a Rhodes Scholar at Oxford University, and with the intention of broadening his service he studied the politics of developing countries. Still this was not
enough for him. As he stared at the pillars around the Rhodes house, he noticed,
etched into the walls, the names of former Rhodes Scholars who had given their lives
in service to their country in the World Wars.

It was at this moment that Greitens recognized that there was more of himself to give. He decided to join the U.S. Navy. When he first enlisted they offered him the small sum of $1,332.60 per month and one chance at Basic Underwater Demolition/SEAL training (BUD/S). He knew his odds of becoming a SEAL were slim. About 80 percent of those who apply to BUD/S drop out because of the almost unbearable training procedures. Yet Greitens recognized that "the military was going to give me very little, but would make me more."

Greitens passed BUD/S and began his career as a SEAL, traveling all over the world for humanitarian work and classified government missions. As *The Heart and the Fist* explains, his job as a SEAL requires both compassion (the heart) and courage (the fist). "Our compassion provides our direction and courage is what we need every day to walk that path," remarked Greitens. "I've also found that my service, and any service that we do to others and for others, also makes us more."

The SEALs bring out the best in men—physically, mentally, and spiritually. "So many of these young men came to BUD/S in a way because they wanted to pass this great test," observed Greitens. "And we live in an America that offers its young men very few tests, very few cultural markers through which they can, to which on the other end they can say, 'You know what, I've become a better person, I've become a man.'"

Men long for ways to prove themselves. If schools, parents, and churches don't find a way to push men, they will push themselves, often into gangs or other unholy alliances.

"Do I have what it takes? Every boy does want to answer that question," said Greitens. "They will find a way to get that answer for themselves and if that means getting themselves in trouble and trying to break the law, they will do that. We have to find a way to channel that energy in a positive way."

The U.S. Navy SEALs are a cultural example our men long for.

"Aristotle talked about the fact that you know what the good thing is by seeing what the good man does," said Greitens. "We need to have those good examples and we need to have those kinds of cultural means and methods for young men to grow into responsible, mature, caring, strong men."

While the SEALs represent the extreme ends of manhood, they exemplify virtues all men can emulate. Greitens's résumé might be awe-inspiring, from Rhodes

Scholar to Navy SEAL, but at his core he is a servant. Loyalty, determination, compassion, and courage—these are just a few of the characteristics that make a SEAL. They are not cold-blooded killers, but a force for good in a world of evil.

"Of the Beginning of Political Societies"

JOHN LOCKE

John Locke (1632-1704) was an English philosopher and writer, regarded as one of the most influential Enlightenment thinkers. His contributions in social contract theory to classical republicanism are reflected heavily in the American Declaration of Independence. Locke's *The Second Treatise of Civil Government* outlines a theory of political or civil society based on natural rights and contract theory—a foundational argument to the idea of a democracy. More hopeful of human nature and community than Thomas Hobbes, he was more influential on our Founders. Here is the argument for the notion that each man has an obligation to the polis.

Men being, as has been said, by nature, all free, equal, and independent, no one can be put out of this estate, and subjected to the political power of another, without his own consent. The only way whereby any one divests himself of his natural liberty, and puts on the bonds of civil society, is by agreeing with other men to join and unite into a community for their comfortable, safe, and peaceable living one amongst another, in a secure enjoyment of their properties, and a greater security against any, that are not of it. This any number of men may do, because it injures not the freedom of the rest; they are left as they were in the liberty of the state of nature. When any number of men have so consented to make one community or government, they are thereby presently incorporated, and make one body politic, wherein the majority have a right to act and conclude the rest.

For when any number of men have, by the consent of every individual, made a community, they have thereby made that community one body, with a power to act as one body, which is only by the will and determination of the majority: for that which acts any community, being only the consent of the individuals of it, and it being necessary to that which is one body to move one way; it is necessary the body should move that way whither the greater force carries it, which is the consent of the majority: or else it is impossible it should act or continue one body, one community, which the consent of every individual that united into it, agreed that it should; and so every one is bound by that consent to be concluded by the majority. And therefore we see, that in assemblies, impowered to act by positive laws, where no number is set by that positive law which impowers them, the act of the majority passes for the act of the whole, and of course determines, as having, by the law of nature and reason, the power of the whole.

And thus every man, by consenting with others to make one body politic under one government, puts himself under an obligation, to every one of that society, to submit to the determination of the majority, and to be concluded by it; or else this original compact, whereby he with others incorporates into one society, would signify nothing, and be no compact, if he be left free, and under no other ties than he was in before in the state of nature. For what appearance would there be of any compact? what new engagement if he were no farther tied by any decrees of the society, than he himself thought fit, and did actually consent to? This would be still as great a liberty, as he himself had before his compact, or any one else in the state of nature hath, who may submit himself, and consent to any acts of it if he thinks fit.

———

Whosoever therefore out of a state of nature unite into a community, must be understood to give up all the power, necessary to the ends for which they unite into society, to the majority of the community, unless they expressly agreed in any number greater than the majority. And this is done by barely agreeing to unite into one political society, which is all the compact that is, or needs be, between the individuals, that enter into, or make up a commonwealth. And thus that, which begins and actually constitutes any political society, is nothing but the consent of any number of freemen capable of a majority to unite and incorporate into such a society. And this is that, and that only, which did, or could give beginning to any lawful government in the world.

Profile: Dave Pereda

Often, the unsung heroes of everyday life are the men and women in uniform who serve their country and fellow man—police, firefighters, soldiers, doctors, nurses, and so on. Without them, our society would descend into chaos and disorder. Men like Dave Pereda protect and defend America's families and homes, both domestically and internation-ally. They are a vital example of service and sacrifice—one that makes our lives better and safer every day. I heard of Dave and his story through my radio show.

From deployment in unstable and war-ridden nations like North Africa, Bosnia, and Israel in the early 1990s, to cleaning up rubble at Ground Zero after September 11, to patrolling the streets of New Orleans after Hurricane Katrina, to running more than two hundred combat missions in Iraq, when his country called, Dave Pereda answered.

Born as an American citizen in Caracas, Venezuela, Pereda spent most of his young life growing up in south Florida as he and his family moved from town to town; his father worked for oil companies. Moving from city to city, Pereda grew up in various high-crime neighborhoods. "Most of my friends that I grew up with are either dead or in jail or on their way to one or the other. A few of them made it out okay," Pereda said. After graduating from high school, Pereda enlisted in the United States Marines. "I had a desire to serve my country and also get out of the environment I grew up in," he said.

Without the money for college, and itching with a desire to serve his country, Pereda began a four-year tour as a corporal in the Marines. In only four years, he traveled the world, serving in North Africa, Israel, Bosnia, the Philippines, and different parts of Europe and the Mediterranean.

In 1994, Pereda left the Marines and started college through the GI Bill. He worked odd jobs, like landscaping and bartending, all the while working toward a career in law enforcement. In January 1998, he was hired by the Clifton, New Jersey, police department.

Since January 5, 1998, Pereda has served the people of New Jersey, sharing time as a detective and an officer on patrol—by "taking out New Jersey's trash" as he likes to say. While working at the bureau, he often investigated as many as forty active cases at the same time. "I'd drive home, walk in the door, and the phone would ring and I'd have to get back in the car and [go] right back to work."

Then in 2007, Pereda did something even more remarkable. He enlisted in the New Jersey Army National Guard Reserve knowing that the probability of getting called up to active duty in either Iraq or Afghanistan was very high. With a wife who was battling medical issues and a six-year-old daughter, Pereda's decision caught his friends and family off guard.

"From the day I got out, I've always kind of had a little draw to continue serving," he said, "but I was working on my career and other issues prevented me. Our country was at war and I believe in our country and I believe in the cause. I've always had that desire to serve, and I finally got an opportunity to join back up. I wanted to do my part in the effort, so I enlisted."

By June 2008, Pereda was activated for deployment to Iraq. As a sergeant and squad leader of the 2nd Battalion, 113th Infantry of the New Jersey Army National Guard, he led a platoon of twelve men. As an ISR (Intelligence Surveillance and Reconnaissance) platoon, Pereda and his men conducted 212 combat missions in the Basra Province in a ten-month period. Despite constant rocket attacks, skirmishes, and IEDs, Pereda's platoon was never hit directly.

While serving in Iraq, Pereda and his men went above and beyond their military obligations. They drove through different cities and neighborhoods and gave Iraqi children school supplies, papers, and soccer balls—often the first toys these boys and girls had ever held. As intelligence officers, Pereda's platoon's job was to cultivate trust with the Iraqi people by interacting with them. After meeting with the Iraqi police and highway patrol, they organized a local platoon used-boot drive to help the Iraqi policemen who were often working checkpoints in torn-up sandals. They repaired one of the local water purification plants and rebuilt one of the Iraqi army outposts.

"Granted, I'm a Christian and they're Muslims, but the bottom line is that most people over there want what we want, and that is a better life for their family and their kids," said Pereda. It turns out his service to the local Iraqis paid off in more ways than he imagined.

On November 10, 2008, a notorious detainee escaped from the detention facility where Pereda was stationed. "This guy was just pure evil," said Pereda. "He was completely fearless and he could care less if he got recaptured." The alarm was quickly spread throughout the area for the escapee, who was known for beheading his victims.

After hitching a ride with a local, the detainee hoped to escape through nearby checkpoints and into the countryside. But through the work of vigilant Iraqi policemen, many of them trained by Pereda and his company, the vehicle was identified and stopped before the detainee could escape.

While stories like this happen every day in Iraq, Pereda will be the first to admit that it's an uphill battle. "I believe in the cause and the effort and my country. I have a lot of pride in serving my country. Even though there's a saying the Marines wrote on a wall during the battle of Fallujah. It said, 'America is not at war; the military is at war; America's at the mall.'"

Whatever the cause and whatever the need, Pereda will continue to serve his country and his community. He said, "I look at it as a blessing. God gave me the ability and put me in the right places to be there to help in whatever capacity I could, as small as it may be in the grand schemes." Ask those Iraqi policemen, a stranded family in New Orleans, or the community of Clifton, New Jersey, and they will tell you that Pereda's service is anything but small.

Yet, as he reflected on society's current psyche, Pereda worried about the attitudes of modern men. He said, "I feel like our society is trending in a direction where it's all about 'me.' It's not about helping others. Instead of it being, what can I do to make my world better? it's, what's in it for me?

"I've served in both the Marines and the army and when I look at some of the values and principles the military tries to instill in their soldiers and Marines, it is integrity, honor, and loyalty. To sum it up, it's someone doing the right thing, selfless service, and always putting others before you."

Looming on the horizon for Pereda is a potential deployment to Afghanistan within the next year. Whether or not the next chapter of his life finds him in Afghanistan or back patrolling the streets of Clifton, Pereda remains a public servant at heart, as evidenced by his words: "I believe a man should be someone who's strong in his convictions and someone who does the right thing even when no one is looking. If I'm not doing the right thing, how can I expect anyone else to do it? It starts with you."

National Greatness

PERICLES

Pericles' famous funeral oration (referenced in the chapter "Man in War") is included in Thucydides' *History of the Peloponnesian War*. Pericles, a prominent Athenian politician, delivered this speech at the end of the first year of the Peloponnesian War (431-404 BC) as a part of the annual public funeral for the war dead. In it Pericles espoused some of the earliest known views on public service and the idea of a man sacrificing himself for his city. The Corinthians, nearby enemies of the Athenians, said of their foes, "An Athenian spends himself in the service of the city, as if his body were not his own, and counts his mind most his own when it is employed upon her business." Following is an excerpt.

Your country has a right to your services in sustaining the glories of her position. These are a common source of pride to you all, and you cannot decline the burdens of empire and still expect to share its honours . . .

I am of the opinion that national greatness is more for the advantage of private citizens, than any individual well-being coupled with public humiliation. A man may be personally ever so well off, and yet if his country be ruined he must be ruined with it; whereas a flourishing commonwealth always affords chances of salvation to unfortunate individuals. A state can support the misfortunes of private citizens, while they cannot support hers.

"Love of Country"

SIR WALTER SCOTT

Sir Walter Scott (1771–1832) was a popular Scottish historical novelist, playwright, and poet. He was considered the first English-language author to have a truly international career in his lifetime, with many contemporary readers in Europe, Australia, and North America. His novels and poetry are still read today, and include famous works like *Ivanhoe* and *Rob Roy*. The following poem affirms that it is not unmanly to be patriotic and love your country.

BREATHES THERE THE MAN, WITH SOUL SO DEAD,
Who never to himself hath said,
   'This is my own, my native land!'
Whose heart hath ne'er within him burn'd
As home his footsteps he hath turn'd
   From wandering on a foreign strand!
If such there breathe, go, mark him well;
For him no Minstrel raptures swell;
High though his titles, proud his name,
Boundless his wealth as wish can claim;
Despite those titles, power, and pelf,
The wretch, concentred all in self,
Living, shall forfeit fair renown,
And, doubly dying, shall go down
To the vile dust, from whence he sprung,
Unwept, unhonour'd, and unsung.

— ❦ —

From *De Officiis* (On Duties)

MARCUS TULLIUS CICERO

In his *De Officiis* (On Duties), Roman philosopher Cicero explains why men join together in bonds to ensure their own survival. He sets forth an early social contract theory on the natural tendency of men to fight for survival by organizing into public assemblies to provide for themselves and the common good, and asserts that "we are not born for ourselves alone."

First of all, Nature has endowed every species of living creature with the instinct of self-preservation, of avoiding what seems likely to cause injury to life or limb, and of procuring and providing everything needful for life—food, shelter, and the like. A common property of all creatures is also the reproductive instinct (the purpose of which is the propagation of the species) and also a certain amount of concern for their offspring. But the most marked difference between man and beast is this: the beast, just as far as it is moved by the senses and with very little perception of past or future, adapts itself to that alone which is present at the moment; while man—because he is endowed with reason, by which he comprehends the chain of consequences, perceives the causes of things, understands the relation of cause to effect and of effect to cause, draws analogies, and connects and associates the present and the future—easily surveys the course of his whole life and makes the necessary preparations for its conduct strangely tender love for his offspring. She also prompts men to meet in companies, to form public assemblies and to take part in them themselves; and she further dictates, as a consequence of this, the effort on man's part to provide a store of things that minister to his comforts and wants—and not for himself alone, but for his wife and children and the others whom he holds dear and for whom he ought to provide; and this responsibility also stimulates his courage and makes it stronger for the active duties of life. Above all, the search after truth and its eager pursuit are peculiar to man. And so, when we have leisure from the demands of business cares, we are eager to see, to hear, to learn something new, and we esteem a desire to know the secrets or wonders of creation as indispensable to a happy life. Thus we come to understand that what is true, simple, and genuine appeals most strongly to a man's nature. To this passion for discovering truth there is added a hungering, as it were, for independence, so that a mind well-moulded by Nature is unwilling to be subject to anybody save one who gives rules of conduct or is a teacher of truth or who, for the general good, rules according to justice and law. From this attitude come greatness of soul and a sense of superiority to worldly conditions.

But since, as Plato has admirably expressed it, we are not born for ourselves alone, but our country claims a share of our being, and our friends a share; and since, as the Stoics hold, everything that the earth produces is created for man's use; and as men, too, are born for the sake of men, that they may be able mutually to help one another; in this direction we ought to follow Nature as our guide, to contribute to the general good by an interchange of acts of kindness, by giving and receiving, and thus by our skill, our industry, and our talents to cement human society more closely together, man to man.

"Power Tends to Corrupt"

LORD ACTON

In April 1887, John Emerich Edward Dalberg Acton penned a letter to the scholar Mandell Creighton. In it he expresses his belief that, more often than not, power leads to corruption in men. When used rightly, power can influence much good in this world, however, we must always be wary of the tendency for men to use their power for their own personal benefit, often to the detriment of others. Lord Acton is often misquoted as saying "power corrupts," when he actually said that "power tends to corrupt." There is a very important difference; power can be used for both good and evil. I have heard more than one young person say they did not want a career in public service or elected office because of reliance on this misquoting of Acton.

I cannot accept your canon that we are to judge Pope and King unlike other men with a favourable presumption that they did no wrong. If there is any presumption, it is the other way, against the holders of power, increasing as the power increases. Historic responsibility has to make up for the want of legal responsibility. Power tends to corrupt, and absolute power corrupts absolutely. Great men are almost always bad men, even when they exercise influence and not authority: still more when you superadd the tendency or certainty of corruption by full authority. There is no worse heresy than the fact that the office sanctifies the holder of it.

Lectures and Miscellanies

Henry James

In the following lectures, the American-born writer and novelist, Henry James (1843–1916), expressed his belief in the transformational power of society. It is through society that man develops identity, manners, and service to the world. Society forces a man to look outside himself and his own interest and focus on serving his fellow man.

The rule or fact in relation to our present social status is undeniable, that an extreme inequality prevails between the public and private element, and that our morality measures accordingly not the reconciliation of these interests, but the degree in which one allows itself to be depressed by the other. In a true fellowship of men, in a society which really deserved its name, the highest morality of course would be to maintain the rigid and undeviating harmony of these two elements. The public conscience in that case would disallow the slightest preponderance to either element, as an instant injury done the other. But our present social adjustment is so imperfect—the public and private interests of mankind are so poorly harmonized in our present society—that a man's morality is high in the exact ratio of his acquiescence in their disparity, in the exact ratio of his acquiescence in the exaltation of the public element over the private one. What enhances my morality, and my consequent claim upon public esteem, is not my genial humanity, or the relations of undeviating justice I maintain in my intercourse with my neighbors; but my willingness to spend and be spent for the interests of society, my willingness to sustain its existing institutions at whatever damage to my private interests ...

Society consequently is the instrument of this unity. It promotes the unity of man's inward and outward life, by enabling him to resist the despotism of the latter. For you all know that so long as one should recognize only sensual and finite good, only that good which stands in the gratification of his natural appetites, he would be utterly blind to infinite and spiritual good, that good which descends into the human mind from God, and inspires human action with a grace, with a dignity, with a beauty unknown to all lower life. In fact he would be a mere brute, minus the instinct which governs the brute, and keeps him sweet and quasi-orderly in his sphere. Society then, as I said, fits man for the recognition of this inward and infinite good, by enabling him to resist the domination of the outward or sensible sphere. The way it enables him to resist this domination, is by gradually supplying all his natural wants. It finds him in want of external blessing, destitute of the supply of his natural wants, and craving consequently above all things and before all things relief in that direction. Society ensures him such relief. Society, or the fellowship of his kind, enables him to overcome the poverty and inclemency of nature. What he could not do by himself, society enables him to do, namely, to achieve the supply of all his natural wants, and so rise above his original brutality, by finding leisure for the culture of his understanding, the refinement of his manners, and the pursuits of science and art ...

Such is the sole function of society, to lift man out of the bondage of nature, that he may become freely subject to God. Its office is not to elevate him out of natural bondage into social bondage, but into the freedom of God, into a life which cannot be corrupted, which cannot be defiled, and which shall never pass away.

"Hávamál"

These lines from the ancient Norse Poetic Edda, or Elder Edda, establish the need for community in the Norse mind. In their mind, no man was worse than he who betrayed his own people; no fate worse than being an outcast.

Young was I once, | and wandered alone,
And nought of the road I knew;
Rich did I feel | when a comrade I found,
For man is man's delight.
. . .

On the hillside drear | the fir-tree dies,
All bootless its needles and bark;
It is like a man | whom no one loves,—
Why should his life be long

From *A Man and His Money*

HARVEY REEVES CALKINS

Harvey Reeves Calkins was a stewardship secretary for the Methodist Episcopal Church. In his book *A Man and His Money*, targeted at clergy and church leaders, he argues that stewardship was "the very kernel of Christ's teaching." In this excerpt he argues that each man is called, first, to care for his family and, second, to tend to his city, state, and country. This excerpt includes something rare, a defense of taxes. Not many today would defend taxes as a way of honoring and maintaining "the glorious institutions of the Republic." Many of us believe there are way too many taxes in our time, but surely at least some few taxes serve this purpose, and we should be mindful of that.

The obligation of life covers a threefold duty of stewardship: First, provision for the family; second, maintenance of the state; third, relief of the poor.

The family must be first. Thus it is written, "God setteth the solitary in families"; and again it is written, "Children are an heritage of the Lord." The question has been carpingly asked, "Would you take bread from the children and give it to the church?" Such a question requires no answer. Rather let it be asked, "Should a man deny himself in order to render acknowledgment unto God, and should he teach fidelity and self-denial to his children?" The sincere question brings its own sincere answer. The only real difficulty that ever comes to a man is his failure to frame the sincere question . . .

The second element of stewardship in a man's obligation of life is maintenance of the state. It was the command of the apostle that "supplications, prayers, intercessions, and giving of thanks be made for all men, for kings, and for all that are in authority; that we may lead a quiet and peaceable life in all godliness and honesty." By "the state" is meant that remarkable fusion of federal, state, county, and municipal government, which, in America, is administered by those "in authority," that is, by the people themselves through their chosen representatives. A citizen's responsibility for taxes, rates, and assessments marks an element of stewardship which is not always recognized as such. Taxes are not infrequently resented as though they were an arbitrary imposition, laid upon one by "an outsider," something which it is a citizen's duty to resist. We pay our grocer bills with a sense of value received, but the cost of maintaining the glorious institutions of the republic is a weariness to us. Some day our citizenship shall be a finer thing. Stewardship is the kingly doorway into all the higher life of our civilization.

From "Acres of Diamonds"

RUSSELL CONWELL

Russell Herman Conwell (1843–1925), born in Massachusetts, was a Baptist minister and orator. He is best remembered as the founder and first president of Temple University in Philadelphia, Pennsylvania, and for his inspirational lecture "Acres of Diamonds," which he delivered more than five thousand times at various times and places between 1900 and 1925. The central idea of his speech is that one need not look elsewhere for opportunity, achievement, or fortune—the resources to achieve all good things are present in one's own community. Conwell elaborated on the theme through examples of success, genius, service, or other virtues involving ordinary Americans contemporary to his audience, culminating in the memorable line: "dig in your own backyard!" It was a speech directed to his backyard, to his fellow Philadelphians. To be great, Conwell says, must mean to be great [even] in Philadelphia! Be true to your city.

Young man, won't you learn a lesson in the primer of politics that it is a prima facie evidence of littleness to hold office under our form of government? Great men get into office sometimes, but what this country needs is men that will do what we tell them to do.

This nation—where the people rule—is governed by the people, for the people, and so long as it is, then the office-holder is but the servant of the people, and the Bible says the servant cannot be greater than the master. The Bible says, "He that is sent cannot be greater than Him who sent Him."

The people rule, or should rule, and if they do, we do not need the greater men in office. If the great men in America took our offices, we would change to an empire in the next ten years.

You think you are going to be made great by an office, but remember that if you are not great before you get the office, you won't be great when you secure it. It will only be a burlesque in that shape.

Greatness consists not in the holding of some future office, but in doing great deeds with little means and the accomplishment of vast purposes from the private ranks of life. To be great at all one must be great here, now, in Philadelphia.

If you wish to be great at all, you must begin where you are and what you are, in Philadelphia, now. He that can give to his city any blessing, he who can be a good citizen while he lives here, he that can make better homes, he that can be a blessing whether he works in the shop or sits behind the counter or keeps house, whatever be his life, he who would be great anywhere must first be great in his own Philadelphia...

Why isn't Philadelphia a greater city in its greater wealth? Why does New York excel Philadelphia? People say, "Because of her harbor." Why do many other cities of the United States get ahead of Philadelphia now? There is only one answer, and that is because our own people talk down their own city.

If there ever was a community on earth that has to be forced ahead, it is the city of Philadelphia. If we are to have a boulevard, talk it down; if we are going to have better schools, talk them down; if you wish to have wise legislation, talk it down; talk all the proposed improvements down. That is the only great wrong that I can lay at the feet of the magnificent Philadelphia that has been so universally kind to me.

I say it is time we turn around in our city and begin to talk up the things that are in our city, and begin to set them before the world as the people of Chicago, New York, St. Louis, and San Francisco do. Oh, if we only could get that spirit out among our people, that we can do things in Philadelphia and do them well!

Arise, ye millions of Philadelphians, trust in God and man, and believe in the great opportunities that are right here not over in New York or Boston, but here—for business, for everything that is worth living for on earth. There was never an opportunity greater. Let us talk up our own city.

Providing Leadership Where Needed Most: America's Youth

ERNEST G. GREEN

Ernest G. "Ernie" Green is the Co-Chairman of Madison Asset Management Group LLC in Washington DC. He is also a member of the "Little Rock Nine," the first group of African-American students to attend an all-white high school in Little Rock, Arkansas, in 1957. He also made history on May 27, 1958, when he became the first African-American to graduate from Little Rock's Central High School at a time when integration was at a crisis stage in this country. Green is a distinguished Eagle Scout and a recipient of the Congressional Gold Medal, the nation's highest civilian award in the United States. Here Green explains how Scouting trains boys to be leaders in their communities.

As a society, we are inundated every day with the notion of leadership to the point that I fear we have become somewhat immune to the true power of the word and what it means to be a "good" leader. Leaders can fall on both sides of the coin—good and evil—history bears witness to that. And just because you are a leader doesn't always mean that you are acting in the best interest of others. It is imperative that this distinction is made to younger generations before the notion of leadership gets further lost in translation.

And what we need more than ever are good leaders. For many, a turbulent economy has thrown any sense of normal family life into turmoil. Those already suffering because of broken homes or unemployment saw any chance of recovery slip even further away. Many of our younger generation have had to fend more for themselves as parents and guardians struggle to provide for the family. We need leaders that have qualities like trustworthy, helpful, kind, courteous, and brave. Do those traits sound familiar? They should because they are part of the foundation of what has been taught by the Boy Scouts of America for the last 100 years—the Scout Law.

Scouting provides that leadership. It is a place for our young people to join others to share life's challenges and learn the skills to improve their health and way of life. It provides a trail for accomplishment and confidence, for values and leadership, and guidance through the Scout Oath and Scout Law that has been the map and compass for young people for almost a century.

I am an Eagle Scout. I achieved the Eagle rank at age fifteen. At a young age, I had tough choices to make. As a member of the "Little Rock Nine," the first nine African-American students to attend Little Rock's all-white Central High School in 1957, I found myself at a crossroads that would greatly impact America as we know it today. At the time I didn't know that I was acting in a leadership capacity, and if it wasn't for Scouting, I may not have had the moral stamina or strength of character to walk up those school steps, enter those unfriendly hallways, and be the subject of curiosity—and yes, sometimes hatred—in those racially divided classrooms.

When I look back at those turbulent times, I will be forever grateful for the lessons Scouting taught me and the leadership skills that have served me well over the years. Those lessons taught me the importance of giving back, respecting myself and others and, today, of providing leadership to other young people who are grasping for some sense of normalcy and direction in their lives. . . .

Eleanor Roosevelt once said: "A good leader inspires people to have confidence in the leader; a great leader inspires people to have confidence in themselves."

It is incumbent upon all of us to follow the Scouting trail that helps build the confidence America's youth needs today. By doing so, we can all proudly take our place in history as supporters of Scouting, knowing that we helped mentor and develop America's next generation of great leaders. Scouting is relevant now more than ever.

The Duties of Citizenship

WILLIAM JENNINGS BRYAN

William Jennings Bryan (1860–1925) ran for the presidency three times yet never won. He is best known for arguing for the prosecution in the famous "Scopes Monkey Trial" of 1925. An ardent populist, Bryan championed the common man and his right to political freedom and economic prosperity.

In this, our land, we are called upon to give but little in return for the advantages which we receive. Shall we give that little grudgingly? Our definition of patriotism is often too narrow. Shall the lover of his country measure his loyalty only by his service as a soldier? No! Patriotism calls for the faithful and conscientious performance of all of the duties of citizenship, in small matters as well as great, at home as well as upon the tented field.

From *The Royal Art*

WILLIAM JENNINGS BRYAN

In his work *The Royal Art* (1914), Bryan outlined his theory of government and the citizen's obligations to it.

The fundamental principles of popular government, as they affect the methods employed and the participation of the people in them, may be set forth as follows:

1. The social ideal towards which the world is moving requires that human institutions shall approximate towards the divine measure of rewards and this can only be realized when each individual is able to draw from society a reward proportionate to his contribution to society.
2. The form of government which gives the best assurance of attaining to this ideal is the form in which the people rule—a government deriving its just powers from the consent of the governed.
3. The chief duty of governments, in so far as they are coercive, is to restrain those who would interfere with the inalienable rights of the individual, among which are the right to life, the right to liberty, the right to the pursuit of happiness, and the right to worship God according to the dictates of one's conscience.
4. In so far as governments are cooperative, they approach perfection in proportion as they adjust with justice the joint burdens which it is necessary to impose and distribute with equity the incidental benefits which come from the disbursement of the money raised by taxation.
5. Competition is so necessary a force in business that public ownership is imperative wherever competition is impossible. A private monopoly is indefensible and intolerable.
6. "Absolute acquiescence in the decision of the majority" is, as Jefferson declares, "the vital principle of republics, from which is no appeal but to force, the vital principle and immediate parent of despotism."
7. As acquiescence in the existence of a wrong is not to be expected, it is the duty of every citizen to assist in securing a free expression of the will of the people. No one can claim to be a good citizen who is indifferent.
8. The government being the people's business, it necessarily follows that its operations should be at all times open to the public view. Publicity is therefore as essential to honest administration as freedom of speech is to representative government. "Equal rights to all and special privileges to none" is the maxim which should control in all departments of government.

9. Each individual finds his greatest security in the intelligence and happiness of his fellows—the welfare of each being the concern of all, and he should therefore exert himself to the utmost to improve conditions and to elevate the level upon which all stand.

10. While scrupulously careful to live up to his responsibilities, the citizen should never forget that the larger part of every human life is lived outside of the domain of government, and that he renders the largest service to others when he brings himself into harmony with the law of God, who has made service the measure of greatness.

Cornerstone School

One of the responsibilities of men in the polis is to educate and nurture those in the community, especially the poor and underprivileged. Nowhere is it needed more than in many of America's large inner cities stricken with poverty and crime. Seeing the dire economic and educational conditions of many people in Washington DC, a group of Capitol Hill staffers took it upon themselves to start their own school. Here is the story of that school, taken from an exclusive interview David Wilezol, associate producer of my radio show, *Morning in America*, did with Cornerstone's executive director. As you will notice, Hanna and his teachers at Cornerstone are lifting up a generation of inner-city children through rigorous academic expectations and character education.

At the edge of a DC city block dotted with mildewed, two-story brick housing projects is Cornerstone School, a private Christian school located in a section of Southeast Washington known as Anacostia, one of the worst neighborhoods in America. Proclaiming its mission to "[bring] a Christ-centered, nurturing, and academically rigorous education to the children of Washington DC," Capitol Hill staffers started the school in 1988, after Congress discarded a report they had written on strategies for successful practices in urban schooling.

Cornerstone now boasts 152 students from pre-K through 10th grade . . .

Its executive director is Clay Hanna, a Bronze Star Army officer who served in more than six hundred combat patrols in Iraq and later trained peacekeepers in Burundi, Nigeria, Togo, and Rwanda. Upon return from Iraq, Hanna initially volunteered at the school part-time. He was hired to lead it full-time in 2009, after several difficult years when it struggled with funding, leadership changes, and the consolidation of two Cornerstone locations into its current one, a space leased from the Catholic church next door. As Hanna welcomed me into his spartan office of white cinder-block walls and seventies orange carpet, I caught sight of his bookshelf, lined with works by Homer, Aristotle, John Stuart Mill, and Jonathan Edwards, and more contemporary writers, like historians Niall Ferguson and Paul Johnson, and the pastor and theologian R. C. Sproul. As we sat down, Hanna, who had been a philosophy major in college, told me that he became captivated by the great thinkers in high school, and that later on, as a result of his leadership experiences in the army and in Africa, he "had [his] eyes opened to the potential of education to transform communities and societies."

Anacostia is a community desperately in need of transformation. Fewer than 10 percent of the students in public high schools go on to college. For black males, it's 5 percent. More troubling, 75 percent of males from Anacostia will spend time in lockup by the time they're 35. Most of Hanna's students live below the poverty line and come from single-parent homes. According to Hanna, "It can be life-threatening simply walking to school. Or they just don't have the support they need at home— the amount of time and effort it takes for that parent to help the student stay on track. But they are willing to not get beaten down by the challenges and are willing to work hard. They serve as an inspiration to me because of their commitment to education."

While Anacostia's problems can be found in nearly any American metropolis, Cornerstone's educational solutions are uncommon. For one thing, Cornerstone is not a charter school, so it accepts no money directly from the government, the better to maintain freedom from government dictums on curriculum. While Hanna acknowledges that fundraising is "always the biggest challenge," Cornerstone is proving that piles of money aren't necessary for student success. Every single child in kindergarten can read, he says, and 90 percent of students who start at Cornerstone in 2nd grade or before pass the Stanford Test, a national English language proficiency assessment test. If students start in 3rd grade or after, 70 percent test at grade level or above. Compare that to 20–30 percent proficiency rates on DC's own CAS test at neighborhood public elementary schools Kimball and Aiton. Cornerstone has also laid the groundwork for a number of students to go on to college over the years, most of whom would otherwise almost certainly never go.

In Hanna's estimation, there are several reasons for the high achievement rate. Chief among them is the curriculum, which emphasizes studying the canon of Western Civilization. Says Hanna, "Exposure to great books is a huge emphasis to us. That's why we are able to outperform the majority of charter schools. Our high school students will read the *Iliad* and the *Odyssey*, and our elementary kids will read *Frog and Toad Are Friends* or *Charlotte's Web*. We try to connnect the ideas of philosophy to history—how did Hegel and Nietzsche shape what happened in pre-war Germany? To be able to think through a time period or idea deeply is a skill that needs to be developed and encouraged. Our curriculum supports the end goal—a leader and thinker who will give to the community and also be able to secure a job."

In the lower grades, where cognitive development is stressed, Hanna is going back to the basics. "When teaching kids how to read, we use phonics. As they get into reading age, we don't just focus on literacy, but literature—how to engage with and appreciate it, not just read words. It pays off when books and ideas become more complicated—they have the tools and interest to approach it. We do this because we *know* reading to kids is the biggest predictor of reading later."

Hanna is against what President Bush described as "soft bigotry of low expectations," and nowhere does this apply more than in Cornerstone's approach to math and science. "We believe children at primary school age should be strong in basic math facts—memorizing times tables, long division in their head, do multidigit subtraction and addition in their heads. That level of familiarity and comfort will set them up for success in algebra and mathematics." ...

———————————

. . . . As Cornerstone's name indicates, Hanna believes a Christ-centered leadership model produces a scholar and citizen-leader who will give sacrificially to the community. "I understand being a leader through the lens of Scripture, specifically,

I'm here to serve, not be served. . . . We aren't a charter school by design. We are able to point to the leadership model Christ provided, which is the way we want our students to study and learn. Education is our primary mission, but part of the role of this school is for the Gospel to go forth in this community. Fifty-two percent of adults in Anacostia are functionally illiterate. How can they hold a pastor accountable? How can they read the Bible? We want to equip our kids to do that."

Walking out of the building, I noticed a bulletin board, covered over with construction paper and glitter glue, with a verse from the book of Isaiah in the center, one of the many that kids at Cornerstone memorize throughout the year. "Behold, I am doing a new thing; now it springs forth, do you not perceive it? I will make a way in the wilderness and rivers in the desert."

The Ethics of Politics

BISHOP CHARLES B. GALLOWAY

In his great survey of American politics, Bishop Galloway (1849–1909) emphasized that as long as America's families are strong and its men are good, the nation will survive. The greatness of America was built on the backs of its men and women, and its future depends on them.

From the depths of my soul and in behalf of American citizenship do I repudiate the doctrine of a distinguished politician who said: "The Decalogue and the Golden Rule have no place in a political campaign." Over against that faithless and blasphemous declaration, which is nothing less than a wanton affront to our national honor, I rejoice to place the eloquent words of the immortal Washington in his farewell address: "Public prosperity has no foundation but morality and religion, and religion is the only security of morality."

In political as in personal conduct there is a right and wrong, and by that divine and universal standard men and measures must stand or fall. It is an eternal decree from which there is neither exemption nor exception. And no brilliancy of genius nor splendor of achievement nor conspicuousness of position can save a man lacking in moral integrity from the merited and irrepealable condemnation of history. There may be a temporary exaltation of wrong and deceit borne upward by a wave of blind popular passion, but the fall is as certain and merciless as the grinding mills of the gods. On the other hand, right doing, buttressed by principle, approved of God, and guarded by the ceaseless vigilance of truth, commands the increasing admiration of the growing years. The genius of history can never be deceived. There was never a man in our American public life of more godlike genius, or varied accomplishments, or irresistible attractiveness, or superb qualities of leadership than Aaron Burr; but for lack of moral fiber he went down to the uttermost humiliation and to an eternal execration . . .

. . . There is an ethical obligation upon every citizen to take an active part in public affairs. Edmund Burke, whose philosophic and political wisdom commands increasing respect, on one occasion uttered these words, which need special emphasis in America to-day: "He transgresses against the law of duty who sleeps upon his watch as well as he who goes over to the enemy." In affairs of State, indifference and neglect are national crimes. One as much betrays his country by disregarding her needs as in the desertion of her colors. Activity in public affairs is the present and imperious demand upon every Christian patriot. It is idle even to criminality to deprecate the course of political events and viciously assail the acts and motives of those in responsible positions when we are doing nothing to elevate the standard of character and wisely guide the affairs of government. The criticisms of a slothful citizen are worse than the emptiest cant. At an important election some years ago in New York—an election involving the interests not only of a great city, but of the entire nation—on Fifth Avenue from Fortieth to Sixty-Eighth Streets, the distance of one mile and a half, just twenty-eight votes were cast. And yet the negligent citizens of that district are they who are loudest in their denunciation of corrupt municipal and national politics.

. . . Our great nation will never lack noble spirits, courageous and unselfish, loving country more than personal gain, who in the hour of trial or peril will point to victory and lead the way. And every such leader becomes an example and inspiration to another generation of patriots. It is wonderful how persuasive and potential is a single act of lofty and heroic service. The midnight ride of Paul Revere from Boston to Lexington at the beginning of the American Revolution, a seemingly unimportant incident in a time of political excitement, will kindle patriotic fires in every brave soul to the latest generation.

That is surely a discouraging picture Lord Byron gives of the rise and fall of nations:

> *Here is the moral of all human tales—*
> *'Tis but the same rehearsal of the past—*
> *First freedom and then glory; when that fails,*
> *Wealth, vice, corruption, barbarism at last;*
> *And history with all her volumes vast,*
> *Hath but one page.*

But I decline to believe that the history of my beloved country will be the rehearsal of such a past. It is built on broad foundations and out of enduring materials, cemented with the richest blood of American freemen. Every living stone has been laid by loving hands and under the blessing of a favoring Providence. It has borne many a wild storm and now seems more solid and majestic than ever before. I ardently believe that it will write a new and brilliant page in history's "volumes vast." So long as our flag flying in the open heavens is the real symbol of a genuine personal and religious liberty, so long as our homes are pure and our women are true and our men are brave, the nation will not deteriorate, but will grow stronger and steadier as it moves majestically through the wide-open gates of every coming century.

———— ❧ ————

"Duties of American Citizenship"

THEODORE ROOSEVELT

At the time of this speech, delivered in Buffalo, New York, in 1883, twenty-four-year-old Theodore Roosevelt was one of the youngest members of the New York State Legislature. His young age, however, did not undermine his authoritative stance on a man's duties to his country, the subject of this speech. At a time when politics leaves a bad odor with many, it is bracing to note Roosevelt's idea that an American citizen's first duty is to be involved in politics.

Of course, in one sense, the first essential for a man's being a good citizen is his possession of the home virtues of which we think when we call a man by the emphatic adjective of manly. No man can be a good citizen who is not a good husband and a good father, who is not honest in his dealings with other men and women, faithful to his friends and fearless in the presence of his foes, who has not got a sound heart, a sound mind, and a sound body; exactly as no amount of attention to civil duties will save a nation if the domestic life is undermined, or there is lack of the rude military virtues which alone can assure a country's position in the world. In a free republic the ideal citizen must be one willing and able to take arms for the defense of the flag, exactly as the ideal citizen must be the father of many healthy children. A race must be strong and vigorous; it must be a race of good fighters and good breeders, else its wisdom will come to naught and its virtue be ineffective; and no sweetness and delicacy, no love for and appreciation of beauty in art or literature, no capacity for building up material prosperity can possibly atone for the lack of the great virile virtues.

But this is aside from my subject, for what I wish to talk of is the attitude of the American citizen in civic life. It ought to be axiomatic in this country that every man must devote a reasonable share of his time to doing his duty in the Political life of the community. No man has a right to shirk his political duties under whatever plea of pleasure or business; and while such shirking may be pardoned in those of small cleans it is entirely unpardonable in those among whom it is most common—in the people whose circumstances give them freedom in the struggle for life. In so far as the community grows to think rightly, it will likewise grow to regard the young man of means who shirks his duty to the State in time of peace as being only one degree worse than the man who thus shirks it in time of war. A great many of our men in business, or of our young men who are bent on enjoying life (as they have a perfect right to do if only they do not sacrifice other things to enjoyment), rather plume themselves upon being good citizens if they even vote; yet voting is the very least of their duties. Nothing worth gaining is ever gained without effort. You can no more have freedom without striving and suffering for it than you can win success as a banker or a lawyer without labor and effort, without self-denial in youth and the display of a ready and alert intelligence in middle age. The people who say that they have not time to attend to politics are simply saying that they are unfit to live in a free community.

The first duty of an American citizen, then, is that he shall work in politics; his second duty is that he shall do that work in a practical manner; and his third is that it shall be done in accord with the highest principles of honor and justice. Of course, it is not possible to define rigidly just the way in which the work shall be made practical. Each man's individual temper and convictions must be taken into account. To a certain extent his work must be done in accordance with his individual beliefs and theories of right and wrong. To a yet greater extent it must be done in combination with others, he yielding or modifying certain of his own theories and beliefs so as to enable him to stand on a common ground with his fellows, who have likewise yielded or modified certain of their theories and beliefs . . .

In facing the future and in striving, each according to the measure of his individual capacity, to work out the salvation of our land, we should be neither timid pessimists nor foolish optimists. We should recognize the dangers that exist and that threaten us: we should neither overestimate them nor shrink from them, but steadily fronting them should set to work to overcome and beat them down. Grave perils are yet to be encountered in the stormy course of the Republic—perils from political corruption, perils from individual laziness, indolence and timidity, perils springing from the greed of the unscrupulous rich, and from the anarchic violence of the thriftless and turbulent poor. There is every reason why we should recognize them, but there is no reason why we should fear them or doubt our capacity to overcome them, if only each will, according to the measure of his ability, do his full duty, and endeavor so to live as to deserve the high praise of being called a good American citizen.

Profiles of Law Enforcement

These accounts of law enforcement officers risking their lives on behalf of public good have been reproduced with the permission of the National Law Enforcement Officers Memorial Fund, an organization dedicated to honoring the sacrifices and heroism of law officers around the country. These men have all been honored with the NLEOMF Officer of the Month award. These gripping accounts not only underscore the dangers of law enforcement work, but also the tremendous courage and commitment to the job, two qualities that have their roots in the honor that accompanies public service.

MAY 2010

On January 21, 2010, Deputy DeGrow was patrolling the area of James Island, South Carolina. Typical of his dedication and thoroughness, he was following up on a residential burglary that he had responded to earlier that morning. When he came upon five subjects walking down the road, they fled immediately upon seeing the deputy's patrol car.

Deputy DeGrow quickly radioed dispatch and gave chase on foot to one of the subjects, who attempted to evade him by circling a house just off the road. With Deputy DeGrow in close pursuit, the subject circled the house twice. Rounding a corner, Deputy DeGrow was met with gunfire. He was shot once, directly below the right eye, by the suspect who lay in wait with the express intent of ambushing and executing the deputy. Deputy DeGrow immediately fell to the ground, dazed. The subject continued to fire on the downed officer, hitting him twice more in the head, twice in his right arm, and once in the left shoulder. Presumably out of ammunition, the gunman ran away.

"As I lay there I could feel the presence of God, and I knew in that moment that I was either leaving this earth or staying. I then had a sense that I was going to be all right and started coming out of the daze," Deputy DeGrow recalled. He rolled to his back, drew his sidearm and quickly scanned the area for the suspect. As he got to his feet, he radioed dispatch again, alerting them that he had been shot and needed medical help immediately. Amazingly, Deputy DeGrow was able to describe the subject who had shot him and informed dispatch that he was going out to the road so that responding officers and medical personnel could find him more easily. Almost passing out a few times on the way back to his cruiser, Deputy DeGrow prayed and kept thinking of his two children.

Officers from the Charleston City (SC) Police Department and Deputy DeGrow's fellow officers from the Charleston County Sheriff's Office were first to arrive on the scene. Deputy DeGrow asked one of his fellow officers to wipe the blood from his right eye. When it didn't work he simply said, "All right guys, take my duty belt and my shirt and vest," as medical personnel were arriving on scene. At the hospital, Deputy DeGrow underwent four hours of emergency surgery to repair the initial damage to his eye. When he awoke, he was surrounded by family, friends, co-workers, and supporters.

In the letter nominating Deputy DeGrow for the Officer of the Month Award, his supervisors stated, "His calm demeanor in the wake of this violent assault and despite grave injury is, quite frankly, of legendary proportions. Jeff continued to perform his duties, until responding officers and emergency medical services arrived to take over the hunt for the subject, and begin to treat Jeff's wounds. His bravery and courageous action directly affected the swift resolution of the case and subsequent arrest of his attacker."

DECEMBER 2009

The flags were flying, spirits were high and traffic was bumper to bumper as the citizens of Elm Grove, Wisconsin, converged on the downtown area for their 2009 Memorial Day Parade this past May. Traffic was beginning to back up in all directions as residents made their way to the parade route. Officer John Krahn, assigned to routine parade traffic control, was doing the best he could to keep the vehicles moving until an unintended guest came along: a 94-car freight train barreling down on the crowded intersection.

With all of the vehicles trying to make their way to the parade, traffic had come to nearly a standstill. As Officer Krahn was directing vehicles through the intersection, the warning lights and gates were activated on the railroad lines in the middle of the intersection. Almost immediately, panic started to set in, as vehicles caught within the railroad gates began scrambling to weave their way off the tracks and around the gates. However, Monica Partenfelder, a mother with her 2-year-old son in the backseat of her minivan, would not be so lucky.

Mrs. Partenfelder began to panic as the seconds ticked away and tried everything she could do to get out of the path of the oncoming train. As she struggled to get out of the way, the tires on her minivan became stuck in the railroad tracks with the front of the minivan facing head on with the multi-ton oncoming train. Witnesses recalled seeing smoke and sparks flying as she tried to free the minivan.

Officer Krahn noticed what was happening and immediately began sprinting toward the minivan screaming for the driver to get out of the car. One witness reported, "At that point I noticed an officer running as fast as I've ever seen anyone run, race to the minivan." The train had begun blaring its horn by the time Officer Krahn reached the vehicle. At the same time, Scott Partenfelder, the father of the 2-year-old boy and Monica's husband who was following them in a separate vehicle, arrived at the minivan and began working to free the child. Officer Krahn opened the driver's side door and was able to unlock the frantic driver's seat belt and get her out of the vehicle. He then began helping Mr. Partenfelder to free the young boy who was still secured in his car seat, risking his life with the imminent impact of the train only seconds away.

The 94-car multi-load train hit the minivan at 40 mph. The brutal force of the impact threw Officer Krahn and Mr. Partenfelder 20 feet through the air, seriously injuring both men. The front of the minivan was demolished as the train pushed it 200 feet down the tracks before finally breaking free and coming to rest on the side of the tracks.

As onlookers ran toward the injured men, Officer Krahn, although severely injured, began yelling for them to check on the child. Amazingly, the child was found to be unharmed in the backseat of the minivan, still in his car seat.

Officer Krahn was transported to the hospital in stable condition, suffering multiple rib fractures, bruising of the lungs, and multiple leg fractures. Mr. Partenfelder was also taken to the hospital in critical condition. Both men recovered and were heralded by the community as heroes.

A few weeks after the incident, Officer Krahn spoke for the first time publicly about his ordeal. He talked about his injuries and how he had become close to the Partenfelder family which had been instrumental in his recovery. He also expressed his appreciation for the incredible amount of support from everyone throughout the process.

Officer John Krahn, a father himself, knew the dangers involved but chose to act above and beyond the call of duty in his actions to rescue a mother and her young child. He is a 17-year law enforcement veteran and continues to serve with the Elm Grove Police Department.

SEPTEMBER 2008

"When lives are at stake, America's first responders do not hesitate to rush directly into harm's way. We do our jobs, searching for, rescuing, and aiding victims regardless of what unseen dangers and health hazards await." Such was the testimony of 22-year veteran Detective Tom McHale of the New York and New Jersey Port Authority Police Department before a Congressional Subcommittee. Few in law enforcement history can match the bravery and determination of Detective McHale whose specialties include solving homicides and fighting terrorism both at home and abroad.

Just seven years after joining the Port Authority Police Department, Tom McHale had his first encounter with terrorism on February 26, 1993, when he was critically injured in the first bombing of the World Trade Center. His heroic efforts during the event, and his investigations afterward, gained him the World Trade Center Individual Acts of Valor Medal and within two years he was assigned to the FBI's elite Joint Terrorism Task Force. So respected would he become within the law enforcement community, that in May 2001, he was also co-assigned to the NYPD Major Case Squad specializing in cold case homicides of fallen police officers.

Three weeks later, NYPD Detectives were investigating an allegation of the sexual molestation of a twelve-year-old. Although the detectives had found an unregistered handgun in the suspect's apartment, he was extremely cooperative during the interview, had been steadily employed for the past 18 years and on the surface, seemed the model citizen. But, the detectives were sure that something was amiss. Why would this gentleman begin rattling off names of former members of the Black Liberation Army (BLA), an ultra-violent splinter group connected to the Black Panthers? Having never heard of the BLA, the detectives did not know that during the early 1970s this home-grown terrorist organization had been responsible for killing and wounding more than two dozen police officers, including Atlanta Police Officer James Richard Greene. Officer Greene had been shot and killed execution style on November 3, 1971. According to Atlanta police, the two gunmen wanted to ingratiate themselves to leaders of the BLA by killing a cop.

It was suggested that the young detectives connect with Detective Tom McHale who had previous experience working on BLA cases. Detective McHale contacted the Atlanta Police Department and the FBI field office and opened a case that had sat cold for thirty years. The team interviewed multiple eyewitnesses and eventually found someone who was able to identify one of the murderers of Officer Greene from a photograph. Few were surprised that the murder suspect was the same person held in the New York molestation case. Despite changing his name and starting a new life, thirty years later the BLA member was extradited to Georgia and was convicted of Officer Greene's murder.

Nine months later, on September 11, 2001, Detective McHale responded to the World Trade Center along with fellow members of the Major Case Squad. While his rescuing efforts were underway, Detective McHale and his team narrowly escaped when the second tower collapsed. He never left the site that day and for the next ten days he was on full-time assignment at Ground Zero as part of the Port Authority Rescue and Recovery Team. Even after he was ordered to return to work with the FBI Joint Terrorism Task Force, Tom McHale returned to the World Trade Center site each evening. As a member of the Ironworkers Union Local 45, Tom McHale volunteered a full shift to assist his fellow ironworkers in their recovery and clean-up efforts. He spent countless hours cutting through steel and recovering remains. He maintained this grueling schedule until the end of January 2002.

In January 2002, Detective McHale and the FBI Joint Terrorism Task Force were sent overseas to continue the search for Osama bin Laden and the Al-Qaeda network. In roughly two months, Detective McHale and his team accomplished miracles. He was instrumental in locating several Al-Qaeda safe houses, identified a possible suicide bomber, and responded to a bombing at a church that took the lives of several people, including two Americans. Before returning to the United States, the detective and his team worked side by side with Special Forces units in Afghanistan to discover a biological weapons factory.

Back in New York, Detective McHale resumed his grueling schedule working a full shift with the Joint Terrorism Task Force followed by a full shift with the Local #45 team. In late May 2002, the honor of cutting down the last steel beam at the World Trade Center was given to Detective McHale in gratitude of his selfless dedication to the more than 2,975 people murdered on September 11th.

— ❧ —

Reflections on the Revolution of France

EDMUND BURKE

Edmund Burke (1729-1797) was a British statesman, author, and political theorist who laid much of the groundwork for modern American social contract theory. He is remembered for his support of the American Revolution and for his opposition to the French Revolution. Since the twentieth century, Burke has been considered a father of the modern conservative movement in political science. Here are men in association for the good of the polis.

To avoid therefore the evils of inconstancy and versatility, ten thousand times worse than those of obstinacy and the blindest prejudice, we have consecrated the state, that no man should approach to look into its defects or corruptions but with due caution; that he should never dream of beginning its reformation by its subversion; that he should approach to the faults of the state as to the wounds of a father, with pious awe and trembling solicitude. By this wise prejudice we are taught to look with horror on those children of their country, who are prompt rashly to hack that aged parent in pieces, and put him into the kettle of magicians, in hopes that by their poisonous weeds, and wild incantations, they may regenerate the paternal constitution, and renovate their father's life.

———

Society is indeed a contract. Subordinate contracts for objects of mere occasional interest may be dissolved at pleasure—but the state ought not to be considered as nothing better than a partnership agreement in a trade of pepper and coffee, calico or tobacco, or some other such low concern, to be taken up for a little temporary interest, and to be dissolved by the fancy of the parties. It is to be looked on with other reverence; because it is not a partnership in things subservient only to the gross animal existence of a temporary and perishable nature. It is a partnership in all science; a partnership in all art; a partnership in every virtue, and in all perfection. As the ends of such a partnership cannot be obtained in many generations, it becomes a partnership not only between those who are living, but between those who are living, those who are dead, and those who are to be born. Each contract of each particular state is but a clause in the great primaeval contract of eternal society, linking the lower with the higher natures, connecting the visible and invisible world, according to a fixed compact sanctioned by the inviolable oath which holds all physical and all moral natures, each in their appointed place. This law is not subject to the will of those, who by an obligation above them, and infinitely superior, are bound to submit their will to that law. The municipal corporations of that universal kingdom are not morally at liberty at their pleasure, and on their speculations of a contingent improvement, wholly to separate and tear asunder the bands of their subordinate community, and to dissolve it into an unsocial, uncivil, unconnected chaos of elementary principles. It is the first and supreme necessity only, a necessity that is not chosen, but chooses, a necessity paramount to deliberation, that admits no discussion, and demands no evidence, which alone can justify a resort to anarchy. This necessity is no exception to the rule; because this necessity itself is a part too of that moral and physical disposition of things, to which man must be obedient by consent or force: but if that which is only submission to necessity should be made the object of choice, the law is broken, nature is disobeyed, and the rebellious are outlawed, cast forth, and exiled, from this world of reason, and order, and peace, and virtue, and fruitful penitence, into the antagonist world of madness, discord, vice, confusion, and unavailing sorrow.

These, my dear Sir, are, were, and, I think, long will be, the sentiments of not the least learned and reflecting part of this kingdom. They, who are included in this description, form their opinions on such grounds as such persons ought to form them. The less inquiring receive them from an authority, which those whom Providence dooms to live on trust need not be ashamed to rely on. These two sorts of men move in the same direction though in a different place. They both move with the order of the universe. They all know or feel this great ancient truth:

*"Quod illi principi et praepotenti Deo qui omnem hunc mundum regit, nihil eorum quae quidem fiant in terris acceptius quam concilia et coetus hominum jure sociati quae civitates appellantur."**

---

* This line comes from Cicero; translated, it means: "There is nothing that pleases the principle and almighty God who oversees this world more than those lawful associations of men that are called states."

Civil and Political Association

ALEXIS DE TOCQUEVILLE

In 1831, the French government sent Alexis de Tocqueville (1805-1859) to study certain aspects of American life. His reports culminated in *Democracy in America*, a classic text about American democracy and economic life from the perspective of an outsider, looking in with admiration. In this powerful description, de Tocqueville captures the very special American practice of "association," men coming together with purpose.

Certain men happen to have a common interest in some concern, either a commercial undertaking is to be managed, or some speculation in manufactures to be tried; they meet, they combine, and thus by degrees they become familiar with the principle of association. The greater is the multiplicity of small affairs, the more do men, even without knowing it, acquire facility in prosecuting great undertakings in common.

Civil associations, therefore, facilitate political association: but on the other hand, political association singularly strengthens and improves associations for civil purposes. In civil life every man may, strictly speaking, fancy that he can provide for his own wants; in politics, he can fancy no such thing. When a people, then, have any knowledge of public life, the notion of association, and the wish to coalesce, present themselves every day to the minds of the whole community: whatever natural repugnance may restrain men from acting in concert, they will always be ready to combine for the sake of a party. Thus political life makes the love and practice of association more general; it imparts a desire of union, and teaches the means of combination to numbers of men who would have always lived apart.

Politics not only give birth to numerous associations, but to associations of great extent. In civil life it seldom happens that any one interest draws a very large number of men to act in concert; much skill is required to bring such an interest into existence: but in politics opportunities present themselves every day. Now it is solely in great associations that the general value of the principle of association is displayed. Citizens who are individually powerless, do not very clearly anticipate the strength which they may acquire by uniting together; it must be shown to them in order to be understood. Hence it is often easier to collect a multitude for a public purpose than a few persons; a thousand citizens do not see what interest they have in combining together—ten thousand will be perfectly aware of it. In politics men combine for great undertakings; and the use they make of the principle of association in important affairs practically teaches them that it is their interest to help each other in those of less moment. A political association draws a number of individuals at the same time out of their own circle; however they may be naturally kept asunder by age, mind, and fortune, it places them nearer together and brings them into contact. Once met, they can always meet again.

Men can embark in few civil partnerships without risking a portion of their possessions; this is the case with all manufacturing and trading companies. When men are as yet but little versed in the art of association, and are unacquainted with its principal rules, they are afraid, when first they combine in this manner, of buying their experience dear. They therefore prefer depriving themselves of a powerful instrument of success, to running the risks which attend the use of it. They are, however, less reluctant to join political associations, which appear to them to be without danger, because they adventure no money in them. But they cannot belong to these associations for any length of time without finding out how order is maintained among a large number of men, and by what contrivance they are made to advance, harmoniously and methodically, to the same object. Thus they learn to surrender their own will to that of all the rest, and to make their own exertions subordinate to the common impulse—things which it is not less necessary to know in civil than in political associations. Political associations may therefore be considered as large free-schools, where all the members of the community go to learn the general theory of association.

But even if political association did not directly contribute to the progress of civil association, to destroy the former would be to impair the latter. When citizens can only meet in public for certain purposes, they regard such meetings as a strange proceeding of rare occurrence, and they rarely think at all about it. When they are allowed to meet freely for all purposes, they ultimately look upon public association as the universal, or in a manner the sole, means which men can employ to accomplish the different purposes they may have in view. Every new want instantly revives the notion. The art of association then becomes, as I have said before, the mother of action, studied and applied by all.

"The Political Duties of Christian Men and Ministers"

Rev. J. S. Smart

In the following sermon, Rev. James Smart (1822–1894) encouraged all men, not just politicians or government workers, to get involved in politics. It is our collective duty, he said, to participate in the state. If men don't represent and protect their interests, they will be sure to lose them.

I am aware that there are those who will be ready, to greet me this evening, with questions like these:—

"Why do you not attend to your own business?" "Why do you meddle with matters that do not concern you?" "Do you intend to mix up politics with religion?" No, I do not intend exactly to mix up politics with religion; but I should like to mix a little more religion with politics, if I could. I humbly conceive that this would be a decided improvement upon the present state of things.

It ought to be understood that the religion of Jesus Christ, which embraces "whatsoever things are true, whatsoever things are honest, whatsoever things are just, whatsoever things are pure, whatsoever things are lovely, and whatsoever things are of good report;" that is, all virtue is the very life-blood of our body politic. It vitalizes and gives efficiency to all our good and wholesome laws; and just in proportion as we banish this religion from our politics, we bleed; we weaken our government.

There can be no government, or nothing worthy of the name, where there is no religion. The truth of this remark is sufficiently attested in the history of infidel France. Indeed, when we consider religion as the embodiment of all virtue, this truth is self-evident.

What is the value of a well-worded law if there be not virtue enough in the community to enforce it? It is not worth the paper upon which it is written. Banish the vitalizing element of religion—that is, all truth, and honesty, and justice, and purity, and love—from any political system, and how long would it exist? Not an hour. But this would simply be banishing religion from politics. Is not the thing absurd? And is not the man who attempts to put asunder what God hath so evidently joined together, an enemy to all good government? I think so. I would not speak thus harshly of any man; but justice demands it.

And now, I would humbly submit the question in reference to our modern politicians: Would it do them any harm to have a little more religion?—a little more of the fear of God before their eyes, and a little less unholy ambition and selfishness?—a little more zeal for right, and a little less for party interest, and party favors? This certainly would do no harm, and in my opinion would mend matters mightily. Then let us not be afraid, my brethren, to mix a little more religion with politics. Let us treat politicians as we are willing to be treated, and as we treat other men. Let us earnestly exhort and entreat them to respect the law of God; and let us try their actions by that law, as revealed in His holy word. And, as in the presence of Jehovah, let us solemnly "protest" against all their wrong doings. Let not their profession as politicians screen them. No man's profession should screen him from the rebukes of the divine law . . .

Let us not shrink from the performance of our duty, because it is an unpleasant task. But we are asked why we meddle with matters which do not concern us. What matters do not concern us? Does not the manner in which the government of the United States is administered, concern us? Indeed it does. I claim that we have, and ought to have, just as much concern in the government of this country, as any other men. This is our right. If any man disputes it, let him show wherein we have forfeited the rights and responsibilities of American citizens. We love our country, and therefore we are deeply concerned in the character of the men chosen to rule over us, for we know, "When the righteous are in authority the people rejoice; but when the wicked bear rule the people mourn." The honor of our country is dear to us, and we know that "Righteousness exalteth a nation, and that sin is a reproach to any people." We are profoundly interested in the prosperity and permanency of this government, and all her virtuous institutions; but we know that any government, and especially a Republic, must stand on virtue, if it stands at all . . .

I remark, in conclusion, that all these political brambles put forth poisonous blossoms, in the form of anti-Christian, anti-temperance, pro-slavery newspapers; and these blossoms, being plucked, will, like the seeds of Canada thistles, fly upon the wines of the wind, and so infectious is their poison, that wherever they fall, if they do not produce nausea, they will infallibly bring forth moral disease. Now, the only sure way to avoid this moral disease, which these blossoms are calculated to produce, is to leave them unplucked to wither upon the branches which bear them. In plain words I mean to say, that it is every Christian man's duty every good citizen's duty, to discountenance a vicious political press;—that it is wrong to encourage, or in any way support or patronize, those papers whose columns are continually filled with low bar-room slang, and whose editors feel themselves at liberty even to attack the private characters of our worthiest citizens, and that, too, in utter disregard of truth, and often in the most scurrilous manner imputing to them words which they never uttered, and sentiments which they never held. Such papers certainly are not fit to be received into Christian families, and read by our children, and I wonder how Christian men can conscientiously subscribe for them, or advertise in them, or in any way countenance or support them. It is our duty to let these bramble blossoms wither upon the branches which bear them. This will not only render the blossoms harmless, but will cause the brambles themselves to wither, and then you will the more easily pluck them up by the roots, and plant the cedars of Lebanon, that is, intellectually tall and morally upright men in their stead—strong men—firm men—honest, uncompromising men, rooted and grounded in their principles, men fitted to be pillars in our political temple, and patterns of virtue to the world. God grant that such men may be promoted to rule over us, and that all political brambles may be plucked up by the roots, that the existence and honor of this republic may be immortal.—Amen.

From "The Capacity for Greatness"

THEODORE ROOSEVELT

The twenty-sixth president of the United States and a hero of the Spanish-American War, Teddy Roosevelt (1858-1919) believed in the capacity of the American people for greatness. Greatness is not based on birth or status or income, but on an attitude of a man's heart to care for and help his fellow man. Roosevelt delivered this address at the beginning of the third session of the fifty-eighth Congress. The last sentence of this excerpt—"Each must stand on his worth as a man and each is entitled to be judged solely thereby"—is a good summary of this entire volume.

To the Senate and House of Representatives:

First and foremost, let us remember that the question of being a good American has nothing whatever to do with a man's birthplace any more than it has to do with his creed. In every generation from the time this Government was founded men of foreign birth have stood in the very foremost rank of good citizenship, and that not merely in one, but in every field of American activity; while to try to draw a distinction between the man whose parents came to this country and the man whose ancestors came to it several generations back is a mere absurdity. Good Americanism is a matter of heart, of conscience, of lofty aspiration, of sound common-sense, but not of birthplace or of creed. The medal of honor, the highest prize to be won by those who serve in the Army and the Navy of the United States, decorates men born here, and it also decorates men born in Great Britain and Ireland, in Germany, in Scandinavia, in France, and doubtless in other countries also. In the field of statesmanship, in the field of business, in the field of philanthropic endeavor, it is equally true that among the men of whom we are most proud as Americans no distinction whatever can be drawn between those who themselves or whose parents came over in sailing ship or steamer from across the water and those whose ancestors stepped ashore into the wooded wilderness at Plymouth or at the mouth of the Hudson, the Delaware, or the James nearly three centuries ago. No fellow-citizen of ours is entitled to any peculiar regard because of the way in which he worships his Maker, or because of the birthplace of himself or his parents, nor should he be in any way discriminated against therefore. Each must stand on his worth as a man and each is entitled to be judged solely thereby.

— ❦ —

Profile: Álvaro Uribe Vélez

Here is a man of unfettered courage and determination. Undaunted by assassination attempts and death threats on his family, Álvaro Uribe Vélez, former president of Colombia, took on the Marxist rebels who undermined the well-being of his country. I interviewed him on my radio show; he is a living hero of mine. Perhaps we can all remember the noble root of the word *politics* more often, and honor it in word and deed as this man did.

In August 2002, Álvaro Uribe Vélez stood proudly in the capital city of Bogotá, Colombia, about to be inaugurated as the fiftieth president of Colombia.

Minutes before the presidential sash was draped around his neck, explosions shook the city of Bogotá, not in celebration of Columbia's new president, but in an attempt to kill him.

The bombings killed twenty-two innocent civilians and injured more than forty people near the national parliament and presidential palace. It was a message from the Marxist, rebel Revolutionary Armed Forces of Colombia (FARC) to President Uribe who had promised, as president, to eviscerate the armed guerrilla drug cartels that were ravaging Colombia.

With the FARC and paramilitary groups hijacking the country for their own drug-powered Marxist regimes, the fate of Colombia's democracy hung in the balance when Uribe took office.

"Half of the people of my country, 50 percent of forty-seven million Colombians, have suffered the same as my family," Uribe told me. "It has been a long nightmare because of narcoterrorists. We have to fight the best we can for the new generations to enjoy the right to live in peace and prosperity."

This was not the first time, nor would it be the last, that the FARC had threatened President Uribe and his family. But it would never be enough to intimidate or stop his mission. The Greek statesman Pericles said that courage was the essence of democracy. Uribe epitomized that courage; he is a man peerless among politicians, a George Washington of Colombia.

Álvaro Uribe Vélez was born in Medellín, Colombia. Widely considered one of the most dangerous cities in the world, Medellín was home to the deadly Medellín Cartel run by the infamous Pablo Escobar, arguably the most elusive and successful drug lord in world history.

After studying law at the University of Antioquia, Uribe began his political career in the Empresas Públicas de Medellín and in the Ministry of Labor and in the Civil Aeronautic. He became the mayor of Medellín in 1982, and he was thrust headfirst into the drug wars.

In 1983, Uribe's father was killed by FARC guerrillas during a kidnapping attempt. After his father's death, Uribe vowed to use his political career, his life in the polis, to protect his family and country from the Marxist rebels. He served as a senator from 1986 to 1994, as governor of Antioquia from 1995 to 1997, and eventually as president of Colombia starting in 2002.

Uribe campaigned for president on the promise of fearlessly fighting the FARC and reclaiming Colombian land from the drug lords. He won the election in a landslide. As president, Uribe took the fight to FARC's doorstep. He forced rebels out of Colombia's cities and back into the countryside, senior rebel commanders were killed, and rebels began to desert. The number of kidnappings and homicides dropped, drug production decreased, and it was safe again for Colombians to travel on the highways. He brought a measure of peace, unknown for more than four decades, back to the lives of everyday Colombians.

In the process, Uribe became the closest ally of the United States in Latin America. In his memoir, *Known and Unknown*, former Secretary of Defense Donald Rumsfeld said, "[I]n President Álvaro Uribe, we had the most skillfull partner we could have hoped for . . . Uribe was unafraid to take on the FARC and reclaim Colombian territory."

Uribe's success didn't come without a fight. During his tenure as president from 2002 to 2010, the rebels tried to assassinate him no less than fifteen times. In April 2002, guerrillas detonated a bomb in a bus along the same route Uribe's convoy was using in the city of Barranquilla. The explosion killed three civilians and injured thirteen, but the armor of his vehicle saved Uribe.

Every day of his presidency Uribe risked life and limb to protect his fellow citizens. In the end, perhaps his greatest accomplishment was restoring the trust of the Colombian people in their own country—their own polis.

"Many Colombians had lost faith," Uribe said. "As president of Colombia, my greatest achievement was to create awareness among the people that the country could be secure, prosperous, and equitable."

When Uribe took office, Rumsfeld wrote that "Colombia was leaning on the verge of becoming a failed state, a haven for drugs and terrorists." After eight years, Uribe transformed Colombia. The economy boomed. International business, which used to avoid Colombia, now considers it one of the top business destinations in Latin America. The investment rate rose from 15 percent of gross domestic product when he took office in 2002 to 25 percent at the end of his second term.

In *Twelfth Night*, William Shakespeare prophesied, "Be not afraid of greatness: some are born great, some achieve greatness and some have greatness thrust upon them."

Álvaro Uribe Vélez both achieved greatness and had it thrust upon him. The people of Colombia, a country on the brink of becoming a failed state, were begging for a leader—a leader who experienced the problem firsthand and understood what it took to overcome the problem.

"This problem is a problem of determination; it's a problem of courage to overcome setbacks and all the difficulties," Uribe told me humbly. "Colombia was at the brink of becoming a failed state. But because of the determination of the Colombian people, the courage of our armed forces, and the help of the United States, Colombia has made significant progress."

Uribe's own ambitions and goals were strong indeed, but they were one with the ends of his society. His was not a sterile or selfish ambition. He was, as Pericles wrote long ago, most about his own business when he was about the business of the city, his polis.

Good Citizenship

GROVER CLEVELAND

Grover Cleveland (1837–1908) was the twenty-second and twenty-fourth president of the United States, the only president to serve two noncon-secutive terms. Known as a reformer and staunch opponent of political corruption, Cleveland believed that America's citizens were the safe-guards of liberty and prosperity, that without active and responsible citizens, the American system of self-government would never survive.

The withdrawal of wholesome sentiment and patriotic activity from political action on the part of those who are indifferent to their duty, or foolhardy in their optimism, opens the way for a ruthless and unrelenting enemy of our free institutions. The abandonment of our country's watch-towers by those who should be on guard, and the slumber of the sentinels who should never sleep, directly invite the stealthy approach and the pillage and loot of the forces of selfish-ness and greed. These baleful enemies of patriotic effort will lurk everywhere as long as human nature remains unregenerate; but nowhere in the world can they create such desolations as in free America, and nowhere can they so cruelly destroy man's highest and best aspirations for self government.

It is useless for us to blink at the fact that our scheme of government is based upon a close interdependence of interest and purpose among those who make up the body of our people. Let us be honest with ourselves. If our nation was built too much upon sentiment, and if the rules of patriotism and benignity that were followed in the con-struction have proved too impractical, let us frankly admit it. But if love of country, equal opportunity and genuine brotherhood in citizenship are worth the pains and trials that gave them birth, and if we still believe them to be worth preservation and that they have the inherent vigor and beneficence to make our republic lasting and our people happy, let us strongly hold them in love and devotion. Then it shall be given us to plainly see that nothing is more unfriendly to the motives that underlie our national edifice than the selfishness and cupidity that look upon freedom and law and order only as so many agencies in aid of their designs. Our government was made by patriotic, unselfish, soberminded men for the control or protection of a patriotic, unselfish and sober-minded people. It is suited to such a people; but for those who are selfish, corrupt and unpatriotic it is the worst government on earth. It is so constructed that it needs for its successful operation the constant care and guiding hand of the people's abiding faith and love, and not only is this unremitting guidance necessary to keep our national mechanism true to its work, but the faith and love which prompt it are the best safeguards against selfish citizenship.

Give to our people something that will concentrate their common affection and solicitous care, and let them be their country's good; give them a purpose that stimulates them to unite in lofty endeavor, and let that purpose be a demonstration of the sufficiency and beneficence of our popular rule, and we shall find that in their political thought there will be no place for the suggestions of sordidness and pelf.

Good Citizenship Dependent Upon Great Citizens

WILLIAM JEWETT TUCKER

The Reverend William Jewett Tucker (1839–1926) served as the ninth president of Dartmouth College from 1893 to 1909. Tucker's obituary notice in the *New York City American*, September 30, 1926, said he "was known in New England as 'the great president,' who brought Dartmouth from the position of a small New Hampshire college to that of a great national educational institution." In many ways it was Tucker's belief in the greatness of the American citizen that led to the success of Dartmouth and Tucker's profound influence on the young men of America. This is an address he gave at the Federation of Churches, Carnegie Hall, New York, November 17, 1905.

As I interpret our present civic conditions the chief fact in evidence is the opportunity for influential and commanding citizenship. I therefore strike at once the note of greatness, not that of mere obligation nor even of necessity, as most in harmony with my subject. The first question about any urgent matter of a public sort is not, how urgent is it, but how great is it? What rank are we ready to assign to it among the subjects which demand our attention? That is the question which I put in regard to citizenship. What rank do we propose to give it among the compelling objects which address themselves to the ambition, the patient endeavor, or the consecrations of men? If we are not prepared to put it in the first rank, to give it a place beside the great constants in the service of state and church, or beside the new and fascinating openings of science and industry, it is quite useless for us to expect any results from our discussion of the need of good citizenship. If we are to have good citizenship, as things are today, we must have great citizens. When we have them in sufficient number, and rightly distributed, we shall have practically settled the question of citizenship. I address myself to one, to my mind the one, solution of our present civic troubles, namely, the presence of men qualified for leadership, whose great qualification is not a sense of duty, but the joy of the task. Nothing short of this will take the men we want away from the fascinations and the rewards of private gain.

What then are the qualities in men which can make them able and willing to achieve greatness by way of citizenship? I name first, without the slightest hesitancy, imagination, the power to see beyond, or even through, wickedness into righteousness. No great cause ever moved far until it had taken possession of the imagination of men. Whatever start the conscience may have given it, it waited for the kindled mind to give it movement. Foreign missions in this country sprang out of as fine a burst of idealism as the republic itself. When young Mills said to his comrades at Williams, "we ought to carry the gospel to dark and heathen lands, and we can do it if we will," the word of duty waited upon the word of inspiration. We have had enough to say about the duty of citizenship. Progress does not lie in any more discussion of duty, or even in the deeper sense of it. It is time for us to change our camping ground—to move out from "we ought" to reform our cities, into "we can do it if we will." What we need in further thought about citizenship is to put more of what Stevenson calls "the purple" into our thinking; or if we are ready for action, to give to that what the *London Spectator* calls the "Nelson touch," the fashion which the old admiral had of doing a great thing in a great way because he saw it in its greatness.

Cato the Younger

PLUTARCH

Cato the Younger (95–46 BC) is remembered as one of the most faithful public servants of the later Roman Republic—a time when corruption and greed were tearing the state apart. In his *Lives*, Plutarch, writing several centuries after Cato, memorialized Cato's stoic morality in public affairs. Here was one noble Roman.

Cato's assiduity also, and indefatigable diligence, won very much upon the people. He always came first of any of his colleagues to the treasury, and away the last. He never missed any assembly of the people, or sitting of the senate; being always anxious and on the watch for those who lightly, or as a matter of interest, passed votes in favour of this or that person, for remitting debts or granting away customs that were owing to the state. And at length, having kept the exchequer pure and clear from base informers, and yet having filled it with treasure, he made it appear that the state might be rich without oppressing the people. At first he excited feelings of dislike and irritation in some of his colleagues, but after a while they were well contented with him, since he was perfectly willing that they should cast all the odium on him, when they declined to gratify their friends with the public money, or to give dishonest judgments in passing their accounts; and when hard-pressed by suitors, they could readily answer it was impossible to do anything unless Cato would consent.

On the last day of his office, he was honourably attended to his house by almost all the people; but on the way he was informed that several powerful friends were in the treasury with Marcellus, using all their interest with him to pass a certain debt to the public revenue, as if it had been a gift. Marcellus had been one of Cato's friends from his childhood, and so long as Cato was with him, was one of the best of his colleagues in this office, but when alone, was unable to resist the importunity of suitors, and prone to do anybody a kindness. So Cato immediately turned back, and finding that Marcellus had yielded to pass the thing, he took the book, and while Marcellus silently stood by and looked on, struck it out. This done, he brought

Marcellus out of the treasury, and took him home with him; who for all this, neither then, nor ever after, complained of him, but always continued his friendship and familiarity with him.

Cato, after he had laid down his office, nonetheless did not cease to keep a watch upon the treasury. He had his servants who continually wrote out the details of the expenditure, and he himself kept always by him certain books, which contained the accounts of the revenue from Sylla's time to his own quaestorship, which he had bought for five talents.

He was always first at the senate, and went out last; and often, while the others were slowly collecting, he would sit and read by himself, holding his gown before his book. He was never once out of town when the senate was to meet. And when afterwards Pompey and his party, finding that he could never be either persuaded or compelled to favour their unjust designs, endeavoured to keep him from the senate, by engaging him in business for his friends, to plead their causes, or arbitrate in their differences, or the like, he quickly discovered the trick, and to defeat it, fairly told all his acquaintance that he would never meddle in any private business when the senate was assembled. Since it was not in the hope of gaining honour or riches, nor out of mere impulse, or by chance that he engaged himself in politics, but he undertook the service of the state as the proper business of honest man, and therefore he thought himself obliged to be as constant to his public duty as the bee to the honeycomb.

Taking Command

GEORGE WASHINGTON

George Washington (1732–1799) composed this letter to his wife, Martha, on June 18, 1775, to inform her that he had reluctantly accepted the Second Continental Congress's request that he command the Revolutionary Army. Although he had not sought the command, he felt it was his duty to serve. Washington's life was marked by his accession to positions he never actively sought—such as the presidency.

Such reticence to obtain power (when his popularity would have easily allowed it) contributed to the national impression of Washington's unparalleled dignity and civil service, so much so that the eulogist at his funeral, Henry Lee, declared him "first in war, first in peace, and first in the hearts of his countrymen." George Washington was a man's man and a man of the polis. If Washington could voluntarily give up power, being victorious over what was then the greatest army in the world, the king of England said he would be the greatest man in the world. Washington did exactly that.

I am now set down to write to you on a subject which fills me with inexpressible concern—and this concern is greatly aggravated and increased when I reflect upon the uneasiness I know it will give you. It has been determined in Congress, that the whole army raised for the defence of the American cause shall be put under my care, and that it is necessary for me to proceed immediately to Boston to take upon me the command of it. You may believe me my dear Patsy, when I assure you in the most solemn manner, that, so far from seeking this appointment, I have used every endeavor in my power to avoid it, not only from my unwillingness to part with you and the family, but from a consciousness of its being a trust too great for my capacity and that I should enjoy more real happiness and felicity in one month with you, at home, than I have the most distant prospect of reaping abroad, if my stay were to be seven times seven years. But as it has been a kind of destiny, that has thrown me upon this service, I shall hope that my undertaking of it is designed to answer some good purpose. You might, and I suppose did perceive, from the tenor of my letters, that I was apprehensive I could not avoid this appointment, as I did not even pretend to intimate when I should return—that was the case—it was utterly out of my power to refuse this appointment without exposing my character to such censures as would have reflected dishonor upon myself, and given pain to my friends. This, I am sure, could not, and ought not to be pleasing to you, and must have lessened me considerably in my own esteem.

— ❧ —

From *Arthur James Balfour*

BERNARD ALDERSON

Arthur Balfour (1848-1930) enjoyed a long and distinguished career in British politics, serving, among other positions, as prime minister from 1902 to 1905 and foreign secretary from 1916 to 1919. Bernard Alderson's 1903 biography of Balfour depicts him as a selfless and dignified public servant who did not seek after his own acclaim—a great example for all men.

Mr Balfour took the most momentous step in his public career when he accepted the post of Irish Secretary, which was destined to be the means of rapidly lifting him into the front rank of British statesmen and leading him eventually to the highest office in the state.

Writing about his political standing at this time, Mr Lucy says: "Up to the day when all the world wondered to hear that Mr Balfour had been appointed Chief Secretary for Ireland, he was a person of no consequence. His rising evoked no interest in the House, and his name would not have drawn a full audience in St James's Hall."

Mr Balfour was himself responsible for this obscurity. He never made any effort to gain prominence, and never indulged in those extraordinary artifices and eccentric attitudes by which some politicians have in their early days endeavoured to attract to themselves public notice. If he had cared, with the aid of his powerful connections, he could easily have acquired an empty notoriety, but nothing would have been more averse to his refined, reserved nature. It may truly be said that popularity, fame, and greatness came upon him unsought. He would never have intrigued for them, and they would never have been his, had they not been found in the path of duty. His hatred of shams was too real and intense; he was steeped too much in the genuineness and the reality of things, and his spirit was too choice to allow him to angle for the fleeting favour of popular applause. It was largely owing to this fine temper of mind, and to this self-effacing attitude, that up to his appointment as Chief Secretary for Ireland he was an unconsidered personality and a negligible quantity in political affairs. To the great masses of the electorate, his name was almost unknown.

— ❧ —

From *Foundations of the Republic*

CALVIN COOLIDGE

"Silent" Calvin Coolidge (1872–1933) assumed the presidency of the United States in 1923 upon the death of President Warren G. Harding, eventually winning election in 1924. Although known for being a man of few words, Coolidge was a prolific author, and his careful adherence to simple yet virtuous living compensated for his lack of bombast on the campaign trail, making him popular with many Americans. Often forgotten in the annals of presidential history, Coolidge believed in a limited government, hoping that a moral and politically robust citizenry would continue to preserve the best characteristics of America and guard against misrule. His 1926 book, *Foundations of the Republic*, reflects these attitudes. He believed, as should we all, that "American citizenship is a high estate" and that service to the polis is an honor.

When each citizen submits himself to the authority of law he does not thereby decrease his independence or freedom, but rather increases it. By recognizing that he is part of a larger body which is banded together for a common purpose, he becomes more than an individual, he rises to a new dignity of citizenship. Instead of finding himself restricted and confined by rendering obedience to public law, he finds himself protected and defended and in the exercise of increased and increasing rights.

—

American citizenship is a high estate. He who holds it is the peer of kings. It has been secured only by untold toil and effort. It will be maintained by no other method. It demands the best that men and women have to give. But it likewise awards to its partakers the best that there is on earth. To attempt to turn it into a thing of ease and inaction would be only to debase it. To cease to toil and struggle and sacrifice for it is to not only cease to be worthy of it but is to start a retreat toward barbarism. No matter what others may say, no matter what others may do, this is the stand that those must maintain who are worthy to be called Americans.

———

I am well aware that it is impossible to maintain in time of peace the same exalted spirit of patriotism that exists in time of war, and yet, although it may be in a less degree, the country has need of devotion to the same ideals. In our land the people rule. The great truth cannot be too often repeated that this nation is exactly what the people make it. It is necessary to realize that our duties are personal. For each of us our country will be about what we make it. The obligation of citizenship is upon each one of us. We must discharge it in the actions of our daily life. If we are employed, we must be true to that employment. If we are in business, then we must be true to that business. What is always of the utmost importance, if we have the privilege to vote we must inform ourselves of the questions at issue and going to the ballot box on election day there vote, as we claim the sacred rights of Americans to live, according to the dictates of our own conscience. You who have offered your blood that these supreme rights and privileges must be maintained as a standard of human conduct on this earth must continue to be their chief exponents by what you say and what you do. The coming generations will reverence your example.

Duty

HORATIO KITCHENER

Sir Horatio Kitchener (1850–1916) spent his life in military service to the British crown, eventually becoming one of the chief architects of Britain's war effort in the first year of World War I. In 1914 Kitchener penned this short tract, which was to be issued to each member of the British

Expeditionary Force, advising him of how he was to act while on campaign. Here is propriety in the service of the polis.

You are ordered abroad as a soldier of the King to help our French comrades against the invasion of a common enemy. You have to perform your task which will need your courage, your energy, your patience. Remember that the honour of the British Army depends on your individual conduct. It will be your duty not only to set an example of discipline and perfect steadiness under fire but also to maintain the most friendly relations with those whom you are helping in this struggle. In this new experience you may find temptations both in wine and women. You must entirely resist both temptations, and, while treating all women with perfect courtesy, you should avoid any intimacy. Do your duty bravely. Fear God. Honor the King.

Profile: Jaime Escalante

In *A Man For All Seasons*, an ambitious young man seeks Thomas More's help in getting a position at court. More thinks otherwise and advises him to be a teacher. "Why not be a teacher? You'd be a fine teacher. Perhaps even a great one," says More. "And if I was, who would know it?" the young man responds. "You, your pupils, your friends, God. Not a bad public, that," answers More.

I think of that exchange when I think of Jaime Escalante. Newspaper publicity, a book, and a Hollywood movie spread his fame, but his influence was most deeply and profoundly felt in the "public" that More describes. Some of my most important conversations with Escalante were recorded in my book, *The De-Valuing of America*, and I reference them here to tell his story. He passed in 2010, a man beloved and sorely missed.

In 1974, Bolivian-born Jaime Escalante began teaching at Garfield High School in East Los Angeles, California. Standing in front of a classroom of inner-city kids, unmotivated and uninterested in learning, Escalante walked out on the very first day and called his former employer at a computer factory and asked for his job back. The only thing that stopped him from quitting was twelve students who expressed interest in learning algebra, Escalante's expertise and passion.

After making special arrangements to teach these few interested minds, Escalante began to form a program to teach disadvantaged Hispanic youngsters higher math, something nearly unheard of in an inner-city school.

His plan was greeted with skepticism and laughter by his colleagues, and he encountered resistance from his students. But he told me that the greatest resistance came not from the students but from others in the profession, other teachers and counselors who urged him not to push so hard. They told him that his plan to teach calculus was a quixotic fantasy. "If you try," some told him, "the students will fail. They can't do it. They will be embarrassed, and their self-esteem will suffer. What you want to do—teach calculus—will be dangerous."

Escalante told me what he told his critics: "If you are fifteen and sixteen years old, in the barrio of East Los Angeles, there are a lot of things that are dangerous. But calculus isn't one of them."

He persisted, and in 1982 eighteen of his students took the Advanced Placement (AP) calculus test. Escalante's success was met with stiff skepticism. The Educational Testing Service doubted the legitimacy of the results and asked fourteen of the students to take the test again. Twelve of the students agreed to take it again (the remaining two decided they didn't need the credit for college), and all twelve scored high enough to have their results validated.

With the skeptics behind him, Escalante continued to expand the scope of his calculus program. In 1983, thirty-three students took the exam and thirty passed, more than double the previous year's success. In 1987, seventy-three students passed the exam, and by 1990 more than four hundred students were enrolled in various Escalante classes, from beginning algebra to advanced calculus. In the heyday of his program, Escalante's efforts were virtually unparalleled anywhere in the country.

Escalante's methods and approach (celebrated in the movie *Stand and Deliver*) were in marked contrast to the theory and practice of pedagogy as taught in most American schools of education. He consistently violated the canard that a teacher shouldn't "impose his values on students." Indeed, he sought every opportunity to impose his ethic of achievement, success, and hard work on them. His reason, as expressed to me, was simple: "My values are better than theirs."

His way of doing this was direct, manly, no-nonsense. In the early days of his career at Garfield, he asked one student whether he wanted to study calculus. "No," said the student, "I want to see my girlfriend."

"Well, then," responded Escalante, "go over to woodworking class on your way out."

"Why?" the student asked.

"So you can learn how to make shoeshine boxes so you can have a career shining the shoes for Anglos as they pass through Los Angeles International Airport on their business trips."

"I don't want to shine Anglos' shoes," protested the student.

"Then study calculus," was Escalante's reply.

Because he genuinely cared about students and because he could see through pedagogical nonsense, Escalante did not assume a fake posture of equality with students; he did not banter in pseudo-Socratic method; he did not cast about his classroom proffering profound doubts and questions about the dilemmas of the age. He took his students where he found them, in a tough barrio of East Los Angeles, and he argued, pulled, cajoled, and exhorted them to the activity of hard work, very hard work, for their own lives, for their own futures.

One story illustrates what manner of man this great teacher Escalante was. Shortly before I left my job as Secretary of Education, I set up a White House luncheon for my "heroes," which President Reagan was gracious enough to host. He was interested in these educators, who briefly told about their schools, their children, their success stories.

After the luncheon, a White House social secretary came up to me and said, "Mr. Secretary, tomorrow night is a state dinner, and we would like to invite Mr. Escalante to sit at the president's table. The president was very impressed with Mr. Escalante."

I said, "Well, that's a great invitation, and I'm sure Jaime will appreciate it. But with all due respect, I doubt that he'll accept. He's already been away from his kids for two days."

The social secretary persisted, "Mr. Secretary, will you *please* ask him? This is, after all, a state dinner with the president."

"I realize you're talking state dinner," I said. "But I'm talking calculus."

I did go to Jaime later that day and told him of the invitation.

"That's a great honor, Bill," he told me. "But I'm sorry, I can't go. I've got to get back to my students."

Jaime Escalante's offer to his students was simple and straightforward: He knew calculus; they didn't. He had what they needed; he would take the time to get them ready, but they had to work, and they had to believe in the watchword of his classroom: *ganas*—desire, effort, perspiration, hard work.

Escalante insisted there is no way around this. He would not let his students avoid it or him. He gave the lie to the proposition that the combination of poverty, disadvantaged background, or color were destiny, that the usual rules of good habits, good behavior, and hard work don't apply.

A Story of Civic Improvement

Benjamin Franklin

Businessman. Publisher. Poet. Postmaster. Inventor. Humorist. Statesman. Diplomat. Benjamin Franklin (1706–1790) is arguably the quintessential figure of colonial America. Among his other accomplishments was his devotion to improving the lives of his fellow citizens, establishing the first library and firehouse in the city of Philadelphia. In this story from his *Memoirs*, which was one of the most popular books of the eighteenth century, Franklin describes his initiative in getting a street paved.

Our city, though laid out with beautiful regularity, the streets large, straight, and crossing each other at right angles, had the disgrace of suffering those streets to remain long unpaved, and in wet weather the wheels of heavy carriages ploughed them into a quagmire, so that it was difficult to cross them; and in dry weather the dust was offensive. I had lived near what was called the

Jersey Market, and saw with pain the inhabitants wading in mud, while purchasing their provisions. A strip of ground down the middle of that market was at length paved with brick, so that, being once in the market, they had firm footing; but were often over shoes in dirt to get there. By talking and writing on the subject, I was at length instrumental in getting the street paved with stone between the market and the brick footpavement, that was on the side next the houses. This, for some time, gave an easy access to the market dry-shod; but, the rest of the street not being paved, whenever a carriage came out of the mud upon this pavement, it shook off and left its dirt upon it, and it was soon covered with mire, which was not removed.

After some inquiry, I found a poor industrious man, who was willing to undertake keeping the pavement clean, by sweeping it twice a week, carrying off the dirt from before all the neighbours' doors, for the sum of sixpence per month, to be paid by each house. I then wrote and printed a paper setting forth the advantages to the neighbourhood, that might be obtained from this small expense; the greater ease in keeping our houses clean, so much dirt not being brought in by people's feet; the benefit to the shops by more custom, as buyers could more easily get at them; and by not having in windy weather the dust blown in upon their goods, &c., &c. I sent one of these papers to each house, and in a day or two went round to see who would subscribe an agreement to pay these sixpences; it was unanimously signed, and for a time well executed. All the inhabitants of the city were delighted with the cleanliness of the pavement that surrounded the market, it being a convenience to all, and this raised a general desire to have all the streets paved; and made the people more willing to submit to a tax for that purpose.

The Story of Cincinnatus

James Baldwin

Lucius Quinctius Cincinnatus (519–438 BC) was an aristocrat and a political figure of the Roman Republic. He served as consul in 460 BC and as the Roman dictator in 458 BC and 439 BC. The clear-headed virtue and simplicity demonstrated by Cincinnatus has made him one of the most highly regarded Roman leaders in all ancient history. Cincinnatus worked on his small farm until he was called upon to defend the Republic from rivaling tribes of the Aequians, Sabinians, and Volscians. He immediately resigned after completing the task. George Washington has been called the "American Cincinnatus" because he, too, served the nation in a position of great power, yet immediately relinquished it to preserve the freedom of the people. Cincinnatus set the example for humble service and selfless leadership. There is a wonderful statue of Cincinnatus near the river in Cincinnati, Ohio. "Is all well with Rome?" might be the slogan of every good citizen.

There was a man named Cincinnatus who lived on a little farm not far from the city of Rome. He had once been rich, and had held the highest office in the land; but in one way or another he had lost all his wealth. He was now so poor that he had to do all the work on his farm with his own hands. But in those days it was thought to be a noble thing to till the soil.

Cincinnatus was so wise and just that everybody trusted him, and asked his advice; and when any one was in trouble, and did not know what to do, his neighbors would say,—

"Go and tell Cincinnatus. He will help you."

Now there lived among the mountains, not far away, a tribe of fierce, half-wild men, who were at war with the Roman people. They persuaded another tribe of bold warriors to help them, and then marched toward the city, plundering and robbing as they came. They boasted that they would tear down the walls of Rome, and burn the houses, and kill all the men, and make slaves of the women and children.

At first the Romans, who were very proud and brave, did not think there was much danger. Every man in Rome was a soldier, and the army which went out to fight the robbers was the finest in the world. No one staid [sic] at home with the women and children and boys but the white-haired "Fathers," as they were called, who made the laws for the city, and a small company of men who guarded the walls. Everybody thought that it would be an easy thing to drive the men of the mountains back to the place where they belonged.

But one morning five horsemen came riding down the road from the mountains. They rode with great speed; and both men and horses were covered with dust and blood. The watchman at the gate knew them, and shouted to them as they galloped in. Why did they ride thus? and what had happened to the Roman army?

They did not answer him, but rode into the city and along the quiet streets; and everybody ran after them, eager to find out what was the matter. Rome was not a large city at that time; and soon they reached the market place where the white-haired Fathers were sitting. Then they leaped from their horses, and told their story.

"Only yesterday," they said, "our army was marching through a narrow valley between two steep mountains. All at once a thousand savage men sprang out from among the rocks before us and above us. They had blocked up the way; and the pass was so narrow that we could not fight. We tried to come back; but they had blocked up the way on this side of us too. The fierce men of the mountains were before us and behind us, and they were throwing rocks down upon us from above. We had been caught in a trap. Then ten of us set spurs to our horses; and five of us forced our way through, but the other five fell before the spears of the mountain men. And now, O Roman Fathers! send help to our army at once, or every man will be slain, and our city will be taken."

"What shall we do?" said the white-haired Fathers. "Whom can we send but the guards and the boys? and who is wise enough to lead them, and thus save Rome?"

All shook their heads and were very grave; for it seemed as if there was no hope. Then one said "Send for Cincinnatus. He will help us."

Cincinnatus was in the field plowing when the men who had been sent to him came in great haste. He stopped and greeted them kindly, and waited for them to speak.

"Put on your cloak, Cincinnatus," they said, "and hear the words of the Roman people."

Then Cincinnatus wondered what they could mean. "Is all well with Rome?" he asked; and he called to his wife to bring him his cloak.

She brought the cloak; and Cincinnatus wiped the dust from his hands and arms, and threw it over his shoulders. Then the men told their errand.

They told him how the army with all the noblest men of Rome had been entrapped in the mountain pass. They told him about the great danger the city was in. Then they said, "The people of Rome make you their ruler and the ruler of their city, to do with everything as you choose; and the Fathers bid you come at once and go out against our enemies, the fierce men of the mountains."

So Cincinnatus left his plow standing where it was, and hurried to the city. When he passed through the streets, and gave orders as to what should be done, some of the people were afraid, for they knew that he had all power in Rome to do what he pleased. But he armed the guards and the boys, and went out at their head to fight the fierce mountain men, and free the Roman army from the trap into which it had fallen.

A few days afterward there was great joy in Rome. There was good news from Cincinnatus. The men of the mountains had been beaten with great loss. They had been driven back into their own place.

And now the Roman army, with the boys and the guards, was coming home with banners flying and shouts of victory; and at their head rode Cincinnatus. He had saved Rome.

Cincinnatus might then have made himself king; for his word was law, and no man dared lift a finger against him. But, before the people could thank him enough for what he had done, he gave back the power to the white-haired Roman Fathers, and went again to his little farm and his plow.

He had been the ruler of Rome for sixteen days.

Compromise

HENRY CLAY SR.

The influential American statesman and politician, Henry Clay Sr. (1777–1852), represented Kentucky in both the Senate and the House of Representatives before going on to serve as the secretary of state of the United States from 1825 to 1829.

Known as the "Great Compromiser," he was invaluable in constructing important compromises on slavery during the Nullification Crisis. Because of his staunch defense of Western interests in America he was commonly called "Henry of the West" and "The Western Star." In 1957, Senator John F. Kennedy chaired a special Senate committee that honored Clay as one of the five greatest senators in American history. Abraham Lincoln paid Clay the greatest of compliments when he said Clay was "my beau ideal of a great man."

Clay appealed to the virtue of "mutual sacrifice" to preserve unity and strength in the nation. Though his convictions did not always make him popular, Clay was committed to acting on good character. He is quoted as once remarking, "I would rather be right than be President." This dedication to doing right motivated his "Compromise" speech as well as his entire political career. Despite the bad reputation of compromise in our time, real men compromise sometimes. There is a difference between a willingness on principle to compromise and a willingness to compromise on principle.

It has been objected against this measure that it is a compromise. It has been said that it is a compromise of principle, or of a principle. Mr. President, what is a compromise? It is a work of mutual concession—an agreement in which there are reciprocal stipulations—a work in which, for the sake of peace and concord, one party abates his extreme demands in consideration of an abatement of extreme demands by the other party: it is a measure of mutual concession—a measure of mutual sacrifice.

Undoubtedly, Mr. President, in all such measures of compromise, one party would be very glad to get what he wants, and reject what he does not desire but which the other party wants. But when he comes to reflect that, from the nature of the government and its operations, and from those with whom he is dealing, it is necessary upon his part, in order to secure what he wants, to grant something to the other side, he should be reconciled to the concession which he has made in consequence of the concession which he is to receive, if there is no great principle involved, such as a violation of the Constitution of the United States. I admit that such a compromise as that ought never to be sanctioned or adopted. But I now call upon any senator in his place to point out from the beginning to the end, from California to New Mexico, a solitary provision in this bill which is violative of the Constitution of the United States.

The responsibility of this great measure passes from the hands of the committee, and from my hands. They know, and I know, that it is an awful and tremendous responsibility. I hope that you will meet it with a just conception and a true appreciation of its magnitude, and the magnitude of the consequences that may ensue from your decision one way or the other. The alternatives, I fear, which the measure presents, are concord and increased discord . . . I believe from the bottom of my soul that the measure is the reunion of this Union. I believe it is the dove of peace, which, taking its aerial flight from the dome of the Capitol, carries the glad tidings of assured peace and restored harmony to all the remotest extremities of this distracted land. I believe that it will be attended with all these beneficent effects. And now let us discard all resentment, all passions, all petty jealousies, all personal desires, all love of place, all hankerings after the gilded crumbs which fall from the table of power. Let us forget popular fears, from whatever quarter they may spring. Let us go to the limpid fountain of unadulterated patriotism, and, performing a solemn lustration, return divested of all selfish, sinister, and sordid impurities, and think alone of our God, our country, our consciences, and our glorious Union—that Union without which we shall be torn into hostile fragments, and sooner or later become the victims of military despotism or foreign domination . . .

Let us look to our country and our cause, elevate ourselves to the dignity of pure and disinterested patriots, and save our country from all impending dangers. What if, in the march of this nation to greatness and power, we should be buried beneath the wheels that propel it onward! . . .

I call upon all the South. Sir, we have had hard words, bitter words, bitter thoughts, unpleasant feelings toward each other in the progress of this great measure. Let us forget them. Let us sacrifice these feelings. Let us go to the altar of our country and swear, as the oath was taken of old, that we will stand by her; that we will support her; that we will uphold her Constitution; that we will preserve her union; and that we will pass this great, comprehensive, and healing system of measures, which will hush all the jarring elements and bring peace and tranquility to our homes.

Let me, Mr. President, in conclusion, say that the most disastrous consequences would occur, in my opinion, were we to go home, doing nothing to satisfy and tranquillize the country upon these great questions. What will be the judgment of mankind, what the judgment of that portion of mankind who are looking upon the progress of this scheme of self-government as being that which holds the highest hopes and expectations of ameliorating the condition of mankind—what will their judgment be? Will not all the monarchs of the Old World pronounce our glorious republic a disgraceful failure? Will you go home and leave all in disorder and confusion—all unsettled—all open? The contentions and agitations of the past will be increased and augmented by the agitations resulting from our neglect to decide them.

Five Keys to Democratic Statesmanship

PAUL JOHNSON

Paul Johnson (1928-) is the author of several best-selling books, includ-
ing *Modern Times: The World from the Twenties to the Nineties* and *A
History of the American People*. In 2006, he received the Presidential
Medal of Freedom. The following is adapted from a lecture delivered on
November 1, 2007, on board the *Crystal Symphony*, during a Hillsdale
College cruise from Montreal to Miami.

The ability to see the world clearly, and to draw the right conclusions from
what is seen, is the foremost lesson which great men and women of state
have to teach us. But there are many more, of which I would single out the
five most important.

First, ideas and beliefs. The best kind of democratic leader has just a few—per-
haps three or four—central principles to which he is passionately attached and will
not sacrifice under any circumstances. This was true, for instance, of Truman, of
Konrad Adenauer of Germany, Alcide de Gasperi of Italy, and Robert Schuman of
France—all the outstanding men who did most to raise Europe from the ashes of the
Second World War and who built up the West as a bulwark against Soviet advance
and a repository of a free civilization. It was also true of Ronald Reagan and Margaret
Thatcher, the two outstanding leaders of the next generation who carried on the
work. I am not impressed by leaders who have definite views on everything. History
teaches it is a mistake to have too many convictions, held with equal certitude and
tenacity. They crowd each other out. A great leader is someone who can distinguish
between the essential and the peripheral—between what must be done and what is
merely desirable. Mrs. Thatcher really had only three musts: uphold the rule of law
at home and abroad; keep government activities to the minimum, and so taxes low;
encourage individuals to do as much as they can, as well as they can.

There are also, of course, statesmen who are necessarily dominated by one
overwhelming object dictated to them by events or destiny. Thus Abraham

Lincoln felt all else had to be sacrificed to the overwhelming necessity of holding the Union together, behind the principles of 1776 . . . Such concentration of effort is itself a product of clarity of vision which includes a strong sense of proportion.

Next comes willpower. I think the history of great men and women teaches that willpower is the most decisive of all qualities in public life. A politician can have immense intelligence and all the other virtues, but if will is lacking he is nothing. Usually a leader has it in abundance. Will springs from unshakeable confidence in being right, but also from a more primitive instinct to dominate events which has little to do with logic or reason. Churchill had it. De Gaulle had it. Margaret Thatcher had it, to an unusual degree. It could be seen that, surrounded by her male Cabinet colleagues—whose knowledge and technical qualifications were often superior— she alone possessed will, and one could almost watch them bowing to it. Of course, will is often in history the source of evil. Hitler came from nothing to power, and the absolute control of a great nation, almost entirely through the force of his will. And it remained in him virtually to the end. Stalin's dictatorship in Russia, and Mao Tse-Tung's in China, were also largely exercises in personal will. Mao's overwhelming will, we now know, led to the deaths of 70 million fellow Chinese. The cost of a misdirected will is almost unimaginably high. Those three or four simple central beliefs behind the will must be right and morally sound.

A third virtue is pertinacity. Mere flashes of will are not enough. The will must be organically linked to resolution, a determination to see the cause through at all costs. There are dark days in every venture, however just. Washington knew this in his long, eight-year war. Lincoln knew this in his long and often agonizing struggle with the South. One aspect of pertinacity is patience. Another is a certain primitive doggedness. One learns a lot about these things by studying Martin Gilbert's magnificent record of Churchill's leadership. "It's dogged as does it" is an old English proverb. True enough. But doggedness should not be confused with blind obstinacy—the obstinacy of a George III or a Jefferson Davis. As with will, resolution must be linked to sound aims.

Fourth is the ability to communicate. The value of possessing a few simple ideas which are true and workable is enormously enhanced if the leader can put them across with equal simplicity. Ronald Reagan had this gift to an unusual degree—quite unlike his co-worker, Margaret Thatcher. While Reagan charmed and mesmerised, she had to bludgeon. There was a comparable contrast between Washington, who had no skill in plausible speechmaking, and Lincoln, not only a great orator for a set occasion, but a man whose everyday remarks carried enormous verbal power. But where words fail, example can take their place. Washington communicated by his actions and his personality. He was followed because Americans could see that he was an honest, incorruptible and decent man. Mrs. Thatcher, too, governed by personality. The Russians called her the Iron Lady. You do not need to charm when you are manifestly made of iron. It is a form of communication in itself.

The fifth and last of the virtues we learn about heroes is magnanimity: greatness of soul. It is not easy to define this supreme quality, which few even among the greatest leaders possess. It is a virtue which makes one warm to its possessor. We not only respect and like, we love Lincoln because he had it to an unusual degree. It was part of his inner being. And Churchill, who also had it, made it one of the top quartet of characteristics which he expected the statesman to show. A passage he penned as the First World War was about to end reads: "In war, resolution. In defeat, defiance. In victory, magnanimity. In peace, good will." This is a sentiment which all those in public life should learn by heart. It encapsulates the lessons of history better than entire books.

"Hello, Freedom Man"

Ronald Reagan

A champion of American exceptionalism and a defender of freedom worldwide, President Ronald Reagan (1911–2004) believed that America was a shining city on a hill whose light guided freedom-loving people all over the world. On January 11, 1989, President Reagan gave his Farewell Address to the American people. He included in his speech a story of American sailors rescuing refugees stranded at sea who were trying to get to America. It is a story about the lengths people will go to taste freedom, something that many countries around the world don't offer. American men in uniform are often the last, best hope of the suffering and oppressed.

This is the 34th time I'll speak to you from the Oval Office and the last. We've been together eight years now, and soon it'll be time for me to go. But before I do, I wanted to share some thoughts, some of which I've been saving for a long time.

It's been the honor of my life to be your president. So many of you have written the past few weeks to say thanks, but I could say as much to you. Nancy and I are grateful for the opportunity you gave us to serve.

One of the things about the presidency is that you're always somewhat apart. You spend a lot of time going by too fast in a car someone else is driving, and seeing the people through tinted glass—the parents holding up a child, and the wave you saw too late and couldn't return. And so many times I wanted to stop and reach out from behind the glass, and connect. Well, maybe I can do a little of that tonight.

People ask how I feel about leaving. And the fact is, "parting is such sweet sorrow." The sweet part is California, and the ranch and freedom. The sorrow—the goodbyes, of course, and leaving this beautiful place.

You know, down the hall and up the stairs from this office is the part of the White House where the president and his family live. There are a few favorite windows I have up there that I like to stand and look out of early in the morning. The view is over the grounds here to the Washington Monument, and then the Mall and the Jefferson Memorial. But on mornings when the humidity is low, you can see past the Jefferson to the river, the Potomac, and the Virginia shore. Someone said that's the view Lincoln had when he saw the smoke rising from the Battle of Bull Run. I see more prosaic things: the grass on the banks, the morning traffic as people make their way to work, now and then a sailboat on the river.

I've been thinking a bit at that window. I've been reflecting on what the past eight years have meant and mean. And the image that comes to mind like a refrain is a nautical one—a small story about a big ship, and a refugee and a sailor. It was back in the early '80s, at the height of the boat people. And the sailor was hard at work on the carrier Midway, which was patrolling the South China Sea. The sailor, like most American servicemen, was young, smart, and fiercely observant. The crew spied on the horizon a leaky little boat. And crammed inside were refugees from Indochina hoping to get to America. The Midway sent a small launch to bring them to the ship and safety. As the refugees made their way through the choppy seas, one spied the sailor on deck and stood up and called out to him. He yelled, "Hello, American sailor. Hello, freedom man."

A small moment with a big meaning, a moment the sailor, who wrote it in a letter, couldn't get out of his mind. And, when I saw it, neither could I. Because that's what it was to be an American in the 1980s. We stood, again, for freedom. I know we always have, but in the past few years the world again, and in a way, we ourselves rediscovered it.

Choosing Just Men

Noah Webster

Noah Webster (1758-1843) has been called the "Father of American Scholarship and Education." In the United States his name has become synonymous with the Merriam-Webster dictionary that was first published in 1828 as "An American Dictionary of the English Language." In this passage he reminds citizens of their political power—the power to vote—and that each man must weigh carefully whom he votes for, because that person will be his elected ruler.

When you become entitled to exercise the right of voting for public officers, let it be impressed on your mind that God commands you to choose for rulers, "just men who will rule in the fear of God." The preservation of government depends on the faithful discharge of this duty; if the citizens neglect their duty and place unprincipled men in office, the government will soon be corrupted; laws will be made, not for the public good so much as for selfish or local purposes; corrupt or incompetent men will be appointed to execute the laws; the public revenues will be squandered on unworthy men; and the rights of the citizens will be violated or disregarded. If a republican government fails to secure public prosperity and happiness, it must be because the citizens neglect the divine commands, and elect bad men to make and administer the laws.

Heroes of Science

ALBERT ROSS VAIL AND EMILY McCLELLAN VAIL

Many of the things we take for granted today—electricity, telephones, airplanes, medicines, computers, and so on—come from the tireless work of scientists and inventors. Some of these men and women are America's great doctors: Dr. Walter Reed and his helpers, Dr. Carrol and Dr. Lazear. Because of their important work, diseases that were once incurable can now be treated. The following passage describes the selfless work of men in the medical community to benefit the lives of thousands of people. Here are people dedicated to the health of the polis, literally understood. Today, many men injured or wounded in the service of America recuperate at Walter Reed Army Medical Center, which is named in honor of Dr. Walter Reed.

A scientist gets his knowledge, first, through hard study. Walter Reed loved his books. He could study twenty hours a day. When he became sleepy he just thought of all there was in the book before him that he did not know; then he set to work again, fresh and vigorous. He was but seventeen years old when he graduated from college at Charlottesville, Virginia, and was given a physician's diploma,—the youngest man who had ever taken a medical degree at the University of Virginia.

He decided at his graduation to give his life to helping those who were sick. He would try to forget himself and his comfort and think only of destroying disease and making sick people well.

For the first six years after his graduation he worked among the poor in the hospitals and the slums of New York City. Then he was appointed by the government to be an army surgeon, and went with a regiment of the government's soldiers out to Arizona.

Some of the western states were very wild in those days. His first post was six hundred miles from a railroad. Indian tribes were all around him, but he was not in the least afraid of them. He took care of them in their illnesses just as he had cared for the poor in Brooklyn. He always gave his best service to those who were poor and could not pay him.

Sometimes he was ill in bed with a fever, but if word came that someone else was ill and needed him he would get up and dress, holding to a chair perhaps to steady himself, and would start off to see his patient.

Once he started out at sundown for the cabin of a sick woman twelve miles away. The temperature was below zero and a storm which had arisen during the day had grown into a blizzard. The blizzard was so terrible that even horses turned and fled before its oncoming fury. Yet he was able to drive his horse through it all, wandering for hours hither and thither in the blinding snow until at last he reached the cabin at midnight.

The Indians soon learned to love him, he was so kind to them. They wanted to show him how much they loved him. So when he and Mrs. Reed were away from home they would creep into their house with presents. When Dr. and Mrs. Reed came back they might find a great piece of venison lying on the dresser in Mrs. Reed's bedroom, or perhaps a picture would have been taken down from the wall and the piece of venison hung on the nail in its place. The Indians would all be gone.

Ever cheerful, useful, undaunted, for eighteen years this soldier-doctor fought weather and disease in frontier camps. Then he was called to be a professor of medicine and a scientific investigator in the United States Army Medical School at Washington. This brought him the chance to do another kind of service to mankind. His training as an unselfish and heroic doctor had prepared him to become a hero in scientific discovery.

There are two ways to insure health to a person. One way is to cure him after he is ill. The other and better way is to destroy the causes of illness and prevent his ever getting sick at all. To find and destroy the cause of disease is the greatest service of medical science.

Between the years 1880 and 1900 wonderful discoveries were made by the scientists who worked in their laboratories about the causes of such diseases as diphtheria, malaria, and pneumonia. These scientists found that people become ill with a fever in the strangest way. Tiny little beings, so small that they can be seen only under a microscope, will enter a man's body when he breathes dust or drinks bad water. These little beings are called germs, or bacteria, and they will stay in his body and often make him ill. One kind of bacteria is the germ of typhoid fever. Another kind causes tuberculosis; another, yellow fever. Now, dust and bad water and bad food are full of such bacteria. So the scientists said people must be careful to breathe pure air, drink clean water, and eat good food, and to keep so vigorous that the body will resist these intruders.

Then they discovered that there are other and still stranger ways by which these germs get into people's bodies. Dr. Reed, in his laboratory work at Washington, found that flies carry the germs, sometimes millions of them, on their legs, and leave them wherever they go. During the Spanish-American war hundreds of soldiers became ill with typhoid fever. Dr. Reed was asked to go to the camps and discover the cause of this spread of typhoid. He found it was because the soldiers ate food over which the flies had crawled. He showed that the men's tents and provisions must be protected by screens; then they would not have these fevers.

Yellow fever was a foe which preyed upon the people of America and Cuba. For years it had devastated Havana. Again and again it swept through America's southern states. One time it caused the death of eight thousand people in New Orleans. Again, it killed one person in every ten in Philadelphia.

Some one had suggested that a mosquito, if it bit a person ill with yellow fever took the fever germs into its body. Then, flying elsewhere, it would bite a well person and with the bite would inject into that person's blood these same germs.

Dr. Reed with four assistants, among whom were Dr. Carrol and Dr. Lazear, decided to prove whether this was true or not. So they went down to Cuba where the yellow fever mosquito, as it is called, was to be found. The best way to study the subject, they decided, would be to let a mosquito which they knew had bitten a yellow fever patient bite them. Of course they might become ill with the fever. Yet what an opportunity for service was theirs! If people could be sure that the mosquito's bite caused yellow fever then they could destroy the yellow fever mosquito and thousands of lives might be saved. So Dr. Reed and his companions, at the risk of their lives, began their investigations.

Quite fearlessly, Dr. Carrol and Dr. Lazear volunteered to try the experiment on themselves and let the mosquito bite them. They knew this bite might cause their death, but they loved the truth and the service of men more than their own lives, and they gladly took the risk.

After receiving the mosquito's bite they both became ill with yellow fever. Dr. Carrol was very, very ill, but recovered. Dr. Lazear died in a few days,—a splendid martyr to science and mankind.

Then two young men, soldiers in the army, came to Dr. Reed and offered to try the experiment. Dr. Reed explained to them the risk and offered to pay them. They replied that they would take no money, they wished to offer their lives "solely in the interest of humanity and the cause of science." Dr. Reed, full of admiration for their nobility of character, touched his cap in military fashion, saying respectfully, "Gentlemen, I salute you." Then he accepted their services. Later he reported: "In my opinion this exhibition of moral courage has never been surpassed in the annals of the Army of the United States."

By their experiments in Cuba Dr. Reed and his devoted companions proved beyond question that yellow fever is transmitted by the mosquito. Soon after, Dr. Reed himself died in Baltimore, at the age of fifty-one. He was worn out by his excessive labors for the sick and the fever-stricken.

As a result of his discoveries the health officers in the South began a war upon the mosquitoes. They dried up pools of water where mosquitoes' eggs were hatched, or killed the eggs by covering the pools with oil. They also screened the houses more carefully than ever, to keep out the mosquitoes which they could not kill. These precautions brought quick results and the yellow fever epidemics disappeared.

Because some men of science were willing to lay down their lives that other people might live, this plague of the centuries was driven out of our southern cities and Cuba, and in time will be driven from the world.

"To Defend and Enjoy His Own"

DANIEL WEBSTER

A free government in America came at an expensive price. The men who stood and fell at Bunker Hill on June 17, 1775, knew the price of resisting British tyranny. For some, it cost their lives. Others fought until running out of ammunition and then retreated to fight another day. These men proved that a ragtag army of farmers could stand up to the military might and discipline of the British army. These men shattered any perception of British invincibility. As the war turned and a new nation was formed, the example of these men was a model for the entire country.

When it came time to remember this pivotal battle, on the fiftieth anniversary, only one man's rhetorical gift could do justice to this noble sacrifice. Daniel Webster (1782–1852) had served a distinguished career as a constitutional lawyer, eloquently arguing numerous cases and bending the fledgling Supreme Court to his will. His career is one of the finest examples of an American statesman. His gift with language and elocution is still an envy of many a silver-tongued rhetorician. He served in the U. S. House of Representatives and the Senate, and as the secretary of state for Millard Fillmore and William Henry Harrison, as well as running for president. While serving in the House of Representatives, Webster was asked to deliver an address marking the sacrifice of Bunker Hill.

Webster's speech is a paean not merely to America, but rather to the virtues and dignity modeled in the government created in this new nation. The necessity of a representative government, the need of safeguards for liberty, and the goodness of the gift handed down by the founders received a stirring rendition. Fifty veterans from that very war sat and listened as Webster called people to service, to live worthy of the gift they had received. When he said, "The *principle* of free government adheres to American soil. It is bedded in it, immovable as its mountains," the very mountains seemed to ring out their affirmation.

Exhibiting leadership in public life, calling others to nobility and action—these are the virtues and God-given talent of someone like Daniel Webster.

A nd, now, let us indulge an honest exultation in the conviction of the benefit which the example of our country has produced, and is likely to produce, on human freedom and human happiness. Let us endeavor to comprehend in all its magnitude, and to feel in all its importance, the part assigned to us in the great drama of human affairs. We are placed at the head of the system of representative and popular governments. Thus far our example shows that such governments are compatible, not only with respectability and power, but with repose, with peace, with security of personal rights, with good laws, and a just administration.

We are not propagandists. Wherever other systems are preferred, either as being thought better in themselves, or as better suited to existing conditions, we leave the preference to be enjoyed. Our history hitherto proves, however, that the popular form is practicable, and that with wisdom and knowledge men may govern themselves; and the duty incumbent on us is, to preserve the consistency of this cheering world. If, in our case, the representative system ultimately fail, popular governments must be pronounced impossible. No combination of circumstances more favorable to the experiment can ever be expected to occur. The last hopes of mankind, therefore, rest with us; and if it should be proclaimed, that our example had become an argument against the experiment, the knell of popular liberty would be sounded throughout the earth.

These are excitements to duty; but they are not suggestions of doubt. Our history and our condition, all that is gone before us and all that surrounds us, authorize the belief, that popular governments, though subject to occasional variations, in form perhaps not always for the better, may yet, in their general character, be as durable and permanent as other systems. We know, indeed, that in our country any other is impossible. The *principle* of free government adheres to American soil. It is bedded in it, immovable as its mountains.

And let the sacred obligation which have devolved on this generation, and on us, sink deep into our hearts. Those who established our liberty and our government are daily dropping from among us. The great trust now descends to new hands. Let us apply ourselves to that which is presented to us, as our appropriate object. We can win no laurels in a war for independence. Earlier and worthier hands have gathered them all. Nor are there places for us by the side of Solon, and Alfred, and other founders of states. Our fathers have filled them. But there remains to us a great duty of defense and preservation, and there is opened to us, also, a noble pursuit, to which the spirit of the times strongly invites us. Our proper business is improvement. Let our age be the age of improvement. In a day of peace, let us advance the arts of peace and the works of peace. Let us develop the resources of our land, call forth its powers, build up its institutions, promote all its great interests, and see whether we also, in our day and generation, may not perform something worthy to be remembered. Let us cultivate a true spirit of union and harmony. In pursuing the great objects which our condition points out to us, let us act under a settled conviction, and a habitual feeling, that these twenty-four States are one country. Let our conception be enlarged to the circle of our duties. Let us extend our ideas over the whole of the vast field in which we are called to act. Let our object be, OUR COUNTRY, OUR WHOLE COUNTRY, AND NOTHING BUT OUR COUNTRY. And, by the blessing of God, may that country itself become a vast and splendid monument, not of oppression and terror, but of Wisdom, of Peace, and of Liberty, upon which the world may gaze with admiration for ever!!

Profile: Marco Rubio

Marco Rubio's journey, from growing up as the son of Cuban exiles to becoming a U.S. Senator, teaches us many things about a man's life in the polis. The sacrifice of a parent can spark an appreciation and gratitude for one's own lot and a desire to return something to the society that has made life better. Rubio's story contrasts two forms of the polis, one in America and one in Cuba, and shows the lengths men will go to join and sustain a polis that is better for themselves and their children.

M ario Rubio was born and raised in Cuba in the 1920s. Fighting poverty like so many of his fellow Cubans, Mario worked for everything he had, often sleeping behind factories on a bed made out of wooden pallets. He met his future wife, Oria Garcia, after working as a guard for a grocery store in exchange for room and board. Oria also came from humble beginnings; as a child, she covered old Coca-Cola bottles with scraps of cloth to use as play dolls. The two married and had their first child, Mario Jr., in 1950.

With the rise of Fidel Castro and the Cuban revolution, the Rubio family fled from Cuba to the United States and settled in Miami. Their work was no easier—they labored in a factory stitching together nylon beach chairs—but at least they had freedom. Like so many American immigrants, Mario and Oria believed in the American dream. They wanted their children to have an opportunity for a better life. So Mario bartended at the popular tourist hotels along the beach, while Oria took various jobs, for example, working as a Kmart stock clerk.

On May 28, 1971, their third child, Marco, was born. In 1979, the family packed up and moved west to Las Vegas. There the Rubio family continued their modest, hardworking life. Oria worked as a housekeeper at the Imperial Palace and Mario Sr. was a bartender at Sam's Town Hotel.

By 1985, the family returned to the Miami area, just in time for Marco to enter South Miami Senior High School. By his junior year he made the varsity football team. He was undersized, but tough and smart on his feet. His teammates quickly recognized him as the mental leader of the team. Marco attended Tarkio College in Missouri on a football scholarship before transferring to Santa Fe Community College. He eventually graduated from the University of Florida with a bachelor's degree in science. He pressed on with his studies and earned his juris doctor from the University of Miami.

In 1996, his final year of law school, Marco worked for the presidential campaign of Bob Dole. With tireless ambition and unmistaken zeal, Rubio distinguished himself early on in politics. Rubio interned for Congresswoman Ileana Ros-Lehtinen and later served on the West Miami City Commission. In 2000, Marco Rubio was elected to the Florida House of Representatives, and in 2006 he became the first Hispanic Speaker of the Florida House. Rubio's meteoric rise continued in 2009 when he announced his election bid for the United States Senate.

Rubio's senate campaign captured the hearts of millions of Americans. Unashamed of his lowly beginnings, Rubio spoke proudly of his parents' journey from Cuba to the United States. As the child of a bartender and a housekeeper, he boasted of the power of the American dream.

In his final campaign video of the election, Rubio said, "America being exceptional is not something I read in a book. As the son of exiles, my parents were born into a society pretty much like every other in the world where if you're not from the right family or with enough money you can only go so far. And that is a very different place from our America—a place where the son of [a] bartender doesn't have to become a bartender and where the son of a maid can achieve any dream."

Rubio believes in the democratic spirit of self-reliance and ingenuity, and he puts that belief into practice. While serving in the Florida House, Rubio traversed the state, hosting townhall forums to listen to the people of Florida and their ideas. Rubio compiled the one hundred best proposals into a book called *100 Innovative Ideas for Florida's Future* and it became the platform of his term. He succeeded in passing all one hundred ideas through the Florida House and fifty-seven of these ideas—from stiffer punishments for gangs and violence to helping small businesses attain health care they can afford—eventually became law.

With a Reagan-like enthusiasm, Rubio promised Florida's voters that he would go to Washington DC to advocate on behalf of their ideas, not his. Rubio won the 2010 Florida Senate election in a landslide.

Sadly, Rubio's father was not there to see his son's historic victory. Mario Sr. passed away in September 2010, only two months before the election, after a long battle with emphysema and lung cancer.

In a statement issued after his father's death, Rubio said, "He was by far the most unselfish person I have ever known, always focused on others, and never on his own well-being. He was especially determined to provide his children opportunities he himself never had."

Rubio added, "My dad worked as a street vendor, security guard, apartment building manager, and crossing guard. But for most of his life he was a bartender, and by all accounts a great one. But his greatest success came from the two most important jobs he ever had: husband and father."

Mario Sr. didn't stop working until he was seventy-eight years old. He and his wife sacrificed everything so that their children might live a better life. Their story and the story of their son Marco illustrate some of the best things about a man's life in the polis. As Aristotle said, because man takes an interest in good and evil and right and wrong, he forms two institutions: the family and the polis (city). A man, like Marco Rubio, who loves his parents and city (or country) is surely twice blessed. Furthermore, the example and power of his parents can make a man engage with another "parent"—the *parens patriae*, Latin for "parent of the nation." Because of the example and sacrifice of his parents, Marco Rubio serves the American people so that others might have the same chance he has.

——— ❧ ———

Profile: Ray Sorensen and the Freedom Rock

Not everyone has to be a soldier to contribute to the well-being of a nation. Contributions can come from the hand holding a rifle or a paintbrush. In an age when many artists provocatively use their talents as a means of criticizing the military, Ray "Bubba" Sorensen is using his talents to honor U.S. veterans. Men should find ways to use their unique gifts in the service of the polis.

Off the side of a highway in Menlo, Iowa (population 365), is a large granite rock, weighing approximately fifty-six tons. It is an unusual sight in the middle of the easy slopes of the Iowa plain, a twelve-foot tall, unshapely lump—a massive piece of stone rising from the prairie, where corn stalks usually dominate the landscape. And if that were not strange enough, it has been painted every Memorial Day by a man named Bubba.

Ray "Bubba" Sorenson II, of nearby Des Moines, watched the movie *Saving Private Ryan* in 1999 as a nineteen-year-old. Moved by a new realization of the sacrifice which war entails, Sorenson decided to utilize his natural gifts as an artist, and made the rock, now dubbed the "Freedom Rock," the canvas on which he would pay tribute to America's veterans.

A graphic designer by vocation, Sorenson's decision to paint the rock was warmly received in the community. Before Sorenson showed up, the Freedom Rock was speckled with the graffiti of local kids. Now, it is covered in beautiful scenes commemorating the American fighting man: Marines raising the flag at Iwo Jima, Washington Crossing the Delaware, a veteran grieving at the Vietnam Wall memorial, a famous depiction of firefighters and police on 9/11, and the bombing of Pearl Harbor have all been represented in great detail. Though he initially decided he would only paint it each year until 2003, Sorenson's work was so warmly received that he has returned each year to paint new scenes, at the urging of local residents and veterans groups.

He took a call from an American Legion Post in Colorado, he told *USA Today* in 2007.

"I had to talk to every legion member. I was probably on the phone for three hours," he says. "They were all giving reasons why I shouldn't quit."

A few years ago, after one California veterans' group wanted to scatter the ashes of some fallen heroes at the rock, Sorenson suggested a better idea. He mixed the ashes into his paint, producing a hauntingly captivating effect. Bone fragments can be seen in the vivid hues coating the crag. "Eight different Vietnam vets ended up in the paint," he said. "It kind of made it a living memorial." The practice continues today.

In 2011 his work commemorated the Navy SEALs in their killing of Osama bin Laden, and the bravery of Army Staff Sgt. Sal Giunta, an Iowa native who was awarded the Congressional Medal of Honor for his heroism in Iraq, the highest honor for valor that can be awarded to a member of the armed forces.

Reverence for our troops is nothing new in America. But in an age when our nation's social fabric is less and less tied together by the bonds of wartime sacrifice, it is easy to be complacent in our tribute to the military. We can donate some money, post a note on Facebook, or stand and clap for the soldiers sitting in a luxury suite at a ballgame and feel good about ourselves. Little is asked of us on behalf of those that gave so much. Sorenson's decision to continue to paint the rock each year speaks of his willingness to use his own talents, time, and money for the service of his country. He is not satisfied with society's *status quo* gestures of honoring our troops.

Sir George Canning, the British Foreign Secretary of the early nineteenth century, once posed the question, "When our perils are past, shall our gratitude sleep?" Let us recall the most praiseworthy members of society with all due honor and respect, through the labors of our hands and our hearts, as does Ray Sorenson.

What You Can Do For Your Country

John F. Kennedy

At his first inaugural address, John F. Kennedy (1917-1963), the thirty-fifth president of the United States, uttered one of the iconic phrases of American political virtue: "Ask not what your country can do for you—ask what you can do for your country." A champion of freedom and individualism, Kennedy believed that the future of America lay in the hands of its citizens, not in government or leaders. Then a high school senior, I was present at this speech.

Vice President Johnson, Mr. Speaker, Mr. Chief Justice, President Eisenhower, Vice President Nixon, President Truman, reverend clergy, fellow citizens, we observe today not a victory of party, but a celebration of freedom—symbolizing an end, as well as a beginning—signifying renewal, as well as change. For I have sworn before you and Almighty God the same solemn oath our forebears prescribed nearly a century and three quarters ago.

The world is very different now. For man holds in his mortal hands the power to abolish all forms of human poverty and all forms of human life. And yet the same revolutionary beliefs for which our forebears fought are still at issue around the globe—the belief that the rights of man come not from the generosity of the state, but from the hand of God.

We dare not forget today that we are the heirs of that first revolution. Let the word go forth from this time and place, to friend and foe alike, that the torch has been passed to a new generation of Americans—born in this century, tempered by war, disciplined by a hard and bitter peace, proud of our ancient heritage—and unwilling to witness or permit the slow undoing of those human rights to which this Nation has always been committed, and to which we are committed today at home and around the world.

Let every nation know, whether it wishes us well or ill, that we shall pay any price, bear any burden, meet any hardship, support any friend, oppose any foe, in order to assure the survival and the success of liberty.

This much we pledge—and more.

To those old allies whose cultural and spiritual origins we share, we pledge the loyalty of faithful friends. United, there is little we cannot do in a host of cooperative ventures. Divided, there is little we can do—for we dare not meet a powerful challenge at odds and split asunder.

To those new States whom we welcome to the ranks of the free, we pledge our word that one form of colonial control shall not have passed away merely to be replaced by a far more iron tyranny. We shall not always expect to find them supporting our view. But we shall always hope to find them strongly supporting their own freedom—and to remember that, in the past, those who foolishly sought power by riding the back of the tiger ended up inside.

To those peoples in the huts and villages across the globe struggling to break the bonds of mass misery, we pledge our best efforts to help them help themselves, for whatever period is required—not because the Communists may be doing it, not because we seek their votes, but because it is right. If a free society cannot help the many who are poor, it cannot save the few who are rich.

To our sister republics south of our border, we offer a special pledge—to convert our good words into good deeds—in a new alliance for progress—to assist free men and free governments in casting off the chains of poverty. But this peaceful revolution of hope cannot become the prey of hostile powers. Let all our neighbours know that we shall join with them to oppose aggression or subversion anywhere in the Americas. And let every other power know that this Hemisphere intends to remain the master of its own house.

To that world assembly of sovereign states, the United Nations, our last best hope in an age where the instruments of war have far outpaced the instruments of peace, we renew our pledge of support—to prevent it from becoming merely a forum for invective—to strengthen its shield of the new and the weak—and to enlarge the area in which its writ may run.

Finally, to those nations who would make themselves our adversary, we offer not a pledge but a request: that both sides begin anew the quest for peace, before the dark powers of destruction unleashed by science engulf all humanity in planned or accidental self-destruction.

We dare not tempt them with weakness. For only when our arms are sufficient beyond doubt can we be certain beyond doubt that they will never be employed.

But neither can two great and powerful groups of nations take comfort from our present course—both sides overburdened by the cost of modern weapons, both rightly alarmed by the steady spread of the deadly atom, yet both racing to alter that uncertain balance of terror that stays the hand of mankind's final war.

So let us begin anew—remembering on both sides that civility is not a sign of weakness, and sincerity is always subject to proof. Let us never negotiate out of fear. But let us never fear to negotiate.

Let both sides explore what problems unite us instead of belabouring those problems which divide us.

Let both sides, for the first time, formulate serious and precise proposals for the inspection and control of arms—and bring the absolute power to destroy other nations under the absolute control of all nations.

Let both sides seek to invoke the wonders of science instead of its terrors. Together let us explore the stars, conquer the deserts, eradicate disease, tap the ocean depths, and encourage the arts and commerce.

Let both sides unite to heed in all corners of the earth the command of Isaiah—to "undo the heavy burdens, and [to] let the oppressed go free."

And if a beachhead of cooperation may push back the jungle of suspicion, let both sides join in creating a new endeavour, not a new balance of power, but a new world of law, where the strong are just and the weak secure and the peace preserved.

All this will not be finished in the first 100 days. Nor will it be finished in the first 1,000 days, nor in the life of this Administration, nor even perhaps in our lifetime on this planet. But let us begin.

In your hands, my fellow citizens, more than in mine, will rest the final success or failure of our course. Since this country was founded, each generation of Americans has been summoned to give testimony to its national loyalty. The graves of young Americans who answered the call to service surround the globe.

Now the trumpet summons us again—not as a call to bear arms, though arms we need; not as a call to battle, though embattled we are—but a call to bear the burden of a long twilight struggle, year in and year out, "rejoicing in hope, patient in tribulation"—a struggle against the common enemies of man: tyranny, poverty, disease, and war itself.

Can we forge against these enemies a grand and global alliance, North and South, East and West, that can assure a more fruitful life for all mankind? Will you join in that historic effort?

In the long history of the world, only a few generations have been granted the role of defending freedom in its hour of maximum danger. I do not shrink from this responsibility—I welcome it. I do not believe that any of us would exchange places with any other people or any other generation. The energy, the faith, the devotion which we bring to this endeavour will light our country and all who serve it—and the glow from that fire can truly light the world.

And so, my fellow Americans: ask not what your country can do for you—ask what you can do for your country.

My fellow citizens of the world: ask not what America will do for you, but what together we can do for the freedom of man.

Finally, whether you are citizens of America or citizens of the world, ask of us the same high standards of strength and sacrifice which we ask of you. With a good conscience our only sure reward, with history the final judge of our deeds, let us go forth to lead the land we love, asking His blessing and His help, but knowing that here on earth God's work must truly be our own.

Tragedy at Little Sioux

AARON DERR

Published in the October 2008 issue of *Boys' Life* magazine, the magazine for all boys (ages 6–17):

> When a tornado strikes a Boy Scout camp in Iowa, dozens of well-prepared Scouts keep a bad situation from getting worse. This story puts you right in the thick of the action as the Scouts work to survive one of nature's worst onslaughts.

At 6:35 p.m. on Wednesday, June 11, 2008, a tornado struck Little Sioux Scout Camp in Iowa, killing four Boy Scouts. Out of the 114 Scouts and youth leaders and 11 adults who were at the camp, nearly 50 were injured. The National Weather Service determined the storm was an EF3 tornado with wind speeds estimated at 145 miles per hour. But thanks to the heroic actions of the campers, youth leaders, and adults, there were no other fatalities.

This is their story.

Bradley Sundsboe, a 17-year-old Eagle Scout from Troop 461, Papillion, Nebraska, is a youth staff member at Little Sioux and was senior patrol leader of the green troop the week of the tornado: "We bring the boys out and divide them into two troops—red and green. We teach them different leadership skills.

"Dinner was at 5 p.m. that day. The weather was overcast but not too bad. All we knew was something big was coming between 2 p.m. and 2 a.m. the next morning."

Jesse Rothgeb, a 15-year-old Life Scout from Troop 331, Omaha, Nebraska, is a youth staff member and worked as Bradley's assistant senior patrol leader for the green troop: "The ranger called us and said there were funnel clouds over Little Sioux. It was really dark. The wind picked up, and it was starting to get worse. So we told Doc [camp doctor Dennis Crabb, M.D.] to hit the sirens. We have a procedure in which each member of the staff runs to the campsites to get the kids to their shelters."

Bradley: "The red guys headed up to their shelter—the north shelter. Our troop—the green troop—was already in the east shelter, but we weren't sure if that shelter was really safe because it's in the middle of a huge valley. So we had to get our guys from the east shelter to the south shelter."

Christian Jones, a 13-year-old Star Scout from Troop 448 in Omaha, Nebraska, was a camper in the red troop: "As I was walking back from my tent to get under the rain fly, I heard the siren, so I yelled to everybody: 'Hey guys, those are tornado sirens. We have to go to the north shelter.' Then the staff comes running down the road yelling, 'Get inside the shelter!'"

Bradley: "I got to the east shelter, popped open the door, and yelled, 'We're going down to the south shelter. Run!' I got near the back to make sure we got all the stragglers. Then the moment we got on the road, the wall of wind and rain just hit us, and it was really intense. I had never been in weather like that.

"As I was running, I heard on the radio the quartermaster, Alex Losen, say, 'There's a tornado on the ground!'

"We were maybe a good 100 feet from the shelter when it got to the point that it was just crazy. I kept looking up . . . I was blinded by the wind and rain, and I was half-expecting to see a tornado bearing down on me. The wind was just terrible.

"Then I heard somebody behind me yell, 'Ditch!' Then I looked behind me and I didn't see anybody there. I just saw trees snapping and falling across the road. The people just weren't there anymore."

Jesse: "We had to dive in a ditch. It was kind of a split-second decision. It was just getting so intense. Trees were falling. We didn't know what direction the tornado was going. We figured it was safest just to get down."

Bradley: "There was a Scout who was having a bit of trouble going up this hill right by the [south] shelter, so I just grabbed him by the neck and threw him in. I was the last person in. I yelled to everybody: 'Shut up! Get down! Cover your heads!'"

Jesse: "It was just roaring. It was really loud. We were just lying in the ditch facedown."

Alex Losen, a 20-year-old Eagle Scout from Omaha, Nebraska, is the quartermaster at Little Sioux: "All these trees were falling down and uprooting. I saw the tornado as it passed by the administration building. Some of the adults and I got inside a large closet in the center of the building. When part of the roof came off, all the air in the building got sucked out. I couldn't even breathe. My ears popped so bad I couldn't hear anything."

Zach Jessen, a 14-year-old Star Scout from Troop 104, Fremont, Nebraska, is a youth staff member and was a troop guide in the red troop taking cover in the north shelter: "It sounded like a freight train going over the top of you. There was stuff flying everywhere. I got under a table. I put a kid's head at my chest to make sure nothing would hit his head, and suddenly the tornado was on top of us."

Christian: "I heard the walls cracking and falling, and I heard the fireplace fall in. The sound was coming from everywhere. It was the worst sound I have ever heard in my life. Like the breaking of a thousand bones . . . crunching and cracking . . . it was terrible."

Zach: "It lasted about eight seconds."

Christian: "They said it lasted eight seconds, but it felt like 100 hours."

Alex: "Kids started running down from the north shelter saying the building got hit and there were injuries. I got my cell phone and called 9-1-1, which was amazing because you can barely get cell-phone service out there but we got it right then."

Christian: "After the tornado passed, I stood up right away and I saw it heading away from us. It was really scary. Then I turned around to look at the shelter, and all I saw was rubble. My friends were lying there. Some of them you could tell were okay and some obviously weren't.

"The first person I saw was my friend Ethan. He had a sprained ankle and head trauma. I could tell he was in pain. He was screaming. A big block was on his foot. So we started moving stuff off of him."

Jesse: "We had to run to the administration building to get first-aid kits, and we had to climb over all these fallen trees just to get there. We grabbed the first-aid kits and started climbing over even more trees. . . . The trees were just littering the ground. It was horrible. It took forever.

"We got up there to the north shelter and saw the devastation. The building was gone. It just wasn't there anymore. It didn't register at first. Then I realized it just wasn't there.

"We dropped our first-aid kits and started moving rubble off people."

Zach: "We took our shirts off and used them as bandages. We were tying them around wounds. One kid had the new Scout zip-off pants, and his leg was really scraped up, so we zipped off the bottom parts of his pants and put them on the wound."

Jesse: "I helped one kid—his leg was crushed. Some kids were bleeding pretty bad. One kid couldn't move at all—debris had hit him in his stomach and chest. There was a broken arm—we splinted that. We used a lot of gauze for the bleeding.

"We worked for about 15 minutes, then we heard the ambulances. I ran down there to tell them what was happening. It took another 20 minutes just to clear a small path so an ambulance could get through."

Zach: "I was still thinking everybody would be okay, but that didn't happen. I saw that one of the kids in my patrol, Ben [Petrzilka], had died.

"I felt helpless. I was really hoping everybody would be okay.

"I didn't see Aaron [Eilerts] anywhere. I figured he had already gone to get help. I didn't realize until the next morning that he had died."

Christian: "Two of the boys who died, Sam [Thomsen] and Josh [Fennen], were in my patrol. I was living with them at camp.

"When the rescuers showed up, we helped them as best we could. We got everybody into groups and herded them across the road and kept them out of the way. Then I carried a couple of stretchers back up the valley to the ambulances."

Steve Foster, paramedic, Burgess Health Center, Onawa, Iowa: "Total devastation is what I saw. I'm surprised there weren't more fatalities. I was so amazed by the composure of the Scouts who were able to help us. They were pulling rubble off other Scouts and trying to find their friends. They were offering first-responder, first-aid services at the scene. It was great to have that much help."

Dr. Peter Daher, emergency physician, Burgess Health Center, Onawa, Iowa: "They were heroes. These kids were so impressive. They were wet, dirty and muddy. Nobody complained, nobody whimpered or cried, even the critically injured ones."

Our Call to Service Can Mean Many Things

RETIRED COL. LEO THORSNESS

Retired Col. Leo Thorsness is a resident of Madison, Alabama, and the current president of the Congressional Medal of Honor Society, whose small membership is made up of recipients of the Medal of Honor—the nation's highest award for military valor. He received the Medal of Honor in 1967 for his heroic actions in the U.S. Air Force during the Vietnam War. Before Col. Thorsness was aware he had received the medal, his plane was shot down over North Vietnam, and he spent six years as a prisoner of war in Hanoi. Col. Thorsness provided this op-ed to *Veterans Today* magazine in March 2011, following the presentation of the American Spirit Award to Boy Scout Jack Pape, upon the 150th anniversary of the Medal of Honor. The American Spirit Award is given by the Congressional Medal of Honor Society to an American citizen who demonstrates extraordinary skill, professionalism, and a spirit of excellence in a challenging situation.

Recent events have reminded me of the power of youth in our country, and how our experiences as young people frame who we become, and how we contribute to the world around us. In my role as president of the Congressional Medal of Honor Society, two key areas of life came together in perfect intersection in Washington DC, on March 25.

There, I had the privilege of seeing the Congressional Medal of Honor Society bestow the American Spirit Award on a Boy Scout from Omaha named Jack Pape. The American Spirit Award recognizes individuals who demonstrate extraordinary skill, professionalism, and a spirit of excellence in a challenging situation. One of the recent recipients was a man by the name of Chesley Sullenberger, who landed his plane on the Hudson River. So you can see, it's a tremendous honor for a seventeen-year-old boy.

In 2008, Jack jumped into action to administer first aid and help save lives at the Little Sioux Scout Ranch, the site of the tornado that tragically killed four Boy

Scouts. A year later, he performed CPR on a young boy who was pulled from a hotel swimming pool.

Many people know that Scouts are trained in first aid. But do you know what else Scouts are trained in? Courage. And leadership. And service. I must say this with some humility, because I, myself, am an Eagle Scout.

Note that I didn't say "was" an Eagle Scout. Being an Eagle, even at the age of 79, is foundational to who I am. I was an Eagle Scout when the badge was pinned on my Scout uniform so many years ago, and I carry those principles with me still today.

Much like Jack never expected to find the circumstances that earned him the American Spirit Award, my Scouting experience benefitted me in unexpected ways. In Scouting, I learned about patriotism, service, courage, and loyalty, and it was during combat in Vietnam, and six years as a prisoner of war in Hanoi that those principles were put to the ultimate test and were proven to be true. I believe they are part of the reason I survived.

When I shook Jack's hand in Washington, I had to share a few words with him. I wanted him to know his experience in Scouting could be both a blessing and a curse. "A curse?" you ask. "Yes, because once people know you are a Scout, so much more is expected of you." I know he can live up to it.

I'm so impressed by what Jack has done in his seventeen years of life. He has taken the words of the Scout Oath to heart, "On my honor, I will do my best to do my duty to God and my country . . ."

He is a reminder that service to our country can come in many forms. We serve our country when we help others in need. We serve our country when we always do our best. We serve our country when we choose to do the right thing.

I look at Jack and marvel at how he could have acted so bravely at such an early age. I believe the answer lies in the values and character he undoubtedly learned at home, and with those he learned with the Scouts.

And while most young people will not face the same type of challenges Jack has faced, the Boy Scouts of America not only prepares young people to act heroically and courageously in times of great crisis, but it also prepares young people for life.

Our country needs more people who will put in more than they will take out. We need more people like Jack Pape. And, perhaps more than ever, we need Scouting.

In Harm's Way for Others

George P. Little

There is no greater public servant than a man who would risk his life for another. This is what many of our firefighters and rescue workers do on a daily basis. As this story of an explosion and fire on Hague Street in New York illustrates, firefighters don't think twice about putting themselves in harm's way to save a person in danger. Written in 1860, the story captures the same readiness for sacrifice shown by New York firefighters on September 11, 2001.

One of the most frightful casualties, attended with an awful destruction of human life, that ever occurred in New York, took place at a quarter to 8 o'clock, Monday morning, Feb. 4, 1850, by the bursting of an eighty horse power boiler, in the printing press and machine shop of Mr. A. B. Taylor, Nos. 5 and 7 Hague street, within a door or two of Pearl street. As soon as the explosion took place, the whole building, which was six stories in height, was actually lifted from its foundation to a height of six feet, and "when it reached that elevation, it tumbled down, crushing in its ruins a vast number. So great was the force of the explosion, that fragments of the building were scattered in every direction; the windows in the neighborhood were broken; and a large part of the front wall of the fated building was thrown with tremendous power into the houses opposite. In fact, the building was completely wrecked, hardly one brick being left standing on another, with the exception of a solitary piece of wall eight or ten feet high, as if to indicate what had been . . .

As near as could be estimated, there were a hundred and twenty persons in the building at the time of the catastrophe, scattered throughout the machine shop, and the hat factory above mentioned, in both of which a great many men and boys are usually employed . . .

It was feared that the large majority of them were either crushed to death, or drowned, from the immense quantity of water poured in. At a quarter to 12 o'clock there were three taken out—Henry Geradet, a man of about forty years of age, residing at Brooklyn, badly bruised, belonging to the hat shop; Frederick Tieman, a boy of about ten years of age, residing at the corner of Park avenue and Division street, Brooklyn, taken out by William Story, of No. 4 (Niagara) engine company, not much hurt; A. Eldridge, of the machine shop, residing at 142 Third Avenue, dangerously bruised. These poor fellows were dripping with wet, and shivering fearfully. The little boy stated there were others alive behind him when he was taken out.

Young Tieman proved himself, as Story stated, "every inch a man;" he did not give way to unnecessary terror and make much noise, when thus confined in the terrible trap. The fire was close to his feet, which were nearly immovable, being jammed in the fallen timbers, when the fireman, Story, reached him, and passing to the boy sufferer his cap, told him to put it over his face, while he (Story) played a stream through the pipe over and around him, for the purpose of quenching the flames. Tieman did as directed, and patiently awaited the hour of deliverance.

Several firemen had been at work some time before Story entered the hole, which was low down, near the engine, in the rear part of the building; and it was only by almost superhuman exertions that he was finally rescued. The voices of several of his companions could be heard in the vicinity, most of them giving way to the impulses of despair, which the little hero endeavored to check by every species of encouragement in his power. "What's the use of crying'?" said he. "The firemen are hard at work; they'll get us out, if anybody can."

It became necessary to saw away a large timber before he could be liberated; and in this and other efforts none evinced a more unflinching determination than Zophar Mills, Esq., who was early on the spot, and worked with a zeal and courage beyond all praise . . .

Towards two o'clock, the multitude became very great, and in fact, all the day, though the cold was so great. The most tremendous excitement prevailed around the tragic scene—women tearing their hair and wringing their hands, as the dead, dragged from out the ruins, proved to be their friends or relatives; while others were in an agony of suspense, almost as bad as a knowledge of the worst.

One man was taken out of the ruins at the rear, after almost superhuman exertions on the part of the firemen, the sufferer having been caught between two beams, and covered with a pile of bricks. The beams had to be sawed, and the poor fellow kept waving his hand, which he had thrust through the aperture, in token that he still survived. More than once the firemen had to stop and play upon the locality where the poor fellow was confined.

Just as they were accomplishing his final release, the fire behind and around him raged fiercely, and the foreman was constrained to call out that the stream must be played upon it. "Oh, stop till we get him out—just a minute—we can stand it—the man's alive," the firemen replied. And they did stand it, and saved the man, though themselves much scorched and nearly suffocated.

Profile: Frank Hall

Chances are, you've never heard of Frank Hall before. He's not a celebrity, actor, or athlete; he's an assistant football coach at Chardon High School in Chardon, Ohio. But Hall did something far more deserving of celebrity status than many cultural icons today—he put his life on the line to save Chardon's students when a gunman entered the school and opened fire. The heroic story of this good, decent man deserves to be told far and wide.

When a gunman entered the Chardon High School cafeteria on February 27, 2012, and opened fire, killing three students and injuring two others, he came face-to-face with Coach Hall, a study hall and cafeteria monitor and the football team's offensive coordinator. Hall didn't back down. When other people panicked and ran away in fear, he confronted the seventeen-year-old suspect and chased him out of the school.

His work didn't end there. He returned to the sides of the victims, Demetrius Hewlin, sixteen; Russell King Jr., seventeen; and Daniel Parmertor, sixteen. And he prayed with them, wiped their tears, and comforted them in their last moments.

In the end, the three boys died of their injuries. But Hall's remarkable courage saved the lives of countless other innocents that tragic winter morning.

At a press conference a few days later, Hall was asked to speak. A man of humility and compassion, Hall said, "I don't know why this happened. I wish I could have done more. I'm not a hero. I'm just a football coach and a study hall teacher." The heroes, he added, were the law enforcement personnel who responded to the shooting.

No, Mr. Hall, you are a hero too. You are a hero to the families and children of Chardon High School, and you are a hero to everyday Americans who long for a Frank Hall of their own in their children's cafeterias, classrooms, and on their sports fields.

Hall, a barrel-chested former lineman and heavyweight wrestler, doesn't have an advanced degree or prolific résumé. A 1992 graduate of Ashtabula Harbor High School, he is a common man who works hard to support his family: a wife, Ashley, and four adopted boys.

Hall is certified to teach social studies but doesn't even have a teaching job. After his heroic effort, he should have teaching offers coming in from all around the country. Why? Because good education is not just about academics; it is also about character, and this man has plenty of it.

Like any great teacher, Hall is well-known and admired by the student body. And what Hall taught the students of Chardon High School transcends the classroom. He taught them what great men, like 9/11 heroes Rick Rescorla and Todd Beamer and Congressional Medal of Honor winner Dakota Meyer, teach us all: that true manhood puts the lives of others before their own. Hall selflessly placed his body between a killer and his targets, a lesson his students will never forget.

"It doesn't surprise me he put his body in front of other people's bodies and saved lives," Chardon assistant football coach Don Navatsyk said in a local interview. "If you talk to 100 kids at school, all 100 would say, 'We love coach Hall.' He's an inspiration."

In an age when our children are increasingly susceptible to mixed signals about manhood and womanhood, Hall stands out. To conclude his emotional press conference, he quoted Matthew 5:14: "You are the light of the world. A town built on a hill cannot be hidden. Neither do people light a lamp and put it under a bowl. Instead they put it on its stand, and it gives light to everyone in the house. In the same way, let your light shine before others, that they may see your good deeds and glorify your Father in heaven" (NIV).

To paraphrase another scripture (Philippians 4:8), whatsoever things are true, whatsoever things are good, think on those things. Moral character is not complicated.

Frank Hall may never be a household name in America, but the students, parents, and teachers of Chardon, Ohio, will never forget him. We should not forget him either. Here is a good, ordinary man who did an extraordinary thing. Our children need heroes like him, who embody the everlasting qualities of manhood: honor, duty, valor, and integrity. We have much to learn from the simple, upstanding life of Frank Hall.

Irrationally Patriotic

G. K. CHESTERTON

G. K. Chesterton (1874–1936) was an English journalist, illustrator, novelist, and writer during the early twentieth century. With an amazing output of novels, essays, poems, and short stories, Chesterton wrote prolifically with great insight, wit, wisdom, joviality, and vigor. Chesterton outlined the irrational roots of patriotism: irrational because these roots precede reason. According to Chesterton, men must not love their native land because it is great; they must make it great because they love it. They must love it because it is theirs. It is this irrational love and loyalty that frees men to see their city as it is—and to praise, critique, and reform it. In the excerpt below, Chesterton focuses on the neighborhood of Pimlico in London, England.

Let us suppose we are confronted with a desperate thing—say Pimlico. If we think what is really best for Pimlico we shall find the thread of thought leads to the throne or the mystic and the arbitrary. It is not enough for a man to disapprove of Pimlico: in that case he will merely cut his throat or move to Chelsea. Nor, certainly, is it enough for a man to approve of Pimlico: for then it will remain Pimlico, which would be awful. The only way out of it seems to be for somebody to love Pimlico: to love it with a transcendental tie and without any earthly reason. If there arose a man who loved Pimlico, then Pimlico would rise into ivory towers and golden pinnacles; Pimlico would attire herself as a woman does when she is loved. For decoration is not given to hide horrible things: but to decorate things already adorable. A mother does not give her child a blue bow because he is so ugly without it. A lover does not give a girl a necklace to hide her neck. If men loved Pimlico as mothers love children, arbitrarily, because it is THEIRS, Pimlico in a year or two might be fairer than Florence. Some readers will say that this is a mere fantasy. I answer that this is the actual history of mankind. This, as a fact, is how cities did grow great. Go back to the darkest roots of civilization and you will find them knotted round some sacred stone or encircling some sacred well. People first paid honour to a spot and afterwards gained glory for it. Men did not love Rome because she was great. She was great because they had loved her.

Abraham Lincoln's Lyceum Address

Abraham Lincoln (1809–1865) is the Shakespeare and the Pericles—the poet laureate and statesman—of the American polis. He believed that America is the last best hope of earth and he fought until his death to preserve the Union. At only twenty-eight years old, Lincoln gave the following speech to the Young Men's Lyceum of Springfield, Illinois, on January 27, 1838. The future of America was in the hands of its citizens, Lincoln said. The end of America would not come from outside threats, but from inside. Lincoln called men to unite in the cause of freedom and equality for the preservation of the nation. The polis, here our beloved country, we truly hold in our own hands. Here is a stern and vivid warning by our greatest statesman and president of why we cannot let it slip from our grasp.

In the great journal of things happening under the sun, we, the American People, find our account running, under date of the nineteenth century of the Christian era.—We find ourselves in the peaceful possession, of the fairest portion of the earth, as regards extent of territory, fertility of soil, and salubrity of climate. We find ourselves under the government of a system of political institutions, conducing more essentially to the ends of civil and religious liberty, than any of which the history of former times tells us. We, when mounting the stage of existence, found ourselves the legal inheritors of these fundamental blessings. We toiled not in the acquirement or establishment of them—they are a legacy bequeathed us, by a once hardy, brave, and patriotic, but now lamented and departed race of ancestors. Theirs was the task (and nobly they performed it) to possess themselves, and through themselves, us, of this goodly land; and to uprear upon its hills and its valleys, a political edifice of liberty and equal rights; 'tis ours only, to transmit these, the former, unprofaned by the foot of an invader; the latter, undecayed by the lapse of time and untorn by usurpation, to the latest generation that fate shall permit the world to know. This task of gratitude to our fathers, justice to ourselves, duty to posterity, and love for our species in general, all imperatively require us faithfully to perform.

How then shall we perform it?—At what point shall we expect the approach of danger? By what means shall we fortify against it?—Shall we expect some transatlantic military giant, to step the Ocean, and crush us at a blow? Never!—All the armies of Europe, Asia and Africa combined, with all the treasure of the earth (our own excepted) in their military chest; with a Buonaparte for a commander, could not by force, take a drink from the Ohio, or make a track on the Blue Ridge, in a trial of a thousand years.

At what point then is the approach of danger to be expected? I answer, if it ever reach us, it must spring up amongst us. It cannot come from abroad. If destruction be our lot, we must ourselves be its author and finisher. As a nation of freemen, we must live through all time, or die by suicide . . .

The question recurs, "how shall we fortify against it?" The answer is simple. Let every American, every lover of liberty, every well wisher to his posterity, swear by the blood of the Revolution, never to violate in the least particular, the laws of the country; and never to tolerate their violation by others. As the patriots of seventy-six did to the support of the Declaration of Independence, so to the support of the Constitution and Laws, let every American pledge his life, his property, and his sacred honor;—let every man remember that to violate the law, is to trample on the blood of his father, and to tear the character of his own, and his children's liberty. Let reverence for the laws, be breathed by every American mother, to the lisping babe, that prattles on her lap—let it be taught in schools, in seminaries, and in colleges; let it be written in Primers, spelling books, and in Almanacs;—let it be preached from the pulpit, proclaimed in legislative halls, and enforced in courts of justice. And, in short, let it become the political religion of the nation; and let the old and the young, the rich and the poor, the grave and the gay, of all sexes and tongues, and colors and conditions, sacrifice unceasingly upon its altars. . . .

Reason, cold, calculating, unimpassioned reason, must furnish all the materials for our future support and defence.—Let those materials be moulded into general intelligence, sound morality, and in particular, a reverence for the Constitution and laws: and, that we improved to the last; that we remained free to the last; that we revered his name to the last; that, during his long sleep, we permitted no hostile foot to pass over or desecrate his resting place; shall be that which to learn the last trump shall awaken our WASHINGTON.

Upon these let the proud fabric of freedom rest, as the rock of its basis; and as truly as has been said of the only greater institution, "the gates of hell shall not prevail against it."

5

Man with Woman and Children

Men are missing from the lives of women and children today in increasing numbers. Almost half of all babies born in the twenty-first century in the United States are born out of wedlock. Single mothers and fatherless children are an increasing phenomena in our culture today. Many women are left on their own to wonder: Where are the good men? Where are the fathers?

The reasons for this sad state of affairs are many: there are massive cultural shifts, there is personal irresponsibility and dereliction, and there is too little education and intentional preparation of boys for manhood. Much too often men perceive fatherhood only as a burden, not a privilege. Fewer and fewer men understand the virtues and rewards of marriage and fatherhood. Since the sexual revolution and our culture's transition into a postmodern, "liberated" society, the ideas of love and marriage have been cheapened, confused, and diluted. Cultural anthropologist David Murray remarked that when you see a young child with a woman walking down the street today it's a natural fact, but when you see a young child with an attentive man it's a cultural achievement.

Let's remember that marriage was originally designed for the benefit of men and women, to advance them, not to hold them back. In the Bible's creation account, woman was created to be a companion to man because God saw that it was not good that man should be alone in the world. Aristotle was one of the first to write that the family is the basic social unit of society. "The family," he said, "is the association established by nature for the supply of men's every day wants." Within a family a man is able to provide for himself, his wife, and his children while helping to sustain mankind. The family is the first form of community, government, and society, and the first and best department of health, education, and welfare.

Marriage provides emotional, physical, and even financial stability that men have difficulty sustaining on their own. But like most things in life, there is no blueprint for a perfect marriage. It is one of life's most complex, beautiful, and yet challenging institutions. Men and woman are independent, unique individuals and like the pieces of a cosmic puzzle, they are joined together in ways that only our Creator knows. C. S. Lewis wrote, "Now Eros [the Greek word for love] makes a man really want, not a woman, but one particular woman. In some mysterious but quite indisputable fashion the lover desires the Beloved herself, not the pleasure she can give."

Call it what you might—love-at-first-sight or falling in love—there is an unexplainable attraction that a man feels toward a woman. From the Bible to Shakespeare to modern cinema, the story of love remains the most powerful story in human life. The famous writer Anton Chekhov said, "He-and-she is the machine that makes fiction work." Victor Hugo, the author of *Les Misérables*, remarked, "The supreme happiness in life is the conviction that we are loved." The trials of courtship and "dating" are the process by which man refines and tests his love, and interest in, a woman and vice versa. It's not an easy task, but approached the right way, namely discerning between physical attraction and real love, a man can ensure himself a long and happy marriage (or avoid the opposite).

A task even more daunting than dating and courting is marriage. One only needs to look at the rising divorce rates, the countless number of self-help books for spouses, and the creation of an entire therapeutic industry for marriage counseling. Men are not entirely to blame for this, but as Joseph Conrad quipped, "Being a woman is a terribly difficult task, since it consists principally in dealing with men." This chapter focuses on ways men can prepare themselves, improve themselves, and be good husbands and fathers.

As you will see in the following passages, the lessons from history and virtuous men teach men to respect women, pursue them for the right reasons, and weigh carefully their actions and words with them. "Love and respect woman," as the Italian philosopher Giuseppe Mazzini said. "Look to her not only for comfort, but for strength and inspiration and the doubling of your intellectual and moral powers."

If a man knows how to treat his wife properly, he will know how to raise his children. The same qualities of a healthy marriage—respect, devotion, loyalty, and compassion—will help a man instill in his children a moral compass that sets them on the right paths in life. Man, woman, and children are the great nucleus of life. And it ripples outward. President Ronald Reagan said, "All great change starts at the dinner table."

❦

Profile: Chris Scott

Here is a look inside the life of a husband and his wife and a father and his children. It's a story most men can relate to: a father with a less-than-generous salary and a wife with her hands full of kids and homework, striving to raise a family of morals, hard work, and responsibility. It's the human condition—spots, blemishes, stains, and imperfections—but it's what makes us better men, fathers, and husbands. I found the extraordinary Chris Scott through my radio show.

The Scott family has a special birthday tradition. When a Scott boy turns five years old, his father, Chris, takes him on a personal father and son fishing trip. At the crack of dawn, Chris and his son set off for a day of fun, laughs, and hopefully fish. It might not seem like much of a birthday present, but when you're competing with seven other siblings for your father's attention, the time is priceless.

For Chris Scott and his wife, Shirley, this is all part of the joy, and inevitable struggle, of raising eight children on a modest middle-class salary. They can't afford the newest toys, the best schools, the big house, or the latest fads. The Scotts don't keep up with the Joneses, but they find a way to make it work. Here's their story:

By day, forty-three-year-old Chris Scott works as a document control coordinator at an engineering firm in Houston, Texas. It's not especially glamorous. Chris said, "I push paper electronically."

But after work is when the real coordination begins—being a husband to his wife and a father to each of his eight children, who range in age from sixteen years to two weeks.

Chris and Shirley never intended to have eight children when they married in 1991. But now they wouldn't have it any other way.

"Children are a blessing from the Lord," Chris said. "We have this idea in our culture that just a few kids is the ideal family. But if you look at Scripture, it says 'blessed is the man whose quiver is full' [Psalm 127:5]. I can't get away from the Scriptures that say it's a good thing to have kids."

It's easy to have children. Raising them is the hard part. Adopted at birth, Chris points to his own parents as a faithful model for his own parenting. Initially, his mother worked, but later decided to stay home to care for Chris and his sister while his father provided for the family. Although this resulted in a drop in the family's income, they decided that it was more important for Chris's mother to be home and keep him out of trouble.

Chris acknowledged how countercultural this approach is in the contemporary landscape of dual-income American families, but he stands by it: "I'm living proof that it doesn't take two incomes to make it—what it takes is living within the means of the income that you have."

Chris also emphasized the importance of Shirley's role as a full-time mother. Originally, as Chris put it, "She was thinking she would work part time, but God changed her heart. Hannah [the oldest] was in her arms not more than sixty seconds and it clicked: 'nobody else is going to raise this little girl.'"

Part of that philosophy of child rearing includes homeschooling their children.

"We're strong proponents of homeschooling—academically the statistics are strong, but we homeschool for character. We want our kids to be trustworthy and honest, loyal and faithful, and to have those character qualities. Eventually the skill or job that God's got for them will come out.

"Our goal and our hope is they will bring glory to God in what they do and go farther and higher than we've gone."

Last November, Chris moved his family from Pearland, Texas, a suburb close to Houston, to Alvin, one a little more distant from the city. As a father to seven boys, Chris sees attending to his property, a fixer-upper on 1.7 acres, as not only an opportunity to show his sons how to work hard, but as a time to bond with them. "Now we've got more room than we know what to do with. We have three push mowers on 1.7 acres. It takes a while, but they get it done. We work on the house, we work on the cars, but we have fun together."

Yet even with a full-time job and the responsibilities of raising eight children, Chris never loses sight of his most important commission—his wife. "God, wife, children, country in that order," he said unflinchingly.

"When my sister and I were little, I remember my parents getting away once in a while. They told me, 'You need to date your spouse. Keep that spark flying. There were two of you before three or four or five of you.' So we try to at least once a week go on a coffee date—run to Starbucks or the store—and have some time together. But even more importantly, we don't let the kids stay up late, they're in bed by 8:30 or 9:30, and afterward we sit and visit for thirty minutes or an hour and discuss what the day entailed and what's on our hearts."

In spite of his convictions, he admitted there are times when he is not the perfect father.

"They know that I get mad sometimes, and I've got to ask for their forgiveness. Sometimes I'll put the wrong priority on stuff—I like fishing—and I'm very project oriented so I'll put things off until I get a project finished."

But he realizes his need for contrition when he slips up.

Inevitably, Chris says, there are times when he questions how he has spent his adulthood, but quickly realizes how blessed and meaningful his life is.

By his own admission, Chris doesn't have the most exciting job, or the nicest car, or the biggest house. But he is molding his children into men and women of moral uprightness, of vocational diligence, of love. He's doing it through yard work, through nightly Bible study, through camping trips—lifetimes of memories that don't depreciate, don't get repossessed, don't get laid off.

"I wouldn't trade that for anything. I prefer the company of my wife and children over anyone else."

"When You Are Old"

W. B. YEATS

W. B. Yeats (1865–1939) was an Irish poet and dramatist. A driving force behind the Irish Literary Revival, Yeats was awarded the Nobel Prize in Literature in 1923, making him the first Irishman so honored. In the following poem, Yeats tells of an old man who recounts the beauty of his wife in her young age. But as her beauty faded and age took its toll, he loved her still.

WHEN YOU ARE OLD AND GREY AND FULL OF SLEEP,
    And nodding by the fire, take down this book,
    And slowly read, and dream of the soft look
Your eyes had once, and of their shadows deep;

How many loved your moments of glad grace,
    And loved your beauty with love false or true,
    But one man loved the pilgrim soul in you,
And loved the sorrows of your changing face;

And bending down beside the glowing bars,
    Murmur, a little sadly, how Love fled
    And paced upon the mountains overhead
And hid his face amid a crowd of stars.

"Down by the Salley Gardens"

W. B. YEATS

At the other end of love in this short, pithy poem, Yeats reflects on falling head over heels in love with a girl when he was young, only to be rejected—a witty reminder to remain levelheaded and realistic about love.

DOWN BY THE SALLEY GARDENS MY LOVE AND I DID MEET;
She passed the salley gardens with little snow-white feet.
She bid me take love easy, as the leaves grow on the tree;
But I, being young and foolish, with her did not agree.

In a field by the river my love and I did stand,
And on my leaning shoulder she placed her snow-white hand.
She bid me take life easy, as the grass grows on the weirs;
But I was young and foolish, and now am full of tears.

Robert E. Lee

ORISON SWETT MARDEN

Robert E. Lee (1807–1870), the famous Confederate general, was a man of virtue and manners. Despite the horrors of the war and the toll it took on the nation, Lee always respected Confederate and Union people alike. As this short story illustrates, he was particularly respectful of women, even when other men weren't.

General Robert E. Lee was on his way to Richmond, and was seated in the extreme end of a railroad car, every seat of which was occupied. At one of the stations, an aged woman of humble appearance entered the car, carrying a large basket. She walked the length of the aisle and not a man offered her a seat. When she was opposite General Lee's seat, he arose promptly and said, "Madam, take this seat." Instantly a score of men were on their feet, and a chorus of voices said, "General, have my seat." "No, gentlemen," he replied, "if there was no seat for this old lady, there is no seat for me." It was not long before the car was almost empty. It was too warm to be comfortable.

"Love Among the Ruins"

ROBERT BROWNING

An English poet and playwright, Robert Browning (1812-1889) is recognized as one of the great Victorian poets. "Love Among the Ruins" comes from a collection of works titled *Men and Women*. The poem itself is based on a contrast between past and present—between a great city that once stood and a pile of rubble that now stands in its place. Kings and wars have come and gone and all that is left among the ruins is love. Love is what Browning says outlasts material objects and natural appetites.

> *Now,—the country does not even boast a tree,*
>   *As you see,*
> *To distinguish slopes of verdure, certain rills*
>   *From the hills*
> *Intersect and give a name to, (else they run*
>   *Into one)*
> *"Where the domed and daring palace shot its spires*
>   *Up like fires*
> *O'er the hundred-gated circuit of a wall*
>   *Bounding all,*
> *Made of marble, men might march on nor be prest,*
>   *Twelve abreast.*

And such plenty and perfection, see, of grass
     Never was!
Such a carpet as, this summer-time, o'erspreads
     And embeds
Every vestige of the city, guessed alone,
     Stock or stone—
Where a multitude of men breathed joy and woe
     Long ago;
Lust of glory pricked their hearts up, dread of shame
     Struck them tame;
And that glory and that shame alike, the gold
     Bought and sold.

Now,—the single little turret that remains
     On the plains,
By the caper overrooted, by the gourd
     Overscored,
While the patching houseleek's head of blossom winks
     Through the chinks—
Marks the basement whence a tower in ancient time
     Sprang sublime,
And a burning ring all round, the chariots traced
     As they raced,
And the monarch and his minions and his dames
     Viewed the games.

And I know, while thus the quiet-coloured eve
     Smiles to leave
To their folding, all our many-tinkling fleece
     In such peace,
And the slopes and rills in undistinguished gray
     Melt away—
That a girl with eager eyes and yellow hair

Waits me there
In the turret, whence the charioteers caught soul
   For the goal,
When the king looked, where she looks now, breathless,
   Till I come.

But he looked upon the city, every side,
   Far and wide,
All the mountains topped with temples, all the glades'
   Colonnades,
All the causeys, bridges, aqueducts,—and then.
   All the men!
When I do come, she will speak not, she will stand,
   Either hand
On my shoulder, give her eyes the first embrace
   Of my face,
Ere we rush, ere we extinguish sight and speech
   Each on each.

In one year they sent a million fighters forth
   South and North,
And they built their gods a brazen pillar high
   As the sky,
Yet reserved a thousand chariots in full force—
   Gold, of course.
Oh, heart! oh, blood that freezes, blood that burns!
   Earth's returns
For whole centuries of folly, noise and sin!
   Shut them in,
With their triumphs and their glories and the rest.
   Love is best!

Duff Cooper's Letter to Diana, His Future Wife

Alfred Duff Cooper (1890-1954) was a British politician, diplomat, and writer. In this letter to his future wife, Diana, Cooper used beautiful and moving prose to express his love for her.

August 20, 1918

Darling, my darling. One line in haste to tell you that I love you more today than ever in my life before, that I never see beauty without thinking of you or scent happiness without thinking of you. You have fulfilled all my ambition, realized all my hopes, made all my dreams come true.

You have set a crown of roses on my youth and fortified me against the disaster of our days. Your courageous gaiety has inspired me with joy. Your tender faithfulness has been a rock of security and comfort. I have felt for you all kinds of love at once.

I have asked much of you and you have never failed me. You have intensified all colours, heightened all beauty, deepened all delight. I love you more than life, my beauty, my wonder.

Leo Tolstoy's Letter to His Fiancée, Valeria Arsenev

In the following letter, Leo Tolstoy (1828-1910), the famous Russian writer, describes his love for his fiancée—a love that surpasses beauty and outside appearance and reaches to the soul.

November 2, 1856

I already love in you your beauty, but I am only beginning to love in you that which is eternal and ever precious—your heart, your soul. Beauty one could get to know and fall in love with in one hour and cease to love it as speedily; but the soul one must learn to know. Believe me, nothing on earth is given without labour, even love, the most beautiful and natural of feelings.

"A Father's Gift to His Son on His Becoming an Apprentice"

ANONYMOUS

The following passage is excerpted from a larger manual of advice from father to son on growing up, finding a job, and raising a family. Here the father offers counseling on which qualities to look for in a woman and which qualities to develop in yourself to prepare for marriage and to make it last. It is old-fashioned indeed, but still mostly applicable today.

With a prospect of success in business, you will naturally turn your thoughts to matrimony. Here, my dear son, be willing to listen to the advice of an old man, anxious for your welfare, in this very important choice, upon which more depends than you are perhaps aware of. It is true the married life has many incumbrances, from which the single is free; but much is to be said on both sides; yet, I must add, a cheerful partner, and a comfortable home, are the strongest incentives a young man can have to a proper attention to business, and to propriety of conduct. No sight is more attractive and gratifying, than a house governed by love and unity, with an active disharge [*sic*] of duty.

Choose a wife whose reputation is pure, and her connections honest and respectable; and whose temper is good. Let your religious principles agree; and let religion, without cant or hypocrisy, regulate all your household.

It is right for a tradesman to select a wife of frugal and industrious habits; for these days afford terrible examples of the neglect of these homely virtues. The happiness of your future life will be increased or diminished by your choice of a partner; therefore, be guided by discretion, as well as by affection; and let her be such an one, in every sense, as you will never be ashamed of.

Call to mind there are as many duties required from the husband as the wife; and a little self-denial and patience on both sides will produce that domestic happiness I pray may be your lot. Let mutual confidence prevail, for concealment between man and wife is a great bar to peace. I shall not enter upon all the duties of the married life, as I rely upon your goodness of heart, that you will not violate any of them.

Should you become a father, your duties and your cares will multiply, but you will also have your comforts: and as you will have been guided by wisdom hither-towards, so here the words of wisdom will assist you still; and the duty of a father is so clearly pointed out both by religion and common sense, that I need not dwell upon it, though it is the most important of all duties.

In your house exercise hospitality, but shun all unnecessary waste, and superflu-ous feasting; these ill agree with the calls of a family, or with the attention we owe to our poor neighbors, who surely have a claim upon our bounty when we are enabled, by Providence, to become bountiful. We find a blessing attending upon charity when it is secret and unostentatious: that charity is best which exercises a spirit of discernment.

Let prudence superintend your househould [sic] in every department, and pro-priety regulate every part.

❧

Advice to Boys

Rev. Lewis Johnston

In the preface to his work of instruction for boys, Rev. Lewis Johnston (1803–1865) dedicated this book, published in 1900, "To the boys of our land in whose keeping the future interests of the country, moral and polit-ical, are to be entrusted." Rev. Johnston understood the importance of educating and training boys to grow up to be responsible men of good character. The following passage lays out his advice for interacting with women.

Shun bad words, obscene books, lustful gestures or actions; light or impudence and imprudent behavior; dishonoring the marriage bed. Excess in eating, drinking, sleeping, keeping lewd company, bad companions, bad luscivious [sic] songs, and vulgar jokes . . .

You must not encourage, but rather give yourself to what is kind and pure, chaste, true, loving, elevating, ennobling, and by all means learn to distinguish between love and lust. This is the switch at which so many are side-tracked to ruin.

Many young boys and girls, and older ones as well, have been thrown in each other's company in private, in the valleys, the mountain tops, on trips to different places, and no thought of wrong action nor improper conduct once crossed the mind.

When you love you seldom think to do anything that will for once bring trouble or cause you to think less of what you love. It will be kept pure and clean. If you truly love a girl she would find favor in your sight. You would cherish and take the utmost care of her. You would see that she was not hurt nor harmed, nor sullied in any way . . .

Lust will degrade you; love will elevate you. Lust will make you vile, selfish, sordid, low; love will make you pure, chaste; lovable, manly. Lust will make you earthly, sensual, devilish; love will make you godlike, continent, noble.

This will help you to examine yourself and restrain many actions that are foreign to true love.

. . . How you are to treat the girls with whom you come in contact. By all means be kind and polite to these young ladies, and if any are tart or sour in her actions or speech you politely pass it by in kindness, never be rude, never, never, never. Do not make any vile advance, getting unpleasantly close up to a young lady, lulling, caressing, fondling, kissing, hugging, every time you meet, placing your hands upon her person or bosom, telling ugly stories, jests that broach on the obscene. Make it a point to be discreet, chaste, pure. Be a man. Be true to your promise. Be honest. Be truthful. Never talk or tell things that will hurt the reputation of a girl. Never say slight things of her, even if she steps out of the way. Have in your mind, she belongs to the sex to which your sister and mother belong, and you are going to respect, even if the sight of her sickens you.

Profile: Nolan Ryan

Here is a man who is not only a bulwark of his own family but an inspiration and model to his community. Great men, like baseball legend

Nolan Ryan, have a positive and lasting impact on the lives of men and women around them. He played the American game of baseball with excellence equaled by only a few other men, and he has lived his life as many should. As this brief story shows, his example was taken to heart.

Nolan Ryan was born to throw a baseball. No one in baseball history threw a baseball harder and longer than "The Ryan Express." The great slugger Reggie Jackson once said that trying to hit a Ryan fastball was "like eating coffee with a fork." With unforgiving power, Ryan and his trademark fastball, often topping 100 mph, embarrassed baseball's best hitters for more than two decades.

Consider Ryan's résumé. His career lasted twenty-seven years, a major league record. He has 5,714 career strikeouts and seven career no-hitters, both major league records. He won 324 games and only Cy Young started more games than his 773. He was an eight-time All-Star and was baseball's first million-dollar man. Other than Jackie Robinson, he is currently the only baseball player to have his jersey number retired by three different teams: the Angels, Astros, and Rangers. In 1999, he was inducted into baseball's Hall of Fame.

From the 1970s to the early 1990s, Nolan Ryan was one of the most popular athletes in America, not just because of his success, but also because of his stature and standing in his local communities. In his home state of Texas, Nolan Ryan is a household name.

In honor of Ryan's retirement in 1993, the Texas Rangers held Nolan Ryan Appreciation Week at Arlington Stadium. Any fan under the age of twenty-seven (the length of his career) who had been named either Nolan or Ryan would be allowed to walk on the field prior to the game. The Rangers' staff expected a hundred or so fans to show up. Instead, close to one thousand Nolans and Ryans (including a few females and a set of twins named Nolan and Ryan) showed up. The response was so overwhelming that the staff gave up on checking IDs and allowed everyone in line to enter. As they circled the field, Ryan sat in the dugout and smiled and waved to each of them. It was one of those great sports moments where the gravitas of human experience transcended mere athleticism.

In this crowd of fans, many of whom had never met Ryan, were people with so much respect for him that they had named their children after him. That surely must be a sign of a great man. Today, a road running in front of Rangers Ballpark and a stretch of highway outside Houston are both called Nolan Ryan Expressway, and he is currently part owner, CEO, and president of the Texas Rangers baseball organization. Ryan will always be remembered as one of baseball's all-time great pitchers, but his legacy as a man and a role model will live on long beyond his baseball days.

From *She Stoops to Conquer*

OLIVER GOLDSMITH

Oliver Goldsmith (1730–1774) was an Anglo-Irish writer and poet. In this short passage from one of his most famous works, *She Stoops to Conquer*, Goldsmith describes old Mr. and Mrs. Hardcastle reflecting on life. Mrs. Hardcastle resents the change in life that comes with age and the boringness that it brings. In a touching moment, Mr. Hardcastle responds that he loves everything that comes with old age, including his old wife.

MRS. HARDCASTLE: Ay, your times were fine times indeed; you have been telling us of them for many a long year. Here we live in an old rumbling mansion, that looks for all the world like an inn, but that we never see company. Our best visitors are old Mrs. Oddfish, the curate's wife, and little Cripplegate, the lame dancing-master; and all our entertainment your old stories of Prince Eugene and the Duke of Marlborough. I hate such old-fashioned trumpery.

MR. HARDCASTLE: And I love it. I love every thing that's old; old friends, old times, old manners, old books, old wine; and I believe, Dorothy [*Taking her hand.*] you'll own I have been pretty fond of an old wife.

Excerpt from *Bleak House*

CHARLES DICKENS

Charles Dickens (1812–1870) was arguably the most popular English writer of the Victorian era, famous for works like *Oliver Twist, A Christmas Carol*, and *Great Expectations*, and perhaps the greatest novelist of all time. In this selection from *Bleak House*, a trooper visiting with Mr. and Mrs. Bagnet remarks on how well they take care of their son, so he turns to the son and instructs him to always obey his parents, with a very specific test in mind.

B oiled beef and greens constitute the day's variety on the former repast of boiled pork and greens, and Mrs. Bagnet serves out the meal in the same way and seasons it with the best of temper, being that rare sort of old girl that she receives Good to her arms without a hint that it might be Better and catches light from any little spot of darkness near her.

. . .

In giving Mrs. Bagnet's hand, with her work in it, a friendly shake—for she took her seat beside him—the trooper's attention is attracted to her face. After looking at it for a little while as she plies her needle, he looks to young Woolwich, sitting on his stool in the corner, and beckons that fifer to him.

"See there, my boy," says George, very gently smoothing the mother's hair with his hand, "there's a good loving forehead for you! All bright with love of you, my boy. A little touched by the sun and the weather through following your father about and taking care of you, but as fresh and wholesome as a ripe apple on a tree."

Mr. Bagnet's face expresses, so far as in its wooden material lies, the highest approbation and acquiescence.

"The time will come, my boy," pursues the trooper, "when this hair of your mother's will be grey, and this forehead all crossed and re-crossed with wrinkles, and a fine old lady she'll be then. Take care, while you are young, that you can think in those days, 'I never whitened a hair of her dear head—I never marked a sorrowful line in her face!' For of all the many things that you can think of when you are a man, you had better have THAT by you, Woolwich!"

Two Poems

ROBERT BROWNING

In addition to "Love Among the Ruins," Robert Browning (1812–1889) penned many other poems about the different facets of love. These two selections highlight Browning's perspective of a man's unique compassion for a woman and a woman's transformative power in a man's life.

"One Word More"

God be thanked, the meanest of his creatures
Boasts two soul-sides, one to face the world with,
One to show a woman when he loves her!

"Summum Bonum"

All the breath and the bloom of the year in the bag of one bee:
All the wonder and wealth of the mine in the heart of one gem:
In the core of one pearl all the shade and the shine of the sea:
Breath and bloom, shade and shine, wonder, wealth, and—how far above
*   them—*
Truth that's brighter than gem,
Trust that's purer than pearl,—
Brightest truth, purest trust in the universe—all were for me
In the kiss of one girl.

From *Don Juan*

LORD BYRON

George Gordon Byron (1788-1824), known more commonly as Lord Byron, was a leading British poet in the Romantic movement. In his narrative poem *Don Juan*, Lord Byron describes man and love from a woman's perspective. She laments that men don't take love seriously and are often preoccupied with fame, glory, and power. It's a cautionary tale that men should not take love lightly, because women don't.

> *Man's love is of man's life a thing apart,*
> *'Tis woman's whole existence: man may range*
> *The court, camp, church, the vessel, and the mart,*
> *Sword, gown, gain, glory, offer in exchange*
> *Pride, fame, ambition, to fill up his heart,*
> *And few there are whom these cannot estrange;*
> *Men have all these resources, we but one,*
> *To love again, and be again undone.*

Penelope

HOMER

The *Odyssey* is an epic Greek poem attributed to the ancient writer Homer. It is one of the first works of Western literature, thought to be written around the eighth century BC. The plot centers on Odysseus and his long journey home after the battle of Troy. While he is gone, it is assumed that he has died, and his wife, Penelope, must fend off suitors who want to marry her. Fighting off temptation after temptation on his journey home, Odysseus remains true to Penelope and returns home to kill the wicked suitors and take his wife's hand again. In this scene,

Odysseus has just returned home and killed the suitors, but Penelope still does not know if this is really Odysseus or a stranger. So she comes up with a test for him to prove his true identity.

A t one moment she looked him full in the face, but then again directly, she was misled by his shabby clothes and failed to recognise him, till Telemachus began to reproach her and said:

"Mother—but you are so hard that I cannot call you by such a name—why do you keep away from my father in this way? Why do you not sit by his side and begin talking to him and asking him questions? No other woman could bear to keep away from her husband when he had come back to her after twenty years of absence, and after having gone through so much; but your heart always was as hard as a stone."

Penelope answered, "My son, I am so lost in astonishment that I can find no words in which either to ask questions or to answer them. I cannot even look him straight in the face. Still, if he really is Ulysses come back to his own home again, we shall get to understand one another better by and by, for there are tokens with which we two are alone acquainted, and which are hidden from all others. . . ."

"My dear," answered Penelope, "I have no wish to set myself up, nor to depreciate you; but I am not struck by your appearance, for I very well remember what kind of a man you were when you set sail from Ithaca. Nevertheless, Euryclea, take his bed outside the bed chamber that he himself built. Bring the bed outside this room, and put bedding upon it with fleeces, good coverlets, and blankets."

She said this to try him, but Ulysses was very angry and said, "Wife, I am much displeased at what you have just been saying. Who has been taking my bed from the place in which I left it? He must have found it a hard task, no matter how skilled a workman he was, unless some god came and helped him to shift it. There is no man living, however strong and in his prime, who could move it from its place, for it is a marvelous curiosity which I made with my very own hands. . . ."

When she heard the sure proofs Ulysses now gave her, she fairly broke down. She flew weeping to his side, flung her arms about his neck, and kissed him, "Do not be angry with me Ulysses," she cried, "you, who are the wisest of mankind. We have suffered, both of us. Heaven has denied us the happiness of spending our youth, and of growing old, together; do not then be aggrieved or take it amiss that I did not embrace you thus as soon as I saw you. I have been shuddering all the time through fear that someone might come here and deceive me with a lying story; for there are many very wicked people going about. . . ."

Then Ulysses in his turn melted, and wept as he clasped his dear and faithful wife to his bosom. As the sight of land is welcome to men who are swimming towards the shore, when Neptune has wrecked their ship with the fury of his winds and waves; a few alone reach the land, and these, covered with brine, are thankful when they find themselves on firm ground and out of danger—even so was her husband welcome to her as she looked upon him, and she could not tear her two fair arms from about his neck.

Telemachus

HOMER

One of the most profound themes of Homer's *Odyssey* is one which every man can relate to: the relationship (or lack thereof) between a son and his father. In the first few books of *The Odyssey*, Odysseus's son, Telemachus, embarks on a quest to discover what has become of his father, who left to fight in the Trojan War when Telemachus was still a baby and has never returned to his wife and son. Eventually, Telemachus and Odysseus reunite and team up to defeat the arrogant and greedy suitors, who have overrun Odysseus's estate in anticipation of marrying Penelope, Odysseus's grieving wife. The moment of reunification between Telemachus and Odysseus is one of the most moving scenes in all of literature, as it depicts the fulfillment of a son's lifelong desire for a relationship with his father. As Waller Newell observed in his essay, "The Crisis of Manliness," too many boys today are like Telemachus, longing for a father who will nurture them and guide them through a hard world. Many boys from broken homes are forced at too-early an age to be their mother's protector from oppressive men while struggling to bring themselves up in a way that their absent father would be proud of. As Waller says, each year that he tells this story to his students the room becomes quieter and quieter because more and more of them realize that they are Telemachus.

S ir," said Telemachus, "as regards your question, so long as my father was here it was well with us and with the house, but the gods in their displeasure have willed it otherwise, and have hidden him away more closely than mortal man was ever yet hidden. I could have borne it better even though he were dead, if he had fallen with his men before Troy, or had died with friends around him when the days of his fighting were done; for then the Acheeans would have built a mound over his ashes, and I should myself have been heir to his renown; but now the storm-winds have spirited him away we know not whither; he is gone without leaving so much as a trace behind him, and I inherit nothing but dismay. . . ."

And Ulysses said, "I am no god, why should you take me for one? I am your father, on whose account you grieve and suffer so much at the hands of lawless men."

As he spoke he kissed his son, and a tear fell from his cheek on to the ground, for he had restrained all tears till now. But Telemachus could not yet believe that it was his father, and said:—"You are not my father, but some god is flattering me with vain hopes that I may grieve the more hereafter; no mortal man could of himself contrive to do as you have been doing, and make yourself old and young at a moment's notice, unless a god were with him. A second ago you were old and all in rags, and now you are like some god come down from heaven."

Ulysses answered, "Telemachus, you ought not to be so immeasurably aston-ished at my being really here. There is no other Ulysses who will come hereafter. Such as I am, it is I, who after long wandering and much hardship have got home in the twentieth year to my own country. What you wonder at is the work of the redoubt-able goddess Minerva, who does with me whatever she will, for she can do what she pleases. At one moment she makes me like a beggar, and the next I am a young man with good clothes on my back; it is an easy matter for the gods who live in heaven to make any man look either rich or poor."

As he spoke he sat down, and Telemachus threw his arms about his father and wept. They were both so much moved that they cried aloud like eagles or vultures with crooked talons that have been robbed of their half fledged young by peasants. Thus piteously did they weep, and the sun would have gone down upon their mourning if Telemachus had not suddenly said, "In what ship, my dear father, did your crew bring you to Ithaca? Of what nation did they declare themselves to be—for you cannot have come by land?"

"I will tell you the truth, my son," replied Ulysses.

—— ❧ ——

Profile: Dr. Ben Carson

Dr. Ben Carson was born into abject poverty, with little, if anything, going for him in life. Today, he is one of the world's foremost neurosurgeons, a man who has made earth-changing advances in medicine and saved many lives. His shift from rags to riches, from poverty to international prominence, is one of the most compelling stories of modern times. As is the case with many great men, he turned his life around through education, diligence, character, and, as we will see, the help of an incredibly devoted mother.

Sonya Carson was one of twenty-four children. She was raised in and out of foster homes and knew little more than poverty and abuse. At age thirteen, she married. Shortly after having her two children, Benjamin and Curtis, she discovered that her husband was a bigamist.

With only a third grade education and hardly anything to her name, she left her husband and raised Ben and Curtis on her own.

Statistics and demographics would predict that young African-American boys in the inner city with a single mother and no money were destined to a life of poverty and misfortune, but Sonya Carson didn't make excuses, and she didn't let her sons make them either. And though she had little formal education herself, she knew the importance of it. She realized that education was the ladder that would lift her sons from poverty to the middle class.

"She recognized the importance of education because she cleaned the homes of very successful people, and then she lived in the neighborhood where we were," Carson told me on my radio show, *Morning in America*. "She was smart enough to say, 'You know, the big difference between these people and these people is not so much the color of their skin but what they do with their minds. You've got one group here just looking at TV and drinking alcohol and out having a good time, and you've got another group here who is reading books and studying and planning and strategizing.'"

So Carson's mother limited the time he and his brother could watch TV to only a couple of shows a week, while many of their friends wasted away their time and future watching TV all day. That made the Carson boys terribly uncool in the neighborhood.

But their mother wasn't concerned about coolness or popularity. Instead of watching TV, Carson and his brother had to check out books from the public library and write regular book reports. (That made them even more uncool.) His mother would grade them, marking them as a teacher would. All along they had no idea she couldn't even read. She did all she could to educate her boys, even with her limited resources and knowledge.

Carson admits that in elementary school he was one of the dumbest students in the class, but by high school, thanks to his mother's tireless work, he started to excel. He went on to Yale University, where he graduated with a degree in psychology. From there he attended the University of Michigan Medical School, where he decided to become a neurosurgeon. In 1977, Carson began a residency at Johns Hopkins University. By 1985, at the ripe age of thirty-three, Carson held the distinguished title of director of pediatric neurosurgery.

In 1987, Carson became the first surgeon ever to successfully separate twins conjoined at the back of the head. The surgery lasted a grueling twenty-two hours, but afterward the twins went on to recover fully and live normal, independent lives. Through this remarkable advance in medicine and surgery, Carson established himself as one of the world's premier surgeons.

In 2008, he was awarded the Presidential Medal of Freedom, the highest civilian award in the United States, by President George W. Bush, for his exemplary accomplishments in medicine. Today, he continues to operate on hundreds of children a year, saving countless lives.

George Washington to Martha

It seems unlikely that a dignified military man like George Washington would pour out his emotions in such a way, but in this September 2, 1758, letter to his future wife, Martha, the twenty-six-year-old Washington expresses his love. The letter culminates in a sly proposal of marriage.

Tis true I profess myself a votary of love. I acknowledge that a lady is in the case and further I confess that this lady is known to you. Yes, Madame, as well as she is to one who is too sensible to her charms to deny the power whose influence he feels and must ever submit to. I feel the force of her amiable beauties and the recollection of a thousand tender passages that I could wish to obliterate till I am bid to revive them. But experience, alas, sadly reminds me how impossible this is . . . You have drawn me, dear Madame, or rather have I drawn myself into an honest confession of a simple fact. Misconstrue not my meaning; doubt it not nor expose it . . . One thing above all things in this world I wish to know, and only one person of your acquaintance can solve me that, or guess my meaning. But adieu to this till happier times, if I shall ever see them.

Pierre Curie

MARIE CURIE

In 1894, a twenty-seven-year-old Polish graduate student studying in Paris, Maria Skłodowska (1867–1934), made the acquaintance of Pierre Curie (1859–1906), who at thirty-five was already an accomplished physicist. Their friendship soon blossomed into a marriage, bound not only by love but by a mutual pursuit of scientific knowledge. As a result, the Curies became renowned as scientists the world over, making landmark contributions in the field of radiation, with the couple winning a Nobel Prize in 1903. In this excerpt from Marie's biography of her husband, published after his death, Marie records Pierre's early pursuit and courtship of her, making evident his need for a wife who could share in his life quest of scientific discovery.

I met Pierre Curie for the first time in the spring of the year 1894 . . . A Polish physicist whom I knew, and who was a great admirer of Pierre Curie, one day invited us together to spend the evening with himself and his wife.

As I entered the room, Pierre Curie was standing in the recess of a French window opening on a balcony. He seemed to me very young, though he was at that time thirty-five years old. I was struck by the open expression of his face and by the slight suggestion of detachment in his whole attitude. His speech, rather slow and deliberate, his simplicity, and his smile, at once grave and youthful, inspired confidence. We began a conversation which soon became friendly. It first concerned certain scientific matters about which I was very glad to be able to ask his opinion. Then we discussed certain social and humanitarian subjects which interested us both. There was, between his conceptions and mine, despite the difference between our native countries, a surprising kinship, no doubt attributable to a certain likeness in the moral atmosphere in which we were both raised by our families.

We met again at the Physics Society and in the laboratory. Then he asked if he might call upon me . . . Pierre Curie came to see me, and showed a simple and sincere sympathy with my student life. Soon he caught the habit of speaking to me of his dream of an existence consecrated entirely to scientific research, and he asked me to share that life. It was not, however, easy for me to make such a decision, for it meant separation from my country and my family, and the renouncement of certain social projects that were dear to me. Having grown up in an atmosphere of patriotism kept alive by the oppression of Poland, I wished, like many other young people of my country, to contribute my effort toward the conservation of our national spirit . . .

During the year 1894 Pierre Curie wrote me letters that seem to me admirable in their form. No one of them was very long, for he had the habit of concise expression, but all were written in a spirit of sincerity and with an evident anxiety to make the one he desired as a companion know him as he was . . . It is appropriate to quote here a few lines which express how he looked on the possibility of our marriage:

"We have promised each other (is it not true?) to have, the one for the other, at least a great affection. Provided that you do not change your mind! For there are no promises which hold; these are things that do not admit of compulsion.

"It would, nevertheless, be a beautiful thing in which I hardly dare believe, to pass through life together hypnotized in our dreams: your dream for your country; our dream for humanity; our dream for science. Of all these dreams, I believe the last, alone, is legitimate. I mean to say by this that we are powerless to change the social order. Even if this were not true we should not know what to do . . . From the point of view of science, on the contrary, we can pretend to accomplish something. The territory here is more solid and obvious, and however small it is, it is truly in our possession."

"Annabel Lee"

EDGAR ALLAN POE

Edgar Allan Poe (1809–1849) was one of the finest American writers of the nineteenth century. Poe focused on morose themes of death, sadness, and loss. Though their speculations have never been confirmed, many scholars believe that Poe wrote this poem in memory of his wife, Virginia, who died in 1847. This poem echoes a distant and dead love gone forever.

It was many and many a year ago,
In a kingdom by the sea,
That a maiden there lived whom you may know
By the name of Annabel Lee;
And this maiden she lived with no other thought
Than to love and be loved by me.

I was a child and she was a child,
In this kingdom by the sea;
But we loved with a love that was more than love—
I and my Annabel Lee;
With a love that the winged seraphs of heaven
Coveted her and me.

And this was the reason that, long ago,
In this kingdom by the sea,
A wind blew out of a cloud, chilling

My beautiful Annabel Lee;
So that her highborn kinsman came
    And bore her away from me,
To shut her up in a sepulcher
    In this kingdom by the sea.

The angels, not half so happy in heaven,
    Went envying her and me
Yes! that was the reason
    (as all men know, In this kingdom by the sea)
That the wind came out of the cloud by night,
    Chilling and killing my Annabel Lee.

But our love was stronger by far than the love
    Of those who were older than we
    Of many far wiser than we
And neither the angels in heaven above,
    Nor the demons down under the sea,
Can ever dissever my soul from the soul
    Of the beautiful Annabel Lee.

For the moon never beams without bringing me dreams
    Of the beautiful Annabel Lee;
And the stars never rise but I feel the bright eyes
    Of the beautiful Annabel Lee;
And so, all the night-tide, I lie down by the side
Of my darling, my darling, my life and my bride,
    In the sepulcher there by the sea,
    In her tomb by the sounding sea.

Antony and Cleopatra

JOHN DRYDEN

John Dryden (1631–1700) was the dominant literary figure of the 1600s in England, winning great acclaim for his works, many of which had classical themes. His translation of the *Aeneid* is still considered a masterpiece. In *All For Love*, Dryden examined the relationship between Mark Antony and Cleopatra. Here, two of Antony's compatriots lament the effect Cleopatra has had on Antony, as they witness the transformation of a Roman warrior into a love-drunk fool. A shallow love can make a man be foolish.

He eats not, drinks not, sleeps not, has no use
Of anything, but thought; or if he talks,
'Tis to himself, and then 'tis perfect raving:
Then he defies the world, and bids it pass,
Sometimes he gnaws his lips, and curses loud
The boy Octavius; then he draws his mouth
Into a scornful smile, and cries, "Take all,
The world's not worth my care."

———

Oh, she has decked his ruin with her love,
Led him in golden bands to gaudy slaughter,
And made perdition pleasing: She has left him
The blank of what he was
. . .
Can any Roman see, and know him now,
Thus altered from the lord of half mankind,
Unbent, unsinewed, made a woman's toy,
Shrunk from the vast extent of all his honours,

And crampt within a corner of the world?
O Antony!
Thou bravest soldier, and thou best of friends!
Bounteous as nature; next to nature's God!
Couldst thou but make new worlds, so wouldst thou give them,
As bounty were thy being! rough in battle,
As the first Romans when they went to war;
Yet after victory more pitiful
Than all their praying virgins left at home!

Abraham Lincoln and Grace Bedell

On October 15, 1860, little Grace Bedell wrote to the Republican candidate for president to encourage him with some advice. This famous presidential candidate ended up taking her advice, and on his way to the White House, he stopped in Westfield, New York, to give little Grace a kiss and thank her for her advice. Here is manliness as gentleness to a child, politeness, and a light touch of humor.

N Y
Westfield Chatauque Co
Oct 15. 1860
Hon A B Lincoln

Dear Sir

My father has just home from the fair and brought home your picture and Mr. Hamlin's. I am a little girl only eleven years old, but want you should be President of the United States very much so I hope you wont think me very bold to write to such a great man as you are. Have you any little girls about as large as I am if so give them my love and tell her to write to me if you cannot answer this letter. I have got 4 brother's [*sic*] and part of them will vote for you any way and if you will let your whiskers grow I will try and get the rest of them to vote for you you would look a great deal better for your face is so thin. All the ladies like whiskers and they would tease their husband's [*sic*] to vote for you and then you would be President. My father is a going to vote for you and if I was a man I would vote for you to [*sic*] but I will try and get every one to vote for you that I can I think that rail fence around your picture makes it look very pretty I have got a little baby sister she is nine weeks old and is just as cunning as can be. When you direct your letter dir[e]ct to Grace Bedell Westfield Chatauque County New York

I must not write any more answer this letter right off

Good bye

Grace Bedell

October 19, 1860

Springfield, Illinois

Miss. Grace Bedell

My dear little Miss.

Your very agreeable letter of the 15th. is received.

I regret the necessity of saying I have no daughters. I have three sons—one seventeen, one nine, and one seven, years of age. They, with their mother, constitute my whole family.

As to the whiskers, having never worn any, do you not think people would call it a piece of silly affection if I were to begin it now? Your very sincere well-wisher

A. Lincoln

Marcus Cato

PLUTARCH

Marcus Cato (95–46 BC) was one of the subjects of Plutarch's *Lives*, a work composed in the first century AD. Although Cato is remembered as one of Rome's greatest and most dignified statesmen, Plutarch here emphasizes Cato's role as a father to his son and shows how raising a child should not be subcontracted to others.

As soon as he had a son born, though he had never such urgent business upon his hands, unless it were some public matter, he would be by when his wife washed it and dressed it in its swaddling clothes ... When he began to come to years of discretion, Cato himself would teach him to read, although he had a servant, a very good grammarian, called Chilo, who taught many others; but he thought it not fit, as he himself said, to have his son reprimanded by a slave, or pulled, it may be, by the ears when found tardy in his lesson: nor would he have him owe to a servant the obligation of so great a thing as his learning; he himself, therefore, taught him his grammar, law, and his gymnastic exercises. Nor did he only show him, too, how to throw a dart, to fight in armor, and to ride, but to box also and to endure both heat and cold, and to swim over the most rapid and rough rivers. He says, likewise, that he wrote histories, in large characters, with his own hand, so that his son, without stirring out of the house, might learn to know about his countrymen and forefathers; nor did he less abstain from speaking anything obscene before his son than if it had been in the presence of the sacred virgins, called vestals.*

---

* The vestal virgins were priestesses of the Roman goddess Vesta, who were required to remain virgins for life, and were considered very holy by Roman society.

The Influence of a Father

JOHN STUART MILL

Remembered as a seminal thinker in the world of political philosophy and economics, John Stuart Mill (1806–1873) was prodigiously gifted intellectually. By age ten he could easily read Plato and Demosthenes in the original Greek. Mill benefited greatly from his father, James Mill, an accomplished intellectual in his own right. In his *Autobiography*, Mill admired his father's patience as he endeavored to master the classical languages.

My father, in all his teaching, demanded of me not only the utmost that I could do, but much that I could by no possibility could have done. What he was himself willing to undergo for the sake of my instruction, may be judged from the fact, that I went through the whole process of preparing my Greek lessons in the same room and at the same table at which he was writing: and as in those days Greek and English lexicons were not, and I could make no more use of a Greek and Latin lexicon than could be made without having yet begun to learn Latin, I was forced to have recourse to him for the meaning of every word which I did not know. This incessant interruption, he, one of the most impatient of men, submitted to, and wrote under that interruption several volumes of his History and all else that he had to write during those years.

The Farmer and His Sons

AESOP

Aesop, a slave and storyteller who lived in ancient Greece, was the author of a collection of stories, or fables, that remain some of the most well-known children's stories in the world. His stories were often parables or allegories tied to moral values. In "The Farmer and His Sons," a dying old man tells his sons of a buried treasure in their fields. While the boys never find a chest of treasure, they discover the real treasure their father was talking about in the hard work of digging and harvesting the fields.

A Farmer had come to the end of his life, and wished his Sons to go on with the care of the farm. So he called them to him, and said:—

"My Sons, I am about to die, but if you will dig up the vineyard, you will find what is hidden there."

They thought there must be a pot of gold there; so, after their father had died, they took spades and dug up all the soil.

The pot of gold, to be sure, they did not find, but the vineyard was so well dug over that it bore more grapes than ever.

This fable teaches that hard work brings the pot of gold.

Things to Tell Your Children or Grandchildren

CHARLES SYKES

The following collection of rules are adapted from *50 Rules Kids Won't Learn in School* by Charles Sykes, modern American writer and radio commentator and author of *Dumbing Down Our Kids: Why American Children Feel Good about Themselves but Can't Read, Write, or Add*. These rules are practical guidelines for how a man should approach life and deal with those around him.

Rule 1: Life is not fair—get used to it!

Rule 2: The world won't care about your self-esteem. The world will expect you to accomplish something before you feel good about yourself.

Rule 3: You will not make $60,000 a year right out of high school. You won't be a vice president with a car phone until you earn both.

Rule 4: If you think your teacher is tough, wait till you get a boss.

Rule 5: Flipping burgers is not beneath your dignity. Your grandparents had a different word for burger flipping. They called it opportunity . . .

Rule 6: If you mess up, it's not your parents' fault, so don't whine about your mistakes, learn from them.

Rule 7: Before you were born, your parents weren't as boring as they are now. They got that way from paying your bills, cleaning your clothes, and listening to you talk about how cool you thought you were. So, before you save the rain forest from the parasites of your parents' generation, try delousing the closet in your own room.

Rule 8: Your school may have done away with winners and losers, but life has not. In some schools they have abolished failing grades and they'll give you as many times as you want to get the right answer. This doesn't bear the slightest resemblance to anything in real life.

Rule 9: Life is not divided into semesters. You don't get summers off and very few employers are interested in helping you find yourself. Do that on your own time.

Rule 10: Television is not real life. In real life people actually have to leave the coffee shop and go to jobs.

Rule 11: Be nice to nerds. Chances are you'll end up working for one!

Fatherhood

RONALD REAGAN

While he is remembered most as the president who won the cold war and renewed the spirit of American exceptionalism, Ronald Reagan (1911–2004) never forgot the importance of family. In his address to the nation on Father's Day 1986, Reagan described the hard work of fatherhood and the undying devotion to one's children.

Fatherhood can sometimes be walking the floor at midnight with a baby that can't sleep. More likely, fatherhood is repairing a bicycle wheel for the umpteenth time, knowing that it won't last the afternoon. Fatherhood is guiding a youth through the wilderness of adolescence toward adulthood. Fatherhood is holding tight when all seems to be falling apart; and it's letting go when it is time to part. Fatherhood is long hours at the blast furnace or in the fields, behind the wheel or in front of a computer screen, working a 12-hour shift or doing a 6-month tour of duty. It's giving one's all, from the break of day to its end, on the job, in the house, but most of all in the heart.

The Best Things in Life

THEODORE ROOSEVELT

President, war hero, author, hunter—the list of President Theodore Roosevelt's accomplishments is unparalleled. Taking all this into account, Roosevelt remarks in his autobiography that there is still nothing like being a father and enjoying the company of your children.

There are many kinds of success in life worth having. It is exceedingly interesting and attractive to be a successful businessman, or railroad man, or farmer, or a successful lawyer, or doctor, or a writer, or a president, or a ranchman, or the colonel of a fighting regiment, or to kill grizzly bears and lions. But for unflagging interest and enjoyment, a household of children, if things go reasonably well, certainly makes all other forms of success and achievement lose their importance by comparison.

Teddy Roosevelt with His Children

ERNEST RUSE

Even those who observed Roosevelt's life from the outside couldn't help but notice his love and care for his children. Here the writer Ernest Ruse describes Roosevelt wrestling and playing with his children behind closed doors during his presidency.

When Mr. Roosevelt has closed the door of his home behind him, says one of his personal friends; the soldier, the statesman, the reformer, the writer, are all shut out, and only the husband and the father enter. His devotion to his wife and children is ideal. To the latter he is not only a father, but also a big, over-grown brother. One of his chief delights is to get down on all-fours in the nursery and play bear with the younger ones. When the little bears tire he sometimes sings old Dutch folksongs for them. Though his voice was never intended for singing, there is a certain quaintness and rough charm about these memories of Holland that greatly delight the children.

Nor is it only his own children who command his devotion. He is emphatically a friend of children. During his campaign he has been known to—catch the eye of a poor little crippled girl in a patched frock, who was making frantic but hopeless efforts to reach him in the outskirts of the crowd, and, pushing aside all the rest, make a way for her, to the great amazement of the curled darlings in the front row.

Jonathan Edwards with His Children

S. E. DWIGHT

Jonathan Edwards (1703–1758), a minister in colonial Massachusetts, was known for his powerful sermons and tireless evangelism. Edwards was one of the most influential and original theologians of the day, and his razor-sharp mind was equaled by his superhuman work ethic. Edwards commonly spent thirteen hours a day in his study, often starting work at 4:30 in the morning, but as S.E. Dwight made clear in his account, he always prioritized his relationship with his family. When we think of Jonathan Edwards we tend to think of his famous sermon "Sinners in the Hands of an Angry God," but when he dealt with his children, Edwards was attentive and loving.

I n his family, he practiced that conscientious exactness which was conspicuous, in all his ways. He maintained a great esteem and regard for his amiable and excellent consort. Much of the tender and kind was expressed in his conversation with her, and conduct towards her. He was wont frequently to admit her into his study, and converse freely with her on matters of religion; and he used commonly to pray with her in his study, at least once a day, unless something extraordinary prevented.

The time for this, commonly, was just before going to bed, after prayer in the family. As he rose very early himself, he was wont to have his family up betimes in the morning; after which, before they entered on the business of the day, he attended on family prayer: when a chapter in the Bible was read, commonly by candle-light in the winter; upon which he asked his children questions according to their age and capacity; and took occasion to explain some passages in it, or enforce any duty recommended, as he thought most proper.

He was careful and thorough in the government of his children; and, as a consequence of this, they reverenced, esteemed, and loved him. He took special care to begin his government of them in good time. When they first discovered any considerable degree of self-will and stubbornness, he would attend to them till he had thoroughly subdued them and brought them to submit. Such prudent discipline, exercised with the greatest calmness, being repeated once or twice, was generally sufficient for that child; and effectually established his parental authority, and produced a cheerful obedience ever after.

He kept a watchful eye over his children, that he might admonish them of the first wrong step, and direct them in the right way. He took opportunities to converse with them in his study, singly and closely, about their souls' concerns; and to give them warning, exhortation, and direction, as he saw need . . .

He was a great enemy to young people's unseasonable associating together for vain amusements, which he regarded as a dangerous step towards corrupting and bringing them to ruin. And he thought the excuse many parents make for tolerating their children in it, (viz. that it is the custom, and the children of others practice it, which renders it difficult, and even impossible to impose restraint,) was insufficient and frivolous; and manifested a great degree of stupidity, on supposition that the practice was hurtful and pernicious to their souls. And when his children grew up, he found no difficulty in restraining them from this mischievous custom; but they cheerfully complied with the will of their parents. He allowed none of his children to be from home after nine o'clock at night, when they went abroad to see their friends and companions; neither were they permitted to sit up much after that time, in his own house, when any came to make them a visit. If any gentleman desired acquaintance with his daughters, after handsomely introducing himself, by properly consulting the parents, he was allowed all proper opportunity for it; but was not to intrude on the proper hours of rest and sleep, nor the religion and order of the family.

"On My First Sonne"

BEN JONSON

Ben Jonson (1572-1637) was an English Renaissance poet, actor, and a contemporary of Shakespeare. "On My First Sonne" was a poem he wrote after the death of his first son, Benjamin, at age seven. The poem is a moving, emotional reflection of a father's pain in his young son's death. There is no pain or suffering like that endured with the death of a child.

> *Farewell, thou child of my right hand, and joy;*
> *My sinne was too much hope of thee, lov'd boy;*
> *Seven yeeres thou' wert lent to me, and I thee pay,*
> *Exacted by thy fate, on the just day.*
> *Oh, I could loose all father, now. For why*
> *Will man lament the state he should envie?*
> *To have so soone scap'd worlds, and fleshes rage.*
> *And, if no other miserie, yet age?*
> *Rest in soft peace, and ask'd, say here doth lye*
> *Ben Jonson his best piece of poetrie.*
> *For whose sake, hence-forth, all his vowes be such,*
> *As what he loves may never like too much.*

"A Boy of Much Promise"

CALVIN COOLIDGE

In this heartrending passage from his autobiography, President Calvin Coolidge (1872–1933) mourns the death of his son Calvin. After his son's death, Coolidge and his presidency were never the same. He would have given it all up—the power, the fame, and the office—to be able to save his son. This is one of the most beautiful, simple, and hardest to read passages I have ever encountered.

My own participation in the campaign was delayed by the death of my son Calvin, which occurred on the seventh of July. He was a boy of much promise, proficient in his studies, with a scholarly mind, who had just turned sixteen.

He had a remarkable insight into things.

The day I became President he had just started to work in a tobacco field. When one of his fellow laborers said to him, if my father was President I would not work in a tobacco field, Calvin replied, If my father were your father, you would.

. . .

We do not know what might have happened to him under other circumstances, but if I had not been President, he would not have raised a blister on his toe, which resulted in blood poisoning, playing lawn tennis in the South Grounds. In his suffering he was asking me to make him well. I could not.

When he went the power and the glory of the Presidency went with him.

The ways of Providence are often beyond our understanding. It seemed to me that the world had need of the work that it was probable he could do.

I do not know why such a price was exacted for occupying the White House.

"Bone of My Bones"

GENESIS 2:19–24 NKJV

In this passage from the creation story in the Bible, God describes the biblical basis of marriage and why he created both man and woman. As recorded in Genesis, woman was formed so that man should not be alone on the earth, and it is through marriage that the two are joined together.

Out of the ground the LORD God formed every beast of the field and every bird of the air, and brought them to Adam to see what he would call them. And whatever Adam called each living creature, that was its name. So Adam gave names to all cattle, to the birds of the air, and to every beast of the field. But for Adam there was not found a helper comparable to him.

And the LORD God caused a deep sleep to fall on Adam, and he slept; and He took one of his ribs, and closed up the flesh in its place. Then the rib which the LORD God had taken from man He made into a woman, and He brought her to the man.

And Adam said:

"This is now bone of my bones
And flesh of my flesh;
She shall be called Woman,
Because she was taken out of Man."

Therefore a man shall leave his father and mother and be joined to his wife, and they shall become one flesh.

Finding a Good Wife

PROVERBS 31:10–31 NKJV

I chose this passage because I think it describes my wife, Elayne. We selected this verse to be read at our wedding and it hangs, framed, in our home today.

Who can find a virtuous wife?
For her worth is far above rubies.
The heart of her husband safely trusts her;
So he will have no lack of gain.
She does him good and not evil
All the days of her life.
She seeks wool and flax,
And willingly works with her hands.
She is like the merchant ships,
She brings her food from afar.
She also rises while it is yet night,
And provides food for her household,
And a portion for her maidservants.
She considers a field and buys it;
From her profits she plants a vineyard.
She girds herself with strength,

And strengthens her arms.
She perceives that her merchandise is good,
And her lamp does not go out by night.
She stretches out her hands to the distaff,
And her hand holds the spindle.
She extends her hand to the poor,
Yes, she reaches out her hands to the needy.
She is not afraid of snow for her household,
For all her household is clothed with scarlet.
She makes tapestry for herself;
Her clothing is fine linen and purple.
Her husband is known in the gates,
When he sits among the elders of the land.
She makes linen garments and sells them,
And supplies sashes for the merchants.
Strength and honor are her clothing;
She shall rejoice in time to come.
She opens her mouth with wisdom,
And on her tongue is the law of kindness.
She watches over the ways of her household,
And does not eat the bread of idleness.
Her children rise up and call her blessed;
Her husband also, and he praises her:
"Many daughters have done well,
But you excel them all."
Charm is deceitful and beauty is passing,
But a woman who fears the LORD, she shall be praised.
Give her of the fruit of her hands,
And let her own works praise her in the gates.

From *Sketches of Young Couples*

CHARLES DICKENS

Charles Dickens (1812–1870) was the most celebrated English novelist of the Victorian era, and he remains popular, responsible for some of English literature's most iconic characters. He published more than a dozen major novels, numerous short stories, a handful of plays, and several nonfiction books. Dickens's *Sketches of Young Couples* contains several short stories of various couples, including the young couple, the formal couple, the nice little couple, and the old couple. Each of the two excerpts here show true-to-life nuances of married couples, whether they are newlywed or well advanced in years together.

THE YOUNG COUPLE

There is to be a wedding this morning at the corner house in the terrace. The pastry-cook's people have been there half-a-dozen times already; all day yesterday there was a great stir and bustle, and they were up this morning as soon as it was light. Miss Emma Fielding is going to be married to young Mr. Harvey . . .

And there, in good truth . . . at the chamber-door—there is Miss Emma 'looking like the sweetest picter,' in a white chip bonnet and orange flowers, and all other elegancies becoming a bride, (with the make, shape, and quality of every article of which the girl is perfectly familiar in one moment, and never forgets to her dying day)—and there is Miss Emma's mamma in tears, and Miss Emma's papa comforting her, and saying how that of course she has been long looking forward to this, and how happy she ought to be—and there too is Miss Emma's sister with her arms round her neck, and the other bridesmaid all smiles and tears, quieting the children, who would cry more but that they are so finely dressed, and yet sob for fear sister Emma should be taken away—and it is all so affecting, that the two servant-girls cry more than anybody . . .

And now the company have gone down to breakfast, and tears have given place to smiles, for all the corks are out of the long-necked bottles, and their contents are disappearing rapidly. Miss Emma's papa is at the top of the table; Miss Emma's mamma at the bottom; and beside the latter are Miss Emma herself and her husband,—admitted on all hands to be the handsomest and most interesting young couple ever known. All down both sides of the table, too, are various young ladies, beautiful to see, and various young gentlemen who seem to think so ...

By this time the merriment and happiness of the feast have gained their height; certain ominous looks begin to be exchanged between the bridesmaids, and somehow it gets whispered about that the carriage which is to take the young couple into the country has arrived ...

Now, for at least six weeks last past it has been solemnly devised and settled that the young couple should go away in secret; but they no sooner appear without the door than the drawing-room windows are blocked up with ladies waving their handkerchiefs and kissing their hands, and the dining-room panes with gentlemen's faces beaming farewell in every queer variety of its expression. The hall and steps are crowded with servants in white favours, mixed up with particular friends and relations who have darted out to say good-bye; and foremost in the group are the tiny lovers arm in arm, thinking, with fluttering hearts, what happiness it would be to dash away together in that gallant coach, and never part again.

The bride has barely time for one hurried glance at her old home, when the steps rattle, the door slams, the horses clatter on the pavement, and they have left it far away.

THE OLD COUPLE

They are grandfather and grandmother to a dozen grown people and have greatgrandchildren besides; their bodies are bent, their hair is grey, their step tottering and infirm. Is this the lightsome pair whose wedding was so merry, and have the young couple indeed grown old so soon!

It seems but yesterday—and yet what a host of cares and griefs are crowded into the intervening time which, reckoned by them, lengthens out into a century! How many new associations have wreathed themselves about their hearts since then! The old time is gone, and a new time has come for others—not for them. They are but the rusting link that feebly joins the two, and is silently loosening its hold and dropping asunder.

It seems but yesterday—and yet how the gay and laughing faces of that bright morning have changed and vanished from above ground! Faint likenesses of some remain about them yet, but they are very faint and scarcely to be traced. The rest are only seen in dreams, and even they are unlike what they were, in eyes so old and dim.

One or two dresses from the bridal wardrobe are yet preserved. They are of a quaint and antique fashion, and seldom seen except in pictures. White has turned yellow, and brighter hues have faded. Do you wonder, child? The wrinkled face was once as smooth as yours, the eyes as bright, the shrivelled skin as fair and delicate. It is the work of hands that have been dust these many years.

Where are the fairy lovers of that happy day whose annual return comes upon the old man and his wife, like the echo of some village bell which has long been silent?

The old gentleman is eighty years old, today . . .

This morning the old couple are cheerful but serious, recalling old times as well as they can remember them, and dwelling upon many passages in their past lives which the day brings to mind. The old lady reads aloud, in a tremulous voice, out of a great Bible, and the old gentleman with his hand to his ear, listens with profound respect. When the book is closed, they sit silent for a short space, and afterwards resume their conversation, with a reference perhaps to their dead children, as a subject not unsuited to that they have just left. By degrees they are led to consider which of those who survive are the most like those dearly-remembered objects, and so they fall into a less solemn strain, and become cheerful again.

. . . The old couple sits side by side, and the old time seems like yesterday indeed. Looking back upon the path they have travelled, its dust and ashes disappear; the flowers that withered long ago, show brightly again upon its borders, and they grow young once more in the youth of those about them.

What Is Love?

GEORGE ELIOT

Mary Ann Evans (1819-1880), known by her pen name George Eliot, was one of the greatest novelists to ever describe and critique the human condition. In her novel *Daniel Deronda*, Evans penned one of the most moving and beautiful explanations of love in all literature, contained in the final lines of this excerpt. Deronda's love for Mirah is an "infolding of immeasurable cares." In real love, the little things done out of devotion and commitment—taking the kids to football practice, going food shopping, cleaning the house—are greater than any happiness found outside of that relationship.

And Deronda was not long before he came to Diplow, which was at a more convenient distance from town than the Abbey. He had wished to carry out a plan for taking Ezra and Mirah to a mild spot on the coast, while he prepared another home that Mirah might enter as his bride, and where they might unitedly watch over her brother. But Ezra begged not to be removed, unless it were to go with them to the East. All outward solicitations were becoming more and more of a burden to him; but his mind dwelt on the possibility of this voyage with a visionary joy. Deronda, in his preparations for the marriage, which he hoped might not be deferred beyond a couple of months, wished to have fuller consultation as to his resources and affairs generally with Sir Hugo, and here was a reason for not delaying his visit to Diplow. But he thought quite as much of another reason—his promise to Gwendolen. The sense of blessedness in his own lot had yet an aching anxiety at its heart: this may be held paradoxical, for the beloved lover is always called happy, and happiness is considered as a wellfleshed indifference to sorrow outside it. But human experience is usually paradoxical, if that means incongruous with the phrases of current talk or even current philosophy. It was no treason to Mirah, but a part of that full nature which made his love for her the more worthy, that his joy in her could hold by its side the care for another. For what is love itself, for the one we love best?—an infolding of immeasurable cares which yet are better than any joys outside our love.

Heroes of Aurora

One test of manhood is how a man responds to evil. Does evil cause you to shrink away and flee, or does it stir up in you courage and valor? For many of the great men of history, evil brought out the best in them: men like Todd Beamer on Flight 93, Medal of Honor recipient Michael Murphy in Afghanistan, and now the Aurora three—the three young men, each in different parts of theater nine at the Century 16 multiplex in Aurora, Colorado, who gave their lives to protect their girlfriends when a gunman opened fire in the crowded theater on July 20, 2012. These three—by all accounts common, everyday men—didn't cower in the face of terrible evil; they conquered it.

Twenty-five-year-old Jon Blunk was sitting next to his girlfriend, Jansen Young, at the midnight premiere of *The Dark Knight Rises* when the deranged gunman (who shall remain nameless) opened fire in the dark theater. Blunk instinctively pushed his girlfriend to the ground and threw his body on top of hers. Blunk, a security guard, served five years in the Navy and was in the process of reenlisting in hopes of becoming a Navy SEAL, family and friends said. He was killed in the gunfire; his girlfriend survived.

Twenty-four-year-old Alex Teves dived on top of his girlfriend, Amanda Lindgren, when the gunfire erupted. Covering her body, he took the bullets so they did not harm her. She survived the massacre; he did not.

Matt McQuinn, twenty-seven, threw his body in front of his girlfriend, Samantha Yowler, as the shooting continued. Yowler survived with a gunshot wound to the knee; McQuinn's body absorbed the fatal shots.

These men were three of twelve innocent people killed early that morning. Their incredible sacrifice leaves us asking, why? Why would a young man with his entire life ahead of him risk everything for a woman to whom he has no legal, financial, or marital obligations?

To call it chivalry would be a tremendous understatement. By all appearances, these men believed that a man has a responsibility to protect a woman, even to the point of death. They believed there are things in life worth dying for, and the innocent women seated next to them were among those things.

They believed, to put it simply, in a code of honor. They put the women's lives before their own—an old-fashioned notion, to be sure, but certainly an honorable one (if you have any doubt, ask the survivors). Their instincts were to protect, not run away.

From all accounts, these young men were average, working men in their twenties. (We know a little about Jon Blunk, but not much, and we know even less about the others.) Like all men, they had their own struggles. After his death we learned that Blunk had an ex-wife and two children living in Nevada. He was scheduled to visit them, to resolve marital issues. This isn't to take anything away from Blunk or the other two heroes, but to illustrate that, in spite of shortcomings, any man can still recognize what it means to be a good man and act like one.

This is especially important given the state of many men today. Record numbers of men aren't working or even looking for work. Neither are they marrying or even acting as fathers to their children. These men need heroes to imitate whom they can relate to in everyday life, not just make-believe superheroes who catch their imagination for an hour or two. Today's men need heroes like the Aurora three.

While much of the media obsesses over the psychology and motivations of the deranged killer, it is the Aurora three whom we should hold high. It is only by telling their story that their code of honor will survive for future generations of men. "The world is forwarded by having its attention fixed on the best things," Matthew Arnold wrote.

In an age when traditional manhood has been increasingly relegated to fiction—capes, masks, and green screens—Blunk, Teves, and McQuinn stand as real-life heroes. Their actions remind us that good triumphs over evil, not just in movies, but also in reality.

"True and False Manliness"

JAMES FREEMAN CLARKE

James Freeman Clarke was a nineteenth-century American preacher and author. He was a staunch abolitionist and fought against many of the social problems of his day. Back then, too, boys had difficulty under-standing manliness, so Clarke thought it expedient to describe his view of proper and improper manliness. This excellent essay clearly demar-cates true manliness from false manliness.

Manliness means perfect manhood, as womanliness implies perfect wom-anhood. Manliness is the character of a man as he ought to be, as he was meant to be. It expresses the qualities which go to make a perfect man,—truth, courage, conscience, freedom, energy, self-possession, self-control. But it does not exclude gentleness, tenderness, compassion, modesty. A man is not less manly, but more so, because he is gentle. In fact, our word "gentleman" shows that a typical man must also be a gentle man.

By manly qualities the world is carried forward. The manly spirit shows itself in enterprise, the love of meeting difficulties and overcoming them,—the resolution which will not yield, which patiently perseveres, and does not admit the possibility of defeat. It enjoys hard toil, rejoices in stern labor, is ready to make sacrifices, to suffer and bear disaster patiently. It is generous, giving itself to a good cause not its own; it is public-spirited, devoting itself to the general good with no expectation of reward. It is ready to defend unpopular truth, to stand by those who are wronged, to uphold the weak. Having resolved, it does not go back, but holds on, through good report and evil, sure that the right must win at last. And so it causes truth to prevail, and keeps up the standard of a noble purpose in the world.

But as most good things have their counterfeits, so there is false manliness which imitates these great qualities, though at heart it is without them. Instead of strength of will, it is only willful; in place of courage, it has audacity. True manliness does what it believes right; false manliness, does what it chooses to do. Freedom, to one, means following his own convictions of truth; to the other it means thinking as he pleases, and doing as he likes. The one is reverent, the other rude; one is courteous, the other overbearing; one is brave, the other foolhardy; one is modest, the other self-assert-ing. False manliness is cynical, contemptuous, and tyrannical to inferiors. The true man has respect for all men, is tender to the sufferer, is modest and kind. The good type uses its strength to maintain good customs, to improve the social condition, to defend order. The other imagines it to be manly to defy law, to be independent of the opinions of the wise, to sneer at moral obligation, to consider itself superior to the established principles of mankind.

A false notion of manliness leads boys astray.

All boys wish to be manly; but they often try to become so by copying the vices of men rather than their virtues. They see men drinking, smoking, swearing; so these poor little fellows sedulously imitate such bad habits, thinking they are making themselves more like men. They mistake rudeness for strength, disrespect to parents for independence. They read wretched stories about boy brigands and boy detectives, and fancy themselves heroes when they break the laws, and become troublesome and mischievous. Out of such false influences the criminal classes are recruited. Many a little boy who only wishes to be manly, becomes corrupted and debased by the bad examples around him and the bad literature which he reads. The cure for this is to give him good books that show him truly noble examples from life and history, and make him understand how infinitely above this mock-manliness is the true courage which ennobles human nature.

In a recent awful disaster, amid the blackness and darkness and tempest, the implacable sea and the pitiless storm,—when men's hearts were failing them from terror, and women and children had no support but faith in a Divine Providence and a coming immortality,—the dreadful scene was illuminated by the courage and manly devotion of those who risked their own lives to save the lives of others. Such heroism is like a sunbeam breaking through the tempest. It shows us the real worth there is in man.

No matter how selfish mankind may seem, whenever hours like these come, which try men's souls, they show that the age of chivalry has not gone; that though "The knights are dust, and their good swords rust," there are as high-hearted heroes now as ever. Firemen rush into a flaming house to save women and children. Sailors take their lives in their hands to rescue their fellow-men from a wreck. They save them at this great risk, not because they are friends or relatives, but because they are fellow-men.

Courage is an element of manliness. It is more than readiness to encounter danger and death, for we are not often called to meet such perils. It is every-day courage which is most needed,—that which shrinks from no duty because it is difficult; which makes one ready to say what he believes, when his opinions are unpopular; which does not allow him to postpone a duty, but makes him ready to encounter it at once; a courage which is not afraid of ridicule when one believes himself right; which is not the slave of custom, the fool of fashion. Such courage as this, in man or woman or child, is true manliness. It is infinitely becoming in all persons. It does not seek display, it is often the courage of silence no less than speech; it is modest courage, unpretending though resolute. It holds fast to its convictions and principles, whether men hear or whether they forbear.

True manliness differs also from the false in its attitude to woman. Its knightly feeling makes it wish to defend her rights, to maintain her claims, to be her protector and advocate. False manliness wishes to show its superiority by treating women as inferiors. It flatters them, but it does not respect them. It fears their competition on equal levels, and wishes to keep them confined, not within walls, as in the Mohammedan regions, but behind the more subtle barriers of opinion, prejudice, and supposed feminine aptitudes. True manliness holds out the hand to woman, and says, "Do whatever you are able to do; whatever God meant you to do. Neither you nor I can tell what that is till all artificial barriers are removed, and you have full opportunity to try." Manly strength respects womanly purity, sympathy, and grace of heart. And this is the real chivalry of the present hour.

From Canal Boy to President

Horatio Alger

In his biography of President James A. Garfield, Horatio Alger describes Garfield's love for his family and friends. A remarkably down-to-earth man, Garfield valued them more than anything else in his life and always made time for them. Charles J. Guiteau, an American lawyer, shot President Garfield, who died weeks later from infection of the gunshot wound. As Alger describes, President Garfield held no anger toward Guiteau, a remarkable example of his forgiveness and love.

In the Milwaukee *Sentinel* of Sept. 22d, I find this tribute by Congressman Williams, of that State:

"Happening to sit within one seat of him for four years in the House, T, with others, perhaps had a better opportunity to see him in all of his moods than those more removed. In action he was a giant; off duty he was a great, noble boy. He never knew what austerity of manner or ceremonious dignity meant. After some of his greatest efforts in the House, such as will live in history, he would turn to me, or any one else, and say: 'Well, old boy, how was that?' Every man was his confidant and friend, so far as the interchange of every-day good feeling was concerned.

"He once told me how he prepared his speeches; that first he filled himself with the subject, massing all the facts and principles involved, so far as he could; then he took pen and paper and wrote down the salient points in what he regarded their logical order. Then he scanned them critically, and fixed them in his memory. 'And then,' said he, 'I leave the paper in my room and trust to the emergency.' He told me that when he spoke at the serenade in New York a year ago, he was so pressed by callers that the only opportunity he had for preparation was, to lock the door and walk three times around the table, when he was called out to the balcony to begin. All the world knows what that speech was.

"He was wrapped up in his family. His two boys would come up to the House just before adjournment, and loiter about his desk with their books in their hands. After the House adjourned, other members would go off in cars or carriages, or walk down the avenue in groups. But Garfield, with a boy on each side of him, would walk down Capitol Hill, as we would say in the country 'cross-lots,' all three chatting together on equal terms.

"He said to me one day during the canvass, while the tears came to his eyes, 'I have done no more in coming up from poverty than hundreds and thousands of others, but I am thankful that I have been able to keep my family by my side, and educate my children.'

"He was a man with whom anybody could differ with impunity. I have said repeatedly, that were Garfield alive and fully recovered, and a dozen of his intimate friends were to go to him, and advise that Guiteau be let off, he would say, 'Yes, let him go.' The man positively knew no malice. And for such a man to be shot and tortured like a dog, and by a dog!

"He was extremely sensitive. I have seen him come into the House in the morning, when some guerrilla of the press had stabbed him deeper in his feelings than Guiteau's bullet did in the body, and when he looked pallid from suffering, and the evident loss of sleep; but he would utter no murmur, and in some short time his great exuberance of spirits would surmount it all, and he would be a boy again.

"He never went to lunch without a troop of friends with him. He loved to talk at table, and there is no gush in saying he talked like a god socially and intellectually. Some of his off-hand expressions were like a burst of inspiration. Like all truly great men, he did not seem to realize his greatness. And, as I have said, he would talk as cordially and confidentially with a child as with a monarch. And I only refer to his conversations with me because you ask me to, and because I think his off-hand conversations with any one reveal his real traits best.

"Coming on the train from Washington, after his nomination, he said: 'Only think of this! I am yet a young man; if elected and I serve my term I shall still be a young man. Then what am I going to do? There seems to be no place in America for an ex-President.'

"And then came in what I thought the extreme simplicity and real nobility of the man. 'Why,' said he, 'I had no thought of being nominated. I had bought me some new books, and was getting ready for the Senate.'"

Thomas Carlyle's Advice to Young Men

THOMAS CARLYLE

The "Great Man" theory was a popular nineteenth-century philosophy, which held that history can be explained by the impact of "great men." Scottish writer Thomas Carlyle (1795–1881) popularized the movement in his writings. Carlyle wrote that "the history of the world is but the biography of great men." Carlyle spent much of his time studying the world's great men and what made them heroes. The following selection is Carlyle's response to a young man who wrote asking what and who he should study. Carlyle encouraged him to study history and learn from the past, but also to digest things that interest him and develop and cultivate those interests. Carlyle concluded by reminding the boy that book learning isn't everything; he must get out in the world and test and refine his learnings. Good mature men should advise young men.

Dear Sir,—Some time ago your letter was delivered me; I take literally the first free half-hour I have had since to write you a word of answer.

It would give me true satisfaction could any advice of mine contribute to forward you in your honourable course of self-improvement, but a long experience has taught me that advice can profit but little—that there is a good reason why advice is so seldom followed; this reason, namely, that it is so seldom, and can almost never be rightly given. No man knows the state of another; it is always to some more or less imaginary man that the wisest and most honest adviser is speaking.

As to the books which you—whom I know so little of—should read, there is hardly any thing definite that can be said. For one thing, you may be strenuously advised to keep reading. Any good book, any book that is wiser than yourself, will teach you something—a great many things indirectly and directly, if your mind be open to learn. This old counsel of Johnson's is also good, and universally applicable—"Read the book you do honestly feel a wish and curiosity to read." The very wish and curiosity indicates that you, then and there, are the person likely to get good of it. "Our wishes are presentiments of our capabilities;" that is a noble saying, of deep encouragement to all true men, applicable to our wishes and efforts in regard to reading as to other things.

Among all the objects that look wonderful and beautiful to you, follow with fresh hope the one which looks wonderfullest, beautifullest. You will gradually find, by various trials (which trials see that you make honest, manful ones, not silly, short, fitful ones), what is for you the wonderfullest, beautifullest—what is your true element and province, and be able to profit by that. True desire, the monition of nature, is much to be attended to. But here, also, you are to discriminate carefully between true desire and false. The medical men tell us we should eat what we truly have an appetite for; but what we only falsely have an appetite for, we should resolutely avoid. It is very true: and flimsy desultory readers, who fly from foolish book to foolish book, and get good of none, and mischief of all—are not these as foolish, unhealthy eaters, who mistake their superficial false desire after spiceries and confectioneries for their real appetite, of which even they are not destitute, though it lies far deeper, far quieter, after solid nutritive food? With these illustrations, I will recommend Johnson's advice to you.

Another thing, and only one other, I will say. All books are properly the record of the history of past men—what thoughts past men had in them—what actions past men did; the summary of all books whatsoever lies there. It is on this ground that the class of books specifically named History can be safely recommended as the basis of all study of books, the preliminary to all right and full understanding of any thing we can expect to find in books. Past history, and especially the past history of one's own native country, every body may be advised to begin with that. Let him study that faithfully; innumerable inquiries will branch out from it; he has a broad beaten highway, from which all the country is more or less visible; there traveling, let him choose where he will dwell.

Neither let mistakes and wrong directions—of which every man, in his studies and elsewhere, falls into many—discourage you. There is precious instruction to be got by finding that we are wrong. Let a man try faithfully, manfully, to be right, he will grow daily more and more right. It is, at bottom, the condition on which all men have to cultivate themselves. Our very walking is an incessant falling—a falling and a catching of ourselves before we come actually to the pavement!—it is emblematic of all things a man does.

In conclusion, I will remind you that it is not books alone, or by books chiefly, that a man becomes in all points a man. Study to do faithfully whatsoever thing in your actual situation, there and now, you find either expressly or tacitly laid to your charge; that is your post; stand in it like a true soldier. Silently devour the many chagrins of it, as all human situations have many; and see you aim not to quit it without doing all that it, at least, required of you. A man perfects himself by work much more than by reading. They are a growing kind of men that can wisely combine the two things—wisely, valiantly, can do what is laid to their hand in their present sphere, and prepare themselves withtal [sic] for doing other wider things, if such lie before them.

With many good wishes and encouragements, I remain, yours sincerely,

Thomas Carlyle

Are You Well Bred?

THE AMERICAN MAGAZINE

The American Magazine was founded in the early 1900s and lasted in various forms until the mid-1900s. In this personal improvement section from a 1921 issue, the author offers self-help in the form of diagnosis and questioning. How you answer these questions will tell a lot about your character and the way you treat women.

A re your actions toward the opposite sex such as to suggest coarseness, over-familiarity, or lack of respect? . . . Do you treat every woman acquaintance as you would have other men treat your sister? Do you confine your demonstrations of affectionate intimacy to your wife, or the woman you wish to make your wife?

Is your self-respect and decent-mindedness such as is apparent from your every-day conduct, or is it the kind you talk about and to which you call attention?

Are you supercilious? Do you always find something to criticize in anybody or anything that is mentioned? Do you rarely find a book, a play, or a person that entirely pleases you? Are you anxious to be thought superior, sophisticated?

Are you cheerful? Are you frequently glum, morose, irritable, petulant? Or are you habitually, and do you constantly study to be, kindly, sympathetic, interested in others?

Are you egotistic? Are you vain, of your appearance, your position, your possessions, your success? Do you talk incessantly about yourself, of what people say of you, of what you think and of what you own?

Are you loyal? Can your friend depend upon you under all circumstances? Do you defend him when others cast aspersion upon him in his absence? Do you speak even more enthusiastically of him behind his back than to his face?

Are you loyal to your wife . . . to your sweetheart? Are you ashamed of your father or mother? Are you loyal to your country? Would you fight for it? Would you refuse to take part in anything that might work harm to your country? Are you interested enough in your country to do your duty as a citizen, or do you shirk your civic obligations?

In using these tests we should not be discouraged if we find many a weak spot in our character. The object is not to encourage morbidity nor to provoke despair. But a right-minded person always wants to know the truth. If he is deficient, he strives to improve; if he is proficient, he goes on to still better things.

Many years ago the Greeks put forward a wise word which we yet may do well to heed. It was, in fact, two words. They were: "Know Thyself!"

Profile: David Gelernter

David Gelernter is a modern intellectual giant. He is a professor of computer science at Yale and his research focuses on computer programming and artificial intelligence. The "tuple space" introduced in his Linda system (1983) is considered the basis of many computer communication systems worldwide. His expertise extends beyond programming—he is the author of seminal works on religion, philosophy, and the arts. He was targeted and attacked by the Unabomber in 1993. He is a survivor and hero and I'm proud to call David Gelernter a friend. Here he offers his thoughts on men, women, and culture.

Ordinary stories would begin with June 24, 1993, describing the moment nails exploded from an envelope—ripping into the torso, the arms, and eye of David Gelernter. They would begin with the bleeding, nearly blinded professor of computer science staggering his way from his office in Watson Hall on the campus of Yale University to a health clinic, arriving with his body torn and no blood pressure.

Targeted by the Unabomber, Gelernter was thrust into the headlines. Films are made out of such violent moments; news revolves around conflict. A victim seeking to overcome tragedy is a hard story line to displace. The brutality screams out and swallows any other accomplishments or nuance. The attack could have been the event that defined Gelernter for the rest of his life.

But Gelernter scoffed at the idea that the knighting of the title "victim" should carry any weight or credence. This is a man who pushed computer science forward, who foresaw the Internet. He paints. He regularly publishes articles and books on culture, philosophy, and religion. His life and his work were far more important than the evil of any deranged man.

And so instead of talking about what he gained in surviving the attack, Gelernter starts with what has been lost. He speaks of the true victims.

"The great disgrace of modern society is the destruction of female self-respect through feminism."

Women have been left vulnerable by the changing expectations. Denied the right to be treated differently—as women—they are forced to hold themselves to the standards and desires of a man. They are left vulnerable, forced to destroy parts of their soul, their innate character, and left cut off from any maternal urge.

This defense of women might seem out of place for a scientist, but Gelernter has never been confined to the lab. Gelernter's work in the field of computer programming saw the shift toward a digital system of information centralization and pushed technology accordingly. The titles of his books attest to his psyche, a kaleidoscope of the perpetually curious conservative thinker: *Americanism: The Fourth Great Western Religion*; *Machine Beauty: Elegance and the Heart of Technology*; *1939: The Lost World of the Fair*; and *Drawing Life: Surviving the Unabomber*. Gelernter also documented the tradition of his faith with *Judaism: A Way of Being*.

It is this holistic approach to life and philosophy pushing him to defend women and the destruction of the first relationship ever created.

Genesis 1:27 says, "So God created mankind in his own image, in the image of God he created them; male and female he created them." Man and woman.

As Gelernter and his wife raised their two sons in the Jewish tradition, they watched that first relationship come under siege.

"The greatest difficulty has to do with relationships between young men and girls. It is to bring young men up to be chivalrous."

Chivalry is an old term. Knights joust for the honor of a fair maiden. Sir Walter Raleigh spreads his cloak across a muddy puddle and allows Queen Elizabeth to cross unscathed. The HMS *Birkenhead* and the iceberg-struck RMS *Titanic* sink as men fill the lifeboats with women and children and sacrifice their lives in the process.

Or it may just be respecting the dignity of a woman and the sanctity of the marriage bed.

"Chivalry is to ask them to make an enormous sacrifice," said Gelernter. "To deny desires and make a sacrifice in a happy-go-lucky atmosphere. But that atmosphere is a systematic attempt to destroy all attempts to reinforce any ideas of a girl's dignity and what she's entitled to ask from a man."

Gelernter is not asking his sons to be angels, but he expects them to rise above the level of animals.

"It's easy for me to say what is required of them; it's hard for them to carry that out. But I'm so very proud of them."

When a young man from the Gelernter household takes a girl "out," there are certain standards that will be part of the evening. He will hold the door open for the young woman. He will pick up the check at dinner. He will treat her with respect. He will walk the young woman home at the end of the night, and if it is a cold night, he will offer to lend her the warmth of his coat. Trifling details to some, nostalgic reminders of a different time to others—but for Gelernter, the small things add up.

"These are tiny things, but they add up. In a larger sense the idea that a man's role in respect to women is to protect, to help, to support, to cherish as opposed to consume. We are a consumer society and the number one consumption is that of women."

The change in role came alongside two developments. Men chose to ignore traditional responsibilities in relationships—forestalling marriage and maintaining a perpetual adolescence. Feminism swept the schools of women's studies, teaching that women should respond and encourage the prolonged independence. By severing the natural progression of relationships and encouraging premarital sexual relationships, women were left defenseless and unable to demand some of their most basic rights.

"It is awful that there are young women who don't feel that they can want what they want, women who want a career, but also want a family and a home. They just do, they feel it. There are so many young women who don't feel entitled to what women in every other generation in human history have. In modern Western society, feminism has abolished it in one generation."

And this ties into deeper urges of the divine.

"Women have an urge to nurture and cherish children; men don't have that, but they can substitute an urge to nurture and cherish women. Men need to turn their sexual interest into something that goes deeper, emotionally and spiritually."

Young men must be taught that their desire for women is something natural, something good. When a beautiful woman walks into the room, there is a stirring deep within the soul that is tied to something more than just the firing of synapses and hormones. When Adam saw Eve in the garden of Eden, he saw that she was good. But Adam did not merely treat Eve as another creation to consume, but rather as part of him to care for and to be joined to. And so that attraction must be properly understood in a way motivating noble action that honors the value and dignity of the women.

Modern society teaches individuals to follow their feelings. Being a man often involves denying those impulses or channeling them in the proper direction, as in the impulse toward doing absurd and dangerous things that captivates boys of all ages. This can either be courage or insanity.

"Courage in the sense that has been abolished for the Hallmark version in modern society," cautioned Gelernter. "Society sees everybody as courageous. A congressman takes a courageous stand, a garbage man takes a courageous stand, or a teacher courageously allows a Christmas card to be shown. All this is nonsense, but men are still capable of being urged to be courageous . . . Bravery is not in all of us, but it is a manly virtue that can also be turned to the benefit of society. One wants to be brave on behalf of one's wife and children or girlfriend for that matter."

By slathering "courageous" across all of society, a casual contempt has been attached to the term, one that undermines the higher meaning of the term. Courage becomes a hollow shell, stripped from the necessary philosophical and religious roots that give strength and meaning.

While Gelernter might cringe from labels like "courageous" or "victim," being the target of such an action, then witnessing—from the inside out—the reaction from society, provides him with a unique perspective on how men act in times of adversity.

"Part of the manly attitude is to keep your feelings to yourself and not visit them upon the world," said Gelernter. "Self-expression is not your goal, except if you're in a very limited part of the world. And even then you'll probably be a pretty lousy artist if you think that self-respect is your goal."

This is not to say that men don't feel emotions; it's just what feelings they choose to share with the world.

"Self-pity—feeling sorry for yourself—well, of course, you bang your foot and of course you feel sorry for yourself. If you see someone who just made a billion dollars and you're just as smart and you didn't make anything, you feel sorry for yourself. That's human, but a man may not control his mental life, but he controls his behavior. It's probably the case that a stiff upper lip—if you keep it to yourself and don't make an issue of whining and expressing the self-pity—that some of that self-pity melts away and you look around and see how much you have."

That type of thinking runs squarely in opposition to what men are trained to believe about life and themselves. Film after film, pop song after pop song preaches the value of "finding oneself" and living in a perpetual state of teary-eyed emotional breakdown. Gelernter taught his boys differently.

"Don't leave it outside. Keep your feelings to yourself. It is unseemly in a man to make a public show of his feelings. You must think about what type of example you're setting for others."

Feelings cannot master the decisions and mental well-being of a man. And when it comes to the issue of getting a job and going to work, Gelernter has a message for men: "Work is not supposed to be fun. You go to work to make money and support you and your family, and to maybe make something productive, not to have fun. We are too easy on ourselves. We are a lazy people."

He lives what he preaches. It might be surprising to discover, but David Gelernter—the man who foresaw the Internet and who can bend technology to his will in a way that most individuals can barely dream of—hates computers.

"One does not have to go into the field that is easiest for one. My own limited successes in computer sciences have been precisely because I don't like computers. I have no patience with them. I'm not willing to play with software. I require it to be simply and elegantly designed so I can figure out how to use it in thirty seconds, because if not, I'm not going to bother."

He was majoring in art, philosophy, and Hebrew, but none of those fulfilled a requirement of his belief system.

"Jewish tradition meant that I had a responsibility to do something that would be worth something to someone and would let me support a family. Computer science interested me, but I don't love it."

Art and science might be opposites for Gelernter, but they aren't mutually exclusive fields. The search for truth is often the search for beauty. A beautiful theorem, a well-constructed dam, or an intricate computer process can reach the limits of poetry. Gelernter keeps painting, keeps writing, and keeps cultivating all sides of his personality and soul.

That development comes hand in hand with Judaism—more a pattern for life than a system of "faith" for Gelernter and his family.

"Judaism makes the texture of life. It's a particular texture of time, a certain feeling at Hanukkah and at the High Holy Days. It's a mood that's constantly changing and gives a certain character to every week and it's more of an approach to life; it isn't as narrow as we often think of it."

His sons were raised with an understanding of that tradition. One wears a yarmulke; the other doesn't. Both are equally Jewish and have their understanding of life shaped by that reality. This belief and practice shapes every part of life, including that fundamental relationship with and protection of women.

"Chivalry is an inherently Judeo-Christian idea. Self-abdication in sake of decency and higher standards is an inherently religious idea. It's a Judeo-Christian idea."

To those who would haggle over the jots and tittles of behavior, asking whether one could be chivalrous without being religious, the reminder from this modern-day prophet is that it is not about the minutiae, but rather about seeking to formulate commandments for living that can be applied across all of life. How can society create men who will protect and serve women?

"Society cannot produce a generation of young men who are gentlemen without a religious context. The idea of a gentleman is very much a Western idea. It is not an Asian idea. It is not an African idea. It is not an Arab idea. The idea of monogamy developed in the West. The idea of the married couple being the fundamental building block of society emerges in the book of Genesis in a startling statement that has no equivalent in other religious traditions. To the extent that society discards its Judeo-Christian framework, it discards the idea of a gentleman."

"Courtship and Matrimony"

ROBERT MORRIS

Marriage is the most sacred and treasured bond between a man and woman. Yet, marriage is not always easy. In this selection from 1858, Robert Morris offers practical advice for recently married couples: don't look for perfection, be flexible and forgiving, and most of all, always strive for affection and compassion.

There are few even of those who have entered the wedded state, who strive from the commencement to soften the ways of life the one to the other, to minister constantly to the comforts and happiness, to remember and discharge all their duties and responsibilities. And when, too, as it often happens, the demon-spirit of an evil temper is constantly manifested, not only in little things but in great, when a shrill, harsh voice of complaint is perpetually ringing in the ears of one or the other—when a disposition to find fault without cause, and thus to annoy and irritate, is constantly apparent; when the husband regards himself as a despot, and treats his wife as a slave; or when the wife, on the other hand, is constantly exacting and never striving to discharge her part in the harmonious obligation, the effects are bitter, painful, and every way melancholy.

And yet there is no relation on this side of the grave, more sacred, more dignified, or more elevated, than that of husband and wife. The parties might be, and should be, to each other, perpetual sources of consolation and pleasure. There should be no distrust, no suspicion, no equivocation between beings so circumstanced. They should live as much as possible as if animated by one soul and aiming at one destiny.

Neither should look for perfection in the other, and yet each should endeavor to excel the other in generous efforts of gentleness, kindness, and affection. It has been well said that "in this world there is nothing of such value as affection, and the most trifling expression thereof, even though it be a single word of endearment, is in the ears that are properly attuned, a pleasanter sound than that of gold pieces." Think of these hints, gentle reader, apply them to your daily practice, and forthwith proceed to correct and amend your many errors of omission and commission.

From *Self-Control, Its Kingship and Majesty*

WILLIAM GEORGE JORDAN

William George Jordan (1864–1928), a favorite American essayist and author, wrote a number of self-help books in the early 1900s. Jordan diagnosed and addressed many of the character problems of men in his day. In this book he focused on self-control and how a man establishes himself in his community and his home by controlling his own virtues and vices.

When a man fails in life he usually says, "I am as God made me." When he succeeds he proudly proclaims himself a "self-made man." Man is placed into this world not as a finality,—but as a possibility. Man's greatest enemy is,—himself. Man in his weakness is the creature of circumstances; man in his strength is the creator of circumstances. Whether he be victim or victor depends largely on himself.

Man is never truly great merely for what he *is*, but ever for what he may become. Until man be truly filled with the knowledge of the majesty of his possibility, until there come to him the glow of realization of his privilege to live the life committed to him, as an individual life for which he is individually responsible, he is merely groping through the years . . .

With this broadening, stimulating view of life, he sees how he may attain his kingship through self-control. And the self-control that is seen in the most spectacular instances in history, and in the simplest phases of daily life, is precisely the same in kind and in quality, differing only in degree. This control man can attain, if he only will; it is but a matter of paying the price.

The power of self-control is one of the great qualities that differentiates man from the lower animals. He is the only animal capable of a moral struggle or a moral conquest.

Every step in the progress of the world has been a new "control." It has been escaping from the tyranny of a fact, to the understanding and mastery of that fact. For ages man looked in terror at the lightning flash; to-day he has begun to understand it as electricity, a force he has mastered and made his slave. The million phases of electrical invention are but manifestations of our control over a great force. But the greatest of all "control" is self-control.

At each moment of man's life he is either a King or a slave. As he surrenders to a wrong appetite, to any human weakness; as he falls prostrate in hopeless subjection to any condition, to any environment, to any failure, he is a slave. As he day by day crushes out human weakness, masters opposing elements within him, and day by day re-creates a new self from the sin and folly of his past,—then he is a King. He is a King ruling with wisdom over himself. Alexander conquered the whole world except,— Alexander. Emperor of the earth, he was the servile slave of his own passions.

We look with envy upon the possessions of others and wish they were our own. Sometimes we feel this in a vague, dreamy way with no thought of real attainment, as when we wish we had Queen Victoria's crown, or Emperor William's self-satisfaction. Sometimes, however, we grow bitter, storm at the wrong distribution of the good things of life, and then relapse into a hopeless fatalistic acceptance of our condition.

We envy the success of others, when we should emulate the process by which that success came. We see the splendid physical development of Sandow, yet we forget that as a babe and child he was so weak there was little hope that his life might be spared . . .

Self-control may be developed in precisely the same manner as we tone up a weak muscle,—by little exercises day by day. Let us each day do, as mere exercises of discipline in moral gymnastics, a few acts that are disagreeable to us, the doing of which will help us in instant action in our hour of need. The exercises may be very simple— dropping for a time an intensely interesting book at the most thrilling page of the story; jumping out of bed at the first moment of waking; walking home when one is perfectly able to do so, but when the temptation is to take a car; talking to some disagreeable person and trying to make the conversation pleasant. These daily exercises in moral discipline will have a wondrous tonic effect on man's whole moral nature.

The individual can attain self-control in great things only through self-control in little things. He must study himself to discover what is the weak point in his armor, what is the element within him that ever keeps him from his fullest success. This is the characteristic upon which he should begin his exercise in self-control. Is it self-ishness, vanity, cowardice, morbidness, temper, laziness, worry, mind-wandering, lack of purpose?—whatever form human weakness assumes in the masquerade of life he must discover. He must then live each day as if his whole existence were telescoped down to the single day before him. With no useless regret for the past, no useless worry for the future, he should live that day as if it were his only day,— the only day left for him to assert all that is best in him, the only day left for him to conquer all that is worst in him. He should master the weak element within him at each slight manifestation from moment to moment. Each moment then must be a victory for it or for him. Will he be King, or will he be slave?—the answer rests with him.

A Father's Legacy

HOMER, TRANSLATED BY SAMUEL BUTLER

In this passage from Homer's epic poem the *Iliad*, the warrior Hector bestows a blessing on his child before he leaves for battle. Hector prays that his son will grow up to surpass him in glory and honor on the battle-field. His words about blood are not something most parents would say to their sons today, but they are emblematic of a father's selfless wish to raise up a son who is better than he.

He stretched his arms towards his child, but the boy cried and nestled in his nurse's bosom, scared at the sight of his father's armour, and at the horse-hair plume that nodded fiercely from his helmet. His father and mother laughed to see him, but Hector took the helmet from his head and laid it all gleaming upon the ground. Then he took his darling child, kissed him, and dandled him in his arms, praying over him the while to Jove and to all the gods. "Jove," he cried, "grant that this my child may be even as myself, chief among the Trojans; let him be not less excellent in strength, and let him rule Ilius with his might. Then may one say of him as he comes from battle, 'The son is far better than the father.' May he bring back the blood-stained spoils of him whom he has laid low, and let his mother's heart be glad."

"A Manly Boy"

ANDREW SLOAN DRAPER

Andrew Sloan Draper (1848-1913) was an American educator, author, and jurist. He served in the New York State Assembly and as a judge of the United States court of Alabama before moving into the field of education and eventually serving as the president and regent of the University of Illinois. Draper focused much of his life on education and training boys to be men. This essay was published in 1907 in *Draper's Self Culture*.

For a boy to be manly, he must act like a man. By this I do not mean that he must no longer be a boy. He must be willing, as far as he is able, to help his parents, and try to assist his brothers and sisters in every way that he can.

There are many things which men do that it would not be right for boys to attempt. But there are also many other things which wise and thoughtful boys will try to do as well as they can, and yet be true boys.

There is an old saying that "you cannot put old heads on young shoulders." This is true to some extent; but when it is given as an excuse for being thoughtless and careless and rude, it is misleading.

We do not want to see our boys going about like little old men, and bearing burdens which their shoulders were never meant to carry. We do not want them to be robbed of the freshness and lightness of youth, while they are yet children but in years.

We believe that "all work and no play makes Jack a dull boy." But it is also true that "all play and no work will give Joe a ragged shirt."

Now a manly boy is as often as fond, if not fonder, of play than a boy who has nothing of a man about him. This is because the work he does gives him a change of employment, which makes play all the pleasenter [*sic*] when he takes part in a game.

In every home there are many things to be done which a boy can do just as well as an older person. He can black boots, mend broken things, run errands, work in the garden, and help his younger brothers and sisters with their lessons.

He can treat his parents with repect, [*sic*] follow their advice, and act in such a manner that they feel they can trust him to do right when he is out of their sight. They know that he is anxious to win their praise, and that he values their esteem.

I remember asking a father if he was not afraid to send a boy of thirteen to pay a large sum of money.

"Oh no," he replied, smiling, "I know it is quite safe with him. You see, he is such a manly boy."

When you are older and read the lives of some men who have risen to high places in the world, you will find that when they were boys they began to act like men. Yet they were just as fond of fun and play as other boys who never tried to give their parents a helping hand.

How often we hear a boy say, "I wish I was a man!" And if we ask why, we often learn that it is because he wants to be able to do as he likes. He is tired of having to obey his parents, and be guided by them. He thinks he knows better than they do what is best for him.

Such a boy is already going wrong, and only wants the chance to break away from the restraints of home. He is not a manly boy. He is often a forward, foolish boy, who can be easily led astray, and who will sooner or later come to grief.

When a manly boy wishes to be a man, it is not that he may have his own way, but that he may be better able to help his parents and be more useful in the world. It is not that he is tired of being a boy, but he is willing to give up youthful pleasures for the sake of those who have done so much for him.

From *The Marriage Guide for Young Men*

George W. Hudson

George W. Hudson wrote *The Marriage Guide for Young Men: A Manual of Courtship and Marriage*, published in 1883, to fill a need in English literature for such a work, claiming that home and society alike were reluctant to talk about the content. If you can overlook the chapter on Hudson's phrenological guidelines for selecting a wife, this is actually an excellent book that plainly explicates the pitfalls and pleasures of courtship and marriage, and how a young man ought to respond.

Always treat ladies with the greatest respect. Do this wherever you meet them. Show them that you regard them not as equals, but as superiors. Bestow upon them those little attentions at home and abroad which go so far toward making them happy. Offer to carry their bundles along the street, to give them a seat in the crowded car, to speak to the conductor for them, and the like; they will appreciate your kindness, and vote you a splendid young man. Do these things in an unselfish spirit, without looking for reward. Show the same attentions to young and old, married and single, you will not miss your reward. Mothers will recommend you to their daughters, and grandmothers to their granddaughters. For your own sake reverence woman wherever you find her; it will confirm you in the habits of a gentleman, and may be the means of winning you a genuine matrimonial prize. But aside from all this, reverence woman for what she is in herself.

Letter to a Sickly Child

Sydney Smith

Sydney Smith (1771–1845), Anglican cleric and English writer, penned the following letter to a sick little boy in 1836. After hearing of his illness,

Smith followed up every day to make sure he was okay. Mixing humor with grace, Smith's letter reflects his compassion and care for the young man.

To Master Humphrey Mildmay

April 30, 1837.

I am very sorry to hear you have been so ill. I have inquired about you every day, till I heard you were better. Mr. Travers is a very skillful surgeon and I have no doubt you will soon be well. In the Trojan war the Greek surgeons used cheese and wine for their ointments and in Henry the Eighth's time cobblers' wax and rust of iron were the ingredients; so you see it is some advantage to live in Berkley Square in the year 1837.

I am going to Holland and I will write to you from thence to tell you all I have seen, and you will take care to read my letter to Mr. Travers. In the meantime, my dear little Humphrey, I wish you most heartily a speedy recovery, and God bless you!

Response to a Fan Letter of Sorts

CHARLES DICKENS

One day Charles Dickens received a letter from a little boy who had been so interested in the story of Nicholas Nickleby that the characters of Smike, Mrs. Squeers, Fanny, and the rest seemed to be really alive. He hated Fanny, and in the spirit of revenge drew an ugly picture of her. Dickens, realizing the little fellow felt so strongly, took time out to write the child in reply.

Respected Sir,—

... Fanny Squeers shall be attended to, depend upon it, Your drawing of her is very like, except that I don't think the hair is quite curly enough. The nose is particularly like hers, and so are the legs. She is a nasty disagreeable thing and I know it will make her very cross when she sees it, and what I say is that I hope it may. You will say the same I know—at least I think you will.

I meant to have written you a long letter but I cannot write very fast when I like the person I am writing to, because that makes me think about them and I like you, and so I tell you. Besides, it is just eight o'clock at night and I always go to bed at eight o'clock except when it is my birthday, and then I sit up to supper, so I will not say anything more besides this, and that is my love to you and Neptune, and if you will drink my health every Christmas Day, I will drink yours.

I am, respected Sir, Your affectionate friend,

Charles Dickens

P.S. I don't write my name very plain but you know what it is, you know, so never mind.

A Father's Prayer

Douglas MacArthur

General Douglas MacArthur (1880–1964) was an outstanding figure in the events during and after the Second World War. He was recognized as a leader and an inspiration to soldiers and civilians alike. His "Father's Prayer" reflects a heart of hope and a vision for the young men of the future. In early 1942, when leading outnumbered United States forces in the Philippines, General MacArthur prayed this prayer many times at morning devotions, according to Major General Courtney Whitney, his longtime military aide. This prayer for his son, Arthur, is a spiritual legacy any son would cherish.

Build me a son, O Lord, who will be strong enough to know when he is weak, and brave enough to face himself when he is afraid; one who will be proud and unbending in honest defeat, and humble and gentle in victory.

Build me a son whose wishes will not take the place of deeds; a son who will know Thee and that to know himself is the foundation stone of knowledge.

Lead him, I pray, not in the path of ease and comfort, but under the stress and spur of difficulties and challenge. Here let him learn to stand up in the storm; here let him learn compassion for those who fail.

Build me a son whose heart will be clear, whose goal will be high; a son who will master himself before he seeks to master other men; one who will reach into the future, yet never forget the past.

And after all these things are his, add, I pray, enough of a sense of humor, so that he may always be serious, yet never take himself too seriously. Give him humility, so that he may always remember the simplicity of true greatness, the open mind of true wisdom, and the meekness of true strength.

Then, I, his father, will dare to whisper, "I have not lived in vain."

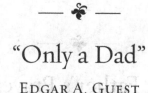

"Only a Dad"

EDGAR A. GUEST

Edgar Guest (1881–1959) was a famous American poet who became known as the "People's Poet" for his practical, common-life stories and imagery. As the title suggests, "Only a Dad" is Guest's ode to things that only fathers can do—a testament to the lengths men will go to take care of their children and families.

Only a dad with a tired face,
Coming home from the daily race,
Bringing little of gold or fame
To show how well he has played the game;
But glad in his heart that his own rejoice
To see him come and to hear his voice.

Only a dad with a brood of four,

One of ten million men or more
Plodding along in the daily strife,
Bearing the whips and the scorns of life,
With never a whimper of pain or hate,
For the sake of those who at home await.

Only a dad, neither rich nor proud,
Merely one of the surging crowd,
Toiling, striving from day to day,
Facing whatever may come his way,
Silent whenever the harsh condemn,
And bearing it all for the love of them.

Only a dad but he gives his all,
To smooth the way for his children small,
Doing with courage stern and grim
The deeds that his father did for him.
This is the line that for him I pen:
Only a dad, but the best of men.

Letter to a Bereaved Husband

SAMUEL JOHNSON

In a heartfelt letter, Samuel Johnson (1709-1784), the renowned English poet and essayist, expressed his condolences to his friend Dr. Lawrence on the loss of his wife. In the following excerpt, Johnson, who also lost his wife, relates his profound loss and emptiness to the unfortunate Dr. Lawrence.

. . . The loss, dear sir, of what you have lately suffered, I felt many years ago, and know therefore how much has been taken from you, and how little can be had from consolation. He that outlives a wife whom he has long loved, sees himself disjointed from the same hopes and fears and interests, from the only companion with whom he has shared much good or evil; and with whom he could set his mind at liberty to retrace the past or anticipate the future. The continuity of being is lacerated; the settled course of sentiment and action stopped; and life stands suspended and motionless, till it is driven by external causes into a new channel. But the time of suspense is dreadful . . .

Nathaniel Hawthorne's Letter to His Daughter

Nathaniel Hawthorne (1804-1864) wrote for grown people and also for children—something that few writers can do. He dearly loved his children and spent much of his time with them. We read in his biography that he made them boats and kites; he took them fishing and flower gathering. In the fall he delighted to plan nut-gathering parties. It is easy to picture the end of that happy day when the children would gather around their father to listen to his stories. Hawthorne wrote this letter to his absent daughter, Una. Here's a different personality than some might associate with the author of *The Scarlet Letter*.

My Dear Little Una,

I have been very much pleased with the letters which you have sent me; and I am glad to find that you do not forget me, for I think of you a great deal. I bring home a great many beautiful flowers, roses and poppies and lilies and harebells and pinks and many more besides, but it makes me feel sad to think that my little Una cannot see them. Your dolly wants to see you very much. She sits up in my study all day long, and has no one to talk with. I try to make her as comfortable as I can, but she does not seem to be in very good spirits. She has been quite good, and has grown very pretty since you went away.

Aunt Louisa and Dora are going to make her a new gown and a new bonnet. I hope you are a good little girl and are kind to your little brother . . . You must not trouble Mamma but must do all you can to help her . . . Do not you wish to come home and see me? I think we shall be very happy when you come, for I am sure you will be a good little girl. Good-by . . .

Your affectionate

Father

— ❦ —

Profile: "A Shau Valley"

War elicits the best of men in the most tragic of ways. Gordon Boucher went off to Vietnam to serve his country. He watched many good men die on the battlefield, including his close friend, Paul Gilbert, who left behind his beautiful fiancée. In the following true story, Boucher recounts the incredible lengths he went to honor Gilbert and his fiancée and the power their love held halfway around the world. If anyone who reads this story knows Georgiana Burke, please write me. I found Gordon through my radio show.

A scream exploded out of the jungle. Captain Gordon Boucher held his breath, burrowing underneath the spreading tree roots that covered him like a skeleton shelter. It was dark. He knew the year, 1972. He knew the date when he had last seen the sun, June 18. But his sense of time had been shattered at 8:30 p.m. when a fiery hell opened in his AC-130 Spectre gunship and he had been blown out of the sky.

He took a deep breath. The jungle crunched and crackled around him.

Animals scratched and clawed their way through the night. The wind blew and halfway up a hill somewhere in A Shau Valley—the pitted, bombed-out underbelly in the north part of South Vietnam—Gordon Boucher waited underneath a tree for the sunrise of June 19 and prayed the jungle would keep screaming.

There's nothing to be scared of in a noisy jungle, the thought looped through Gordon's head. *It's the quiet ones you have to worry about.*

When the night grew quiet, the vines and leaves quit sweating and the animals were still, it meant the North Vietnamese soldiers were close, clicking their way through the valley. Somewhere, soldiers hunted for the fire control officer of the U.S.

Air Force—for anyone who had survived the fiery ball engulfing the massive plane. But among the roots, Gordon listened to the screeches and growls.

How he was alive, he couldn't quite say. The last thing he remembered was the flame burning inside the plane and Captain Paul Faris Gilbert yelling, "Wait and jump only after I pull the alarm bell!"

Gordon waited.

In the darkness, sitting and listening, Gordon remembered the math major from Plainview, Texas. An ache mixed with the pounding in his chest. Paul was as good a man as Gordon had ever known. A man who stood tall with brown hair combed over, a gentle smile, and—tucked inside his jacket—a black-and-white photograph of a beautiful girl.

That smiling girl was Ms. Georgiana Burke. Gordon knew about Georgiana because Paul loved this woman wholly; she pervaded his conversation. And this woman loved her Air Force captain.

Love struggled to live in Vietnam as a faithful man was hard to find. Temptation called from the broken street corners. Fidelity was a virtue suspended and promiscuity infected even the cleanest of the American GIs. A man with a fiancée stood on a shaky pedestal.

But Paul never wilted under the gaze of his men. Gordon watched his life and listened to the way he spoke of Georgiana. The two never contradicted each other.

He was nothing to Gordon; the two men didn't know each other but war throws together whom it will and they ended up talking. Paul was involved in student government, a three-year member of the Latin Club, and the band president. He attended an Episcopal church. Gordon was a boy from Brooklyn, New York, who found peace at synagogue. Their upbringings, interests, and views on life were polar opposites but the men shared one trait—they both chose to serve. Each could have had their pick of professions; they were hardworking and bright. Yes, the draft was whisking men from the classroom to the front line, but Gordon and Paul could have played the odds and kept their heads down. Instead they chose to volunteer.

Gordon even went a step further.

After joining in 1968 he had felt something in his throat—cancer of the thyroid. He was rushed into surgery. Doctors removed his thyroid in a radical procedure and he received a medical discharge in 1970. He was put on a temporary retirement list.

He could have stayed on that list, dodged combat, and stayed off the front line with dignity and respect.

But Gordon wasn't content with that.

He started exercising; slowly at first, tiptoeing his way back into shape. While teaching math at a private school, Gordon heard of a program meant to bring cancer survivors back to active duty.

He called the flight surgeon's office in San Antonio. "I want in."

The office seemed interested but school break came and Gordon had a trip lined up to Paris.

"If the Air Force wants me, let me know," Gordon told his mother before he flew out. "I'll check at the American Express office once a week. Tell them to leave word there if they want me. I'll be waiting."

In August, the message came, and Gordon caught the next plane home.

Thrown back into the mix, he was forced to pass two physicals. Then came the orders, handed directly down from the president of the United States: "Come off the temporary disability retirement list and join the 16th SOS, flying C-130 gunships."

The boy from Brooklyn didn't hesitate.

"My country spent $200,000 to $300,000 training me. I owe it to them. I've got a mission to do, and if I don't go back, I'll have a bad taste in my mouth forever."

Trained as a navigator, Gordon learned the art of being a fire control officer, of directing the destruction and force of this plane. Dragons might cut a less menacing presence than the AC-130 Spectre as it glided through the night, searchlights blazing through the sky as crew scurried inside, promising the type of awful vengeance this craft could unleash. The soldiers called it "the ranger of the sky."

Arriving in the maw of Vietnam, Gordon was thrown straight into the missions. Bombing runs, rescue operations, and between the wheels of the ship touching down and taking off, there were the conversations with Paul Faris Gilbert.

The conversations rarely trifled in the mundane. Jumping from philosophy to politics and religion, Gordon and Paul stayed up late, sitting around the fire each night in the A Shau Valley.

Gordon had been at Ohio State University before enlisting; Paul finished at the University of Texas. Choosing the Air Force, he was stationed at Dyess Air Force Base, on the dusty outskirts of Abilene, Texas. Whatever it was that pushed him to fly, he loved it, soloing in a T-37 and training above Mach 1 levels. He cut a sharp figure in the dress whites of the U.S. Air Force. And one woman liked what she had seen.

Gordon only saw Georgiana once, when Paul took the picture out one night, and handed it over. "She's one of the most beautiful women I've ever seen." The words jumped off Gordon's tongue. Paul knew. He was going to marry her.

Not all women have to be met to be known. Their presence touches all parts of life. It transforms the men who love them. The gracious beauty of Georgiana Burke perfumed the life of Paul Gilbert, and anyone who met the boy from Plainview knew there was something special about her. While the beauty of Helen may have led to the downfall of Paris, Georgiana inspired Paul to become something greater.

When a truly great love is discovered, when a man meets a woman of value, fireworks do not always explode. The sun does not set into a Monet painting and there may not be a string quartet softly lilting in the background, but something changes. The movies can't quite capture the whole arc of true love, but meet a man who loves, and is loved by, a great woman and there is something different. It is like the sun, warming all parts of life and causing seeds of courage, dignity, and virtue to grow. All parts of his life and those around him are touched by the light.

Gordon could see Georgiana's light in Paul.

In 1972, as the end of the war could be seen grinding closer, the Vietnamese soldiers were clawing for a bargaining chip. The AC-130 was a fine prize filled with highly skilled soldiers who could be used as leverage during the eventual negotiations for peace.

On the night of June 18, Paul wasn't scheduled to fly. He just wanted to eat dinner. Sitting with pilot Peter Marx, the call came for a volunteer to pilot the 16th SOS and take over for an ill pilot.

Paul jumped up, canceled his order and headed out the door.

"He never hesitated, no questions asked, just ready to serve," said Marx.

The plane took off. It wasn't long before the crew saw a flash and knew that a surface-to-air missile, a SA7, a heat seeker, was coming at them. The fifteen-man crew tried to dodge but misread the missile. They took a wrong turn, and the number three engine went out in a tremendous crash. The plane burned, one-hundred-foot flames extending out past the fuselage.

Paul took control of the plane, and the two other men in the booth moved toward the back. Staying in his station, Gordon felt the plane shudder and then drop. It dove down, down, down. Paul desperately tried to put out the fire. It kept burning.

Paul screamed, "Don't jump until I ring the alarm bell!"

Gordon's entire body willed him out of the plane. *Jump. There may not be another chance.* Other crew members threw themselves into the blackness, but Paul had told him to wait, and Gordon trusted his captain.

The alarm bell rang. Gordon pushed himself through his booth, but as he pushed himself into the starboard side of the plane, the right wing burned off, and then the plane was spinning.

He tried to move, but his entire body was paralyzed, watching the door, the exit, but unable to reach it—11 to 13 Gs of force, pressing down.

Gordon craned his head. All he could see were bodies, gunners still wearing their flight suits, no parachutes. And it was burning red. Everything was red and on fire.

Looking out over the ship, frozen as the flames came closer, a thought ran through Gordon's head, a quote from Tolkien's *Lord of the Rings*, at the moment where Sam and Frodo peer at a burning Mount Doom: "I'm glad to be with you . . . Here at the end of all things."

The heat picked up, and then the world went white, black, and then cool. Gordon's eyes flicked open. "Where am I?"

He didn't feel anything, but then looked down. There was a light, trees, flames, and it was all coming closer.

He ripped the ring of his parachute and the canvas billowed over his head. Five seconds later and he hit the tree line. Gordon made his way through the trees, pushing through the branches and finally reaching the ground. He unhooked the chute, headed up the hill, found a tree to hide underneath, and then waited.

With his gun tightly held to his chest, Gordon listened for any sound to indicate that he might not be alone.

"If anyone pops their head through here, I'm taking them with me."

The minutes had ticked into hours when Gordon realized the night had quieted. Twenty minutes passed and then there were Vietnamese forces on either side of Gordon, coming only ten feet from the hiding soldier. He kept his finger on the trigger and his body completely still.

He waited.

The noise picked back up in the jungle. Gordon stayed where he was until the sunrise exposed his position, and then he moved. He found a briar patch, thought, *No one will stick their hand in here*, and submerged himself in the prickly thorns.

He had a radio and had been talking quietly as he reached out to the planes and choppers searching for him. It took time for them to find his position and even longer for them to rescue him, but about 9:00 a.m., the choppers lowered a "tree penetrator"; Gordon wrapped the cable around him and was jerked into the air.

Fifteen men had flown out on the original mission; three men survived.

After arriving back on the base, Gordon was grounded for ten days. He then went on to fly seventy-five more missions before the end of his term. He earned multiple medals, including two distinguished flying crosses, eight air medals, one combination medal, and the Purple Heart.

Gordon knew that he lived through the war only because of Paul's bravery. The sacrifice shook him and the knowledge of what Paul had lost could not be forgotten.

So he wrote a letter to Paul's family. He told them what Paul had meant to him, the sacrifices Paul had made, and the honor with which he had conducted his duty.

"Paul was a man who was faithful to the woman he loved, the men he served, the country who sent him, and the God who made him," he remembered.

He posted the letter. He wasn't sure if he'd get a response from the family, but after a little waiting, he opened the mail to discover a letter from a different person.

"Knowing that you will not recognize the name on this letter; first let me tell you that I am Paul Gilbert's fiancée."

The Gilberts had passed Gordon's letter on to Ms. Georgiana Burke, and the woman who Paul had loved so much proved to be as gracious in grieving as she had been in the stories Paul told.

"I know that the past few months have been very difficult for you, but I'm sure you have executed your work admirably."

Georgiana was a woman of few words and when she wrote to Gordon, the tragedy of Paul's death hung over each line. The words spoke of loss, but they also were filled with the thoughts of a woman whose care for others far outweighed any pity she might have had for herself. Serenity hung over the words as she passed encouragement to Gordon, a reminder that things would get better.

But there was still a reminder of what love she had lost.

"That I love Paul more than I am capable of expressing cannot be denied. To consider spending the rest of my life without him is sometimes most unendurable. But most of all the beauty of the things we experienced together and the joy we shared will live forever."

Gordon never heard from Ms. Burke again, but he kept her letter and treasured it. The love she had lost and the sacrifice Paul had made stayed with Gordon throughout his life. After the war, it wasn't an easy transition back to the world of civilians. There were things he had seen in the jungles that didn't go away with the ceasefire.

But Gordon remembered Paul and Georgiana. It gave him hope, and when Betsy came along, Gordon, at the age of forty, gave a love of his own a chance. Betsy proved to be Gordon's own angel and she helped shepherd him out of the darkness that too often envelops combat veterans.

"I've got all these memories," said Gordon. "They make living with a guy like me nothing like a piece of cake. It felt like I'd be in two places at once—with my wife and still back in Vietnam. But Betsy never gave up on me and stayed patient."

Three years after they were married, Betsy found out she was pregnant. It was not guaranteed to be a safe pregnancy. The toxins Gordon had been exposed to in Vietnam meant that carrying this baby to term came with more than one risk. But Gordon and Betsy stayed hopeful and when they found out their baby was a boy, Gordon knew the name of his son.

"We named him Joshua Paul Boucher," said Gordon. "Joshua after my father and Paul after the man who saved my life."

Fathers carry a responsibility to teach their sons from birth, to speak with them often and tell them what they must know about being a man. From a young age Josh heard the story of the man who died so that his father might live. His days are lived out in the shadow of Paul's memory.

Matthew wrote, "Greater love has no man than this, than he who laid down his life for his friends" and those men of great love will continue to emerge in times of combat. The crucible of the battlefield tests the purity of convictions and the depth of each man's beliefs, and while many break, men like Paul leave a legacy that inspires and challenges generations to come.

And those generations cannot and should not shrug off such a sacrifice. Countless are blessed by such self-sacrifice and must not be overlooked, but the ones left behind still linger. Gordon told Josh of Georgiana's love—the letter from the bereaved fiancée will be passed down as his inheritance—and the model of love lived out in her life and in the life of his mother, Betsy, affects Josh to this day. With such a model of gracious femininity and self-denying masculinity, the young man learned early the beauty of a noble relationship between a man and a woman.

Gordon tried to reach out to Georgiana and let her know about his son and the name that he carries but he could never find her.

On November 17, 1994, Gordon stood with Betsy and Josh at Arlington National Cemetery. Remains had been found that the U.S. government claimed were those of the thirteen men lost in the crash of the AC130 Spectre gunship and the time had come for these men to be given the funeral and honor they so fully earned.

Guns were raised and fired, twenty-one times. The coffin was lowered into the ground and a C130 gunship flew overhead in tribute.

Young Josh watched quietly.

"What does it mean to be a man?" Gordon would later reflect. "It seems like something simple. It means being faithful and doing your duty."

Paul lived that life out, Gordon followed his example, and Josh seems cut from that same cloth as he excelled in school, worked hard, and went to Brown University. His father speaks of him with warmth and pride, and never forgets the gift of life that he was given. Gordon lives with a fervor and gratefulness, still very much in love with his wife, Betsy. He lives in Virginia and can be found serving and working around the synagogue or working on a small book on economics for the common American.

But he's still looking for Georgiana Burke, to thank her one more time and introduce her to the boy who carries the name of the man she loved.

Thomas Jefferson's Letter to Thomas Jefferson Smith

Parenting is not just limited to mothers and fathers—a woman shouts at a child to stop him from dangerously crossing a street; a father coaches the local Little League team. Communication from outside influences can mean a lot in a child's life, as evidenced by this February 21, 1825, letter from Thomas Jefferson to young Thomas Jefferson Smith. It is great advice from an old man to a young boy.

This letter will, to you, be as one from the dead. The writer will be in the grave before you can weigh its counsels. Your affectionate and excellent father, has requested that I would address to you something which might possibly have a favorable influence on the course of life you have to run, and I too, as a namesake, feel an interest in that course. Few words will be necessary, with good dispositions on your part. Adore God. Reverence and cherish your parents. Love your neighbor as yourself, and your country more than yourself. Be just. Be true. Murmur not at the ways of Providence. So shall the life into which you have entered, be the portal to one of eternal and ineffable bliss. And if to the dead it is permitted to care for the things of this world, every action of your life will be under my regard. Farewell.

The man, who, by his steady course, has happiness insur'd.
When earth's foundations shake, shall stand, by Providence secur'd.

A DECALOGUE OF CANONS FOR OBSERVATION IN PRACTICAL LIFE.

1. Never put off till to-morrow what you can do to-day.
2. Never trouble another for what you can do yourself.
3. Never spend your money before you have it.

4. Never buy what you do not want, because it is cheap; it will be dear to you.
5. Pride costs us more than hunger, thirst and cold.
6. We never repent of having eaten too little.
7. Nothing is troublesome that we do willingly.
8. How much pain have cost us the evils which have never happened.
9. Take things always by their smooth handle.
10. When angry, count ten, before you speak; if very angry, an hundred.

"Dr. Johnson and His Father"

In this touching story about the famous English poet and essayist, Samuel Johnson (1709-1784) and his father, Johnson reflects on a mistake he made in his younger days and the regret it caused him later in life. The realization of this missed opportunity for love caused Johnson anguish and remorse. To fathers and sons and fathers and daughters: take the time to be together—now.

It is in a little bookshop in the city of Lichfield, England. The floor has just been swept and the shutter taken down from the one small window. The hour is early, and customers have not yet begun to drop in. Out of doors the rain is falling.

At a small table near the door, a feeble, white-haired old man is making up some packages of books. As he arranges them in a large basket, he stops now and then as though disturbed by pain. He puts his hand to his side; he coughs in a most distressing way; then he sits down and rests himself, leaning his elbows upon the table.

"Samuel!" he calls.

In the farther corner of the room there is a young man busily reading from a large book that is spread open before him. He is a very odd-looking fellow, perhaps eighteen years of age, but you would take him to be older. He is large and awkward, with a great round face, scarred and marked by a strange disease. His eyesight must be poor, for, as he reads, he bends down until his face is quite near the printed page.

"Samuel!" again the old man calls.

But Samuel makes no reply. He is so deeply interested in his book that he does not hear. The old man rests himself a little longer and then finishes tying his packages. He lifts the heavy basket and sets it on the table. The exertion brings on another fit of coughing; and when it is over he calls for the third time, "Samuel!"

"What is it, father?" This time the call is heard.

"You know, Samuel," he says, "that to-morrow is market day at Uttoxeter, and our stall must be attended to. Some of our friends will be there to look at the new books which they expect me to bring. One of us must go down on the stage this morning and get everything in readiness. But I hardly feel able for the journey. My cough troubles me quite a little, and you see that it is raining very hard."

"Yes, father; I am sorry," answers Samuel; and his face is again bent over the book.

"I thought perhaps you would go down to the market, and that I might stay here at the shop," says his father. But Samuel does not hear. He is deep in the study of some Latin classic.

The old man goes to the door and looks out. The rain is still falling. He shivers, and buttons his coat.

It is a twenty-mile ride to Uttoxeter. In five minutes the stage will pass the door.

"Samuel, will you not go down to the market for me this time?"

The old man is putting on his great coat.

He is reaching for his hat.

The basket is on his arm.

He casts a beseeching glance at his son, hoping that he will relent at the last moment.

"Here comes the coach, Samuel;" and the old man is choked by another fit of coughing.

Whether Samuel hears or not, I do not know. He is still reading, and he makes no sign nor motion.

The stage comes rattling down the street.

The old man with his basket of books staggers out of the door. The stage halts for a moment while he climbs inside. Then the driver swings his whip, and all are away.

Samuel, in the shop, still bends over his book.

Out of doors the rain is falling.

Just fifty years have passed, and again it is market day at Uttoxeter.

The rain is falling in the streets. The people who have wares to sell huddle under the eaves and in the stalls and booths that have roofs above them.

A chaise from Lichfield pulls up at the entrance to the market square.

An old man alights. One would guess him to be seventy years of age. He is large and not well-shaped. His face is seamed and scarred, and he makes strange grimaces as he clambers out of the chaise. He wheezes and puffs as though afflicted with asthma. He walks with the aid of a heavy stick.

With slow but ponderous strides he enters the market place and looks around. He seems not to know that the rain is falling.

He looks at the little stalls ranged along the walls of the market place. Some have roofs over them and are the centers of noisy trade. Others have fallen into disuse and are empty.

The stranger halts before one of the latter. "Yes, this is it," he says. He has a strange habit of talking aloud to himself. "I remember it well. It was here that my father, on certain market days, sold books to the clergy of the county. The good men came from every parish to see his wares and to hear him describe their contents."

He turns abruptly around. "Yes, this is the place," he repeats.

He stands quite still and upright, directly in front of the little old stall. He takes off his hat and holds it beneath his arm. His great walking stick has fallen into the gutter. He bows his head and clasps his hands. He does not seem to know that the rain is falling.

The clock in the tower above the market strikes eleven. The passers-by stop and gaze at the stranger. The market people peer at him from their booths and stalls. Some laugh as the rain runs in streams down his scarred old cheeks. Rain is it? Or can it be tears?

Boys hoot at him. Some of the ruder ones even hint at throwing mud; but a sense of shame withholds them from the act.

"He is a poor lunatic. Let him alone," say the more compassionate.

The rain falls upon his bare head and his broad shoulders. He is drenched and chilled. But he stands motionless and silent, looking neither to the right nor to the left.

"Who is that old fool?" asks a thoughtless young man who chances to be passing.

"Do you ask who he is?" answers a gentleman from London. "Why, he is Dr. Samuel Johnson, the most famous man in England. It was he who wrote Rasselas and the Lives of the Poets and Irene and many another work which all men are praising. It was he who made the great English Dictionary, the most wonderful book of our times. In London, the noblest lords and ladies take pleasure in doing him honor. He is the literary lion of England."

"Then why does he come to Uttoxeter and stand thus in the pouring rain?"

"I cannot tell you; but doubtless he has reasons for doing so;" and the gentleman passes on.

At length there is a lull in the storm. The birds are chirping among the house-tops. The people wonder if the rain is over, and venture out into the slippery street.

The clock in the tower above the market strikes twelve. The renowned stranger has stood a whole hour motionless in the market place. And again the rain is falling.

Slowly now he returns his hat to his head. He finds his walking stick where it had fallen. He lifts his eyes reverently for a moment, and then, with a lordly, lumbering motion, walks down the street to meet the chaise which is ready to return to Lichfield.

We follow him through the pattering rain to his native town.

"Why, Dr. Johnson!" exclaims his hostess; "we have missed you all day. And you are so wet and chilled! Where have you been?"

"Madam," says the great man, "fifty years ago, this very day, I tacitly refused to oblige or obey my father. The thought of the pain which I must have caused him has haunted me ever since. To do away the sin of that hour, I this morning went in a chaise to Uttoxeter and did do penance publicly before the stall which my father had formerly used."

The great man bows his head upon his hands and sobs.

Out of doors the rain is falling.

Profile: Bill Phillips

My friend Bill Phillips was a man who dedicated his life to his family, his community, and his work. Despite working long, hard hours, Phillips always made time for the most important things in life—his sons and his wife. Men like Phillips make a lasting impact on the people around them, and when Bill passed away in a tragic accident in 2010 we all felt the loss.

Football games in America are filled and surrounded with rituals. There can be the tailgate before the game—throngs of people surrounding the stadium with food and drink—the pregame speech from the coach, the run out onto the field, and there is the coin toss. But before the whistle sounds, and the kicker makes the slow loping run to send the ball to the other end of the field, one more tradition must happen. Boys look for their fathers.

It may not be much. A quick glance into the stands, a scan of the rows before turning back to the field, but the question stays the same: Will he be there? Sons want to play beneath the gaze of their father and no matter how much the attention of anyone else—even that smiling young lady—might thrill the heart of a teenager, there is one member of the audience whose attention boys innately crave. But sometimes work runs late and he isn't sitting there. He may have had "better things" to do. He just couldn't make it or, sadly, there may be a split that means it's not the father's turn to be at the game. And still others have had that primary relationship with their father damaged to such a point that they would cringe to see him anywhere near their lives. It can be sad.

But for Andrew, Colter, and Paul Phillips, they always knew that—barring some type of extraordinary disruption—William (Bill) Phillips Sr. would be sitting up in the stands when they ran out on the field. They loved their father, and he loved supporting them in whatever they were doing.

Competition ran in the Phillipses' blood, and the boys took a page from their father's path in life. The six-foot-seven-tall Bill played defensive tackle at Evansville from 1972 to 1976, while his wife Janet swam in college. The boys went to Georgetown Preparatory School in Bethesda, Maryland, and were separated by a few years. Andrew took his place on the offensive line while Colter and Paul lined up as tight ends.

Bill loved his boys and those boys excelled on the field. As each came to his final year, the scholarship offers started coming in. Andrew left first to attend Stanford University. Colter entered the University of Virginia and Paul accepted an offer to play at the University of Indiana.

These boys were no slouches on the field, and their father was no slouch off the field, serving as the legislative director and chief of staff to Alaskan senator Ted Stevens and working as a highly successful attorney and lobbyist. It was the type of job that could make it hard to make it out on Friday nights to the lights of the stadium—but Bill did everything he could to be there each week.

For Bill, football wasn't just about the score when the referee finally blew his whistle.

"My dad was really a huge fan of what football can do for you in your life, and the life lessons you can learn from playing the game," said Colter. "He said that if you can be a good football player, not having good skill, but being a good teammate and really learn the game—you can really be successful in life."

And Bill was so proud of his boys. Even when Andrew was on the West Coast, Bill would do everything in his power to make the games, leaving Colter's high school games on a Friday night and catching a red-eye flight so as not to miss the college game on Saturday. He made attending his sons' games a priority, even when it meant moving his work schedule around.

When Colter ran out on the field, he'd go through a routine, running to the bench, saying a prayer, then looking to the stands for his mother and father.

All of the boys knew that football wasn't just a game; it taught the boys how to live as a man. They were taught to act with courage, conviction, and with clarity of purpose despite any difficulties. They watched their father and they loved him.

He made spending time with each of them a priority, and when Senator Ted Stevens wanted Bill to head to Alaska with him for a salmon fishing trip in August 2010, Bill decided to take his youngest son, thirteen-year-old William Jr. or "Willy" as he was called. It was supposed to be a wonderful adventure for father and son.

But something went wrong and the 1957 De Havilland DHC-3 Otter floatplane they were flying slammed into the side of a mountain in Dillingham, Alaska, with tremendous force, leaving a three-hundred-foot gash in the hillside. Bill died. Senator Stevens and three others were also killed.

Oil and wreckage caked the slope as cold rain and wind gusted about the wreckage. Willy was injured, trapped in the plane. Three other travelers were still alive, but it was a cold night. A helicopter finally circled overhead, and Willy knew he had to flag it down or more people might not make it. Willy was injured, but he waved at the helicopter and tried to jump out of the crashed plane to get their attention. He broke his leg.

There were no complaints from the thirteen-year-old. Rescuers had seen them, but it would still be a few hours before any help could make it through the treacherous Alaskan countryside to the plane. Willy tended to the other injured survivors in the plane, trying to keep them warm and protected. Two volunteer emergency technicians, a doctor and a nurse, were dropped into the region by plane and hiked the thousand feet up to the wreckage.

The plane was resting on a thirty-degree slope. The doctor and the nurse performed emergency treatment on the wounded, but there was no way for the injured to be extracted until morning.

The survivors were taken to Providence Alaska Medical Center. Willy had cuts across his body and injuries to his hands and legs.

The news of Senator Stevens's death was a shock, but the news that Bill Phillips' life had ended spread fast as well.

Gregg Renkes, Janet's brother-in-law, released a statement saying that Bill Phillips "was a man of deep faith who lived for his family, was kind, generous and believed in the goodness of every individual. Bill was a successful entrepreneur and a gifted attorney whose wisdom and insights into life, law and public policy were sought by many."

Bill was loved by many. The man lived a life that was hard to ignore. A quiet life, marked by integrity and uncluttered by any presumption or affected importance.

On the twentieth of August, a funeral mass was held at Our Lady of Mercy Catholic Church in Potomac, Maryland. Hundreds of people paid tribute to the life of Bill Phillips in a two-hour service. The football team from the University of Virginia attended.

Willy stayed quietly in a wheelchair, but each of the other sons spoke.

They remembered the life of their father as one marked by a commitment to his faith and his family. He was a man with a great love of family, but his love extended outside of his family, even to strangers, and he never looked for thanks or recognition for his actions. He loved Alaska and the wilderness of that state.

The sons were prepared to sit out the 2010 football season, to come home and support their mother. But Janet would have none of that and told the boys that they still needed to "be kids" and that their father would have wanted them to play.

While Bill might have passed and finally been unable to make it to the football games of the boys he loved so much, his spirit lived on after his coffin was lowered into the ground. His was a spirit that gave Willy strength to serve others, even in the horrors of the crash, and a spirit that kept Andrew, Colter, and Paul smiling and able to run onto the field.

For the Phillips family, football wasn't just a game and when the boys look up into the stands, they will still feel their father watching. And maybe others will be watching, too, for in the funeral program on that August day, the football schedules for the three boys were printed on the back of the program, with an encouragement from Janet to friends and family to attend and stand in for Bill.

6

Man in Prayer and Reflection

I t is natural to think of men first as physical beings and to describe manhood as muscle, strength, power, and actions—whether heroic and courageous or weak and timid. But the true root of a man's existence is his ability to think and reflect. In the Bible, God's first task for man was to name creation and be its caretaker—an internal, reflective activity. And in another tradition Socrates famously explained, "The unexamined life is not worth living."

Reflection and contemplation separate men from the rest of creation. "There is one art of which every man should be a master—the art of reflection—if you are not a thinking man, to what purpose are you a man at all?" asked English poet and philosopher Samuel Coleridge. And said English writer Robert Dodsley, "Reflection is the business of man; a sense of his state is his first duty."

Without reflection men would be nothing more than walking appetites, driven to and fro by natural instincts. Reflection allows us to weigh our actions, judge the consequences, and proceed circumspectly. It is how a man evaluates and determines his fortune and future.

Some self-reflection helps in leading a good and joyful life. As the twentieth-century American historian, William L. Shirer, said, "Most true happiness comes from one's inner life, from the disposition of the mind and soul." How does a man cultivate such a disposition? "It takes reflection and contemplation and self-discipline," he said.

Admittedly, that doesn't come easily. Some of us men are not readily inclined to reflection, contemplation, and self-discipline. But a life without some reflection and self-examination is incomplete. It is like a house built on sand, easily destroyed by the slightest of life's storms—or like a house left unmaintained. As English poet Edward Young put it, "A soul without reflection, like a pile without inhabitant, to ruin runs."

A man sharpens and strengthens his body through exercise; he sharpens and strengthens his mind through thought and reflection—like spiritual calisthenics and study. Much like a body goes to waste without exercise, so, too, will a thoughtless mind.

While you can judge a man's physical manhood by the weight he can lift or the pace of his sprint, his "mental manhood" is more elusive. The development of the mind is a nonlinear event, with no specific milestones or checkpoints. It's an internal struggle—a push and a pull that's often two steps forward and one step back. But we welcome the fight. "The real man smiles in trouble," said American pamphleteer Thomas Paine, "gathers strength from distress, and grows brave by reflection."

Reflection goes hand in hand with, and is not the opposite of, faith. Most Jews and Christians embrace both reason and revelation. Broadly defined, prayer is personal communication with God. Prayer is the bridge from ephemeral reflection to eternal contemplation. In the act of prayer, man studies and dissects his own soul while recognizing that there is an order and a power greater than himself to whom he is accountable. Prayer brings us closer to God in the same way that engaging in conversation with another human strengthens our relationship with that person.

What we consider prayer typically includes petition, intercession, confession of sin, praise, and thanksgiving. Any conversation with God, however, can be considered prayer. Said Victor Hugo, author of Les Misérables, "Certain thoughts are prayers. There are moments when, whatever be the attitude of the body, the soul is on its knees."

In any discussion of prayer, the question naturally arises: If God knows everything, then why pray? We pray because it is a demonstration of trust and faith in God. Through prayer we are dependent on the goodness of God and confess our conviction in his goodness. It's not for him, it's for us.

We also keep watch of ourselves through prayer. George Herbert, a Welsh poet and Anglican priest, said it best: "Sum up at night what thou hast done by day, and in the morning what thou hast to do.—Dress and undress thy soul; mark the decay and growth of it.—If with thy watch, that too be down, then wind up both; since we shall be most surely judged, make thine accounts agree."

And beyond an exercise of our faith, prayer may even influence God's actions. James tells us, "You do not have because you do not ask" (James 4:2 NKJV). Jesus himself said, "And whatever things you ask in prayer, believing, you will receive" (Matthew 21:22 NKJV). The Bible makes it very clear that when we ask, God answers. As you will see throughout this chapter, men who prayed incessantly believed that God would answer—and he often did in powerful ways. On the other hand, if you pray very little or not at all, it is a sign that you believe prayer accomplishes little or nothing at all.

I fear that this is the place we find a majority of men today. According to Gallup polling in 2010, only 39 percent of men attend church regularly (compared to 47 percent of women). Church is often the punch line of television-show jokes or only appears relevant around the holiday season. It seems that modern man spends less time in prayer and reflection than many of the generations before him.

Whether an athlete or a construction worker or a doctor, a man is better off if he is a thinking man and a prayerful man. Reflection and prayer are a man's internal GPS system, and to neglect this part of life would be like going on a journey without a map or a compass. A man may not see where he is headed in life without first realizing where he has been and how he got there, and attaining the wisdom to know that he depends on a power greater than himself. In this chapter we see famous and unfamous men thinking and praying. Men—good men from all stations of life—do both.

The Our Father (or the Lord's Prayer)

The Our Father is the oldest of Christian prayers, going back to Jesus Christ himself, who, as it says in the gospel of Matthew, taught his disciples to pray in these words. Because the prayer came from Christ, it is used in every mass and liturgy and recited by billions of people every day. In thinking about "our Father," we should recognize that there are two Latin words for "father," *pater* and *genitor*. The latter refers to the biological act of fathering. The former, and the more important, *pater* refers to the

protective and guiding acts of a father. The Lord's prayer in Latin begins
"Pater Noster."

> *Our Father in heaven,*
> *Hallowed be Your name.*
> *Your kingdom come.*
> *Your will be done*
> *On earth as it is in heaven.*
> *Give us this day our daily bread.*
> *And forgive us our debts,*
> *As we forgive our debtors.*
> *And do not lead us into temptation,*
> *But deliver us from the evil one.*
> *For Yours is the kingdom and the power and the glory forever. Amen.*

The Glory Be

The Glory Be, also known as the doxology, is one of the earliest-known
prayers to refer to the holy Trinity. In Eastern Rite Catholic churches (as
well as Eastern Orthodox ones), the Sign of the Cross is made while the
Glory Be is recited.

Glory be to the Father, and to the Son, and to the Holy Ghost, as it was in the
beginning, is now, and ever shall be, world without end. Amen.

A Child's Grace

Praying before a meal is a great way to remind children to thank God for
their daily blessings. This is a heartfelt personal favorite at many tables
across the country.

God is great and God is Good,
And we thank Him for this food;
By His hand must all be fed,
Give us Lord, our daily bread. Amen.

"We Thank Thee"

REBECCA WESTON

There is never a bad time to pray. Men should thank God for all we have, whether it's morning, noon, or night.

Father, we thank thee for the night,
And for the pleasant morning light;
For rest and food and loving care,
And all that makes the world so fair.

Help us to do the things we should,
To be to others kind and good;
In all we do, in work or play,
To grow more loving every day.

Profile: Os Guinness

In many countries around the world, the free exercise of religion is prohibited. In America, we often take for granted the ability to gather in the churches of our choice when and wherever we want. In countries like China, this would be a crime. Os Guinness, one of the great modern evangelists and social commentators, was raised as a missionary child in China. Here is a man who experienced religious persecution firsthand, but it only made his faith stronger and his will more determined.

Church services stop being interesting after the first two hours—especially to an eight-year-old Irish boy living in a foreign country.

The teaching, prayer, and singing started as in all services, but one, two, three, four, five hours later, and young Os Guinness lost all attention and finally turned to his father,

"When's this going to be over? Why are they still talking?"

His father answered quietly.

"They're preparing for persecution."

Os tried to keep listening, but the sermons were dense, filled with hours of Scripture and theology. Like a general preparing his troops for the final siege, this pastor sought to prepare his congregation to withstand hardship.

And in 1948, persecution and suffering strode toward the church of the Chinese people, in the form of Chairman Mao and the "People's Army." Even at the age of eight, Os knew what it meant to endure trials. His parents were medical missionaries, two selfless individuals who lived their lives on call for the Chinese people, thinking nothing of pulling teeth, amputating limbs, or of cycling one hundred miles to deliver a baby.

The service in China was not without cost. The Henan Famine of 1943 killed five million people. Two of those graves were filled by Os' brothers.

Though many tears were shed, the Guinness family hadn't lost their faith. Rooted in the tradition of evangelicals, the faithful line stretched back to Arthur Guinness and the Guinness Brewing Company. Generation after generation grounded themselves on the Word of God, leaving the children with a solid foundation.

But now another gale approached, and it struck with a fury.

"In the morning there were trials," said Guinness. "And in the afternoon, there were executions."

———

From his first days, Os saw faith rooted realistically in his parents' lives. The way of Christ was never painted as easy, but it never was seen as joyless. Os was away from his parents. They were imprisoned throughout his teenage years. Faith meant more than a simple rejection of other ideas, it embraced the way of Christ, and joyfully applied that to all parts of life.

But in those days of China, Os witnessed a living definition of what it meant to be a Christian and live out a faith that breathes. It was a faith viewing the world for all its blackness, but a faith refusing to retreat.

"People often see doubt as the opposite of faith, and that's not true," said Os. "The opposite of faith is unbelief. Doubt is a halfway stage. It's being of two minds; you half believe and you half don't believe. Like a spinning coin, it's going to come down one way or the other. Doubt is either going to be resolved and go back to faith or be left unresolved and move on to unbelief."

"I came of faith and came of age in the 1960s, in what was called 'Swinging London,'" said Os. "It was the beginnings of the counterculture, so it was an incredible challenge to relate my faith to everything going on around me, and most Christians didn't."

And so, the great-great-grandson of a man who was friends with John Wesley and George Whitfield and a supporter of William Wilberforce picked up the mantle of his family, and spent the next fifty years serving the twin roles of an apologist for the verity of his faith and a keen analyst of the times.

The two tie together. Os tells people that he's always had a keen sense of the times, but that his understanding of the times stems from his understanding of Truth—the truth of the Scriptures. And that's one that Os reinforces by returning to the source, practicing private devotion and worship—spending forty minutes reading and studying and twenty minutes praying, each day.

"I've now been reading the Scriptures for fifty years," said Os. "There's never a day when I don't see something new, not last year, or the previous forty-nine years . . . the old Puritan John Robinson was right when he said, 'the Lord has yet more truth and light to break out of the Word.' We should expect that."

And it's against that standard that Os holds all trends in Christendom—are we living as Christ called us to live?

"Why do we take Scripture seriously?" asked Os. "We take it seriously, because Jesus did. For instance, what's his answer to the evil one? Every temptation, 'it is written.' Clearly for him, Scripture was the final absolute authority for his life, and so for his followers it must be the same, for all their lives. That's why we're evangelicals."

When he thinks back to his time in China, Guinness can remember walking down the streets of Nanjing after the invasion, unable to escape the loudspeakers.

Blaring, screeching—the propaganda spewed across the Chinese city, enveloping marching Communist soldiers and the cowering people, as the swinging red and yellow banners hung high over one eight-year-old boy.

Os kept walking. He didn't know much about Mao or the People's Army. When the invasion of 1949 came, sweeping around the son of medical missionaries, infiltrating and touching every part of his life—the little Irish boy was left feeling more than a bit alone.

But there was a face coming toward him—a neighbor, a classmate, a close friend—and Os started to smile. But when little Os looked up into the eyes of these people, he saw nothing. It didn't matter whether it was a girl or boy; young or old—the reaction repeated itself each time. Turn the head, and keep walking.

"They just looked right past me, as if I didn't exist."

Trust was deadly in these days of terror. Public discussion and debate suffocated. Parents informed on their children, children on their parents, and friends were a deadly luxury. Even the slightest of eye contact could be enough to turn a suspicious Communist tribunal to imprison a person or issue the death sentence.

Against this army, the Guinness family stood, unafraid, even when they were put under house arrest—given only a change of clothes, a Bible, and a hymnbook.

"I never saw them complain or lift an eyebrow of disagreement with each other," said Os, "and I certainly never saw in them anything but pure dedication to Christ and Christ's work for the Chinese people."

His parents memorized three-fourths of the Bible during this arrest and never gave up hope, and Os was sent to a boarding school in England. At the end of a long odyssey of reading and thinking, at the age of eighteen, Os found faith for himself.

"The Nietzsches and Sartres and Camuses were on one side," said Os. "And on the other side, Dostoyevsky, Pascal, C. S. Lewis, and G. K. Chesterton. I was convinced that the Christian faith was true, for me, and that's where it became true and not just coming out of my family heritage."

Cataloging the breadth of his work is exhausting. Os says he's "not a prophet," but the Irishman's quiet clarity has served the church and society well throughout the years.

He criticized the free-flowing "Jesus Movement" of the sixties and seventies for its shallow transience. He was the first to dissect the prosperity-driven megachurches in his book *Dining with the Devil*—with a gentle but sharp and cutting eye.

"The danger of the health and wealth gospel is not just that it's strong here," said Os. "But that it's affecting other countries. It's vile here, but when it's used in Africa to oppress poor people and make a few pastors immensely rich, it's trebly vile."

But there's something about those days in China, watching true oppression and totalitarian abuse, which seemed to help Os see the need for space and discussion. Christianity is free of the fear of differing ideas and values. Paul met the Athenians in debate, challenging their presuppositions in love and truth. A desire for that same type of discourse has driven much of Os' energy in the last thirty years.

"How do we forge a civil public square?" asked Os. "America has the key, but they're not living up to it."

There is a commitment to freedom of expression and worship, within certain boundaries, at the foundations of America. This is uniquely suited to host discussion in a global society wrestling with the interaction of Christianity, Judaism, Islam, and the pantheon of Eastern-based belief systems.

"America has to be true to its own values and history and core—the true remedy—and create a tough, civil public square," said Os. "In other words, when Muslims come . . . they come, to put it in their terms, within our tent. And we should teach them, 'This is the way that we do it in America. Everyone has religious liberty, we respect them, freedom of conscience is ultimate, but we teach them the American way' . . . Take your motto, *E Pluribus Unum*—'out of the many, one.' It's not just a motto, it's your greatest accomplishment. But to keep that going, you have to know what the *Unum* is."

It's a big goal. One that can seem to be progressing slowly in this anger-charged climate, and whether this public square will ever be created can be difficult to see at times.

But from his time in China, Guinness learned that growth isn't always measured in the short term.

When his parents were released from prison in the 1950s, people would come up and say, "I'm so sorry your life's work has been wasted."

But his parents responded, "No, no, we trust God, the seeds have been sown."

The year before Os' father died, he went back to China, the epicenter of the fastest growth of the Christian church in two thousand years of history. The seeds had been sown.

"Now I Lay Me Down to Sleep"

Teaching your child to pray can be a joyous task. The easiest place to start is with short, simple prayers that can be recited daily and memorized easily. You will find that children love to say prayers, especially ones with rhythm and rhyme. The message is simple, yet heartfelt, and even adults remember the prayers they recited every day as a child. The first several selections included below contain great verses with which to start.

"Now I lay me down to sleep" is a classic children's prayer from the eighteenth century. It was first found in print in Thomas Fleet's *New England Primer*, the first edition dating back to 1737. It is reported that John Adams, second president of the United States, recited this prayer every day of his life. Some things from boyhood grow into manhood.

Now I lay me down to sleep,
I pray the Lord my soul to keep;
If I should die before I wake,
I pray the Lord my soul to take.

Tuning the Soul

ROBERT MURRAY M'CHEYNE

Scottish preacher, missionary, and poet Robert Murray M'Cheyne (1813–1843) died at the age of twenty-nine. His short life was one marked by piety and prayer. His was a man's full life, a short one, but a rich one.

I ought to pray before seeing any one. Often when I sleep long, or meet with others early, it is eleven or twelve o'clock before I begin secret prayer. This is a wretched system. It is unscriptural. Christ arose before day and went into a solitary place. David says: "Early will I seek thee"; "Thou shalt early hear my voice." Family prayer loses much of its power and sweetness, and I can do no good to those who come to seek from me. The conscience feels guilty, the soul unfed, the lamp not trimmed. Then when in secret prayer the soul is often out of tune, I feel it is far better to begin with God—to see his face first, to get my soul near him before it is near another.

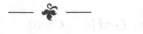

Unspoken Prayer

ANONYMOUS

Sometimes God doesn't answer the prayers of men the way men want him to. As this prayer illustrates—one found in the pocket of an unknown Confederate soldier at the end of the Civil War—what we ask from God might be given to us in a way we never imagined. In the end, God knows what is best for us and works all things for our good.

I asked God for strength, that I might achieve;
I was made weak, that I might learn to humbly obey.
I asked for health, that I might do greater things;
I was given infirmity, that I might do better things.
I asked for riches, that I might be happy;
I was given poverty, that I might be wise.
I asked for power, that I might have the praise of men;
I was given weakness, that I might feel the need of God.
I asked for all things that I might enjoy life;
I was given life, that I might enjoy all things.
I got nothing I asked for but everything I had hoped for.
Almost despite myself, my unspoken prayers were answered.
I am, among men, most richly blessed.

"May I Know Thee More Clearly"

SAINT RICHARD

Richard of Chichester (1197-1253) was bishop in Chichester, a cathedral city in West Sussex, South East England. Throughout his life Richard worked to bring order to the church and was made a saint in 1262.

Thanks be to thee, my Lord Jesus Christ,
For all the benefits Thou has given me,
For all the pains and insults Thou has borne for me.
O most merciful Redeemer, friend and brother,
May I know Thee more clearly,
Love Thee more dearly,
Follow Thee more nearly.

Harry S. Truman's Daily Prayer

Harry S. Truman (1884-1972) rose from humble origins in rural Missouri to become the thirty-third president of the United States. Throughout his life, Truman endeavored to conduct himself with integrity and always do right by others. Truman learned this prayer as a young man and repeated it to himself throughout his life. This excerpt comes from his own diary, dated August 15, 1950, a day on which Truman happened to meet with General Omar Bradley, the mayor of New York, the secretary of defense, the attorney general, his cabinet, a senator, a representative, another general, and some personal friends. Many men in the highest of offices have found comfort in prayer.

The prayer on this page has been said by me—by Harry S. Truman—from high school days, as a window washer, bottle duster, floor scrubber in an Independence, Mo., drugstore, as a timekeeper on a railroad contract gang, as an employee of a newspaper, as a bank clerk, as a farmer riding a gang plow behind four horses and mules, as a fraternity official learning to say nothing at all if good could not be said of a man, as public official judging the weaknesses and shortcomings of constituents, and as President of the United States of America.

Oh! Almighty and Everlasting God, Creator of Heaven, Earth and the Universe: Help me to be, to think, to act what is right, because it is right; make me truthful, honest and honorable in all things; make me intellectually honest for the sake of right and honor and without thought of reward to me. Give me the ability to be charitable, forgiving and patient with my fellowmen—help me to understand their motives and their shortcomings—even as Thou understandest mine!

Amen, Amen, Amen.

"On Self-Improvement"

LORD ROBERT BADEN POWELL OF GILWELL

To the founder of the modern Boy Scouts movement, men of honor were men of religion and faith. But while Lord Powell may have said that "no man is good unless he obeys God and his laws," what that meant for Powell was a very practical and tangible experience.

There was a required aspect of faith to nobility and virtue in life, but this virtue was predicated upon the expression of good works. One did not simply read the Bible, go to church, and then walk out— for Powell, what was done outside the church doors seemed more important than what was taught inside the church. But there was also a very classic understanding of the presence of God in the natural world. There could be no separation between the study of Scripture and the study of biology—exploring God's character could come in a meadow or wood as easily as on a pew. God's image was in all creation, and Powell desired his young scouts to dive deep into that image. At the heart those British values of no-nonsense common sense and hard work—fleshed out in instruction on piety—are clearly seen in Powell's instructions to his young listeners in this campyard yarn, entitled "On Self-Improvement."

The prevailing want of religion should be remedied by a practical working religion rather than a too spiritual one at first.

Self-Education, that is, what a boy learns for himself is what is going to stick by him and guide him later on in life far more than anything that is imposed on him through "instruction" by a teacher.

This is true of Religion as of secular subjects. The work of a teacher, or a Scoutmaster, is merely to encourage him in his effort and to suggest the right direction for it.

The boy is naturally inclined to religion, but to instruct him in the Point which may appeal to the adult has often the result of either boring him off it or of making him a prig.

A sure way to gain his whole-hearted realization of God is through Nature Study, and of his Christian duties through the Scout's practice of Good Turns, the Missioner's Badge work, etc.

Sunday Scouting—In Christian countries Boy Scouts should, without fail, attend church or chapel, on Sundays. The afternoon walk might then be devoted to quiet scouting practices such as "Nature Study" by exploring for plants or insects, observing animals or birds; or in town or bad weather visiting good picture galleries, museums, etc.; "Knight Errantry," doing good turns by good collecting flowers and taking them to the patients and so on. Sunday is a day of rest; loafing is not rest. Change of occupation from the workshop to the fields is rest; but the Sabbath is too often a day of loafing, and, morally made the worst day in the whole week for our lads and girls. Combine with the instruction of your Church the study of God in Nature, and the practice of good turns on God's day.

No man is much good unless he believes in God and obeys his laws. So every Scout should have a religion.

Religion seems a very simple thing: First: *Love and Serve God.* Second: *Love and serve your neighbor.*

In doing your duty to God, you must always be grateful to him. Whenever you enjoy a pleasure or a good game, or succeed in doing a good thing, thank Him for it, if only with a word or two, just as you say grace at a meal. And it is a good thing to bless other people. For instance, if you see a train starting off, just pray for God's blessing on all that are in the train.

In doing your duty towards man, be helpful and generous, and also always be grateful for any kindness done to you, and be careful to show that you are grateful. Remember again that a present given to you is not yours until you have thanked the giver for it.

While you are living your life on this earth, try to do something good which may remain after you.

It is something to *be* good, but it is far better to *do* good.

Matins (Morning Prayer)

ROBERT HERRICK

The term *matins* is Latin for "morning prayer." In this short supplication, the seventeenth-century English poet Robert Herrick (1591-1674) asks God to cleanse his soul with the morning light and let him begin anew each day.

When with the virgin morning thou dost rise,
Crossing thyself come thus to sacrifice;
First wash thy heart in innocence; then bring
Pure hands, pure habits, pure, pure every thing.
Next to the altar humbly kneel, and thence
Give up thy soul in clouds of frankincense.
Thy golden censers fill'd with odours sweet
Shall make thy actions with their ends to meet.

A Prayer for Guidance

George Washington

The first pilgrims to the shores of America began their life in the New World with a bended knee and prayer. Since the landing of the *Mayflower*, the leaders of the country have been lifting the nation up in prayer. In both public addresses and private journals, many presidents of the United States have prayed for guidance, strength, and comfort for the people of the nation. The next several prayers—from George Washington, Abraham Lincoln, Franklin D. Roosevelt, John F. Kennedy, Jimmy Carter, Ronald Reagan, George H. W. Bush, and George W. Bush—reflect the reverent perspective that is unique to our country. This first selection is an undated prayer from Washington's prayer journal at Mount Vernon.

O eternal and everlasting God, I presume to present myself this morning before thy Divine majesty, beseeching thee to accept of my humble and hearty thanks, that it hath pleased thy great goodness to keep and preserve me the night past from all the dangers poor mortals are subject to, and has given me sweet and pleasant sleep, whereby I find my body refreshed and comforted for performing the duties of this day, in which I beseech thee to defend me from all perils of body and soul . . .

Increase my faith in the sweet promises of the gospel; give me repentance from dead works; pardon my wanderings, and direct my thoughts unto thyself, the God of my salvation; teach me how to live in thy fear, labor in thy service, and ever to run in the ways of thy commandments; make me always watchful over my heart, that neither the terrors of conscience, the loathing of holy duties, the love of sin, nor an unwillingness to depart this life, may cast me into a spiritual slumber, but daily frame me more and more into the likeness of thy son Jesus Christ, that living in thy fear, and dying in thy favor, I may in thy appointed time attain the resurrection of the just unto eternal life bless my family, friends, and kindred.

A Prayer for Peace

Abraham Lincoln

From the second inaugural address, March 4, 1865, by the nation's "poet president," as great a man as ever seen.

Fondly do we hope, fervently do we pray, that this mighty scourge of war may speedily pass away. Yet if God wills that it continues . . . until every drop of blood drawn with the lash shall be paid another drawn with the sword . . . so still it must be said that the judgments of the Lord are true and righteous altogether.

With malice toward none, with charity for all, with firmness in the right as God gives us to see the right, let us finish the work we are in, to bind up the nation's wounds, to care for him who shall have borne the battle, and for his widow and for his orphans, to do all which may achieve and cherish a just and a lasting peace among ourselves and with all nations.

A Prayer in Dark Times

Franklin D. Roosevelt

This prayer was offered on D-day, June 6, 1944. It is manly to pray, and it is manly for a leader to lead us in prayer.

Almighty God: Our sons, pride of our nation, this day have set upon a mighty endeavor, a struggle to preserve our Republic, our religion and our civilization, and to set free a suffering humanity . . .

Lead them straight and true; give strength to their arms, stoutness to their hearts, steadfastness in their faith. They will need Thy blessings. Their road will be long and hard. For the enemy is strong. He may hurl back our forces. Success may not come with rushing speed, but we shall return again and again; and we know by Thy grace, and by the righteousness of our cause, our sons will triumph . . .

Embrace these, Father, and receive them, Thy heroic servants, into Thy kingdom. And for us at home—fathers, mothers, children, wives, sisters, and brothers of brave men overseas, whose thoughts and prayers are ever with them—help us, Almighty God, to rededicate ourselves in renewed faith in Thee in this hour of great sacrifice . . . Give us strength, too—strength in our daily tasks, to redouble the contributions we make in the physical and the material support of our armed forces.

With Thy blessing, we shall prevail over the unholy forces of our enemy. Help us to conquer the apostles of greed and racial arrogances. Lead us to the saving of our country, and with our sister nations into a world unity that will spell a sure peace—a peace invulnerable to the schemings of unworthy men. And a peace that will let all men live in freedom, reaping the just rewards of their honest toil.

A Prayer of Gratitude

JOHN F. KENNEDY

A prayer offered Thanksgiving Day 1963.

Let us therefore proclaim our gratitude to Providence for manifold blessings— let us be humbly thankful for inherited ideals—and let us resolve to share those blessings and those ideals with our fellow human beings throughout the world.

On that day let us gather in sanctuaries dedicated to worship and in homes blessed by family affection to express our gratitude for the glorious gifts of God; and let us earnestly and humbly pray that He will continue to guide and sustain us in the great unfinished tasks of achieving peace, justice, and understanding among all men and nations and of ending misery and suffering wherever they exist.

A Prayer for a Meaningful Life

JIMMY CARTER

The following are two separate prayers: a prayer from Carter's inaugural address, January 20, 1977, and a prayer from his Thanksgiving speech to the nation, November 27, 1980.

JANUARY 20, 1977

I would like to have my frequent prayer answered that God let my life be meaningful in the enhancement of His kingdom and that my life might be meaningful in the enhancement of the lives of my fellow human beings.

NOVEMBER 27, 1980

I call upon all the people of our Nation to give thanks on that day for the blessings Almighty God has bestowed upon us, and to join the fervent prayer of George Washington who as President asked God to "impart all the blessings we possess, or ask for ourselves to the whole family of mankind."

A Prayer for Healing

RONALD REAGAN

From a speech to the American people, February 6, 1986.

To preserve our blessed land we must look to God . . . It is time to realize that we need God more than He needs us . . . We also have His promise that we could take to heart with regard to our country, that "If my people, which are called by my name shall humble themselves, and pray and seek my face, and turn from their wicked ways; then I will hear from heaven and will forgive their sin, and will heal their land."

Let us, young and old, join together, as did the First Continental Congress, in the first step, in humble heartfelt prayer. Let us do so for the love of God and His great goodness, in search of His guidance and the grace of repentance, in seeking His blessings, His peace, and the resting of His kind and holy hands on ourselves, our nation, our friends in the defense of freedom, and all mankind, now and always.

The time has come to turn to God and reassert our trust in Him for the healing of America . . . Our country is in need of and ready for a spiritual renewal. Today, we utter no prayer more fervently than the ancient prayer for peace on Earth.

If I had a prayer for you today, among those that have all been uttered, it is that one we're so familiar with: "The Lord bless you and keep you; the Lord make His face to shine upon you and be gracious unto you; the Lord lift up His countenance upon you and give you peace . . ." And God bless you all.

A Prayer to Help Others

GEORGE H. W. BUSH

A prayer offered in George H. W. Bush's inaugural address, January 20, 1989.

Heavenly Father, we bow our heads and thank You for Your love. Accept our thanks for the peace that yields this day and the shared faith that makes its continuance likely. Make us strong to do Your work, willing to heed and hear Your will, and write on our hearts these words: "Use power to help people."

For we are given power not to advance our own purposes, nor to make a great show in the world, nor a name. There is but one just use of power, and it is to serve people. Help us to remember it, Lord.

The Lord our God be with us, as He was with our fathers; may He not leave us or forsake us; so that He may incline our hearts to Him, to walk in all His ways . . . that all peoples of the earth may know that the Lord is God; there is no other.

A Prayer for the Departed

George W. Bush

From George W. Bush's address to the nation after the World Trade Center attacks, September 14, 2001.

We come before God to pray for the missing and the dead, and for those who love them . . . On this national day of prayer and remembrance, we ask Almighty God to watch over our nation, and grant us patience and resolve in all that is to come. We pray that He will comfort and console those who now walk in sorrow. We thank Him for each life we now must mourn, and the promise of a life to come.

As we have been assured, neither death nor life, nor angels nor principalities nor powers, nor things present nor things to come, nor height nor depth, can separate us from God's love. May He bless the souls of the departed. May He comfort our own. And may He always guide our country.

"The Examined Life"

Plato

Plato was a classical Greek philosopher, mathematician, and founder of the Academy in Athens—the first institution of higher learning in the Western world. Told through the life and actions of Socrates, Plato's discourse in his *Apology* on introspection and the contemplative life is a cornerstone of philosophy and science. According to Plato, the good life was one of reflection and introspection. The personal and public discussion of truth is a vital part of any man's life; it is the measure of his soul. In the following excerpt, Socrates famously declares that "an unexamined life is not worth living." Even after a jury had convicted him, Socrates would not abandon his quest for truth, declaring that he would rather die than give up philosophy. It is not unmanly to think and meditate on life.

Far from it, men of Athens; a fine life indeed would it be for a man of my age, having gone into exile, to live changing from one city to another and being expelled. For I know well that, wherever I go, the young will listen to me discoursing, as they do here; and, if I drive them away, they will themselves expel me, persuading their elders; but if I do not drive them away, their fathers and kinsmen will expel me—for their sakes.

Perhaps then someone would say, "But will you not be able, Socrates, having gone into exile, to live being silent and remaining quiet?" It is just this, of which it is the hardest of all to convince some of you. For if on the one hand I say that this is to disobey the god and that for this reason it is impossible to remain quiet, you will not believe me, thinking that I am dissembling; or if on the other hand I say that this happens also to be a very great blessing to a man, to discourse each day on virtue and the other matters, about which you hear me conversing and examining myself and others, and that an unexamined life is not worth living, when I say this still less will you believe me. The facts are indeed as I say, men of Athens, but to convince you is no easy matter.

Aids to Reflection

Samuel Taylor Coleridge

An English poet and philosopher, Samuel Taylor Coleridge (1772-1834), along with his friend William Wordsworth, were founders of the Romantic movement in England. While not receiving the same recognition as Wordsworth, Coleridge was a foundational figure in English poetry. As you will see in the following excerpt, Coleridge believed that the key to any pursuit was reflection and making yourself a "thinking man."

R eader!—You have been bred in a land abounding with men, able in arts, learning, and knowledges manifold, this man in one, this in another, few in many, none in all. But there is one art, of which every man should be master, the art of Reflection. If you are not a thinking man, to what purpose are you a man at all? In like manner, there is one knowledge, which it is every man's interest and duty to acquire, namely, Self-knowledge: or to what end was man alone, of all animals, endued by the Creator with the faculty of self-consciousness . . .

But you are likewise born in a Christian land: and Revelation has provided for you new subjects for reflection, and new treasures of knowledge, never to be unlocked by him who remains self-ignorant. Self-knowledge is the key to this casket; and by reflection alone can it be obtained. Reflect on your own thoughts, actions, circumstances, and—which will be of especial aid to you in forming a habit of reflection—accustom yourself to reflect on the words you use, hear, or read, their birth, derivation, and history. For if words are not Things, they are Living Powers, by which the things of most importance to mankind are actuated, combined, and humanized. Finally, by reflection you may draw from the fleeting facts of your worldly trade, art, or profession, a science permanent as your immortal soul; and make even these subsidiary and preparative to the reception of spiritual truth, "doing as the dyers do, who having first dipt their silks in colours of less value, then give them the last tincture of crimson in grain."

"A Student's Prayer"

Saint Thomas Aquinas

Saint Thomas Aquinas was an Italian priest of the Catholic Church in the Dominican order and one of history's preeminent theologians and philosophers. He was the foremost classical proponent of natural theology, and the father of the Thomistic school of philosophy and theology. Aquinas is held in the Catholic Church to be the model teacher for those studying for the priesthood. The works for which he is best known are the *Summa Theologica* and the *Summa Contra Gentiles*. One of the thirty-three

Doctors of the Church, he is considered the church's greatest theologian and philosopher. Pope Benedict XV said: "The Church has declared Thomas' doctrine to be her own." Here is a prayer of his.

Ineffably wise and good Creator, illustrious Original, true fountain of light and wisdom, vouchsafe to infuse into my understanding some ray of Thy brightness, thereby removing that twofold darkness under which I was born, of sin and ignorance. Thou that makest the tongues of infants eloquent, instruct, I pray Thee, my tongue likewise; and pour upon my lips the grace of Thy benediction. Give me quickness to comprehend and memory to retain; give me happiness in expounding and a facility in learning, and copious eloquence in speaking. Prepare my entrance on the road of science, direct me in my journey, and bring me safely to the end of it, even happiness and glory, in Thine eternal kingdom, through Jesus Christ our Lord. Amen.

"That Which . . . Had Been Long Looked For"

GEORGE MÜLLER

George Müller (1805–1898) exercised an audacious faith. It was a faith that started with the German evangelist's total belief in the sufficiency and power of his God. For Müller that belief inspired him to pray for everything that he needed in life. Never has the command of Christ in prayer—"and give us this day, our daily bread"—been more completely obeyed and trusted in an individual's life.

And it wasn't just in Müller's personal life and church that these prayers came to bear fruit. In 1836, alongside his wife Susannah, Müller established the Ashley Downs orphanage in Bristol, England. While it was an uncommon thing for a minister to offer such kind treatment to orphans, the uncommon character of Müller went further than defying the norms of society. Müller didn't believe in asking for financial support or entering into debt; rather, the kindly preacher would get down on his knees, close his eyes, and begin praying.

It might come in a milkman unexpectedly bringing milk by for the children, a rich woman feeling compelled to send a donation, or any of the other hundred acts of providence that supplied and sustained Müller's years of service. He kept a detailed diary of his prayers, charting out his requests and anxieties, then waiting to watch God answer his prayers.

It's a remarkable and expansive document, charting years of prayers and years of answers. Times were not always easy for Müller. Many occasions saw the orphan staring at empty cupboards, wondering where the next meal was going to come from. And while some of the donations came from rich individuals, the majority of the gifts seem to have come from, what Müller calls, "laborers." These were the individuals toiling in the fields, working with their hands, and who took seriously the command to "lay up not treasures for yourself here on earth" and gave their last alms to the poor.

He kept detailed records of the gifts, showing where each shilling and pence was spent—he took seriously the call to steward well what he had been given. In the end, Müller watched as more than £100,000 came in to build the five orphanages. He cared for more than 10,000 orphans in his lifetime and established 117 schools that offered Christian educations to more than 120,000 children. Here is a man's life of good works, anchored in his faith.

Feb. 7. This day has been one of the most remarkable days as it regards the funds. There was no money in hand. I was waiting upon God. I had asked him repeatedly, but no supplies came. Brother T. called, between eleven and twelve o'clock, to tell me that about one pound two shillings would be needed, to take in bread for the three houses and to meet the other expenses; but we had only two shillings ninepence, which yesterday had been taken out of the boxes in the Orphan Houses. He went to Clifton to make arrangements for the reception of the three orphans of our sister Loader, who fell asleep on the 4th; for, though we have no funds in hand, the work goes on, and our confidence is not diminished. I therefore requested him to call, on his way back from Clifton, to see whether the Lord might have sent any money in the mean time.

When he came I had received nothing, but one of the laborers, having five shillings of his own, gave it. It was now four o'clock. I knew not how the sisters had got through the day. Toward the close of the day I went to the Girls' Orphan House, to meet with the brethren for prayer. When I arrived there I found that a box had come for me from Barnstable. The carriage was paid, else there would have been no money to pay for it. (See how the Lord's hand is in the smallest matters!) The box was opened, and it contained, in a letter from a sister, ten pounds, of which eight pounds was for the orphans, and two pounds for the Bible Fund; from brethren at Barnstable, two pounds eleven shillings two pence; and from another brother, five shillings. Besides this, there were in the box four yards of merino, three pairs of new shoes, two pairs of new socks; also six books for sale; likewise a gold pencil-case, two gold rings, two gold drops of earrings, a necklace, and a silver pencil-case . . .

August 22. In my morning walk, when I was reminding the Lord of our need, I felt assured that he would send help this day. My assurance sprang from our need; for there seemed no way to get through the day without help being sent. After breakfast I considered whether there was anything which might be turned into money for the dear children. Among other things there came under my hands a number of religious pamphlets which had been given for the benefit of the orphans; but all seemed not nearly enough to meet the necessities of the day. In this our deep poverty, after I had gathered together the few things for sale, a sister, *who earns her bread by the labor of her hands*, brought eighty-two pounds. This sister had seen it to be binding upon believers in our Lord Jesus to act out his commandments: "Sell that ye have [sell your possessions] and give alms," Luke xii. 33; and "Lay not up for yourselves treasures upon earth," Matt. vi. 19. Accordingly, she had drawn her money out of the bank and stocks, being two hundred and fifty pounds, and had brought it to me at three different times, for the benefit of the orphans, the Bible, missionary, and school fund, and the poor saints. About two months ago she brought me one hundred pounds more, being the produce of some other possession which she had sold, the half of which was to be used for the school Bible, and missionary fund, and the other half for the poor saints. This eighty-two pounds which she has brought to-day is the produce of the sale of her last earthly possession. [At the time I am preparing this fifth edition for the press, more than sixteen years have passed away, and this sister has never expressed the least regret as to the step she took, but goes on quietly laboring with her hands to earn her bread.]

An Instrument of Peace

SAINT FRANCIS OF ASSISI

Saint Francis of Assisi (1181 or 1182-1226) was the son of a wealthy cloth merchant in Assisi, Italy. Francis later rejected the worldly, materialistic life he had previously led, and became a Catholic friar. He founded the Franciscan order, the women's Order of Saint Clare, and the lay Third Order of Saint Francis. Saint Francis is one of the most venerated religious figures in Roman Catholic history, recognized for his humble devotion to God. Real men know humility.

Lord, make me an instrument of your peace;
Where there is hatred, let me sow love.
Where there is injury, pardon.
Where there is doubt, faith.
Where there is despair, hope.
Where there is darkness, light.
Where there is sadness, joy.

O Divine Master,
grant that I may not so much seek to be consoled, as to console;
to be understood, as to understand;
to be loved, as to love;

For it is in giving that we receive,
it is in pardoning that we are pardoned,
and it is in dying that we are born to Eternal Life.
Amen.

— ❧ —

Profile: Saint Damien de Veuster

Great men of faith risk life and limb to serve and minister to others, and for this they deserve to be honored and remembered. Damien de Veuster (1840–1889) was a missionary who moved to Hawaii to aid a leper colony. As a result, he contracted leprosy and lost his life. For many years Damien was unjustly ridiculed by other ministers. One unlikely man came to his defense, and today Damien is remembered as Saint Damien de Veuster.

A curious figure inhabits the halls of the U.S. Capitol—a square statue, with glasses that stick out and a cassock covering the beaten body. This man is Saint Damien de Veuster, the only saint to be honored with a place in the Capitol. Born in Flanders, Belgium, when Damien turned twenty-three, he followed Christ's call to evangelize to the "furthermost parts of the earth," and moved to Hawaii. When Hawaii took the drastic measure of sequestering the growing number of lepers on the far end of the island of Molokai—divided from the rest of civilization by a mountain—Damien volunteered to serve them.

Damien arrived at the settlement in 1873. He knew he would encounter squalor, lawlessness, and a horrifying disease, and was most likely signing his death sentence. But he stood strong, writing his brother to say, "I make myself a leper with the lepers to gain all to Jesus Christ."

Damien implemented basic law and order. Under his direction, shacks received a coat of paint, farms were organized, and a school was built. Then in 1884, Damien contracted leprosy himself. He worked diligently to continue his reforms, enlarge orphanages, and serve. When he died five years later, Damien was forty-nine.

"Were it not for the constant presence of our divine Master in our humble chapel," said Damien, "I would not have found it possible to persevere in sharing the lot of the lepers in Molokai . . . Here I am a priest, dear parents, here I am a missionary in a corrupt, heretical, idolatrous country. How great my obligations are! Ah! do not forget this poor priest running night and day over the volcanoes night and day in search of strayed sheep. Pray night and day for me, I beg You."

After his death the Catholic Church moved to honor this brave man, but other ministers leveled scurrilous accusations. One Presbyterian minister, C. M. Hyde, delivered a particularly vicious condemnation.

In response, none other than the famed author Robert Louis Stevenson stood up to defend Damien's reputation and memory, helping to preserve the possibility of sainthood for the quiet priest. He wrote,

> We are not all expected to be Damiens; a man may conceive his duty more narrowly, he may love his comforts better, and none will cast a stone at him for that . . . But, sir, when we have failed, and another has succeeded; when we have stood by, and another has stepped in; when we sit and grow bulky in our charming mansions, and a plain, uncouth peasant steps into the battle, under the eyes of God, and succors the afflicted, and consoles the dying, and is himself afflicted in his turn, and dies upon the field of honour—the battle cannot be retrieved as your unhappy irritation has suggested. It is a lost battle, and lost for ever. One thing remained to you in your defeat—some rags of common honour; and these you have made haste to cast away.

In 1995, Damien was beatified, and in 2009, he finally received sainthood.

"The servant of the Word consequently became a suffering servant, a leper with the lepers, for the last four years of his life," said Pope Benedict XVI. "In order to follow Christ, Fr Damien not only left his homeland but also risked his health: therefore as the word of Jesus proclaimed to us in today's Gospel says he received eternal life."

Call to Prayer

GENERAL ROBERT E. LEE

General Robert E. Lee (1807–1870) is a legendary figure as a dedicated servant and devoted Christian. His life greatly affected both the North and the South. After his death a Northern newspaper wrote of him: "We have long since ceased to look upon him as the Confederate leader, but have claimed him as one of ourselves; have cherished and felt proud of his military genius; have recounted and recorded his triumphs as our own; have extolled his virtue as reflecting upon us—for Robert Edward Lee was an American, and the great nation which gave him birth would be today unworthy of such a son if she regarded him lightly." Lee encouraged spiritual strength in his men and made a habit of daily prayer. His call to prayer was a reminder to his men of their obligation to the Lord for success and victory. If Lee was not embarrassed to pray, no man should be.

Soldiers! We have sinned against Almighty God. We have forgotten his signal mercies, and have cultivated a revengeful, haughty, and boastful spirit. We have not remembered that the defenders of a just cause should be pure in His eyes; that "our times are in His Hands," and we have relied too much on our own arms for the achievement of our independence. God is our only refuge and our strength. Let us humble ourselves before Him. Let us confess our many sins, and beseech Him to give us a higher courage, a purer patriotism, and more determined will; that He will convert the hearts of our enemies; that He will hasten the time when war, with its sorrows and sufferings, shall cease, and that He will give us a name and a place among the nations of the earth.

Times That Try Men's Souls

THOMAS PAINE

During the birth of America, Thomas Paine (1737-1809) was an author, pamphleteer, inventor, intellectual, and revolutionary. He wrote the famous, widely read pamphlet "Common Sense," which was instrumental in advocating the colonies' independence from Britain. He also authored "The American Crisis," excerpted below, in support of the American Revolution. He is considered one of the Founding Fathers of the United States and his work was so influential during the Revolution that John Adams once remarked, "Without the pen of the author of 'Common

Sense,' the sword of Washington would have been raised in vain." Despite being an agnostic, Paine frequently referenced God and Providence in his works and believed that reflection and contemplation were a necessity in any man's life.

These are the times that try men's souls.

The summer soldier and the sunshine patriot will, in this crisis, shrink from the service of their country; but he that stands it now, deserves the love and thanks of man and woman.

Tyranny, like hell, is not easily conquered; yet we have this consolation with us, that the harder the conflict, the more glorious the triumph.

What we obtain too cheap, we esteem too lightly: it is dearness only that gives every thing its value . . .

Quitting this class of men, I turn with the warm ardor of a friend to those who have nobly stood, and are yet determined to stand the matter out: I call not upon a few, but upon all: not on this state or that state, but on every state: up and help us; lay your shoulders to the wheel; better have too much force than too little, when so great an object is at stake.

Let it be told to the future world, that in the depth of winter, when nothing but hope and virtue could survive, that the city and the country, alarmed at one common danger, came forth to meet and to repulse it.

Say not that thousands are gone, turn out your tens of thousands; throw not the burden of the day upon Providence, but "show your faith by your works," that God may bless you. It matters not where you live, or what rank of life you hold, the evil or the blessing will reach you all. The far and the near, the home counties and the back, the rich and the poor, will suffer or rejoice alike. The heart that feels not now is dead; the blood of his children will curse his cowardice, who shrinks back at a time when a little might have saved the whole, and made them happy. I love the man that can smile in trouble, that can gather strength from distress, and grow brave by reflection. 'Tis the business of little minds to shrink; but he whose heart is firm, and whose conscience approves his conduct, will pursue his principles unto death.

"Forms of Prayer at Sea"

WILLIAM WORDSWORTH

William Wordsworth (1770-1850) was an English poet who, along with Samuel Taylor Coleridge, began the Romantic movement in English literature. Wordsworth was Britain's poet laureate from 1843 until his death in 1850. He remains one of the most widely recognized and influential poets in the history of literature. Two poems follow, "Forms of Prayer at Sea" and "The Pilgrim Fathers."

> *To kneeling Worshippers no earthly floor*
> *Gives holier invitation than the deck*
> *Of a storm-shattered Vessel saved from Wreck*
> *(When all that Man could do availed no more)*
> *By him who raised the Tempest and restrains:*
> *Happy the crew who this have felt, and pour*
> *Forth for his mercy, as the Church ordains,*
> *Solemn thanksgiving. Nor will 'they' implore*
> *In vain who, for a rightful cause, give breath*
> *To words the Church prescribes aiding the lip*
> *For the heart's sake, ere ship with hostile ship*
> *Encounters, armed for work of pain and death.*
> *Suppliants! the God to whom your cause ye trust*
> *Will listen, and ye know that He is just.*

"The Pilgrim Fathers"

WILLIAM WORDSWORTH

WELL WORTHY TO BE MAGNIFIED ARE THEY
Who, with sad hearts, of friends and country took
A last farewell, their loved abodes forsook,
And hallowed ground in which their fathers lay;
Then to the new-found World explored their way,
That so a Church, unforced, uncalled to brook
Ritual restraints, within some sheltering nook
Her Lord might worship and his word obey
In freedom. Men they were who could not bend;
Blest Pilgrims, surely, as they took for guide
A will by sovereign Conscience sanctified;
Blest while their Spirits from the woods ascend
Along a Galaxy that knows no end,
But in His glory who for Sinners died.

The *Amidah*

The *Amidah*, also called the *Shmoneh Esreh,* is the central prayer of the Jewish liturgy. As Judaism's prayer par excellence, the *Amidah* is often designated simply as *tfila* (prayer) in rabbinic literature. Observant Jews recite the *Amidah* at each of three prayer services in a typical weekday: morning, afternoon, and evening. A special abbreviated *Amidah* is also the core of the *Mussaf* (Additional) service that is recited on *Shabbat* (the Jewish Sabbath), *Rosh Chodesh* (the day of the New Moon), and Jewish festivals, after the morning Torah reading, with additional various forms of the *Amidah* that depend on the occasion. The typical weekday

Amidah consists of nineteen blessings; following are several selections. Many old prayers still move men of all ages.

THE GOD OF HISTORY

Blessed are you, O Lord our God and God of our fathers, the God of Abraham, the God of Isaac and the God of Jacob, the great, mighty and revered God, the Most High God who bestows lovingkindnesses, the creator of all things, who remembers the good deeds of the patriarchs and in love will bring a redeemer to their children's children for his name's sake. O king, helper, savior and shield. Blessed are you, O Lord, the shield of Abraham.

THE GOD OF NATURE

You, O Lord, are mighty forever, you revive the dead, you have the power to save. [From the end of Sukkot until the eve of Passover, insert: You cause the wind to blow and the rain to fall.] You sustain the living with loving kindness, you revive the dead with great mercy, you support the falling, heal the sick, set free the bound and keep faith with those who sleep in the dust. Who is like you, O doer of mighty acts? Who resembles you, a king who puts to death and restores to life, and causes salvation to flourish? And you are certain to revive the dead. Blessed are you, O Lord, who revives the dead.

FOR REPENTANCE

Bring us back, O our father, to your Instruction; draw us near, O our King, to your service; and cause us to return to you in perfect repentance. Blessed are you, O Lord, who delights in repentance.

For Forgiveness

Forgive us, O our Father, for we have sinned; pardon us, O our King, for we have transgressed; for you pardon and forgive. Blessed are you, O Lord, who is merciful and always ready to forgive.

For the Answering of Prayer

Hear our voice, O Lord our God; spare us and have pity on us. Accept our prayer in mercy and with favor, for you are a God who hears prayers and supplications. O our King, do not turn us away from your presence empty-handed, for you hear the prayers of your people Israel with compassion. Blessed are you, O Lord, who hears prayer.

Thanksgiving for God's Unfailing Mercies

We give thanks to you that you are the Lord our God and the God of our fathers forever and ever. Through every generation you have been the rock of our lives, the shield of our salvation. We will give you thanks and declare your praise for our lives that are committed into your hands, for our souls that are entrusted to you, for your miracles that are daily with us, and for your wonders and your benefits that are with us at all times, evening, morning and noon. O beneficent one, your mercies never fail; O merciful one, your lovingkindnesses never cease. We have always put our hope in you. For all these acts may your name be blessed and exalted continually, O our King, forever and ever. Let every living thing give thanks to you and praise your name in truth, O God, our salvation and our help. (Selah.) Blessed are you, O Lord, whose Name is the Beneficent One, and to whom it is fitting to give thanks.

A Soldier's Prayer

This prayer is printed on the Veterans' Wall at Hodgeman County Court-house in Jetmore, Kansas. It communicates the determination, dedication, and valor of soldiers, and serves as a memorial to those who have served our nation so well. For many, faith is the father of courage.

We Will Not Forget

When I am called to serve, dear Lord,
Wherever war may be,
Give me courage to fight battles,
My country may ask of me.

Grace me with your presence,
And know that I love you,
While I fight the enemy,
My country needs me to.

I want to do my duty,
And to give the best in me,
To do what I've been called to do,
And protect our liberty.

And if, according to your will,
I must give up my life,
Please bless with your protecting hand,
My family I leave behind.

Thanksgiving Proclamation

George Washington

George Washington (1732–1799), the first president of the United States, was a deeply religious man. The famous portrait of Washington kneeling in prayer at Valley Forge captures his religious zeal and the role faith played in his personal and political life. He famously proclaimed in his 1796 Farewell Address, "Of all the dispositions and habits, which lead to political prosperity, Religion and Morality are indispensable supports."

While the Pilgrims had started the tradition of Thanksgiving many years earlier, George Washington was responsible for its status as a significant day of remembrance. His October 3, 1789, proclamation was sent to the governors of each of the states, and assigned the day upon which the American people devote themselves in service to "that great and glorious Being who is the beneficent author of all the good that was, that is, or that will be." It exhorts the people in the young country to express their gratitude to God for his protection throughout the Revolutionary War and the peace they had experienced since and for allowing the Constitution to be composed in a peaceful and rational manner. George Washington was often on his knees praying, as great men often are.

By the President of the United States of America, a Proclamation.

Whereas it is the duty of all Nations to acknowledge the providence of Almighty God, to obey his will, to be grateful for his benefits, and humbly to implore his protection and favor—and whereas both Houses of Congress have by their joint Committee requested me to recommend to the People of the United States a day of public thanksgiving and prayer to be observed by acknowledging with grateful hearts the many signal favors of Almighty God especially by affording them an opportunity peaceably to establish a form of government for their safety and happiness.

Now therefore I do recommend and assign Thursday the 26th day of November next to be devoted by the People of these States to the service of that great and glorious Being, who is the beneficent Author of all the good that was, that is, or that will be—That we may then all unite in rendering unto him our sincere and humble thanks—for his kind care and protection of the People of this Country previous to their becoming a Nation—for the signal and manifold mercies, and the favorable interpositions of his Providence which we experienced in the course and conclusion of the late war—for the great degree of tranquility, union, and plenty, which we have since enjoyed—for the peaceable and rational manner, in which we have been enabled to establish constitutions of government for our safety and happiness, and particularly the national One now lately instituted—for the civil and religious liberty with which we are blessed; and the means we have of acquiring and diffusing useful knowledge; and in general for all the great and various favors which he hath been pleased to confer upon us.

And also that we may then unite in most humbly offering our prayers and supplications to the great Lord and Ruler of Nations and beseech him to pardon our national and other transgressions—to enable us all, whether in public or private stations, to perform our several and relative duties properly and punctually—to render our national government a blessing to all the people, by constantly being a Government of wise, just, and constitutional laws, discreetly and faithfully executed and obeyed—to protect and guide all Sovereigns and Nations (especially such as have shewn kindness unto us) and to bless them with good government, peace, and concord—To promote the knowledge and practice of true religion and virtue, and the encrease of science among them and us—and generally to grant unto all Mankind such a degree of temporal prosperity as he alone knows to be best.

Given under my hand at the City of New York the third day of October in the year of our Lord 1789.

"My God Shall Raise Me Up"

SIR WALTER RALEIGH

Sir Walter Raleigh (1552–1618), British statesman, explorer, and poet of the late sixteenth and early seventeenth century, was executed by the court of King James I, after the death of Queen Elizabeth. This prayer—this meditation on the immutability of the grave, and the hope of resurrection—was written the night before his beheading, and was his final poem and epitaph.

EVEN SUCH IS TIME, THAT TAKES IN TRUST
Our youth, our joys, our all we have,
And pays us but with earth and dust;
*   Who, in the dark and silent grave,*
When we have wandered all our ways,
Shuts up the story of our days:
But from this earth, this grave, this dust
My God shall raise me up, I trust!

From *The Power of Prayer*

SAMUEL PRIME

Samuel Prime (1812–1885) was a Presbyterian minister in New York City and the author of *The Power of Prayer*, a volume that chronicles a series of prayer meetings from 1857 to 1858 on New York's Fulton Street. The popularity of the Fulton Street prayer meetings grew during hard economic times and fostered similar prayer meetings in churches around the city and eventually the nation. In this episode, prayer convicts a dishonest businessman of his need to right a wrong. More than once, prayer has stimulated a man's conscience.

It was often made the subject of daily prayer, that none who came there to pray might go away to do business according to what was commonly denominated "the laws of trade." We remember that the men of business prayed that they might be always enabled to do business on Christian principles, and go from the prayer-meeting to carry out the principles of the gospel into daily life. We have often heard men exhorted to do their business on Christian principles. There has been a great quickening of the consciences of men in regard to this matter. Much that was done in business was considered to be in direct contravention of the laws of Christ's house. Many have had great trials in their own minds in regard to their business. Some have felt that they must give up their pursuits or lose their souls; many have felt that if they carried the gospel into all their business relations they must *fail*; as they would stand no chance in the trade if they were scrupulously honest. An extensive hardware merchant made an earnest address in the Fulton street prayer-meeting on this very subject. He appealed to his brethren to set a holy example in this business, to have the same religion for "down-town" which they had for "up-town"—the same for the week-day that they have for the Sabbath—the same for the counting-room as for the communion-table. This address was four or five minutes in length, and was very effective. He was followed to his store by a well-known manufacturer with whom he had had dealings for many years, and of whom he had bought largely.

"You did not know," said the manufacturer, "that I was in the meeting, and heard your remarks. But I was there. Now, sir, I have for the last five years been in the habit of charging you more for goods than other purchasers. I want you to take your books and charge back to me so much per cent on every bill of goods you have had of me for the five years last past."

The merchant came into the prayer-meeting the next day and told what had transpired, and made another exhortation to the same effect—on doing business on Christian principles.

"Matins"

GEORGE HERBERT

George Herbert was an Anglican clergyman and Welshman who lived during the early seventeenth century. He was a faithful and much-loved parish priest and wrote beautiful religious poetry, which was published after his death. This poem reminds men of what is most important.

I cannot ope mine eyes,

But thou art ready there to catch
My morning-soul and sacrifice:
Then we must needs for that day make a match.

———

My God, what is a heart?

Silver, or gold, or precious stone,
Or starre, or rainbow, or a part
Of all these things, or all of them in one?

———

My God, what is a heart?

That thou shouldst it so eye, and wooe,
Powring upon it all thy art,
As if that thou hadst nothing els to do?

———

Indeed mans whole estate

Amounts (and richly) to serve thee:
He did not heav'n and earth create,
Yet studies them, not him by whom they be.

———

Teach me thy love to know;

That this new light, which now I see,
May both the work and workman show:
Then by a sunne-beam I will climbe to thee.

Eulogy for Abraham Lincoln

MATTHEW SIMPSON

The following excerpt is from the funeral address delivered at the burial of Abraham Lincoln by Bishop Matthew Simpson, May 5, 1865. During the Civil War, Simpson's influence in the church did much to unite the support of Northern Methodists. For this reason, Lincoln and Simpson became close friends. Here, in very few words, he offers an inside look at Linclon's life of faith, one all men should seek to emulate.

As a ruler I doubt if any president has ever shown such trust in God, or in public documents so frequently referred to Divine aid. Often did he remark to friends and to delegations that his hope for our success rested in his conviction that God would bless our efforts, because we were trying to do right. To the address of a large religious body he replied, "Thanks be unto God, who, in our national trials, giveth us the Churches." To a minister who said he hoped the Lord was on our side, he replied that it gave him no concern whether the Lord was on our side or not "For," he added, "I know the Lord is always on the side of right;" and with deep feeling added, "But God is my witness that it is my constant anxiety and prayer that both myself and this nation should be on the Lord's side."

"In Prayer"

EDITED BY ARTHUR BENNETT

The Puritans were an important group of Protestants in the sixteenth and seventeenth centuries who started a movement within the English church to "purify" it. Among the first settlers to come to America, through faith and hard work they established one of the first long-standing colonies. The Puritans were a deeply religious people and their faith is evident in their teachings and work ethic. In this popular Puritan prayer, the reader can see the power of prayer and how it sustained these brave settlers of a new world. The Puritans were tough men, brimming with faith.

O Lord, in prayer I launch far out into the eternal world, and on that broad ocean my soul triumphs over all evils on the shores of mortality. Time, with its gay amusements and cruel disappointments never appears so inconsiderate as then.

In prayer I see myself as nothing; I find my heart going after Thee with intensity, and long with vehement thirst to live to Thee. Blessed be the strong gales of the Spirit that speed me on my way to the New Jerusalem.

In prayer all things here below vanish, and nothing seems important but holiness of heart and the salvation of others.

In prayer all my worldly cares, fears, anxieties disappear, and are of as little significance as a puff of wind.

In prayer my soul inwardly exults with lively thoughts at what Thou art doing for Thy church, and I long that Thou shouldest get Thyself a great name from sinners returning to Zion.

In prayer I am lifted above the frowns and flatteries of life, and taste heavenly joys; entering into the eternal world I can give myself to Thee with all my heart, to be Thine forever.

In prayer I can place all my concerns in Thy hands, to be entirely at Thy disposal, having no will or interest of my own.

In prayer I can intercede for my friends, ministers, sinners, the church, Thy kingdom to come, with greatest freedom, ardent hopes, as a son to his father, as a lover to the beloved.

Help me to be all prayer and never to cease praying.

Prayer and the Individual Life

Henry B. F. MacFarland

This selection is taken from a collection of writings, *Men and Religion*, by early leaders of the Young Men's Christian Association (YMCA). Founded on June 6, 1844, in London, England, by George Williams, the goal of the organization was to put Christian principles into practice, achieved by developing "a healthy spirit, mind, and body." Today the YMCA is a worldwide movement of more than forty-five million members from 125 national federations affiliated through the World Alliance of YMCAs. Written a hundred years ago, *Men and Religion* emphasizes the importance of personal devotion and internal faith in a young man's life. From day one, the founders of the YMCA perceived that the way to make an impact on culture is to be firmly established in one's spiritual life. In these writings they shared their hopes for young men seeking God. It is a powerful message for men.

Whatever form our work for the Kingdom may take, we are very sure of one thing, and that is its success will depend on prayer. And it will depend not only upon corporate prayer, the prayer of the Church, of the Brotherhood, of the Association, but it will depend upon prayer in the individual life. If it does not succeed, it will not be the fault of the millions of men outside the Church. We shall be responsible for its failure, if it falls. We have taken the solemn responsibility, all of us. No one else is apparently so deeply interested as we are; no one else can be expected to pray for it as we are expected to pray for it. The responsibility is beyond the power of human speech to express . . .

I should not be willing to admit that we are better or that we are greater than the men who have gone before us, but I should be willing to say that there is a greater responsibility upon us than upon the men who have gone before us, just because there has been a greater opportunity pointed out. That responsibility has to be met by individual prayer for the salvation of individual men, and all the other desired consequences will follow. I like for myself in such cases to make the matter very practical, by bringing before my mind some one man who shall stand to me for these millions who are outside the Church. The only way that I can see that one man is by looking into my own heart, for there I find every man of our time, and of all times, human nature always being the same. And there I see that there is no new man and no new need, but that just exactly the same human nature is there today that was here when Jesus Christ walked about in Galilee; the same need, the same desire, even though it is not known to the man himself; the same response when the good news comes to him, and the same results when he expects it . . .

Let us not suppose—we do not suppose—that any plan, however wisely laid, however strongly backed by men and money and everything that our modern business world-sense gives us, can succeed in or of itself. We know very well that with all that kind of support we may defeat the plan ourselves if we have not this prayer-life, this individual, definite, continuous, persistent, importunate prayer which has always availed and which always will avail . . .

How long is it since you spent an hour in prayer, or since I did? How long is it since we were in a prayer meeting that lasted two hours—not a midweek service with a lecture that took most of the time and a prayer by the pastor and a reluctant, extorted prayer from one or two of the other church leaders, but a real meeting for prayer?

. . . Nothing can be done with the men outside until we ourselves are right with God and with men, and able to pray . . . If we could have in every one of our hearts such a searching examination as we have not had in many years, such a personal determination to so live that we can pray, our brightest hopes would be more than fulfilled . . .

We take prayer for granted. We are like the miner who stuck the Lord's Prayer up on his bedpost, tumbled into bed at night and said, "Them's my sentiments." A hurried prayer in the morning, a hurried prayer with the family . . . a hurried prayer in the evening, most of it on the order of Cromwell's man who went into battle saying, "Lord, if I forget thee today, forget not Thou me." If we witness the power of Jesus Christ in our lives and faithfully pray, the men outside, who believe in the reality of what they see and in nothing else, will believe in the reality of this gospel and will respond to it.

Four Thoughts on Prayer

SAINT AUGUSTINE OF HIPPO

Augustine (354–430), a Latin Church father, is one of the most important figures in the development of Western Christianity. When the Western Roman Empire was starting to disintegrate, Augustine developed the concept of the church as a spiritual City of God, after which he authored a book by the same name. In the Catholic Church and the Anglican Communion, he is a saint and preeminent Doctor of the Church, and the patron of the Augustinian religious order. His memorial is celebrated August 28, the day of his death. Among the Orthodox, he is called "Blessed Augustine," or "Saint Augustine the Blessed." His spiritual challenges are familiar to many men.

Holy prayer is the column of all virtues; a ladder to God; the support of widows, the foundation of faith; the crown of religious; the sweetness of the married life.

Prayer is the protection of holy souls; a consolation for the guardian angel; an insupportable torment to the devil; a most acceptable homage to God; the best and most perfect praise for penitents and religious; the greatest honor and glory; the preserver of spiritual health.

What can be more excellent than prayer; what is more profitable to our life; what sweeter to our souls; what more sublime, in the course of our whole life, than the practice of prayer!

He whose attitude towards Christ is correct does indeed ask "in his name" and receives what he asks for, if it is something which does not stand in the way of his salvation. He gets it, however, only when he ought to receive it, for certain things are not refused us, but their granting is delayed to a fitting time.

From *Confessions*

Saint Augustine of Hippo

Confessions is Augustine's autobiographical work, often considered the first Western autobiography. Consisting of thirteen books, Augustine's *Confessions* recounts his sinful youth and his conversion to Christianity. Here reflection and prayer combine to help a young man find his way.

Great art Thou, O Lord, and greatly to be praised; great is Thy power, and Thy wisdom infinite. And Thee would man praise; man, but a particle of Thy creation; man, that bears about him his mortality, the witness of his sin, the witness that Thou resistest the proud: yet would man praise Thee; he, but a particle of Thy creation. Thou awakest us to delight in Thy praise; for Thou madest us for Thyself, and our heart is restless, until it repose in Thee. Grant me, Lord, to know and understand which is first, to call on Thee or to praise Thee? and, again, to know Thee or to call on Thee? for who can call on Thee, not knowing Thee? for he that knoweth Thee not, may call on Thee as other than Thou art. Or, is it rather, that we call on Thee that we may know Thee? but how shall they call on Him in whom they have not believed? or how shall they believe without a preacher? and they that seek the Lord shall praise Him: for they that seek shall find Him, and they that find shall praise Him. I will seek Thee, Lord, by calling on Thee; and will call on Thee, believing in Thee; for to us hast Thou been preached. My faith, Lord, shall call on Thee, which Thou hast given me, wherewith Thou hast inspired me, through the Incarnation of Thy Son, through the ministry of the Preacher.

And how shall I call upon my God, my God and Lord, since, when I call for Him, I shall be calling Him to myself? and what room is there within me, whither my God can come into me? whither can God come into me, God who made heaven and earth? is there, indeed, O Lord my God, aught in me that can contain Thee? do then heaven and earth, which Thou hast made, and wherein Thou hast made me, contain Thee? or, because nothing which exists could exist without Thee, doth therefore whatever exists contain Thee? Since, then, I too exist, why do I seek that Thou shouldest enter into me, who were not, wert Thou not in me? Why? because I am not gone down in hell, and yet Thou art there also. For if I go down into hell, Thou art there. I could not be then, O my God, could not be at all, wert Thou not in me; or, rather, unless I were in Thee, of whom are all things, by whom are all things, in whom are all things? Even so, Lord, even so. Whither do I call Thee, since I am in Thee? or whence canst Thou enter into me? for whither can I go beyond heaven and earth, that thence my God should come into me, who hath said, I fill the heaven and the earth.

Prayer of Saint Benedict

Saint Benedict of Nursia (480–547) is honored by the Roman Catholic Church as the patron saint of Europe and students. Benedict established twelve communities for monks at Subiaco, about forty miles to the east of Rome. He is considered the founder of Western Christian monasticism.

O gracious and Holy Father, give us wisdom to perceive Thee, intelligence to understand Thee, diligence to seek Thee, patience to wait for Thee, eyes to behold Thee, a heart to meditate upon Thee, and a life to proclaim Thee; through the power of the Spirit of Jesus Christ our Lord, amen.

Homily 6 on Prayer

SAINT JOHN CHRYSOSTOM

One of the most eloquent preachers of the early church, John Chrysostom's work is still widely studied and used as the standard liturgy of the Orthodox Church. The word *chrysostom* translates as "golden-mouthed" in Greek. In this homily he makes clear in what way prayer is to be done, and the benefits it will render to the man who so petitions.

There is nothing more worthwhile than to pray to God and to converse with him, for prayer unites us with God as his companions. As our bodily eyes are illuminated by seeing the light, so in contemplating God our soul is illuminated by him. Of course the prayer I have in mind is no matter of routine, it is deliberate and earnest. It is not tied down to a fixed timetable; rather it is a state which endures by night and day.

Our soul should be directed in God, not merely when we suddenly think of prayer, but even when we are concerned with something else. If we are looking after the poor, if we are busy in some other way, or if we are doing any type of good work, we should season our actions with the desire and the remembrance of God. Through this salt of the love of God we can all become a sweet dish for the Lord. If we are generous in giving time to prayer, we will experience its benefits throughout our life.

Prayer is the light of the soul, giving us true knowledge of God. It is a link mediating between God and man. By prayer the soul is borne up to heaven and in a marvelous way embraces the Lord. This meeting is like that of an infant crying on its mother, and seeking the best of milk. The soul longs for its own needs and what it receives is better than anything to be seen in the world.

"Universal Prayer"

Alexander Pope

Widely known for his philosophical poem *Essay on Man*, Alexander Pope (1688-1744) was a renowned eighteenth-century English poet. His "Universal Prayer" masterfully traces the history and purpose of God through creation to Pope's own personal struggles as he tries to find his place in the universe and make himself a better man.

Father of all! In every age,
In ev'ry clime ador'd,
By saint, by savage, and by sage,
Jehovah, Jove, or Lord!

Thou Great First Cause, least understood,
Who all my sense confin'd
To know but this, that Thou art good,
And that myself am blind:

Yet gave me, in this dark estate,
To see the good from ill;
And, binding Nature fast in Fate,
Left free the human Will.

What Conscience dictates to be done,
Or warns me not to do;
This teach me more than Hell to shun,
That more than Heav'n pursue.

What blessings thy free bounty gives
Let me not cast away;
For God is paid when man receives;
T' enjoy is to obey.

Yet not to earth's contracted span
Thy goodness let me bound,
Or think thee Lord alone of man,
When thousand worlds are round.

Let not this weak, unknowing hand

Presume thy bolts to throw,
And teach damnation round the land
On each I judge thy foe.

If I am right, thy grace impart,
Still in the right to stay;
If I am wrong, O teach my heart
To find that better way.

Save me alike from foolish Pride
Or impious Discontent,
At aught thy wisdom has denied,
Or aught that goodness lent.

Teach me to feel another's woe,
To right the fault I see:
That mercy I to others show,
That mercy show to me.

Mean tho' I am, not wholly so,
Since quicken'd by thy breath;
O lead me whereso'er I go,
Thro' this day's life or death!

This day be bread and peace my lot:
All else beneath the sun
Though know'st if best bestow'd or not,
And let Thy will be done.

To Thee, whose temple is of Space,
Whose altar earth, sea, skies,
One chorus let all Beings raise!
All Nature's incense rise!

— ❧ —

National Day of Prayer

ABRAHAM LINCOLN

On March 30, 1863, President Abraham Lincoln issued the following proclamation declaring April 30, 1863, to be a day of national fasting, repentance, and prayer. It was the middle of the American Civil War, the bloodiest war to that date on American soil. Being a man of great faith himself, President Lincoln recognized that the country would never be healed and joined together again without the blessing of God. Lincoln went on to proclaim that men must confess their sins and transgressions if the United States would once again be a nation blessed by God. Lincoln's proclamation laid the groundwork for the National Day of Prayer, which we still celebrate in America today.

Whereas the Senate of the United States, devoutly recognizing the supreme authority and just government of Almighty God in all the affairs of men and of nations, has by a resolution requested the President to designate and set apart a day for national prayer and humiliation; and

Whereas it is the duty of nations as well as of men to own their dependence upon the overruling power of God, to confess their sins and transgressions in humble sorrow, yet with assured hope that genuine repentance will lead to mercy and pardon, and to recognize the sublime truth, announced in the Holy Scriptures and proven by all history, that those nations only are blessed whose God is the Lord;

And, insomuch as we know that by His divine law nations, like individuals, are subjected to punishments and chastisements in this world, may we not justly fear that the awful calamity of civil war which now desolates the land may be but a punishment inflicted upon us for our presumptuous sins, to the needful end of our national reformation as a whole people? We have been the recipients of the choicest bounties of Heaven; we have been preserved these many years in peace and prosperity; we have grown in numbers, wealth, and power as no other nation has ever grown. But we have forgotten God. We have forgotten the gracious hand which preserved us in peace and multiplied and enriched and strengthened us, and we have vainly imagined, in the deceitfulness of our hearts, that all these blessings were produced by some superior wisdom and virtue of our own. Intoxicated with unbroken success, we have become too self-sufficient to feel the necessity of redeeming and preserving grace, too proud to pray to the God that made us.

It behooves us, then, to humble ourselves before the offended Power, to confess our national sins, and to pray for clemency and forgiveness.

Now, therefore, in compliance with the request, and fully concurring in the views of the Senate, I do by this my proclamation designate and set apart Thursday, the 30th day of April, 1863, as a day of national humiliation, fasting, and prayer. And I do hereby request all the people to abstain on that day from their ordinary secular pursuits, and to unite at their several places of public worship and their respective homes in keeping the day holy to the Lord and devoted to the humble discharge of the religious duties proper to that solemn occasion.

All this being done in sincerity and truth, let us then rest humbly in the hope authorized by the divine teachings that the united cry of the nation will be heard on high and answered with blessings no less than the pardon of our national sins and the restoration of our now divided and suffering country to its former happy condition of unity and peace. In witness whereof I have hereunto set my hand and caused the seal of the United States to be affixed.

Done at the city of Washington, this 30th day of March, A. D. 1863, and of the Independence of the United States the eighty-seventh.

ABRAHAM LINCOLN.
By the President:
WILLIAM H. SEWARD, Secretary of State.

"A Prayer Under the Pressure of Violent Anguish"

ROBERT BURNS

Prayer is a conversation with God and, as we see in the following prayer by Robert Burns (1759–1796), it is not always joy and happiness. Like the apostle Paul crying out in Romans for relief from the thorn in his body, prayer can be an honest pleading to God in time of need or suffering. Robert Burns, also known as "Scotland's favorite son," was a poet and a lyricist. Burns is widely regarded as the national poet of Scotland and a pioneer of the Romantic Movement. In this prayer, Burns begs God to deliver him from his anguish, but reminds God that if he must bear it, he will do it without complaining.

O Thou Great Being! what Thou art,
    Surpasses me to know;
Yet sure I am, that known to Thee
    Are all Thy works below.
Thy creature here before Thee stands,
    All wretched and distrest;
Yet sure those ills that wring my soul
    Obey Thy high behest.
Sure, Thou, Almighty, canst not act
    From cruelty or wrath!
O, free my weary eyes from tears,
    Or close them fast in death!
But, if I must afflicted be,
    To suit some wise design,
Then man my soul with firm resolves,
    To bear and not repine!

Begin the Day with Prayer

Edward McKendree Bounds

E. M. Bounds (1835–1913) was a Methodist minister and devotional writer, born in Shelby County, Missouri. He studied law growing up and was admitted to the bar at age twenty-one. After practicing law for three years, he began preaching for the Methodist Episcopal Church, South. At the time of his pastorate in Brunswick, Missouri, war was declared, and he was made a prisoner of war for refusing to take the oath of allegiance to the federal government. After release he served as chaplain of the 5th Missouri Regiment (of the Confederate Army) until the close of the war. After the war ended, Bounds served as pastor of churches in Tennessee, Alabama, and St. Louis, Missouri.

He spent the last seventeen years of his life with his family in Washington, Georgia, writing his "Spiritual Life Books." His book *Power Through Prayer* is called by some the greatest book on prayer ever written. It is said that he prayed daily for three hours before he would begin work on his writings. Following are excerpts from *Power Through Prayer* and his sermon "Praying Men Are God's Mightiest Leaders."

The men who have done the most for God in this world have been early on their knees. He who fritters away the early morning, its opportunity and freshness, in other pursuits than seeking God will make poor headway seeking him the rest of the day. If God is not first in our thoughts and efforts in the morning, he will be in the last place the remainder of the day.

Behind this early rising and early praying is the ardent desire which presses us into this pursuit after God. Morning listlessness is the index to a listless heart. The heart which is behindhand in seeking God in the morning has lost its relish for God. David's heart was ardent after God. He hungered and thirsted after God, and so he sought God early, before daylight. The bed and sleep could not chain his soul in its eagerness after God. Christ longed for communion with God; and so, rising a great while before day, he would go out into the mountain to pray. The disciples, when fully awake and ashamed of their indulgence, would know where to find him. We might go through the list of men who have mightily impressed the world for God, and we would find them early after God.

———— ❧ ————

From "Praying Men Are God's Mightiest Leaders"

EDWARD MCKENDREE BOUNDS

Praying men are the men who spend much time with God. Praying men always feel a great need and desire to be alone with God. Though very busy men, they always stop at some appointed time for communion with God. They have spent much time alone with Him and have found that the secret of wise and powerful leadership for God is in these seasons of special access and grace.

Praying men are men of the single eye. They have been so much alone with God, have seen so much of His glory, have learned so much of His will, have been fashioned so strongly after His image that He fixes and fills their gaze. All else is too insignificant to engage their attention, too little to catch their eye. A double vision—one for self, and the other for God—mightily hinders prayer. Praying men are men of one book; they feed on God's Word; it lives in them in vitalizing force and abides in them in full authority and faith. They are Bible men. The Bible inspires their prayers and quickens their faith. They rest on its promises as on a globe of granite.

Praying men are the only productive workers for God. True prayer is a working force, a divine energy that must come out, that is too strong to be still. The work of praying men achieves the best results because it is done by God's energy. Praying men have His direction and do His work for His glory, under the full and cheering beam of His presence, His Word, and His Spirit.

Praying men are the men who have done so much for God in the past. They are the ones who have won the victories for God and spoiled His foes. They are the ones who have set up His kingdom in the very camps of His enemies. There are no other conditions for success today. This century has not suspended the necessity or force of prayer. There is no substitute by which its gracious ends can be secured.

Only praying hands can build for God. Men of prayer are God's mighty ones on earth, His master builders. They may be destitute of all else, but with the wrestlings and prevailings of a simple-hearted faith they are mighty—the mightiest for God. Church leaders may be gifted in all else, but without this greatest of gifts they are as

Samson shorn of his locks, or as the altars of the temple where heavenly flame has died without the divine presence.

"A Prayer in Darkness"

G. K. CHESTERTON

Gilbert Keith Chesterton (1874–1936), the famous English writer, was known best for his keen eye in social commentary. When the *Times* invited several prominent authors to write essays on the theme "What's Wrong with the World?" Chesterton's contribution was as short as it was to the point: "Dear Sirs, I am. Sincerely yours, G. K. Chesterton." Chesterton combined wit with a cultural diagnosis—that of sinful man and his fallen nature. In much the same way, this prayer by Chesterton thanks God, that despite man's sin and evil intentions, God has granted the world grace and redemption. Men, like Chesterton, who have a sense of their own deep imperfections some-times turn away from God and prayer. They should not.

THIS MUCH, O HEAVEN—IF I SHOULD BROOD OR RAVE,
 Pity me not; but let the world be fed,
 Yea, in my madness if I strike me dead,
Heed you the grass that grows upon my grave.
 If I dare snarl between this sun and sod,
 Whimper and clamour, give me grace to own,
In sun and rain and fruit in season shown,
 The shining silence of the scorn of God.
 Thank God the stars are set beyond my power,
If I must travail in a night of wrath,
 Thank God my tears will never vex a moth,
 Nor any curse of mine cut down a flower.
Men say the sun was darkened: yet I had
 Thought it beat brightly, even on—Calvary:

And He that hung upon the Torturing Tree
Heard all the crickets singing, and was glad.

Address at the Episcopal National Cathedral

REV. BILLY GRAHAM

The morning of September 11, 2001, was a beautiful fall day with blue skies and balmy temperatures. Students filled classroom seats and workers started another nine to five in the same fashion as any innocent American morning. In a matter of minutes, as the planes hurtled toward the Twin Towers, the Pentagon, and the peaceful fields of Shanksville, Pennsylvania, America was about to be changed forever. Would our nation be crushed by the worst attack of all time on our soil or would we rise and rebuild stronger than ever? In the face of fathomless mourning and tragedy, the American people were angry, hurt, and confused. I was informed permission has never before been granted to republish this speech in a book. Thanks to the Graham family I am able to feature it here.

President George W. Bush called the nation together in a day of prayer and remembrance three days later, on September 14. Addressing the country on behalf of the president was the famous evangelist, Rev. Billy Graham. In this speech, Graham reminded Americans of their ability to overcome the greatest of catastrophes. Underneath the rubble, he said, lay an indestructible foundation—one of American faith, determination, and trust in a God who would never abandon his children. This prayer rallied many American men.

P resident and Mrs. Bush, I want to say a personal word on behalf of many people. Thank you, Mr. President, for calling this day of prayer and remembrance. We needed it at this time.

We come together today to affirm our conviction that God cares for us, whatever our ethnic, religious, or political background may be. The Bible says that He's the God of all comfort, who comforts us in our troubles. No matter how hard we try, words simply cannot express the horror, the shock, and the revulsion we all feel over what took place in this nation on Tuesday morning. September eleven will go down in our history as a day to remember.

Today we say to those who masterminded this cruel plot, and to those who carried it out, that the spirit of this nation will not be defeated by their twisted and diabolical schemes. Someday, those responsible will be brought to justice, as President Bush and our Congress have so forcefully stated. But today we especially come together in this service to confess our need of God.

We've always needed God from the very beginning of this nation, but today we need Him especially. We're facing a new kind of enemy. We're involved in a new kind of warfare. And we need the help of the Spirit of God. The Bible words are our hope: God is our refuge and strength; an ever present help in trouble. Therefore we will not fear, though the earth give way, and the mountains fall into the heart of the sea.

But how do we understand something like this? Why does God allow evil like this to take place? Perhaps that is what you are asking now. You may even be angry at God. I want to assure you that God understands these feelings that you may have. We've seen so much on our television, heard on our radio, stories that bring tears to our eyes and make us all feel a sense of anger. But God can be trusted, even when life seems at its darkest.

But what are some of the lessons we can learn? First, we are reminded of the mystery and reality of evil. I've been asked hundreds of times in my life why God allows tragedy and suffering. I have to confess that I really do not know the answer totally, even to my own satisfaction. I have to accept by faith that God is sovereign, and He's a God of love and mercy and compassion in the midst of suffering. The Bible says that God is not the author of evil. It speaks of evil as a mystery. In 1 Thessalonians 2:7 it talks about the mystery of iniquity. The Old Testament prophet Jeremiah said "The heart is deceitful above all things and beyond cure. Who can understand it?" He asked that question, "Who can understand it?" And that's one reason we each need God in our lives.

The lesson of this event is not only about the mystery of iniquity and evil, but secondly it's a lesson about our need for each other. What an example New York and Washington have been to the world these past few days. None of us will ever forget the pictures of our courageous firefighters and police, many of whom have lost friends and colleagues; or the hundreds of people attending or standing patiently in line to donate blood. A tragedy like this could have torn our country apart. But instead it has united us, and we've become a family. So those perpetrators who took this on to tear us apart, it has worked the other way—it's backlashed. It's backfired. We are more united than ever before. I think this was exemplified in a very moving way when the members of our Congress stood shoulder to shoulder the other day and sang "God Bless America."

Finally, difficult as it may be for us to see right now, this event can give a message of hope—hope for the present, and hope for the future. Yes, there is hope. There's hope for the present, because I believe the stage has already been set for a new spirit in our nation. One of the things we desperately need is a spiritual renewal in this country. We need a spiritual revival in America. And God has told us in His word, time after time, that we are to repent of our sins and return to Him, and He will bless us in a new way. But there's also hope for the future because of God's promises. As a Christian, I hope not for just this life, but for heaven and the life to come. And many of those people who died this past week are in heaven right now. And they wouldn't want to come back. It's so glorious and so wonderful. And that's the hope for all of us who put our faith in God. I pray that you will have this hope in your heart.

This event reminds us of the brevity and the uncertainty of life. We never know when we too will be called into eternity. I doubt if even one [of] those people who got on those planes, or walked into the World Trade Center or the Pentagon last Tuesday morning thought it would be the last day of their lives. It didn't occur to them. And that's why each of us needs to face our own spiritual need and commit ourselves to God and His will now.

Here in this majestic National Cathedral we see all around us symbols of the cross. For the Christian—I'm speaking for the Christian now—the cross tells us that God understands our sin and our suffering. For He took upon himself, in the person of Jesus Christ, our sins and our suffering. And from the cross, God declares "I love you. I know the heartaches, and the sorrows, and the pains that you feel, but I love you." The story does not end with the cross, for Easter points us beyond the tragedy of the cross to the empty tomb. It tells us that there is hope for eternal life, for Christ has conquered evil, and death, and hell. Yes, there's hope.

I've become an old man now. And I've preached all over the world. And the older I get, the more I cling to that hope that I started with many years ago, and proclaimed it in many languages to many parts of the world. Several years ago at the National Prayer Breakfast here in Washington, Ambassador Andrew Young, who had just gone through the tragic death of his wife, closed his talk with a quote from the old hymn, "How Firm A Foundation." We all watched in horror as planes crashed into the steel and glass of the World Trade Center. Those majestic towers, built on solid foundations, were examples of the prosperity and creativity of America. When damaged, those buildings eventually plummeted to the ground, imploding in upon themselves. Yet underneath the debris is a foundation that was not destroyed. Therein lies the truth of that old hymn that Andrew Young quoted: "How Firm a Foundation."

Yes, our nation has been attacked. Buildings destroyed. Lives lost. But now we have a choice: Whether to implode and disintegrate emotionally and spiritually as a people, and a nation, or, whether we choose to become stronger through all of the struggle to rebuild on a solid foundation. And I believe that we're in the process of starting to rebuild on that foundation. That foundation is our trust in God. That's what this service is all about. And in that faith we have the strength to endure something as difficult and horrendous as what we've experienced this week.

This has been a terrible week with many tears. But also it's been a week of great faith. Churches all across the country have called prayer meetings. And today is a day that they're celebrating not only in this country, but in many parts of the world. And the words of that familiar hymn that Andrew Young quoted, it says, "Fear not, I am with thee. Oh be not dismayed for I am thy God and will give thee aid. I'll strengthen thee, help thee, and cause thee to stand upon" my righteous—on "thy righteous, omnipotent hand."

My prayer today is that we will feel the loving arms of God wrapped around us and will know in our hearts that He will never forsake us as we trust in Him. We also know that God is going to give wisdom, and courage, and strength to the President, and those around him. And this is going to be a day that we will remember as a day of victory. May God bless you all.

"Let My Thoughts Abide in Thee"

ROBERT LOUIS STEVENSON

Robert Louis Stevenson (1850–1894) was a Scottish novelist, poet, essayist, and travel writer. His most well-known books include *Treasure Island*, *Kidnapped*, and *The Strange Case of Dr. Jekyll and Mr. Hyde*. This prayer comes from a collection of his many short works and poems.

> *I ask good things that I detest,*
> *With speeches fair;*
> *Heed not, I pray Thee, Lord, my breast,*
> *But hear my prayer.*
>
> *I say ill things I would not say—*
> *Things unaware:*
> *Regard my breast, Lord, in Thy day,*
> *And not my prayer.*
>
> *My heart is evil in Thy sight:*
> *My good thoughts flee:*
> *O Lord, I cannot wish aright—*
> *Wish Thou for me.*
>
> *O bend my words and acts to Thee,*
> *However ill,*
> *That I, whate'er I say or be,*
> *May serve Thee still.*
>
> *O let my thoughts abide in Thee*
> *Lest I should fall:*
> *Show me Thyself in all I see,*
> *Thou Lord of all.*

New Year's Prayer

Samuel Johnson

Samuel Johnson (1709-1784) is one of the greatest men of letters in the history of the English language. Most famous for his *Dictionary*, which was instantly a landmark work upon its publication, Johnson also gained acclaim as a humorist, essayist, poet, translator, and literary critic. Johnson was a devout Christian, as his prayers attest. This one was prayed in the wee hours of January 1, 1773.

Almighty God, by whose mercy my life has been yet prolonged to another year, grant that thy mercy may not be vain. Let not my years be multiplied to increase my guilt; but as age advances, let me become more pure in my thoughts, more regular in my desires, and more obedient to thy laws. Let not the cares of the world distract me, nor the evils of age overwhelm me. But continue and increase thy loving kindness towards me; and when Thou shalt call me hence, receive me to everlasting happiness, for the sake of Jesus Christ our Lord. Amen.

Resolutions

Samuel Johnson

My purpose is:

To avoid idleness.
To regulate my sleep as to length and choice of hours.
To set down every day what shall be done the day following.
To keep a journal.
To worship God more diligently.
To go to church every Sunday.

To study the Scriptures.
To read a certain portion every week.

The Martyrdom of Polycarp of Smyrna

Violence against Christians was common in the Roman Empire, as Christians refused to worship the Caesars as gods. Polycarp (ca. AD 69–155) a bishop of Smyrna, now the city of Izmir in modern-day Turkey, had served the Lord for eighty-six years (by his own account) at the time of his death through burning at the stake. Although the author of the account is unknown, he vividly captures Polycarp's fervent turn to prayer in the face of his own martyrdom, as Polycarp not only prays for his own captors, but also prayerfully rejoices to be counted a martyr for God's glory. More than one estimable man has died for his faith.

B ut the most admirable Polycarp, when he first heard that he was sought for, was in no measure disturbed, but resolved to continue in the city. However, in deference to the wish of many, he was persuaded to leave it. He departed, therefore, to a country house not far distant from the city. There he stayed with a few friends, engaged in nothing else night and day than praying for all men, and for the churches throughout the world, according to his usual custom . . .

And when those who sought for him were at hand, he departed to another dwelling, whither his pursuers immediately came after him. And when they found him not, they seized upon two youths that were there, one of whom, being subjected to torture, confessed. It was thus impossible that he should continue hid, since those that betrayed him were of his own household . . .

His pursuers then, along with horsemen, and taking the youth with them, went forth at supper-time on the day of the preparation with their usual weapons, as if going out against a robber. And having come about evening, they found him lying down in the upper room of a certain little house, from which he might have escaped into another place; but he refused, saying, "The will of God be done." So when he heard that they had come, he went down and spoke with them. And as those that were present marvelled at his age and constancy, some of them said, "Was so much effort made to capture such a venerable man?" Immediately then, in that very hour, Polycarp ordered that something to eat and drink should be set before them, as much indeed as they cared for, while he besought them to allow him an hour to pray without disturbance. And on their giving him leave, he stood and prayed, being full of the grace of God, so that he could not cease for two full hours, to the astonishment of those who heard him, insomuch that many began to repent that they had come forth against so godly and venerable an old man.

Now, as soon as he had ceased praying, having made mention of all that had at any time come in contact with him, both small and great, illustrious and obscure, as well as the whole catholic church throughout the world, the time of his departure having arrived, they set him upon an ass, and conducted him into the city, the day being that of the great Sabbath. And the Irenarch Herod, accompanied by his father Nicetes (both riding in a chariot), met him, and taking him up into the chariot, they seated themselves beside him, and endeavoured to persuade him, saying, "What harm is there in saying, Lord Caesar, and in sacrificing, with the other ceremonies observed on such occasions, and so make sure of safety?" But he at first gave them no answer; and when they continued to urge him, he said, "I shall not do as you advise me." So they, having no hope of persuading him, began to speak bitter words unto him, and cast him with violence out of the chariot, insomuch that, in getting down from the carriage, he dislocated his leg . . . But without being disturbed, and as if suffering nothing, he went eagerly forward with all haste, and was conducted to the stadium, where the tumult was so great, that there was no possibility of being heard . . .

Immediately then they surrounded him with those substances which had been prepared for the funeral pile. But when they were about also to fix him with nails, he said, "Leave me as I am; for He that gives me strength to endure the fire, will also enable me, without your securing me by nails, to remain without moving in the pile."

They did not nail him then, but simply bound him. And he, placing his hands behind him, and being bound like a distinguished ram taken out of a great flock for sacrifice, and prepared to be an acceptable burnt-offering unto God, looked up to heaven, and said,

O Lord God Almighty, the Father of your beloved and blessed Son Jesus Christ, by whom we have received the knowledge of You, the God of angels and powers, and of every creature, and of the whole race of the righteous who live before you, I give You thanks that You have counted me, worthy of this day and this hour, that I should have a part in the number of Your martyrs, in the cup of your Christ, to the resurrection of eternal life, both of soul and body, through the incorruption imparted by the Holy Ghost. Among whom may I be accepted this day before You as a fat and acceptable sacrifice, according as You, the ever-truthful God, have fore-ordained, have revealed beforehand to me, and now have fulfilled. Wherefore also I praise You for all things, I bless You, I glorify You, along with the everlasting and heavenly Jesus Christ, Your beloved Son, with whom, to You, and the Holy Ghost, be glory both now and to all coming ages. Amen.

"The Upward Look"

BOETHIUS

Boethius, sixth-century Christian philosopher and martyr, met his tragic end after court favor turned against him. In 525, King Theodoric the Great suspected him of sympathizing with his political rival, Emperor Justin. Although Boethius never betrayed his king, he was imprisoned and beaten to death. While in prison, Boethius reflected on the fickle nature of Fortune, writing his great work *The Consolation of Philosophy*, which served as the primary text concerning matters of chance and free will for the next one thousand years. In this poem, Boethius counsels men not only to contrast the world around them to the perfect order of the stars, but to lift their souls heavenward, so that in conforming their souls to divine love, men may find peace—not in a perfectly ordered world, but in an ordered soul.

In what divers shapes and fashions do the creatures great and small
Over wide earth's teeming surface skim, or scud, or walk, or crawl!
Some with elongated body sweep the ground, and, as they move,

Trail perforce with writhing belly in the dust a sinuous groove;
Some, on light wing upward soaring, swiftly do the winds divide,
And through heaven's ample spaces in free motion smoothly glide;
These earth's solid surface pressing, with firm paces onward rove,
Ranging through the verdant meadows, crouching in the woodland grove.
Great and wondrous is their variance! Yet in all the head low-bent
Dulls the soul and blunts the senses, though their forms be different.
Man alone, erect, aspiring, lifts his forehead to the skies,
And in upright posture steadfast seems earth's baseness to despise.
If with earth not all besotted, to this parable give ear,
Thou whose gaze is fixed on heaven, who thy face on high dost rear:
Lift thy soul, too, heavenward; haply lest it stain its heavenly worth,
And thine eyes alone look upward, while thy mind cleaves to the earth!

"Prayer of Columbus"

WALT WHITMAN

On his fateful journey of 1492, Christopher Columbus encountered the New World of North America. His feats and accomplishments are often well remembered, although of late he has been much maligned and criticized, some of it fair. Perhaps less noted are the worries and discouragement that Columbus battled throughout the journey. This poem by Walt Whitman (1819–1892) articulates the persevering, prayerful spirit of this adventurer in the midst of hardships.

A batter'd, wreck'd old man,
Thrown on this savage shore, far, far from home,
Pent by the sea and dark rebellious brows, twelve dreary months,
Sore, stiff with many toils, sicken'd and nigh to death,
I take my way along the island's edge,
Venting a heavy heart.

I am too full of woe!
Haply I may not live another day;
I cannot rest O God—I cannot eat or drink or sleep,
Till I put forth myself, my prayer, once more to Thee,
Breathe, bathe myself once more in Thee—commune with Thee,
Report myself once more to Thee.

Thou knowest my years entire, my life,
(My long and crowded life of active work—not adoration merely;)
Thou knowest the prayers and vigils of my youth,
Thou knowest my manhood's solemn and visionary meditations,
Thou knowest how before I commenced I devoted all to come to Thee,
Thou knowest I have in age ratified all those vows and strictly kept them,
Thou knowest I have not once lost nor faith nor ecstasy in Thee,
(In shackles, prison'd, in disgrace, repining not,
Accepting all from Thee, as duly come from Thee.)

All my emprises have been fill'd with Thee,
My speculations, plans, begun and carried on in thoughts of Thee,
Sailing the deep or journeying the land for Thee;
Intentions, purports, aspirations mine—leaving results to Thee.

O I am sure they really came from Thee,
The urge, the ardor, the unconquerable will,
The potent, felt, interior command, stronger than words,
A message from the Heavens whispering to me even in sleep,
These sped me on.

By me and these the work so far accomplish'd,
By me earth's elder cloy'd and stifled lands uncloy'd, unloos'd,
By me the hemispheres rounded and tied—the unknown to the
known.

The end I know not—it is all in Thee,
Or small or great I know not—haply what broad fields, what lands,
Haply the brutish measureless human undergrowth I know,
Transplanted there may rise to stature, knowledge worthy Thee,
Haply the swords I know may there indeed be turn'd to reaping-tools,
Haply the lifeless cross I know—Europe's dead cross—may bud and
blossom there.

One effort more—my altar this bleak sand;
That Thou O God my life hast lighted,
With ray of light, steady, ineffable, vouchsafed of Thee,
(Light rare untellable—lighting the very light,
Beyond all signs, descriptions, languages!)
For that O God—be it my latest word—here on my knees,
Old, poor, and paralyzed—I thank Thee.

My terminus near,
The clouds already closing in upon me,
The voyage balk'd—the course disputed, lost,
I yield my ships to Thee.

My hands, my limbs grow nerveless,
My brain feels rack'd, bewilder'd,
Let the old timbers part, I will not part,
I will cling fast to Thee, O God, though the waves buffet me,
Thee, Thee at least I know.

Is it the prophet's thought I speak, or am I raving?
What do I know of life? what of myself
I know not even my own work past or present,
Dim ever-shifting guesses of it spread before me,

Of newer better worlds, their mighty parturition,
Mocking, perplexing me.

And these things I see suddenly—what mean they?
As if some miracle, some hand divine unseal'd my eyes,
Shadowy vast shapes smile through the air and sky,
And on the distant waves sail countless ships,
And anthems in new tongues I hear saluting me.

Litany of Humility

RAFAEL CARDINAL MERRY DEL VAL

The following prayer is a favorite of one of the great men I know, Clarence Thomas, Associate Justice of the Supreme Court of the United States. The intent of these words of Rafael Cardinal Merry del Val, Secretary of State for Pope Saint Pius X, is to put off pride and selfish ambition and to humble one's self before God. The repetition in this prayer makes the message ever more powerful.

O Jesus, gentle and humble of heart, hear me!
From the desire of being esteemed,
From the desire of being loved,
From the desire to be sought,
   Deliver me, Jesus.
From the desire to be mourned,
From the desire of praise,
From the desire of preference,
From the desire of influence,
From the desire of approval,
From the desire of authority,
From the fear of humiliation,

From the fear of being despised,

From the fear of repulse,

From the fear of calumny,

From the fear of oblivion,

From the fear of ridicule,

From the fear of injury,

From the fear of suspicion,

That others may be loved more than myself. Jesus grant this desire.

That others may be more highly esteemed.

That others may grow and increase in honour, and I decrease. Jesus grant me to desire it.

That others may be employed, and I set aside. Jesus, grant me to desire this.

That others may attract the praise, and myself be forgotten.

That others may be preferred in all.

Grant me the utmost holiness of which I am capable, then let others be holier than myself. Jesus, grant me to desire it!

Praying in Faith

Martin Luther

Martin Luther (1483–1546) is best known as the father of the Protestant Reformation. Born into a peasant family in Eisleben, Germany, Luther sought to better himself by becoming a scholar. At the age of twenty he entered a monastery and soon afterward he was ordained as a priest. In 1517 he composed his famous Ninety-five Theses and nailed them on the door of the castle church in Wittenberg, registering his complaints with the Roman Catholic Church and providing the impetus for the Protestant Reformation.

Luther was not only a revolutionary theologian but also a man of deep respect for religion. His Protestant views were condemned as heretical and he was summoned to denounce them at the Diet of Worms on April

17, 1521. Facing the leaders of the Roman Catholic Church, Luther boldly stood by his writings. "Unless I am convinced by proofs from Scriptures or by plain and clear reasons and arguments, I can and will not retract, for it is neither safe nor wise to do anything against conscience. Here I stand. I can do no other. God help me. Amen." What follows are two excerpts from his writings, the first from *Treatise on Good Works* and the second from *Table Talk*. Faith is often the cornerstone of conviction.

Prayer is, therefore, a special exercise of faith, and faith makes the prayer so acceptable that either it will surely be granted, or something better than we ask will be given in its stead. So also says St. James: "Let him who asketh of God not waver in faith; for if he wavers, let not that man think that he shall receive any thing of the Lord." This is a clear statement, which says directly: he who does not trust, receives nothing, neither that which he asks, nor anything better.

What a Great Gift We Have in Prayer

MARTIN LUTHER

No human creature can believe, how powerful prayer is, and what it is able to effect, but only those that have learned it by experience.

It is a great matter when in extreme need, as then one can take hold on prayer. I know, as often as I have earnestly prayed, that I have been richly heard, and have obtained more than I prayed for; indeed God sometimes deferred, but notwithstanding he came.

O how great an upright and godly Christian's prayer is! how powerful with God; that a poor human creature should speak with God's high Majesty in heaven, and not be affrighted?

Therefore the ancients finely described prayer, namely, that it is, a climbing up of the heart unto God. . . .

A Prayer for a Good Death

Thomas More

Sir Thomas More (1478–1535), known by Catholics as Saint Thomas More, was a famous English philosopher, writer, and statesman. He served as a close counselor to Henry VIII of England and was later appointed Lord Chancellor. He is remembered by the Catholic Church for his opposition to the Protestant Reformation, especially the work of Martin Luther and William Tyndale. In 1886, More was beatified by the Catholic Church and in 1935 he was canonized.

In 1535, More was imprisoned in the Tower of London for refusing to condone Henry VIII's marriage to Anne Boleyn after Henry divorced his first wife. As a result, in 1535, he was tried for treason and executed by beheading. More's virtue followed him even to death. He is reported to have declared while on the scaffold that he died "the king's good servant, but God's first." His prayer for a "good death" reflects his determined strong spirituality. He was one of the most excellent of men. A play and movie about his life—*A Man for All Seasons*—is well worth the time.

Good Lord,
Give me the grace so to spend my life,
That when the day of my death shall come,
Though I may feel pain in my body,
I may feel comfort in soul;
And with faithful hope in thy mercy,
In due love towards thee
And charity towards the world,
I may, through thy grace,
Part hence into thy glory.

Prayer Found in the Heart

C. H. SPURGEON

Charles Haddon Spurgeon (1834-1892) was a British Baptist preacher widely regarded among many Christian denominations for his profound work within the British community. In his lifetime, Spurgeon preached to around ten million people, often as many as ten times each week at different places. In 1857, he started a charity organization called Spurgeon's, which now works globally. He also founded Spurgeon's College, which was named after him posthumously. His life is a testament to the power of prayer and faith.

How many men seem to begin to pray without really thinking about prayer! They rush, without preparation or thought, into this presence of God. Now, no loyal subject, would seek an audience of his sovereign, to present a petition, without having first carefully prepared it; but many seem to think there is no need to look for a prayer, or to find one, when they approach the mercy-seat. They appear to imagine that they have only just to repeat certain words, and to stand or kneel in a certain attitude, and that is prayer. But David did not make that mistake; he found his prayer in his heart. David and his heart were well acquainted; he had long been accustomed to talk with himself. There are some men, who know a thousand other people, but who do not know their own selves; the greatest stranger to them, in the whole world, is their own heart. They have never looked into it, never talked with it, never examined it, never questioned it. They follow its evil devices, but they scarcely know that they have a heart, they so seldom look into it. But David, when he wanted to pray, went and looked in his heart to see what he could find there, and he found in his heart to pray this prayer to God.

This leads me to say, dear friends, that the best place in which to find a prayer is to find it in your heart. Some would have fetched down a book, and they would have said, "Let us see; what is the day of the month,—how many Sundays after Advent? This is the proper prayer for to-day." But David did not go to a book for his prayer, he turned to his heart to see what he could find there that he might pray unto God. Others of us would, perhaps, have been content to find a prayer in our heads. We have been accustomed to extemporize in prayer, and so, perhaps, bowing the knee, we should have felt that the stream of supplication would flow because we are so habituated to speaking with God in prayer. Ah, dear friend, it is no worse to find a prayer in a book than to find it in your head! It is very much the same thing whether the prayer be printed or be extemporized; unless it comes from the heart, it is equally dead in either case . . .

How was it that David found this prayer in his heart? I think it was because his heart had been renewed by divine grace. Prayer is a living thing; you cannot find a living prayer in a dead heart. Why seek ye the living among the dead, or search the sepulcher to find the signs and tokens of life? No, sir, if you have not been made alive by the grace of God, you cannot pray.

The dead cannot pray, and the spiritually dead cannot pray; but the moment you begin to pray, it is a sign that life has been given to you. Ananias knew that Saul was a living soul when God said to him, "Behold, he prayeth." "It is all right," said Ananias; "for the Lord must have quickened his heart." David found this prayer in his heart because his was a living heart.

And he found it there, also, because his was a believing heart. How can a man pray if he does not believe in God, or if he merely thinks that there may be a supernatural Being, somewhere or other in the universe, but that he is not within hail,—and cannot be made to hear,—or is not a living personality, or, if he is, he is too great to care about us, or to listen to the words of a man. But, when the Lord has taught you the truth about his own existence, and his real character, when he has come so near to you that you know that he is the Rewarder of them that diligently seek him, then, in that believing heart of yours prayer will spring up as the corn springs up in the furrows of the field.

I pause here a moment just to ask each one,—Do you pray? Do you present to God prayers that come from your heart? I do not ask whether you use a form of prayer, or not; but does your heart really go with the prayer you offer? . . .

So, the Lord puts prayer into our heart by instructing us how to pray and by inclining us to pray . . .

How are you to get into this state? Well, I cannot tell you, except this; live near to God. If you live near to God, you must pray. He that learns how to live near to God will learn how to pray, and to give thanks to God. Look into your hearts, also, as David did. You cannot find prayer there if you do not look for it. Think much of your own needs, for a realization of how many and how great they are will make you pray. When you see the falls of others, recollect that you also will fall unless God holds you up; so make that a reason and subject for prayer. When you see others who are slack in devotion, or who have become cold in heart remember you will be as they are if grace does not prevent. So, let your own needs drive you to prayer.

The *Anima Christi*

The *Anima Christi* is an ancient prayer that is still often recited at Holy Communion. It reminds me of what is most important.

Soul of Christ, sanctify me
Body of Christ, save me
Blood of Christ, inebriate me
Water from Christ's side, wash me
Passion of Christ, strengthen me
O good Jesus, hear me
Within Thy wounds hide me
Suffer me not to be separated from Thee
From the malicious enemy defend me
In the hour of my death call me
And bid me come unto Thee
That I may praise Thee with Thy saints
and with Thy angels
Forever and ever
Amen

Agnus Dei

Agnus Dei is a Latin term meaning "Lamb of God" and was originally used to refer to Jesus Christ in his role of the perfect sacrificial offering that atones for the sins of humanity. In the mass of the Roman rite and also in the Eucharist of the Anglican Communion, the Lutheran Church, and the Western rite of the Orthodox Church the *Agnus Dei* is the invocation to the Lamb of God sung or recited during the fraction of the Host. It is said to have been introduced into the mass by Pope Sergius I (687–701). The text of the invocation is based upon John the Baptist's reference in John 1:29 to Jesus, "Behold the Lamb of God that taketh away the sin of the world." It is one of my favorite prayers. It asks God for that final gift of peace. Following is the text, first in Latin, then English:

Agnus Dei, qui tollis peccata mundi, miserere nobis.
Agnus Dei, qui tollis peccata mundi, miserere nobis.
Agnus Dei, qui tollis peccata mundi, dona nobis pacem. Amen.
Lamb of God, who takes away the sins of the world, have mercy on us.
Lamb of God, who takes away the sins of the world, have mercy on us.
Lamb of God, who takes away the sins of the world, grant us peace. Amen.

Man: At the End

This book is very large, with many movements describing the different aspects of a man's life. Now here is the final selection, a man's life—in brief, in sum—from beginning to end.

Clarence E. Glover was a man: a father, husband, neighbor, and friend. From family to work, to faith, to service to polis and country, and even to hobbies and leisure, Clarence Glover lived as a man should.

He was well-off and well-known in his community—not fabulously rich or famous—but he lived a life that every man can and ought. From the prosaic prose of his obituary to the eloquence of his funeral sermon, this selection captures Clarence Glover's entire journey through life, from birth to death.

One story in particular is evidence of the type of man Clarence Glover was. On the bed where Clarence slept beside Dorothy, his wife of thirty-nine years, was a white tapestry bedspread. As he went to his knees every night and in times of need, Clarence rested his arms in the same spot on the bedspread. Over the course of many years, the bedspread was worn down from the pressure of his arms in prayer. When Clarence died suddenly at age sixty-four, his daughters, Elayne and Diane, and his son, Elliott, found great comfort in praying in their father's "place" on that bedspread. Now ninety-two, Dorothy has never parted with that bed covering.

Clarence E. Glover was my father-in-law.

— ❧ —

Obituary

Mr. Clarence E. Glover of 2400 Red Fox Trail, Charlotte, died Monday, October 1, 1984, in Charlotte Memorial Hospital. He was born March 10, 1920, in Livingston, SC, son of the late Clarence Lesterjett Glover and Ida Carson Glover.

Mr. Glover retired in November, 1983 as the Regional Vice-President of Commercial Credit Corporation, headquartered in Charlotte. He was responsible for ninety-four offices of Commercial Credit Corp in five states: Kentucky, West Virginia, Virginia, North and South Carolina. He was responsible for marketing, operations and personnel in these offices. He had been associated with the company for 36 years.

On June 2, 1947 he was transferred from active duty in the U.S. Navy to the U.S. Naval Reserve Program. He retired from the U.S. Naval Reserve 38 years later as Lieutenant Commander. He was a 1941 graduate of the University of South Carolina with a Bachelor of Science degree in Business Administration. He was a member of Dilworth United Methodist Church, where he had served as President of the Men's Bible Class and on the Administrative Board of the church. Mr. Glover was Past Commodore of the River Hills Yacht Club and Past President and former Board member of the Navy League of Charlotte. He was a member of the Charlotte Rotary Club. He had served on the Board of Directors of the N.C. Consumer Finance Association. He was an avid sports fan and a member of the Gamecock Club.

Funeral services will be at 2:00 PM Wednesday, October 3, 1984, in Dilworth United Methodist Church, conducted by minister, Dr. Edgar Nease, Jr. Interment will be in Sharon Memorial Park. Surviving are his wife, Mrs. Dorothy Glover; son, Clarence "Elliott" Glover of Charlotte; two daughters, Mrs. Elayne Glover Bennett of Washington, DC and Mrs. Diane Glover Cook of Charlotte; three grandchildren, John Robert Bennett, Molly Whiting Glover and Dorothy Carson Cook; four sisters, Mrs. Melba Wyndham of Orangeburg, SC, Mrs. Corinne Cardwell of Charleston, SC, Mrs. Freddie Phillips of Orangeburg, SC and Mrs. Julia Livingston of Livingston, SC. Friends may send memorials to Men's Bible Class, Dilworth United Methodist Church, 605 East Boulevard, Charlotte, NC 28203. Honorary pallbearers will be members of the Men's Bible Class. Harry & Bryant Co. is serving the family of Mr. Glover.

— ❦ —

Funeral Meditation

The beauty of this earth is not only found in earth, and skies and seas; it is found in people and in human relationships. Folliot Pierpoint spoke of this in his beautiful hymn that was just played in our midst a few moments ago. The words of that hymn that ring out so prominently for me so often are

> For the joy of human love,
> Brother, sister, parent, child,
> Friends on earth, and friends above,
> For all gentle thoughts and mild;
> Lord of all, to thee we raise
> This our hymn of grateful praise.

While we can enjoy the lakes that look like a mirror in the fall, the snow-capped hills in the winter, or the flowering shrubs in the springtime, the greater joys of life are found in relationships, and Clarence Glover discovered this.

If you traced his life from birth to death, one has to sense that the one word that assumed prominence in his total life was the word *family*. His early years were never forgotten. They were not easy years. They were years of struggle and hard work, of tilling the soil on the farm of his parents in South Carolina. But he looked back on these years with pride for they were years when his family grew together and he never lost sight of his family from whence he came. His roots meant much to him. His own family, the one that he begot himself, was precious in his sight. I dare say there was not an hour in the day when each of his family members was not thought of by their father. His happiest hours were those that he spent with his family. No grandchild was ever born but what you would think it was the culmination of World War II and that the bands ought to be out and the banners unfurled because there was a new Glover grandchild. He never hesitated to call me and tell me of the newest member of his family. You might say he was foolishly delightful as a grandfather. Oh, what memories his children have of his love, of his attention, and of his support.

And Christmas! Well that was the greatest day of the year for him for he had prepared through the months to give the presents to his children and his family. He reminded me of my father, for my father began the day after Christmas to prepare for the next Christmas and to do those things that would bring joy to his family.

Friends were important to Clarence Glover. People were not to be used as stepping stones. They were to be helped to step higher in their life and that was his feeling and he had a sense of calling to make this happen. No one of us here this afternoon knows how many young people he helped to get a start in life, to make a gainful step, to have an education, to get over a hard place. He did this without any publicity. He did it because he believed in people and he loved people. Yes, he enjoyed people. One of his favorite activities was his Men's Bible Class, a class which he served as president at least two terms. These were his friends. They were not just people who came to the class. They were people he knew and loved, and he enjoyed every minute with them. It should be noted that his friends were not regulated to one class or one color or one place. The people with whom he worked at Commercial Credit were not really employees in his sight. Even though he was Regional Vice-President, they were his friends. And whenever I visited there with him, I always sensed that these were people with whom he worked, not people who worked for him. He was concerned about their future and he cared for them. Furthermore, he even made friends with people who attended Clemson University! Being a rabid Gamecock graduate that might not have been the easiest thing he ever did—to be a friend with a Tiger from Clemson; but he enjoyed thoroughly his banter with Jim Foster and others who attended Clemson and this fall he was especially happy because his team was undefeated. He walked a little more cockily than the rest of us could.

Ah, yes, family, friends and work were all important to him; but let's not overlook his faithfulness to God and country. Clarence was a true patriot. When World War II broke out he joined the Navy and was in some of the stiffest battles the Navy fought during that war. He was a part of nine invasions. For thirty-eight years he remained a part of the service of his country and he rose to the rank of Lieutenant Commander. He believed in America and the American way of life. There was nothing artificial about his patriotism. There was nothing superficial about his love for his country. These were as much a part of his life as his own very breath. If ever a flag was appropriately draped over the casket of a citizen of this country it is so today, for his country counted.

And in all of this God was not forgotten. He was committed to the principles of the Christian faith. He loved his church and his Sunday school class. Let me share with you something that many of you might not have ever suspected. He believed in prayer. On several occasions he called me and asked me to pray for him or for someone he loved. God was not some far-off entity to Clarence Glover. God was personal. He was one to be talked with.

Too soon he passed from our midst. Yet, what a mark he made. Now he has passed on the torch to us that we most assuredly must carry into the future. His belief in God, in country, in family must be our banners too.

Dr. Edgar H. Nease, Jr.
October 4, 1984
Dilworth United Methodist Church

Acknowledgments

As with any project I complete, I am indebted to many:

To my editor, Joel Miller, and the entire team at Thomas Nelson: I am grateful to be at home with a publisher. Your patience, encouragement, and support make these projects a pleasure. You are a good man, Joel.

To Brian Kennedy and the Claremont Institute: thanks for your encouragement and support of my writing and speaking on a variety of topics connected to the health of our Republic.

To my new team of researchers who provided invaluable contributions to this book throughout the entire process: Olivia Linde, Brian Dutze, Shane Ayers, and David Carver. The future looks better in your capable hands.

Thanks to David Wilezol for his in-depth knowledge of the classics and all his assistance. And also, David Nathan Martin, whose creativity and skill inspired and created many of the fascinating profiles in this book.

Special thanks to the leader of this team—Christopher Beach—chief engineer of this project, who put many of the pieces together.

I thank John Cribb, a longtime friend, collaborator, and coauthor for looking over and improving the nearly complete manuscript.

For keeping me up-to-date on other jobs and responsibilities while writing this book, I owe thanks to Noreen Burns, who has dedicated herself to my projects and my family (and its projects) for more than twenty years.

Also, to Seth Leibsohn, my friend, who was ready to help at the beginning, and did, and stood at the ready throughout.

I also want to thank my friends Kathryn Lopez and Claude Jennings for their contributions along the way.

And thanks to the many men featured in this book who allowed us an inside look at their worlds and beliefs. I hope our words do justice to your wisdom and actions. I must also thank the great callers on my radio show, *Morning in America*, who inspired much of the content of this book.

Most importantly, to my wife, Elayne: many of the best notions expressed in this book are ones you work to instill in our sons and other young men in our community. For that I am eternally grateful. Great women raise up real men.

To my sons, John and Joe: I've watched you grow from boys into men and I couldn't be more proud. You are on your way and are your father's pride.

Credits

I: MAN IN WAR

Profile: Donovan Campbell by David Wilezol.

"St. Crispin's Day Speech" from *Henry V* in *The Works of William Shakespeare* by William Shakespeare, edited by Charles and Mary Cowden Clarke. London: Bickers and Son, 1864.

Response to the Archbishop of Canterbury by Secretary of State Colin Powell from the World Economic Forum in Davos, Switzerland, January 26, 2003.

"Character of the Happy Warrior" from *The Complete Poetical Works of William Wordsworth* by William Wordsworth, edited by Henry Reed. Philadelphia: Hayes and Zell, 1854.

"The Campaigns of Alexander the Great" by Alexander the Great, told by Arrian, the Roman Historian, from *The Anabasis of Alexander; or, The History of the Wars and Conquests of Alexander the Great*, translated with commentary by E. J. Chinnock. London: Hodder and Stroughton, 1884.

Profile: Joshua Marcellino by Nathan Martin.

"Concord Hymn" from *The Complete Works of Ralph Waldo Emerson* by Ralph Waldo Emerson, edited by Edward Waldo Emerson. Boston and New York: Houghton, Mifflin and Company, 1904.

"This Was Their Finest Hour" by Winston Churchill, speech delivered to the House of Commons of the Parliament of the United Kingdom on June 18, 1940.

David and Goliath: 1 Samuel 17:1–58 NKJV.

Profile: Rick Rescorla by Christopher Beach.

Funeral Oration by Pericles. Thucydides: II 34–46, The Funeral Oration of Pericles.

"Before Action" from *Treasury of War Poetry: British and American Poems of the World War 1914–1917* by W. N. Hodgson, edited by George Herbert Clarke. Boston and New York: Houghton Mifflin Company, 1917.

"Battle Is a Joyous Thing" by Jean de Brueil.

The Navy SEAL Creed reprinted with permission from www.navyseals.com and Navy SEALs Special Warfare Command.

"Bivouac of the Dead" by Theodore O'Hara, from *The Bivouac of the Dead and Its Author* by George Washington Ranck and Theodore O'Hara. Cincinnati: The Robert Clarke Company, 1898.

Profile: Red Falvey by Nathan Martin.

"Be Ye the Avengers of Noble Blood" by William the Conqueror from *British historical & political orations: From the XIIth to the XXth century*, edited by Ernest Rhys. London: J. M. Dent & Sons; New York: E. P. Dutton & Co., 1915.

Profile: Alvin York by Christopher Beach, compiled from historical sources: The Alvin C. York Institute. http://www2.york.k12.tn.us/YorkHome.html; *Uncle Sam Wants You: World War I and the Making of the Modern American Citizen* by Christopher Capozzola. New York: Oxford University Press, 2008; http://www.practicalmanliness.com/alvin-york-%E2%80%93-hero-of-world-war-i/.

Remarks on the Fortieth Anniversary of D-Day by Ronald Reagan, delivered at Pointe du Hoc, France, on June 6, 1984.

From *The Apology* from *The Dialogues of Plato*, vol. 1, by Plato. New York: Scribner, Armstrong, and Co., 1873.

"The Soldier's Faith" from *Speeches*, by Oliver Wendell Holmes. Boston: Little, Brown and Company, 1896.

"Of Man" from *Leviathan* by Thomas Hobbes, reprinted in "English Prose (1137–1890)" by John Matthews Manly. Boston: Ginn and Company, 1909.

"The Charge of the Light Brigade" by Lord Alfred Tennyson. London: Gale House, 1857.

"We Shall Fight Them on the Beaches" by Winston Churchill, delivered to the House of Commons of the Parliament of the United Kingdom on June 4, 1940.

The Iliad of Homer with a Verse Translation by W. C. Green. London: Longmans and Co., 1884.

Profile: John Leone by Nathan Martin.

Beowulf translated by Francis B Gummere. http://www.gutenberg.org/files/981/981.txt.

"In Flanders Fields" from *In Flanders Fields: and Other Poems* by John McCrae. New York, London: G. P. Putnam's Sons, 1910.

Horatius at the Bridge from *The History of Rome*, vol. 1 by Titus Livius Livy. Translated by D. Spillan. New York: Harper and Brothers, 1879.

"Duty, Honor, Country" by General Douglas MacArthur. Published with the approval of the General Douglas MacArthur Foundation, MacArthur Square, Norfolk, Virginia.

"The War Sonnets" from *The Collected Poems of Rupert Brooke* by Rupert Brooke. New York: John Lane Company, 1920.

Profile: Audie Murphy reprinted with the permission of the Arlington National Cemetery, http://www.arlingtoncemetery.mil/historical_information/audie_murphy.html.

2: MAN AT WORK

Profile: Terry Toussaint by Christopher Beach.

"Work" by Eliza Cook from *McGuffey's Fifth Eclectic Reader* by William Holmes McGuffey. Cincinnati: American Book Company, 1879.

"The Plough Boy" by Kate Douglas Wiggin and Nora Archibald Smith, from *Parley's Poetical Present*. Worcester: J. Grout, Jr., ca. 1800.

"How Do You Tackle Your Work?" by Edgar Guest, published in "A Heap o' Livin.'" Chicago: The Reilly and Lee Co., 1916.

The Gift of God: Ecclesiastes 3:10–15 NKJV.

From *Two Years Before the Mast: A Personal Narrative of Life at Sea,* by Richard Henry Dana, New York: Harper and Brothers, 1842.

"The Parable of the Talents": Matthew 25:14–30 NKJV.

Profile: Gac Filipaj, the Janitor Turned Classicist by [[TK]]. "Custodian Graduates from Columbia University After 19 Years, Columbia School of General Studies website, May 7, 2012, http://gs.columbia.edu/news-press?article=custodian-graduates-columbia-university-after-19-years-2012. "Columbia University janitor graduates with degree in Classics," Public Radio International, May 14, 2012, http://www.pri.org/stories/business/social-entrepreneurs/tt-columbia-university-janitor-graduates-with-degree-in-classics-9870.html. The remaining facts and quotes in this story are from "Gac Filipaj, Columbia University Custodian, Earns Degree After Working Way Through School," *Huffington Post,* May 8, 2012, http://www.huffingtonpost.com/2012/05/08/gac-filipaj-custodian-columbia-degree-graduates_n_1500953.html.

"The Strenuous Life" by Theodore Roosevelt from *The Strenuous Life: Essays and Addresses.* New York: The Century Co., 1902.

"The Work Is What Counts" by Theodore Roosevelt, from *Presidential Addresses and State Papers: February 19, 1902 to May 13, 1903* by Theodore Roosevelt. New York: The Review of Reviews Company, 1910.

"No Man Is Happy If He Does Not Work" by Theodore Roosevelt from *A Compilation of the Messages and Speeches of Theodore Roosevelt, 1901–1905* by Theodore Roosevelt, edited by Alfred Henry Lewis. Bureau of National Literature and Art, 1906.

Saving Time from *Ad Lucilium epistulae morales,* Books I–LXI by Seneca. Cambridge, MA: Harvard University Press, 1917.

Profile: Incwell by Nathan Martin.

"Works and Days" from *The Homeric Hymns and Homerica* by Hesiod. London: Heinemann, 1920.

From *The Sea-Wolf* by Jack London. New York: The Macmillan Company, 1904.

Profile: Coach Ken by Nathan Martin.

"A Humorist's Confession" by Mark Twain, from *The New York Times,* November 26, 1905. http://query.nytimes.com/gst/abstract.html?res=FB0612FF3F5C1A728DDDAF0A94D9415B858CF1D3.

"Psalm of Life" by Henry Wadsworth Longfellow, from *The Code Poetical Reader, for School and Home Use* by A Teacher. London: Burns and Oats, 1877.

"The Spiritual Value of Work" by Mark Judge. Reprinted with the permission of the author. http://onfaith.washingtonpost.com/onfaith/guestvoices/2009/12/the_spiritual_value_of_work.html.

From *The Future of the American Negro* by Booker T. Washington. Boston: Small, Maynard and Company, 1900.

From *Up From Slavery* by Booker T. Washington. New York: Doubleday, Page and Co., 1907.

The Way to Wealth by Benjamin Franklin, from *The Life of Benjamin Franklin* by Leonard Woods. London: Printed for Hunt and Clarke, 1826.

"Charmides" from *The Dialogues of Plato* by Plato. New York: Oxford University Press, American branch, 1892.

Profile: George Gershwin: Merle Armitage, *George Gershwin*. Emeryville, CA: Da Capo Press, 1995. William Hyland, *George Gershwin: A New Biography*. Westport, CT: Praeger Publishers, 2003. Howard Pollack, *George Gershwin: His Life and Work*. Berkeley, CA: UC Press, 2006. Walter Rimley, *George Gershwin, An Intimate Portrait*. Champagin, IL: University of Illinois Press, 2009.

"Chuck Yeager Breaks Sound Barrier" from *The American Patriot's Almanac* by William Bennett and John Cribb. Nashville: Thomas Nelson, 2008.

From *Democracy in America*, vol. 2, by Alexis de Tocqueville. New York: J. and H. G. Langley, 1840.

Profile: Michel Faulkner by David Wilezol and Christopher Beach.

From *Middlemarch: a Study of Provincial Life* by George Eliot. New York: Harper and Brothers, 1873.

"The Four Chaplains of World War II" from *The American Patriot's Almanac* by William Bennett and John Cribb. Nashville: Thomas Nelson, 2008.

Paradise Lost by John Milton, from *The Works of the English Poets from Chaucer to Cowper*, edited by Samuel Johnson and Alexander Chalmers. London: Printed for J. Johnson, J. Nichols and Son, 1810.

From *True Tales of Arctic Heroism in the New World* by Adolphus Washington Greely. New York: Charles Scribner's Sons, 1912.

"Men Wanted for Hazardous Journey" by Christopher Beach, written from historical sources: http://en.m.wikipedia.org/wiki/Ernest_Shackleton; *Literature of Travel and Exploration: An Encyclopedia* by Jennifer Speake. New York: Taylor & Francis, 2003.

"Inaugural Address at Edinburgh" by Thomas Carlyle, from *Autobiography: Essay on Liberty* by John Stuart Mill and Thomas Carlyle. New York: P.F. Collier and Son Company, 1909.

"On the Elevation of the Laboring Classes" by William Ellery Channing, from *The Works of William E. Channing* by William Ellery Channing. Boston: James Munroe and Company, 1845.

Profile: David Aikman by Nathan Martin.

Emerson on Labor from *Works of Ralph Waldo Emerson* by Ralph Waldo Emerson. London: George Routledge and Sons, 1883.

Some Fruits of Solitude from *The Select Works of William Penn* by William Penn. London: Printed and sold by J.Phillips, 1782.

Selections from *Meditations* in *The Thoughts of the Emperor Marcus Aurelius Antoninus* by Marcus Aurelius. Translated by George Long. Boston: Little, Brown and Company, 1889.

Pensées in *Thoughts* by Blaise Pascal. New York: P. F. Collier and Son Company, 1910.

3: MAN IN PLAY, SPORTS, AND LEISURE

Profile: "Pistol" Pete Maravich, rewritten from sources by Christopher Beach: http://www.pistol-pete-videos.com/maravich_biography.htm; http://www.pistolpete23.com/Pistol_Lived_Up_In_End.htm.

"Do You Fear the Wind?" by Hamlin Garland, from *The Home Book of Verse, American and English, 1580–1912*, vol. 4, 1253–1648. New York: H. Holt and company, 1915.

"It Is a Pleasant Day" by Peter Parley, from *Parley's Poetical Present*. Worcester: J. Grout, Jr., ca. 1800.

"The Answer" from *Songs of the Stalwart* by Grantland Rice. New York: D. Appleton and company, 1917.

"Playing the Game" by Anonymous.

"The Quitter" by Robert W. Service, appearing in *Public Service*, vol. 22. H. J. Gonden, 1917.

Profile: Eddie Aikau by Christopher Beach.

"The American Boy" by Theodore Roosevelt, from an essay published in *St. Nicholas*, May, 1900. http://www.foundationsmag.com/americanboy-com.html.

"A President and His Leisure" from *An Autobiography* by Theodore Roosevelt. New York: Charles Scribner's Sons, 1913.

"Coin Collecting" from *The Numismatist*, vols. 12–13. American Numismatic Association, 1899.

"The New Coney Island" from *The Century Illustrated Magazine*, Vol. 68. New York: The Century Co., 1904.

"A Nation's Pastime" from *America's National Game* by Albert Goodwill Spalding. American Sports Publishing Company, 1911.

"Leisure" by William Henry Davies, from *The Living Age*, vol. 274. Boston: Littell, Son and Co., 1912.

On Gardening by Francis Bacon, appearing in *The American Cotton Planter: a Monthly Journal Devoted to Improved Plantation Economy*, vol. 2, edited by N. B. Cloud. Published by the Cleveland Academy of Natural Science, 1854.

"Finding Troy" from *Troy and Its Remains: a Narrative of Researches and Discoveries Made on the Site of Ilium, and in the Trojan Plain* by Heinrich Schliemann. New York: J. Murray, 1875.

"A Father to His Son, Upon Leaving for College" from *A Father to His Son: A Letter to an Undergraduate upon His Entering College* by John D. Swain. New Haven: Yale publishing association, 1912.

Profile: Tim Tebow from "Coaching character," Suzy A. Richardson. *The Gainesville Sun*, October 7, 2007, http://www.webcitation.org/6C3RRbZ4e. "SAHS' Wiles, Nease's Tebow win state football awards," Justin Barney. *St Augustine Record*, December 9, 2005, http://www.staugustine.com/stories/120905/spo_3507267.shtml. "Tim Tebow Says He's Still a Virgin, Saving Himself for Marriage," Clay Travis. AOL News, July 23, 2009, http://www.aolnews.com/2009/07/23/tim-tebow-says-hes-still-a-virgin-saving-himself-for-marriage/. "Ravens trade 25th overall pick to Denver Broncos," Associated Press, April 22, 2010, Cbssports.com http://www.cbssports.com/nfl/story/13275408/ravens-trade-25th-overall-pick-to-denver-broncos. Denver Broncos 2011 Schedule and Results http://www.denverpost.com/broncos/ci_18554685.

Tragedy on K2, rewritten from historical sources by Christopher Beach.

Abe Lincoln Wrestles Jack Armstrong from *Abraham Lincoln: A History*, vol. 1, by John G. Nicolay and John Hay. New York: The Century Co., 1890.

From *War and Peace* by Leo Tolstoy. New York: The Modern Library, 2002.

"The Traffic Guard" by Christopher Beach, published in *Surfer* magazine, June 2010.

"The Art of Fencing" by Louis and Regis Senac, from *The Art of Fencing by* Regis Senac, Louis Senac, and Edward Breck. New York: American Sports Publishing Co., 1915.

A Day At the Ancient Olympic Games by Anacharsis of Scythia, appearing in *The Dictionary of Useful Knowledge* by R.K. Philp. London: Houlston and Wright, 1861.

Learning Languages for Fun by Benjamin Franklin, from *Memoirs of Benjamin Franklin*, vol. 1, by Benjamin Franklin, William Temple Franklin, and William Duane. Philadelphia: M'Carty and Davis, 1834.

"An Autumn Effect" from *The Works of Robert Louis Stevenson*, vol. 4, by Robert Louis Stevenson.

Edinburgh: printed by T. and A. Constable for Longmans Green and Co. and sold by Chatto and Windus, London, 1896.

Filling Days and Finding Relaxation from *The Letters of the Younger Pliny* by Pliny the Younger. K. Paul, Trench, Trübner and Co., Ltd., 1890.

"Angler Grove Cleveland" by A. M. Stoddart from *The Oregon Sportsman*, vols. 3–5. Portland: Published under the Fish and Game Commission, 1915.

Profile: Milan High School and the 1953 Indiana State Championship by David Wilezol: Greg Guffey, *The Greatest Basketball Story Ever Told: The 1954 Milan Miracle*. Bloomington, IN.: Indiana University Press, 2003, xi. Phillip M. Hoose, "Indiana's Cinderella Basketball Team," in Ralph Gray, *Indiana History: A Book of Readings*. Bloomington, IN: IUP, 408–410.

Leo Tolstoy the Chess Player by Edward Winter, from *The British Chess Magazine*, vol. 17. London: Trubner and Co., 1897.

Profile: Cal Ripken, Jr., the Iron Man of Baseball by Christopher Beach: http://www.baseball-almanac.com/quotes/quoripk.shtml. *What They Said in 1995: The Yearbook of World Opinion* compiled and edited by Alan F. Pater, Jason R. Pater. Palm Springs, CA: Monitor Book Co, 1996.

"In Defense of Sports" by William J. Bennett, from *Commentary Magazine*. New York: Feb. 1976.

Buster Douglas Defeats Mike Tyson by David Wilezol: Bryan Armen Graham, "Douglas reflects on upset, talks Pacquiao-Mayweather, MMA," *Sports Illustrated*. Online Edition. Feb. 11, 2010. Jemele Hill, "Buster Douglas: The Upset's Other Side." ESPN.com, Feb. 12, 2010. Accessed June 13, 2011. "The Moments: Mike Tyson vs. Buster Douglas." East Side Boxing.com. December 12, 2005. Richard O'Brien, "Douglas' Knockout of Tyson Still Resonates 20 Years Later," *Sports Illustrated*. Online Edition. Feb. 11, 2010. Jeremy Schapp, "Busting the Myths of Tyson-Douglas." ESPN.com, February 12, 2010. Accessed June 13, 2011.

"The National Game" from *The Book of American Pastimes: Containing a History of the Principal Base Ball, Cricket, Rowing, and Yachting Clubs of the United States* by Charles Peverelly. New York: Published by the author, 1866.

Practice Makes Perfect by Christopher Beach: Bill Hillman, "Reeperbahn." http://hillmanweb.com/BEATLES/reeper.html. Accessed May 15, 2009.

Profile: Aaron Rodgers by Christopher Beach: http://espn.go.com/blog/rick-reilly-go-fish/post/_/id/826/aaron-rodgers-unforgettable-forgiveness.

"Little Bob's First Bass" from *Tragic Fishing Moments* by Will H. Dilg. Chicago: Reilly and Lee, 1922.

"Hunting the Grisly" from *Hunting the Grisly: and Other Sketches* by Theodore Roosevelt. New York: Review of Reviews, 1910.

1980 U.S. Ice Hockey Team Miracle on Ice, rewritten from historical sources by David Wilezol: Dave Anderson, "Ice Hockey, the Russian Way," *New York Times*. Feb. 18, 1980; Wayne Coffey, *The Boys of Winter*. New York City: Crown Publishers, 2005; Gerald Eskenazi, "U.S. Defeats Soviet Squad in Olympic Hockey by 4-3," *New York Times*. Feb. 23, 1980; Leonard Shapiro, "U.S. Shocks Soviets in Ice Hockey, 4-3," *Washington Post*. Feb. 23, 1980: D1.

Profile: Jeremy Lin from "Lin makes Lakers believe the hype," Christopher Hunt. ESPN, February 11, 2012, http://www.webcitation.org/65R1h4iIH. "Lin Gets His All-Star Weekend Closeup," Steve Aschburner on the NBA's *Sekou Smith's Hangtime Blog*, February 24, 2012, http://www.

webcitation.org/65hoNwHbW. "Exclusive: Jeremy Lin says 'Lin-sanity' was triggered by a leap of faith," Marcus Thompson II. *San Jose Mercury News*, February 13, 2012.

On Leisure from *Ad Lucilium epistulae morales*, Books LXCI–XCII by Lucius Annaeus Seneca. Cambridge, MA: Harvard University Press, 1920.

The Thrilla in Manila, rewritten from historical sources by David Wilezol: "Ali, Frazier Make $1 Million Side Bet," *New York Times*. July 2, 1975: 23. Dave Anderson, "Ali Retains Title as Fight is Stopped in 14th," *New York Times*. Oct. 1, 1975: 93. Joel Dreyfuss, "Float Like a Butterfly, Sting Like A Bee," *The Washington Post*. Sept. 2, 1975. William Barry Furlong, "This Morning," *The Washington Post*. Sept. 24, 1975: D1. ———, "This Morning," *The Washington Post*. Sept. 30. 1975: D1. Glen Schouw, "Greatest heavyweight fight!" *The Daily News (Natal)*, Oct. 6, 2005. Wilfred Sheed, "Boxing Fans Violently Split," *The Washington Post*. Sept. 24, 1975: F1.

"Prepared for a Rain" from *Tragic Fishing Moments* by Will H. Dilg. Chicago: Reilly and Lee, 1922.

Profile: Mario Andretti, rewritten from historical sources by David Wilezol: "Interview with Mario Andretti and Tom Lee," *Auto Racing Daily*. Autoracingdaily.com. Nov. 10, 2010. Accessed June 13, 2011. Larry Schwartz, "Super Mario Had Speed to Burn." ESPN.com. June 14, 2007. Accessed June 13, 2011.

Piers Paul Read's *Alive: The Story of the Andes Survivors* by William J. Bennett. *Commentary Magazine*, August 1974.

4: MAN IN THE POLIS

"Not Yours to Give" by David Crockett, from *The Life of Colonel David Crockett* by Edward S. Ellis. Philadelphia: Porter and Coates, 1884.

Profile: Zudhi Jasser by Nathan Martin.

The Athenian Oath from *The Civic Searchlight*. Detroit: Detroit Citizens League, 1915.

"A Politician and a Hero" by Richard J. Hinton from *True Stories of Heroic Lives: Stirring Tales of Courage and Devotion of Men and Women of the Nineteenth Century*. New York: Funk and Wagnalls Company, 1899.

From *Politics* by Aristotle, in *The Library of Original Sources: The Greek World*, edited by Oliver Joseph Thatcher. New York: University Research Extension, 1907.

"A Nation's Strength" by Ralph Waldo Emerson, from *Carpenter*, vol. 25. United Brotherhood of Carpenters and Joiners of America, 1905.

Profile: A Navy SEAL by Christopher Beach.

"Of the Beginning of Political Societies" from *Second Treatise of Government* by John Locke. Project Gutenberg, 1690. http://www.gutenberg.org/files/7370/7370-h/7370-h.htm.

Profile: Dave Pereda by Christopher Beach.

National Greatness by Pericles, from *History of the Peloponnesian War* translated into English by Richard Crawley. London: J.M. Dent and Sons, Ltd., 1914.

"Love of Country" by Sir Walter Scott, from *Choice Literature*, Book 7. American Book Co., 1912.

From *De Officiis* (On Duties) by Marcus Tullius Cicero. Translated by Walter Miller. Cambridge, MA: Harvard University Press, 1913.

"Power Tends to Corrupt" by Lord Acton from *Historical Essays and Studies* by Baron John Emerich Edward Dalberg Acton. London: Macmillan and Co., Limited, 1907.

Lectures and Miscellanies from *Lectures and Miscellanies* by Henry James. New York: Redfield, 1852.

"Hávamál" from *The Poetic Edda*, translated by Henry Adams Bellows. Princeton, NJ: Princeton University Press, 1936.

From *A Man and His Money* by Harvey Reeves Calkins. New York and Cincinnati: The Methodist Book Concern, 1914.

From "Acres of Diamonds" in *Acres of Diamonds* by Russell Herman Conwell. New York: Harper and Brothers, 1915.

The Duties of Citizenship by William Jennings Bryan, from *The First Battle: A Story of the Campaign of 1896*, vol. 3. Chicago: W. B. Conkey Company, 1896.

From *The Royal Art* by William Jennings Bryan. New York: Fleming H. Revell, 1914.

Cornerstone School from "A Way in the Wilderness," David Wilezol. *Doublethink* magazine, February 6, 2012, http://americasfuture.org/doublethink/2012/02/a-way-in-the-wilderness/.

The Ethics of Politics from *Great Men and Great Movements: a Volume of Addresses* by Charles Betts Galloway. Nashville, TN: Publishing House Methodist Episcopal Church, South, Smith and Lamar, agents, 1914.

"Duties of American Citizenship" by Theodore Roosevelt. A speech delivered in Buffalo, New York, Jan. 26, 1883.

Profiles of Law Enforcement, printed with permission from the National Law Enforcement Officers Memorial Fund.

Reflections on the Revolution of France from *The Works of the Right Honourable Edmund Burke*, vols. 5–6, by Edmund Burke. London: Printed for C. and J. Rivington, 1826.

Civil and Political Association from *Democracy in America*, vol. 2, by Alexis de Tocqueville. New York: Colonial Press, 1899.

"The Political Duties of Christian Men and Ministers: a Sermon for the Times Delivered at Jackson, July 28, 1854" by James S. Smart. Detroit: Baker and Conover, 1854.

From "The Capacity for Greatness" by Theodore Roosevelt, in *A Compilation of the Messages and Speeches of Theodore Roosevelt, 1901–1905, Vol. 2*. Bureau of National Literature and Art, 1906.

Profile: Álvaro Uribe Vélez by Christopher Beach.

Good Citizenship from *Good Citizenship* by Grover Cleveland. Philadelphia: H. Altemus, 1908.

Good Citizenship Dependent upon Great Citizens from *Public Mindedness: an Aspect of Citizenship Considered in Various Addresses Given While President of Dartmouth College* by William Jewett Tucker. Concord: The Rumford press, 1909.

Cato the Younger by Plutarch, from *Plutarch's Lives of Illustrious Men*, translated from the Greek and revised by A. H. Clough. Boston: Little, Brown and Company, 1880.

Taking Command by George Washington, from *The Story-Life of Washington: a Life-history in Five Hundred True Stories* by Wayne Whipple. Philadelphia: The John C. Winston Co., 1911.

From *Arthur James Balfour: the Man and His Work* by Bernard Alderson. London: G. Richards, 1903.

From *Foundations of the Republic* by Calvin Coolidge, reprinted with permission from the University of the Pacific Press. Originally published by University of the Pacific Press, 1926.

Duty by Horatio Kitchener, from *Life of Lord Kitchener*, vol. 3, by Sir George Arthur. New York: The Macmillan Company, 1920.

Profile: Jaime Escalante by Christopher Beach, written from *The De-Valuing of America: the Fight for Our Culture and Our Children* by William J. Bennett. New York: Simon and Schuster, 1992

A Story of Civic Improvement from *Memoirs of Benjamin Franklin*, vol. 1, by Benjamin Franklin. Philadelphia: M'Carty and Davis, 1834.

The Story of Cincinnatus, retold by James Baldwin. Reprinted from *The Book of Virtues* by William John Bennett. New York: Simon and Schuster, 1993.

Compromise from *The Works of Henry Clay: Speeches* by Henry Clay, edited by Calvin Colton, LL.D. New York: G. P. Putnam's Sons, 1904.

Five Keys to Democratic Statesmanship from *Heroes: What Great Statesmen Have to Teach Us* by Paul Johnson. Imprimis, December 2007. Reprinted by permission from Imprimis, a publication of Hillsdale College.

"Hello, Freedom Man" by Ronald Reagan, from his Farewell Address to the Nation delivered Jan. 11, 1989, Washington D.C.

Choosing Just Men from *History of the United States* by Noah Webster. New Haven: S. Babcock, 1837.

Heroes of Science from *Heroic Lives* by Albert Ross Vail and Emily McClellan Vail. Boston: Beacon Press, 1917.

"To Defend and Enjoy His Own" from *The Great Orations and Senatorial Speech of Daniel Webster* by Rochester: W. M. Hayward, 1853.

Profile: Marco Rubio, rewritten from historical sources by Christopher Beach.

Profile: Ray Sorensen and the Freedom Rock by David Wilezol, compiled from: "Artist Turns Iowa Graffiti Rock into Military Tribute" by John D. Banusiewicz. Armed Forces Press Service, Nov. 17, 2003. http://www.defense.gov/news/newsarticle.aspx?id=27770; "Message Takes Shape on Freedom Rock" by Kyle Munson. *Des Moines Register*. May 24, 2011. http://www.desmoinesregister.com/article/20110504/NEWS03/105040345/Munson-Message-takes-shape-Freedom-Rock-; "Artist's Tribute Has Become Sacred to Vets." *USA Today*, May 22, 2007. http://www.usatoday.com/news/nation/2007-05-21-rock-art_N.htm.

What You Can Do for Your Country by John F. Kennedy, from his Inaugural Address, delivered Jan. 20, 1961.

In Harm's Way for Others from *The Fireman's Own Book* by George P. Little. Boston: Dillingham and Bragg, 1860.

Profile: Frank Hall adapted from William J. Bennett's CNN column titled "Let's teach our students about character," March 6, 2012, http://www.cnn.com/2012/03/06/opinion/bennett-chardon-shooting.

Irrationally Patriotic from *Orthodoxy* by G. K. Chesterton. New York: John Lane Company, 1909.

Abraham Lincoln's Lyceum Address, "Address Before the Young Men's Lyceum of Springfield, Illinois, Jan. 27, 1838" from *Abraham Lincoln: Complete Works, Comprising His Speeches, State Papers, and Miscellaneous Writings*, vol. 1, edited by John G. Nicholay and John Hay. New York: The Century Co., 1920.

5: MAN WITH WOMAN AND CHILDREN

Profile: Chris Scott by David Wilezol.

"When You Are Old" from *Selected Poems* by William Butler Yeats. New York: The Macmillan Company, 1921.

"Down by the Salley Gardens" from *Selected Poems* by William Butler Yeats. New York: The Macmillan Company, 1921.

Robert E. Lee from *Success: A Book of Ideals, Helps, and Examples for All Desiring to Make the Most of Life* by Orison Swett Marden. Boston and Chicago: W. A. Wilde and Company, 1897.

"Love Among the Ruins" from *The Poetic and Dramatic Works of Robert Browning*, vol. 2, by Robert Browning. Boston and New York: Houghton, Mifflin and Company, 1895.

Duff Cooper's Letter to Diana, His Future Wife, Aug. 20, 1918.

Leo Tolstoy's Letter to His Fiancée, Valeria Arsenev, Nov. 2, 1856.

"A Father's Gift to His Son, on His Becoming an Apprentice: to Which Is Added Dr. Franklin's Way to Wealth," author unknown. New York: Samuel Wood and Sons, 1821.

Advice to Boys from *Advice to Boys* by Lewis Johnston. Pine Bluff: Richard Allen Institute, ca. 1900.

Profile: Nolan Ryan by Christopher Beach.

From *She Stoops to Conquer* by Oliver Goldsmith, in *The Miscellaneous Works of Oliver Goldsmith: With an Account of His Life and Writings*, edited by Washington Irving. Philadelphia: J. Crissy and J. Grigg, 1830.

Excerpt from *Bleak House* in *The Writings of Charles Dickens: Bleak House* by Charles Dickens. Boston and New York: Houghton, Mifflin and Company, 1894.

Two Poems by Robert Browning, from *The Robert Browning Year-Book: a Selection of Passages for Every Day in the Year from His Writings, in Verse and Prose*. Compiled by J. R. Tutin. Edinburgh: W. P. Nimmo, Hay and Mitchell, 1890. *The Poetical Works of Robert Browning*, vol. 9, by Robert Browning. New York: Macmillan and Co., 1894.

From *Don Juan* in *The Works of Lord Byron Complete in One Volume* by Baron George Gordon Byron. Francfort, O. M.: H. L. Broenner, 1837.

Penelope by Homer from *The Odyssey* edited and translated by Samuel Butler. London: A.C. Fifield, 1900.

Telemachus by Homer from *The Odyssey* edited and translated by Samuel Butler. London: A.C. Fifield, 1900.

Profile: Dr. Ben Carson by Christopher Beach.

George Washington to Martha from *The Story-Life of Washington: A Life-History in Five Hundred True Stories* by Wayne Whipple. Philadelphia: The John C. Winston Co., 1911.

Pierre Curie by Marie Curie from *Pierre Curie* by Marie Curie, with autobiographical notes by Marie Curie. Translated by Charlotte and Vernon Kellogg. New York: Macmillan, 1923.

"Annabel Lee" from *The Works of Edgar Allan Poe*, vol. 2, by Edgar Allan Poe. New York: W. J. Widdleton, 1863.

Antony and Cleopatra from *The Works of John Dryden*, vol. 5, by John Dryden, edited by Walter Scott. London: James Ballentyne and Co. Edinburgh, 1808.

Abraham Lincoln and Grace Bedell, from *The American Patriot's Almanac* by William Bennett and John Cribb. Nashville: Thomas Nelson, 2008.

Marcus Cato from *Plutarch's Lives of Illustrious Men* by Plutarch, translated from the Greek and revised by A. H. Clough. Boston: Little, Brown and Company, 1880.

The Influence of a Father from *Autobiography* by John Stuart Mill. New York: P. F. Collier and Son, 1909.

The Farmer and His Sons from *The Book of Fables: Chiefly from Aesop* by Aesop; Chosen and phrased by Horace E. Scudder. Boston: Houghton, Mifflin and Company, 1882.

Things to Tell Your Children or Grandchildren from *50 Rules Kids Won't Learn in School* by Charles J. Sykes, printed with permission from Charles J. Sykes. New York: St. Martin's Press, 2007.

Fatherhood by Ronald Reagan, Presidential Radio Address, June 14, 1986.

The Best Things in Life from *Theodore Roosevelt: an Autobiography* by Theodore Roosevelt. New York: The Macmillan Company, 1913.

Teddy Roosevelt with His Children from *Selections from Roosevelt* by Theodore Roosevelt, edited by Ernest Ruse. Tokyo: Uchida Rokakuho, 1906.

Jonathan Edwards with His Children from *The Life of President Edwards* by Sereno Edwards Dwight. New York: G. and C. and H. Carvill, 1830.

"On My First Sonne" by Ben Jonson, from *The Works of the English Poets, from Chaucer to Cowper,* edited by Samuel Johnson and Alexander Chalmers. London: Printed for J. Johnson, J. Nichols and Son, 1810.

"A Boy of Much Promise" by Calvin Coolidge, from *The Autobiography* by Calvin Coolidge Cosmopolitan Book Corporation, 1929. Reprinted with permission from the Calvin Coolidge Memorial Foundation and the great-grandchildren of Calvin Coolidge.

"Bone of My Bones": Genesis 2:19–24 NKJV.

Finding a Good Wife: Proverbs 31:10–31 NKJV.

From *Sketches of Young Couples* in *The Works of Charles Dickens* by Charles Dickens. London: Chapman and Hall, Limited; and Henry Frowde, 1908.

What is Love? from *Daniel Deronda* by George Eliot. Montreal: Dawson Brothers, 1876.

Heroes of Aurora adapted from Bennett's CNN column titled "Aurora heroes: Three who gave their lives," July 29, 2012, CNN, http://www.cnn.com/2012/07/25/opinion/bennett-aurora-three.

"True and False Manliness" by James Freeman Clarke, appearing in *The Christian Life*, vol. 10. London: Jan. 5, 1884.

From Canal Boy to President in *From Canal Boy to President: or the Boyhood and Manhood of James A. Garfield* by Horatio Alger, Jr. Boston: DeWolfe, Fiske, and Co., 1881.

Thomas Carlyle's Advice to Young Men, appearing in *The Treasury of Modern Biography*, compiled by R. Cochrane. London and Edinburgh: William P. Nimmo, 1878.

Are You Well Bred? From *The American Magazine*, vol. 92. New York: The Crowell Publishing Company, 1921.

Profile: David Gelernter by Nathan Martin.

"Courtship and Matrimony" from *Courtship and Matrimony: With Other Sketches from Scenes and Experiences in Social Life: Particularly Adapted for Every-day Reading* by Robert Morris. Philadelphia: T. B. Peterson, 1858.

From *Self-Control, Its Kingship and Majesty* in *The Kingship of Self-Control: Individual Problems and Possibilities* by William George Jordan. New York: F. H. Revell, 1899.

A Father's Legacy from *The Iliad* by Homer, translated by Samuel Butler, 1898.

"A Manly Boy" from *Draper's Self Culture* by Andrew Sloan Draper. New York: Ferd Kaiser, 1907.

From *The Marriage Guide for Young Men: A Manual of Courtship and Marriage* by George W. Hudson. Ellsworth, ME: Published by the author, 1883.

Letter to a Sickly Child from *A Memoir of the Reverend Sydney Smith*, vol. 2, by Sydney Smith. London: Longman, Brown, Green, and Longmans, 1855.

Response to a Fan Letter of Sorts from *The Letters of Charles Dickens: 1833–1856* by Charles Dickens, edited by Georgina Hogarth and Mamie Dickens. New York: Charles Scribner's Sons, 1879.

A Father's Prayer by Douglas MacArthur, published with the approval of the General Douglas MacArthur Foundation, MacArthur Square, Norfolk, Virginia.

"Only a Dad" by Edgar Guest, appearing in *The Book of Virtues: a Treasury of Great Moral Stories* by William John Bennett. New York: Simon and Schuster, 1993. Reprinted with permission of the author.

Letter to a Bereaved Husband by Samuel Johnson, from *Life of Johnson* by James Boswell, edited by John Wilson Croker. London: John Murray, 1876.

Nathaniel Hawthorne's Letter to His Daughter from *Nathaniel Hawthorne and His Wife: a Biography*, vol. 1, by Julian Hawthorne. Boston and New York: Houghton Mifflin Company, 1884.

Profile: "A Shau Valley" by Nathan Martin.

Thomas Jefferson's Letter to Thomas Jefferson Smith from *Memoir, Correspondence, and Miscellanies: from the Papers of Thomas Jefferson vol. 4* by Thomas Jefferson, edited by Thomas Jefferson Randolph. Charlottesville: F. Carr, and Co., 1829.

"Dr. Johnson and His Father" from *Thirty More Famous Stories Retold* by James Baldwin. London: American Book Company, 1905.

Profile: Bill Phillips by Nathan Martin: http://www.washingtonpost.com/wpdyn/content/article/2010/08/11/AR2010081106502.html; http://www.washingtonpost.com/wpdyn/content/article/2010/11/24/AR2010112403208.html.

6: MAN IN PRAYER AND REFLECTION

The Our Father (or the Lord's Prayer): Matthew 6:9–13 NKJV.

The Glory Be from *Congregational Church Hymnal*, edited by George S. Barrett. London: Hodder and Stoughton, 1887.

A Child's Grace from *Wonders of Providence: Remarkable and Authentic Providential Stories*, compiled by Rev. J Martin Rohde. Chicago: The Evangelical Publishing Co., 1911.

"We Thank Thee" by Rebecca Weston, from *The Character Building Readers*, Part 2, by Ellen E. Kenyon-Warner. New York, Philadelphia: Hinds, Noble and Eldredge, 1910.

Profile: Os Guinness by Nathan Martin.

"Now I Lay Me Down to Sleep" from *The New-England Primer: a History of Its Origin and Development*, edited by Paul Leicester Ford. New York: Dodd, Mead and Company, 1897.

Tuning the Soul by Robert Murray M'Cheyne, from *Moody Bible Institute Monthly*, vol. 21, by Moody Bible Institute. Chicago: The Moody Bible Institute, 1920.

Unspoken Prayer by Anonymous.

"May I Know Thee More Clearly" by Saint Richard, from *The Churchman's Prayer Manual* by G. R. Bullock-Webster, 31, Acts and Devotion. Prayer 48, 1913.

Harry S. Truman's Daily Prayer, reprinted with permission of the Harry S. Truman Library.

"On Self-Improvement" from *Scouting for Boys* (first published ed.) by Lord Robert Baden Powell, London, Windsor House, Bream's Buildings, E.C.: Horace Cox (printer for C.A. Pearson). January–March 1908.

Matins (Morning Prayer) from Hesperides: The Poems and Other Remains of Robert Herrick Now First Collected, by Robert Herrick, edited by W. Carew Hazlitt. London: John Russell Smith, 1869.

A Prayer for Guidance by George Washington, from *Washington's Prayers*, edited by W. Herbert Buck. Norristown, PA: 1907.

A Prayer for Peace by Abraham Lincoln, from *The History of Abraham Lincoln and the Overthrow of Slavery* by Isaac D. Arnold. Chicago, Clarke and Co., 1866.

A Prayer in Dark Times by Franklin D. Roosevelt, from the U.S. Congressional Record, 110th Congress, First Session, 2009. Vol. 153. Pt. II.

A Prayer of Gratitude by John F. Kennedy, from "Thanksgiving Day 1963, Proclamation 3560." Federal Register, Title 3-The President, 1959–1963: 313.

A Prayer for a Meaningful Life by Jimmy Carter, from his Inaugural Address. http://en.wikisource. org/wiki/Jimmy_Carter%27s_Inaugural_Address. Accessed June 20, 2011 and "Thanksgiving Day, 1980, Proclamation 4803." Federal Register, Title 3-The President, 1980: 118.

A Prayer for Healing by Ronald Reagan, from a speech delivered Feb. 6, 1980.

A Prayer to Help Others by George H. W. Bush, from his "Inaugural Address," Washington DC, January 20, 1989.

A Prayer for the Departed by George W. Bush, from "Address on the National Day of Prayer and Remembrance for the Victims of the Terrorist Attacks on September 11, 2001," Washington DC, Sept. 14, 2001.

"The Examined Life" by Plato, from *The Apology of Socrates*, edited and translated by D. F. Nevill. London: F. E. Robinson and Co., 1901.

Aids to Reflection by Samuel Taylor Coleridge, from *The Complete Works of Samuel Taylor Coleridge*, edited by W. G. T. Shedd. New York: Harper and Bros., 1884.

"A Student's Prayer" by Thomas Aquinas, from *Prayers of the Ages*, edited by Caroline S. Whitmarsh. Boston: Ticknor and Fields, 1868.

"That Which . . . Had Been Long Looked For" from *A Narrative of Some of the Lord's Dealings with George Müller*, Part II, by George Müller. London: J. Nisbet and Co., 1855.

An Instrument of Peace by St. Francis of Assisi, originally published in French in La Clochette, n° 12, déc. 1912: 285.

Profile: Saint Damien de Veuster: *The American Catholic Quarterly Review*, vol. 15. Philadelphia: Hardy and Mahony, 1890. "Father Damien: an Open Letter to the Reverend Doctor Hyde of Honolulu" by Robert Louis Stevenson. London: Chatto and Windus, 1890. http://www. stdamiens.org/02stdamienbiography.html.

Call to Prayer by General Robert E. Lee, from *Life and Letters of Robert Edward Lee: Soldier and Man* by John William Jones. New York and Washington: The Neale Publishing Company, 1906.

Times That Try Men's Souls by Thomas Paine, from *Selections from Early American Writers: 1607–1800* by William B. Cairns. New York: Macmillan, 1912.

"Forms of Prayer at Sea" from *The Poetical Works of William Wordsworth*, vol. 4, by William Wordsworth. London: Edward Moxon, 1846.

"The Pilgrim Fathers" by William Wordsworth, from *The Complete Poetical Works of William Wordsworth*, edited by Henry Reed. Philadelphia: Troutman and Hayes, 1851.

The *Amidah* translated by David Bivin, in *Jerusalem Perspective* (see also New Light on the Difficult Worlds of Jesus, Insights from His Jewish Context by David Bivin) quoted from CBN.com.

A Soldier's Prayer, reprinted with permission of the Hodgeman County Courthouse. http://www.hodgemancountyks.com/courthouse.html.

Thanksgiving Proclamation by George Washington from the George Washington Papers at the Library of Congress. New York, Oct. 3, 1789, http://memory.loc.gov/ammem/GW/gw004.html.

"My God Shall Raise Me Up" by Sir Walter Raleigh, from *Flowers of the Cave* by Laurie Magnus and Cecil Headlam. Edinburgh and London: William Blackwood and Sons, 1901.

From *The Power of Prayer: Illustrated in the Wonderful Displays of Divine Grace at the Fulton Street and Other Meetings in New York and Elsewhere, in 1857 and 1858* by Samuel Irenaeus Prime. New York: Charles Scribner, 1859.

"Matins" from *The Temple* by George Herbert. London: Pickering, 1838.

Eulogy for Abraham Lincoln by Matthew Simpson from *Memorial Record of the Nation's Tribute to Abraham Lincoln*, compiled by B. F. Morris. Washington DC: W. H. and O. H. Morrison, 1865.

"In Prayer" from *The Valley of Vision: A Collection of Puritan Prayers*, edited by Arthur Bennett. Carlisle, PA: Banner of Truth, 1975.

Prayer and the Individual Life by Henry B. F. MacFarland, from *Men and Religion*, published for the Men and Religion Forward Movement. New York: Young Men's Christian Association Press, 1911.

Four Thoughts on Prayer by Saint Augustine of Hippo, from *Prayer: the Key of Salvation* by Michael Müller. Baltimore: Kelly and Piet, 1868.

From *The Confessions of Saint Augustine* by Saint Augustine, Bishop of Hippo; Translated by E. B. Pusey. Chatto and Windus, 1921, http://www.gutenberg.org/cache/epub/3296/pg3296.html.

Prayer of Saint Benedict. The Benedictine Fellowship of Saint Laurence, http://saintlaurenceosb.org/prayer.html.

Homily 6 on Prayer by Saint John Chrysostom. http://www.vatican.va/spirit/documents/spirit_20010302_giovanni-crisostomo_en.html.

"Universal Prayer" from *The Poetical Works of Alexander Pope*, vol. 3, by Alexander Pope. London: F. J. Du Roveray, 1804.

National Day of Prayer by Abraham Lincoln, Proclamation 97. Appointing a Day of National Humiliation, Fasting, and Prayer, March 30, 1863.

"A Prayer Under the Pressure of Violent Anguish" from *The Works of Robert Burns: Poetry* by Robert Burns. Edinburgh: William Paterson, 1877.

Begin the Day with Prayer from *Preacher and Prayer* by Edward McKendree Bounds. Nashville and Dallas: Publishing House of the M.E. Church, South, 1907.

From "Praying Men Are God's Mightiest Leaders" from *Purpose in Prayer* by Edward McKendree Bounds. New York: Fleming H. Revell Co., 1920.

"A Prayer in Darkness" by G. K. Chesterton, from *Modern British Poetry*, edited by Louis Untermeyer. New York: Harcourt, Brace and Company, 1920.

Address at the Episcopal National Cathedral by Rev. Billy Graham, delivered September 14, 2001. Printed with Permission from Franklin Graham and The Billy Graham Evangelistic Association.

"Let My Thoughts Abide in Thee" from *The Works of Robert Louis Stevenson*, vol. 8, by Robert Louis Stevenson. London: William Heinemann in association with Chatto and Windus; Cassell and Company Limited; and Longmans, Green and Company; New York: Charles Scribner's Sons, 1922.

New Year's Prayer from *The Works of Samuel Johnson*, vol. 2, by Samuel Johnson. New York: George Dearborn, 1837.

Resolutions from *The Works of Samuel Johnson*, vol. 2, by Samuel Johnson. New York: George Dearborn, 1837.

The Martyrdom of Polycarp of Smyrna from *The Writings of the Apostolic Fathers*, translated by Alexander Roberts and Sir James Donaldson. Edinburgh: T. and T. Clark, 1867.

"The Upward Look" by Boethius, from *King Alfred's Books* by G. F. Browne. London: Society for Promoting Christian Knowledge, 1920.

"Prayer of Columbus" from *Leaves of Grass* by Walt Whitman. Philadelphia: David McKay, 1884.

Litany of Humility by Rafael Cardinal Merry del Val, from *Gold Dust: a Collection of Golden Counsels for the Sanctification of Daily Life*, translated and abridged from the French by C. M. Yonge. London: J. Masters and Co., 1880.

Praying in Faith from *A Treatise on Good Works* by Martin Luther, 1520, http://www.gutenberg.org/files/418/418-h/418-h.htm.

What a Great Gift We Have in Prayer by Martin Luther, from *The Familiar Discourses of Dr. Martin Luther* by Captain Henry Bell. Lewes: Sussex Press, 1818.

A Prayer for a Good Death from *English Prayers and Treatise on the Holy Eucharist* by Thomas More, edited by Philip E. Hallett. London: Oates and Washbourne, 1938.

Prayer Found in the Heart by C. H. Spurgeon, delivered at the Metropolitan Tabernacle in Newington, Jan. 16, 1876. Published Thursday, Feb. 4, 1904.

The *Anima Christi* from *Blessed Sacrament Book* by Francis Xavier Lasance. New York: Benziger Brothers, 1913.

Agnus Dei from *The Prayer Book Dictionary*, edited by George Harford, Morley Stevenson, and John Walton Tyrer. New York: Longmans, Green and Company, 1912.

Index

About the Author

D r. William J. Bennett is a No. 1 *New York Times* best-selling author, radio talk show host of *Morning in America,* and political television commentator on CNN. He served as Secretary of Education under President Ronald Reagan and Drug Czar under President George H. W. Bush. His previous bestsellers include *The Book of Virtues, The American Patriot's Almanac,* and his three-volume history *America: The Last Best Hope.* An educator and dynamic speaker, he is the Washington Fellow of the Claremont Institute. Find him online at BillBennett.com.